COMPUTER ARCHITECTURE

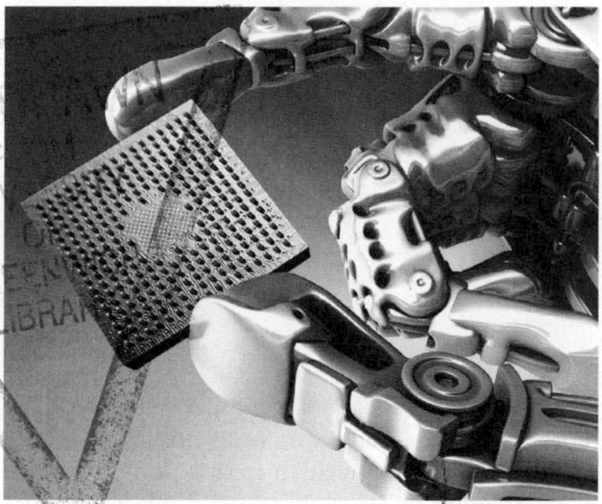

An **Embedded** Approach

Ian McLoughlin

School of Computer Engineering
Nanyang Technological University

Mc Graw Hill

Singapore • Boston • Burr Ridge, IL • Dubuque, IA • Madison, WI • New York • San Francisco
St. Louis • Bangkok • Kuala Lumpur • Lisbon • London • Madrid
Mexico City • Milan • Montreal • New Delhi • Seoul • Sydney • Taipei • Toronto

The McGraw-Hill Companies

Computer Architecture: An Embedded Approach

Higher Education

10 9 8 7 6 5 4 3 2
CTP MPM
20 13 12 11

When ordering this title, use **ISBN 978-007-131118-2** or **MHID 0-007-131118-1**

Printed in Singapore

About the Author

Ian McLoughlin is an Associate Professor in the School of Computer Engineering, Nanyang Technological University, Singapore. His background includes work for industry, government and academia across three continents over the past 20 years. He is an engineer, and has designed or worked on systems that can be found in space, flying in the troposphere, empowering the global telecommunications network, underwater, in daily use by emergency services and embedded within consumer devices. For his work on rural telecommunications solutions, he won the inaugural IEE Innovation in Engineering Award in 2005 with his team from Tait Electronics Ltd, Christchurch, New Zealand. He is a member of IET, senior member of IEEE, a Chartered Engineer in the UK and an Ingenieur Europeen (Eur. Ing.)

Contents

List of Boxes xiv

Preface xvii

Acknowledgments xix

Walk Through xx

Chapter 1: Introduction **1**

1.1 Book Organisation 1

1.2 Evolution 2

1.3 Computer Generations 5

1.3.1 First Generation 6

1.3.2 Second Generation 7

1.3.3 Third Generation 7

1.3.4 Fourth Generation 8

1.3.5 Fifth Generation 9

1.4 Cloud, Pervasive, Grid and Massively Parallel Computers 10

1.5 Where To From Here? 11

1.6 Summary 14

Chapter 2: Foundations **15**

2.1 Computer Organisation 15

2.1.1 Flynn's Classification 16

2.1.2 Connection Arrangements 17

2.1.3 Layered View of Computer Organisation 18

2.2 Computer Fundamentals 18

2.3 Number Formats 23

2.3.1 Unsigned Binary 23

2.3.2 Sign-Magnitude 24

2.3.3 One's Complement 24

2.3.4 Two's Complement 24

2.3.5 Excess-n 24

2.3.6 Binary-Coded Decimal 26

2.3.7 Fractional Notation 26

2.3.8 Sign Extension 27

2.4 Arithmetic 29
2.4.1 Addition 29
2.4.2 The Parallel Carry-Propagate Adder 29
2.4.3 Carry Look-Ahead 30
2.4.4 Subtraction 30
2.5 Multiplication 34
2.5.1 Repeated Addition 34
2.5.2 Partial Products 35
2.5.3 Shift-Add Method 38
2.5.4 Booth and Robertson's Methods 38
2.6 Division 41
2.6.1 Repeated Subtraction 41
2.7 Working with Fractional Number Formats 43
2.7.1 Arithmetic with Fractional Numbers 44
2.7.2 Multiplication and Division of Fractional Numbers 45
2.8 Floating Point 46
2.8.1 Generalised Floating Point 46
2.8.2 IEEE754 Floating Point 46
2.8.3 IEEE754 Modes 47
2.8.4 IEEE754 Number Ranges 51
2.9 Floating Point Processing 54
2.9.1 Addition and Subtraction of IEEE754 Numbers 55
2.9.2 Multiplication and Division of IEEE754 Numbers 56
2.9.3 IEEE754 Intermediate Formats 56
2.9.4 Rounding 60
2.10 Summary 60

Chapter 3: CPU Basics **66**

3.1 What Is a Computer? 66
3.2 Making the Computer Work for You 67
3.2.1 Program Storage 67
3.2.2 Memory Hierarchy 68
3.2.3 Program Transfer 69
3.2.4 Control Unit 70
3.2.5 Microcode 75
3.2.6 RISC vs CISC Approaches 77
3.2.7 Example Processors 79
3.3 Instruction Handling 81
3.3.1 The Instruction Set 81
3.3.2 Instruction Fetch and Decode 84
3.3.3 Compressed Instruction Sets 90
3.3.4 Addressing Modes 93
3.3.5 Stack Machines and Reverse Polish Notation 96

3.4 Data Handling 98
3.4.1 Data Formats and Representations 99
3.4.2 Data Flows 103
3.4.3 Data Storage 104
3.4.4 Internal Data 105
3.4.5 Data Processing 105
3.5 A Top-Down View 109
3.5.1 Computer Capabilities 109
3.5.2 Performance Measures, Statistics and Lies 111
3.5.3 Assessing Performance 113
3.6 Summary 115

Chapter 4: Processor Internals **121**
4.1 Internal Bus Architecture 121
4.1.1 A Programmer's Perspective 121
4.1.2 Split Interconnection Arrangements 122
4.1.3 ADSP21xx Bus Arrangement 124
4.1.4 Simultaneous Data and Program Memory Access 125
4.1.5 Dual-Bus Architectures 127
4.1.6 Single-Bus Architectures 129
4.2 Arithmetic Logic Unit 130
4.2.1 ALU Functionality 130
4.2.2 ALU Design 131
4.3 Memory Management Unit 132
4.3.1 The Need for Virtual Memory 132
4.3.2 MMU Operation 133
4.3.3 Retirement Algorithms 137
4.3.4 Internal Fragmentation and Segmentation 138
4.3.5 External Fragmentation 138
4.3.6 Advanced MMUs 139
4.3.7 Memory Protection 140
4.4 Cache 143
4.4.1 Direct Cache 144
4.4.2 Set-Associative Cache 145
4.4.3 Full-Associative Cache 147
4.4.4 Locality Principles 148
4.4.5 Cache Replacement Algorithms 149
4.4.6 Cache Performance 153
4.4.7 Cache Coherency 155
4.5 Co-Processors 157
4.6 Floating Point Unit 158
4.6.1 Floating Point Emulation 159

4.7 Streaming SIMD Extensions (SSE) and Multimedia Extensions 161
4.7.1 Multimedia Extensions (MMX) 162
4.7.2 MMX Implementation 162
4.7.3 Use of MMX 163
4.7.4 Streaming SIMD Extensions (SSE) 164
4.7.5 Using SSE and MMX 164
4.8 Co-Processing in Embedded Systems 165
4.9 Summary 166

Chapter 5: Enhancing CPU Performance **172**
5.1 Speed-Ups 173
5.2 Pipelining 173
5.2.1 Multi-Function Pipelines 175
5.2.2 Dynamic Pipelines 177
5.2.3 Changing Mode in a Pipeline 177
5.2.4 Data Dependency Hazard 179
5.2.5 Conditional Hazards 180
5.2.6 Conditional Branches 183
5.2.7 Compile-Time Pipeline Remedies 185
5.2.8 Relative Branching 187
5.2.9 Instruction-Set Pipeline Remedies 189
5.2.10 Runtime Pipeline Remedies 190
5.3 Complex and Reduced Instruction Set Computers 193
5.4 Superscalar Architectures 194
5.4.1 Simple Superscalar 194
5.4.2 Multiple-Issue Superscalar 197
5.4.3 Superscalar Performance 198
5.5 Instructions Per Cycle 198
5.5.1 IPC of Difference Architectures 199
5.5.2 Measuring IPC 201
5.6 Hardware Acceleration 201
5.6.1 Zero-Overhead Loops 202
5.6.2 Address Handling Hardware 205
5.6.3 Shadow Registers 209
5.7 Branch Prediction 209
5.7.1 The Need for Branch Prediction 210
5.7.2 Single T-bit Predictor 212
5.7.3 Two-Bit Predictor 214
5.7.4 The Counter and Shift Registers as Predictors 215
5.7.5 Local Branch Predictor 216
5.7.6 Global Branch Predictor 218
5.7.7 The Gselect Predictor 221
5.7.8 The Gshare Predictor 222

5.7.9 Hybrid Predictors 223
5.7.10 Branch Target Buffer 226
5.7.11 Basic Blocks 228
5.7.12 Branch Prediction Summary 229
5.8 Parallel Machines 230
5.8.1 Evolution of SISD to MIMD 231
5.8.2 Parallelism for Raw Performance 235
5.8.3 More on Parallel Processing 237
5.9 Tomasulo's Algorithm 240
5.9.1 The Rationale Behind Tomasulo's Algorithm 240
5.9.2 An Example Tomasulo System 241
5.9.3 Tomasulo's Algorithm in Embedded Systems 246
5.10 Summary 247

Chapter 6: Externals **252**
6.1 Interfacing Using a Bus 252
6.1.1 Bus Control Signals 253
6.1.2 Direct Memory Access 254
6.2 Parallel Bus Specifications 255
6.3 Standard Interfaces 257
6.3.1 System Control Interfaces 257
6.3.2 System Data Buses 258
6.3.3 Input/Output Buses 264
6.3.4 Peripheral Device Buses 265
6.3.5 Interface to Networking Devices 266
6.4 Real-Time Issues 266
6.4.1 External Stimuli 267
6.4.2 Interrupts 267
6.4.3 Real-Time Definitions 267
6.4.4 Temporal Scope 268
6.4.5 Hardware Architecture Support for Real-Time Operating Systems 270
6.5 Interrupts and Interrupt Handling 271
6.5.1 The Importance of Interrupts 271
6.5.2 The Interrupt Process 272
6.5.3 Advanced Interrupt Handling 278
6.5.4 Sharing Interrupts 278
6.5.5 Re-Entrant Code 279
6.5.6 Software Interrupts 279
6.6 Wireless 280
6.6.1 Wireless Technology 280
6.6.2 Wireless Interfacing 282
6.6.3 Issues Relating to Wireless 282
6.7 Summary 284

Chapter 7: Practical Embedded CPUs **291**
7.1 Introduction 291
7.2 Microprocessors are Core Plus More 291
7.3 Required Functionality 294
7.4 Clocking 300
7.4.1 Clock Generation 301
7.5 Clocks and Power 302
7.5.1 Propagation Delay 303
7.5.2 The Trouble with Current 304
7.5.3 Solutions for Clock Issues 305
7.5.4 Low-Power Design 305
7.6 Memory 307
7.6.1 Early Computer Memory 308
7.6.2 Read-Only Memory 308
7.6.3 Random Access Memory 314
7.7 Pages and Overlays 323
7.8 Memory in Embedded Systems 325
7.8.1 Non-Volatile Memory 326
7.8.2 Volatile Memory 328
7.8.3 Other Memory 329
7.9 Test and Verification 332
7.9.1 Integrated Circuit Design and Manufacture Problems 332
7.9.2 Built-in Self-Test 334
7.9.3 Joint Test Action Group 337
7.10 Error Detection and Correction 340
7.11 Watchdog Timers and Reset Supervision 345
7.11.1 Reset Supervisors and Brownout Detectors 346
7.12 Reverse Engineering 348
7.12.1 The Reverse Engineering Process 349
7.12.2 Detailed Physical Layout 353
7.13 Preventing Reverse Engineering 359
7.13.1 Passive Obfuscation of Stored Programs 361
7.13.2 Programmable Logic Families 362
7.13.3 Active RE Mitigation 363
7.13.4 Active RE Mitigation Classification 363
7.14 Summary 365

Chapter 8: CPU Design **369**
8.1 Soft-Core Processors 369
8.1.1 Microprocessors are More Than Cores 370
8.1.2 The Advantages of Soft-Core Processors 370
8.2 Hardware-Software Co-Design 373

8.3 Off-The-Shelf Cores 377
8.4 Making Our Own Soft Core 379
8.5 CPU Design Specification 380
8.5.1 CPU Architecture 381
8.5.2 Buses 381
8.5.3 Storage of Program and Data 382
8.5.4 Logical Operations 383
8.5.5 Instruction Handling 384
8.5.6 System Control 385
8.6 Instruction Set 386
8.6.1 CPU Control 388
8.7 CPU Implementation 390
8.7.1 The Importance of Testing 391
8.7.2 Defining Operations and States: defs.v 391
8.7.3 Starting Small: counter.v 391
8.7.4 CPU Control: state.v 394
8.7.5 Program and Variable Storage: ram.v 396
8.7.6 The Stack: stack.v 399
8.7.7 Arithmetic, Logic and Multiply Unit: alu.v 401
8.7.8 Tying It All Together: tinycpu.v 403
8.8 CPU Testing and Operation 408
8.9 CPU Programming and Use 409
8.9.1 Writing TinyCPU Programs 409
8.9.2 TinyCPU Programming Tools 413
8.10 Summary 415

Chapter 9: The Future 419
9.1 Single-Bit Architectures 419
9.1.1 Bit-Serial Addition 420
9.1.2 Bit-Serial Subtraction 421
9.1.3 Bit-Serial Logic and Processing 422
9.2 Very-Long Instruction Word Architectures 422
9.2.1 The VLIW Rationale 422
9.2.2 Difficulties with VLIW 424
9.3 Parallel and Massively Parallel Machines 425
9.3.1 Clusters of Big Machines 426
9.3.2 Clusters of Small Machines 426
9.3.3 Parallel and Cluster Processing Considerations 431
9.3.4 Interconnection Strategies 432
9.4 Asynchronous Processors 434
9.4.1 Data Flow Control 437
9.4.2 Avoiding Pipeline Hazards 437

9.5 Alternative Number Format Systems 438
9.5.1 Multiple-Valued Logic 438
9.5.2 Signed Digit Number Representation 439
9.6 Optical Computation 442
9.6.1 The Electro-Optical Full Adder 442
9.6.2 The Electro-Optical Backplane 443
9.7 Science Fiction or Future Reality? 444
9.7.1 Distributed Computing 444
9.7.2 Wetware 445
9.8 Summary 446

Appendix A: Standard Notation for Memory Size **447**
Examples 448

Appendix B: Open Systems Interconnection Model **449**
B.1 Introduction 449
B.2 The OSI Layers 449
B.3 Summary 451

Appendix C: Exploring Trade-Offs in Cache Size and Arrangement **452**
C.1 Introduction 452
C.2 Preparation 452
C.3 Installing Cacti and Dinero 453
C.4 Meet the Tools 453
C.5 Experimenting with Different Trade-Offs 454
C.6 Further Information in Cache Design 455

Appendix D: Wireless Technology for Embedded Computers **459**
D.1 Introduction 459
D.2 802.11a, b and g 460
D.2.1 802.11a/b/g Solutions for Embedded Systems 460
D.3 802.11n 460
D.3.1 Draft 802.11n Solutions for Embedded Systems 460
D.4 802.20 461
D.5 802.16 461
D.5.1 802.16 Solutions 461
D.6 Bluetooth 462
D.6.1 Bluetooth Solutions 462
D.7 GSM 463
D.7.1 GSM Solutions 463
D.8 GPRS 464
D.9 ZigBee 464
D.9.1 ZigBee Solutions 465

D.10 Wireless USB 466
D.10.1 Wireless USB Solutions 466
D.11 Near Field Communication 466
D.11.1 NFC Solutions 467
D.12 WiBro 467
D.13 Wireless Device Summary 468
D.14 Application Example 468
D.15 Summary 470

Appendix E: Tools for Compiling and Simulating TinyCPU 471
E.1 Preparation and Obtaining Software 471
E.2 How to Compile and Simulate Your Verilog 472
E.3 How to View Simulation Outputs 475
E.4 Advanced Test Benches 482
E.5 Summary 483

Appendix F: Tools for Compiling and Assembling Code for TinyCPU 484
F.1 Introduction 484
F.2 The Assembly Process 484
F.3 The Assembler 485
F.4 Example Program Assembly 488
F.5 The Compiler 489
F.6 Summary 490

Index 491

List of Boxes

2.1	Worked endiness example 1	20
2.2	Worked endiness example 2	21
2.3	Worked endiness example 3	21
2.4	Worked endiness example 4	22
2.5	What is a number format?	23
2.6	Negative two's complement numbers	25
2.7	Worked examples of number conversion	25
2.8	Is binary a fractional number format?	27
2.9	Fractional format worked example	27
2.10	Sign extension worked example	28
2.11	Exercise for the reader	30
2.12	Worked example	31
2.13	Exercise for the reader	32
2.14	Exercise for the reader	33
2.15	Worked examples of two's complement multiplication	37
2.16	Exercise for the reader	39
2.17	Booth's method worked example	40
2.18	Long division worked example	42
2.19	Worked examples of fractional representation	44
2.20	Worked example of fractional division	45
2.21	IEEE754 normalised mode worked example 1	48
2.22	IEEE754 normalised mode worked example 2	49
2.23	Exercise for the reader	49
2.24	IEEE754 denormalised mode worked example	50
2.25	IEEE754 infinity and other 'numbers'	51
2.26	Worked example: converting decimal to floating point	54
2.27	Floating point arithmetic worked example	57
2.28	IEEE754 arithmetic worked example	58
3.1	How the ARM was designed	79
3.2	Illustrating conditionals and the S bit in the ARM	85
3.3	Condition codes in the ARM processor	87
3.4	Understanding the MOV instruction in the ARM	89
3.5	A Huffman coding illustration	91
3.6	Recoding RPN instructions to minimise stack space	98

3.7	Data types in embedded systems	101
3.8	Standardised performance	112
4.1	Exploring ALU propagation delays	134
4.2	MMU worked example	137
4.3	Trapping software errors in the C programming language	142
4.4	Cache example: the Intel Pentium Pro	144
4.5	Direct cache example	146
4.6	Set-associative cache example	147
4.7	Cache replacement algorithm worked example 1	151
4.8	Cache replacement algorithm worked example 2	152
4.9	Access efficiency example	154
4.10	MESI protocol worked example	157
4.11	An alternative approach: FPU on the ARM processor	159
5.1	Pipeline speed-up	175
5.2	WAW hazard	181
5.3	Conditional flags	182
5.4	Branch prediction	185
5.5	Speculative execution	186
5.6	Relative branching	188
5.7	Scoreboarding	196
5.8	ZOL worked examples	207
5.9	Address generation in the ARM	208
5.10	Aliasing in local prediction	219
6.1	DMA in a commercial processor	255
6.2	Bus settings for peripheral connectivity	257
6.3	The trouble with ISA	260
6.4	Scheduling priorities	270
6.5	ARM interrupt timing calculation	275
6.6	Memory remapping during boot	277
7.1	Configurable I/O pins on the MSP430	296
7.2	Pin control on the MSP430	297
7.3	NAND and NOR flash memory	311
7.4	Memory map in the MSP430	330
7.5	Using JTAG for finding a soldering fault	338
7.6	Using JTAG for booting a CPU	339
7.7	Hamming (7, 4) encoding example	343
7.8	Hamming (7, 4) encoding example using matrices	344
7.9	Bus line pin swapping	358
9.1	Example of a VLIW hardware	424
9.2	Examples of parallel processing machines	435
9.3	Example of a CSD number	442

Preface

There are a great deal of computer architecture texts in print at any one time. Many famous authors have tried their hands at writing in this area, however, computers constitute a rapidly advancing and fluid field, so few books can hope to keep up without constant revisions. Above all, the rapidity of the shift towards embedded computing systems has left many authors, and texts, foundering in the wake. Some texts persist in regarding computers in the same light as the room-sized machines of the 1950s and 1960s. Many more view computers in the light of the desktop and server machines of the 1980s and 1990s. A handful acknowledge that the vast majority of computers in modern use are embedded within everyday objects. Few acknowledge that the future is embedded: there will come a time when the concept of a desktop computer seems as anachronistic as the punched card machines of 50 years ago.

This text is facing squarely towards the embedded future. Topics related to embedded processors are handled alongside the more traditional topics of other texts and, wherever possible, examples from the embedded world are highlighted.

The target audience for this book consists of three groups of people. Firstly, undergraduate students of computer architecture-related courses, typically those in their third year. Secondly, master's level students requiring a refresher in computer architecture before embarking on a more in-depth study. Thirdly, industrial engineers. As reconfigurable logic circuits, especially FPGAs (field programmable gate arrays) are becoming larger, faster and cheaper, there is increasing interest in soft-core computers – that is CPUs designed by engineers for specific tasks. For perhaps the first time in history, these tools allow ordinary engineers the opportunity to design and build their own custom computers. Digesting this text will provide engineers with a solid platform of knowledge to understand the traditional and contemporary techniques and trade-offs in computer architecture – the art of computer design.

This text has been written from the bottom up without basing it on an existing book. This allows it to avoid many of the historical blind alleys and irrelevant side shows in computer evolution, leading to a more precisely defined focus. This is not just a computer architecture book with an extra chapter on embedded systems. It is a fresh and integrated look at the computer architecture of today, which is built upon the foundation and history of bigger and older machines, but which is definitely driving towards greater levels of integration within embedded systems.

This book aims to be an easy-access and readable text. Plenty of diagrams are given to explain tricky concepts, and many explanatory boxes are provided throughout, containing extra worked examples, interesting snippets of information and additional explanations to augment the main text. Apart from covering all of the main items in the typical computer architecture theory curriculum that are of relevance to embedded engineers (but excluding tape storage, Winchester drives and supercomputer design), the book contains a wealth of practical information for the target audience – even the opportunity to build and test out a custom soft-core processor.

SI units are used throughout the book, including the newer 'kibibyte' and 'mebibyte' measures for computer memory (explained in Appendix A). Each of the main curriculum chapters includes end-of-chapter problems, with answers available in an instructor's manual. All examples, and much more material including recommendations for further reading, are available on the associated website at www.mheducation.asia/olc/mcloughlin.

Ian McLoughlin

Acknowledgements

Thanks are due most of all to my patient wife, Kwai Yoke, and children Wesley and Vanessa for allowing me the time to write this book. Tom Scott, Benjamin Premkumar, Stefan Lendnal and Adrian Busch gave me plenty of encouragement at times when I needed it (this text took form over a long drawn out five-year period). Doug McConnell was an inspiration as was the late Sir Angus Tait – most of the book was written while I worked as Principal Engineer in Group Research, Tait Electronics Ltd, Christchurch, New Zealand. This company is the largest electronics research and development company in Oceania, founded 30 years ago by Angus Tait at age 55 – an age at which most people wind down to retirement. Not Angus Tait: he still went to work every day to guide the company, until he passed away in August 2007.

Thanks are also reluctantly given to my computer architecture, advanced computer architecture and computer peripherals students at Nanyang Technological University (NTU), for asking me difficult questions, stretching my knowledge and through that motivating me to teach better. Associate Professor Lee Keok Kee kick-started me into gathering materials for this book, and I would also like to acknowledge my many other friends and colleagues in NTU, and also past colleagues in Tait Electronics Ltd, Simoco, The University of Birmingham, HMGCC and GEC Hirst Research Centre. Thanks are also due to Gerald Bok and colleagues at McGraw-Hill, especially to Doreen Ng and the editorial team for their professionalism and hard work in turning the manuscript into a beautiful book.

Most importantly, I wish to acknowledge my mother who constantly encouraged me along the way – not just of writing this book, but throughout my entire lifetime. Her high expectations led, eventually to my entering academia, and she has always been most enthusiastic regarding my forays into writing; thank you Mum. However, above all I want to give glory to the God who made me, protected me, nurtured me, gave his son to save me, and will eventually welcome me into His presence. All that I am, accomplish, obtain and achieve, I owe to Him.

WALK THROUGH

***Explanatory boxes** containing extra **worked examples** and **interesting snippets of information** to augment main text*

40

Chapter 2

Box 2.17

Booth's method worked example

Consider -9×11 (signed):

```
 11110111    multiplicand -9
 00001011    multiplier 11
-11110111    (i=0, subtract multiplicand since bit pair=10)
 0000000     (i=1, no action since bit pair=11)
+110111      (i=2, add multiplicand << 2 since bit pair = 01)
-10111       (i=3, subtract multiplicand << 3 since bit pair=10)
+0111        (i=4, add multiplicand << 2 since bit pair=01)
 000         (i=5 and onwards, no action since all bit pairs=00)
```

The result is therefore obtained as the summation of the following:

```
-11110111
+11011100
-10111000
+01110000
```

Or by converting the subtractions into additions (see Section 2.4.4):

```
 00001001
+11011100
+01001000
+01110000
=10011101    + Carry
```

Result:

10011101 = −128 + 16 + 8 + 4 + 1 = −99 (correct)

It is important to note that when i = 0, the bits considered are the least significant bit of the multiplier and a hidden zero. Thus, when the least significant bit of the multiplier is a '1', the multiplicand must be subtracted (i.e. treated as a '10' instead). This can be seen in the second worked example (Box 2.17).

There are two points worth mentioning here. First, when dealing with two's complement signed operands, the partial products must be sign extended in the same way as the full partial product multiplier.

Second, when scanning from right to left, the hidden bit at the right-hand side means that the first pair of non-equal bits that is encountered will always be a '10', indicating a subtraction. This regularity may be useful when designing a hardware implementation.

Even for someone who has been doing binary arithmetic for many years, the preparation of this book highlighted how easy it can be to make very trivial binary addition mistakes. If you are required to do this as part of an examination, always

Multiplication

79

CPU Basics

Box 3.1

How the ARM was designed

In the mid-1980s, groundbreaking British computer company Acorn, with a contract from the British Broadcasting Corporation (BBC) to design and market BBC microcomputers was looking for a way to move beyond their hugely successful 8-bit BBC microcomputers. These were powered by the lean and efficient Rockwell 6502 processors. The BBC initiatives had encouraged computer use in the UK so much that there were reportedly far more computers per capita in England than anywhere else in the world. Sir Clive Sinclair's ZX Spectrum for example, had sold 4 million units by the time sales of the IBM PC had reached 1 million units. Acorn is also reputed to have sold over 1 million BBC computers overall.

In the early explosion of the 'computer revolution' it quickly became apparent to Acorn that 16-bit processors from companies such as Intel and Motorola were not powerful enough to meet their projected future needs – needs which included releasing the world's first multi-tasking graphical desktop operating system in the late 1980s (later some observers would conclude that this was copied by Microsoft as the basis for Windows 95, XP and beyond).

In typical pioneering fashion, Acorn decided that, since nothing good enough was available, they would create their own processor. They designed the ARM1 and its support ICs (such as MEMC and VIDC) within two years despite having never developed any silicon previously.

Acorn wanted a machine with a regular architecture – similar to the 6502, but vastly more powerful. They chose to use the RISC approach, but revisited their software needs by analysing operating system code to determine most used instructions which they then optimised for the ARM processor. The same approach yielded an instruction set (see Section 3.3) and its coding. Later, much needed additions were the multiply and multiply-accumulate instructions.

This heritage leaves the globally successful ARM processor with a direct link back to the UK Government-funded BBC initiatives: the ARM software interrupt, supervisor modes, fast interrupt, no microcode, static pipeline, load-store architecture are all derived either from the hardware or the software architectures adopted by Acorn.

inside almost every electronic product and most of these are ARM-based. Meanwhile, Acorn itself no longer exists, having self-destructed in 1999.

3.2.7 **Example Processors**

Over the years, since the IBM research group published their initial results, the RISC approach has impacted almost every sphere of processor design. In particular, the ARM RISC processor family now dominates the world of embedded systems. Therefore, in this book almost all assembly language code examples are given in ARM assembler format. For example:

```
ADD R0, R1, R2
```

Making the Computer Work for You

*A wealth of practical information including the opportunity **to build and test out a custom soft-core processor***

379

CPU Design

determine the amount of CPU time spent within each function, the program trace and the number of loops executed).

An operating system, particularly a real-time operating system (RTOS), is often required in many developments. Unfortunately, it can be difficult writing or porting an OS to a new processor, and this is one major argument in favour of choosing a core that is already supported by a good OS such as embedded Linux. Despite this, there are reasons to custom design a soft core, for example, when only small items c such as hand-written assembly language are used.

In fact, over the next few sections of this book, we will create a custom s and later develop an assembler for this (we will also introduce a basic C-like co

8.4 **Making Our Own Soft Core**

In this section, and those following, we will cement together much of the kno gained up to this point, by following the design of a simple CPU. Actually, we w the design of this, and then create a real Verilog executable which can be used in FPGA. The CPU which we will describe is in fact named TinyCPU, and is the in of Professor Koji Nakano[4] of the Department of Information Engineering, Sc Engineering, Hiroshima University, Japan. TinyCPU consists of only about 420 Verilog hardware description language source code.

Although this design is included here specifically for the purpose of teachi illustrating basic computer architecture features, TinyCPU is a fully working CPU it is written in Verilog it can be included inside most common FPGAs, such a from Altera, Xilinx and Actel and programmed to perform real-world tasks. Pr Nakano and his team have also released both a simple assembler for TinyCI a compiler for a subset of the C programming language (i.e. basic C comma supported but not some of the esoteric and advanced features).

For readers who are seeking a processing core for their FPGA designs, Ti may well work. However, far better would be for readers to first understand, a experiment with TinyCPU: rather than adopt this design as-is for a project, w extend it or use this knowledge to create or choose a custom processing core? Ti may not be the most efficient or suitable design for a particular application, b the practical CPU design knowledge that this chapter presents plus the found material presented in earlier chapters, readers will have the skills needed to c custom solution or to choose from existing available solutions.

A word of warning though – sometimes it will be better to use a common pro core for several designs, even when the core is clearly sub-optimal, because of the benefits that this allows: the possibility of code/library reuse, shared devel

[4] The source code and design of TinyCPU are used with the kind permission of Professor Nak More information relating to TinyCPU can be found on his HDL wiki pages at http://www.cs.hiroshima-u.ac.jp/~nakano/wiki/

385

CPU Design

Figure 8.8

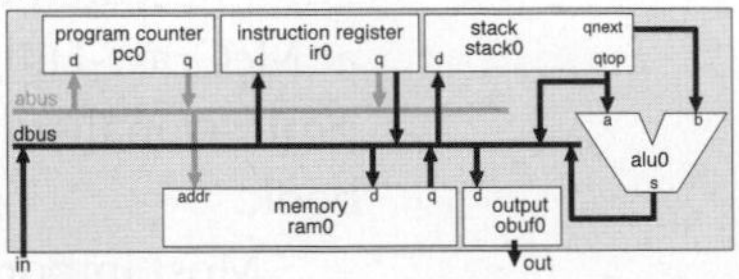

A block diagram of TinyCPU now showing an instruction register (ir0) and a program counter (pc0).

tion register requires the ability to output to either the data bus or address bus at the appropriate times. This structure can be seen in Figure 8.8.

8.5.6 **System Control**

TinyCPU is almost complete – at least as far as the data and address path are concerned. However, there are several items that are still necessary for CPU operation. These are the control buses to turn buffers and latches on and off (which we omit for clarity) and a controller to use these to regulate the sequence of operations within the CPU.

The diagram in Figure 8.9 thus contains one more block, the state machine controller (state0). It is shown unconnected to the other units within the CPU, and it is true that state0 does not connect to the data or address buses. However, it does connect widely to almost every unit and bus driver within TinyCPU.

Figure 8.9

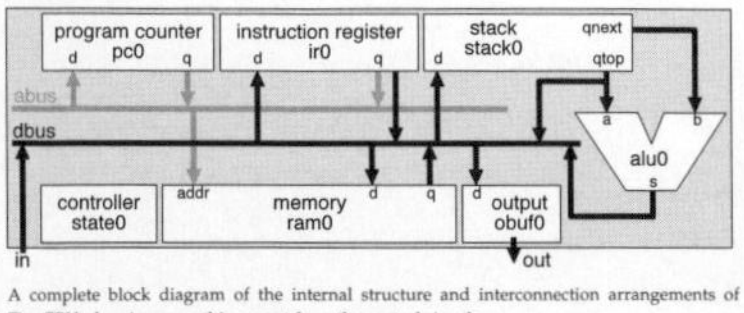

A complete block diagram of the internal structure and interconnection arrangements of TinyCPU, showing everything apart from the control signals.

CPU Design Specification

Each chapter ends with a set of ***20 problems***

Attention is given to ***industrially-relevant embedded systems*** *and* ***issues relating to modern microprocessors and system-on-chip devices***

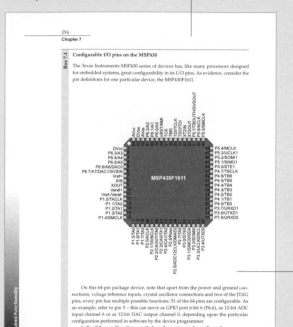

Box 7.1 Configurable I/O pins on the MSP430

The Texas Instruments MSP430 series of devices has, like many processors designed for embedded systems, great configurability in its I/O pins. As evidence, consider the pin definitions for one particular device, the MSP430F1611.

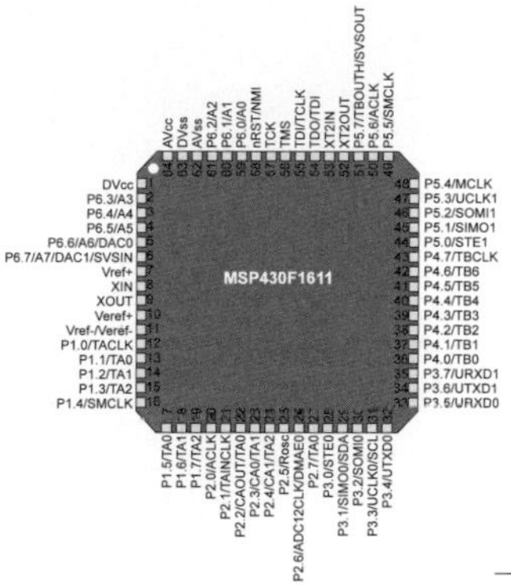

On this 64-pin package device, note that apart from the power and ground connections, voltage reference inputs, crystal oscillator connections and two of the JTAG pins, every pin has multiple possible functions: 51 of the 64 pins are configurable. As an example, refer to pin 5 – this can serve as GPIO port 6-bit 6 (P6.6), as 12-bit ADC input channel 6 or as 12-bit DAC output channel 0, depending upon the particular configuration performed in software by the device programmer.

In Box 7.2, we will explore exactly how these pins can be configured.

Required Functionality

Problems

Determine whether, in the time interval shown, all tasks meet their respective deadlines.

6.11 Repeat Problem 6.10. The only difference is that the tasks are now ordered using rate monotonic scheduling. Does this change make any difference in terms of tasks meeting their deadlines over the first $t = 40$ ms of operation?

6.12 A consumer electronics device requires a small, low-power and medium-speed CPU controller. Discuss whether a parallel-connected data memory storage system or a series-connected data memory storage system would be more appropriate.

6.13 If the system of Problem 6.12 was 'souped up' so that performance and speed became more important than size and power consumption, would that affect the choice of bus you would choose?

6.14 Figure 6.9 shows the timing diagram for the Atmel AT29LV512 flash memory device. The timing parameters shown have the following values from the Atmel datasheet:

Figure 6.9

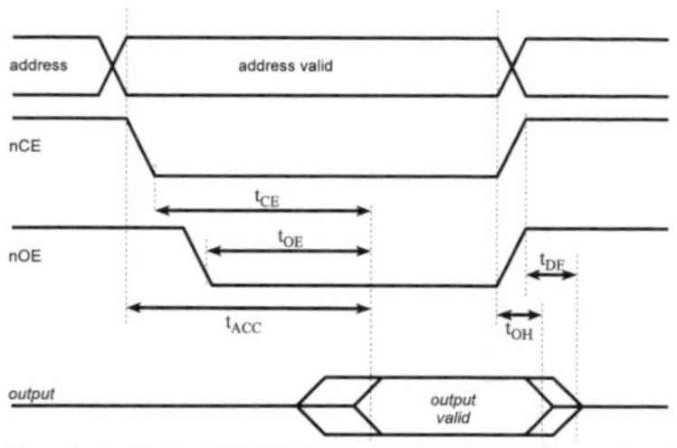

The read cycle of the Atmel AT29LV512 flash memory device (this waveform was drawn from inspection of the Atmel AT29LV512 datasheet).

Plenty of diagrams *to explain tricky concepts*

Appendices E and F on ***TinyCPU***

APPENDIX F

Tools for Compiling and Assembling Code for TinyCPU

F.1 Introduction

We have seen in Section 8.9 how to write code for, and program, TinyCPU. We developed a very small example which performed a simple integer subtraction. This was then assembled by hand into a machine code program which was inserted into the Verilog code of TinyCPU (specifically, within `ram.v`). The main message from that exercise was how tedious and longwinded such a process is when performed by hand.

In Section 8.9.2, we discussed in passing the assembler and compiler released by Professor Nakano for TinyCPU,[1] but did not provide any details.

In this appendix, we will present the entire assembler, explain its workings and demonstrate its use on the same subtract example from Section 8.9. We will also discuss the C compiler briefly.

F.2 The Assembly Process

The assembler is presented with a program consisting of assembly language mnemonics, labels, constants and other information. A simple TinyCPU program, illustrating the syntax and format, copied from Section 8.9.1, is shown in Listing F.1.

Listing F.1 subtract.asm

```
        IN
        PUSH cnst
        SUB
        OUT
        HALT
cnst: 3
```

[1] Both are available from `http://www.cs.hiroshima-u.ac.jp/~nakano/wiki/`. In addition, the assembler source code will be given in full in this appendix.

APPENDIX E

Tools for Compiling and Simulating TinyCPU

Many advanced tools exist currently for FPGA development. The main FPGA vendors provide their own software, often with a web version freely available for download, while the professional chip development companies supply their own tools, which are often used in industry, running on UNIX and Linux workstations, to develop the most advanced projects. Mentor Graphics ModelSim is perhaps the most common of these tools.

It is the author's recommendation that ModelSim be chosen for larger or more critical design projects. However, for rapid evaluation and lightweight testing we will present here a simple open source solution: Icarus Verilog,[1] combined with GTKwave[2] waveform viewer. Alternative options, especially for the waveform viewer, are also available.

E.1 Preparation and Obtaining Software

The software runs best, and of course fastest, on a Linux computer, preferably running `Kubuntu` or `Ubuntu` Linux. Since some readers may not have upgraded their PCs from Windows to Linux, they can first install `Wubi`[3] – this will create a large file on their 'C' drive and add an option to the Windows bootup menu, so that next time they reboot they can choose to run `Kubuntu`. To uninstall is equally easy. The large file can simply be deleted to remove the software. Mac operating system users can obtain and run both versions on their computers, or more competent users could simply build the software from source.

At this point, it is assumed that readers have a working Linux distribution or similar. `Kubuntu/Ubuntu` users can now proceed to install both items of software. At a shell window, type the following:

```
sudo apt-get install verilog gtkwave
```

[1] `http://www.icarus.com/eda/verilog/`

[2] `http://gtkwave.sourceforge.net/`

[3] Simply download and run the `wubi` installer from `http://wubi-installer.org`, and then follow all instructions, choosing `kubuntu` or `ubuntu` as the distribution to install.

Preparation and Obtaining Software

CHAPTER 1

Introduction

1.1 Book Organisation

Computers have evolved a long way: from Charles Babbage's analytical machine of 1834 (Figure 1.1 shows a drawing of his difference engine, an earlier, fully working mathematical processing machine of similar design) to the supercomputers of today, the story has been one of ever-increasing processing power, complexity and miniaturisation.

Surprisingly, many techniques of Babbage's day (as well as the early electrical computers of the 1940s) can still be found in today's systems, demonstrating the amazing foresight of those early pioneers. Unfortunately, these links with the past are not always positive – today's Intel desktop processors contain performance-limiting evolutionary throwbacks to the 8086 processor and beyond. With the benefit of hindsight, we have the opportunity to look back through computing history, and identify many short-lived evolutionary branches that seemed, at the time, to be promising paths to future progress, but which quickly disappeared. Sometimes these may reappear years later in specialised machines, but more often they are little more than historical curiosities.

What seems likely then is that the computers of tomorrow will be built on the techniques used in those of today. A snapshot of current techniques (as any computing text has to be) needs to recognise this fact, rather than presenting the technology as being set in stone.

This book will loosely follow the evolutionary trend. Early chapters will focus on computer fundamentals. Mastery of these fundamentals will allow a student to construct a working computer on paper, however slow and inefficient their design might be if constructed. These early chapters will be followed by a consideration of the architectural speed-ups and advanced techniques in use today. These are separated from the fundamentals because some of them may turn out to be the current 'evolutionary blind alleys', but nevertheless they are some of the techniques currently driving Moore's Law so quickly forward.

Every now and then something completely revolutionary happens in computer architecture – these break the evolutionary trend and consign many past techniques that gave incremental performance increases,

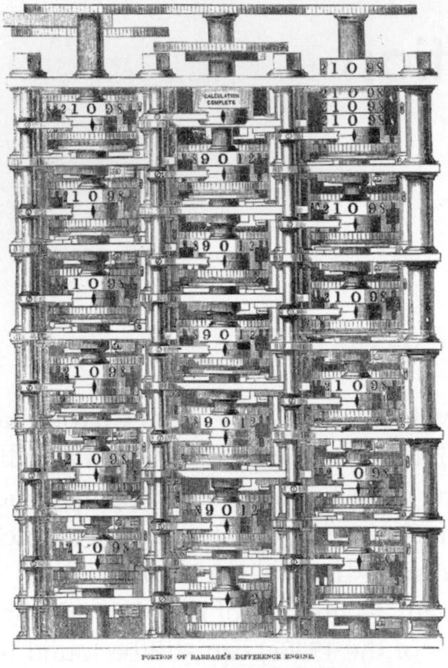

Figure 1.1 A portion of Babbage's analytical difference engine, as drawn in Harper's new monthly magazine Vol. 30, Issue 175, p. 34, 1864. The original engine documents, and a working reconstruction, can be seen today in the London Science Museum.

to oblivion. Without a crystal ball this book will not attempt to identify these technologies, but that will not prevent us from making an informed guess, in the final chapter, about advanced technologies which may spark a revolution in the field of computing over the next few decades.

1.2 Evolution

The concept of evolution of animals is controversial: to date there has been no scientific proof of the theory, yet many choose to believe in it. Some prefer a 'wait and see' approach, hoping that science will eventually catch up, while others choose to believe in an all-powerful yet unseen creator. Moving away from animals, to man-made devices, the fact that computers have followed an evolutionary path of improvement is quite obvious and unquestioned. While there have been rare disruptive breakthroughs, computing history is full of many small incremental improvements over the years.

Of course, something as complex as a computer requires an intelligent engineer to have designed it. We can often identify the engineers by name, especially those who have made significant improvements (a few of them are still alive today to tell us about it). Furthermore, the design and history of the pioneering machines, often constructed at great expense, should have been very well documented.

So in computing, one would expect the history of development to be very definite; there should be little confusion and controversy regarding the pioneering machines from half a century ago. Unfortunately, that is not the case: there exists a very wide range of opinions, with little agreements upon exact dates, contributions and 'firsts'.

Figure 1.2

One of ten Colossus computers in use during the Second World War (courtesy of the Bletchley Park Trust: `www.bletchleypark.org.uk`).

Just pick up any two books on computer architecture or computer history and compare them. For our present purposes, we will begin the modern era of computing with the invisible giant, Colossus.

Colossus (shown in Figure 1.2), built by engineer Tommy Flowers in 1943 and programmed by Alan Turing and colleagues in Bletchley Park, is now generally credited with being the world's first programmable electronic computer. This was built in England during the Second World War as part of the (ultimately successful) code-breaking effort against the German Enigma code. Unfortunately, Colossus fell under the British Official Secrets Act and remained hidden for 50 years. All papers relating to it were ordered destroyed after the war, when Prime Minister Winston Churchill (with a typically descriptive – although secret – pronouncement) ordered the machines to be 'broken into pieces no larger than a man's hand'. Plans and schematics were burned by the designers and its codebreaker operators sworn to secrecy under peril of imprisonment, or worse, for treason.

The action to hide this machine was successful. Despite the occasional unverified rumour over the years, the existence of Colossus was only revealed publicly when the few remaining documents were de-classified in the year 2000 and a government report containing the information was released. For this reason, Colossus is not even mentioned in many descriptions of computer history: an entire generation of computer architects had never even heard about it.

However, there were other very well-known and reported machines of similar vintage to Colossus that began operation in the years that followed. One of the most famous, ENIAC (Electronic Numerical Integrator And Computer), was commissioned and built in the USA. While Colossus remained totally hidden, ENIAC, operational by 1944, apparently snapped up worldwide patents to digital computing devices. Many textbook authors, not knowing anything about Colossus, have hailed ENIAC as the first modern computer. In fact, apart from being operational earlier, Colossus, being binary, was more like today's computers than ENIAC, which was decimal. However, neither were easily reprogrammable, requiring adjustments to switch settings and change wire plug positions, respectively.

Amazingly, Charles Babbage's analytical engine of over a century earlier, being digital rather than analogue and fully programmable, was in some ways more advanced than these first electronic computers. Babbage even designed a printer peripheral that could literally 'write out' the results of numerical computations. Babbage's machine also had a full programming language that could handle loops and conditional branching. This led Babbage's friend, Ada Byron, Countess of Lovelace (the child of famous poet Lord Byron), who worked on the machine, to write the world's first computer program. Possibly the first and last time in history that poetry and programming came together.

Between the difference engine and Colossus, the computing field was not totally deserted: German Konrad Zuse had an electrical computer working around 1940/1941, based on relays (therefore classified as electrical rather than electronic). Another creditable early attempt at building an electronic computer was the construction of the Atanasoff-Berry machine at Iowa State College, USA in 1941. Although not programmable and plagued by unreliability, this demonstrated several early concepts and undoubtedly advanced the state of the art in computing.

The advent of the transistorised computer is a similar area of confusion. The transistor, invented at Bell Labs, USA in 1948, was low power and small – ideal characteristics for building a computer (although the early transistors were somewhat less reliable than valves[1]). The first transistor-based machine was actually Manchester University's Transistor Computer running in 1953, although several texts again mis-attribute this honour to the TX-0 at Massachusetts Institute of Technology, USA in 1956.

Finally, confusion reigns over the first stored-program computer (as opposed to the ones programmed by plugging wires in different holes or flipping switches). This was probably Manchester University's Small-Scale Experimental Machine or SSEM (known affectionately as the 'Baby'), which successfully ran a stored program in 1948.

Another early stored-program computer, Maurice Wilkes' EDSAC (Electronic Delay Storage Automatic Calculator), began operation at Cambridge University in May 1949. The equally famous US Army EDVAC (Electronic Discrete Variable Automatic Computer) machine it was also a stored-program binary device of the same era, although it was not operational until 1951–1952 (despite construction starting in 1944).

[1] Glass thermionic valves containing tiny filament electrodes in a partial vacuum were the basic logic switches used in most early computers. Valves are known as 'vacuum tubes' or simply 'tubes' in North America. Interestingly, although they are now defunct in computing, today they are sought-after items for very high-end audio amplification equipment.

Table 1.1

Prominent machines in the evolution of computer technology.

Year	Location	Name	First
1834	Cambridge	Difference engine	Programmable computer
1943	Bletchley	Colossus	Electronic computer
1948	Manchester	SSEM (Baby)	Stored-program computer
1951	MIT	Whirlwind 1	Real-time I/O computer
1953	Manchester	The transistor computer	Transistorised computer
1971	California	Intel 4004	Mass-market CPU & IC
1979	Cambridge	Sinclair ZX-79	Mass-market home computer
1981	New York	IBM PC	Personal computer
1987	Cambridge	Acorn A400 series	High-street RISC PC sales
1990	New York	IBM RS6000	Superscalar RISC processor
1998	California	Sun picoJAVA	Computer based on a language

Clearly then, given the three areas of confusion, the history of computers is not as straightforward as it seems. Manchester University played a prominent but very low-key role and has been overlooked by many computer historians. Manchester also produced the world's first commercial computer, the Ferranti Mark 1 in 1951[2] but ultimately, the computer business became centred elsewhere.

Table 1.1 identifies a handful of world firsts in computing, along with the year they were reported to have become operational.

The table shows the progression in computer technology and goes a long way towards explaining how today's computer is very much evolutionary rather than revolutionary, although one wonders what happened to the 1960s.

1.3 Computer Generations

Sometimes computers, just like humans, are described in terms of their generation. This is a classification built up over the years, based mostly around the construction method, computing logic devices and usage of computers.

Anyone who saw computer magazine advertisements in the 1980s may remember how manufacturers cashed in on these generations and repeatedly advertised new

[2] The Ferranti Mark 1 was followed closely by the LEO computer (which was derived from EDSAC), running accounting programs for the ubiquitous Lyons Tea Houses from Spring 1951 onwards.

products as fifth generation. Thankfully this practice has abated, and it seems that, in terms of generations at least, the computing world is going through a plateau at the moment. In the following sections, we will examine the five generations of computers.

1.3.1 First Generation

- Based on vacuum tubes, usually occupying an entire room.
- Short MTBF (Mean Time Between Failures); only a few minutes between failures.
- Used base-10 arithmetic.
- Programming maybe by switch or cable, or hard wired.
- No programming languages above basic machine code.
- Many were stored program. Introduction of von Neumann architecture.

The best known example, the ENIAC, consumed over 100 kW of power yet could only deliver around 500 additions per second. This monster used 1800 valves, weighed 30 tonnes and occupied 1300 square metres. The user interface (typical for machines of this generation) is shown in Figure 1.3. ENIAC was designed by the US Army for solving ballistic equations as a means of calculating artillery firing tables.

The Colossus computer was equally vast and was dedicated – at least in its early years – to code breaking: number crunching that broke the powerful and secret Enigma code, contributing to the Allied victory in the Second World War. However, it is sad that one of the first German messages decoded was something like 'we're going to bomb Coventry'. Not wanting to alert the enemy that the code had been cracked, the government decided not to warn the inhabitants, many of whom were later killed or injured as the bombs rained down over that city.

Figure 1.3

Two women operating the ENIAC's main control panel (US Army photo).

1.3.2 Second Generation

- Transistor-based, but still heavy and large.
- Much better reliability.
- Generally used binary logic.
- Punched card or tape used for program entry.
- Support for early high-level languages.
- Often bus-based systems.

The CDC6000 of the time was renowned for its intelligent peripherals. But it is another example, the PDP-1 with 4 Ki words of RAM running at up to 0.2 MHz, that is perhaps the best known. This remarkable machine led the now sadly defunct Digital Equipment Corporation (DEC) to prominence. The PDP-1 was available at a price tag of around US$100k, but had available an impressive array of peripherals: light pen, EYEBALL digital camera, quadrophonic sound output, telephone interface, several disc storage devices, a printer, keyboard interface and a console display. The PDP-1 with several of its peripherals are shown occupying almost an entire room in Figure 1.4.

1.3.3 Third Generation

- Utilised integrated circuits.
- Good reliability.
- Emulation possible (microprograms).
- Multi-programming, multi-tasking and time sharing.

Figure 1.4

PDP-1 (photograph courtesy of Lawrence Livermore National Laboratory and found on www.computer-history.info).

- High-level languages common, some attempts at user interface design.
- Use of virtual memory and operating systems.

The very popular and versatile IBM System/360 boasted up to 512 kibibytes of 8-bit memory and ran at 4 MHz. It was a register-based computer with a pipelined central processing unit (CPU) architecture and memory access scheme that would probably appear familiar to programmers today. IBM constructed many variants of the basic machine for different users, and most importantly opted for a microcode design that could easily emulate other instruction sets: this guaranteed backwards compatibility for users of second generation computers (users who had invested very significant sums of money in their machines). Modified and miniaturised, five of these computers perform number crunching in the NASA space shuttles.

Although not quite room-sized, the basic S/360 was still a physically large device as Figure 1.5 illustrates.

1.3.4 Fourth Generation

- Used VLSI (very large-scale integration) integrated circuits.
- Highly reliable and fast.
- Possible to integrate the entire CPU on a single chip.
- DOS and CP/M operating systems and beyond.
- These are today's computers.

Examples are profuse, including all desktop and notebook computers. The Phoebe, a culmination of Acorn's innovative RISC-based architecture and advanced windowing operating system, is shown in Figure 1.6. Sadly, the company did not survive long

Figure 1.5

IBM System/360 (photograph by Ben Franske, from the Wikipedia IBM System/360 page).

Figure 1.6 Acorn Phoebe (picture from publicity material © Acorn Computers, 1998–http://acorn.chriswhy.co.uk/AcornPics/phoeb2.html).

enough to market this machine – perhaps a consequence of making the machine bright yellow. Apple, by contrast, displayed more marketing genius by originally releasing their 333 MHz iMac with a choice of five flavours (colours), although more recently they have reverted to an all-white, black or aluminium product line-up (some of the newer range of iMacs are shown in Figure 1.7).

1.3.5 Fifth Generation

- Natural interaction between humans and computers.
- Very high-level programming languages – maybe even programming in English.
- May appear intelligent to the user.

Figure 1.7

The Apple iMac range: stylish and user-friendly machines running a reliable UNIX-based operating system (photograph courtesy of Apple).

There are no confirmed examples at the time of writing. When such examples arrive, it is quite possible that there will be nothing worth photographing: hundreds of tiny embedded computers distributed around us and not a beige (or yellow) box in sight.

Not really fifth generation, but the selection of the desirable and well-engineered Apple iMac computers (see Figure 1.7) may indicate the future: stylish and user-centric machines. Or, perhaps it is Apple's smaller but equally desirable iPhone (shown in Figure 1.9), reputed to contain eight separate ARM processor cores, or their equally impressive iPad, that will herald the coming of the fifth generation?

1.4 Cloud, Pervasive, Grid and Massively Parallel Computers

Consider the history of computers. In the beginning these were room-sized machines, whether mechanical or electrical, serviced by a dedicated staff of technicians. Relentless technological progress allowed electrical valve-based hardware to be replaced with smaller transistors. The room-sized computer started to shrink. Integrated circuits were then invented to carry multiple transistors, starting with hundreds, then thousands and beyond. The 8-bit MOS Technology Inc./Rockwell 6502 processor released in 1975 contained around 4000 transistors in a 40-pin dual in line package (DIP). By 2008, Intel had reached 2 billion transistors on a single chip.

The story thus far, has been room-sized computers shrinking, first to several refrigerator-sized units, then to a single unit. Further shrinkage into a desktop box heralded the era of the personal computer (PC). PCs in turn became smaller. 'Luggables' appeared in the early 1980s, then portables, laptops, notebooks and palm computers. Today, it is possible to purchase a fully embedded computer with sensors and CMOS camera within a capsule that can be swallowed to aid in medical diagnosis.

So is this a story of one-way miniaturisation? Well, the answer has to be 'no' because computers have also become larger in some respects. The benefits of networking, such as Internet access, allow computers to easily link up, and potentially to share computation resource between themselves. What were once single computing jobs can now be parallelised across multiple computing elements or computer clusters, even in geographically diverse configurations (this type of massive parallelism will be discussed in Section 9.3).

So, given that the tasks that we need to have performed can either be executed on a single small box or spread around and shared among several machines surrounding us (including embedded ones), the question becomes, how do we define 'a computer' – is it the box itself, or is it the 'thing' that executes the task?

Fifty years ago, it was easy to define because 'the computer' was in the computer room. Today, a single beige box resting on my desk may well contain two or more CPUs, each of which may contain several computing cores and yet I refer to that box in the singular as my 'computer'. When I perform a web search query, it will probably be sent to Google where it is processed by a 'server farm' containing upwards of 10,000 computer elements (each one just like my desktop PC). When such a server

Figure 1.8

The beautiful MareNostrum installation developed by the Barcelona Supercomputing Center in the Torre Girona chapel (picture courtesy of Barcelona Supercomputing Center, `www.bsc.es`).

farm co-operates to perform processing, it is classed as a supercomputer, again in the singular.

So the computer has become large again, and yet consists of many smaller individual computing elements. One leading example of a large collection of computers working together is the Barcelona Supercomputer, the MareNostrum, installed in the Torre Girona chapel in Barcelona, and shown in Figure 1.8.

1.5 Where To From Here?

The process of miniaturisation is set to continue. More and more products, devices and systems contain embedded computers and there is no sign that this trend will die out. Computer speeds also will continue to increase. After all, there is a pretty amazing track record to this: consider the numbers in Table 1.2, showing how computers have progressed in speed since the earliest days – remembering of course that the various definitions of the word 'computer' have changed several times throughout.

Pause for a moment and consider the sheer magnitude of this progress. In almost no other sphere of life can we see such an incredible, and sustained, performance improvement. Given this track record, we can probably safely leave the miniaturisation and performance improvement process to major industry players such as ARM, Intel and AMD.

Table 1.2

The amazing progression of computer calculating speeds from the earliest days (data provided courtesy of Professor Jack Dongarra, University of Tennessee, USA).

Year	Floating point operations per second, FLOPS
1941	1
1945	100
1949	1000 (1 KiloFLOPS, kFLOPS)
1951	10,000
1961	100,000
1964	1,000,000 (1 MegaFLOPS, MFLOPS)
1968	10,000,000
1975	100,000,000
1987	1,000,000,000 (1 GigaFLOPS, GFLOPS)
1992	10,000,000,000
1993	100,000,000,000
1997	1,000,000,000,000 (1 TeraFLOPS, TFLOPS)
2000	10,000,000,000,000
2007	478,000,000,000,000 (478 TFLOPS)
2009	1,100,000,000,000,000 (1.1 PetaFLOPS)

Or can we? Despite the miniaturisation, we have seen that (super) computers are getting bigger – and more power hungry. Parallel computing has emerged as the main technique of choice in building the world's fastest computers. The days of a central computer facility, the mainframe, could well be returning. The difference being that the mainframe may now be located in a different country to its users, with mixed wireless and Internet accessibility to those users. Perhaps the mainframes should be located in cold countries where excess heat can go towards warming nearby homes?

Since the technology to separate bulk computing from the point at which that computer power is needed mostly exists today, and with the possible exception of wireless connectivity, is now mature, the controlling factors in the continued advance of this model are services and software.

However, this does not mean that it is time to abandon the advance and improvement of computers and their architecture (which would mean you can stop reading here), but it does mean that the focus may change. From big and powerful to small and low power. From large-scale number crunching to embedded and application specific.

Returning to the educational aims of this book for a moment, engineers working on computer systems have traditionally asked questions such as 'what processor shall I use in my system?' and 'how do I get this processor to work in my system?' This book provides the background necessary to enable answers to be found to both of these questions. In addition, it allows new questions to be asked, and answered, such as: 'Should I create a new processor specifically for my system, and if so, how?' or 'Should I use a simple CPU and connect to a remote server, or do all processing internally?'

That computing is now primarily an embedded engineering discipline, despite the existence of many huge supercomputers like the MareNostrum, is due to the pervasiveness of computer technology within embedded and consumer devices. Consider the case of the iPhone, shown in Figure 1.9, which reportedly contains something like nine separate microprocessors, with eight of them ARM-based. So in answer to the question of where to from here, we can predict two ongoing trends: towards fewer but bigger clusters of large computers, and towards more and smaller personalised computing devices.

Also, it would probably help your career prospects to learn a little about the ubiquitous ARM along the way.

Figure 1.9 The Apple iPhone, reputed to contain eight separate ARM processors in a sleek body with integral touch-screen (photograph courtesy of Apple).

1.6 Summary

You, the reader, may not build the world's fastest supercomputer (or maybe you will, who knows?), but hopefully you will be designing or programming some amazing embedded systems in future.

This chapter has presented a historical perspective of computing: relentless forward progress, many huge leaps in technology and understanding, but millions of small incremental improvements. Isaac Newton famously remarked in a letter to his rival Robert Hooke that, 'if I have seen further it is by standing on ye shoulders of Giants'.

This could not be more true of most computer designers. You cannot really get closer to standing on the shoulders of giants than when you use an existing computer to design the next one!

With this perspective behind you, and confident of ongoing future progress in this field, it is now time to learn the techniques (and some secrets) from the designers of the computing systems of the past few decades. The following chapters will begin this process by covering basic and foundational techniques, before considering speed-ups and performance enhancing techniques of computers – whether desktop machines or embedded systems. Later, we will spend more time investigating embedded systems themselves, even taking the opportunity to build our own embedded CPU. Finally, we will look further into the future to try and identify some promising, but unusual, techniques on the horizon of the computing world.

CHAPTER 2

Foundations

This chapter introduces the background information needed to appreciate the design of a modern central processing unit (CPU). We will consider formalised methods of computer organisation and classification, define many of the terms used to describe computer systems, discuss computer arithmetic and data representation, and look at a few of the structural building blocks we will encounter later when analysing computer systems.

2.1 Computer Organisation

What does a computer consist of? How are the elements connected? In order to answer these questions, we need to first recognise that there exists a vast range of possibilities inherent in the structure of a computer. Looking at some of today's desktop computers many of the peripheral elements traditionally connected around a CPU are subsumed within the same Integrated Circuit (IC) package; this would not be recognisable as a computer to the early pioneers. However the main, historic, computer elements are usually still present – even if they are not at first immediately identifiable. In embedded systems the trend is more apparent – system-on-chip (SoC) processors that integrate almost all required functions on a single chip are now predominant.

Secondly, not all computers are organised in the same way, or have the same requirements. After all, they could range in size from a room-sized supercomputer, to a wristwatch-based personal digital assistant (PDA) or smaller.

Despite the range of possibilities, most systems comprise functional blocks with a degree of similarity. The placement of these blocks inside or outside the CPU chip is a design or cost consideration, and the interconnections between them (both internal and external) are generally parallel buses, the width and speed of which are also design or cost considerations.

There may be multiple copies of each functional block present or multiple interconnections between some blocks.

With such variety, there is a need to classify the range of architectural possibilities in some way. It was Michael Flynn who first devised a comprehensive classification scheme for describing such systems in 1966.

Figure 2.1

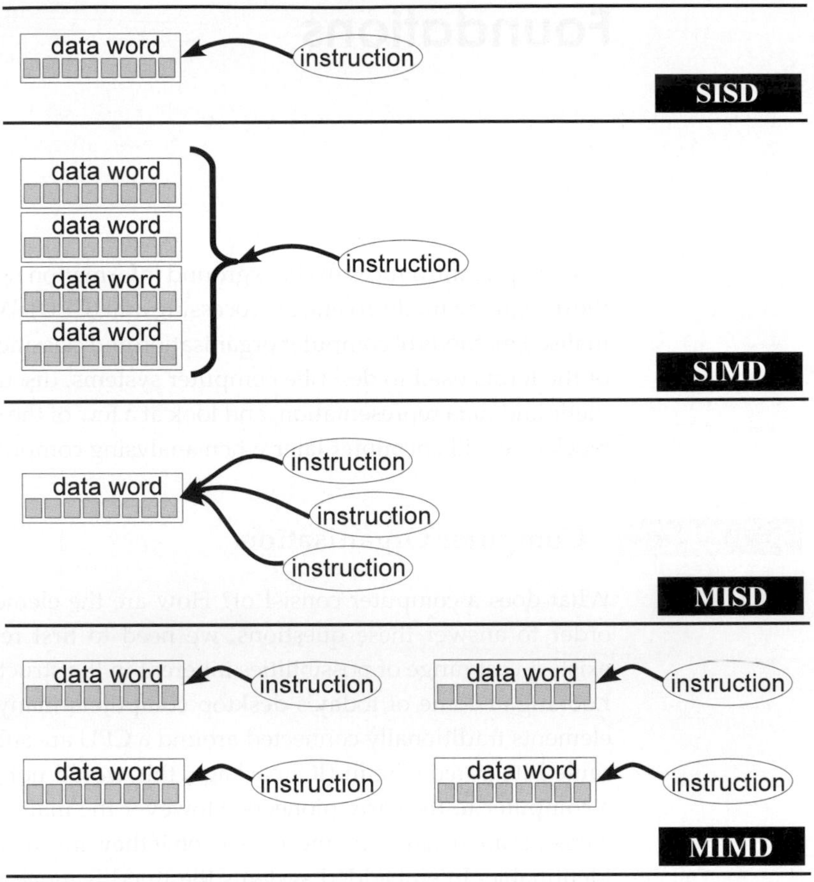

An illustration of Flynn's taxonomy of SISD, SIMD, MISD and MIMD processing. These four classifications show the relationship between instructions and data being acted upon at a snapshot in time (because the taxonomy actually refers to streams of data and instructions rather than individual items).

2.1.1 Flynn's Classification

The widely used *Flynn's Classification* scheme categorises computers based on the number of instruction streams and the number of data streams that are present.

An instruction stream can be thought of as a command to a data processing unit to modify data (in a data stream) passing through the unit. This is represented diagrammatically in Figure 2.1 which shows four examples of different connection arrangements. These are namely:

- **Single instruction, single data stream** (SISD) – A traditional computer containing a single CPU receiving its instructions from a stored program in memory and acting on a single data stream (shown in this case as one instruction acting upon one item of data).

- **Single instruction, multiple data streams** (SIMD) – A single instruction stream acting on more than one item of data. For example, given the numbers 4, 5 and 3, 2, a single instruction to perform two separate additions of $4 + 5$ and $3 + 2$ would be SIMD. An example of this arrangement is an array or vector processing system which can perform identical operations on different data items in parallel.
- **Multiple instruction, single data stream** (MISD) – A rare combination of overspecified multiple instructions acting on a single data stream. This redundancy could possibly be useful in fault-tolerant systems.
- **Multiple instruction, multiple data streams** (MIMD) – These systems are arranged similarly to multiple SISD systems. In fact, a common example of an MIMD system is a multi-processor computer such as the Sun Enterprise servers.

Although Flynn originally designed his taxonomy to describe processor-level arrangements, the same considerations can equally be applied to units within a processor. For example, Intel's multimedia extensions (MMX) found on Pentium processors and later as streaming SIMD extensions (SSE), is an example of a SIMD arrangement. It allows a single instruction to be issued which can cause an operation on multiple data items (such as eight simultaneous additions on different pairs of data). We will cover MMX along with SSE later in Section 4.7.

2.1.2 Connection Arrangements

Another common description of processor architectures is based on whether the program instructions and data are handled together or separately.

- **Von Neumann** systems are those that share resources for storage and transfer of data and instructions. Many modern computers fall into this category by virtue of storing programs and data in shared memory, and using a single bus to transfer them from memory to the CPU. Shared bus bandwidth tends to mean that such a system has limited performance, but its advantages are simpler design and lower cost.
- **Harvard architecture** systems have separate data and instruction storage and transfer. Since instruction and data transfer can be simultaneous, such systems can offer high performance.
- Other architectures include systems with multiple dedicated buses (such as the ADSP2181 internal buses), shared data/instruction address bus but separate data buses or similar. Chapter 4 will introduce and explain internal bus arrangements further.

Some CPUs such as the DEC/Intel StrongARM are advertised as being Harvard architecture, although they interface to shared memory via a single bus. In this case, the StrongARM is a Harvard architecture internally because it contains separate blocks of

Figure 2.2

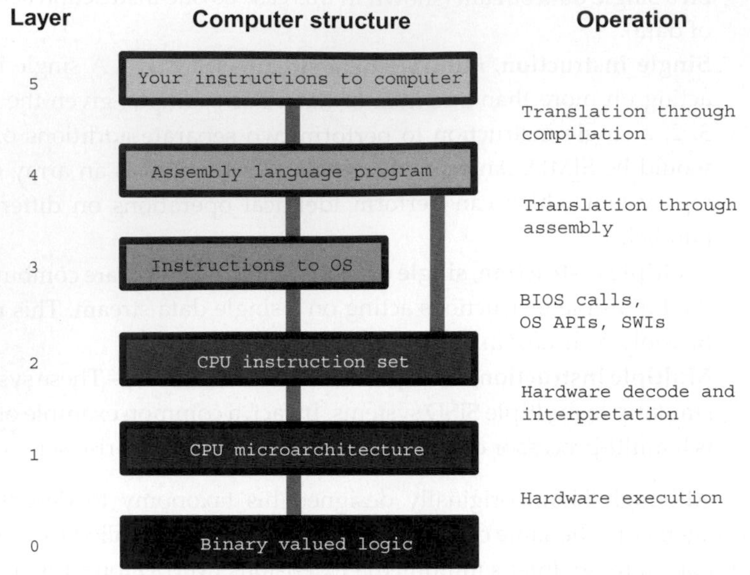

A layered view of computer organisation and structure.

internal data and instruction cache memory, although it has an external von Neumann connection arrangement.

2.1.3 Layered View of Computer Organisation

It is sometimes useful to consider a computer system as a number of interlinked layers. This is illustrated in Figure 2.2 in which the operation of connecting between layers is described, also as a hierarchy of operations.

From the bottom up, any CPU can be viewed as a collection of gates performing logical operations. These logical operations must be controlled to perform the required function by microprograms or a state machine, where the sequence of micro-operations is specified by one or more instructions from the instruction set. Instructions are issued either directly from a user program or from predefined basic input output system (BIOS) or operating system functions.

Interestingly, this layer-like model is a reflection of the Open Systems Interconnection (OSI) model, applied to computer hardware and software (the OSI model is covered in Appendix B).

2.2 Computer Fundamentals

The computer systems described in this book, such as the SISD machine discussed in Section 2.1.1, generally comprise a number of discrete functional units interconnected by buses. Some of these units will now be briefly introduced, before being covered in detail in subsequent chapters:

- Central processing unit (CPU) – The part of a computer that controls operation through interpretation of instructions and through built-in behaviour. It handles input/output functions and performs arithmetical and logical operations on data (in other words, contains an ALU). In recent times, CPU has begun to refer to a physical IC which, in some cases actually constrains all parts necessary to function as a standalone computer.
- Arithmetic logic unit (ALU) – This component of the CPU performs simple arithmetic and logical operations such as add, subtract, AND, OR. It is an asynchronous unit which takes two data inputs from parallel connected registers or bus(es) and outputs either direct to a register or is connected through a tristate buffer to a bus. In addition, it has a control input to select which function to perform, and interfaces to a status register. It handles fixed point binary (and occasionally BCD) numbers only and is located on-chip in modern processors.
- Floating point unit (FPU) – Either an on-chip or an external co-processor, it performs arithmetic on floating point numbers. The particular floating point format supported in most modern FPUs is called IEEE754. It is usually comparatively slow (can take tens or hundreds of instruction cycles to perform a calculation) and its interface is to the main CPU through special floating point registers.
- Memory management unit (MMU) – This component provides a layer of abstraction between how the processor addresses memory and how that memory is physically arranged. This abstraction is termed *virtual memory*. The MMU translates a *virtual address* that the processor needs to access into a real *physical address* in memory. The processor typically sees a large linear continuous address space in memory, with the MMU hiding a physical memory organisation which may be of different sizes (larger or smaller), non-continuous or consisting partly of RAM and partly of hard disc storage.

In addition, there are a number of items that we will include in our discussion that are useful to define now, prior to being covered in detail later:

- Register – On-chip[1] storage locations that are directly wired to internal CPU buses to allow extremely fast access (often in one instruction cycle). The distinction blurs between this and on-chip memory for some CPUs and the stack in the picoJavaII processor.
- Tristate buffer – A device to enable or disable driving a bus. It is usually placed between a register and a bus to control when the bus will be driven by that register. The first two states are when the tristate drives the bus voltage to be either logic high or logic low; the third (tri-) state is high impedance, meaning that the device does *not* drive the bus at all.

[1] Originally, these were separate hardware devices, but are now exclusively incorporated on-chip for convenience and access speed reasons.

- Complex Instruction Set Computer (CISC) – Think of any useful operation and directly insert this into the CPU hardware. Do not worry how big, power hungry or slow this will make the CPU; you will end up with a CISC machine. Early VAX machines reputedly included instructions that could take over 2000 clock cycles to execute.
- Reduced Instruction Set Computer (RISC) – CPUs are limited by their slowest internal components and by silicon size. Based on the premise that 80% of instructions use only 20% execution time and the remaining 20% use up 80% of the chip area, CPUs are reduced to contain the 80% most useful instructions. Sometimes a working definition of RISC means 'supporting a set of less than 100 instructions'. It is also significant to note an emerging trend where a RISC CPU core emulates a CISC machine.
- Instruction cycle – This refers to the time taken to fetch an instruction, decode it, process it and return the result. This may be one or more periods of the main clock cycle (derived from an external oscillator). For RISC processors, instructions typically execute in a single clock cycle. For CISC processors, some instructions take a lot longer.
- Big or little endian – Big endian means that the most significant byte is presented first. It is used in processors such as 68000 and SPARC. Little endian means that

Box 2.1

Worked endiness example 1

Q. Given a 32-bit word stored in a 16-bit architecture memory system as shown below, and given that the stored word is made up of least significant byte (LSB), second byte (B1), third byte (B2) and most significant byte (MSB), is the following a little or big endian representation?

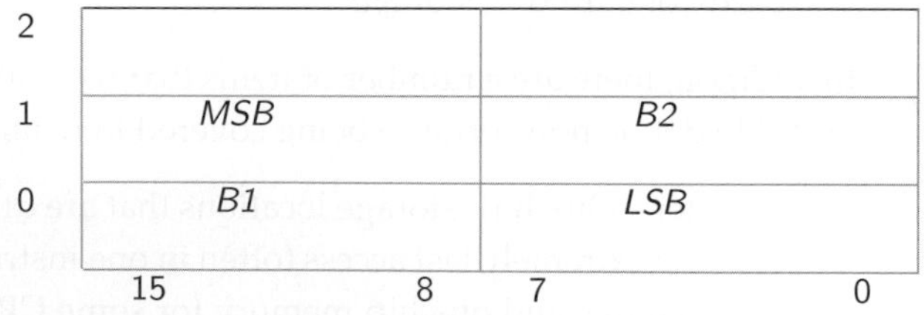

In the diagram, the memory line (in 16-bit words) is given on the left, and the bit positions are shown below.

A. Checking for little endian first, we identify the lowest byte-wise memory address and count upwards. In this case, the lowest address line is 0 and the lowest byte starts at bit 0. The next byte up in memory starts at bit 8 and is still at line 0. This is followed by line 1 bit 0 and finally line 1 bit 8. Counting the contents from lowest byte address upwards, we get $\{LSB, B1, B2, MSB\}$. Since this order DOES follow the least-to-most byte format it must be little endian.

Box 2.2

Worked endiness example 2

Q. A 32-bit word is stored as shown below. Is this a little or big endian representation?

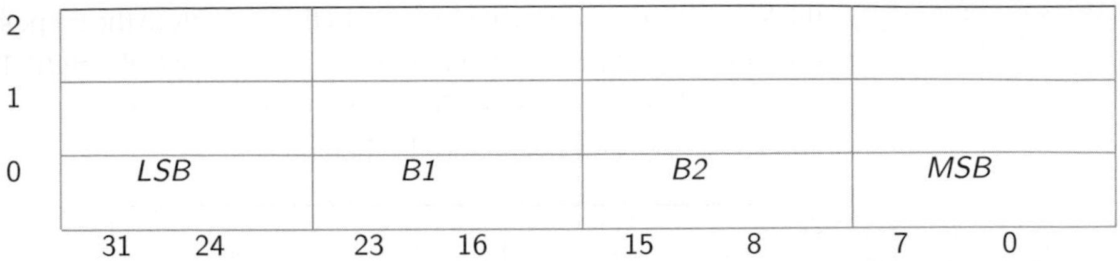

A. First identify the lowest byte-wise memory address. This is clearly address line 0, starting at bit 0. Next is address line 0, bit 8 and so on. Counting from least to most and writing out the contents we get {*MSB*, *B2*, *B1*, *LSB*}. This order does NOT follow the least-to-most byte format, so it is not little endian. Therefore it must be big endian.

the least significant byte is presented first, as used by the Intel x86 family. Some processors (such as the ARM7) allow for switchable 'endiness'.

Unfortunately, endiness is complicated by the variable memory-width of modern computers. It was easier when everything was byte-wide, but now there is an added dimension of difficulty. Given an unknown system, it is probably easier to check first whether it is little endian, and if not, classify it as big endian, rather than working the other way around. Boxes 2.1, 2.2, 2.3 and 2.4 explore this issue in detail.

Box 2.3

Worked endiness example 3

Q. Given the memory map shown below, write in the boxes the 32-bit number represented by MSB, B1, B2 and LSB bytes using a little endian representation.

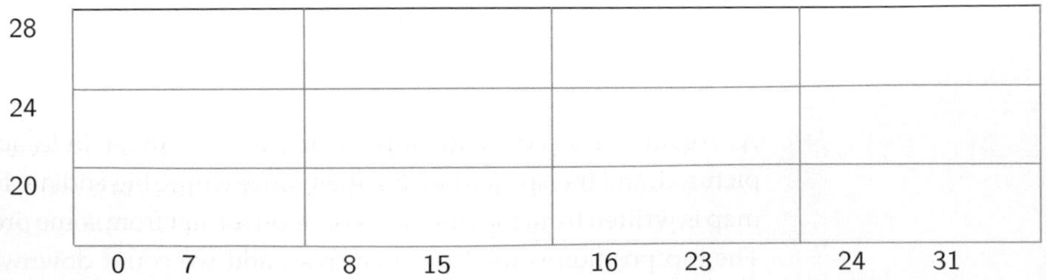

(Continued)

Box 2.3

Worked endiness example 3 (*Continued*)

A. Little endian is always easier: its LSB is at the lowest byte-address and then we count upwards in memory to the MSB. First, we need to identify the location of the lowest byte-address in memory. In this case, note the bit positions written along the bottom – they start from left and increment towards the right. Lowest address of those shown is therefore address 20 and bit 0. Next byte will be address 20, bit 8 onwards and so on. The end result should then be:

28				
24				
20	*LSB*	*B1*	*B2*	*MSB*
	0 7	8 15	16 23	24 31

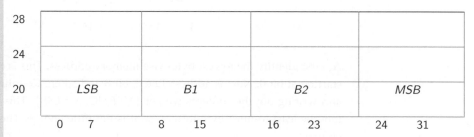

Note: Look also at the addresses. Instead of being consecutive locations, incrementing by one each line (as the other examples showed), these addresses jump by 4 bytes each line. This indicates that memory is byte-addressed instead of word-addressed. This is typical of ARM processors which, despite having a 32-bit wide memory, address each byte in memory separately.

Box 2.4

Worked endiness example 4

Q. Given the memory map shown below, write in the boxes the 16-bit number represented by MSB and LSB bytes using a big endian representation.

50	
51	
52	
	7 0

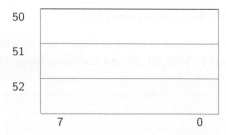

A. Again, we need to identify which is the lowest byte address in the memory pictured, and then place the MSB there since we are big endian. In this case, the memory map is written from top down – a common format from some processor manufacturers. The top position is the lowest address, and we count downwards. Since memory is byte-wide, this is relatively easy. The answer is thus:

(*Continued*)

Box 2.4

Worked endiness example 4 (*Continued*)

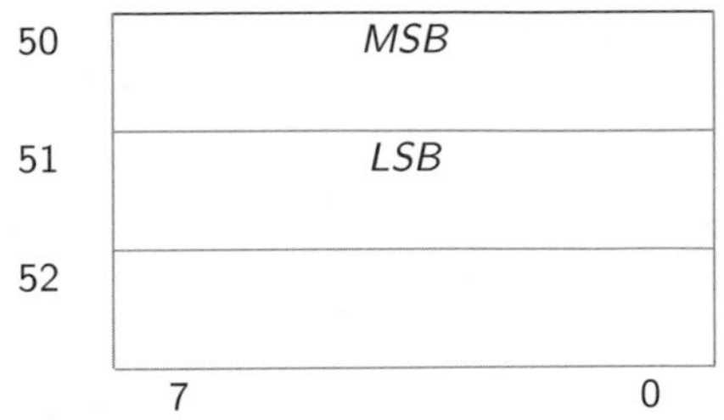

Box 2.5

What is a number format?

We are all aware of decimal format, either integer as in the number 123 or fractional as in 1.23, which are both examples of base 10.

In fact, there are an infinite number of ways to represent any number (an infinite number of different bases), but only a few of these are common. Apart from decimal, the hexadecimal format (base 16) is used frequently in software, as is binary (base 2) in hardware, and which we employ in all examples here.

2.3 Number Formats

Modern computers are remarkably homogeneous in their approach to arithmetic and logical data processing: most utilise the same number format and can be classified by how many bits of data are operated on simultaneously (known as the *data width*). They even tend to employ similar techniques for number handling. This was not the case in early computers where a profusion of non-standard data widths and formats abounded, most of which are purely of historical significance today.

It could be argued that seven (or fewer) binary number formats remain in use today. Box 2.5 discusses exactly what constitutes a number format, but in order for us to consider processing hardware later in this chapter, it is useful to now review the main formats that we will be encountering as we progress through the book.

2.3.1 Unsigned Binary

In unsigned binary, each bit in a data word is weighted by the appropriate power of two corresponding to its position. For example, the 8-bit binary word `00110101b` is equivalent to 53 decimal. The trailing b is sometimes present to indicate it is a binary number; reading from the right to the left, the number evaluates to

$$1(2^0) + 0(2^1) + 1(2^2) + 0(2^3) + 1(2^4) + 1(2^5) + 0(2^6) + 0(2^7)$$

In general, the value, v of a n-bit binary number x, where x[i] is the ith bit reading from the right to the left, starting from bit 0, is

$$v = \sum_{i=0}^{n} x[i] \cdot 2^i$$

The unsigned binary format is easy for humans to read after a little practice, and is handled efficiently by computer.

2.3.2 Sign-Magnitude

This format reserves the most significant bit (MSB) to convey polarity (called the 'sign bit'), and then uses unsigned binary notation for its remaining least significant bits to convey magnitude. By convention, an MSB of 0 indicates a positive number while an MSB of 1 indicates a negative number.

For example, the 4-bit sign-magnitude number `1001` is −1 and the 8-bit number `10001111b` is equivalent to $8 + 4 + 2 + 1 = -15$ decimal.

2.3.3 One's Complement

This format has largely been replaced by two's complement but can still occasionally be found. Again, the MSB conveys polarity while the remaining bits indicate magnitude. However, if the number is negative (i.e. the sign bit is 1), the polarity of the magnitude bits is reversed.

For example, the 8-bit one's complement number `1110111` is equal to −8 decimal.

2.3.4 Two's Complement

This is undoubtedly the most common signed number format in modern computers. It has achieved predominance for efficiency reasons: identical digital hardware for arithmetic handling of unsigned numbers can be used for two's complement numbers. Again, the MSB conveys polarity, and positive numbers are similar in form to unsigned binary. However a negative two's complement number has magnitude bits that are formed by taking the one's complement and adding 1 (Box 2.6 provides a binary example of this method which is literally 'taking the two's complement of a number').

For example, the 4-bit two's complement number represented by binary digits `1011` is equal to $-8 + 2 + 1 = -5$ decimal, and the 8-bit two's complement number `10001010` is equal to $-128 + 8 + 2 = -118$ decimal.

It is undoubtedly harder for humans to read negative two's complement numbers than some of the other formats mentioned above, but this is a small price to pay for reduced hardware complexity. Box 2.7 provides some examples of two's complement number formation, for both positive and negative values.

2.3.5 Excess-n

This representation will crop up later when we discuss floating point. In this format, a number v is stored as the unsigned binary value $v + n$. An example is the

Box 2.6

Negative two's complement numbers

Negative two's complement numbers can be easily formed in practice by taking the one's complement of the binary magnitude then adding 1. As an example, suppose we wish to write −44 in 8-bit two's complement:

Start by writing +44 in 7-bit binary:	010 1100
Next, flip all bits (take the one's complement):	101 0011
Add 1 to the least significant bit position:	101 0100
Finally, insert the sign bit (1 for negative):	1101 0100

If you are not used to writing binary numbers, try to write them in groups of 4. That way it is easier to line up the columns, and it aids in the conversion to hexadecimal (since a group of 4 bits corresponds to a single hex digit).

Box 2.7

Worked examples of number conversion

Q1. Write the decimal value 23 as a two's complement 8-bit binary number.

A1. We can start by drawing the bit weightings of an 8-bit two's complement number. Starting from the left, we begin with the sign bit.

−128	64	32	16	8	4	2	1

The sign bit is only set if the number we want to write is negative. In this case, it is positive so write a zero there. Next we look at 64. If our number is greater than 64 we would write a '1' here, but it is not so we write a zero. The same goes for 32, so now we have:

0	0	0	16	8	4	2	1

Moving on to 16, we find that our number (23) *is* bigger than 16, and so we subtract 16 from the number to leave 23 − 16 = 7. A '1' goes in the 16 box.

Next, we compare our remainder with 8. The remainder is smaller so a '0' goes in the 8 box. Moving on to 4, our remainder is bigger than this so we subtract 4 to make a new remainder 7 − 4 = 3 and write a '1' in the 4 box. Continuing with 2 and 1, both get '1's in their boxes. The final answer is thus:

0	0	0	1	0	1	1	1

Q2. Write the decimal value −100 as a two's complement 8-bit binary number.

A2. Again looking at the number line above, we realise that, as a negative number, we need a '1' in the −128 box. Doing the sum −100 − (−128) or −100 + 128 leaves a

(Continued)

Box 2.7

Worked examples of number conversion (*Continued*)

remainder of 28. The rest of the numbers act as normal – a '0' in the 64 box, a '0' in 32 box, then a '1' in the 16 box. The remainder will then be 28 − 16 = 12. Continuing, there will be '1' in the 8 box, remainder 4, then a '1' in the 4 box and '0's beyond that:

1	0	0	1	1	1	0	0

Note: The only really easy things to see, at a glance, about two's complement numbers are whether they are negative or not (a '1' in the most significant position) and whether they are odd or not (a '1' in the least significant position).

the excess-127 representation in 8 bits, which can represent any number between −127 and +128 (stored in binary bit-patterns that look like the unsigned values 0 and 255 respectively).

This format can be a little confusing to students. As examples, the 8-bit excess-127 binary number `00000000` equals −127 (which is found by working out the unsigned binary value, in this case zero, and then subtracting 127 from it). Another example is `11000010` which in binary would be 128 + 64 + 2 = 194, but since it is excess-127 we subtract 127 from the result to give 194 − 127 = 67 decimal.

2.3.6 Binary-Coded Decimal

Binary-coded decimal (BCD) was used extensively in early computers. It is fairly easy for humans to read in practice, because each decimal digit (0 to 9) of a number to be stored in BCD is encoded using a group of four binary digits. Thus, 73 in decimal is stored as `0111 0011` in BCD. Four binary digits can store a value from 0 to 15 so there are also some binary patterns that are not used in BCD. Ultimately, BCD has been superseded because it is neither efficient in storage nor easy to design hardware for.

2.3.7 Fractional Notation

This can actually apply to any binary notation (in fact to decimal too – see Box 2.8) but usually applies to unsigned or two's complement numbers within the computer architecture field. It is strictly a conceptual interpretation of the numbers where the usual bit weighting of 2^0 for the LSB, 2^1 for the next bit, 2^2 for the 3rd bit and so on is replaced by a scaled weighting pattern. In some digital signal processing (DSP) circles, fractional notation is described as *Q-format*. Otherwise, fractional notation binary is typically described as $(m.n)$ format where m is the number of digits before the imaginary radix (in decimal, the radix is known as the decimal point, but when dealing with another number base we cannot refer to it as a 'decimal' point, so we call it the radix) and n is the number of digits after it.

Box 2.8

Is binary a fractional number format?

Remember that there is nothing special about binary – it is simply a way of writing a number in base 2 instead of base 10 (decimal) that we are familiar with.

Just as we can write fractional numbers in decimal (such as 9.54) as well as integers (such as 19), we can also write any other base number in fractional as well as integer format. So far, we have only considered integer binary format, however, it is also important to realise that fractional binary format is used extensively in areas such as digital signal processing.

Box 2.9

Fractional format worked example

Q: Write the decimal value 12.625 as a (7.9) fractional format two's complement binary number.

A: First, start by looking at the bit weightings of the (7.9) format:

−64	32	16	8	4	2	1	1/2	1/4	1/8						

where the weightings below 1/8 have been removed for space reasons. Next, we realise that the number is positive, so there is a '0' in the −64 box. We then scan from left to right in exactly the same way as for a standard two's complement representation (or unsigned binary for that matter), using the weights shown above.

It turns out that $12.625 = 8 + 4 + 0.5 + 0.125$ and so the result will be:

0	0	0	1	1	0	0	1	0	1	0	0	0	0	0	0

An example of two 8-bit binary number arrangements in unsigned and (6.2) format are shown below:

unsigned	2^7	2^6	2^5	2^4	2^3	2^2	2^1	2^0
(6.2) format	2^5	2^4	2^3	2^2	2^1	2^0	2^{-1}	2^{-2}

Refer to Box 2.9 for more examples of fractional format numbers in binary.

The beauty of fractional notation applied to unsigned or two's complement numbers is that the values are handled in hardware exactly the same way as the non-fractional equivalents: it is simply a programming abstraction.

2.3.8 Sign Extension

This is the name given to the process by which a signed two's complement number of a particular width is extended in width to a larger number of bits. For example, converting an 8-bit number to a 16-bit number. While this is done occasionally as an explicit operation specified by a programmer, it is more commonly performed as part of operations such as addition and multiplication.

Sign extension can be illustrated in the case of moving from a 4-bit to an 8-bit two's complement binary number. First, write the 4-bit two's complement number `1010` in 8-bit two's complement.

If we are considering signed numbers, we know that the 4-bit number involves bit weightings of $[-8, 4, 2, 1]$ while the 8-bit weightings are $[-128, 64, 32, 16, 8, 4, 2, 1]$. For the 4-bit number, the value `1010` is clearly

$$-8 + 2 = -6$$

If we were to simply write the 8-bit value as a 4-bit number padded with zeros as in `00001010`, then, referring to the 8-bit weightings, the value that this represents would be

$$8 + 2 = 10$$

This is clearly incorrect. If we were then to note that a negative number requires the sign bit set and responded by simply toggling the sign bit to give `10001010` then the value would become

$$-128 + 8 + 2 = -118$$

This is again incorrect. In fact, in order to achieve the extension from 4 to 8 bits correctly, it is necessary that not only the original MSB must be set correctly, but every additional bit that we have added (every bit to the left of the original MSB) must also be set to the same value as the original MSB. The sign bit has thus been extended to give **`1111`**`1010` with a value of

$$-128 + 64 + 32 + 16 + 8 + 2 = -6$$

Finally, a correct result is achieved. Another example of sign extension is given in Box 2.10.

There is evidently no difficulty with positive two's complement numbers, but the sign extension rule can still be applied (it has no effect, but makes a hardware design easier if it applies to *all* numbers rather than just *some*).

Box 2.10

Sign extension worked example

Q: Write the value -4 in 4-bit two's complement notation. Copy the most significant bit (MSB) four times to the left. Read off the result as an 8-bit two's complement number.

A: `1100` $(-8 + 4 + 0 + 0)$

MSB is 1, so copying this to the left four times gives **`1111`**`1100`.

Reading off in 8-bit signed binary, $(-128 + 64 + 32 + 16 + 8 + 4) = -4$.

For further thought: Repeat the exercise with a positive number such as 3. Does the method still apply equally for positive numbers?

2.4 Arithmetic

This section considers the hardware capable of performing the addition or subtraction of two binary numbers. This functionality is used within the arithmetic logic unit (ALU) in almost all processors, which also handles basic logic functions such as AND, OR, NOT and so on. The ALU is described as a CPU functional unit later in Section 4.2.

2.4.1 Addition

Binary arithmetic is accomplished bitwise with a possible carry from the adjacent less significant bit calculation. In hardware, a *full adder* calculates the addition of two bits and a carry in and generates a result with an additional carry output.

A full adder is shown symbolically in Figure 2.3, where each arrow represents a single logic bit. A half adder is similar, but does not have any provision for the carry in.

2.4.2 The Parallel Carry-Propagate Adder

To create an 8-bit parallel adder, the full adder hardware would typically be repeated eight times for each of the input bits although the least significant bit position could use the slightly simpler half adder, as shown in Figure 2.4.

In Figure 2.4, x[7:0] and y[7:0] are the two input bytes and z[7:0] is the output byte. Cout is the final carry output. For the case of adding unsigned numbers, when Cout is set it indicates that the calculation has resulted in a number that is too large to be represented in 8 bits. For example, we know that the largest magnitude unsigned number that can be represented in 8 bits is $2^8 - 1 = 255$. If two large numbers such as 200 and 100 are added together, the result (300) cannot fit into 8 bits. In this case, the carry would be set on the adder and the result (z) would hold the remainder $300 - 256 = 44$.

The topmost Cout therefore doubles as an overflow indicator when adding unsigned numbers: if it is set following a calculation, this indicates that the result cannot be represented using the number of bits present in the adder. Some further thoughts on this are explored in Box 2.11.

Figure 2.3 A full adder, showing two bits being added, together with a carry in, and the output of a single bit with carry.

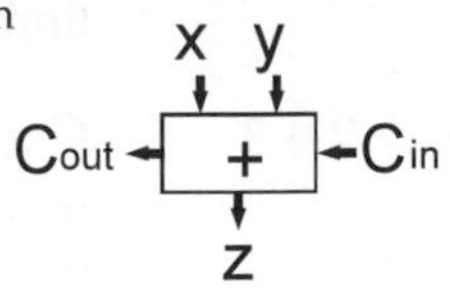

Figure 2.4

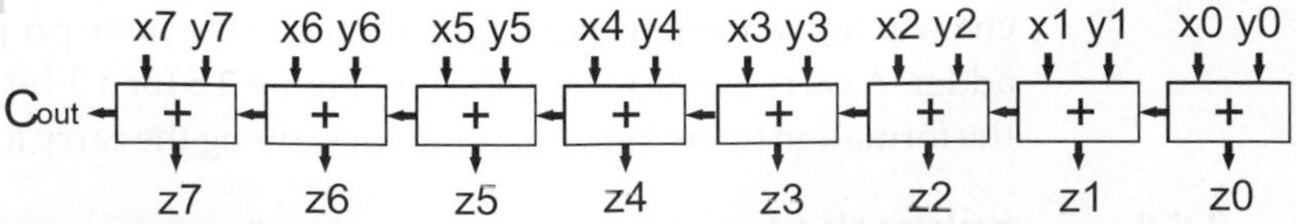

The carry-propagate or ripple-carry adder constructed from a sequence of full adders plus one half adder.

Arithmetic

Box 2.11

Exercise for the reader

How does the topmost Cout signal from an adder behave when adding signed two's complement numbers?

1. Try working by hand using a 4-bit adder. With 4-bit two's complement numbers the representable range is -8 to $+7$.
2. Try adding some values such as $2+8=?, 2+(-8)=?, 7+7=?$ and $(-8)+(-8)=?$
3. What do you conclude about the Cout signal: does it mean the same for signed two's complement numbers as it does when adding unsigned numbers?

This behaviour and the add mechanism is common to almost any binary adder. Although the parallel adder appears to be a relatively efficient structure and even works in a similar way to a human calculating binary addition by hand (or perhaps using an abacus), it suffers from a major speed limitation that bars its use in most microprocessor ALUs: carry propagation.

Given that the input numbers are presented to the adder simultaneously, one measure of the adder speed is the length of time required to calculate the output. Each full or half adder in the chain is relatively quick: both the carry out and the result will be available a few nanoseconds after the carry in and input bits are presented (for modern hardware). The problem is that the least significant half adder (adder 0) must finish calculating before the next bit calculation (adder 1) can start. This is because adder 1 needs to get the carry from adder 0 before it can complete its calculation, and that carry is not valid until adder 0 finishes. Adder 1 then supplies its carry to adder 2 and so on. Further up the chain, adder 6 will only supply its carry to adder 7 a significant length of time after the input words were first presented to the adder.

A worked example of calculating an entire ripple-carry adder propagation delay is presented in Box 2.12. It is important because, if such an adder were present in a synchronous machine, this propagation delay may well be the part of the system that limits the maximum system clock speed.

2.4.3 Carry Look-Ahead

In order to speed up the parallel adder described above, a method is required to supply the carry inputs to adders as early as possible.

This is achieved with a carry predictor, which is a piece of combinational logic that calculates the carry values directly. In fact, it can supply carry values to each adder in the chain at the same time, with approximately the same propagation delay as a single half adder. A carry predictor is shown in Figure 2.5 for a 3-bit adder. It is interesting to note the formation of the logic equations describing the carry look-ahead units (see Box 2.13).

2.4.4 Subtraction

Similar to addition, subtraction is performed bitwise. But when performing subtraction, do we need to consider the result from neighbouring bits? The answer is yes, but these

Box 2.12

Worked example

Q: The adders and half adders used in a 4-bit parallel carry-propagate adder are specified as follows:

Time from last input bit (x or y) or carry in to result z: 15 ns
Time from last input bit (x or y) or carry in to carry out: 12 ns
If input words x[3:0] and y[3:0] are presented and stable at time 0, how long will it be before the 4-bit output of the adder is guaranteed stable and correct?

A: Starting from the least significant end of the chain, adder 0 receives stable inputs at time 0. Its result z is then ready at 15 ns and its carry is ready at 12 ns. Adder 1 requires this carry in order to begin its own calculation, so this only starts at 12 ns. It takes until 24 ns before it can provide a correct carry result to adder 2 and this will not provide a carry to adder 3 until 36 ns. Adder 3 then begins its calculation. Its output z is then ready at 51 ns and its carry out is ready at 48 ns. So even though the adders themselves are fairly quick, when chained, they require 51 ns to calculate the result.

Note: The phrase 'begins its calculation' when applied to the full or half adders may be misleading. They are actually combinational logic blocks. A change of state at the input will take some time (up to 15 ns in this case) to propagate through to the output. Since they are combinational logic, they are always 'processing' input data and their outputs are always active. However, from the specification, we know that the outputs are only guaranteed correct 15 ns or 12 ns after the inputs are correctly presented (for result z and carry out respectively).

are now linked through 'borrows' from higher bits, rather than 'carries' from lower bits. This is problematic in the same way as addition.

In terms of computational hardware, a specialised subtracter would be required if it were not for the fact that addition and subtraction can be interchanged in many

Figure 2.5

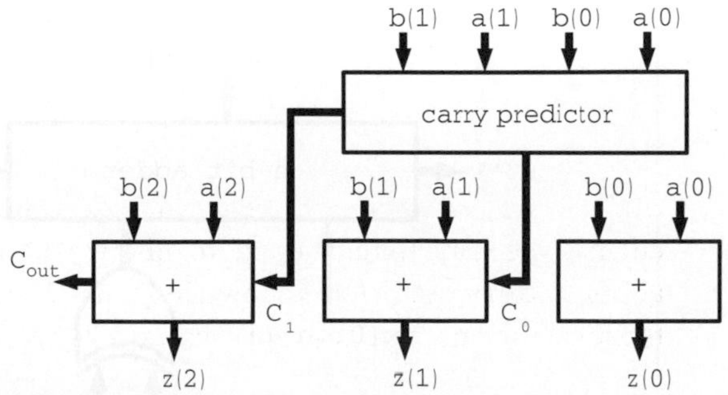

The carry look-ahead adder constructed from several full adders and carry predict logic.

Box 2.13

Exercise for the reader

1. Write the logic equation of a single-bit full adder.
2. Extend this to a 3-bit adder as shown above.
3. Re-arrange the equations to give C_0 and C_1 in terms of the input (rather than any carry ins). Note that the number of basic calculations required to give C_1 is small, and thus the propagation delay through gates required to do this calculation is also small.
4. Now extend the equations to derive C_2. How many calculation steps are needed for this? Is it more than for C_1? Can you deduce anything about the scaling of this method to longer adder chains (thinking in terms of propagation delay and also logic complexity)?

number formats. As an example, consider the decimal calculation $99 - 23 = 76$ which can be written in an alternative arrangement as $99 + (-23)$ giving an identical result.

Although the result is identical, it is achieved by performing an addition rather than a subtraction, and changing the sign of the second operand. Many commercial ALUs work in a similar fashion: they contain only adding circuitry and a mechanism to change the sign of one operand. As we have seen in Section 2.3.4, changing the sign of a two's complement number is relatively easy: first, change the sign of every bit and then add 1 to the least significant bit position. Adding 1 to the LSB is the same as setting the carry input for that adder to 1.

Needless to say, this is easily achieved in hardware with a circuit such as the subtraction logic shown in Figure 2.6. In this circuit, the exclusive-OR gate acting on input operand y is used to change the sign of each bit (an exclusive-OR acts as a switched inverter in that if one input is held high, every bit present on the other input will be inverted, otherwise it will be unchanged). If the circuit is performing a subtraction, the add/subtract line is held high, one operand is negated and C_{in} is also set high – this has the effect of adding 1 to the least significant bit.

Figure 2.6

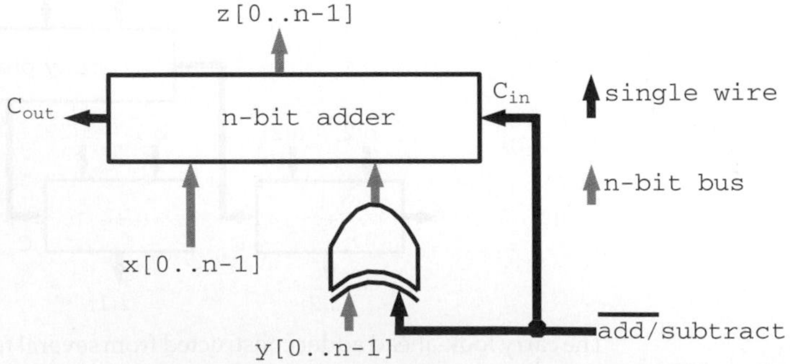

Subtraction logic consisting basically of an adder with external exclusive-OR gates.

There is one further area of subtraction that needs to be explored, and that is overflow: when performing an addition, you will recall that the topmost *Cout* can be used to indicate an overflow condition. This is no longer true when performing subtractions as some examples on 4-bit two's complement numbers will reveal:

```
0010 + 1110 = ?
0010 + 1110 = 0000 + Cout
```

$2 + (-2) = ?$

Clearly, the result should be an easily-represented zero, and yet the *Cout* signal is set. Consider another example where we would normally expect an overflow:

```
0111 + 0110 = ?
0111 + 0110 = 1101          Answer = -3 ?
```

$7 + 6 = ?$

Again, the result should not be −3, it should be 13. Evidently, the circuitry shown is not sufficient alone, and some account needs to be taken of the values being processed. The answer is that the sign bits must be examined prior to adding, and the result checked based on this. This is not computationally hard – a simple look-up table will suffice:

$$\begin{aligned} &\textit{positive} + \textit{positive} = \textit{positive}\\ &\textit{positive} + \textit{negative} = \textit{unknown}\\ &\textit{negative} + \textit{positive} = \textit{unknown}\\ &\textit{negative} + \textit{negative} = \textit{negative} \end{aligned}$$

For the mixed calculation (one positive and one negative number), the sign of the answer is unknown, but is not problematic since by definition it can never result in an overflow (think of it this way: the negative number will reduce the size of the positive number, but the most it can do would be if the positive number is zero, in which case the answer is the same as the negative input, and the inputs themselves do not include carry flags).

For the case of two positive numbers being added, the result sign bit should be 0. If it is not, then an overflow has occurred. For the case of two negative numbers, the result sign bit should be 1, and if it is not an overflow has occurred. It can be seen therefore that the value of *Cout* alone is not enough to indicate that an overflow has occurred. In most processors, a separate overflow flag is provided, set through consideration of the sign bits as we have seen. Consider the worked example in Box 2.14.

Box 2.14

Exercise for the reader

Try extending the argument in the text to a subtraction. Using 4-bit two's complement signed number format, perform a few additions, then a few subtractions. Verify that all of the subtractions $a - b$ can be performed in binary as $a + (-b)$. Verify that the *Cout* signal does not indicate an overflow condition.

Perform the additions $-5 + -5$ and $-5 + -1$ and look at the sign bit and carry bits of the result. Can you conclude that the *Cout* signal is useless, or can it be used to increase the bit range of the result?

2.5 Multiplication

In the early days of microprocessors, multiplication was too complex to be performed in logic within the CPU and hence required an external unit. Even when it was finally squeezed onto the same piece of silicon, it was a tight fit: the multiply hardware in early ARM processors occupied more silicon area than the entire ARM CPU core.

In more recent times, however, manufacturers have tuned multipliers to the target application. For fast real-time embedded processors (perhaps an ARM7 in a GSM cell-phone handling speech coding), there is a need to perform multiplications as quickly as possible and hence a fast multiplier will be used. This will evidently occupy a large silicon area compared to a slower multi-cycle multiplier used on a non real-time processor (such as the ARM610 which was designed to power desktop computers in the early 1990s, and to be the brains of the Apple Newton – the world's first PDA).

There are many methods of performing the multiplication $m \times n$ at various rates (and with various complexities). Some of the more typical methods are listed here:

1. Repeated addition (add m to itself n times).
2. Add shifted partial products.
3. Split n into a sequence of adds and left shifts applied to m.
4. Booth and Robertson's methods.

Each of these will be considered in the following subsections in turn. There are, of course, other more esoteric methods as this is an active research area. Interestingly, some methods may perform estimation rather than calculation, or involve loss of precision in the result. These would include converting operands to the logarithmic domain and then adding them, or using an alternative or redundant number format.

Alternative number formats are briefly described in Section 9.5, but when it comes to hardware for performing binary calculations, there are so many alternatives that it will be impossible to describe them all.

2.5.1 Repeated Addition

The simplest method of performing a multiplication is one of the smallest in implementation complexity and silicon area but at the cost of being slow. When multiplying integers $m \times n$ the pseudo-code looks like:

set register A $\leftarrow m$
set register B $\leftarrow 0$
loop while (A $\leftarrow$ A $-$ 1) ≥ 0
  B $\leftarrow$ B $+ n$

Since this involves a loop that repeats n times then the execution time is dependent on the value of n. However, if n is small, the result, B, is formed early.

If we consider that a 32-bit number can represent an integer with value in excess of two billion, we realise that many iterations of the loop might be necessary: it could imply a rather long execution time.

2.5.2 Partial Products

Instead of iterating based on the magnitude of n (as in the repeated addition method above), the partial products method iterates based on the number of bits in number n.

Each bit in the number n is examined in turn, from least to most significant. If a bit is set, then a partial product derived from number m shifted left to line up with the bit being examined, is accumulated. In multiplier terminology, the two numbers are termed *multiplier* and *multiplicand* although we also know for decimal numbers that it does not matter which way the multiplication is performed since $(m \times n) = (n \times m)$.

Here is a partial products example:

1001	multiplicand 9
1011	multiplier 11
1001	(since multiplier bit 0 = 1, write 9 shifted left by 0 bit)
1001	(since multiplier bit 1 = 1, write 9 shifted left by 1 bit)
0000	(since multiplier bit 2 = 0, write 0 shifted left by 2 bits)
1001	(since multiplier bit 3 = 1, write 9 shifted left by 3 bits)
01100011	result = 99 (sum of the partial products)

The situation is complicated slightly when it comes to working with two's complement signed numbers, firstly in that the most significant bit of the multiplier represents sign, and secondly in that sign extension must be used (see Section 2.3.4).

For the signed case, all partial products have to be sign extended to the length of the result (which by default would be the sum of the lengths of the input representations minus 1 to account for the sign bit, such that a 6-bit signed number plus a 7-bit signed number would require 12 bits to represent the result).

Since each partial product corresponds to one bit of the multiplier and is shifted to account for the multiplier bit weighting, the partial product corresponding to the MSB is a special case: the bit weighting is negative and this partial product must therefore be subtracted from the accumulator rather than added. This is shown in the flowchart of Figure 2.7, where it is assumed that the grey-coloured two's complement accumulate blocks are able to take account of sign extension.

To understand the process better, it is useful to attempt some simple binary multiplication by hand using those methods; the reader can follow some examples in Box 2.15.

In reality, the accumulation of partial products may be more efficiently performed in the reverse direction (i.e. looping down rather than looping up). In the best case this would also remove the need to treat the partial product of the multiplier sign bit differently (since this is not accumulated, it is merely the value in the accumulator before additions begin, thus allowing its sign to be negated during the load-in process).

Figure 2.8 illustrates a block diagram of an alternative partial product multiplication method for unsigned numbers only (although extending this method to two's complement is a relatively simple task). The figure shows the sequence of operations to be taken once the set-up (operand loading) is complete.

The set-up phase resets the accumulator Q to zero and loads both multiplier and multiplicand into the correct locations. In step 1 the least significant bit of the multiplier is tested. If this is a 1 (step 2) then the multiplicand is added to the accumulator (step 3).

Figure 2.7

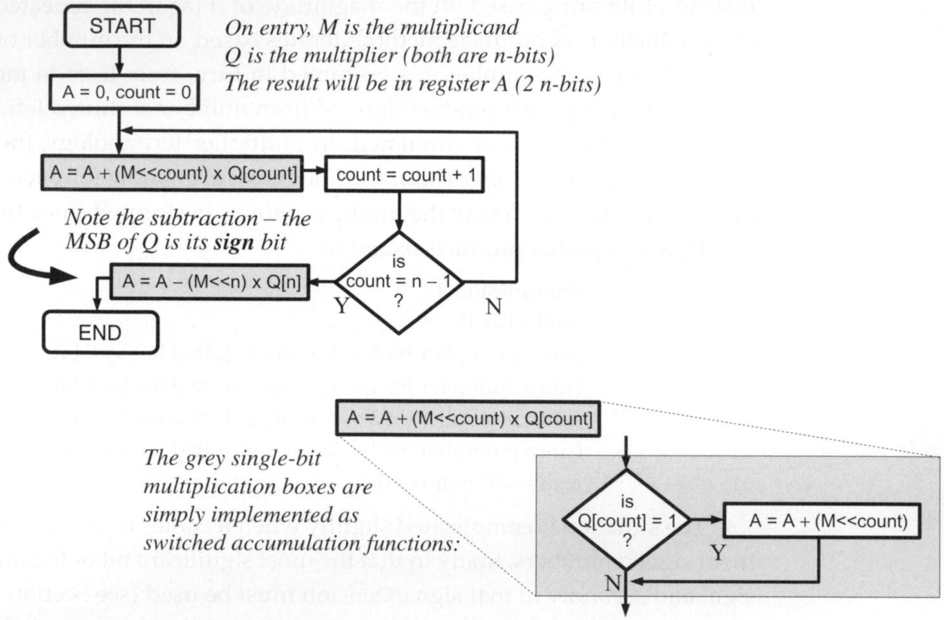

A flowchart showing the steps for performing partial product multiplication.

Step 4 occurs regardless of the two previous conditional steps, and shifts the entire accumulator one bit to the right. The system loops n times (using control logic which is not shown) before terminating with the answer in the long register.

Consider the differences between this and the original flowchart of Figure 2.7 in terms of the number of registers needed, bus wires, connections, switches, adder size and control logic involved.

Figure 2.8

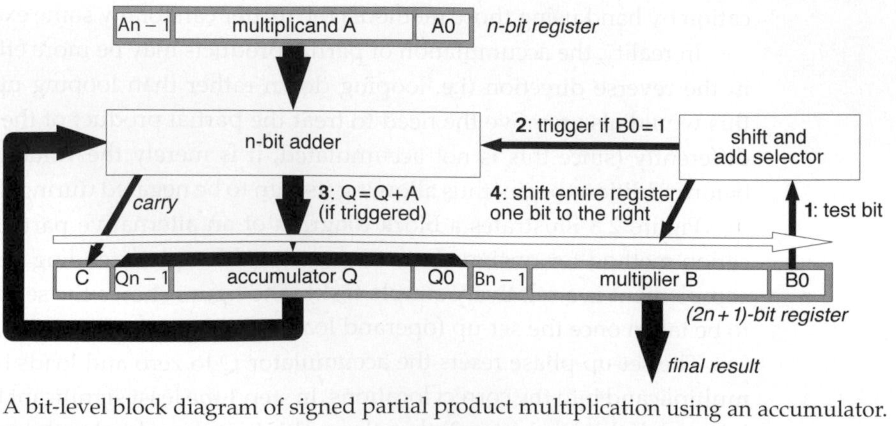

A bit-level block diagram of signed partial product multiplication using an accumulator.

Box 2.15

Worked examples of two's complement multiplication

Look at -5×4 (signed):

1011	multiplicand −5
0100	multiplier 4
00000000	(since multiplier bit 0 = 0, write 0 shifted left by 0 bit & sign extend)
+0000000	(since multiplier bit 1 = 1, write 0 shifted left by 1 bit & sign extend)
+111011	(since multiplier bit 2 = 0, write −5 shifted left by 1 bit & sign extend)
+00000	(since multiplier bit 3 = 0, write 0 shifted left by 1 bit & sign extend)
=11101100	result = $-128 + 64 + 32 + 8 + 4 = -20$

Similarly, let us look at 4×-5 (signed):

0100	multiplicand 4
1011	multiplier −5
00000100	(since multiplier bit 0 = 1, write 4 shifted left by 0 bit & sign extend)
+0000100	(since multiplier bit 1 = 1, write 4 shifted left by 1 bit & sign extend)
+000000	(since multiplier bit 2 = 0, write 0 shifted left by 2 bits & sign extend)
+00100	(since multiplier bit 3 = 1, write 0 shifted left by 3 bits & sign extend)
=11101100	result = $-128 + 64 + 32 + 8 + 4 = -20$

But the last term needs to be subtracted. What we will do is change the sign by flipping all the bits and adding 1(00100000 → flip → 11011111 → +1 → 11100000). We then simply add the sum to the other partial products. This gives:

00000100	
+0000100	
+000000	
+11100	
=11101100	result = −20

As we can see the result is the same. We have illustrated the cases of needing sign extension and of handling a negative multiplier causing the final partial product to be subtracted instead of added.

Interestingly, this method of multiplication, including the right shift method (which divides a number by two), was reportedly used by Russian peasants for hundreds of years, allowing them to perform quite complex decimal multiplies with ease. The algorithm starts with the two numbers to be multiplied, A and B, written at the head of two columns respectively. We will give as an example, 31 multiplied by 17:

$$B = 17 \quad A = 31$$

Working downwards, divide the B column by two each line, discarding the fractional part until 1 is reached. Fill the A column similarly, but double the number on each successive line:

$B = 17$	$A = 31$
8	62
4	124
2	248
1	496

Next, simply add up all of the numbers in the A column that correspond to *odd* numbers in the B column. In this example, only 17 and 1 are odd in the B column, therefore the final answer will be $31 + 496 = 527$, which is of course correct.

Note that the alternatives given in this section are by no means the only partial product hardware designs available, and far from being the only multiplication methods available (even among Russian peasants).

2.5.3 Shift-Add Method

The shift-add method relies on the fact that, for binary numbers, a shift left by one bit is equivalent to multiplying by two. A shift left by two bits is equivalent to multiplying by four and so on.

Using this property to perform a multiply operation will not avert the issue encountered when applying the repeated addition method in that the number of operations depends on the *value* of the multiplier rather than the number of bits in the multiplier word. For this reason, this method is not normally found as a general multiplier in commercial processors. However, it can be very efficient where the multiplier is fixed and close to a power of two. For this reason, it is often used in digital filters (devices that perform a sequence of multiplications) with predetermined multiplier values.

This method is also easy to implement as a fixed filter in FPGA[2]-based designs since in this case moving from one adder to the next is simply wiring up two logic elements (logic cells), and a right shift can be accomplished simply by wiring output bits 0, 1, 2 . . . of one cell to input bits 1, 2, 3 . . . on the next.

2.5.4 Booth and Robertson's Methods

Booth's method, is similar to partial products in that the multiplier bits are scanned from right to left and a shifted version of the multiplicand added or subtracted depending on the value of the multiplier bits. The difference is that the multiplier bits are examined in pairs rather than singly. An extension of this method examines 4 bits in parallel, and in Robertson's method, an entire byte in parallel.

The advantage of these methods is that they are extremely fast. However, the logic required becomes complex as the number of bits considered in parallel increases.

The trick in Booth's method is to define a rule by which the multiplicand is subtracted or added depending on the values of each pair of bits in the multiplier. If two consecutive bits from the multiplier are designated as X_i and X_{i-1}, when the multiplier is scanned from $i = 0$, then the action taken upon detecting each possible combination of two bits is as shown in Table 2.1.

[2] FPGA: field programmable gate array: a flexible, programmable logic device.

Table 2.1

Predefined rules for bit-pair scanning in Booth's method.

X_i	X_{i-1}	rule
0	0	no action
0	1	add shifted multiplicand
1	0	subtract shifted multiplicand
1	1	no action

When a multiplicand is added or subtracted to/from an accumulator, it is first shifted left by i bit positions, just as it is done in partial products. This process can be examined in detail by following the examples in Boxes 2.16 and 2.17.

Box 2.16

Exercise for the reader

Consider 9 × 10 (unsigned):

```
    1001   multiplicand 9
    1010   multiplier 10
    ----
    0000   (i = 0, no action since bit pair = 0 and a hidden zero)
   -1001   (i = 1, subtract multiplicand since bit pair = 10)
  +1001    (i = 2, add multiplicand << 2 since bit pair = 01)
 -1001     (i = 3, subtract multiplicand << 3 since bit pair = 10)
+1001      (i = 4, add multiplicand << 2 since bit pair = 01)
           (i = 5 and onwards, no action since all bit pairs = 00)
----
```

The result is therefore obtained as the summation of the following:

```
 10010000
-1001000
 +100100
  -10010
```

Or by converting the subtractions into additions (see Section 2.4.4):

```
 10010000
+10111000
  +100100
+11101110
=01011010
```

Result:

1011010 = 64 + 16 + 8 + 2 = 90 (correct)

Multiplication

Box 2.17

Booth's method worked example

Consider -9×11 (signed):

```
 11110111   multiplicand -9
 00001011   multiplier 11
-11110111   (i=0, subtract multiplicand since bit pair=10)
 0000000    (i=1, no action since bit pair=11)
+110111     (i=2, add multiplicand << 2 since bit pair = 01)
-10111      (i=3, subtract multiplicand << 3 since bit pair=10)
+0111       (i=4, add multiplicand << 2 since bit pair=01)
 000        (i=5 and onwards, no action since all bit pairs=00)
```

The result is therefore obtained as the summation of the following:

```
-11110111
+11011100
-10111000
+01110000
```

Or by converting the subtractions into additions (see Section 2.4.4):

```
 00001001
+11011100
+01001000
+01110000
=10011101    + Carry
```

Result:

10011101 $= -128 + 16 + 8 + 4 + 1 = -99$ (correct)

It is important to note that when $i = 0$, the bits considered are the least significant bit of the multiplier and a hidden zero. Thus, when the least significant bit of the multiplier is a '1', the multiplicand must be subtracted (i.e. treated as a '10' instead). This can be seen in the second worked example (Box 2.17).

There are two points worth mentioning here. First, when dealing with two's complement signed operands, the partial products must be sign extended in the same way as the full partial product multiplier.

Second, when scanning from right to left, the hidden bit at the right-hand side means that the first pair of non-equal bits that is encountered will always be a '10', indicating a subtraction. This regularity may be useful when designing a hardware implementation.

Even for someone who has been doing binary arithmetic for many years, the preparation of this book highlighted how easy it can be to make very trivial binary addition mistakes. If you are required to do this as part of an examination, always double-check your binary arithmetic. Getting it right the first time is not as simple as it may seem.

As mentioned previously, Booth extended his method into examination of 4 bits at a time, using a look-up-table type approach, and Robertson took this one step further by building an 8-bit look-up table. These methods are in fact common in various modern processors, although they require considerable resources in silicon.

2.6 Division

For many years, commodity CPUs and even DSPs did not implement hardware division due to the complexity of silicon required to implement it. Analog Devices DSPs and several others did include a DIV instruction, but this was generally only a hardware assistance for the very basic primary-school method of repeated subtraction.

2.6.1 Repeated Subtraction

Since division is the process of deciding how many times a divisor M 'goes' into a dividend Q (where the answer is the quotient Q/M), then it is possible to simply count how many times M can be subtracted from Q until the remainder is less than M.

For example, in performing 13/4, we could illustrate this loop:

iteration i = 1, remainder r = 13 − 4 = 9;
iteration i = 2, remainder r = 9 − 4 = 5;
iteration i = 3, remainder r = 5 − 4 = 1;
Remainder 1 is less than divisor 4 so the answer is 3 with remainder 1.

When working in binary the process is identical and perhaps best performed as long division as in the worked example in Box 2.18.

So now the question is, how to handle signed integer division? Answer: The most efficient method is probably to note the signs of both operands, convert both to unsigned integers, perform the division and then apply the correct sign afterwards. Division uses the same sign rules as multiplication in that the answer is only negative if the signs of the operands differ.

The division process for one popular microprocessor can be seen in the flowchart of Figure 2.9. A close examination of this may prompt some questions such as: 'Why shift *both* A and Q left at each iteration?' and 'Why perform an addition of Q = Q + M inside the loop?' These questions may be answered by considering how the operations are performed using registers within a CPU. This will be left as a pencil-and-paper exercise for the reader to follow the operation of the algorithm for one example division, perhaps of two 6-bit numbers: this exercise will help to clarify how this system works.

Just note that at the completion of the algorithm, register A holds the answer, with any remainder being in register Q. The algorithm will have iterated for n cycles where n is the number of bits in the input words. As always, it is entirely possible to derive other flowcharts that work differently, for example, some will even iterate and scan through the bits in the opposite direction.

Box 2.18

Long division worked example

Consider 23 ÷ 5 (unsigned).
First, write the values in the long division format:

```
        101 | 010111

    divisor   dividend
```

Then, starting from the most significant end (left) and working towards the least significant end (right), scan each bit position in the dividend to see if the divisor can be 'found' in the dividend. In each case if it is not found, write a '0' in the corresponding position above the dividend, and look at the next bit. After three iterations, we would have:

```
              000    (quotient)
        101 | 010111
```

But now, at the current bit position in the dividend, `101` can be found. We thus write `101` below the dividend and a '1' above the dividend at the correct bit position. Then subtract the divisor (at that bit position) from the dividend to form a new dividend:

```
              0001
        101 | 010111
          –    101
              000011
```

Next, we continue working from left to right but this time looking at the new dividend for the divisor. In this case it is not found; after scanning all bit positions we are left with:

```
              000100
        101 | 010111
          –    101
              000011
```

The answer is seen above: the quotient is `000100` with a remainder of `000011`. Since we were dividing 23 by 5, we expect an answer of 4 (correct) and a remainder of 3 (also correct).

Figure 2.9 A flowchart of a division algorithm.

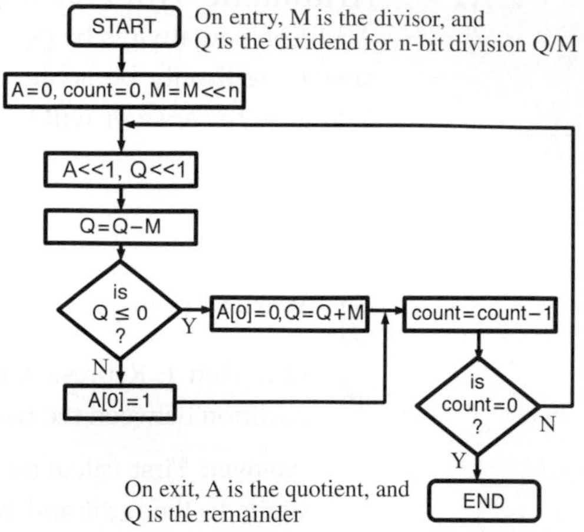

2.7 Working with Fractional Number Formats

Section 2.3.7 introduced the representation of fractional numbers using Q-format notation. Although there are many reasons for requiring fractional notation, one major reason is in digital signal processing, where a long digital filter may require hundreds or thousands of multiply-accumulate operations before a result is determined.

Imagine if some of the filter 'weights' (the fixed values in the filter that the input numbers are multiplied by) are very small. In this case, after multiplying by these small values many times, the result could be tiny, rounded down to zero by the number format used. On the other hand, if some filter weights are large, the result of many multiplications could be huge, resulting in an overflow. Understandably, this makes designing such filters a very sensitive balancing act.

Fortunately, there is a reasonable and efficient solution: ensure that the operands used are in fractional format, and are less than, but as close to, 1.0 as possible. The rationale being that anything multiplied by a number that is less than or equal to 1.0 cannot be greater than itself. We are thus assured that the result of multiplying two of these numbers will never result in an overflow. Similarly, anything multiplied by a value slightly less than 1.0 does not become significantly smaller, hence results are less likely to quickly round down to zero.

This is possible numerically because we are only multiplying and adding in a filter and these are linear processes: $(a \times b + c)$ has the same result as $(10a \times b + 10c)/10$.

Remember again that the actual fractional format used is not relevant to the hardware used to perform the calculations. It is only an abstraction that the software engineer must keep in mind. This will be illustrated with various examples as we progress through this chapter.

2.7.1 Arithmetic with Fractional Numbers

Addition can always be performed on two fractional format numbers, but the correct answer will only be achieved when the formats of each operand are identical. The format of the answer will be that of the operands:

$$(m.n) + (m.n) = (m.n)$$
$$(m.n) - (m.n) = (m.n)$$

Box 2.19

Worked examples of fractional representation

Question 1: Represent 1.75 and 1.25 in (2.2) format fractional notation, perform an addition between the two and determine the result.

Answer: First calculate the bit weightings for (2.2) format notation: we need two digits to the right and two digits to the left of the radix point. Digits to the left are integer weighting, are powers of 2 and start with 1. Digits to the right are fractional, are 1 over powers of 2 and start with 1/2:

2^1	2^0	2^{-1}	2^{-2}

We can decompose 1.75 into $1+0.5+0.25$ and 1.25 into $1+0.25$ and write them in (2.2) binary format as `0111` and `0101`.

The binary addition of these operands results in `1100`. Is this correct? `1100` in (2.2) format equals $2+1=3$. Of course $1.75+1.25=3$ so yes, the answer is correct.

Next, we will illustrate what happens when something goes wrong.

Question 2: Represent 1.75 in (2.2) format fractional notation, represent 0.625 in (1.3) format fractional notation, perform an addition between the two and determine the result.

Answer: 1.75 was represented in question 1 and is `0111`.
(1.3) format fractional notation has weightings 1, 0.5, 0.25, 0.125 and thus if we decompose 0.625 into $0.5+0.125$ we get a binary pattern `0101`.

Next, we perform the addition `0111 + 0101` which gives the answer `1100`.

However, we do not know the fractional format of the result. Let us speculate whether this is (2.2) or (1.3) format by working out the decimal value in each case.

In (2.2) format the result is $2+1=3$ and in (1.3) the result is $1+0.5=1.5$. However, the answer should be $1.75+0.625=2.375$. Clearly, this does not match either of the potential answers.

What we should have done was change one of them so they were both in the same format before we performed the addition.

Note: Did you see that the binary patterns of both examples are identical? It is only our interpretation of those bit-patterns that changed between examples. Using different interpretations in this way can cause the same bit-pattern to have multiple meanings – but the hardware used to perform the calculation does not need to change.

The arithmetic of such fractional format numbers is illustrated with two examples in Box 2.19.

2.7.2 Multiplication and Division of Fractional Numbers

In the case of multiplication, there is more flexibility in that the operands can have different fractional formats, and the fractional format of the answer is derived from those of the operands:

$$(m.n) \times (p.q) = (m + p) \times (n + q)$$

It is evident that the number of bits in the answer of the multiplication will be the sum of the number of bits in the two operands, and this is expected from what we already know of multiplier hardware from Section 2.5.

Division is rather more complex. In fact, the best way to perform division is first to remove the radix points of both numbers by shifting both radix positions, in step, digit by digit to the right until they are below the least significant digit of the largest operand, extending the smaller operand where appropriate. The division then occurs in standard binary fashion.

The worked example in Box 2.20 illustrates how fractional division is done.

Box 2.20

Worked example of fractional division

Consider `11.000` ÷ `01.00` (unsigned).

This has the trivial meaning of 3 ÷ 1. The first step in performing this operation is to shift the radix point in step to the right by one position:

`110.00 ÷ 010.0`

This is insufficient since the numbers still contain the radix so we repeat one step:

`1100.0 ÷ 0100.`

This is still insufficient so we perform the step again, extending the `0100` as a side-effect of removing radix from `1100.0` as follows:

`11000. ÷ 01000.`

The division then occurs as a standard binary division:

```
01000 | 11000
```

Continuing the long-hand binary division:

```
          00011
01000 |   11000
      −   1000
          -----
          01000
      −   01000
          -----
          00000
```

The answer is `11`, which as decimal value 3, is correct.

Looking at the worked example, it is clear that the actual division is no more complex than standard binary arithmetic; however, consideration of the radix position may be problematic. In fact, it requires some careful coding on the part of the programmer.

2.8 Floating Point

Floating point numbers are similar to fractional format binary but they have additional flexibility in that the position of the radix point is variable (and is stored as part of the number itself). It is this flexibility that allows floating point numbers to encode an enormous range of values with relatively few bits.

2.8.1 Generalised Floating Point

A floating point number is one which has a mantissa S (or fractional part) and an exponent E (or power). There is probably also a sign (σ) such that the value of the number represented in base B is given as:

$$n = \sigma \times S \times B^E$$

Or more correctly considering the sign to be binary, with 1 indicating negative and 0 indicating positive, such that:

$$n = (-1)^\sigma \times S \times B^E$$

An example in base 10 would be 2.3×10^6 which we know is just a shorthand method of writing 2,300,000. In fact, this illustrates one of the main benefits of floating point: floating point numbers generally require less writing (and in binary require fewer digits) than the decimal (or binary) values they represent.

In binary the difference is that $B = 2$ rather than 10 and thus the example will typically be something like `01001111` $\times 2^6$ which, if the mantissa (`01001111`) is unsigned, becomes:

$$\texttt{01001111} \times 2^6 = 79_{10} \times 64_{10} = 5056_{10} = \texttt{1001111000000}$$

where the subscript 10 indicates a decimal value.

Of course, the final value is the same as the mantissa, but shifted by the exponent (in the same way that we added five-zeros to the base 10 example above).

Normally, all the bits that constitute a floating point number (σ, S and E) are stored in the same location such that they total a convenient number of bits such as 16, 32, 64 or 128. Some bit-level manipulation is therefore required when processing them to separate out the three different parts from the full stored number.

2.8.2 IEEE754 Floating Point

Although there are many possible floating point formats and various implemented examples scattered through computing history, IEEE standard 754 which emerged in the 1970s, has become by far the most popular, adopted by all major CPU manufacturers. It is generally considered in the trade that IEEE754 is a well thought-out and efficient floating point format, and as a consequence is highly regarded.

It is not the intention of this text to describe the entire IEEE754 standard, but we will cover some of its more common features. We will consider single and double precision formats which fit into 32-bit and 64-bit storage locations respectively. In the C programming language these would normally correspond to *float* and *double* data types:

Name	**Bits**	**Sign, σ**	**Exponent, E**	**Mantissa, S**
Single precision	32	1	8	23
Double precision	64	1	11	52

In addition, further bits can be added to the representation during intermediate calculation stages (in a hardware floating point unit) to ensure overall accuracy is maintained, as will be described later in Section 2.9.3.

Despite all 32 bits or 64 bits being used for sign, mantissa and exponent, the IEEE754 format manages to cleverly signify four alternative states using unique bit-patterns that do not occur for normal numbers. These are shown in the following table, beginning with the default state called 'normalised':

Name	σ	E	S
Normalised	1 or 0	not all zero or all one	any
Zero	1 or 0	all zero	all zero
Infinity	1 or 0	all one	all zero
Not a Number (NaN)	1 or 0	all one	non-zero
Denormalised	1 or 0	all zero	non-zero

When an IEEE754 number is written, we typically write the bits from left to right in the order (σ, E, S) as shown below:

σ	E	S

where the box represents a 32-bit or 64-bit binary number that we know, or are told, contains an IEEE754 format value. All examples given in this book will only use the 32-bit single-precision format to save paper.

2.8.3 IEEE754 Modes

In the discussion that follows, we will use **S** to represent the mantissa bit-pattern in unsigned fractional (0.23) or (0.52) format, **E** to represent the exponent bit-pattern in unsigned two's complement format and σ to represent the sign. Note that they have different meanings in the five IEEE754 modes.

In this way, an IEEE754 number written in a box such as this:

0	10110010	11100000000000000000000

would be said to have $\sigma = 0$ and therefore positive sign,

$$E = 128 + 32 + 16 + 2 = 178 \text{ and}$$

$$S = 0.5 + 0.25 + 0.125 = 0.875$$

We will maintain this naming convention for E and S throughout. So henceforth the words 'mantissa' and 'exponent' are used to indicate the *meaning* of the written bit-pattern, whereas S and E are the actual values written down in binary.

For example, an S of `10110010`b = 0.875d might mean the mantissa is 0.875 or is 1.875 or is irrelevant (not a number, *NaN*). The actual meaning of the written bit-patterns changes with mode as we shall see below.

2.8.3.1 Normalised Mode

This is the number format that most non-zero numbers will be represented in. It is the one mode whereby the number format can truly be called 'floating point'. In this mode, the number represented by the bit-patterns (σ, E, S) is given by:

$$n = (-1)^{\sigma} \times (1 + S) \times 2^{E-127}$$

where it can be seen firstly that the exponent is in an excess-127 notation (introduced in Section 2.3.5) and secondly that the mantissa needs to have a '1' added to it. In other words, the mantissa is equal to $S + 1$ and we know that S was written in (0.23) format.

All this may be very confusing, so we will return to the example IEEE754 number and use it in the worked example in Box 2.21, and give a second example in Box 2.22.

Many of our example numbers have long tails of zeros. We can obtain an idea about the basic precision of IEEE754 by considering what difference would result if the least significant bit at the end of one of those tails is flipped from a '0' to a '1'. Box 2.23 provides a guide as to how we can investigate the effect.

Box 2.21

IEEE754 normalised mode worked example 1

Given the following binary value representing an IEEE754 number, determine its decimal value.

`0`	`10110010`	`11100000000000000000000`

First of all, we note that here $\sigma = 0$ and therefore the value has positive sign. We also note that the number is in normalised mode. Therefore:

$$E = 128 + 32 + 16 + 2 = 178 \text{ and}$$

$$S = 0.5 + 0.25 + 0.125 = 0.875$$

Using the formula for normalised mode numbers, we can calculate the value that this conveys:

$$n = (-1)^0 \times (1 + 0.875) \times 2^{178-127}$$

$$= 1.875 \times 2^{51}$$

$$= 4.222 \times 10^{15}$$

As we can see, the result of the worked example is a fairly large number, illustrating the ability of floating point formats to represent some quite big values.

Box 2.22

IEEE754 normalised mode worked example 2

Given the following binary value representing an IEEE754 number, determine its decimal value.

1	00001100	01010000000000000000000

In this case, $\sigma = 1$ and therefore has negative sign, and remaining bit-patterns give:

$$E = 8 + 4 = 12 \text{ and}$$

$$S = 1/4 + 1/16 = 0.3125$$

Using the formula for normalised mode numbers, we can calculate the value that this conveys:

$$\begin{aligned} n &= (-1)^1 \times (1 + 0.3125) \times 2^{12-127} \\ &= -1.3125 \times 2^{-115} \\ &= -3.1597 \times 10^{-35} \end{aligned}$$

This time the result is a very small number. This illustrates the enormous range of numbers possible with floating point, and also the fact that all through the represented number range (explored further in Section 2.8.4), precision is maintained.

Box 2.23

Exercise for the reader

Notice in the worked examples (Boxes 2.21 and 2.22) that our 23-bit long mantissa values began with a few 1's but tailed off to a long string of 0's at the end. This was done to reduce the difficulty in calculating the value of the mantissa because, as a (0.23) fractional format number, the weightings at the left-hand end are easier to deal with, having value 0.5, 0.25, 0.125 and so on. In fact, as we move to the right the bit weights quickly become quite difficult to write down.

The exercise in this case is to repeat one of the worked examples, but with the least significant bit of the mantissa set to 1. If the weighting for the most significant mantissa bit, bit 23, is $2^{-1}(0.5)$ and for the next bit, bit 22, is $2^{-2}(0.25)$, what will be the weighting for bit 0?

When this is added into the answer, what difference if any does it make to the written result?

The real question now is, does this indicate anything about the precision of IEEE754 numbers?

2.8.3.2 Denormalised Mode

Some numbers have such small magnitude that IEEE754 cannot represent them. Generalised floating point would round these values down to zero, but IEEE754 has a special denormalised mode that is able to extend the represented numbers downwards in magnitude towards zero – gracefully decreasing precision until zero is reached.

Denormalised mode is not actually floating point because the exponent (which is the part of the number that specifies the radix point) is set to all zeros and thus no longer 'floats'. However, this mode, in allowing range extension is an important advantage of IEEE754 numbers.

In this mode, the number represented by the bit-patterns (σ, E, S) is given by:

$$n = (-1)^{\sigma} \times S \times 2^{-126}$$

It can be seen firstly that the exponent is fixed as mentioned above, and secondly that we no longer need to add a '1' to the mantissa. The reason for this will be apparent when we explore number ranges in Section 2.8.4.

Since the exponent is fixed, the bit-pattern is always all-zero and the mantissa non-zero. A worked example will help to clear up any confusion, and this is provided in Box 2.24.

Since denormalised numbers extend the range of IEEE754 downwards, they will always have very small magnitude.

2.8.3.3 Other Mode Numbers

Zero, infinity and *NaN* are identified by their special bit-patterns. These can all be positive as well as negative, and require special handling in hardware (see Box 2.25).

Box 2.24

IEEE754 denormalised mode worked example

Given the following binary value representing an IEEE754 number, determine its decimal value.

0	00000000	11010000000000000000000

Firstly, we note that since $\sigma = 0$, the number represented by these bit-patterns therefore has positive sign.

$E = 0$ so we look at the mode table in Section 2.8.2 to see whether we are dealing with a zero or a denormalised number. We actually need to examine the mantissa to decide which it is (a zero must have a zero mantissa, otherwise it is a denormalised number).

Looking at the mantissa we see it is non-zero and therefore a denormalised mode number:

$$S = 0.5 + 0.25 + 0.0625 = 0.8125$$

Using the formula for denormalised mode numbers, we can calculate the value that this conveys:

$$n = (-1)^0 \times 0.8125 \times 2^{-126}$$

$$= 9.5509 \times 10^{-39}$$

Box 2.25

IEEE754 infinity and other 'numbers'

Infinity is most commonly generated by a divide-by-zero or by a normalised mode overflow. Infinity can be positive or negative to indicate the direction from which the overflow occurs.

NaN, indicating Not-a-Number, is generated by an undefined mathematical operation such as infinity multiplied by zero or zero divided by zero.

Zero itself may indicate an operation that really did result in zero, for example (2−2), or it could result from an underflow, when the result is too small to be represented even by denormalised mode, in which case the meaning of +/− zero indicates whether the un-representable number was slightly above or slightly below zero.

2.8.4 IEEE754 Number Ranges

One excellent way of understanding IEEE754 is through the construction of a number line that represents the ranges possible in the format. The following number line, representing an unsigned 8-bit number, will illustrate what this involves:

Minimum magnitude = 0		Maximum magnitude = $2^8 - 1 =$ 255
<——————————————————————>		
Accuracy (distance between number steps) = 1.0		

Three parameters are indicated which describe the format. The first is the smallest magnitude number (`0000 0000`), the second is the largest magnitude number (`1111 1111`) and the final is the accuracy. Accuracy is defined as the distance between steps in the format. In this case, the numbers count upwards as integers: 1, 2, 3, 4, 5, . . . 255 and so the step size is simply 1.

Now, we will undertake to define a number line for IEEE754 format in the same way. To simplify matters we will consider positive numbers, but we will look at both normalised and denormalised modes although only for the single-precision case.

Normalised mode requires that E is not all-zero or all-one, but S can take any value and the actual value represented is:

$$n = (-1)^{\sigma} \times (1 + S) \times 2^{E-127}$$

If we look for the smallest magnitude normalised mode number, we need to find the smallest S and smallest E possible. The smallest S is simply 0, but the smallest E cannot be 0 (because that would denote denormalised or zero mode), so it has to be `00000001` instead:

0	00000001	00000000000000000000000

Floating Point

Inserting these values into the formula and assuming a positive sign gives us:

$$minnorm = (1+0) \times 2^{1-127} = 1 \times 2^{-126} = 1.175 \times 10^{-38}$$

Next, looking for the largest magnitude number, we remember that S can be anything, but E cannot be `11111111` (because that would put it into infinity or *NaN* modes). So we choose the largest E as `11111110` and the largest S as being all-one.

Considering E first, the value equates to 254. However, S is slightly harder to evaluate:

```
111 1111 1111 1111 1111 1111
```

But realising that this is (0.23) format and is slightly less than 1.0 in value, we can see that if we add a binary 1 to the least significant digit then all the binary 1's in the word would ripple-carry to zero as the carry is passed up the chain and we would get a value like this:

```
 111 1111 1111 1111 1111 1111
+000 0000 0000 0000 0000 0001
=1000 0000 0000 0000 0000 0000
```

We can use this fact; knowing that there are 23 bits, the bit weight of the first most significant bit is 2^{-1}, the weight of the second most significant bit is 2^{-2} and so on. Then the twenty-third most significant bit (which is actually the least significant bit) must have a weight of 2^{-23}.

Therefore, the value of S has to be $(1.0 - 2^{-23})$ since adding 2^{-23} to it would make it exactly equal 1.0:

0	11111110	11111111111111111111111

Putting all that into the formula we have:

$$max\ norm = (1 + 1 - 2^{-23}) \times 2^{254-127} = (2 - 2^{-23}) \times 2^{127} = 3.403 \times 10^{38}$$

What about number accuracy? If we look at the numbers we have found we will realise that accuracy is not constant. The smallest bit is always 2^{-23} times the exponent across the entire range.

Finally, starting a number line for normalised mode, we get:

min 1.175×10^{-38}		max 3.403×10^{38}
<——————————————————————————>		
Accuracy (distance between number steps) = 2^{-23} of the exponent		

Since the sign bit changes only the sign and does not affect the magnitude, the range line must be a mirror image for negative numbers.

Denormalised mode can be handled in a similar way, although by definition the exponent is always zero and the value of the number represented is:

$$n = (-1)^{\sigma} \times S \times 2^{-126}$$

Remembering that a mantissa of zero is disallowed, the smallest denormalised number has just the least significant mantissa bit set:

0	00000000	00000000000000000000001

And therefore a value of 2^{-23} following the argument for normalised mode maximum number. The formula becomes:

$$min\ denorm = 2^{-23} \times 2^{-126} = 2^{-149} = 1.401 \times 10^{-45}$$

As for the largest denormalised number, this is simply the number where S is a maximum. Looking at the mode table in Section 2.8.2 we see it can be all-ones:

0	00000000	11111111111111111111111

Again using the same argument as the normalised maximum value case, this has a meaning of $(1 - 2^{-23})$, giving a value of:

$$max\ denorm = (1 - 2^{-23}) \times 2^{-126} = 2^{-149} = 1.175 \times 10^{-38}$$

Now to work out the number accuracy: in this case since the exponent is fixed, the accuracy is simply given by the value of the mantissa least significant bit multiplied by the exponent:

$$2^{-23} \times 2^{-126}$$

min 1.401×10^{-45}		max 1.175×10^{-38}
<——————————————————————————>		
Accuracy (distance between number steps) = $2^{-23} \times 2^{-126}$		

Putting the number lines together, we see the huge range spanned by IEEE754 single-precision numbers. Remember that this is actually only half of the real number line that has positive as well as negative sides:

Zero	**Denormalised**		**Normalised**	
0	1.401×10^{-45}	1.175×10^{-38}	1.175×10^{-38}	3.403×10^{38}
0	<——————————>		<——————————>	
0	Accuracy $2^{-23} \times 2^{-126}$		Accuracy $2^{-23} \times 2^{E-127}$	

The number line becomes useful when we want to convert decimal numbers to IEEE754 floating point. It tells us which mode we should use, whether zero, denormalised, normalised or infinity. To illustrate this, follow a worked example of conversion from decimal to floating point in Box 2.26.

There will be more examples of such conversions in Sections 2.9.1 and 2.9.2.

Box 2.26

Worked example: converting decimal to floating point

Q. Write decimal value 11 in IEEE754 single-precision format

A. Looking at our number line in Section 2.8.4 we can see that this value lies squarely in the normalised number range, so we are looking for a normalised number of the form:

$$n = (-1)^{\sigma} \times (1 + S) \times 2^{E-127}$$

To obtain this, it is first necessary to write $N = 11$ decimal as A $\times 2^B$ where A is equivalent to (1 + S). Knowing that $0 \geq S \leq 1$ it follows that $1 \geq A \leq 2$. Probably the easiest way is to take the number N and repeatedly halve it until we get a value A between 1 and 2:

This gives 11 followed by 5.5 followed by 2.75 and finally 1.375.

So $A = 1.375$ and therefore $N = 1.375 \times 2^B$ and it does not take too much work to see that B is determined by the number of times we had to halve the original number, N in this case, 3. Therefore our number is: $n = (-1)^0 \times (1.375) \times 2^3$

Examining the formula for normalised numbers, we see that this requires:

$$\sigma = 0$$
$$E = 130 \text{ (so that } E - 127 = 3)$$
$$S = 0.375 \text{ (so that } 1 + S = 1.375)$$

Finding a binary bit-pattern for E gives 128 + 2 or `10000010` and since 0.375 is easily represented as 0.25 + 0.125 then the full number is:

0	10000010	01100000000000000000000

2.9 Floating Point Processing

Up to now we have considered only the representation of floating point numbers, in particular the IEEE754 standard. Such a representation is only useful if it is possible to process the numbers to perform tasks, and this is considered further here.

In many computer systems, floating point processing is accomplished through the use of special-purpose hardware called a floating point co-processor or floating point unit (FPU). In fact, even though this is often included on-chip in commercial CPUs, it is normally still accessed as a co-processor rather than as part of the main processor.

For computers that do not have hardware floating point support, software emulation is widely available, and apart from longer execution times (refer to Section 4.6.1), the user may be unaware of where the float calculations are being done, whether in hardware or software. Most floating point support (whether hardware or software) is based on the IEEE754 standard although there are occasional software options to increase calculation speed at the expense of the full IEEE754 accuracy.

IEEE754 number processing involves the following steps:

1. Receive operands.
2. Check for number format modes. If the value is fixed, immediately generate the answer from a look-up table.
3. Convert exponents and mantissas if necessary.
4. Perform operation.
5. Convert back to valid IEEE754 number format. Keep the most significant 1 of the mantissa as close to the left as possible, for reasons of maintaining maximum precision.

2.9.1 Addition and Subtraction of IEEE754 Numbers

In generalised floating point, the exponents of the numbers must all be the same before addition or subtraction can occur. This is similar to ensuring fractional format *(n.m)* + *(r.s)* has $n = r$ and $m = s$ before adding as we saw in Section 2.7.1.

For example, consider the decimal numbers $0.824 \times 10^2 + 0.992 \times 10^4$. In order to do this addition easily, we must have both exponents equal – then we simply add the mantissas. But do we convert both exponents to be 10^2 or do we convert both to be 10^4, or even choose something in between such as 10^3?

In answering this question, first, let us consider how to convert an exponent downwards. We know that 10^3 is the same as 10×10^2 and 10^4 is the same as 100×10^2. Since we are talking about decimal, we multiply the mantissa by the base value of 10 every time we decrement the exponent. Performing this in our calculation would give us the sum:

$$0.824 \times 10^2 + 99.2 \times 10^2$$

Converting up is the converse: 10^2 is the same as 0.01×10^4 and would result in the sum:

$$0.00824 \times 10^4 + 0.992 \times 10^4$$

On paper, in decimal, the value of both expressions is identical, but in binary, in hardware, this may not be true. So the question remains: which action do we take? Do we convert the smaller exponent to match the bigger one or the bigger exponent to match the smaller one, or move to something in the middle?

The answer is, firstly, we do not want to convert both numbers because that is introducing extra work, and secondly when we consider the bit-fields of binary numbers and knowing that by making an exponent smaller the mantissa has to get bigger it becomes evident that there is a danger of the mantissa overflowing if it becomes too big. We therefore opt to never increase a mantissa. This means we have to increase the smaller exponent and scale its mantissa correspondingly:

$$0.00824 \times 10^4 + 0.992 \times 10^4$$

This is termed equalising the exponents or normalising the operands. Later, we will see that methods exist to help prevent the mantissa from disappearing by being rounded down to zero during this process.

Once the exponents are equal, we can perform an addition on the mantissas:

$$0.00824 \times 10^4 + 0.992 \times 10^4 = (0.00824 + 0.992) \times 10^4$$

IEEE754 addition and subtraction are similar to the decimal case except that since the base is 2, the action of increasing one exponent to be the same value as the other causes the mantissa of that number to be reduced by a factor of 2 for each integer increase in exponent. The reduction by a factor of 2, in binary, is accomplished by a right shift.

There is also one other factor we must consider and that is the format of the resulting number. Remember that in normalised mode the mantissa bit-pattern cannot be greater than 1. Well, if the result of a calculation on the mantissa becomes too big then we must right shift the mantissa and consequently increment the exponent.

Similarly, if the mantissa becomes small it must be shifted left and the exponent decremented. These factors will be explored through a worked example in Box 2.27.

We can now take the process further. Having determined how to equate the exponents prior to performing arithmetic, we can tie that in with our knowledge of IEEE754 format and perform these operations directly on IEEE754 format numbers themselves.

Referring to the worked example in Box 2.27, we can now write the IEEE754 bit-patterns of the numbers and perform the conversion in Box 2.28.

Subtraction is similar to addition – all steps remain the same except the mantissas are subtracted as appropriate. Of course, we still have to consider overflow on the result mantissa because we could be subtracting two negative numbers, such that the result is larger than either original operand.

2.9.2 Multiplication and Division of IEEE754 Numbers

For multiplication and division we do not need to normalise the operands first, but we do need to perform two calculations on the numbers, one for the mantissas and one for the exponents. The following relationships hold for these operations on base B numbers:

$$(A \times B^C) \times (D \times B^E) = (A \times D) \times B^{(C+E)}$$

$$(A \times B^C)/(D \times B^E) = (A/D) \times B^{(C-E)}$$

Another decimal example will illustrate the point:

$$(0.824 \times 10^2) \times (0.992 \times 10^4)$$
$$= (0.824 \times 0.992) \times 10^{(2+4)} = 0.817408 \times 10^6$$

Once again, in the case of IEEE754 format numbers the result must be converted to a correct representation and special results (zero, infinity, *NaN*) checked for.

2.9.3 IEEE754 Intermediate Formats

Although a particular IEEE754 calculation may have IEEE754 operands as input and as output, there are cases where the output will be numerically incorrect unless there is greater precision within the calculation. A short example subtraction on 9-bit numbers

Box 2.27

Floating point arithmetic worked example

Q. Convert decimal values 20 and 120 to IEEE754 format, add them and convert the result back to decimal.

A. Looking at our number line from Section 2.8.4 we realise that both values lie in the normalised number range of IEEE754, but initially we will simply consider a generic $A \times 2^B$ format. Furthermore, we will not look at the exact IEEE754 bit-patterns here. Simply remember that $A = (1 + S)$ and $B = (E - 127)$.

Starting with 20 we divide repeatedly by 2 until we get a remainder between 1 and 2: 10, 5, 2.5, 1.25 and so $A = 1.25$. We divided four times so $B = 4$.

120 similarly divides down to 60, 30, 15, 7.5, 3.75, 1.875 so $A = 1.875$. Since we divided six times, $B = 6$.

The information is inserted into the following table. We do not need to derive the E and S bit-patterns at this stage; we are more concerned with their interpretation:

σ	B	A	Binary value	Decimal value
0	4	1.25	1.25×2^4	20
0	6	1.875	1.875×2^6	120

Next step is to equalise the exponents. As discussed in the text, we have to make both equal the largest exponent value, reducing the mantissa of the smaller number as appropriate.

1.25×2^4 thus becomes 0.625×2^5 and then 0.3125×2^6 to reform the operands into the following:

σ	B	A	Binary value	Decimal value
0	6	0.3125	0.3125×2^6	20
0	6	1.875	1.875×2^6	120

Since both exponents are identical, it is now possible to proceed by adding the mantissas to form a result:

σ	B	A	Binary value	Decimal value
0	6	2.1875	2.1875×2^6	?

However, this is not a valid representation for IEEE754 because the mantissa value is too large. Remember the (1 + S) in the formula? Well, $A = (1 + S) \leq 2$ is our constraint. If both operands were IEEE754-compliant then we should be able to guarantee that no more than one shift is needed to put it right, so we shift the A value right by one binary digit and then increment B:

σ	B	A	Binary value	Decimal value
0	7	1.09375	1.09375×2^7	?

A check on a calculator will reveal that 1.09375×2^7 is indeed the correct answer giving us a decimal value of 140.

Box 2.28

IEEE754 arithmetic worked example

First, we begin with the normalised mode formula:

$$n = (-1)^{\sigma} \times (1 + S) \times 2^{E-127}$$

Begin with the value of 20 decimal. In the previous worked example, it was determined to be 1.25×10^4. Slotting this into the formula reveals that $(1 + S) = 1.25$ and so $S = 0.25$, $(E - 127) = 4$ and thus $E = 131$. This is represented below:

0	10000011	01000000000000000000000

120 decimal was 1.875×2^6 which gives us $S = 0.875$ and $E = 133$:

0	10000101	11100000000000000000000

The result of the addition was 1.09375×2^7 such that $S = 0.09375$ and $E = 134$.

Since 0.09375 is not an obvious fraction of 2, we can use a longhand method to determine the bit-patterns. In this, we repeatedly multiply the value by 2, subtracting 1 whenever the result is equal to or bigger than 1, and ending when the remainder is zero:

$0 : 0.09375$
$1 : 0.0187$
$2 : 0.375$
$3 : 0.75$
$4 : 1.5 - 1 = 0.5$
$5 : 1 - 1 = 0$

We subtracted 1 on iterations 4 and 5. We make use of this by setting the fourth and fifth bits from the left to 1. In fact, we could have used this method for the first two numbers, but they were too easy:

0	10000110	00011000000000000000000

will illustrate this:

1.0000 0000	$\times 2^1$	A
− 1.1111 1111	$\times 2^0$	B

Before we can proceed with the subtraction it will of course be necessary to normalise the numbers to the same exponent. We do this by increasing the smaller one as we have done in Section 2.9.1:

1.0000 0000	$\times 2^1$	A
− 0.1111 1111	$\times 2^1$	B

Now we can proceed with the calculation. The result:

0.0000 0001	$\times 2^1$	C

Then shift the mantissa left as far as possible:

1.0000 0000 $\times 2^{-7}$

Let us look at the actual numbers that we have used. Operand A has value 2.0 and operand B has value $(2.0 - 2^{-8})$ which in decimal is 1.99609375. So the result should be:

$$2.0 - 1.99609375 = 0.00390625$$

However, the result from our calculation is 1×2^{-7} or 0.0078125. There is obviously a problem somewhere.

Now let us repeat the calculation but this time adding something called a *guard bit* during the intermediate stages. This effectively extends the length of the mantissa by adding another digit at the least significant end. We start at the point where the numbers have been normalised. Note the extra digit:

1.0000 0000 **0**	$\times 2^1$	A
– 1.1111 1111 **0**	$\times 2^0$	B

Next shifting to normalise the exponents, the LSB of B shifts into the guard bit when we shift the number right by 1 bit:

1.0000 0000 **0**	$\times 2^1$	A
– 0.1111 1111 **1**	$\times 2^1$	B

and subtract to get the following result:

0.0000 0000 **1** $\times 2^1$ C

Then shift the mantissa left as far as possible:

1.0000 0000 **0** $\times 2^{-8}$

Notice that in line C this time the most significant (only) 1 occurred in the guard bit whereas previously it was located at the bit above that. The normalised value is now 1×2^{-8} or 0.00039065, a correct answer this time.

Although this example showed generalised 8-bit floating point numbers, the principle is the same for IEEE754 numbers.

The example above showed a loss of precision error causing an incorrect result during a subtraction. Of course, the same error could occur during an addition since A – B is the same as A + (–B). But can it also occur during multiplication and division? It is left as an exercise for the reader to try and find a simple example that demonstrates this.

In IEEE754 terminology, more than one guard bit is used and the method is called extended intermediate format. It is standardised with the following bit widths:

Name	Bits	σ	Exponent E	Mantissa S
Extended single precision	43	1	11	31
Extended double precision	79	1	15	63

Obviously it becomes awkward to handle 43-bit and 79-bit numbers in computers that are based around 8-bit binary number sizes, but this should not normally be an issue because extended intermediate format is designed for use within a hardware floating point unit during a calculation. The input numbers and output numbers will still be 32 bits or 64 bits only.

2.9.4 Rounding

Sometimes an extended intermediate value needs to be rounded in order to represent it in a desired output format. At other times a format conversion from double to single precision may require rounding. Rounding can be necessary for both fixed and floating point number calculations at times.

There is more than one method of performing numeric rounding and many computer systems will support one or more of these methods under operating system control:

- Round to nearest (most common) – Round to the nearest representable value and if two values are equally near, default to the one with LSB = 0, for example 1.1 to 1, 1.9 to 2 and 1.5 to 2.
- Round towards +ve – Round towards the most positive number, for example −1.2 to −1 and 2.2 to 3.
- Round towards −ve – Round towards the most negative number, for example −1.2 to −2 and 2.2 to 2.
- Round towards 0 – Equivalent to always truncating the number, for example −1.2 to −1 and 2.2 to 2.

For very high-precision computation, it is possible to perform each calculation twice, rounding towards negative and rounding towards positive respectively during each iteration. The average of the two results could be the answer (at least in a linear system). Even if a high-precision answer is not obtained using this method, the difference between the two answers obtained will give a good indication of the numerical accuracy involved in the calculations.

2.10 Summary

This chapter, entitled 'Foundations', has really begun our journey inside the computer – whether that is a room-sized mainframe, a grey desktop box or a tiny embedded system. It is foundational too, since almost all computers, whatever their size, are based upon similar principles. They use the same number formats, perform the same type of calculations such as addition, subtraction, multiplication and division. The main differences that we have seen are that there exist some faster methods to carry out these operations, but at the cost of increased complexity, size and usually power consumption.

We began the chapter by considering the definition of a computer and what it contains. We introduced the useful classification of computer types (or CPUs) by Flynn, viewed them in terms of their connectivity and the layers of functionality that they contain. We then refreshed our knowledge of number formats and the basic operations, before going into a little more detail about how these calculations are achieved.

Having covered the foundations here, the next chapter will focus on how to achieve the connectivity and calculations that we know are required – how to fit these functional units together, write and store a program and control the internal operation required in a working CPU.

Problems

2.1 A programmer wrote a C language program to store 4 bytes (b0, b1, b2, b3) to consecutive memory locations and ran this on a little endian computer with 32-bit wide memory. If he examined the memory after running his program, would he see something like A or B in the diagrams below?

	bit 31			*bit 0*
A:	b3	b2	b1	b0
B:	b0	b1	b2	b3

2.2 Complete the following table (for 8-bit binary numbers), indicating any instances where conversion is impossible for the given value:

Value	*Unsigned*	*Two's complement*	*Sign-magnitude*	*Excess-127*
123				
−15				
193				
−127				

2.3 With a two's complement (2.30) format number, how do we represent the value 0.783203125? Can this be represented exactly with (a) 32 bits, (b) 16 bits and (c) 8 bits?

2.4 One BCD digit consists of 4 bits. Starting with a 4-bit ripple-carry adder, modify this with extra single-bit adders and logic gates to create an adder that can add two BCD digits and produce a BCD sum. Extend the design so that it can add two 4-digit BCD numbers.

2.5 Using partial products (long multiplication), manually multiply the two 4-bit binary numbers X = `1011` and Y = `1101` assuming they are unsigned numbers.

2.6 Repeat the previous multiplication using Booth's algorithm.

2.7 If ADD, SHIFT and compare operations each require a single CPU cycle to complete, how many CPU cycles are needed to perform the calculation in Problem 2.5? Compare this with the steps of Booth's method in Problem 2.6. Also would Booth's algorithm become more efficient for a larger word width?

2.8 Consider a RISC CPU that has an instruction named 'MUL' that can multiply the contents of two registers and store the result into a third register. The registers are 32-bits wide, and the stored result is the top 32 bits of the 64-bit logical result

Problems

(remember that 32 bits $\times$ 32 bits should give 64 bits). However, the programmer wants to determine the full 64-bit result. How can he obtain this? (*Hint: You will need to do more than one multiply, and also a few ANDs and adds to get the result*). Verify your method, and determine how many instructions are needed.

2.9 If we multiply the two (2.6) format unsigned numbers X = 11010000 and Y = 01110000 then we should get a (4.12) format result. We can shift the result two digits left, giving (2.14) [i.e. effectively removing the top 2 bits] and then truncate it to (2.6) [by discarding the lower 8 bits]. Will this cause an overflow, and will the truncation lose any bits?

2.10 Consider the IEEE754 single-precision floating point standard.

(a) Express the value of the stored number N in terms of its storage bits (σ, E, S) for the following cases:

i. $E = 255, S \neq 0$
ii. $E = 255, S = 0$ successfully
iii. $0 < E < 255$
iv. $E = 0, S \neq 0$
v. $E = 0, S = 0$

(b) Express the following values in IEEE754 single-precision normalised format:

i. -1.25
ii. $1/32$

2.11 Can a standard exponent/mantissa floating point number format represent zero in more than one way? Can IEEE754 represent zero in more than one way? If so, explain any differences between the representations.

2.12 Use the division flowchart of Figure 2.9 to obtain the quotient and remainder values for the unsigned 5-bit binary division Q/M where Q = 10101b and M = 00011b.

2.13 Use the multiplication flowchart from Figure 2.7 to perform partial product multiplication of two 5-bit unsigned binary numbers 00110 and 00101. Determine the number of registers used, their sizes and their content during each iteration.

2.14 Repeat the previous problem using the multiplication block diagram of Figure 2.8, to compare and contrast the two approaches in terms of efficiency, number of steps, number of registers and so on.

Problems

2.15 Consider the following calculation in the C programming language:

$$0.25 + (float)(9 \times 43)$$

Assuming that integers are represented by 16-bit binary numbers and the floats are in 32-bit IEEE754 single-precision representation, follow the numerical steps involved in performing this calculation to yield a result in IEEE754 format.

2.16 How would Michael Flynn classify a processor that has an instruction able to simultaneously right shift by one bit position every byte stored in a group of five internal registers?

2.17 Justify whether self-modifying code (that is, software that can modify its own instructions by rewriting part of its code) would fit better in a von Neumann or Harvard architecture system.

2.18 Using a 16-bit processor and only a single result register, follow the process to add the (2.14) format unsigned number X = `01.11000000000000` and the (1.15) format unsigned number Y = `0.110000000000000`. What format would the result need to be in to avoid overflow? Is there any loss of precision caused by the calculation in this case?

2.19 Identify the IEEE754 modes of the following numbers:

1	10100010	10100000000000000000000000
0	00000000	10100000000000000000000000
0	11111111	00000000000000000000000000

2.20 What would be the mantissa and the exponent of the result of the following base 7 calculation, expressed in base 7?

$$(3 \times 7^8)/(6 \times 7^4)$$

Hint: You do not need to use a calculator to obtain the answer.

2.21 Using partial products (long multiplication), manually multiply the two 6-bit binary numbers X = `100100` and Y = `101010` assuming they are signed.

2.22 Repeat the previous multiplication by swapping the multiplier and multiplicand (i.e. multiply the two 6-bit signed binary numbers X = `101010` and Y = `100100`). Compare the number of additions that are required to perform

Problems

the partial product summation. Is it possible to simplify the process by swapping multiplier and multiplicand, and if so why?

2.23 Repeat the previous two multiplications using Booth's method. Is there any difference in the number of partial product additions when the multiplier and multiplicand are swapped?

2.24 Referring to Section 2.9, determine the number of basic integer addition, shift and multiplication operations required to perform a single-precision IEE754 floating point normalised mode multiply, and compare this with the basic operations required to perform a (2.30) $\times$ (2.30) multiply. Ignore extended intermediate mode, overflow and saturation effects and assume the floating point numbers have different exponent values.

2.25 How many computational operations are required to perform an 8-bit division using repeated subtraction?

CHAPTER 3

CPU Basics

In this chapter, we begin looking at a cohesive unit which we can call a computer – specifically its brains, the central processing unit (CPU). This chapter will very much present a traditional view of computer architecture. It will neither consider state-of-the-art extensions and speed-ups which Chapter 5 will cover nor look too deeply at individual functional units within a computer which Chapter 4 will cover.

Rather, this chapter will concentrate on what a computer is comprised of, how it is organised and controlled and how it is programmed.

3.1 What Is a Computer?

When the general public refer to a computer, they generally envisage a beige-coloured box with monitor, keyboard and mouse. While the box they imagine does contain a computer, we know there is a whole lot more in there.

The 'computer' part of the system is the CPU, memory subsystem and any required buses – in fact those items that allow it to function as a stored-program digital computer. It does not require a graphics card, wireless interface card, hard disc or sound system in order to compute and execute stored programs.

The stored-program digital computer is basically just a very flexible, but generally quite basic, calculating and data transfer machine that is programmable to perform the required functions.

These days, most people in the developed world will be surrounded by tens, if not hundreds, of computers. These may be inside microwaves, toasters, cellphones, MP3 players, even electronic door locks. It has been estimated that a luxury car contains well over 100 processors, and even an entry model may contain over 40 separate devices. In one surprising example encountered recently, a new double-sized electric blanket was promoted as containing four dedicated microprocessors – one active and one backup device for dual independent controls on each side. With usage on this scale it becomes easy to imagine that the 'future is embedded'. The contents of this chapter apply whether the computer is room-size or the size of an ant.

3.2 Making the Computer Work for You

As we have seen, at its most basic level a computer is simply a unit able to transfer data and perform logical operations. All higher-level computational functions are a sequence or combination of these basic data moves and logic operations. Various units inside the computer are dedicated to performing different tasks, and these are fairly standard building blocks used by most computers. For example, an arithmetic logic unit (ALU) performs arithmetic operations, while a bus transfers data from one point to another. Obviously, some method is needed for directing the computer – deciding when and where to move data and which logic operations to perform using these building blocks. The computer (comprising its internal units and buses) must be *programmed* to perform the work that we wish it to undertake.

As a first step, the work required needs to be divided into a sequence of available operations. Such a sequence is called a *program* and each operation is commanded through an *instruction* plus operands. The list of supported operations in a computer defines its *instruction set*.

3.2.1 Program Storage

Instructions clustered into a program need to be stored in a way that is accessible to the computer. The very first electronic computers were programmed by plugging wires into different holes. Later, manual switches were used and then automated with punched card readers. Punched and then magnetic tape were invented, but whatever the storage format a new program was entered by hand each time after power-up.

Modern computers store programs on magnetic disc, ROM, EEPROM, flash memory or similar media. Programs are often read from their storage device into RAM before execution for performance reasons: RAM is faster than most mass-storage devices.

Items stored in memory need to have a location that is accessible. Their storage place also needs to be identified in order to be accessed. Early computer designers termed the storage location an *address*, since this allows the CPU to select and access any particular item of information or program code which reside at unique addresses. The most efficient way to do this has been for the CPU to notify the memory storage device of the address it requires, wait for the content of that address to be accessed and then read in the value from the device interface some time later.

As you may know, CPUs are programmed at the lowest level in machine code instructions which are fixed (in most RISC devices such as ARM, PIC or MIPS), or variable length sequences of bytes (as in several CISC devices such as Motorola 68000). It is a bunch of these instructions, in some particular program sequence, that instructs a computer to perform required tasks.

For these sequences of instructions to do something useful, they probably require access to some data which requires processing. This historically encouraged a separation between program and data storage spaces, particularly since the two types of information have different characteristics: programs are typically sequential and read-only whereas data may require read/write access and may be accessed either sequentially or in a random fashion.

3.2.2 Memory Hierarchy

Storage locations within a computer can all be defined as 'memory', because once written to they remember the value written. Often, however, we reserve this term for referring to solid-state RAM and ROM rather than registers, CDs and so on. Whatever the naming convention, storage is defined by various trade-offs and technology choices that include the following characteristics:

- Cost.
- Density (bytes per cm^3).
- Power efficiency (nanojules per write, read or second of storage time).
- Access speed (including seek time and average access time).
- Access size (byte, word, page, etc.).
- Volatility (i.e. data lost when the device is unpowered).
- Reliability (does it have moving parts? does it age?).
- CPU overhead to manage it.

These factors lead to a hierarchy of memory as shown in the pyramid in Figure 3.1, for both a large desktop/server and a typical embedded system. Two items shown will be explored subsequently in Chapter 4: the memory management unit (MMU) and cache. However, for the present discussion notice that registers – temporary storage locations very close to the CPU functional units – are the fastest, but most expensive

Figure 3.1

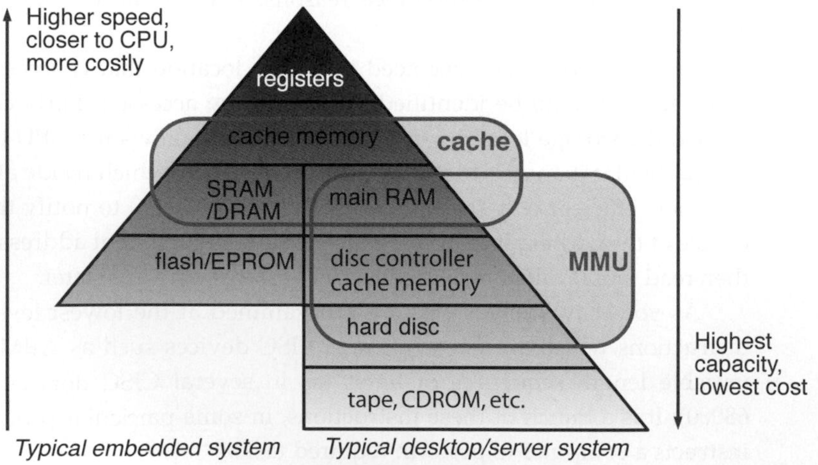

A pyramidal diagram illustrating the hierarchy of memory in terms of speed, size, cost and so on for embedded systems (on the left) and traditional desktop computers (on the right).

resource (and are therefore generally few in number, ranging from 1, 2 or 3 in simple microcontrollers up to 128 or more in some large UNIX servers).

Moving down the pyramid, cost per byte decreases (and thus the amount provided tends to increase), but the penalty is that access speed also decreases. A computer, whether embedded, desktop or supercomputer, almost always comprises several of the levels in the hierarchy:

- **Registers** – Store temporary program variables, counters, status information, return addresses, stack pointers and so on.
- **RAM** – Hold stack, variables, data to be processed and often a temporary store of program code itself.
- **Non-volatile memory** such as flash, EPROM or hard disc – Store programs to be executed – particularly important after initial power-up *boot time* when volatile RAM memory would be empty.

Other levels are there for convenience or speed reasons, and since there are so many levels in the hierarchy, there are several places capable of storing required items of information. Thus, a convenient means is required to transfer information between locations as and when required.

3.2.3 Program Transfer

For reading a program from external storage into RAM, an I/O interface such as IDE (integrated drive electronics – a very popular interface for hard discs), SCSI (small computer systems interface – which can address discs, scanners and many other devices), other parallel buses or serial buses (such as USB) are used (these interfaces will be explained later in Sections 6.3.2 and 6.3.4).

The connection between the RAM and CPU, and also between CPU and I/O devices is via a bus, and this transfers a program, a byte or word at a time. RAM may be external or internal to the physical integrated circuit (IC) on which the CPU resides.

When an instruction from a program is read from RAM into a CPU it needs to be decoded and then executed. Since different units inside the CPU perform different tasks, data to be processed needs to be directed to a unit able to perform the required function. To convey information around the inner parts of a CPU, there needs to be an internal bus between an instruction fetch/decode unit and the various processing units, and perhaps a bus to collect the result from each processing unit, and place it somewhere.

Often, data to be processed is already available in internal registers (and in particular, many modern CPUs, called *load-store*, constrain their architecture so data being processed must come from registers). This data is transported from registers to processing units via buses. Results will then be sent back to registers, again by bus. It is often convenient to group all internal registers together into a bank. In addition, in a *regular architecture* machine every processing unit will be connected to this bank of registers, again using a bus.

In Chapter 4, we will look at computer buses in a different way as we examine many of the functional blocks found in modern CPUs and consider the effect of different bus arrangements on performance. Here, we can be content with the assumption that such things as internal buses do exist.

Given a (possibly quite complex) bus interconnection network inside a CPU, plus multiple internal functional units and registers that connect to this, the question arises as to what arbitrates and controls data transfers across and between the buses.

3.2.4 Control Unit

Multiple buses, registers, various functional units, memories, I/O ports and so on, need to be controlled. This is the job of the imaginatively named *control unit*. Most operations require there to be a well-defined process flow within a CPU, such as:

- Fetch instruction.
- Decode instruction.
- Execute instruction.
- Save result (if any) of instruction.

Furthermore, there needs to be a method of ensuring that these steps occur and do so in the correct order. This presupposes the need to have a set of control wires and signals within a device from some control unit to each of the on-chip units that must be controlled.

In early processors, the control unit was a simple finite state machine (FSM) endlessly stepping through one of several predefined states. Control wires ran from this to each of the endpoints requiring control in a spider-web of wires and interconnects. We will see this method in more detail when we design our own processor in Chapter 8.

Control is not only needed to fetch and distribute instructions, it is also needed for carrying out the actions of single instructions. Consider the case of performing a simple data transfer from register A to register B (LDR B, A) across a single 32-bit bus as shown in Figure 3.2.

The two triangles within the figure are tristate buffers – devices similar to a switch in that when the control signal is enabled, signals can pass through the buffer but when the control signal is disabled, signals do not pass through the buffer. This is used in a bus (for example) to decide which register is allowed to drive the bus wires. Only a single register can drive a bus at any one time, so all other tristates connected to that bus must remain turned off.

Bearing this in mind, the actions that need to be taken for a data transfer are summarised here:

1. Turn off any tristate buffers driving the bus (in this case de-assert *ena1 to 4*).

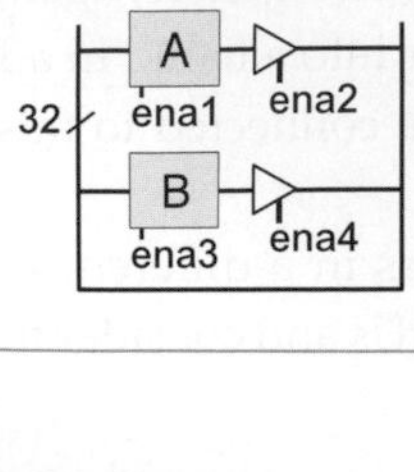

A block diagram of a very simple computer control unit showing two registers, each with selectable tristate buffers and a single 32-bit bus connecting all ports. **Figure 3.2**

2. Assert *ena2* to turn on the 32-bit tristate, driving the content of register A onto t shared bus.
3. Assert *ena3* to feed the bus data into register B.
4. De-assert *ena3* to lock the bus data into register B.
5. De-assert *ena2* to free up the bus for other operations.

Perhaps the details of the process will differ from device to device (in particular the enable signals are usually edge-triggered on different clock edges), but something like this process is needed – in the order given – and more importantly sufficient time is required between stages for:

- 1 to 2 – Wait for the 'off' signal to propagate along the control wires, hit the tristate buffers and for them to act on it.
- 2 to 3 – Wait for the bus voltage to stabilise (i.e. the content of register A to be reflected by the bus voltage levels).
- 3 to 4 – Give the register sufficient time to capture the bus value.
- 4 to 5 – Wait for the control signal to hit the register and the register to stop 'looking at the bus' before the bus can be freed for another purpose.

Sometimes the waiting time is most important. In modern processors it is counted in system clock cycles, with each stage of the process being allocated a single or potentially more cycles.

Figure 3.3 illustrates cycle-by-cycle timing for the case of one clock between actions, showing the sequence of events at each stage in the process. It is evident that a synchronous control system is needed to carry out a sequence of actions involved in even the most simple of CPU instructions.

Not all instructions need to step through the same states. Some instructions, such as those that return no result, can be terminated early. Those instructions could either be supported by allowing a state machine to continue running through all states (but with dummy actions for the unused states), or be supported by early termination or custom state transitions. In the example given, such an instruction would not need to complete five states before finishing.

Figure 3.3

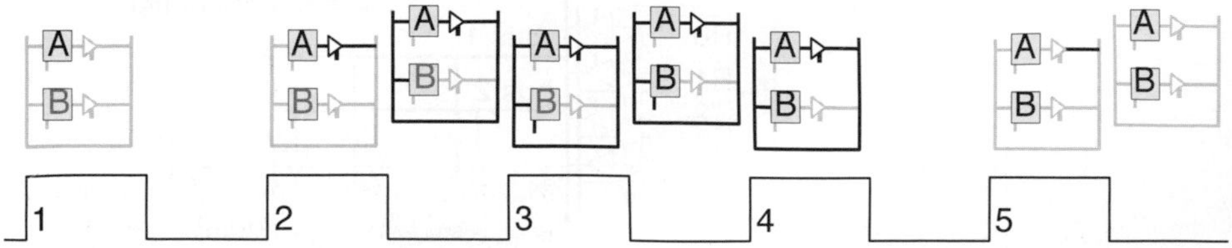

An illustration of the cycle-by-cycle timing of the simple control unit that was shown in Figure 3.2 as it transfers data from register A to register B. Darker lines indicate that the particular bus or signal is active at that time.

Some instructions are likely to need specialised handling that extends the state machine further. CPU designers generally cater for this by increasing the complexity of the state machine to handle such exceptions to the rule, all in the quest to increase runtime efficiency.

Over the years, more and more weird and wonderful instructions have been introduced. It does not take a genius to figure out where they all have ended up – more and more complex state machines! In some cases, the CPU control unit became the most complex part of the design and required up to half of the on-chip area. In other cases, the state machine was so complex that it was itself implemented as another CPU – in effect a simpler processor handling the control needs of a larger and more complex one. In IC design terms (as in many other fields), complexity is known to lead to errors and for these reasons alternatives were researched.

So far, we have only considered the case of handling different instructions within a processor. Now, let us consider the actual task of distributing the control signals across larger and ever-growing IC sizes with increasing numbers of internal bus interconnects, larger register banks, more functional units and a larger degree of clocking complexity and flexibility. It is to be expected that a larger degree of the internal processor routing logic (i.e. wires that traverse the device from one side to another) is going to be needed. This presents difficulties beyond the complexity of instruction control. It turns out that in a silicon IC, the interconnects that can reach across an entire chip are a scarce resource: these are normally reserved for fast data buses. The need to utilise more and more of these for dedicated control purposes has provided another impetus to the research of alternative control strategies.

Three general methodologies resulted, namely *distributed control*, *self-timed control* and *simplification* (increased regularity). The main example of distributed control is in the use of microcode, explored in Section 3.2.5. An example of simplification is in the move to RISC processors, explored in Section 3.2.6. Let us briefly examine each control method.

Figure 3.4 shows part of the internals of a very simple CPU. There are four registers in a bank and two arithmetic logic units (ALUs) all connected through two

Figure 3.4

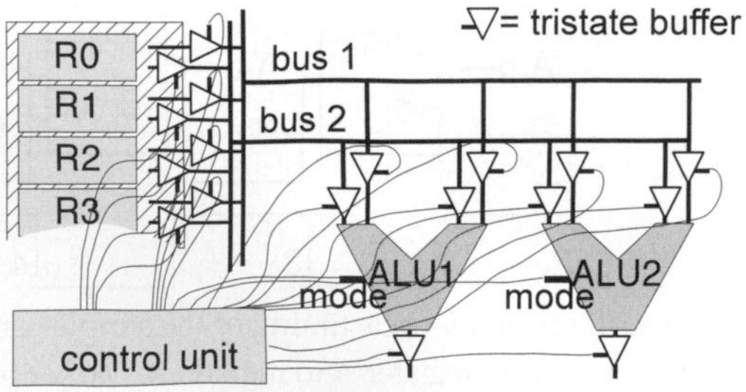

A block diagram of the centralised control wiring required for a very simple CPU.

Figure 3.5 A small control unit is shown in this diagram wired to the input-select logic for a bank of four registers.

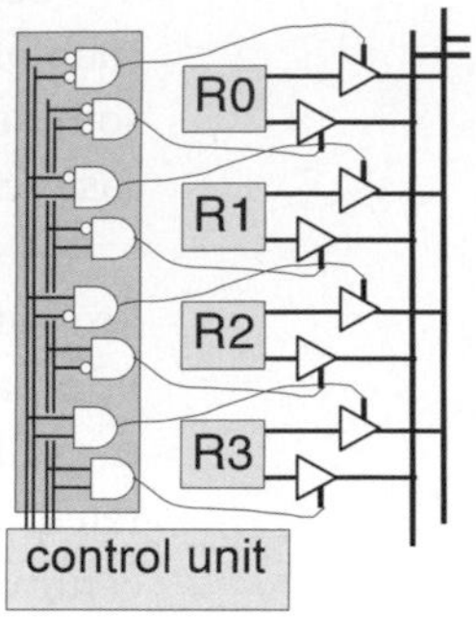

shared data buses. At each point of bus entry/exit there is a tristate buffer. Each bus, tristate, register and ALU port is several bits wide.

Evidently, the thin control wires emanating from the control unit are many, even for such a simple system. These are used to control each of the tristate buffers and the mode of the ALUs (which can perform several selectable functions). Some, such as register-select logic, are not shown. In Chapter 4 and beyond, different bus arrangements will be discussed, but control signals such as these will not be shown in subsequent chapters: diagrams simply become too complicated.

One simplification that can be introduced is the use of a control bus or several control buses. Instead of two control signals needed for each register as in Figure 3.4, the fact that each data bus can only carry a single value at a time can be exploited to need only a 2-bit selection bus to drive each data bus (i.e. 4-bit total control for the system shown). This is termed a *register-select* bus. Such an approach may not seem particularly beneficial in a four-register system, but with 32 registers it would reduce the number of register-select control wires from 64 to 6. A small example is shown in Figure 3.5.

The number of wires emanating from the control unit to the register bank in Figure 3.5 is four. These are decoded *in the register bank itself* to select the appropriate register. This is not necessarily minimising logic, but is minimising the number of connections around the CPU.

To summarise, control is needed for arbitration of internal buses, for initiating the fetch, decoding and handling of instructions, for interactions with the outside world (such as I/O interfacing) and pretty much everything sequential in a CPU, which is a great deal. Control may even extend to handling external memory, and the next chapter carries an important example of this in the memory management unit.

Self-timed control is an alternative strategy that distributes control throughout a CPU, following from the observation that most instructions need to follow a common 'control path' through a processor – fetch, decode, execute and store. And during execution, the process is also fairly common – drive some registers onto buses, drive values from buses into one or more functional units, then some time later allow the result to be collected (again using one or more buses) and latched back into registers.

Self-timed control in this instance does not imply an asynchronous system since each block is synchronous, albeit to a faster clock (note that self-timing *is* used within some esoteric asynchronous systems which we will explore in Chapter 9, but in this case we are only dealing with synchronous logic).

A centralised control unit could specify in turn 'fetch now' then 'decode now' then 'execute now' and finally 'store now'. This would require control connections from the IC areas responsible for each of these tasks, back to the central control unit. However, the self-timed strategy requires the control unit to simply start the process of instruction fetch. The signal 'decode now' would be triggered from the fetch unit and not from a central location. Similarly, 'execute now' would be a signal generated by the decode unit and passed to the execute unit. In this way, a control interconnect is needed from each unit to the next unit, but not all going to a single central location. In effect, the control signals are actually following the data paths, something that becomes even more effective in a pipelined machine (which will be covered in Chapter 5).

The two alternative approaches of centralised and self-timed control are shown in the flowcharts of Figure 3.6. In this case, data buses are not shown which would originate from external memory and traverse the fetch, decode, execute and store (FDES) string. On the left is shown a control unit with four control buses, each one linked to the enable inputs of the four separate units. At the relevant times as specified in an internal state machine, the control unit will initiate operations in the FDES units.

Depending upon the instruction being processed, the control unit state machine may need to operate the FDES differently (perhaps a longer execution stage or skip the store). This knowledge must be encoded within the control unit, which must remember every combination of operations for every unit connected to it.

The state machine must firstly contain detailed information on the timings and requirements of each unit. It must also keep track of potentially multiple instructions progressing simultaneously through these units.

On the right-hand side, a self-timed system is shown: the control unit still initiates the process, but in this case each subsequent unit is initiated from the previous unit as

Figure 3.6

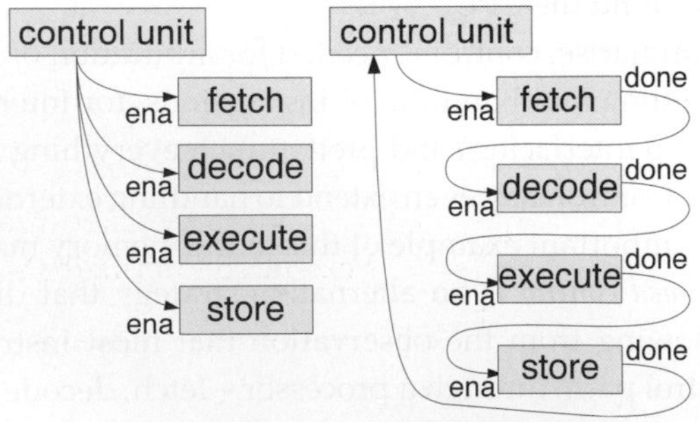

Control flowcharts of the alternative strategies of centralised control (left) and self-timed control (right).

and when necessary. Since the units themselves initiate the next step, the data buses (not shown) are assumed to have the correct information at the correct times.

Depending upon the instruction being processed, units may decide to skip themselves and pass the request directly to the next unit. Each unit must thus encode the knowledge of its own responsibilities and timings.

Perhaps more problematic is the need to convey different information to the various units. For example, the execute unit needs to know what function is to be performed – is it an AND, OR, SUB and so on. It does not need to know where to store the result from the execution – this information is needed by the store unit which in turn does not need to know what function was performed. In the self-timed case, either a full record of needed information is passed between units, with units only reading the items relevant to them, or there is a centralised store for such information. The choice of implementation strategy depends upon complexity and performance requirements.

3.2.5 Microcode

As CPUs grew and became more complex, they ended up as an amalgamation of basic required functionality, with assorted customised one-off instructions, some of which were past their sell-by-date, an example from the 1980s being the binary-coded-decimal handling instructions of the Intel 8086, 80386, 80486 processors required for backwards compatibility with several decades-old legacy business software. The commercial drive was for greater processing speed, and that was achieved partly through increasing clock rates and partly through performing more functions with a single instruction.

Much of this drive for complex instructions came from the disparity between the speed of external and internal memory. Internal memory cost an enormous amount of money, but was up to 1000 times faster than external memory. A big bottleneck was dragging an instruction from external memory into the processor. It therefore made perfect sense to create a single complex instruction that replaced a sequence of 100 separate smaller instructions.

In fact, it was possible to think in terms of tokens. The external program was written in tokens (instructions), fed slowly into the CPU, each causing a longer sequence of internal operations. Each token could launch a sequence of internal operations, and these internal operations in turn were really programs, written in microcode. Microcode was the basic instruction set of these processors, but often did not particularly resemble the external instructions. Every external instruction would be translated into a microcode program or microprogram, upon entering the CPU.

Microprogramming, as a technique, was actually invented by Maurice Wilkes in the early 1950s at Cambridge University, although one of the IBM System/360 family of computers was probably the first commercial machine to implement this technology.

Some of the microcoding concepts are illustrated in Figure 3.7 where an external program in slow memory is being executed by the CPU. The current program counter (PC) is pointing at the instruction DEC A, presumably a command to decrement register A. This is fetched by the CPU and decoded into a sequence of microcode instructions

Figure 3.7

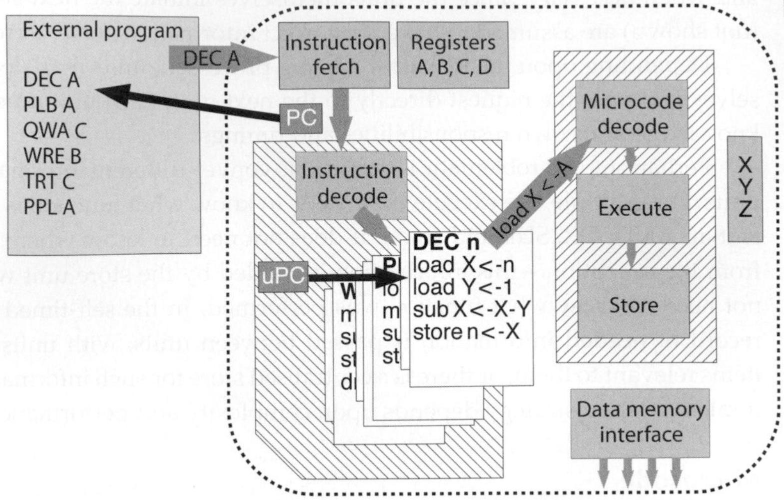

A block diagram of an instruction being fetched from slow external memory, decoded inside a CPU and executed as a sequence of much simpler microcode instructions.

to load register X from A, then load register Y with 1, then subtract Y from X and finally to store the result back in A.

The small four-instruction microprogram that the DEC instruction launches is contained entirely inside the CPU, in fast, on-chip read only memory (ROM), and requires an internal microprogram counter. None of this is visible from the 'outside world' of the external program which may not even know that registers X, Y and Z exist inside the CPU.

Extending this approach further led to a processor which used nanocode: external programs would be converted to a microprogram of microcode instructions, each of which would in turn translate to a nanoprogram of nanocode instructions! Despite the elegance of this Cat-in-the-Hat technique, there were decreasing returns with the microcode approach. It relied upon the fact that external memory was a bottleneck. In the days when external random access memory (RAM) was expensive and slow, but internal ROM was very fast, this was undoubtedly true. But then advances in RAM technology, including static RAM (SRAM), dynamic RAM (DRAM) and then synchronous dynamic ram (SDRAM) all chipped away at the speed advantages of ROM that by the 1990s there was little difference between the technologies.

With minimal speed advantage, the popularity of microcode began to wane.

An exception was where the benefits of *instruction translation* were required. This feature is inherent in the microcode approach, and allows a CPU of one type to use the instruction set of another machine.

In the late 1990s, processors were being developed that were internally RISC machines, but which could execute CISC instruction sets (see next section). Nowhere was this advantage more clear than with the humble x86 series of processors. With a design heritage harking back to 1971, these CPUs had to not only guarantee backwards code compatibility by executing an ancient and poorly-optimised CISC instruction set, but had to do this faster than competing processors. The old-fashioned CISC instructions that entered some of these processors would be translated into sequences of much faster optimised RISC-style assembler. The RISC instructions thus took the place of modern-day microcode.

A further advantage of the microcode translation was the design of a processor that could mimic other devices. Such a device could execute an ARM program as if it were a native ARM processor, and then switch to executing Texas Instruments DSP code as if it were a TI DSP: the ultimate approach to being all CPUs to all programmers.

Despite such niche markets, the driving factors behind microcode disappeared, and it became less popular in the 1980s. The trend was constantly towards doing more, and doing it faster: Moore's Law in full swing.

3.2.6 RISC vs CISC Approaches

The ideas behind RISC (Reduced Instruction Set Computer) and CISC (Complex Instruction Set Computer) have been mentioned briefly in Section 2.2. The CISC architecture encompasses many complicated and powerful instructions, whereas the RISC architecture concentrates on a smaller subset of common useful instructions which it handles extremely fast. Even when complex operations are synthesised through multiple RISC instructions they will be as fast, or faster, than if encoded directly as a CISC instruction.

This concept is illustrated in Figure 3.8 showing two programs – one running on a RISC machine, with its fast one-cycle per instruction operation completing a program of 12 instructions (A to L) in 12 clock cycles. Below that is a CISC computer with its longer clock cycle (because the hardware is more complicated and thus slower) completing the same process in roughly the same number of clock cycles, but in this case using only five complex instructions instead of the 12 in the RISC machine. Since the clock cycles are longer, it completes the task slower than the RISC machine. This is typically the case, although conditions do sometimes exist, especially for smaller programs, where the CISC processor can complete its program faster.

Figure 3.8

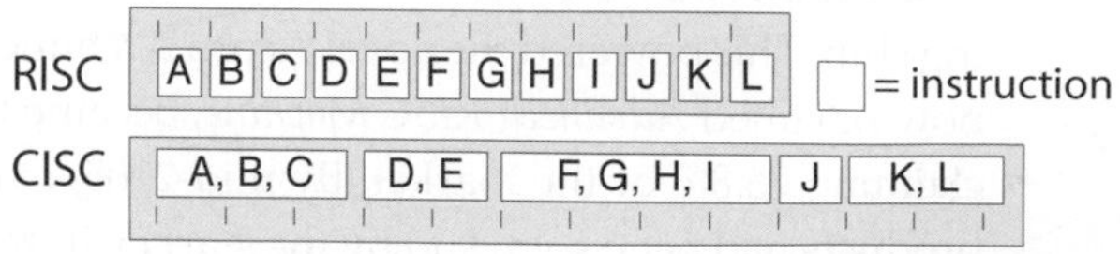

A diagram illustrating the difference in size, speed and functionality of CISC and RISC instructions. RISC instructions (top) are uniformly small, each occupying a single CPU cycle, indicated by the vertical tick marks. By contrast, the CISC instructions (bottom) require multiple cycles to execute and often accomplish more per instruction than in the RISC case.

However, this account does not quite describe the two approaches in context and for that we require a little hindsight. Taking a historical perspective, early computers were operated by the designers of the machines themselves. Designers knew what basic operations were required in their programs and catered for these directly in hardware. As hardware became more capable, it became possible to add instructions to the computer that could perform functions that would otherwise require time-consuming strings of instructions.

As time progressed, computer programmers concentrated on software development, and computer architects specialised in the hardware aspects. Programmers would then approach architects asking for custom instructions to make their programs faster. Architects often complied, but sometimes took the initiative to add what they imagined were useful instructions, but which left the programmers scratching their heads.

By the mid-1980s, various design groups, most notably at Berkeley and then Stanford universities in the USA, began to question the prevailing design ethos. They were probably prompted in this by groundbreaking work performed quietly at IBM, in which less complex machines that could clock much faster because of simple and regular design, were investigated. These machines demonstrated that simple instructions could be processed very quickly. Even though sometimes a few RISC instructions were needed to perform the same operation as a single-CISC instruction, a RISC program was typically still significantly faster overall.

The name Reduced Instruction Set Computer pays tribute to the simplicity of the original designs, although there was no actual reason to reduce the size of the instruction set, just to reduce the complexity of the instructions. Groups that popularised RISC technology produced, in turn the RISC I, RISC II and MIPS processors. These evolved into commercial devices delivering powerful workstation performance where backwards compatibility with x86 code was not required, namely the SPARC and MIPS devices.

In the meantime, over in Cambridge in the UK, a tiny design group at Acorn Computers Ltd, the highly successful producer of the 6502-powered BBC microcomputer range (that contributed to the UK having the highest rate of computer ownership in the world), had designed their own processor, based on the earliest Berkeley work. This *Acorn RISC Machine*, the ARM1, was designed on a 2-MHz BBC microcomputer running BASIC. Acorn wrote their own silicon design tools for this processor which was very soon followed by the ARM2, which became the world's first commercial RISC processing chip. This powered the novel Acorn Archimedes range of computers. By 2002, ARM, now renamed *Advanced RISC Machine*, became the world's top-selling 32-bit processor claiming 76.8% of the market. By mid-2005, over 2.5 billion ARM processor-powered products had been sold, and by the start of 2009 that had increased to be more than one sold for every person on the planet. The popularity of the ARM processor continues to increase. Box 3.1 briefly explores the background to the development of the amazing ARM processor.

While Intel rode the wave of the desktop personal computer boom, the ARM architecture is riding the much larger wave of the embedded processor boom. CPUs are now

Box 3.1

How the ARM was designed

In the mid-1980s, groundbreaking British computer company Acorn, with a contract from the British Broadcasting Corporation (BBC) to design and market BBC microcomputers was looking for a way to move beyond their hugely successful 8-bit BBC microcomputers. These were powered by the lean and efficient Rockwell 6502 processors. The BBC initiatives had encouraged computer use in the UK so much that there were reportedly far more computers per capita in England than anywhere else in the world. Sir Clive Sinclair's ZX Spectrum for example, had sold 4 million units by the time sales of the IBM PC had reached 1 million units. Acorn is also reputed to have sold over 1 million BBC computers overall.

In the early explosion of the 'computer revolution' it quickly became apparent to Acorn that 16-bit processors from companies such as Intel and Motorola were not powerful enough to meet their projected future needs – needs which included releasing the world's first multi-tasking graphical desktop operating system in the late 1980s (later some observers would conclude that this was copied by Microsoft as the basis for Windows 95, XP and beyond).

In typical pioneering fashion, Acorn decided that, since nothing good enough was available, they would create their own processor. They designed the ARM1 and its support ICs (such as MEMC and VIDC) within two years despite having never developed any silicon previously.

Acorn wanted a machine with a regular architecture – similar to the 6502, but vastly more powerful. They chose to use the RISC approach, but revisited their software needs by analysing operating system code to determine most used instructions which they then optimised for the ARM processor. The same approach yielded an instruction set (see Section 3.3) and its coding. Later, much needed additions were the multiply and multiply-accumulate instructions.

This heritage leaves the globally successful ARM processor with a direct link back to the UK Government-funded BBC initiatives: the ARM software interrupt, supervisor modes, fast interrupt, no microcode, static pipeline, load-store architecture are all derived either from the hardware or the software architectures adopted by Acorn.

inside almost every electronic product and most of these are ARM-based. Meanwhile, Acorn itself no longer exists, having self-destructed in 1999.

3.2.7 Example Processors

Over the years, since the IBM research group published their initial results, the RISC approach has impacted almost every sphere of processor design. In particular, the ARM RISC processor family now dominates the world of embedded systems. Therefore, in this book almost all assembly language code examples are given in ARM assembler format. For example:

```
ADD R0, R1, R2
```

adds together the contents of registers R1 and R2 and stores the result in register R0.

Today, although it is easy to find examples of 'pure' RISC processors such as the ARM and MIPS, even the die-hard CISC devices (such as Motorola/Freescale 68000/Coldfire and some of the Intel x86 range) are now implemented with CISC-to-RISC hardware translators and internal RISC cores. Pure CISC processors do not seem to be popular these days. For this reason, when referring to CISC processors we define a pseudo-ARM assembler format, rather than use the format from any particular CISC device:

```
ADD  A, B, C
```

adds together registers B and C, placing the result in register A. Usually, examples in this text are identified as being RISC or CISC, and can otherwise be differentiated because the RISC examples use ARM-style registers R0 to R15 whereas CISC examples use alphabetical registers A, B, C and so on. Some special-purpose registers are also mentioned in later sections; SP is the stack pointer, LR is the link register.

The only exception to the use of pseudo-ARM instructions in this book is in discussions relating to the Analog Devices ADSP21xx processor and a single Texas Instruments TMS320 example. The ADSP in particular uses an assembly language that is structurally similar to the C programming language, and therefore quite easily readable. These exceptions will be highlighted at the time the code segments are presented.

Note that some processors, most notably the 68000, would actually specify the *destination* register last instead of first as in the ARM. However, in this book the destination register is always specified ARM style, and any comment is written following a semicolon (';'):

```
SUB  R3,  R2,  R1;  R3 = R2 - R1
```

Sometimes the destination and first source register are the same:

```
ADD  C,  D;  C = C + D
```

or perhaps there is only a single source register:

```
NOT  E,  F;  E = not F
```

or maybe no source register:

```
B  R3;  jump to address contained in R3
```

Generally the instructions themselves are self-explanatory (`ADD, AND, SUB` and so on). The following section will provide more examples and detail on the ARM instruction format, including a list of all instruction families.

Beware, in the ARM, the destination register is specified first for all instructions *apart from* the store to memory instruction and its variants:

```
STR  R1,  [R3]
```

This would store the content of register R1 into the memory address held in R3.

3.3 Instruction Handling

As mentioned in Section 3.2, computers are operated through sequences of instructions known as *programs*. The generic term for such programs is *software*. Various schemes exist for creating software through writing in high-level languages (HLL), where each HLL command is made up of a sequence of perhaps several tens of CPU instructions. In low-level languages, typically each command invokes few, or perhaps only a single CPU operation.

If we define a CPU operation to be some data move or logical transaction by the CPU, an instruction is a command to the CPU from a program (which results in one or more CPU operations). A HLL command is made up of one or more instructions, and a stored program is a list of such instructions.

In some computers, a single instruction can be used to invoke multiple CPU operations. This may be required for performance reasons, especially where the rate at which a program can be read from external memory is far slower than the speed at which the processor can execute the operations. In fact, this thinking led in the past to the idea of microcode (explored in Section 3.2.5).

Machine code is the name given to (usually) binary numerical identifiers that correspond to known actions in a CPU. This may mean, for example, that when examining program memory, hexadecimal byte `0x4E` followed by byte `0xA8` might represent two instructions in an 8-bit processor, or a single instruction, `0x4EA8`, in a 16-bit processor. In modern processors, programmers are very rarely required to deal with the underlying binary numerical identifiers that the processor understands, but handle these through a set of abbreviated mnemonics called *assembly language* or *assembly code*. It is this code that is produced and stored when compiling a HLL into an executable.

The instruction set is a list of the possible assembly language mnemonics. It is a list of all instructions supported by a particular CPU.

3.3.1 The Instruction Set

The instruction set describes the set of operations that the CPU is capable of performing, with each operation being encoded through an instruction which is part of the set. Some instructions require one or more operands (for example, ADD A, B, C where A, B and C are called the source and destination operands and may be immediate values, registers, memory locations or others depending on the addressing modes available – see Section 3.3.4). Often, there is a restriction placed on operand type or range, for example, a shift instruction may be limited to the maximum shift allowed by the shift hardware.

The instruction set contains every instruction and thus describes the full capability of the processor hardware. The set may be broken into groups based upon which processor unit they involve such as the following defined for the ADSP2181 processor:

Instruction group	Example operations within the group
ALU	add, subtract, AND, OR, etc.
MAC	multiply, multiply-accumulate, etc.
SHIFT	arithmetic/logical shift left/right, derive exponent, etc.
MOVE	register/register, memory/register, register/memory, I/O, etc.
PROGRAM FLOW	branch/jump, call, return, do loops, etc.
MISC	idle mode, NOP, stack control, configuration, etc.

Many processors would add an FPU or MMX group to those defined, but the ADSP2181 is a fixed point only processor with no multimedia extensions.

The instruction set for the ARM processor, specifically the ARM7, is shown for reference in Figure 3.9 (note this shows the ARM mode instructions and does not include the 16-bit Thumb mode that many ARM processors also support). Notations used in the instruction set table include the following:

- **S** in bit 20 indicates instruction should update condition flags upon completion (see Box 3.2).
- **S** in bit 6/22 indicates transfer instruction should restore status register.
- **U** signed/unsigned for multiply and up/down for data transfer index modifications.
- **I** an indicator bit used to select immediate addressing.

Figure 3.9

<table>
<tr><th>31 30 29 28</th><th>27</th><th>26</th><th>25</th><th>24</th><th>23</th><th>22</th><th>21</th><th>20</th><th>19</th><th>18</th><th>17</th><th>16</th><th>15</th><th>14</th><th>13</th><th>12</th><th>11</th><th>10</th><th>9</th><th>8</th><th>7</th><th>6</th><th>5</th><th>4</th><th>3</th><th>2</th><th>1</th><th>0</th><th></th></tr>
<tr><td>conditions</td><td>0</td><td>1</td><td>1</td><td>X</td><td>X</td><td>X</td><td>X</td><td>X</td><td>X</td><td>X</td><td>X</td><td>X</td><td>X</td><td>X</td><td>X</td><td>X</td><td>X</td><td>X</td><td>X</td><td>X</td><td>X</td><td>X</td><td>X</td><td>1</td><td>X</td><td>X</td><td>X</td><td>X</td><td>undefined</td></tr>
<tr><td>conditions</td><td>0</td><td>0</td><td>I</td><td colspan="4">opcode</td><td>S</td><td colspan="4">Rn</td><td colspan="4">Rd</td><td colspan="12">second operand</td><td>data processing</td></tr>
<tr><td>conditions</td><td>1</td><td>0</td><td>1</td><td>L</td><td colspan="24">address offset to destination</td><td>branch</td></tr>
<tr><td>conditions</td><td>0</td><td>0</td><td>0</td><td>0</td><td>0</td><td>0</td><td>A</td><td>S</td><td colspan="4">Rn</td><td colspan="4">Rd</td><td colspan="4">Rs</td><td>1</td><td>0</td><td>0</td><td>1</td><td colspan="4">Rm</td><td>MUL</td></tr>
<tr><td>conditions</td><td>0</td><td>0</td><td>0</td><td>0</td><td>1</td><td>U</td><td>A</td><td>S</td><td colspan="4">RdHi</td><td colspan="4">RdLow</td><td colspan="4">Rn</td><td>1</td><td>0</td><td>0</td><td>1</td><td colspan="4">Rm</td><td>long multiply</td></tr>
<tr><td>conditions</td><td>0</td><td>1</td><td>I</td><td>P</td><td>U</td><td>B</td><td>WL</td><td></td><td colspan="4">Rn</td><td colspan="4">Rd</td><td colspan="12">address offset</td><td>LDR/STR</td></tr>
<tr><td>conditions</td><td>0</td><td>0</td><td>0</td><td>P</td><td>U</td><td>1</td><td>WL</td><td></td><td colspan="4">Rn</td><td colspan="4">Rd</td><td colspan="4">offset</td><td>1</td><td>S</td><td>H</td><td>1</td><td colspan="4">offset</td><td>halfword transfer</td></tr>
<tr><td>conditions</td><td>0</td><td>0</td><td>0</td><td>P</td><td>U</td><td>0</td><td>WL</td><td></td><td colspan="4">Rn</td><td colspan="4">Rd</td><td>0</td><td>0</td><td>0</td><td>0</td><td>1</td><td>S</td><td>H</td><td>1</td><td colspan="4">Rm</td><td>halfword transfer</td></tr>
<tr><td>conditions</td><td>1</td><td>0</td><td>0</td><td>P</td><td>U</td><td>S</td><td>WL</td><td></td><td colspan="4">Rn</td><td colspan="16">list of registers</td><td>block transfer</td></tr>
<tr><td>conditions</td><td>0</td><td>0</td><td>0</td><td>1</td><td>0</td><td>0</td><td>1</td><td>0</td><td>1</td><td>1</td><td>1</td><td>1</td><td>1</td><td>1</td><td>1</td><td>1</td><td>1</td><td>1</td><td>1</td><td>1</td><td>0</td><td>0</td><td>0</td><td>1</td><td colspan="4">Rn</td><td>BX</td></tr>
<tr><td>conditions</td><td>0</td><td>0</td><td>0</td><td>1</td><td>0</td><td>B</td><td>0</td><td>0</td><td colspan="4">Rn</td><td colspan="4">Rd</td><td>0</td><td>0</td><td>0</td><td>0</td><td>1</td><td>0</td><td>0</td><td>1</td><td colspan="4">Rm</td><td>single data swap</td></tr>
<tr><td>conditions</td><td>1</td><td>1</td><td>0</td><td>P</td><td>U</td><td>N</td><td>WL</td><td></td><td colspan="4">Rn</td><td colspan="4">CRd</td><td colspan="4">CP no.</td><td colspan="8">offset</td><td>LDC</td></tr>
<tr><td>conditions</td><td>1</td><td>1</td><td>1</td><td>0</td><td colspan="4">CP opcode</td><td colspan="4">CRn</td><td colspan="4">CRd</td><td colspan="4">CP no.</td><td colspan="3">CP</td><td>0</td><td colspan="4">CRm</td><td>CDP</td></tr>
<tr><td>conditions</td><td>1</td><td>1</td><td>1</td><td>0</td><td colspan="3">CP opcode</td><td>L</td><td colspan="4">CRn</td><td colspan="4">Rd</td><td colspan="4">CP no.</td><td colspan="3">CP</td><td>2</td><td colspan="4">CRm</td><td>MCR</td></tr>
</table>

The ARM instruction set in a tabulated format. Columns are headed by the instruction word bit they contain. All 14 classes of instruction available in this version of the ARM instruction set are shown.

- **A** accumulate/do not accumulate answer.
- **B** unsigned byte/word.
- **W** write back.
- **L** load/store.
- **P** pre- and post-increment and decrement operators.
- **R** indicates one of the 16 registers.
- **CR** indicates a co-processor register (one of eight co-processors that can be identified).

Many of these modifiers are specific to the ARM processor and will not be considered further in the text. However, we shall look in more detail at the 'S' bit and the addressing capabilities (see Section 3.3.4). The interested reader is referred to the ARM Ltd website[1] where further explanations and documents are available. The instruction set varies slightly among ARM processors. The version shown above is the more common ARM7TDMI version.[2]

Recently, ARM have completed a rebranding exercise in which their processors are now known as Cortex devices. The original ARM7, ARM9 and ARM11 devices are termed 'classic'. Most likely, this move has been an effort to counter the fragmentation of the huge ARM market in which one basic architecture (the ARM) was required to span a very wide and diverse set of needs, ranging from tiny and slow sensor systems to larger and faster handheld computers. At the time of writing, the new processors are classed into three ranges which better subdivide the traditional strength areas for ARM devices:

Cortex-A series processors are application-oriented. They have the in-built hardware support suited for running rich modern operating systems such as Linux, with graphically rich user interfaces such as Apple's iOS and Google's Android. The processing power of these runs from the efficient Cortex-A5, through the A8, A9 and up to the highest performance Cortex-A15 device. All support ARM, Thumb and Thumb-2 instructions sets (Thumb-2 reportedly improves upon Thumb in terms of performance and compactness).

Cortex-R series devices are targeted to real-time systems that also have significant performance requirements. These include smartphone handsets, media players and cameras. The ARM company is also promoting Cortex-R for automotive and medical systems; ones in which reliability and hard real-time response are often important. These probably do not require complex and rich operating systems, just small, hard and fast real-time arrangements. At the time of writing, only the Cortex-R4 is available, and has already found its way into many real-time systems in use worldwide.

Cortex-M family processors are at the lower end of the range for use in very cost-sensitive and low power systems. It could be argued that these are for traditional microcontroller-type applications that probably do not need advanced operating

[1] `http://www.arm.com`

[2] This information was extracted from ARM Ltd Open Access document DDI 0029E.

system support (and possibly do not need any OS). These are for applications that do not have rich user interface requirements, and for which the clock speed will be no more than several tens of MHz. At the time of writing, the Cortex-M0 is the entry device, beyond which the M3 and M4 provide increasing levels of performance.

Although most variants of the ARM7 support a 16-bit Thumb mode (see Section 3.3.3), all ARM7 devices support the standard fixed length 32-bit instructions shown above. It can be seen that, as in the ADSP21xx, there are various groups of instructions, such as data processing, multiply or branch. With 15 instruction groups, 4 bits are needed to represent the instruction group and further bits are used within this to represent the exact instruction in each group.

Notice the fixed condition bits available for every instruction. No matter which instruction is being used, these bits are located at the same position in the instruction word. This regularity aids in instruction decoding within the processor. It is important to note that the consequence of this is that every instruction can operate conditionally. This is unusual, and among common modern processors is found only in the ARM: most other processors support conditional branch instructions only. In the ARM, the S bit within many instruction words controls whether that instruction can change condition codes on completion (see Box 3.2). These two features, when used in conjunction with each other, are very flexible and efficient.

Also, note that for every instruction, the destination register (if required) is in the same place in the instruction word. This further regularity also simplifies the decoding process.

3.3.2 Instruction Fetch and Decode

In a modern computer system, programs being executed normally reside in RAM (they may have been copied there from hard disc or flash memory). A memory controller, usually part of a memory management unit that we will explore in Section 4.3, controls external RAM and handles memory accesses on behalf of the CPU.

Within the CPU, an instruction fetch and decode unit (IFDU or simply IFU) retrieves the next instruction to be executed at each instruction cycle. The next instruction is identified by an address pointer, which is held in a program counter (PC) in nearly every processor in use today. This program counter is normally incremented automatically after an instruction is retrieved, but is overridden with a new value when a jump or a branch occurs. These items are illustrated in Figure 3.10.

Figure 3.10

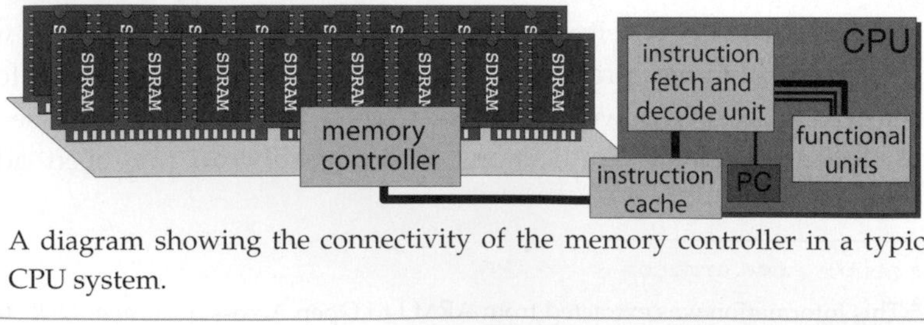

A diagram showing the connectivity of the memory controller in a typical CPU system.

Box 3.2

Illustrating conditionals and the S bit in the ARM

Consider the efficiency of the ARM processor compared to a mythical standard RISC processor that does not allow conditional operation for every instruction.

The instruction mnemonics used are similar to those of the ARM (but not completely realistic). First, we will examine the program on the standard RISC processor that adds the numbers in registers R0 and R1 and then, depending on the answer, either places a 0 in register R2 (if the result is less than 0) or places a 1 in register R2 otherwise.

```
        ADDS R0, R0, R1
        BLT pos1    (branch if less than 0)
        MOV R2, #1
        B pos2
pos1 MOV R2, #0
pos2 .....
```

The program occupies five instructions and will always require a branch no matter what registers R0 and R1 contain on entry.

The following code segment reproduces the same behaviour for the ARM processor, but uses conditional moves to replace the branch. In this case, R0 and R1 are added. The S after the ADD mnemonic indicates that the result of the addition should update the internal condition flags. Next, a value 1 is loaded into R2 if the result of the last condition-code-setting instruction is less than 0. A value 0 is loaded into R2 if the result is greater than or equal to 0.

```
ADDS  R0, R0, R1
MOVLT R2, #1
MOVGE R2, #0
.....
```

The ARM version is obviously shorter – only three instructions are required, and in this case no branches are needed. It is this mechanism that allows ARM programs to be efficient whereas RISC processors are traditionally known for less efficient code density. In higher level languages, the structure that leads to this code arrangement is very common:

```
IF condition THEN
   action 1
ELSE
   action 2
```

Once the instruction fetch and decode unit reads an instruction, it begins to decode that instruction which then flows through steps as shown in the flowchart of Figure 3.11.

Figure 3.11

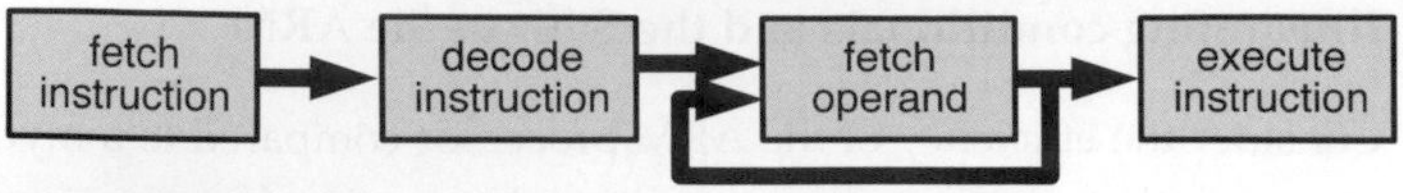

A flowchart of instruction processing for a typical processor.

3.3.2.1 Instruction Decode

In the ARM, because all instructions can be conditional, the IFU first looks at the condition code bits encoded in the instruction and compares these bitwise with the current condition flags in the processor status register. If the conditions required by the instruction do not match the current condition flags, then the instruction is dumped and the next one retrieved instead.

In the ARM, the simplicity of the instruction set means that the conditional bits of each retrieved word can simply be ANDed with status register bits 28 to 31 (that encode the current condition flags). Box 3.3 explains the quite extensive set of conditional codes available in the ARM.

Looking again at the ARM instruction set, it can be seen that the destination register (for instructions that have a destination) is located in the same place in each instruction word. On decode, the IFU simply takes these 4 bits (used to address the 16 registers) and applies them as a register bank destination address.

3.3.2.2 Fetch Operand

Evidently, the value of the operand is not always encoded in the instruction word itself. The ARM and many other RISC processors are simplified by being *load-store* architectures where operands in memory cannot be used directly in an operation – they have to be transferred into a register first. The exception is with immediate values which are encoded as part of several data processing instructions, such as `MOV` (see the example in Box 3.4).

So the ARM normally prepares operands for an operation either by decoding an immediate value from the instruction word or by selecting one or more source, and one destination register. The exception is the load (`LDR`) and store (`STR`) instructions that explicitly move 32-bit values between memory and a register.

In many other processors, normally CISC rather than RISC, it is possible to execute an instruction that performs some operation on the contents of a memory address and stores the result back into another memory address. Evidently in such a processor, the action of moving operands around will require one or two memory accesses. Since RISC processors aim to complete each instruction within a single clock cycle if possible, this has been disallowed.

3.3.2.3 Branching

The branch instruction group in the ARM instruction set is, as expected, all conditional – as indeed are branch instructions in nearly all other processors. In a branch instruction, bits 24 to 27 are the unique identifiers that indicate an instruction in the branch group.

Box 3.3

Condition codes in the ARM processor

The ARM, as we have seen in Figure 3.9, reserves 4 bits (bits 31, 30, 29 and 28) for condition codes in every instruction. This means that every machine code instruction can be conditional (although when written in assembly language there may be some instructions which do not take conditionals).

Normally, the condition code is appended to the instruction. Thus, an `ADDGT` is an `ADD` instruction that only executes when the condition flags in the processor indicate that the result of the last instruction which set the condition flags is greater than 0.

The full set of ARM conditionals is shown in the table below (although strictly the last two are unconditional conditionals!).

Condition nibble	Condition code	Meaning	Conditional on
0000	EQ	equal	$Z=1$
0001	NE	not equal	$Z=0$
0010	CS	carry set	$C=1$
0011	CC	carry clear	$C=0$
0100	MI	minus	$N=1$
0101	PL	plus	$N=0$
0110	VS	overflow set	$V=1$
0111	VC	overflow clear	$V=0$
1000	HI	higher	$C=1, Z=0$
1001	LS	lower or same	$C=0, Z=1$
1010	GE	greater or equal	$N=V$
1011	LT	less than	$N=\sim V$
1100	GT	greater than	$N=V, Z=0$
1101	LE	less than or equal	$(N=\sim V)$ or $Z=1$
1110	AL	always	–
1111	NV	never	–

The L bit distinguishes between a jump or a call (branch-and-link in ARM terminology, where *link* means that the address to return to is placed in the link register LR, which is R14, when the branch occurs). Apart from the 4 bits needed to define the instruction type, 4 bits are needed for condition codes. So there are only 24 bits remaining. These 24 bits are called the *offset*. They indicate where to branch to – which instruction address should be placed in the program counter.

Since the ARM is a 32-bit processor, instruction words are 32 bits wide. However, memory is only byte wide, such that one instruction spans four consecutive memory locations. The ARM designers have specified that instructions cannot start just anywhere, they can only start on 4-byte boundaries: addresses 0, 4, 8, 12 and so on. So the *offset* refers to blocks of 4 bytes.

Now there are two general methods of indicating addresses to branch to in computer architecture; these are *absolute* and *relative*. Absolute specifies a complete memory address, whereas relative specifies a certain number of locations forwards or backwards from the current position. As computer memory spaces have become larger, specifying absolute addresses has become inefficient – the principle of locality (Section 4.4.4) indicates that branch distances will usually be quite small, requiring fewer bits to specify than an entire absolute jump address (which would in fact take 28 bits in the ARM).

Back to the ARM, the jump address is termed an offset, which means it must be a jump relative to the current program counter location. With a 24-bit offset, a branch can indicate a jump range of 2^{24} words in memory which is 64 MiB. Of course, the offset has to be signed to allow a jump backwards (as in a loop) as well as forwards, and so this means a $+/-$ 32 MiB jump span.

Is the limited branch range a limitation? Not normally. Despite rampant code bloat, even at the time of writing, single programs are not usually 64 MiB long. It is thus likely that the ARM's designers have catered for the vast majority of jump requirements with the instruction.

However, a 32-bit memory bus allows up to 4 GiB of memory space to be addressed, which is far larger than the capability of address jumps. So, if a 70 MiB jump is required, how could it be accomplished?

In this case, the ARM has a *branch and exchange* instruction. To use this, the destination address is first loaded into a register (which is 32 bits in size), and then this instruction can be issued to jump to the address held in that register. Of course, the question arises as to how the register itself can be loaded with a 32-bit number. Section 3.3.4 will discuss addressing modes, one of which is the immediate constant – a number encoded as part of the instruction. Box 3.4 will also consider how immediate values can be loaded with the MOV instruction.

3.3.2.4 Immediate Constant

The issue is that, with a 32-bit instruction word, it is not possible to convey a 32-bit constant as well as bits specifying condition, destination register, S bit and so on. An immediate constant (a value encoded within the instruction word) has to be less than 32 bits.

Box 3.4

Understanding the MOV instruction in the ARM

The MOV is 32-bits long like all ARM instructions. Its structure is shown below.

4-bit cond	0	0	1	opcode	S	Rn	Rd	4-bit rotation	8-bit value

or

4-bit cond	0	0	0	opcode	S	Rn	Rd	immediate/register shift & Rm

The 4-bit condition code is common with all other ARM instructions, the opcode defines the exact instruction in the data processing class, Rn is the first operand register, Rd is the second operand register and, selected through bit 25 = 1, Rm is the third.

We will concentrate on the top form of the command, where an 8-bit immediate constant and 4-bit rotation are supplied (the actual rotation to be applied is twice the value supplied here). Where the opcode specifies a MOV instruction, the immediate, rotated by the degree specified is loaded into the destination register. Here are some examples:

```
MOV R5, #0xFF      ; Rd = 5, Rn = 0, rotation = 0, value = 0xFF
MOV R2, #0x2180    ; Rd = 2, Rn = 0, rotation = 2, value = 0x43 (loads 0x43<<4)
```

Note: For these MOV instructions, Rn is always set to 0 since it is unused.

Question: How can the processor set a register to 0xF0FFFFFF?

Answer: The programmer would probably write:

```
MOV R0, #0xF0FFFFFF
```

However, the assembler would be likely to complain ('number too big for immediate constant' or similar) since the 32-bit value that is specified cannot fit into an 8-bit register no matter what degree of shift is required. Some assemblers and more experienced programmers would know that they can simply convert the instruction to a 'move NOT' instead:

```
MVN R0, #0x0F000000    ; Rd = 0, Rn = 0, rotation = 12, value = 0x0F
```

As you can see, despite the relatively small immediate value size that can be accommodated within the instruction field, this allied with the instruction flexibility and shift value, can actually encode quite a wide variety of constants.

In the case of the ARM, immediate constants are loaded into a register with the MOV instruction (in the data processing instruction group). An immediate value can be located inside the section labelled 'Operand 2' in the ARM instruction set (Figure 3.9). However, not all of the operand is used for holding the constant. In fact, only an 8-bit immediate value is catered for, with the remaining 4 bits used to specify a rotation.

So, although the processor has 32-bit registers, only an 8-bit number can be loaded. However, due to the rotation mechanism (with 4 bits for rotation this can specify 15 positions either left or right), a large variety of numbers can result. Box 3.4 looks in detail at the bitfields present in the ARM processor MOV instruction, to see how these impact the flexibility of one variant of the instruction.

Many processors work differently. They generally allow at least a 16-bit constant to be loaded immediately and the 16 bits are encoded as part of the instruction word. CISC processors often have variable length instructions or use two consecutive instructions. A variable length instruction may be 16-bits long when only an 8-bit constant is to be loaded, or 32-bits long when a 16-bit or 24-bit constant is loaded. Variable length instructions require the instruction fetch unit to be fairly complex, and thus a more simple method of achieving a similar result is to use two consecutive instructions. The first instruction may mean 'load the next instruction value to register R2' so that the IFU simply reads the next value directly into the register rather than trying to decode it. This evidently means that some instructions require two instruction cycles to execute, and imposes a timing penalty, especially in pipelined processors (Section 5.2).

For the example of the ARM processor, although the restriction in immediate values exists, in practice many constants can be encoded with an 8-bit value and a shift so that this does not translate into a significant performance bottleneck. The ADSP2181 handles immediate loads in a similar fashion and has been designed for high-speed single-cycle operation.

3.3.3 Compressed Instruction Sets

Especially in processors with variable length instructions, *Huffman encoding* is used to improve processor efficiency. In fact, as we shall see later, similar ideas can be used even within a fixed length processor, but in this case not for efficiency reasons.

Huffman encoding is based on the principle of reducing the size of the most common instructions and increasing the size of the least common instructions to result in an average size reduction. Obviously, this requires knowledge of the probability of instructions occurring and then allowing the size of the encoded word used to represent those instructions to be inversely proportional to their probability. An example of Huffman coding applied to instruction set design is provided in Box 3.5.

It should be noted that in the real world, one particular application may exhibit very different instruction probability statistics compared to the average.

Many ARM processors contain an alternative 16-bit instruction set called the Thumb. This was designed to improve code density. Note however that even though a given memory size can support twice as many Thumb instructions compared to 32-bit ARM instructions, on average more Thumb instructions are required to perform the same function as the underlying ARM instructions which they map to once decoded (this is mainly because there are fewer different Thumb instructions to choose from).

The process by which ARM engineers designed the Thumb instruction set is noteworthy since they used a similar idea to Huffman coding. ARM engineers examined a database of example application code and calculated the number of uses of each

Box 3.5

A Huffman coding illustration

An example processor has five instructions for which an analysis of the 1000 instruction software program that it runs reveals the following occurrences:

```
CALL 60, ADD 300, SUB 80, AND 60, MOV 500
```

If an equal number of bits were used to represent each instruction in this instruction set, 3 bits would be needed (since that would allow up to seven possibilities). Ignoring any operands, 1000×3 bits $= 3000$ bits are required to represent that program.

The processor designers wish to use Huffman coding to reduce the program size. First, they calculate the probability of each instruction (by dividing each occurrence by the total number of instructions):

```
CALL 0.06, ADD 0.3, SUB 0.08, AND 0.06, MOV 0.5
```

Next, these are ordered in a list in terms of probability. The lowest two probabilities are combined and the list re-ordered:

MOV 0.5	MOV 0.5
ADD 0.3	ADD 0.3
SUB 0.08	**C/A** 0.12
CALL 0.06	SUB 0.08
AND 0.06	

This process is then repeated until finally there are only two choices left:

MOV 0.5	MOV 0.5	MOV 0.5	MOV 0.5
ADD 0.3	ADD 0.3	ADD 0.3	**C/A/S/A** 0.5
SUB 0.08	**C/A** 0.12	**C/A/S** 0.2	
CALL 0.06	SUB 0.08		
AND 0.06			

Next, traverse the tree from right to left. The bottom two entires in each column are numbered: the upper value is designated binary '1' and the lower is binary '0', and these numbers must be written down when tracing through. Any other column entry can simply be followed left without writing anything more until the original instruction on the left-hand side is reached.

For example, in the right-hand column, a '1' indicates MOV, a '0' indicates any one of CALL/AND/SUB/ADD. Moving left, a '01' now indicates an ADD whereas a '00' is the prefix for any of CALL/AND/SUB. In the next column, '001' indicates either CALL or AND and '000' indicates SUB. Writing all of these out gives the following:

(Continued)

Box 3.5

A Huffman coding illustration (*Continued*)

MOV is '1', ADD is '01', SUB is '000', CALL is '0011', and AND is '0010'. If we look at the number of bits used to represent each instruction, we can see that the most common instruction (MOV) is represented by a single bit whereas the least common (AND) needs 4 bits, so the encoding method seems to have worked in representing the most common instructions with fewer bits. Using the original number of occurrences of each instruction and the number of Huffman bits, we can calculate the new program size:

$$(500 \times 1) + (300 \times 2) + (80 \times 3) + (60 \times 4) + (60 \times 4) = 1820$$

Which is significantly fewer than the 3000 bits we calculated for a fixed 3-bit representation.

instruction. Only the most common instructions were made available in Thumb mode. The binary encoding within the fixed 16-bit word used to represent an instruction is length coded based on the number of bits required for the other operands.

Some features of the Thumb instruction set are as follows:

- There is only one conditional instruction (an offset branch).
- There is no 'S' flag. Most Thumb instructions will update condition flags automatically.
- The destination register is usually the same as one of the source registers (in ARM mode the destination and source are almost always specified separately).
- All instructions are 16 bits (but register and internal bus width is still 32 bits).
- The addressing mode for immediate and offset addresses is significantly limited.
- Most instructions can only access the lower 8 registers (of 16).

The Thumb instruction set is significantly more complicated than the ARM instruction set, although the decoding process (from Thumb instruction fetched from memory to ARM instruction ready to be executed inside the processor) is automatic and very fast. The following are some example instructions:

16-bit binary instruction bit pattern			**Instruction name**	**Example**
1101	Condition (4 bits)	Offset (8 bits)	Conditional branch	BLT loop
11100	Offset (11 bits)		Branch	B main
01001	Destination register (4 bits)	Offset (8 bits)	Load memory to register	LDR R3, [PC, #10]
101100001	Immediate (7 bits)		Add to stack	ADD SP, SP, #23

From the limited examples shown here, it can be seen that the few most significant bits identify the instruction. These actually range from 3 bits to 9 bits in length across the entire instruction set. In the case of the ADD instruction shown, the register it operates on is fixed: it is an add to stack only – the flexibility and regularity of the ARM instruction set, where almost all instructions operate on any registers, is lost – but the most common operations found in software *are* catered for.

It should be noted at this point that the Thumb instruction set, being 16 bits wide, really operates at its best when the interface to external memory is 16 bits, in which case each ARM instruction would require two memory cycles to be retrieved (and thus the processor would run half as fast as it should), whereas the Thumb code could be executed at full speed.

3.3.4 Addressing Modes

Addressing modes describe the various methods of identifying an operand within an instruction. Instructions specify many operations, which may have no operands, one, two or three operands. There may, very exceptionally, be instructions with greater than three operands. In most modern processors, common examples of non-zero operands are as follows:

Type	Examples	Operand
Single operand	B address	Address, may be given directly, may be an offset from current position or may be an address in a register or memory location.
Two operands	NOT destination, source	Destination or source may be registers, memory addresses or memory locations specified by registers. The source may also be a numeric value.
Three operands	ADD destination, source, source	Destination or source may be registers, memory addresses or memory locations specified by registers. The source may also be a numeric value.

Of course, not all possible operand types are suitable for all instructions, and even so may not be available on some processors (for example RISC processors, being *load-store*, typically limit the operands of arithmetic instructions to registers, whereas in CISC processors they may be located in memory or elsewhere). A final point to note is the assumption in the two bottom examples above that the first operand written is the destination – which is true for ARM assembly language, but is reversed for some other processors (see Section 3.2.7). This can be a real cause for confusion when writing assembler code for different processors (and is an occupational hazard for computer architecture lecturers/authors).

The term *addressing mode* refers to the method of specifying a load or store address, using one of several different techniques. The following table lists the common addressing modes, with ARM-style assembly language examples (although it should be noted that PUSH does not exist in the ARM instruction set, only in the Thumb).

Name	Example	Explanation
Immediate addressing	MOV R0, **#0x1000**	Move hexadecimal value 0x1000 to register R0
Absolute addressing	LDR R0, **#0x20**	Load whatever is in memory at address 0x20 into R0
Register direct addressing	NOT R0, **R1**	Take content of R1, NOT it and store inside R0
Register indirect addressing	LDR R0, **[R1]**	If R1 contains value 0x123, then retrieve contents of memory location 0x123, and place it in R0
Stack addressing	PUSH R0	In this case, the contents of R0 are pushed onto the stack (and the assumption is of only one stack)

The following extensions and combinations of the basic idea are also common:

Name	Example	Explanation if R1 = 1 & R2 = 2
Register indirect with immediate offset	LDR R0, **[R1, #5]**	The second operand is the memory address $1 + 5 = 6$
Register indirect with register indirect index	STR R0, **[R1, R2]**	The second operand is the memory address $1 + 2 = 3$
Register indirect with register indirect index and immediate offset	LDR R0, **[R1, R2, #3]**	The second operand is the memory address $1 + 2 + 3 = 6$
Register indirect with immediate scaled register indirect index	STR R0, **[R1, R2, LSL #2]**	The second operand is the memory address $1 + (2 \ll 2) = 9$

Various processors, including the ARM and the ADSP2181, also offer an automatic way to update registers after they have been used to perform offset addressing. For example, a register indirect access with immediate offset could leave the register used in the access updated after addition of the offset. This is shown in the following examples where R1 = 22:

`LDR R0, [R1], #5`	*Load R0 with content of memory address 22 and then set R1 = 22 + 5 = 27*
`LDR R0, [R1, #5]!`	*Set R1 = 22 + 5 = 27 and then load R0 with content of memory address 27*

Note that it is not our intention here to teach the details of the ARM instruction set, but merely to use it as a teaching aid for the underlying addressing techniques.[3]

It is instructive to analyse the limitations that caused CPU designers to provide certain levels of functionality within a processor – and this is rarely more revealing than in the consideration of the instruction set. In this regard, CISC processors are more interesting. Some examples are given below from an imaginary CISC processor, where main memory locations mA, mB and mC are used for absolute operand storage, and a RISC processor, where registers R0, R1 and R2 are used for register direct addressing:

- **CISC processor:** `ADD mA, mB, mC` ; mA = mB + mC

  In this case, once the CPU has read and decoded the instruction, it must read the content of two further memory locations to retrieve the operand values mB and mC, and this probably requires two memory bus cycles. These values must then be transferred by internal bus to the ALU as they are retrieved (and since this is sequential, only one bus is needed). Once the ALU has calculated the result, this is transferred by bus to a memory interface for writing back to main memory location mA.

  The instruction overhead is three external memory cycles in addition to the ALU operation time. External memory cycles are usually far slower than internal ALU operations, and so this is clearly a bottleneck. There is only a need for one internal bus in this processor.

  The instruction word must hold three absolute addresses. With 32-bit memory, this equates to 96 bits, making a very long instruction word. This could be reduced through offset/relative addressing, but would probably still be too big for a 32-bit instruction word.

- **RISC processor:** `ADD R0, R1, R2` ; R0 = R1 + R2

  The same operation is now performed with registers. All of the operand values are already inside the CPU, which means they can be accessed quickly. Once the instruction has been read and decoded, register R1 is allowed to drive one internal operand bus and register R2 is allowed to drive the other internal operand bus simultaneously. Both operands are thus conveyed to the ALU in a single very fast internal bus cycle. Once the ALU has calculated the result, an internal results bus will collect the result. R0 will be listening to this bus and, at the appropriate time, latch the result value from the bus.

  The instruction overhead is two fast internal bus cycles in addition to the ALU operation time. In our example description, the CPU must contain three internal buses: two to simultaneously transfer both operands and one to collect the result. Other alternative arrangements are equally possible.

---

[3] Those who *do* wish to learn the ARM instruction set are recommended to refer to the book *ARM System Architecture*, by Steve Furber (one of the original inventors of the ARM processor).

The instruction word needs to contain three register values. However, with a bank of 32 registers, only 5 bits are needed to specify each register, and so 15 bits are used in total. This would easily allow the operation to be encoded in a 32-bit instruction.

- **CISC processor:** `ADD mA, mB` ; mA = mA + mB

  Similar to the first example, the CPU must read two external memory locations to retrieve the operand values, requiring two memory bus cycles. It also needs to transfer the result back to memory and thus execution time is unchanged.

  However, the instruction word this time only needs to contain two absolute addresses instead of three. This would be achievable in a real system, especially if an absolute value is used for the first operand address and an offset used for the second one.

- **CISC processor:** `ADD mB` ; ACC = mB + ACC

  The CISC processors of the 1980s and earlier commonly utilised accumulators. These were general-purpose registers (the forerunners of the register bank) that were used as an operand for all arithmetic and data mode operations and to hold the result of those operations. The other operand was almost always an absolute value from memory. In this case, the instruction requires a single value to be loaded from memory prior to the addition and thus involves a single external memory bus cycle.

  The instruction word needs to only contain a single absolute memory value, which could be achieved by loading a second instruction word containing the address (thus requiring two instruction fetches to be performed prior to instruction execution).

- **Stack processor:** `ADD`

  This is a special case (that will be explored further in the next section and specifically in Chapter 8) where a CPU pops the top two stack entries, adds them together and pushes the result back onto the stack. This needs to access a stack which would be quick if it were an internal memory storage block, however, a stack would more normally be located in off-chip memory. The main benefit with the stack approach is that the instruction does not need to encode any absolute memory addresses. Theoretically, this can make for an extremely small instruction width.

3.3.5 Stack Machines and Reverse Polish Notation

People generally employ *infix* notation to represent an operation written on paper (such as $a + b \div c$), where an agreed fixed precedence[4] of operators (that can be overridden using parentheses) determines the order in which the various operations occur. Polish notation (note: not *reverse* Polish notation) was invented by Polish mathematician Jan

[4] Many readers may remember being taught the BODMAS acronym as an aid to remembering precedence during primary school mathematics. BODMAS stands for **B**rackets, **O**rders (e.g. powers and square roots), **D**ivision, **M**ultiplication, **A**ddition and **S**ubtraction: see `http://www.malton.n-yorks.sch.uk/MathsWeb/reference/bodmas.html`

Lukasiewicz in the 1920s to place the operator before the operands, thus it is a *prefix* notation. By specifying the operand in this way, operator precedence is unimportant and parentheses are not required.

Reverse Polish notation (RPN) by contrast is a *postfix* notation where the order of the equation completely defines the precedence. This was created during the 1950s and 1960s as an aid to working with a stack-based architecture. It was subsequently introduced and loved (or hated) by two generations of Hewett-Packard electronic calculator users.

An example of RPN is $bc \div a +$, where the operands b and c are given first followed by the command to divide them and hold the result. Then operand a is loaded followed by the command to add the previous result to a and store the new result somewhere. Some further examples are shown below and in Figure 3.12.

Infix	**Postfix**
a × b	ab ×
a + b − c	ab + c −
(a + b) ÷ c	ab + c ÷

Considering the operations taking place, it becomes evident that using a stack is a very efficient method of performing RPN operations. A stack in this case is a storage device with a single entry/exit point. Numbers can be pushed onto the 'top' of the stack and then popped back off the 'top' of it. It is a last-in first-out (LIFO) construct.

An example of a stack operation performing *ab* + is shown in Figure 3.12, reading from left to right. Some things to note are that only a single push occurs in each step (likely to each take a single cycle in a stack-based processor) although the number of pops required to feed an operation is determined by the number of operands required. For example, an ADD requires two operands, so two POPs are used to load those to the ALU. The result of each operation is PUSHed back onto the top of the stack.

Figure 3.12

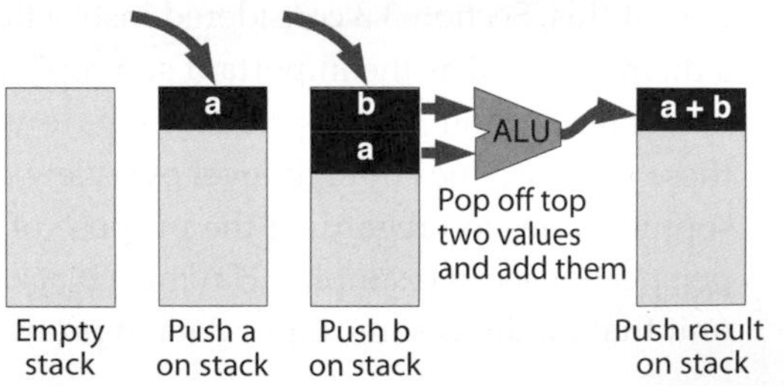

An illustration of the concept of stack processing. Two operands are pushed in turn onto the stack and ALU then executes, popping the operands, calculating the sum and then pushing the result back onto the stack.

Box 3.6

Recoding RPN instructions to minimise stack space

Consider the infix expression `a + (b × c)` which can also be written as `(b × c) + a` since the order of addition is unimportant to the final result.

For each expression, write the equation in postfix notation and write out the sequence of stack operations that would be required to execute it. Consider the stack usage for each expression.

It should be clear that writing the equation one way involves the use of a maximum stack depth of three locations, whereas the alternative way results in a stack depth of only two locations.

It appears that the order of the postfix expression can have a significant impact on the stack resources (and hence hardware resources) needed, although it will not alter the number of steps needed to find a solution.

Not all infix expressions are insensitive to order. Addition and multiplication are, whereas division and subtraction are most definitely not.

It is also interesting to consider the use of such a stack machine performing complex programming tasks. It seems efficient for simple operations, but sometimes it is possible that the final state of the stack after a sequence of operations may not have the correct results located on the top of the stack. This may be exacerbated by multi-tasking or interrupt service routines. There must be a way of re-ordering the stack, such as popping items out and storing into main memory, and then pushing them back in a different order. This could be a very time-consuming process and impacts heavily on the overall performance of a stack machine. This process is also explored in Box 3.6 where re-ordering is performed to minimise stack usage.

3.4 Data Handling

This chapter, up to now, has concentrated on CPU basics – what a computer is and what it fundamentally consists of. We have mentioned instructions, programs and so on. As part of this, Section 3.3 considered instruction handling, including some variations on a theme, as well as the important sub-topic of addressing modes.

Later, Section 3.5 will present a top-down view of computers. However, in between these two extremes of high-level overview and low-level detail, there is a more philosophical question regarding the purpose of computers. We can consider a 'black box' perspective as an example.[5] Having a black box perspective, we view a computer as a unit that modifies some input data to produce some output data.

[5] For those who have not encountered this term, a 'black box' is the name given to something that, when considered as a unit, is defined solely in terms of its inputs and outputs. It does not matter what is inside the box as long as it produces the correct output given the correct input.

Both input and output data could take many forms: commands, knowledge, sensor data, multimedia and so on. For some systems, input data could consist of a single trigger event. Output data could likewise consist of an actuator switch signal. This is the case in control systems, which often operate with a need for real-time processing of data (real-time issues are considered in depth in Section 6.4). Some systems are data rich – either input or output may consist of dense streams of data, such as digital audio or video. These systems may also need to operate in real time. However, the majority of computer systems are probably general-purpose machines capable of performing both control and data processing tasks with little regard to real-time issues.

The common theme here is clearly data: computers process data, whether that is a single bit trigger for which timing is critical, or a 1 Tbyte block of multimedia data that completes processing in several minutes. This section is dedicated to this important aspect of computers: what data is, how it is presented, stored and processed.

3.4.1 Data Formats and Representations

We have discussed number formats in general in Section 2.3, including those of most relevance to computers (unsigned binary, two's complement and so on). Whatever format is in use, the *width* of the number – the number of bits occupied by one number – can be adjusted by computer architects to either increase the largest magnitude number that can be stored or to increase the precision. Typically, since computers are byte-based, number sizes are in multiples of 8 bits.

Most CPUs have a natural size data format which is determined by the width of the internal buses, for example byte-wide in the old 6502 processor and 32-bits wide in the ARM. Although the ARM can also handle bytes and 16-bit half-words, it accesses main memory in 32-bit units, and thus handles 32-bit values no slower than the handing of bytes. Registers, memory locations, most operands and so on are 32 bits in the ARM.

Programmers typically handle data in memory or in registers through a high-level language such as C. Although some programming languages tightly define the number format used by data types within the language, that is not really the case for the C programming language, apart from the definition of a byte, which is always 8-bits in size.

Usually, although it is actually at the discretion of the particular C compiler in use, the `int` data type generally matches the natural size of the processor for machines of 16-bit word size and above. Thus, an `int` in a 16-bit machine will normally be a 16-bit number, whereas it will tend to be 64 bits in a 64-bit machine.

Programmers beware: if you wish to write portable code, ensure that there are no assumptions made about the exact size of a `int`, `short` and so on. Table 3.1 illustrates the width of several data types for the common gcc compiler targeting different processors.[6] Concerns over the changing nature of some of the original C language data

[6] Note that some compiler implementations will differ, or may not comply to ISO or ANSI C language specifications.

Table 3.1

Comparison of C programming language data type sizes for CPUs ranging from 8 bits to 64 bits. Note how some of the data types change size between processors, while others remain the same. For a particular implementation, these sizes are usually defined by maximum and minimum representable number specifications in the configuration header file *types.h*. Remember also that the byte order may change between big and little endian processors (see Section 2.2).

C name	8-bit CPU	16-bit CPU	32-bit CPU	64-bit CPU
char	8	8	8	8
byte	8	8	8	8
short	16	16	16	16
int	16	16	32	64
long int	32	32	32	64
long long int	64	64	64	64
float	32	32	32	32
double	64	64	64	64
long double	*compiler specific – may be 128, 96, 80 or 64 bits*			

types has led to many developers adopting specific-sized data types, described further in Box 3.7.

Of course, experienced programmers will know that any integer data type in the C programming language (i.e. the top six rows in the table) can be specified as either signed or unsigned. The default (if neither is specified) data types are signed two's complement.

The `long int` and `long long int` can also be specified as just `long` and `long long` respectively. On all but the largest machines these will require multiple memory locations for storage.

The char type normally contains a 7-bit useful value, complying with the ASCII standard (American Standard Code for Information Interchange), shown in Table 3.2. Any top-bit-set character (i.e. a char where bit 8 is non-zero) would be interpreted as an extended ASCII character (ASCII characters that are not shown in the figure). Interestingly, characters lower than decimal 32 (space) and including decimal 127 (delete), are non-printable characters having special values related to their original definitions for teletype terminals. For example, ASCII character 8, \b is the bell character, which would cause a 'beep' sound when printed. A brief web search can easily reveal the meanings of other special ASCII characters.

ASCII was excellent when computers were effectively confined to English (or American) speakers, but not particularly useful for other languages. Hence, significant effort

Box 3.7

Data types in embedded systems

Although general programs written in languages such as C and C++ will make use of the standard data types shown in Table 3.1, this can cause confusion when porting code. If a programmer makes an implicit assumption regarding the size of a particular data type, this assumption may no longer be correct when the code is compiled on a different processor.

The situation was actually far worse in the days before the widespread adoption of the gcc compiler – many compilers had different compilation modes such as 'large memory model' and 'small memory model' which could result in the number of bits used to represent variables changing (even gcc has command switches which can change this, but are not often used). Cross compiling for embedded systems, where the target machine may differ from the host compilation machine, makes it doubly important to ensure that any code tested on the host performs similarly on the target.

Perhaps the simplest way to achieve this, and to remain mindful of the limitations of different data types, is to directly specify the size of each type when declaring variables. In the C99 programming language (the version of C formalised in 1999) the definitions have been made for us in the `<stdint.h>` header file:

Size	Unsigned	Signed
8	`int8_t`	`uint8_t`
16	`int16_t`	`uint16_t`
32	`int32_t`	`uint32_t`
64	`int64_t`	`uint64_t`

The 64-bit definitions (and other odd sizes such as 24 bits) may exist for a particular processor implementation but not for others. Of course, if it exists, it will occupy the sizes given, but otherwise these are optional, so for some machines the compiler will not support anything but the main 8-, 16- and 32-bit definitions. Writers of code for embedded systems will likely encounter these safer type declarations more often than those writing desktop machine software. The author would encourage embedded systems developers to use the specific-sized types wherever possible.

has been paid over many years to define different character encodings for other languages. Perhaps the ultimate challenge has been Chinese which has around 13,000 pictograms (individual 'letters'): clearly an 8-bit data type is not able to encode written Chinese. Many solutions have appeared over the past two decades, most of which use

Table 3.2

The American Standard Code for Information Interchange, 7-bit ASCII table, showing the character (or name/identifier for non-printable characters) and the representative code in decimal and hexadecimal.

Char	Dec	Hex	Char	Dec	Hex	Char	Dec	Hex	Char	Dec	Hex
\0	0	0x00	(spc)	32	0x20	@	64	0x40	`	96	0x60
(soh)	1	0x01	!	33	0x21	A	65	0x41	a	97	0x61
(stx)	2	0x02	"	34	0x22	B	66	0x42	b	98	0x62
(etx)	3	0x03	#	35	0x23	C	67	0x43	c	99	0x63
(eot)	4	0x04	$	36	0x24	D	68	0x44	d	100	0x64
(enq)	5	0x05	%	37	0x25	E	69	0x45	e	101	0x65
(ack)	6	0x06	&	38	0x26	F	70	0x46	f	102	0x66
\a	7	0x07	'	39	0x27	G	71	0x47	g	103	0x67
\b	8	0x08	(	40	0x28	H	72	0x48	h	104	0x68
\t	9	0x09	)	41	0x29	I	73	0x49	i	105	0x69
\n	10	0x0a	*	42	0x2a	J	74	0x4a	j	106	0x6a
(vt)	11	0x0b	+	43	0x2b	K	75	0x4b	k	107	0x6b
\f	12	0x0c	,	44	0x2c	L	76	0x4c	l	108	0x6c
\r	13	0x0d	–	45	0x2d	M	77	0x4d	m	109	0x6d
(so)	14	0x0e	.	46	0x2e	N	78	0x4e	n	110	0x6e
(si)	15	0x0f	/	47	0x2f	O	79	0x4f	o	111	0x6f
(dle)	16	0x10	0	48	0x30	P	80	0x50	p	112	0x70
(dc1)	17	0x11	1	49	0x31	Q	81	0x51	q	113	0x71
(dc2)	18	0x12	2	50	0x32	R	82	0x52	r	114	0x72
(dc3)	19	0x13	3	51	0x33	S	83	0x53	s	115	0x73
(dc4)	20	0x14	4	52	0x34	T	84	0x54	t	116	0x74
(nak)	21	0x15	5	53	0x35	U	85	0x55	u	117	0x75
(syn)	22	0x16	6	54	0x36	V	86	0x56	v	118	0x76
(etb)	23	0x17	7	55	0x37	W	87	0x57	w	119	0x77
(can)	24	0x18	8	56	0x38	X	88	0x58	x	120	0x78

Table 3.2

(Continued)

Char	Dec	Hex	Char	Dec	Hex	Char	Dec	Hex	Char	Dec	Hex
(em)	25	0x19	9	57	0x39	Y	89	0x59	y	121	0x79
(sub)	26	0x1a	:	58	0x3a	Z	90	0x5a	z	122	0x7a
(esc)	27	0x1b	;	59	0x3b	[	91	0x5b	{	123	0x7b
(fs)	28	0x1c	<	60	0x3c	\	92	0x5c	|	124	0x7c
(gs)	29	0x1d	=	61	0x3d	]	93	0x5d	}	125	0x7d
(rs)	30	0x1e	>	62	0x3e	^	94	0x5e	~	126	0x7e
(us)	31	0x1f	?	63	0x3f	_	95	0x5f	(del)	127	0x7f

two or more sequential bytes to hold a single character. The current de-facto standard encoding is called *unicode*, which has various 'flavours' but which can use up to four sequential bytes to encode the vast majority of characters, including Chinese, Japanese, Korean and so on.

Although the detail of this encoding system is beyond the scope of this book, the implications are not: early computers were byte-sized and were naturally able to handle byte-sized ASCII characters. These days, it requires a 32-bit machine to handle a 4-byte unicode character in a single operation. Similarly, early interfacing methods such as the PC parallel and serial ports (see Chapter 6) were byte-based. Memory accesses have often been byte-based. The argument has been that a byte is a convenient size for simple counting and for text processing. However, this argument no longer applies in many cases. Where non-English alphabet systems are concerned, a byte-sized processing system is nothing more than a historical curiosity.

One final point to note concerning data sizes is the uniformity of the `float` and `double` types. This uniformity is related to the ubiquity of the IEEE754 standard, and the fact that the majority of hardware floating point units comply with the standard (this will be explained a little more in Section 4.6).

3.4.2 Data Flows

Again adopting a black-box view, a computer takes input, processes it and generates output. Evidently the requirements of that data are important, in terms of timeliness, quantity, quality and so on.

Today's computers, and especially many consumer electronic embedded systems, are heavily user-centric. This means that input, output or both need to interact with a human being. Some data also tends to be quite voluminous (video, audio and so on). Buses, which we will consider more fully in Section 6.1, need to be sized to cope with the required data flows, and systems should also consider human needs. For example, the human sensory organs are often far more sensitive to sudden discontinuities than they are to continuous errors (noise). It is usually more annoying for listeners to hear music from a CD player which skips than it is to listen to music in the presence of background noise. Similarly with video: skipped frames can be more annoying than a slightly noisy picture.

Most of the important real-time issues will be explored in Section 6.4. However, at this point, we need to stress that computer architects should bear in mind the use to which their systems will be put. Embedded computer architects may have an advantage in that their systems are less flexible and more generic, and thus better able to satisfy users. Unfortunately, they also suffer the considerable disadvantage that size, cost and power limitations are more severe, and thus require finer balancing of trade-offs in design.

Technically speaking, data flows through computers on pathways called buses. This data may originate from external devices or some form of data store, be processed in some way by a CPU or co-processor, and then output similarly either to another external device or data store.

3.4.3 Data Storage

The memory hierarchy of Figure 3.1 highlights the difference in memory provision between embedded systems and typical desktop or server systems: with the exception of some iPod-like devices, data storage in embedded systems is usually flash-memory-based. In desktop systems it is often stored on hard disc (for short-term storage), or tape/CDROM or DVD (for backup storage).

Data 'inside' a computer is located within RAM, cache memory, registers and so on. From a programmer's perspective it is either in registers or in main memory (since cache memory is usually deliberately invisible to a programmer). Data enters memory from external devices or hard discs over buses (Section 6.1) either individually a byte or word at a time, or in bursts, perhaps using a scheme such as direct memory access (DMA – see Section 6.1.2). Large amounts of data occupy pages of memory, handled by a memory management unit (MMU – covered in Section 4.3), and small amounts may exist in fixed variable locations or in a system stack. Since embedded systems often use parallel bus-connected flash memory devices, data in such systems is already directly accessible by the main processor and thus is considered already 'inside' the computer.

Data is brought into a CPU from memory for processing, and again may be conveyed as individual items or as a block. For load-store machines (Section 3.2.3), data to be processed must first be loaded into individual registers since all processing operations take input only from registers and output only to registers. Some specialised machines (such as vector processors) can handle blocks of data directly and some machines have dedicated co-processing units that can access memory directly, without requiring the CPU to handle loading and storing.

3.4.4 Internal Data

When compiling C code, the compiler decides how to handle program variables. Some variables, usually the most often accessed ones, will occupy registers during the time that they are being accessed. However, most processors have insufficient registers for more than a handful of variables to be catered for in this way.

Global variables have a dedicated memory address during the execution of a program, but other variables are stored in a memory stack. That means that when a program contains a statement such as '`i++`' and `i` is a local variable which the compiler decides cannot remain in a register, the compiler dedicates a particular location in the stack to the variable. The pseudo-machine code instructions to execute this statement on a load-store machine would thus be as follows:

1. Load the data item at the particular stack offset corresponding to variable `i` into a register.
2. Increment the value stored in that register.
3. Save that register content to the stack offset that it was retrieved from.

If there was a subsequent decision to be made on variable `i` (such as `if i > 100 then ....`) the compiler knows that `i` is already occupying a register, so it will re-use that register in the subsequent comparison and decision. Some variables, as we have mentioned, can remain in registers throughout a calculation. It all depends upon how many registers are available, how many variables are in use and how frequently these are accessed.

Actually the programmer has little control over which variables are to be stored in registers and which are to be kept in a stack, although the C programming language keyword `register` asks the compiler to keep a variable in a register if possible. For example, if we wanted to maintain `i` in a register (if possible), we would have declared `i` as:

```
register int i=0;
```

Spill code is the name given to the few machine code instructions that a compiler adds to a program to load-store variables between memory and registers. Since memory accesses are far slower than register accesses, spill code not only slightly increases the size of a program, it also adversely affects execution speed. Minimising spill code has long been a target of compiler researchers and computer architects worldwide.

3.4.5 Data Processing

Adding two 8-bit integers in an 8-bit processor is always going to be a simple proposition, and adding two 8-bit numbers in a 32-bit processor is also relatively simple[7] since both arithmetic operations can be performed with a single instruction.

[7] Remember though that sign extension (Section 2.3.8) would need to be performed when placing 8-bit values into 32-bit registers; otherwise negative two's complement numbers may be incorrectly interpreted in the ALU!

This single instruction is normally accomplished very easily in hardware: send the two operands from registers to an ALU and then load the result back into another register.

The situation becomes more interesting when processing larger numbers in a smaller processor and when performing more complex processing. Let us consider three possibilities in turn: operating on numbers that are larger than the width of the processor, floating point in a fixed point CPU and complex numbers.

3.4.5.1 Big Numbers on Small CPUs

Since the C programming language can define 32-bit or even 64-bit data types, it follows that any C compiler for 8-bit, 16-bit or even 32-bit CPUs must be able to support arithmetic and logical operations on numbers larger than the natural size of the processor.

First of all, note that many processors with a certain data bus width actually support higher precision arithmetic. For example, most ARM processors are able to perform a multiplication between two 32-bit numbers. We know that the maximum size of the result of such an operation could be 64 bits. The original ARM multiplier would allow only the lower 32-bit part of that result to be stored to the destination register. However, a 'long multiply' instruction on newer ARM processors allows the full 64-bit result to be stored to two 32-bit destination registers. Evidently, the operation to store the results will take twice as long to complete (but this is a lot less time than trying to determine the upper 32 bits from the operation using other methods).

Let us examine how we can perform a 64-bit multiply on an ARM processor that does not have a 'long' multiply instruction (although please note that this may not be the fastest way to do it):

1. Load operand 1 lower 16 bits to R1
2. Load operand 1 upper 16 bits to R2
3. Load operand 2 lower 16 bits to R3
4. Load operand 2 upper 16 bits to R4
5. $R0 = R1 \times R3$
6. $R0 = R0 + (R2 \times R3) \ll 16$
7. $R0 = R0 + (R1 \times R4) \ll 16$
8. $R0 = R0 + (R2 \times R4) \ll 32$

This is illustrated diagrammatically in Figure 3.13, where the loading is shown as a set-up stage and the multiplication and adding are shown as an operation stage. Within this stage, four multiplications, three shifts and three additions need to be performed to calculate the result.

The clear message here is that the lack of a single 'long' multiply instruction will entail several additional operations, and possibly registers, to replace it. Of course, there are slightly faster or lower-overhead schemes than the particular one shown, that can work in certain cases. However, for general-purpose multiplication none of these can better the use of a single instruction.

Figure 3.13

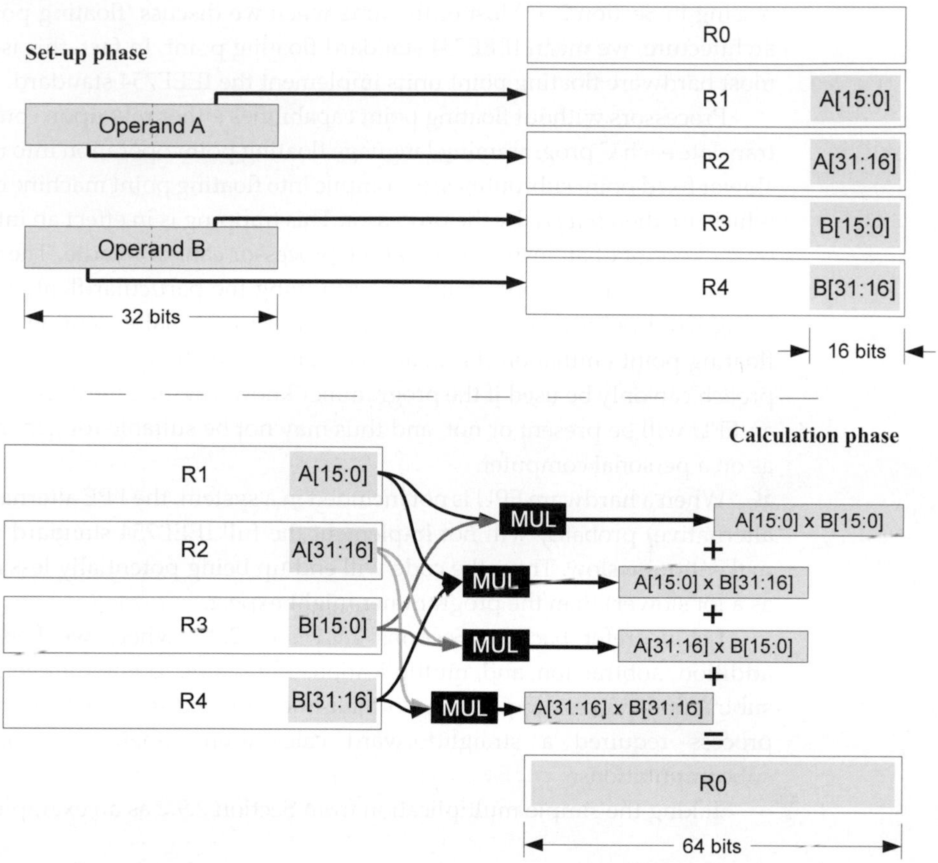

A block diagram illustrating the set-up and calculation stages of the multi-step procedure necessary to perform a 32-bit × 32-bit = 64-bit multiplication using multiply hardware only capable of returning a 32-bit result (i.e. 16-bit × 16-bit = 32-bit hardware).

Logical operations on longer data words are quite simple: split the operands, process the logical operations on each part separately and then re-assemble the result. This is because a logical operation on one bit in a binary word does not have any impact upon the neighbouring bits.

Arithmetic operations require a little more thought than logical operations (but are simpler than multiplication or division). The issue with arithmetic operations is that of overflow: the result of adding two 16-bit numbers may be 17 bits in length. The extra bit (carry) must therefore be taken into consideration when performing the addition of the split numbers. Usually, that will involve calculating the lower half of the split first and then adding this (with carry) to the result of the upper half.

3.4.5.2 Floating Point on Fixed Point CPUs

We discussed floating point numbers extensively in Section 2.8 and floating point processing in Section 2.9. Most of the time when we discuss 'floating point' in computer architecture, we mean IEEE754 standard floating point. In fact, this is natural because most hardware floating point units implement the IEEE754 standard.

Processors without floating point capabilities either rely upon compiler support to translate each C programming language floating point operation into much longer and slower fixed point subroutines, or compile into floating point machine code instructions which are then *trapped* by the processor. This trapping is in effect an interrupt triggered by the receipt of an instruction that the processor cannot handle. The interrupt service code then has the responsibility of performing the particular floating point operation using fixed point code before returning back to normal execution. This is known as floating point emulation (FPE), and is examined further in Section 4.6.1. The first approach can only be used if the programmer knows, at the time of compilation, whether an FPU will be present or not, and thus may not be suitable for general software such as on a personal computer.

When a hardware FPU is not included in a system, the FPE alternative (or compiler alternative) probably will not implement the full IEEE754 standard since this would make it quite slow. Thus, the code will end up being potentially less accurate (as well as a lot slower) than the programmer might expect.

Let us refer back to Sections 2.9.1 and 2.9.2 where we had considered the addition/subtraction and multiplication of floating point numbers: the addition/subtraction process required a normalisation procedure, whereas the multiplication process required a straightforward calculation, albeit one containing several subcomputations.

Taking the simple multiplication from Section 2.9.2 as an example:

$$(A \times B^{C}) \times (D \times B^{E}) = (A \times D) \times B^{(C+E)}$$

For a machine equipped with FPU, $(A \times B^{C})$ and $(D \times B^{E})$ would be single 32-bit (for float) or 64-bit (for double) values. These would be loaded into two FPU registers, a single instruction issued to perform the multiplication and the answer retrieved from a destination FPU register. By contrast, for a machine without FPU, several fixed point operations would be required instead:

1. Split off mantissa and exponent A and C and store in R1 and R2 respectively.
2. Split off mantissa and exponent D and E and store in R3 and R4 respectively.
3. Calculate the new mantissa: R1 × R3.
4. Calculate the new exponent: R2 + R4.
5. Normalise exponents.
6. Recombine and store in IEEE754 format.

Clearly, the single FPU instruction is preferable to the several fixed point operations that are needed to replace it.

3.4.5.3 Complex Numbers

Complex numbers, of the form $(a+j.b)$ where $j = \sqrt{-1}$, are frequently used in scientific systems and also in radio communications systems. Almost all CPUs lack support for complex numbers and few programming languages cater for them.[8]

Complex number calculations on a system with hardware handling only real numbers, just like floating point performed with fixed precision arithmetic, requires a few steps. Consider the multiplication and addition of two complex numbers:

$$(a + j.b) \times (c + j.d) = (a.c - d.b) + j(a.d + b.c)$$
$$(a + j.b) + (c + j.d) = (a + c) + j(b + d)$$

The complex multiplication needs four real multiplications and two additions. The complex addition is a little simpler, requiring only two real additions. This will require the programmer (or compiler) splitting the operation into steps of several simpler instructions.

A processor with hardware support for complex numbers would possess a single instruction capable of performing these operations. The underlying hardware architecture would actually need to perform all of the splitting, suboperations and separate multiplies, but this would be handled very quickly within the CPU without requiring separate loads, stores and data moves.

3.5 A Top-Down View

3.5.1 Computer Capabilities

Looking at various processors available today, there are a profusion of features, clock speeds, bit widths, instruction sets and so on. The question arises as to what is needed in a particular computer. Some capabilities are examined below.

3.5.1.1 Functionality

Given that all computable functions can be performed by some sequence of logic operations, the main reason why not all functions are computed in such a way (i.e. as a possibly long sequence of logical operations), is related to efficiency – how long does such a function take to complete, and what hardware resources are required? There is some trade-off in that making a computer simpler can allow faster clock speeds. This argument led to the advent of RISC processors which, being simpler, clock faster – at the expense of having to perform some functions longhand that would be built into a CISC computer as single instructions.

[8] The notable exception is FORTRAN (FORmula TRANslation), the general-purpose compiled language introduced by IBM in the mid-1950s. FORTAN, updated several times since (the latest being 2003), has natively supported a complex number data type for over 50 years. Among modern languages, there has been some promotion of Java as a scientific language, with a complex number extension. Unfortunately, Java is currently significantly slower to execute than FORTRAN.

However, it is generally pragmatic to consider how often a particular function is required in software when deciding how to implement it. Put simply, if a function is required very frequently during everyday use, then maybe it is useful to build a dedicated hardware unit to handle it quickly. In this way, an ALU is included in all modern processors and almost all have hardware multiplier units.

Not only functional operations, but flexibility in the instruction set is an important feature. For example, there may be time-saving instructions available in one design but not another, even when these do not require large amounts of hardware support. Examples are the universality of conditional instructions in the ARM instruction set (Section 3.3.1) and zero-overhead loop instructions in some digital signal processors (shown later in Section 5.6.1).

The internal architecture of a CPU – namely the number of buses, registers and their organisation, is also an important consideration for performance. Generally speaking, more buses means more data items can travel around a device simultaneously, and thus better performance. Likewise, more registers support more software variables that would otherwise need to be stored in slower memory, and again improves performance.

3.5.1.2 Clock Speed

A higher clock speed does not always mean faster operation. For example, it is relatively easy to design a fast ALU, but not at all trivial to design a fast multiply unit. When comparing two processors, clock speed alone is not sufficient to decide which is faster. There are many factors such as functionality, bus bandwidth, memory speeds and so on, which must be considered: in effect, asking 'what can be accomplished each clock cycle?' This question is considered in the next section.

3.5.1.3 Bit Widths

Until recently, the vast majority of CPU sales were for 4-bit processors, destined to be used in watches, calculators and so on. These days the profusion of mostly 32-bit processors (generally ARM-based) used in cellphones and network appliances, is tipping the balance towards *wider* processors.

Although it might seem a wider processor will result in faster computation, this is only true if the data types being computed make use of the extra width. High-end servers with 64-bit or even 128-bit architectures are available, but if these are being used to handle text (such as 7-bit or 8-bit ASCII or even 16-bit Unicode), the extra width may well be wasted.

3.5.1.4 Memory Provision

The memory connected to a processor is often critical in determining operation speed. Not only the speed of memory access, but the width (together specifying a bandwidth in bits per second) and technology are just as important. Other aspects include burst mode access, paging or packetisation and single-edged or double-edged clocking.

On-chip memory also may not always be single-cycle access, but it is likely to be faster than off-chip memory. Given a particular software task that must be run, the amount of memory provided on-chip, and off-chip, must be considered. A cache (Section 4.4) in particular is used to maximise the use of faster memory, and the complexity of hardware memory units tends to influence how well memory use is optimised. In terms of memory, the way software is written and compiled can also result in more efficient use of hardware resources.

3.5.2 Performance Measures, Statistics and Lies

In order to determine exactly how fast a computer operates, the simplest general-purpose measure is simply how many instructions it can process per second.

MIPS (millions of instructions per second) measures the speed at which instructions or operations, can be handled. This is a useful low-level measure, but it does not really relate to how powerful a computer is: the operations themselves may be very simple such that multiple operations are required to perform a useful task. In other words, a simple computer with a high MIPS rating (such as a RISC processor) may handle real-world tasks slower than a computer with a lower MIPS rating but with instructions that each can perform more work (such as a CISC processor). The *bogomips* rating, calculated at boot-up on Linux PCs, is a famous attempt to gauge a MIPS score in software – but is unfortunately notoriously inaccurate.

MIPS as a measure is therefore made up of two components, clock frequency f (in Hz) and *CPI* (cycles per instruction) such that:

$$MIPS = f/CPI$$

More generally, for a particular program containing P instructions, the completion time is going to be:

$$T_{complete} = (P \times CPI)/f$$

So completion time reduces when CPI is low, f is high or most obviously P is low (i.e. a shorter program will probably execute faster than a longer one). The trade-off between P and CPI in computer architecture is a revisit of the RISC vs CISC debate, while ever-increasing clock frequency is the story of modern CPUs.

The task of minimising CPI is another aspect of modern computer systems. Up until the 1980s, CPI would be greater than 2, perhaps as much as several hundreds in CISC machines. The RISC approach began to shift CPI downwards, with the aim of achieving a CPI of unity. The ARM family of processors typically achieve a CPI of about 1.1, and other RISC processors can do a little better than this.

Later, the advent of superscaler architectures led to CPI values of below unity, through allowing several instructions to execute simultaneously. This, and the inverse of CPI (called *IPC*) will be explored later in Section 5.5.1.

Sometimes floating point performance is an important attribute and this is measured in *MFLOPS* (millions of floating point operations per second). In recent times, GFLOPS readings are more commonly quoted, meaning thousands of MFLOPS and even petaFLOPS, PFLOPS. These values are more indicative of actual performance than MIPS since we are counting useful calculation operations rather than the low-level instructions which comprise them.

Box 3.8

Standardised performance

In the mid-1980s, the computer industry worldwide saw an unprecedented level of competition between vendors. This was not simply a two-entry race between AMD and Intel. It included thousands of manufacturers selling enormously differing machines – alternative architectures, different memory, tens of CPU types, custom operating systems, 8 bits, 16 bits and even some more unusual choices.

In the UK, companies such as Sinclair, Acorn, Oric, Amstrad, Research Machines, Apricot, Dragon, ICL, Ferranti, Tandy, Triumf-Adler and more battled in the marketplace against IBM, Apple, Compaq, DEC, Atari, Commodore and others. Claims and counterclaims regarding performance littered the advertisements and sales brochures available at that time. However, with no standard and no baseline, claims were often dubious to say the least.

In response, the British Standards Institute (BSI) published a performance standard for computers – testing useful tasks such as integer calculation, floating point calculation, branching performance and graphics as well as disc reads and writes. However, at that time the programming language of choice was BASIC (Beginners All-purpose Symbolic Instruction Set), and hence the standards were written in this language! From today's point of view, the graphics and disc tests are also dated: the 'graphics' test was actually text being written to the screen or VDU (visual display unit) in the parlance of the time. This was important for many users interested in nothing more than word-processing. Also disc reads and writes were to floppy discs – a great advance on the tape drives used for most home computers at the time – hard discs (usually known as Winchester drives in those days) were simply too expensive and not even supported on most machines available at the time. Far more common was saving programs to cassette tape.

Today, computer magazines and websites test new hardware and software with a battery of tests far removed from the BSI standard, but following the same rationale. Thus, measures such as 'refresh rate for playing Quake III' and 'time taken to sort 1 million rows of random numbers in a spreadsheet' are to be found. Other more standard, but often not freely available, tests exist but these are less commonly applied: after all, most users are more interested in playing Quake than in how quickly they can calculate π to 100 decimal places.

Benchmarks are so important that several companies exist to provide such services (Box 3.8 explores the background and necessity of having such benchmarks). *BDTi* is one example which publishes comparative speeds for several digital signal processors (DSPs). Their measures are skewed towards outright calculating performance, something which is the mainstay of the DSP market.

Otherwise, *SPECint* and *SPECfp* benchmarks compute integer and floating point performance directly. These are obtainable in source code format from the Standard Performance Evaluation Corporation (SPEC) for a fee, and can be compiled on an architecture to assess its performance. Each measure is calculated from a set of algorithms that have to be run, and results combined. Generally, a year is provided to indicate test version. Thus, SPECint92 is the 1992 version of the integer standard.

The SPEC measures themselves incorporate two earlier measures known as *Dhrystone* and *Whetstone*, both originating in the 1970s and measuring integer and floating point performance respectively. Many other performance metrics exist and may be used to assess performance for various tasks (such as graphics rendering, real-time performance, byte handling and so on).

Unfortunately, it is a well-known fact that, given any single performance measure, computer architects can tweak an architecture to yield a high score at the expense of other, unmeasured, operations. Furthermore, none of these measures really reflect the overall completion time of anything but the simplest tasks running in isolation. So many issues intervene in the real world to confuse results, such as interrupted tasks, operating system calls, varying memory speeds, disc speeds, multi-tasking and cache.

In computing, a cache (covered in detail in Section 4.4) is a small block of very fast memory provided on a system which has far slower main memory. Any program running directly from the cache will obviously execute quicker than one running from slow main memory. Why this is relevant is that in the past, at least one processor vendor has deliberately designed a cache just big enough to hold an entire performance measure algorithm (i.e. the entire SPECint or Dhrystone program) so that it runs much faster than it does on a competitor's machine.

In such an example, if the main memory were set to run ten times slower, the performance measure result would not change since the measuring program runs from the cache, not main memory. Obviously, such a performance measure is not realistic. In fact, such a machine would yield a faster performance score than a competitor with a smaller cache but significantly faster main memory – one which would in reality probably perform real-world tasks much quicker.

Given significant performance-altering factors such as those we have mentioned, it is clear that the world of benchmarking is fraught with difficulty. A system designer is thus urged to be careful. In practice, this may mean understanding device operation in detail, building in large safety margins or testing final code in-situ before committing to a device. Although it is rare in industrial projects for software to be available and working before hardware is complete, if such an opportunity arises, the approach of in-situ testing is very much recommended.

3.5.3 Assessing Performance

Section 6.4.4 will discuss completion times and execution performance for real-time and multi-tasking systems, but here we consider estimation of performance. In order to underscore the need for accurate performance estimation, here is an example from industry:

> Several years ago, an embedded design group needed hardware to run an algorithm requiring 12 MIPS of processing power. A 32-bit CPU rated at providing 40 MIPS when clocked at 40 MHz was chosen to execute this. In an attempt to reduce design risks, the

designers obtained a development board, loaded a Dhrystone measure on to this and checked actual performance themselves before committing to that processor as the design choice.

During the design process, they realised that on-chip memory was insufficient for the needs of their software and hence added external DRAM memory. Due to the small size of the CPU package and the low number of pins, the external memory bus was limited to being 16-bits wide. External memory accesses were therefore 16-bits wide instead of 32-bits wide.

Having completed their hardware design and built the system, they loaded up the code and found it would not execute in the time required. Where had they gone wrong?

Firstly, the Dhrystone measure fitted into fast on-chip memory and so could run at full speed, whereas their wanted algorithm was too large to fit into on-chip memory and therefore had to be stored in DRAM instead. Not only were the DRAM accesses themselves slower than internal memory accesses, but DRAM needed a 'time out' occasionally to refresh itself. During that time-out, all memory accesses by the CPU were stalled.

Finally, the 16-bit interface meant that two memory reads were now required to fetch each 32-bit instruction – two 16-bit accesses were also required to read in every 32-bit data word. This meant that, when executing a program from DRAM, the CPU needed to spend half of its time idle. Every even cycle it would fetch the first half of the instruction. In the odd cycle it would fetch the second half of the instruction, and only then begin to process it.

The 16-bit interface effectively dropped the 40 MIPS down to 20 MIPS, and the lower speed of the DRAM accesses plus refresh time reduced the 20 MIPS performance further to around 9 MIPS.

The solutions were unpleasant: either switch to using very fast external memory (SRAM) which was perhaps 20 times as expensive, or upgrade to another CPU with either faster speed or a wider external memory interface, or both. Designers chose neither – they added a *second* CPU alongside the first to handle some of the processing tasks.

This example underscores the necessity of matching performance requirements to hardware. In general, there are two approaches to this. The first one is through a *clear understanding* of the architecture, and the second is through *careful evaluation* of the architecture. In both cases, the architecture referred to is not only that of a central processor; it includes other important peripheral elements.

Gaining a *clear understanding* of software requirements means having fixed software that needs to be run on a system, analysing that software to identify its contents (particularly any bottlenecks) and then matching the results of that analysis to available hardware. At the simplest level this might mean avoiding an integer-only CPU when most calculations need to be done in floating point.

This approach is commonly taken for DSP systems, and will include a close look at memory transfers, placement of variable blocks into different memory areas that can be accessed simultaneously (Section 4.1.4), input and output bottlenecks and mathematical operations which are typically the major strength of such processors. Slow set-up, user interface and control code are generally ignored in such calculations, except in the sizing of overall program memory requirements.

At this point it is useful to note that most, if not all, software developments end up overrunning initial program memory use estimates. Clever coding can often bring down data memory use and can reduce processing requirements, but can seldom save significant amounts of program memory. Unlike desktop computer designers, embedded designers do not have the luxury of providing for RAM expansion: this must be fixed at design time. In such cases, it is wise to significantly overestimate memory needs up-front.

The second approach mentioned of matching required performance to hardware, is through *careful evaluation*. This does not require detailed architectural understanding, but does require detailed levels of testing. Ideally, the final runtime software should be executed on candidate hardware to evaluate how much CPU time it requires. A list of other tasks to be performed should also be made and checked to see whether those can fit into whatever spare processing time remains. Software profiling tools (such as GNU *gprof*) will identify any bottlenecks in the runtime code and make clear which software routines require large amounts of CPU time.

It is important to run any test a number of times (but do not average the results if timing is critical – take the maximum worst case), to increase program size sufficiently to force it out of the cache or on-chip memory, if appropriate, and to enable whatever interrupts and ancillary tasks might be needed in the final system.

If, as is sometimes the case, the target software is already running on another machine, it is possible to compare its execution on that machine to execution on another – but only after considering all important architectural factors as discussed in these last two chapters. In such instances, compiling and comparing a suite of standard benchmarks on both machines will help, assuming that the benchmarks chosen are ones of relevance to the target software.

The world is full of examples where designers have estimated processor performance and/or memory requirements incorrectly (including one example designed for an Asian industrial manufacturer in 1999 by the author: a portable MP3 player that could only replay seven seconds of MP3 audio at a time, due to unexpectedly low memory bus bandwidth. Luckily, a faster speed grade processor became available).

You have been warned! Beware the pitfalls of performance estimation, evaluation and measurement. Above all, remember to read the small print below manufacturers' performance claims.

3.6 Summary

In this chapter, the basics of the microprocessor have been covered, starting with the functionality of a CPU, the ability to control this with a program and the need to transfer this program (and store it somewhere).

A control unit needs to keep a processor on track, managing operations and exceptions, and being directed in turn by the computer program through a sequence of instructions. Control units can be centralised, or distributed with timing from a state machine, a microcode engine or using self-timed logic.

Each instruction in a program is part of an allowable instruction set that (depending on your point of view) describes the operations capable of being performed by that processor, or which specifies the microprocessor behaviour. Such behaviour includes data transfer through internal buses to various functional units. Having laid the foundation for CPU design here and in the previous chapter, in Chapter 4, we will delve into the internal arrangements and functional units of most mainstream CPUs and attempt to relate that to the programmer's experience.

Problems

3.1 If the assembler instruction LSL means 'logical shift left', LSR means 'logical shift right', ASL means 'arithmetic shift left' and ASR means 'arithmetic shift right' then what are the results of performing these operations on the following signed 16-bit numbers?

a. `0x00CA   ASR 1`
b. `0x0101   LSR 12`
c. `0xFF0F   LSL 2`
d. `0xFF0F   LSR 2`
e. `0xFF0F   ASR 3`
f. `0xFF0F   ASL 3`

3.2 An analysis of representative code for a RISC processor with only eight instructions finds the following occurrences of those instructions:

Instruction	Number of occurrences
ADD	30
AND	22
LDR	68
MOV	100
NOT	15
ORR	10
STR	60
SUB	6

a. If each instruction (excluding operands) is 6-bits long, how many bits does the program occupy?
b. Use the information in the table to design a Huffman coding for the processor.

Calculate the number of bits needed to store the program using the Huffman coded instruction set.

3.3 Show the sequence of stack PUSHes and POPs during the execution of the following Reverse Polish notation (RPN) operations and translate each into infix notation:

a. ab +
b. ab + c×
c. ab × cd*sin* + −

Consider the maximum depth of stack required to perform these operations.

Problems

3.4 A ROT (rotate) instruction is similar to a shift, except that it wraps around – when shifting right, each bit that drops off the LSB end of the word is moved around to become the new MSB. When shifting left, each MSB that drops off is moved around to become the new LSB.

The ROT argument is positive for left shifts and negative for right shifts.

So, imagine a processor that has a ROT instruction but no shift. How can we do arithmetic and logical shifting?

3.5 Translate the following infix operations to Reverse Polish notation (RPN):

a. (A and B) or C
b. (A and B) or (C and D)
c. ((A or B) and C) + D
d. C + {pow(A, B) × D}
e. See if you can perform the following translation in three different ways:

$$\{C + \text{pow}(A, B)\} \times D$$

3.6 Calculate the maximum stack usage (depth) for each of the three answers to part (e) above.

3.7 Translate the following Reverse Polish notations to infix:

a. AB + C + D ×
b. ABCDE + × ×−
c. DC not and BA ++

3.8 Given the following segment of ARM assembler, rewrite the code to use conditional ADDS to remove the need for any branch instructions.

```
        ADDS R0, R1, R3
        BGE step2
        ADD R2, R1, R6
        BLT step3
step2   ADD R2, R3, R6
step3   NOP
```

3.9 In ARM assembly language, determine the least number of instructions in each case to perform the following immediate loads (hint: use the MOV instruction):

a. Load a value 0x12340001 to register R0
b. Load a value 0x00000700 to register R1
c. Load a value 0xFFFF0FF0 to register R2

Problems

3.10 Identify the sequence of operations in a RISC processor that is required to add the contents of two memory addresses $m1$ and $m2$ and store the result to a third address $m3$.

3.11 Scientists discover a new type of silicon memory cell. Semiconductor engineers design this into a new memory chip. Identify six factors that computer architects would look at when deciding whether to adopt this new technology for mass storage in an embedded video player.

3.12 Consider the following instructions and decide whether they are from a RISC or CISC processor:

a. MPX: Multiply the content of two memory locations, then add the result to an accumulator.
b. BCDD: Perform a binary-coded decimal division on two registers, format the result in scientific notation and store as ASCII to a memory block ready for display to the screen.
c. SUB: Subtract one operand from another and return the result as a third operand. The operands and result are register contents only.
d. LDIV Rc, Ra, Rb: Perform a 100-cycle-long division of Ra/Rb and place the result in register Rc.

3.13 Write an approximate microcode program sequence to perform any two of the instructions from the previous problem. Assume an internal RISC-style architecture.

3.14 What is a load-store architecture? Why would computer designers adopt such an idea?

3.15 In a simple computer pipeline, what process normally follows the instruction fetch stage?

3.16 For a fictitious 32-bit processor, the hexadecimal machine code instruction for the assembler command to store a word `0x1234` in memory location `0x9876` looks like this:

```
0x0F00 1234 088D 9876
```

By examining the machine code instruction, determine whether this processor is likely to be capable of absolute addressing. Justify your answer.

3.17 Another fictitious processor, this time an 8-bit CPU, has eight registers. Is it possible to have instructions in this processor that specify two operand registers and a separate result register?

Problems

3.18 Assuming ARM-style assembly language (but not necessarily an ARM processor), identify the type of addressing represented in the following instructions:

a. `MOV R8, #0x128`
b. `AND`
c. `STR R12, [R1]`
d. `AND R4, R5, R4`
e. `LDR R6, [R3, R0, LSL #2]`
f. `LDR R2, [R1, R0, #8]`
g. `STR R6, [R3, R0]`

3.19 Which processor is likely to be faster at processing 32-bit floating point data: a 900 MHz 32-bit floating point CPU or a 2 GHz 16-bit integer-only CPU?

3.20 When writing code in the C programming language on different processors, is a `byte` always represented as 8 bits? How about the `short` and `int` – what size are these, and are they always the same?

CHAPTER 4

Processor Internals

Chapter 2 has covered much of the low-level numerical calculations performed by computer and also dealt with the definitions of computer functional units and classifications of some connectivities. In Chapter 3, this information has been formed into cohesive units with different functions that are able to execute sequences of instructions as specified by a programmer, since we know that computers, and indeed CPUs, can be divided logically into a number of functional units performing different tasks.

This chapter will extend beyond the basic high-level discussion of what goes into a CPU and focus on the largest, most prominent and most important of the internal units that are commonly found in modern processors. We will look in more detail at what tasks those units perform and how they are able to do so. This discussion mainly covers the ALU, FPU, MMU and memory cache unit. However, before embarking upon that discussion, we will first consider the issue of how the units are wired up through buses.

It is time to assess the actual architecture – specifically the interconnected bus structure – of units within a CPU.

4.1 Internal Bus Architecture

4.1.1 A Programmer's Perspective

From a programmer's perspective, the internal bus architecture of a processor can be seen in two main, but related, ways. The first is in the degree of flexibility of register use. This is evident in the set of possible registers that can be used as operands in a particular instruction: in the ARM for instance, where a register operand is allowed, *any* register from its register bank can be named:

```
ADD R0, R1, R2  ;R0 = R1 + R2
```

Any register could be used – we could even use the same register:

```
ADD R0, R0, R0  ;R0 = R0 + R0
```

Many processors do not have this flexibility or are less *regular*. Secondly, there is the issue of how much work can be performed in a single instruction cycle. This is normally implicit in the instruction set itself.

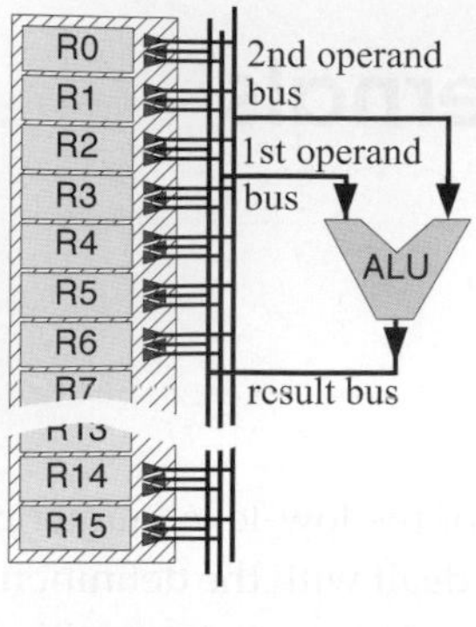

Figure 4.1 A schematic diagram of an ALU and a bank of registers interconnected with a three-bus arrangement.

Again looking at the ARM, there are at most two register input operands and a single register result operand associated with any arithmetic or logic instruction:

```
ADD R0, R1, R2  ;R0 = R1 + R2
```

With regard to the means of transporting data from a register to the ALU and back again: if this all happens in a single cycle, it implies that both the input and the output have their own buses (since only one operand can travel along one bus at any time). One bus will convey the content of R1, another will convey the content of R2 and yet another will convey the result from the ALU back to register R0.

Taking the two observations together implies that all registers connect to all buses, and there are at least three main internal buses.

The arrangement concerning registers and ALU that we can deduce from a brief examination of the instruction set is shown in Figure 4.1. This is actually a simplified schematic of the ARM processor internal interconnection arrangement. The arrows indicate controllable tristate buffers, acting as gates controlling read and write access between the registers and the buses. Control logic (described in Section 3.2.4) is not shown.

4.1.2 Split Interconnection Arrangements

The ARM is justly famed for its regularity and simplicity. Some other processors are less friendly to low-level programmers: where the ARM has a bank of 16 identical registers with identical connectivity,[1] it is more usual to assign special meanings to sets of registers. One common arrangement is to dedicate several *address registers* to holding and handling addresses, whereas the remainder are *data registers*. It is easy where there is such a split to imagine an internal address bus that only connects to those registers dedicated to handling addresses. In the ARM, where every register can hold an address (since it uses indirect addressing, explained in Section 3.3.4), every register must also have connectivity to the internal address bus.

[1] In fact, registers R14 and R15 are the link register and program counter respectively. These understandably require connections that other registers will lack which are not really evident through examining the instruction set. Registers also vary in their shadowing arrangements.

Figure 4.2

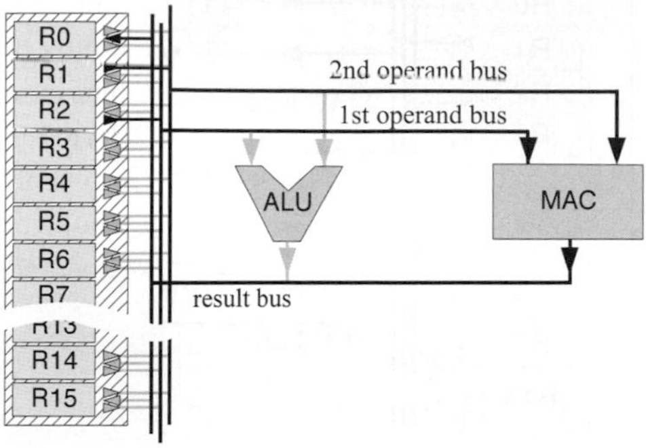

A schematic diagram of an ALU, a MAC and a bank of registers interconnected with a three-bus arrangement. The ability to convey two operands simultaneously to a single functional unit is highlighted.

In some processors, such as the ADSP21xx, there is no bank of registers – there are instead specific registers associated with the input and output of each processing element. This means that when using a particular instruction, the low-level programmer has to remember (or look up in the programming manual) which registers are allowed. Sometimes an instruction has to be wasted to switch a value from one register to another to perform a particular function – although clever instruction set design means that these inefficiencies are quite rare. These days, such architectures are uncommon among general-purpose processors, but are still found in some digital signal processors (DSPs) such as the ADSP21xx[2] family.

So, why would designers go to such trouble and complicate the instruction set? The answer requires us to take a snapshot of the internals of a processor as it performs some function. In this case, we will look at the ARM as it performs the following two instructions, using hardware which is shown diagrammatically in Figure 4.2.

```
MUL R0, R1, R2  ;R0 = R1 + R2
ADD R4, R5, R6  ;R4 = R5 + R6
```

The snapshot of time represented in Figure 4.2 shows data being output from R1 and R2 simultaneously on the two operand buses (indicated in dark colour), flowing into the multiply-accumulate unit (MAC), and the result flowing over the results bus back into register R0.

The thing to note during this snapshot is that, the registers from R3 onwards and the ALU are all sitting idle. When CPU designers see resources sitting idle, they tend to wonder if it is possible to utilise them – in this instance, to see if there is a way of using the ALU and the MAC simultaneously. One answer is to partition the design as shown in Figure 4.3.

[2] The 'xx' means that there are various serial numbers in the ADSP21 family which share these characteristics, such as the ADSP2181, ADSP2191 and so on.

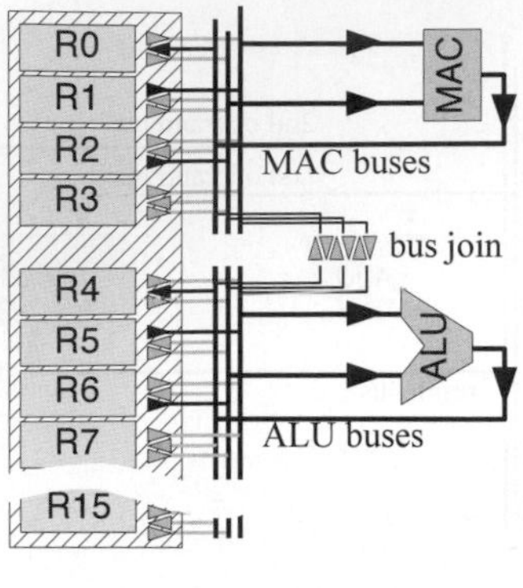

Figure 4.3 A schematic diagram of an ALU, a MAC and a bank of registers interconnected with a three-bus arrangement. This is similar in resource use to the hardware illustrated in Figure 4.2 although in this case bus partitioning has been used to allow the two functional units to transfer their operands simultaneously.

In the arrangement shown, both the MAC and the ALU have their own buses – both input and result, and by extension, their own set of preferred registers. Thus, as long as the programmer remembers to use R0 to R3 when dealing with the MAC, and R4 to R7 when dealing with the ALU, both of the example instructions:

```
MUL R0, R1, R2  ; R0 = R1 + R2
ADD R4, R5, R6  ; R4 = R5 + R6
```

can be performed simultaneously in a single cycle.

This process is probably the underlying thinking below the design of the ADSP21xx hardware, squeezed by designers for every last drop of performance gain.

4.1.3 ADSP21xx Bus Arrangement

In the ADSP21xx hardware, every processing element is limited to receiving its input from only a few registers and outputting a result to another small set. This means there are many internal buses and many operations can be performed very quickly in parallel.

A simplified diagram of some of the many internal buses within the ADSP21xx is shown in Figure 4.4. In this figure, PMA is program memory address and DMA is

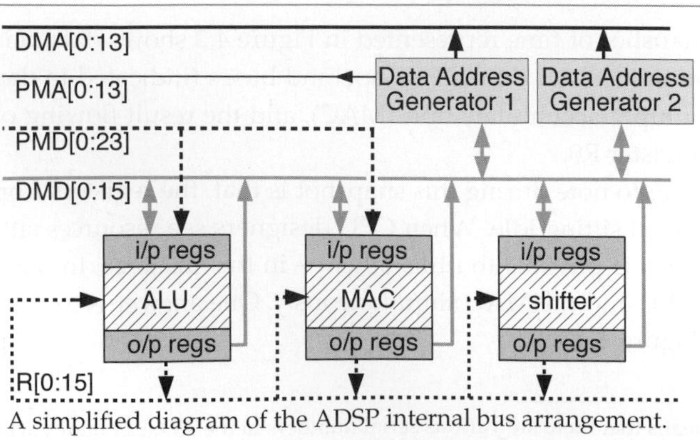

Figure 4.4 A simplified diagram of the ADSP internal bus arrangement.

data memory address. Both are address buses that index into the two blocks of memory (program and data) which also indicate that this is basically a Harvard architecture processor (see Section 2.1.2). However, it actually goes a step further in its partitioning of address spaces. PMD and DMD are program and data memory data buses respectively. Note the bus sizes: not only does this ADSP have a complex internal bus interconnection arrangement, but the bus width and width of the interconnects differ.

The diagram shows that the ALU and the MAC, but not the shifter, can receive input operands from the 24-bit PMD bus, but all can receive input and output from the 16-bit DMD bus.

4.1.4 Simultaneous Data and Program Memory Access

A topic that is very important in areas such as signal processing is the consideration of how fast external data can be brought into a computer, processed and then output. Signal processors typically operate on streams of such data, whether such data is high-fidelity audio or wideband wireless signals.

Signal processing operations tend to be some form of digital filter. This can be considered as a time series of samples, *x[0]*, *x[1]*, *x[2]* and so on, being the input values at time instant 0 (which we can think of as 'now'), one sample previously and two samples previously respectively. *y[0]*, *y[1]*, *y[2]* are the output values at those corresponding times. If this were audio data, then *x* and *y* would be audio samples, probably 16 bits and if they were sampled at 48 kHz the time instants would each be $1/48000 = 21\mu s$ apart.

Without delving too deeply into digital signal processing (DSP), we can say there are two general filter equations: the finite impulse response (FIR) filter and the infinite impulse response filter (IIR). FIR outputs are obtained by multiplying each of the previous n samples by some predetermined values and then adding them up. Mathematically, this is written:

$$y[0] = \sum_{i=0}^{n-1} a[i] \times x[i]$$

So the current output *y[0]* depends on n previous input values multiplied by the filter coefficients *a[]* and then summed together. The number of previous values defines the *order* of the filter. A tenth order filter would be defined by setting $n = 10$ and predetermining ten *a[]* values. An *adaptive FIR filter* would be the one in which the *a[]* values are changed from time to time.

The IIR filter, by contrast, makes the output value dependent upon all previous outputs as well as previous inputs:

$$y[0] = \sum_{i=0}^{n-1} a[i] \times x[i] + \sum_{i=1}^{n-1} b[i] \times y[i]$$

This includes the use of a further set of filter coefficients, *b[]*. IIR filters can also be adaptive and are generally able to perform the same work as FIR filters but with a lower *order* (which means a smaller value of n). This strong filtering action comes at a price, and that is mainly observed by IIR filters becoming unstable, if not designed carefully.

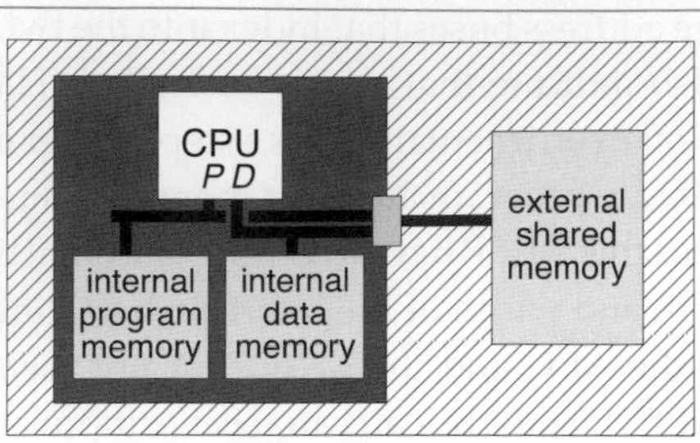

A block diagram of Harvard architecture internal memory access in a DSP augmented by the ability to add external shared memory.

Figure 4.5

The art of designing high-performance digital signal processors is to make these equations able to operate as quickly as possible, with the goal of being able to calculate a value *y[0]* in as few clock cycles as possible. Looking back at the equation for the FIR filter, we can see that most of the work is done by the following low-level operation:

```
ACC:= ACC + (a[i] × [i])
```

The act of multiplying two values and adding to something already there is called multiply-accumulate, which uses an accumulator, usually abbreviated to 'ACC'.

Now we need to relate that function to the hardware of a digital signal processor. There are many subtleties that could be discussed here, and using this operation, but in this case one of the most important aspects is the memory access arrangements.

Consider the block diagram in Figure 4.5 showing a digital signal processor containing a CPU, two memory blocks and a block of external shared memory. The device seems to have an internal Harvard architecture (separate program and data memory and buses), but connects externally to a block of shared memory. This type of arrangement is very common, with the internal memory being static RAM (SRAM), and sometimes having SDRAM (synchronous dynamic RAM) externally for the main reason that it is far less expensive than SRAM (refer to Section 7.6 for details on memory technologies and their features).

On-chip memory uses short internal buses and is generally extremely fast, sometimes accessing instructions in a single cycle. Occasionally, a block of two-cycle memory is also provided. This is twice as slow as single-cycle memory since it requires two clock cycles between requesting data and it being made available.

Ignoring the memory speed for now, and referring back to the multiply-accumulate example, we need to feed the multiplier with two values: one being a predetermined coefficient, *a[]* and the other being an input data value *x[]*. Given a shared bus, these two values cannot be obtained / transferred simultaneously. However, given the internal spilt buses in the diagram, they can both be fetched together and begin to be multiplied in a single cycle – if obtained from the separate on-chip memory blocks. Overall, this will probably be a multi-cycle operation: one cycle to load and decode the instruction, the cycle following that to load the operands, and then one or more cycles to operate on those. However, given fast single-cycle on-chip memory it is possible for the operand fetch to occur as part of an internal instruction cycle.

Usually, anything that traverses an off-chip bus is slow compared to data following on-chip paths, and this is one major driving factor behind the use of cache memory (explored later in Section 4.4). Where the external memory device is SDRAM there will almost always be an on-chip cache to alleviate the issue so that however fast SDRAM is, there is always a two- or three-cycle latency between requesting a single memory value and it being provided.

4.1.5 Dual-Bus Architectures

Taking a step backwards, a large hardware saving is made by minimising the number of buses: buses are bundles of parallel wires that must be routed through an integrated circuit, which cost in terms of buffers, registers and interconnects. They are expensive in silicon area and consume prime 'real estate' on chip. It is entirely possible to reduce area (and thus cost) by moving to a two-bus architecture and beyond that to a single-bus architecture (Section 4.1.6).

This is one case where our investigation does not parallel computer architecture evolution. The reason is that using a three-bus architecture is actually more sensible than using a single bus and easier to explain. Tricks are required when buses are fewer – tricks that have been used in silicon before the 1980s but which nevertheless complicate the simple view of a bus as a path between the source and destination of operands and results. All examples in this section and the next are fictitious: they present something like the ARM architecture, but with different bus arrangements. Original reduced bus designs, such as the venerable 6502 processor, did not have the luxury of a register bank, let alone a multiplier. Therein lies the problem: silicon area was too limited to allow a nice architecture or sometimes even a time-efficient architecture. In many cases, it was simply sufficient that the design could be manufactured and could work. With space for only three general registers, the 6502 designers were never going to be able to shoehorn in another parallel bus – they would have added some more registers instead.

Figure 4.6 presents a register bank connected to an ALU using a two-bus arrangement. There are three registers or latches shown clustered around the ALU (actually making this very similar to the 6502 – ignoring the larger register bank of course).

In order for this, and the following examples to make sense, it is necessary to remember something about the ALU. That is the propagation delay timings. When we

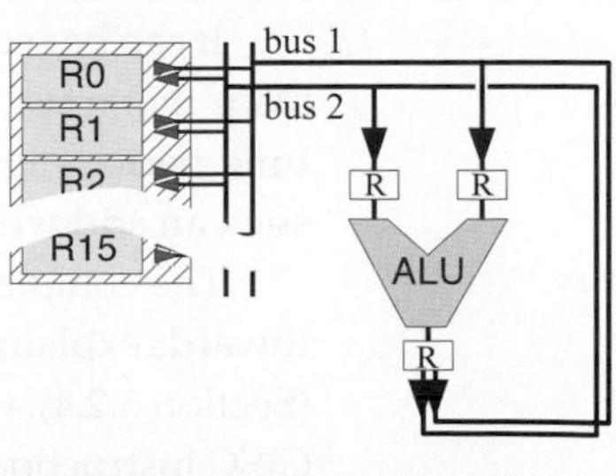

Figure 4.6 A dual-bus connection between an ALU and a register bank.

present stable electrical signals at the two input arms of the ALU, we need to wait for a certain length of time before the answer appearing at the bottom of the ALU is valid. Some control logic (not shown) would be present to instruct the ALU as to exactly what arithmetic or logic operation it should be performing, and this is assumed constant here. But the length of time we have to wait depends on the exact operation being performed – and the maximum (worst case) time is the one that determines how fast we can clock the circuitry based around this ALU. In a modern system, this delay may be something like one or two nanoseconds.

That delay is accounted for, but the problem here is that there is effectively no minimum delay: what this means is that as soon as one of the input signals is removed or changes, the result can start to become corrupted. The consequence of this is that the input operands must remain in place driving the ALU as the result is collected and stored. Only then can the input operands change, or be removed.

Hence, the registers on the ALU input arms. Without at least one register there is no way for a two-bus architecture to drive an ALU with input operands and simultaneously collect the result. With one or two registers present there are several alternatives that may save on hardware slightly, but the more general is the following sequence of events performing:

```
ADD R0, R1, R2  ;R0 = R1 + R2
```

Each numbered step is at a monotonically increasing time instant:

1. Set up system, clear buses and set ALU functionality switch to 'ADD'.
2. Allow register R1 to drive bus 1 (by turning on register output buffer) and register R2 to drive bus 2 (by turning on register output buffer).
3. Latch bus 1 value into first ALU operand register and bus 2 value into second ALU operand register.
4. Turn off R1 register output buffer (bus 1 becomes free) and R2 register output buffer (bus 2 becomes free).
5. Wait for worst case propagation delay through ALU.
6. Latch ALU result into ALU output buffer.
7. Allow ALU output buffer to drive one bus.
8. Latch content of that bus into register R0.
9. Turn off ALU output buffer (both buses become free and the system is ready to perform the next operation).

It can be seen that the very simple ADD command actually comprises a number of steps that must be performed in hardware. These steps add up to something like eight time periods ignoring ALU propagation delay. In a three-bus design (Section 4.1.1), such an add would require only three time periods.

The complexity of these steps even for a simple ADD instruction goes some way towards explaining the importance of a control unit inside a CPU to manage this process (Section 3.2.4). Can you imagine the control complexity needed for a large multi-cycle CISC instruction?

Figure 4.7 A single-bus connection between an ALU and a register bank.

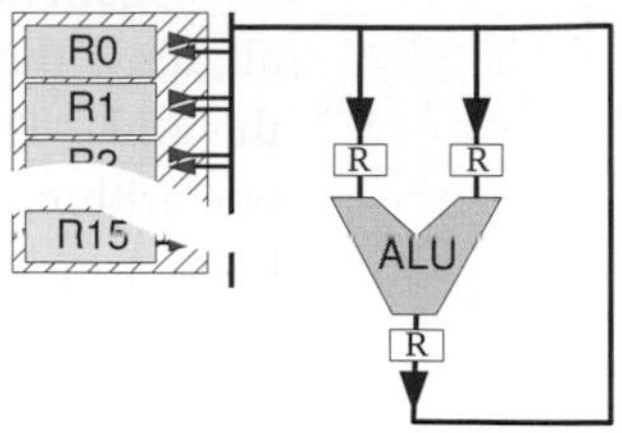

4.1.6 Single-Bus Architectures

The case of a single-bus architecture can be extrapolated from the section above. Again using a fictitious ARM-style processor as an example, the architecture may look similar to that shown in Figure 4.7.

Note the architectural simplicity of the design, which belies the operational complexity of the multi-step operation of such a system. Again we consider adding `R0 = R1 + R2` with each numbered step being at a monotonically increasing time instant.

1. Set up system and set ALU functionality switch to 'ADD'.
2. Allow register R1 to drive bus (by turning on the register output buffer).
3. Latch bus value into the first ALU operand register.
4. Turn off register output buffer for R1.
   Allow register R2 to drive bus (by turning on the register output buffer).
5. Latch bus value into the second ALU operand register.
6. Turn off register output buffer for R1.
   Wait for worst-case propagation delay through ALU.
7. Latch ALU result into ALU output buffer.
8. Allow ALU output buffer to drive the bus.
9. Latch content of the bus into register R0.
10. Turn off ALU output buffer (bus becomes free and the system is ready to perform the next operation).

Comparing the sequence above to that for a two-bus system in Section 4.1.5, the two extra steps and the resulting reduction in efficiency are noticeable. One common improvement made historically to single-bus architectures was the addition of a very short and inexpensive result feedback bus as shown Figure 4.8.

Figure 4.8 A single-bus connection between an ALU and a register bank as in Figure 4.7 but augmented with a single feedback link from ALU output to one of the ALU input latches.

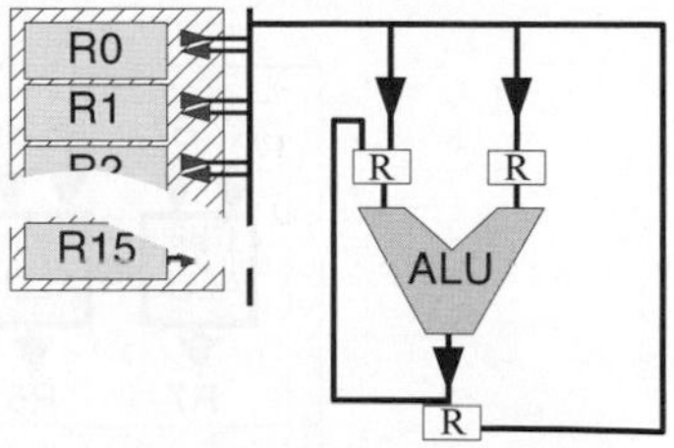

Again there are several alternative arrangements to perform this functionality, but all allow the result of an ALU calculation to be fed back to the input of one arm of the ALU. This would be useful when performing accumulation or when following one arithmetic or logical operation after another. In this case, the register on the left-hand arm of the ALU became known as the *accumulator*. It was the basis for almost every operation, the most used register in the entire system, the programmer's friend. Older low-level programmers came to know and love the accumulator: many mourned its death, killed by RISC and CISC advancements alike. This quote from well-known New Zealand engineering management guru Adrian Busch sums it all up: 'If it hasn't got an accumulator, it isn't a real CPU.'

4.2 Arithmetic Logic Unit

4.2.1 ALU Functionality

Clearly, an arithmetic logic unit (ALU) is the part of a computer capable of performing arithmetic and logical operations. But what exactly are these? An example of ALU operations defined from the instruction sets of two common processors may give some indication:

- ADSP2181 – Add, subtract, increment, decrement, AND, OR, EOR, pass/clear, negate, NOT, absolute, set bit, test bit, toggle bit. There are limits on which registers can be used as input and only two registers are available for output.
- ARM7 – Add, subtract, increment, decrement, AND, OR, EOR, pass/clear, NOT. Any register can be used as input and any register as output.

In general, the ALU performs bitwise logical operations, tests and addition or subtraction. There may be other functions performed by the ALU that are derivatives of these, and using multiple ALU operations a great deal of other functions could be performed.

A basic ALU, performing addition or subtraction, can be constructed from a number of single-bit slices operating in a chain, similar (in the add/subtract case) to the carry-propagate adder of Section 2.4.2 and illustrated in Figure 4.9. In this case, where control or function-select logic is not shown, eight separate single-bit ALUs operate bit-wise with carry on two input bytes to generate a result byte. The operation being performed is:

```
R = ALU_op(A, B)
```

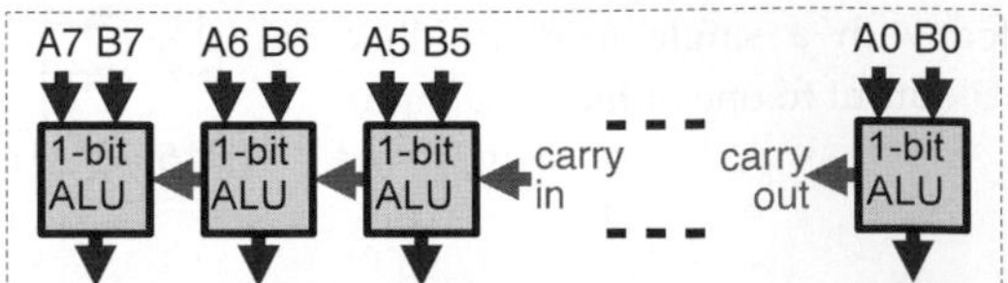

Figure 4.9 A block diagram of the parallel bitwise functional chain of parallel 1-bit units that comprise a byte wide ALU.

Some 4-bit examples of ALU operations are given below:

1001	AND	1110	=	1000	Bitwise and
0011	AND	1010	=	0010	Bitwise and
1100	OR	0001	=	1101	Bitwise or
0001	OR	1001	=	1001	Bitwise or
0001	ADD	0001	=	0010	Addition
0100	ADD	1000	=	1100	Addition
0111	ADD	0001	=	1000	Addition
	NOT	1001	=	0110	Negation
0101	SUB	0001	=	0100	Subtraction
0110	EOR	1100	=	1010	Exclusive-OR

From the background work in Chapter 2, we know that addition and subtraction are not parallel bit-wise operations. By that, we mean the nth bit result of an addition depends not only on the nth bits of each input operand, but also on all previous bits, n, $n-1, n-2 \ldots 0$. In fact, arithmetic operations between two values in general are not accomplished in a bit-parallel manner, but logical operations between two values are.

Knowing what types of functions an ALU performs in typical devices and having looked at some examples, it may now be instructive to perform a low-level design of an ALU to explore how it operates.

4.2.2 ALU Design

The block symbol traditionally used for an ALU is shown in Figure 4.10 with n-bit input operands A and B and n-bit result output indicated.

Function select is normally a bit-parallel control interface that identifies with the ALU operation being performed. Status information includes whether the answer is positive, negative, equal to zero, includes a carry or is an overflow. In some processors, these values are abbreviated to N, Z, O[3] and C.

Before		**Operation**	**Afterwards**	
R1	**R2**		**R0**	**Flags**
5	5	SUB R0, R1, R2	0	Z
8	10	SUB R0, R1, R2	−2	N
Assume that the registers are 8 bits for the next two. An 8-bit register can store numbers from 0 to 255 unsigned or −128 to 127 in two's complement signed binary.				
255	1	ADD R0, R1, R2	0	C
127	1	ADD R0, R1, R2	128 (unsigned), −128 (signed)	O, N
−1	1	ADD R0, R1, R2	0	Z, C

[3] 'V' is often used to represent the overflow flag instead of 'O', which might be confused with a zero.

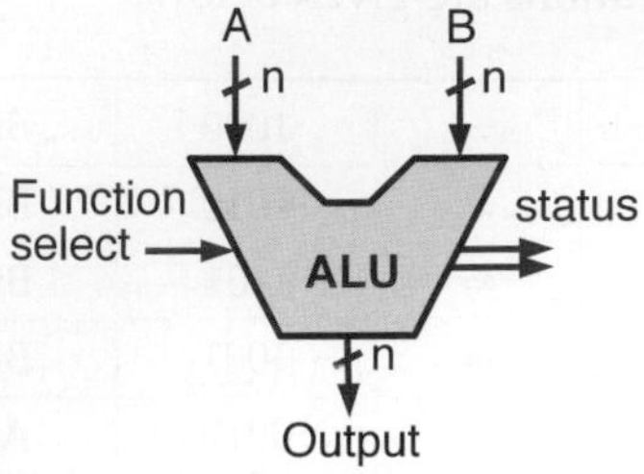

Figure 4.10 The block symbol normally used to represent an ALU showing *n*-bit operand inputs A and B, function-select logic and finally both *n*-bit result output and status flag output.

Remember: For 8-bit numbers, 01111111 + 0000001 will always equal 10000000 in binary. The question is how you interpret this. The input numbers are 127 and 1, but the output is −128 if interpreted in two's complement or +128 if interpreted as an unsigned number. Without any further information, only the programmer will know which meaning is intended.

The overflow (O) flag is intended as a help when using two's complement numbers. To the ALU there is no difference between these and unsigned numbers. However, the ALU will inform the programmer using the O status flag whenever a calculation has resulted in a potential two's complement overflow. If the programmer is dealing with unsigned numbers, it is safe to ignore this. However, when the numbers are two's complement, this has to be taken as an indication that the answer cannot be represented in this number of bits: it is too large in magnitude.

For the ALU that we will design here, we will ignore the status apart from a simple carry indication, and will perform AND, OR and ADD only. We will consider that it is a bit-parallel ALU and design just a single bit in the chain (since all the bits should be equal).

The resulting design, drawn in logic would look similar to the schematic representation in Figure 4.11. Box 4.1 builds upon this design to calculate the propagation delay that such a device would exhibit.

4.3 Memory Management Unit

A memory management unit (MMU) allows the physical memory available to a computer to be organised in a different logical arrangement as far as the CPU is concerned. The hardware resides between CPU and main memory, on the memory access bus and the logical memory arrangement is also known as *virtual memory*. This was invented at Manchester University in 1962 and is sometimes called *paging* memory.

4.3.1 The Need for Virtual Memory

Virtual memory provides the CPU with a very large space of memory that user programs can access. In reality, the physical memory is much smaller and the current *page* of memory being used by the CPU must be loaded into the physical memory on demand. Many modern operating systems, such as Linux, rely on virtual memory.

Figure 4.11

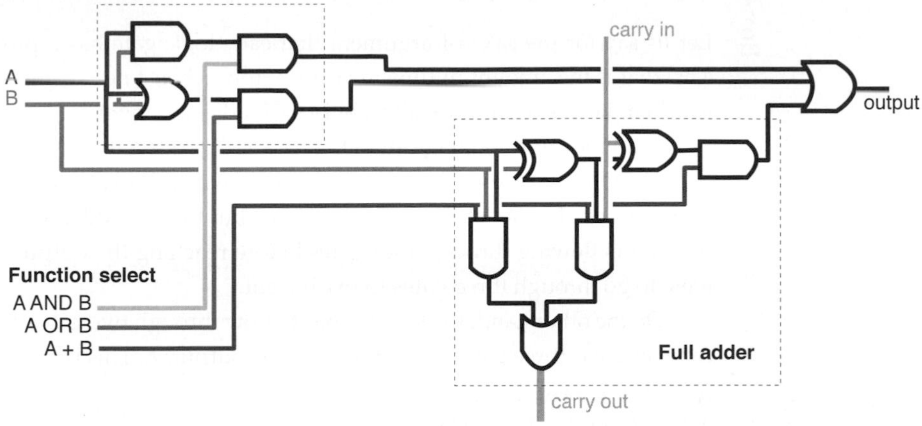

A schematic representation of the logic devices and connectivities within a single-bit slice of a typical ALU.

Virtual memory allows a program or sequence of programs that are larger than available RAM to be executed on a computer. Of course this could be accomplished with clever programming and access to a large memory space such as hard disc. However, an MMU allows programs to be written as if memory is continuous and large. The MMU takes care of where, exactly, a program is to be located and is responsible for managing the physical RAM in a computer.

The original rationale for virtual memory was the great disparity in cost between fast expensive RAM and slow inexpensive hard disc. Using virtual memory allows a lower cost computer with smaller RAM to behave as if it were a higher cost machine with more memory, the only difference being that sometimes memory accesses are slower.

With an active MMU, the average memory access speed will reduce as compared to pure RAM, and that is because hard disc is far slower. This is seen as an acceptable penalty to pay in order to have a large memory space.

Note that the secondary storage is not necessarily hard disc. It could be any storage media that is more spacious and slower than the main RAM, including slower flash memory.

4.3.2 MMU Operation

In modern MMU systems, unused pages are usually stored on hard disc, which is far larger than the physical memory but much slower.

An example of simple MMU connectivity is shown in Figure 4.12. In this figure, as far as the CPU is concerned, the system has a 32-bit address space (and can therefore address something like 2^{32} memory locations or 4 Gibytes of memory); however, the memory in our example is only 20-bits wide (2^{20} memory locations or 1 Mibytes). The MMU hides this from the CPU.

Box 4.1

Exploring ALU propagation delays

Let us say for the sake of argument that each logic gate has a propagation delay of 4 ns: that is the amount of time measured from when a new value is input to the gate to when the new output result stabilises (if it does change).

Examine the ALU diagram in Figure 4.11 (ignoring the function-select signals) to look for worst-case longest paths. Both inputs A and B go through two blocks of gates. The block on the top left has only two rows, but the full adder at the bottom right has the inputs flowing through four gates before reaching the output on the right. They have to go through three gates to reach Cout.

On the other hand, the carry in has to flow through two gates before it reaches the carry out and three gates until it reaches the output, Z. This is summed up as:

A/B to Z: $4 \times 4\,\text{ns} = 16\,\text{ns}$
A/B to Cout: $3 \times 4\,\text{ns} = 12\,\text{ns}$
Cin to Z: $3 \times 4\,\text{ns} = 12\,\text{ns}$
Cin to Cout: $2 \times 4\,\text{ns} = 8\,\text{ns}$

Let us use these figures to find a worst-case propagation delay (and hence maximum operating speed) for a 4-bit ALU performing as addition:

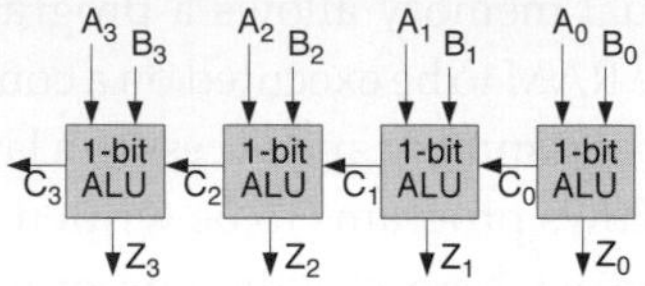

This is $A + B = Z$, and since it is an add, we need to account for the carry propagate. We can now trace the worst-case propagation path which is the input at the right-hand side of the ALU, through each carry in turn, to the most significant ALU. Since the delay from any input to the Z output is more than the delay to the carry out, the worst case is thus the sum of:

Bit 0: A/B to Cout 12 ns
Bit 1: Cin to Cout 8 ns
Bit 2: Cin to Cout 8 ns
Bit 3: Cin to Z 12 ns
Total: 40 ns

If this is being clocked at maximum rate, the clock period cannot exceed 40 ns to ensure that a correct and final output is generated for each input. Of course, sometimes the correct output appears much sooner than that, but there is no easy way to determine in advance whether the output will appear quickly or slowly. It is therefore necessary to always wait for the known worst-case delay of $1/40\,\text{ns} = 25\,\text{MHz}$.

This is not a fast clock rate for a modern processor. It may therefore be necessary to either use faster gates, allow the adder to take two clock cycles to complete, or employ some tricks to speed up the adder. One such trick is the carry predictor or look-ahead unit that was introduced in Section 2.4.3. This is quick, but can occupy a significant amount of logic when the number of bits that the adder operates on is large.

Figure 4.12

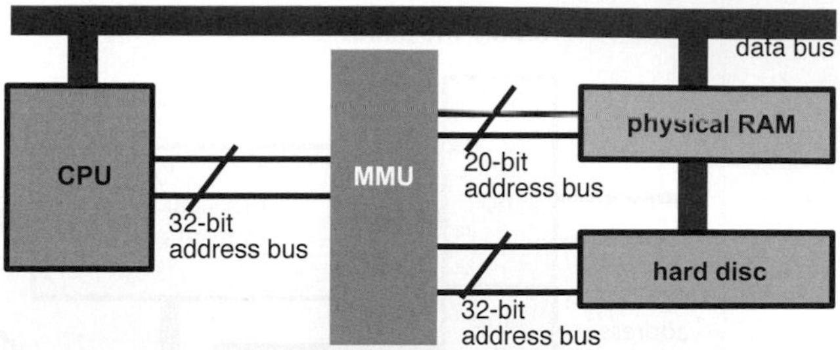

A memory management unit (MMU) is shown connected between a CPU and both physical RAM and a hard disc. While the data bus connects these elements directly, the MMU adjusts the address-bus signals 'visible' to the various components.

Memory is split into *pages*. If we assume that a page is 256 kibytes in length (a typical value), then main memory can hold 4 pages, but the CPU can access up to 16,384 pages.

The MMU loads new pages into RAM and stores unused pages to hard disc (which is big enough to hold all of the logical memory). If the CPU requests a page that is not loaded, then the MMU first retires an unused page from RAM (stores it back to hard disc) and then loads in the requested page from hard disc.

To know which page to retire, the MMU needs to track which pages are being used and ideally chooses an unused page for retirement. This is a similar idea to what happens in memory caching (described later in Section 4.4). Two look-up tables are used to keep track of what is currently in RAM and what is currently on hard disc. These are known as physical RAM contents table and disc memory contents table respectively.

Within the MMU, if the CPU requests look-up of a memory location that resides on a page that is already in RAM, this is known as a hit. If the page containing that memory location is not already in RAM, this is a page fault or miss. This operation can be seen in Figure 4.13 (also refer to the worked example in Box 4.2).

The sequence of events needed when a CPU is requesting a read from memory location X is shown below:

1. CPU places address X on the address bus, then asserts a read signal.
2. MMU signals CPU to wait while it retrieves the contents of address X.
3. MMU splits address X into page number and line number within that page.
4. MMU interrogates physical RAM contents table.
   - If the required page is loaded (a hit), this block outputs the physical RAM address of that block. The physical RAM address, combined with the line number within the block, forms the address in physical RAM to be retrieved.
   - If the required page is not loaded (page fault), then the page number is passed to the disc memory contents table. This looks up the hard disc address of

Figure 4.13

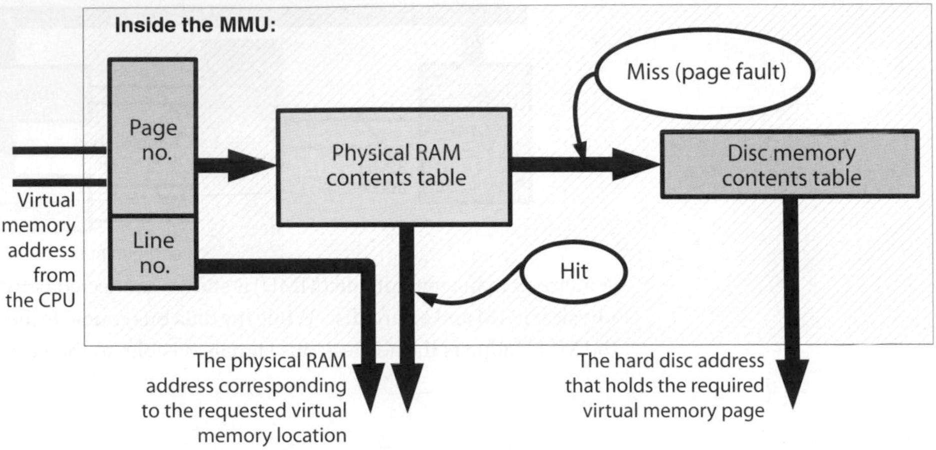

A block diagram of a simple MMU, illustrating the internal units and connectivity between them and showing the consequence of a miss and a hit respectively.

that page, and then loads the entire page into RAM. Since the page is now in RAM, the contents of address X are not retrieved in the same way as for a page hit.

- Note that since physical RAM is not infinite in size, there must be a process to retire pages back into hard disc. Indeed, a process tracks the usage of pages to know which page is to be retired.

5. The MMU outputs the contents of memory location X on the data bus and signals to the CPU that the data is ready.

The CPU clearly must wait for a longer time to retrieve a value from memory when a page fault occurs. Hard disc may be hundreds of times slower than RAM and the look-up process itself may be relatively slow despite manufacturers' best efforts to create a fast system. This wait is sometimes called a *stall time*.

It should be noted that sometimes a programmer will not want to wait for a page fault to resolve. In that case, the variables or programs that are speed-critical can be placed into a special page that is locked into physical RAM; in fact, page attributes allow advanced MMUs to handle pages in several ways. Most modern operating systems locate interrupt service routines and low-level scheduling code in such locked pages.

The method of storing pages of memory on slow hard disc for use later and loading them into RAM as required, seems a logical method of allowing users to experience a larger memory than they actually have available. However, the difficulties lie in actually implementing such a system: what methods to use to indicate which page gets retired when a new one needs loading and how big the pages should be. The next two sections consider these problems.

Box 4.2

MMU worked example

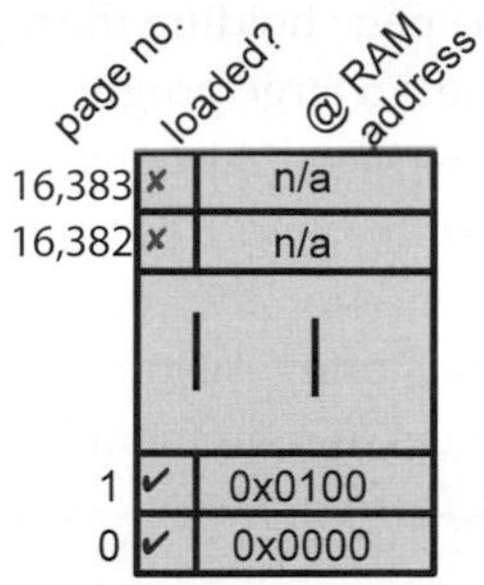

The physical RAM contents table in a simple CPU probably looks similar to the figure shown above. In this case, there is a line in the table corresponding to every logical page address in the computer. A parameter indicates which of these pages is currently loaded into RAM and, if so, at what RAM address.

Notice in the example table that page 0 is at RAM address 0 and page 1 is at RAM address `0x0100`. Now, we know that the pages can be placed anywhere within RAM, but in this case we can see that the page size may be `0x0100` locations (256). This corresponds to 8 bits of the address bus and would allow the 8-bit line number to be anything between 0 and 255.

We can also see that there are 16,384 pages: we would need 14 bits to represent this many pages. This gives us an indication of the memory size on the CPU: $14 + 8 = 22$ bits. Eight bits of the address represent the line number and the remaining 14 bits the page number. With 22 bits there will be $2^{22} = 4$ Mibytes of memory (assuming each location is a byte). We can confirm that, since $16{,}384 \times 256 = 4{,}194{,}304$ as expected.

Note: This also tells us that in such a computer the conversion from CPU logical address to line and page number is simple: the bottom 8 bits are the line number while the top 14 bits are the page number.

4.3.3 Retirement Algorithms

If a new page is loaded from hard disc to physical RAM, unless RAM happens to be empty, space has to be made by saving one of the pages that is already loaded, back to hard disc (and then updating the physical RAM contents table).

Different algorithms can be used to decide which page is to be *retired* back to the hard disc:

- **LRU** or least recently used, where the least recently used page is retired.
- **FIFO** or first-in first-out, where the oldest loaded page is retired.

Both algorithms have their advantages and disadvantages. Users of Microsoft windows operating systems on smaller machines may be familiar with disc thrashing – the process whereby the hard disc seems to be continually operating. This is said to be due to the choice of a particularly bad algorithm for retiring pages. Consider a program loop that is so large its code is spread across multiple pages. In this case, just moving from the bottom of the loop back to the top of the loop may result in a page fault if, in the meantime, the page holding the top of the loop has been retired.

Worst case is a large program with variables scattered across many pages. If a short piece of code writes single values to each of those variables, then the pages containing them will have to be in RAM, maybe having to be loaded in specially, just for a single write. In this case, the compiler and operating system have failed to optimise the program by clustering memory locations.

The problem of retirement is similar to that faced by the memory cache, discussed in Section 4.4.

4.3.4 Internal Fragmentation and Segmentation

Inefficiency results if an entire page needs to be reserved for a single memory location within that page. Or worse if a program is slightly larger than one page so that just a few lines of code are stored on an otherwise empty page such that the program takes up two memory pages but is actually more like one-page long.

In both cases, the precious fast RAM of the computer will be made to contain unused spaces. Furthermore, the long and slow process of retiring pages and loading new ones will be performed each time for mostly meaningless data. This is termed internal fragmentation.

One response to internal fragmentation has been to reduce the size of pages. However, that makes the look-up tables in the MMU large and eventually causes the look-up process itself to become a bottleneck to MMU operation.

A more recent response has been to introduce memory segments – variable length pages, but also pages that are able to grow and (in some cases) shrink on demand during program execution. A C language program may use one segment for local function variables and one for global variables. Another segment could contain the program stack. Although the C programmer need not be concerned with low-level details, the underlying operations would be to access variables by segment number and location within that segment (line). This is called a two-dimensional memory.

One advantage of such segmentation is that segments can be protected from each other. Program memory segments may be executable whereas data memory segments are not, such that erroneous attempts to branch into data memory would result in an error (rather than the total machine crash common of older operating systems and computers). Similarly, a rogue program storing variables to an incorrect location would not be allowed to overwrite the memory of another application.

4.3.5 External Fragmentation

Segmented memory spaces are more complicated because they need routines to keep track of both the size and the contents of each segment in addition to the various location contents tables. However, they are more efficient than the original paged systems because they do not suffer from internal fragmentation in the way mentioned in Section 4.3.4.

Figure 4.14

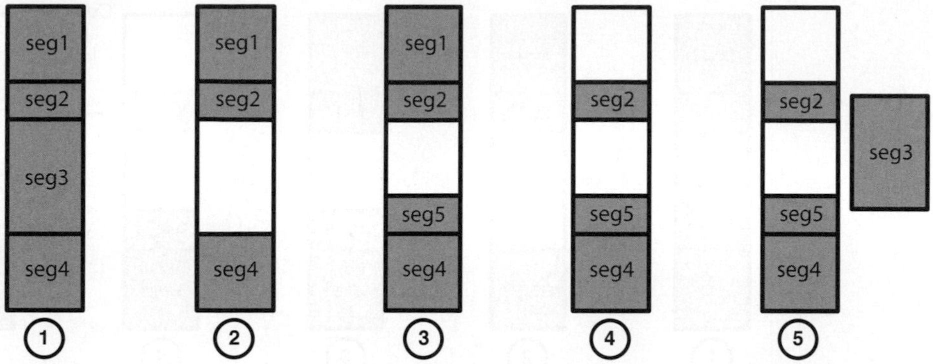

An illustration of external fragmentation: five steps in memory segment loading and unloading result in a memory map having sufficient free space but insufficient contiguous free space to reload segment seg3.

Unfortunately, they suffer from *external* fragmentation instead as shown in Figure 4.14. Working from left to right, an original program is loaded (1), occupying four segments in memory. In (2), the operating system wants to access some new memory in segment 5 so it retires a segment (in this case it chooses segment 3). Segment 5 is then loaded (3).

In (4), segment 1 is retired to hard disc and in (5) the operating system wishes to access segment 3 and thus has to reload it.

At this point, there is clearly sufficient empty space in RAM for segment 3, but it is not continuous empty space. There are two responses possible. One is to split segment 3 into two parts and load wherever it can be fitted in, and the second is to tidy up memory and then load segment 3. The first response would work in this instance, but could quite quickly become very complex and would in time actually contribute to the problem because there will be more and more smaller and smaller segment-parts. For that reason, the second response is used. The tidying process is called compaction and it is performed before loading segment 3, as illustrated in Figure 4.15.

Since compaction obviously takes some time, it should be performed only when necessary.

There are a profusion of segment management algorithms available as this has been an active research field for many years. Common among them is the need to track used and unused portions of memory, and the ability in some way to perform compaction. Some of the simpler algorithms default to always performing compaction if a gap appears.

4.3.6 Advanced MMUs

The MMU hardware shown in Section 4.3.2 works well for fixed page sizes, but what about with segmented memory? Remember that the speed of the physical RAM contents

Figure 4.15

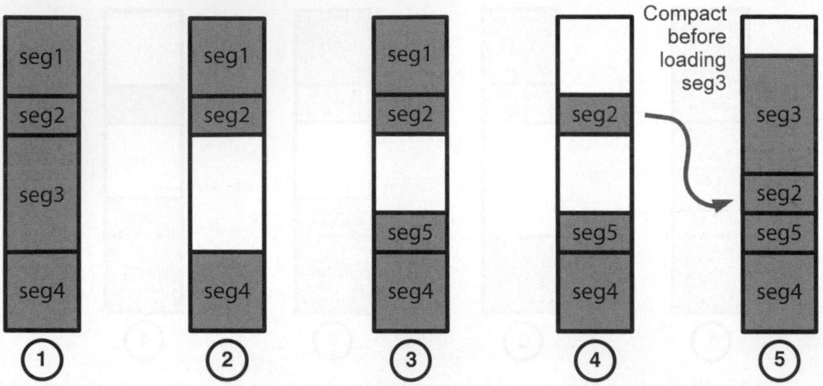

The same series of memory operations are performed as in Figure 4.14 but in this case a compaction operation before reloading seg3 allows reorganisation of memory contents sufficient to allow the segment to be loaded.

table in particular is very important to overall memory access speed – all requested locations must be searched for in this block. For segmented memory it is not sufficient any longer to simply divide the address bus into two and consider the bottom few bits to be line and the top few bits to be page, because now the pages have different sizes. This means that the contents table becomes a complex contents-addressable look-up table (LUT).

Such LUTs have look-up time proportional to size, and so the bigger the table gets, the slower it is. The problem is that, in order to reduce external fragmentation, the system needs to cope with some fairly small segment/page sizes. Consider the example of the UltraSPARC II. This supports up to 2200 Gbytes of RAM, but has a minimum page size of 8 kbytes. This means in a worst case there could be 200,000 pages in the system. A LUT capable of storing information on each of these pages would be very slow: it would mean that all memory accesses, in physical RAM or not, would be considerably slowed down by the look-up process.

The solution is to introduce a small, fast look-up table for commonly used pages, and store the less commonly used pages in a slower look-up table (or RAM). This is effectively caching the contents table, and is termed a translation look-aside buffer (TLB). It has other names such as Translation Buffer (TB), Directory Look-aside Table (DLT) and Address Translation Cache (ATC). It is shown in Figure 4.16.

At the time of writing, UltraSPARC II and MIPS R3000 processors use this technique, but not the ARM 7, x86 series or digital signal processors. It is generally reserved for very fast workstation-class processors.

4.3.7 Memory Protection

There are some remaining benefits that an MMU can provide the system designer beyond the ability to swap pages into and out of physical memory and store them on

Figure 4.16

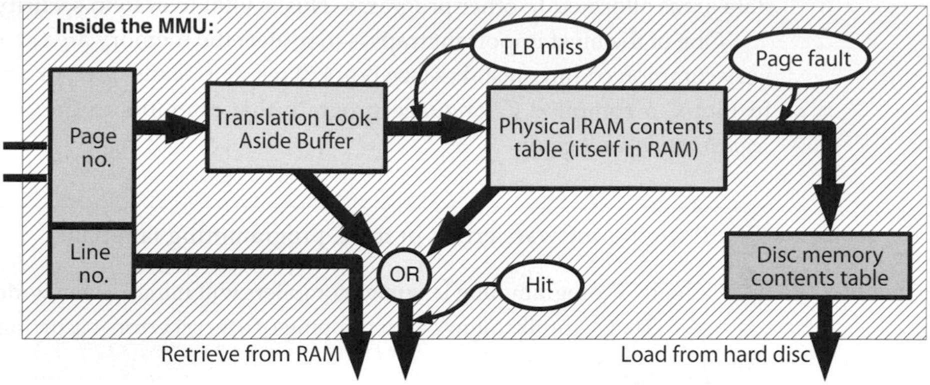

A block diagram of MMU operation using a TLB. Contrast this to the non-TLB case in Figure 4.13 on page 136.

hard disc. Actually, the price of RAM has dropped year-by-year to the point where very few software applications require more RAM than can be fitted inexpensively into a desktop computer (despite the best efforts of code-bloating software writers). For embedded processors too, the MMU is often still present even when there is no physical off-line storage space, such as hard disc. The question is, why do system designers persist in building memory management units when the original purpose of these has largely disappeared?

The main reason is memory protection. Since the MMU sits between main memory and the processor, it is capable of scanning and modifying addresses very quickly without processor intervention. The MMU is capable of raising a signal to the processor alerting it to any problems (such as 'you have asked for an address that does not exist'). In the ARM, for example, this would be through an interrupt signal called *data abort* for a data fetch or *prefetch abort* if it happened when requesting an instruction. Special low-level handlers would be written as part of an operating system to (attempt to) deal with these if and when they occur.

Looking at the issue from a software perspective, the system programmer can set up the memory management unit to restrict access to various portions of memory or flag other portions of memory as allocated or not allocated. Compiled code usually has a number of program and data areas – program areas are not usually writeable but data areas are. When applied to a memory management unit, a given program area that is currently being executed from will have a certain set of other memory areas it can read from and write to.

In most modern operating systems, user code does not have indiscriminate access to write to every memory location – it can only write to its own allocated memory areas. This prevents, for example, a mistake in user code from corrupting the operating system and crashing the computer.

Non-OS code cannot write to system control registers and cannot overwrite the data areas allocated to other programs. This is vital to system security and reliability.

One of the most important traps is to protect the memory area at address 0. Several very common coding mistakes (see Box 4.3) result in reads from, or writes to, address 0. In Linux, a compiled C language program that attempts to do this will exit with a *segmentation fault* error.

Box 4.3

Trapping software errors in the C programming language

Usually C programming language compilers will initialise newly-defined variables to zero. This helpfully allows easy trapping of several errors occurring at zero:

```
int *p;
int x;
x=*p; //since p is set to NULL (0), a read from here will
trigger a data abort
```

Defining a block of memory with library function `malloc()` will fail if, for example, there is insufficient memory space left to claim. On failure, malloc will return NULL.

```
void *ptr=malloc(16384);
//we forgot to check the return address to see if malloc failed
*ptr=20;
//since ptr holds NULL (0), this will trigger a data abort
```

Similarly, there is the issue of calling a function which has a runtime allocation;

```
boot_now()
{
      void (*theKernel)(int zero, int arch);
      ...
      ...
      printf("Launching kernel\n");
      theKernel(0, 9);
}
```

In this code (taken from an embedded system bootloader), the function theKernel() is defined in the first line and should point to a memory address where the OS kernel has been loaded; however, the programmer has forgotten to add this in. By default, it will thus be set to zero. Launching the kernel will jump the code execution to address 0, resulting in a prefetch abort.

Note that the values 0 and 9 passed to the function (for an ARM) are simply going to be stored into registers R0 and R1 before the branch occurs. If the kernel does reside at the address specified and is embedded Linux, it would execute – decompressing itself, and then set up the system based on these values that it finds in R0 and R1.

4.4 Cache

Cache memory is close to the CPU, has very fast access speed, but is usually expensive. If cost were not an issue, computer designers would employ only fast memory in their systems. As it is, this would be uneconomical for all but the most expensive supercomputers.

Cache fits into the memory hierarchy shown in Section 3.2.2. Memory near the top of the hierarchy is fastest, smallest and most expensive while memory towards the bottom is slowest, largest (in storage terms) and cheapest.

Cache attempts to increase average access speed for memory accesses whereas MMU tries to allow a larger memory space to be accessed, but in so doing, actually reduces average access speed. Unlike the MMU, a cache does not require any operating system intervention. However, like the MMU, it is transparent to the applications programmer.

There need not only be a single cache – there can in fact be different levels of cache operating at different speeds. The highest level caches (close to the CPU) are usually implemented as fast on-chip memory. These tend to be small (8k for some ARMs and the 80486) and the size tends to increase as the caches approach main RAM. A good illustration of the concept of a cache in a real (but now outdated) system is in the Pentium Pro processor, described in Box 4.4.

Split caches can be used separately for data and instructions, necessary for caching in Harvard architecture processors (those that have separate memory for data and program storage, see Section 2.1.2), but often advantageous for von Neumann architecture processors too. For example, the innovative DEC StrongARM processors (long since replaced by Intel XScale ARM-based architecture) were ARM-based and therefore had an internal von Neumann architecture; however, they used a Harvard architecture cache. This allowed the two cache parts to be optimised for different behaviour: program memory accesses tend to be sequential in nature whereas data memory accesses tend to jump among clusters of locations and different caching schemes and architectures suit each behaviour differently.

Similar to virtual memory, a cache miss occurs when the required data is not in the cache and has to be fetched from slower memory. As before, some data has to be retired first and possibly some compaction takes place.

The hit ratio is the proportion of requested locations that can be found in the cache, and is therefore the primary measure of cache performance. This can be maximised by good cache organisation and an efficient caching algorithm, based on the use of the cache.

There are a number of different forms of cache organisation that significantly affect the cost and performance of the cache. Three of the more common ones, the *direct cache*, *set-associative cache* and *full-associative cache* are outlined in the following sections.

Note that in modern CPUs, caches actually read blocks of memory, perhaps 32 or 64 bytes at a time, rather than single memory locations. For simplicity, most of the examples given in this section will consider that a cache entry holds only a single

Box 4.4

Cache example: the Intel Pentium Pro

Intel's Pentium Pro was innovative in its day, packaged with a 256-kibyte cache in the same chip package as the CPU but on separate silicon. Unfortunately, this approach, shown diagrammatically below, was found to be unreliable and ultimately led to the failure of the Pentium Pro as an enduring product line.

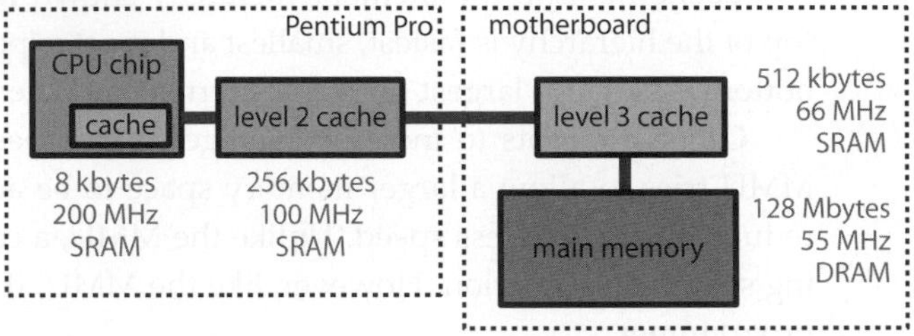

In the diagram, it can be seen that the relatively fast CPU has a small amount of level 1 cache (8 kbytes) built in. Level 2 cache is in the same package, roughly half the speed but 32 times as large. Level 3 cache is fast SRAM located on the motherboard, slower still and larger than Level 2 cache. Finally, main memory capacity is huge by comparison, but significantly slower. It is implemented in DRAM (dynamic RAM), a low-cost high density technology that is typically much slower than SRAM.

Note: Today, cache systems will still look quite similar but there may be extra zeros on each of the RAM sizes and perhaps even another level of cache. Main memory would have transitioned through SDRAM (Synchronous DRAM) to RDRAM (Rambus), or DDR (double data rate) RAM or beyond (see Section 7.6).

memory location. In the more realistic case of memory blocks, the tag address in cache is the start address of the block, and the cache controller knows that *m* consecutive memory locations must be cached in one cache line. The advantage of caching blocks in this way is that modern memory such as SDRAM or RDRAM is much more efficient when asked to load or save blocks of sequential memory locations than it is when handling multiple single addresses.

4.4.1 Direct Cache

In this scheme, each cache location can hold one line of data from memory. Each memory address corresponds to a fixed cache location, and as the cache is much smaller than the memory, each cache location corresponds in turn to many memory locations.

Therefore, when the direct cache is requested to return a particular memory address content, it only needs to check in one cache location for the correct tag. The cache location is taken from the lowest *n* bits of the memory address (assuming the cache and memory widths are equal) such as the 32-bit example below:

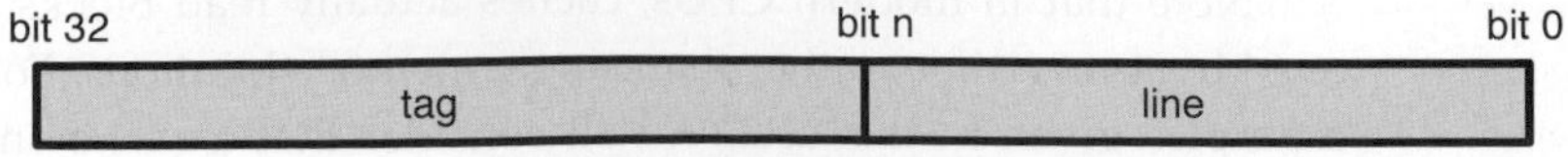

The split between tag and line is conceptually similar to the page and line split in the MMU (Section 4.3). The number of locations in the direct cache is equal to the number of lines. Every page (tag) has the same number of lines, so if a value from one page (tag) is cached, it is placed in cache at the location specified by the line.

Each cache location actually contains a number of fields: a dirty/clean flag indicates if the cache value has been updated (but not yet stored in main memory). A valid bit indicates if the location is occupied. A tag entry indicates which of the possible memory pages is actually being cached in that line. Finally, the cache stores the data word that it is caching from RAM.

So the direct cache algorithm is:

- **CPU Reads from memory** – Split the required address into TAG and LINE. Check the cache at the LINE location and see if the TAG entry matches the requested one. If it does, read the value from the cache. If the TAGs do not match then look at the dirty flag. If this is set, first store the current cache entry on that line back to main memory. Then read the main memory value at the required address into that cache line. Clear the dirty flag, set the valid flag and update the TAG entry.
- **CPU Writes to memory** – There is a choice depending on exactly how the cache is set up to operate:
  - *write through* writes the value into the cache line (first storing any dirty entry that is already there) and also writes the value into main memory.
  - *write back* does not store into main memory (this will only happen next time another memory location needs to use the same line), just stores to cache.
  - *write deferred* allows the write into the cache and some time later (presumably when there is time available and the CPU is not waiting) the cache line is written back to main memory.

Whenever the cache value is written to main memory, the dirty flag is cleared to indicate that the main memory value and cache value are the same, called cache-memory coherence.

With the *write through* scheme, if the memory location being written to is not already in the cache, it is possible to directly store the data to memory, hence bypassing the cache. This is called *write through with no write allocate* (WTNA). Where the value is *always* stored to cache irrespective of whether it has been written to memory as well, it is termed *write through with write allocate* (WTWA).

The main advantage of the direct cache is its look-up speed. For every memory address in main RAM, there is only a single location in cache that needs to be interrogated to decide whether that address is being cached. Unfortunately, this very advantage is also a problem – every cache line corresponds to many real memory locations. Box 4.5 presents an example of the direct cache access.

4.4.2 Set-Associative Cache

The problem with the direct cache is that address locations 0, 1024, 2048, 3072 . . . etc. all compete for one cache line. If we run software that happens to use addresses 0,

Box 4.5

Direct cache example

The diagram below represents a direct cache currently in use within a simple microcomputer system.

	valid	dirty	tag	data
line 1023	✔	☹	0000	0000 2001
line 1022	✔	☺	0001	FFFF FFF1
line 2	✔	☺	0100	0000 0051
line 1	✗	☺	XXXX	XXXX XXXX
line 0	✔	☹	0000	1A23 2351

The cache has 1024 lines (corresponding to ten bits of the address bus), and each line stores two flags, a tag entry and the actual cached data. The smiley characters indicate dirty (sad) and clean (happy) entries respectively.

On system start-up, all entries are clean but invalid, like line 1. This probably means that line 1 has not been used in this cache since the system last reset.

Line 0 on the other hand is valid, so it must be caching real data. It is dirty, so the data must have changed recently and the new data not yet been written back to main RAM. With a tag of 0, line 0 must hold the cached value for CPU address 0, and the latest content for that location is the 32-bit value `0x1A23 2351`.

Since there are 1023 lines in cache, line 0 could have been caching addresses `0x400` (1024), `0x800`, `0xC00` instead, but since the tag is 0, we know it represents address 0 instead.

Line 2 is also valid but clean, meaning that the data it holds is the same as the data in main RAM that it is caching. The location it is caching is line 2 from page (tag) `0x100`. Since the line indicates the bottom ten bits of the address bus, the actual address being cached in that line is `(0x100 << 10) + 2 = 0x40002`, and the data there (also that in main RAM currently) is `0x51`.

Finally, line 1023 is valid but dirty, meaning that the data it holds has been changed since the last write to main RAM. With a tag of 0, this is caching address location `(0x0 << 10) + 1023 = 0x003FF`.

1024 and 2048 to store data, then only one of these data items can be cached at any one time.

To improve on this, an n-way *set-associative cache* allows n entries to each line. In some ways it looks like n banks of direct cache operating in parallel.

In a 2-way set-associative cache, there are two possible locations that can cache any main memory address (this type of cache is illustrated through an example in Box 4.6).

Box 4.6

Set-associative cache example

The diagram below represents a two-way set-associative cache currently in use within a simple microcomputer system.

line	valid	dirty	tag	data	valid	dirty	tag	data
1023	✔	☹	0000	0000 2001	✔	☺	0015	0110 2409
1022	✔	☺	0001	FFFF FFF1	✔	☺	0002	0000 0003
2	✔	☺	0100	0000 0051	✗	☺	XXXX	XXXX XXXX
1	✗	☺	XXXX	XXXX XXXX	✔	☹	0006	FFF1 3060
0	✔	☹	0000	1A23 2351	✔	☺	0004	4A93 B35F

This cache bears a strong resemblance to the direct cache of Box 4.5, but with two entries for each line (being two-way set-associative). The cache has 1024 lines (corresponding to 10 bits of the address bus).The smiley characters as before indicate dirty (sad) and clean (happy) entries respectively.

On system start-up, all entries are clean but invalid, like line 1 on the left-hand side and line 2 on the right-hand side. This probably means that those entries have not been used since the system was last reset.

The difference between direct and set-associative caches can be illustrated with reference to line 0. On the left it holds the same as in the direct cache example of Section 4.4.1. However, in this case, the same line is simultaneously caching a memory location from page (tag) 4. This entry is dirty-valid, indicating the value has changed in cache and has not been written back to main RAM. The cached data is the 32-bit value *0x4A93 B35F* and this is the latest available content for address $(0x004 << 10) + 0 = 0x1000$.

When reading from such a cache, the process can still be quick – equivalent to interrogating two look-up tables (and in fact the interrogation can be performed in parallel). This technique is commonly used, for example the original StrongARM processor from Digital Equipment Corporation contained a 32-way set-associative cache.

As with all caches, values may need to be retired before a new location is cached. The question is, which way of the *n*-ways is chosen for retirement? This can be seen to be similar to the choice given in the MMU case, and again there are a choice of algorithms for retirement, covered in Section 4.4.4.

4.4.3 Full-Associative Cache

If we run software that happens to use addresses 0, 1024 and 2048 but does not use addresses 1, 1025 and 2049, then direct or set-associative caches line 0 will always be busy, with cached locations being swapped in and out. Cache line 1 will by contrast always be empty.

A full-associative cache improves on this because it allows any memory location to be mapped into any cache location. In this case, the cache TAG holds the full address of its content (rather than just the page).

The problem is that when this cache is asked to retrieve a location, every cache entry TAG must be checked. In other words, every line in the cache needs to be examined. In the direct case, only one TAG needed to be checked. In the n-way set-associative cache, only n TAGs had to be checked.

So, although the chances of getting a good hit/miss ratio are better with a full-associative cache, the operation of the cache itself is slower due to the increased checking required. This problem is similar to that faced by the physical RAM contents table in an MMU.

4.4.4 Locality Principles

The storage patterns of variables being loaded and unloaded are heavily dependent on the use to which the cache is put, but in general, in a computer with a few general-purpose programs running, there are two-well defined characteristics: those for data memory and program memory. These lead to a well-known term in computer architecture, which is the *principle of locality*. There are actually two locality principles, the first being *spatial locality*, which refers to items clustered by address. The second, *temporal locality*, refers to items clustered in time.

These can be visualised by looking at a computer memory map and colouring data variables used within the past few thousand clock cycles. If a computer is frozen during operation, there will probably be a few very well-defined clusters of highlighted memory addresses and large areas of currently unused memory. Freezing again after a few seconds would show different clustered areas of active memory. The operation of a good cache would attempt to place as much as possible of the highlighted clusters into fast cache memory and thus speed up average program execution time.

If the visualisation method were applied to program memory instead, there would be some sequential blocks of highlighted memory flowing like ribbons through memory.

The principle of *spatial locality* states that at any one time, active items are probably located near each other by memory address. For program memory this is due to the sequential nature of program instructions, and for data memory due to the way a compiler will cluster defined variables into the same memory segment.

The principle of *temporal locality* states that an item that has recently been accessed is more likely to be accessed again than any other locations. For program memory this can be explained through looping constructs whereas for data memory, this may be the repetitive use of some variables throughout a program.

Both principles of locality are illustrated in Figure 4.17 where three memory pages are shown, as snapshots of memory usage, at several instants progressing through time. The density of memory usage is shown by the shading of the rectangular blocks within the pages. The memory addresses are indicated by the position within the rectangular

Figure 4.17

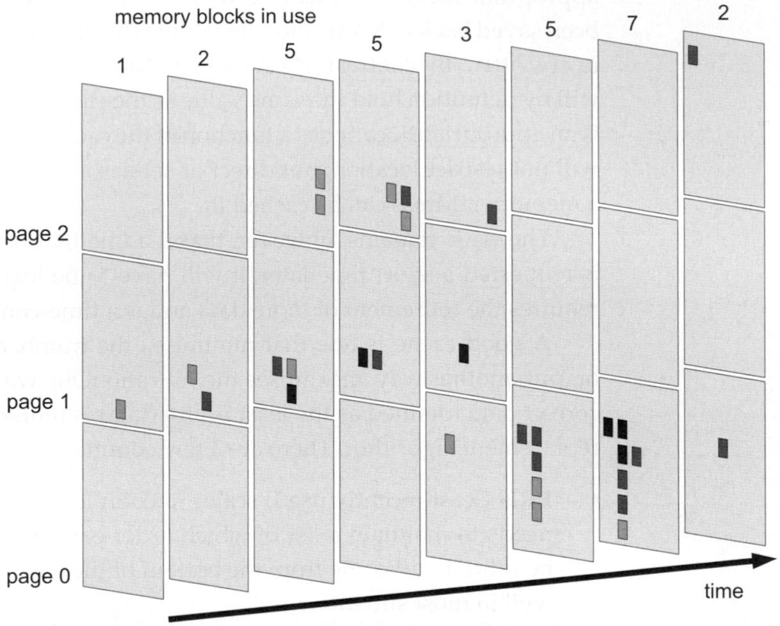

An illustration of the principles of spatial and temporal locality, showing how memory use (indicated by the dark blocks of memory on several memory pages) changes over time. Temporal locality is illustrated by the way clusters of memory that are active at one time tend to also be in use during the next time instant, but differ from those in use at a much later time. Spatial locality is illustrated by the way clusters of active memory reside in particular areas within each page, rather than being scattered evenly. The number of blocks within the pages that are used at any one time is shown at the top of the figure.

page. It can be seen that temporal locality results in a gradual move between different memory clusters as time progresses. Spatial locality means that memory accesses tend to cluster together. Note that variables (or stack items) stored across several pages may be active at any one time. This is because different types of item could reside in different pages (in particular, data and program items would be unlikely to share a memory page).

The implication of locality is that in general it is possible to predict roughly which memory locations are likely to be accessed in future. The function of a good cache is to use this information to cache those locations and therefore to increase average access speed.

4.4.5 Cache Replacement Algorithms

A replacement algorithm keeps track of locations within an operating cache. It operates when a new location is requested but the appropriate parts of cache are full, meaning that some location already in cache must be replaced by the new location. If the appropriate location in cache is 'dirty' (in other words it has been written to but has not been saved back to RAM since then), then the data must be saved to RAM prior to being overwritten. By contrast, clean cache entries can be replaced straight away since they will by definition hold the same value as the cached location in RAM. Of course, which is an appropriate location is a function of the cache organisation: a full-associative cache will not restrict location, but direct or set-associative caches limit which line (or lines) a memory address can be cached in.

The issue remains, however, that if a line that has just been retired back to RAM is requested a short time later, it will have to be loaded back in again. This possibly requires the retirement of more data and is a time-consuming process.

A good cache is one that minimises the number of loads and unloads required or, put another way, maximises the hit ratio. One way to do this is to ensure that the correct data (defined as the least useful data) is retired, and this is the job of the cache replacement algorithm. There are a few common algorithms worthy of mention:

- **LRU** (least recently used) scales in complexity with the size of the cache, since it needs to maintain a list of which order each entry was used in. The next item to be retired will come from the bottom of the list. LRU tends to perform reasonably well in most situations.
- **FIFO** (first-in first-out) replaces the location that has been longest in the cache. It is very easy to implement in hardware since each loaded line identifier simply goes into a FIFO and when an item needs to be retired, the identifier at the output of the FIFO is the next one chosen. It is less effective than LRU in cases where some memory location is repeatedly used for a long time while other locations are used only for a short time.
- **LFU** (least frequently used) replaces the least frequently used location. It is more difficult to implement since each cache entry needs to have some form of counter and circuitry to compare all the counters. However, LFU performs very well in most situations.
- **Random** is very easy to implement in hardware: just pick a (pseudo-) random location. Surprisingly, this technique actually performs reasonably well.
- **Round robin** (or **cyclic**) will take turns retiring cache lines. It is common in n-way set-associative caches where each of the n-ways is retired in turn. Its chief advantage is ease of implementation, but performance is poor for smaller caches.

Remember that caches must be *FAST*, and since these algorithms will need to keep track of which lines have been accessed and will be called when a replacement is needed, they need to be implemented in such a way that they do not limit the performance of the cache: a perfect replacement algorithm is no use if it slows the cache down to the same speed as main RAM. These algorithms will need to be implemented in fast hardware rather than software. The implementation complexity is therefore an issue.

Boxes 4.7 and 4.8 present worked examples of how cache replacement algorithms operate for some example sequences of reads and writes.

Box 4.7

Cache replacement algorithm worked example 1

Q. A computer system has cache and main memory states as shown in the diagram on the right. At reset, the cache is entirely empty but the main memory has locations filled with the values *aa*, *bb*, *cc* and up to *ii* as shown. Each cache line can cache one memory address.

If the LRU replacement algorithm is used with a write back system and the cache is full associative (and filled from the bottom up), trace the actions required and draw the final state of the cache after the following sequence of operations:

(1) Read from address 0.
(2) Read from address 1.
(3) Read from address 0.
(4) Read from address 2.
(5) Read from address 3.
(6) Read from address 4.
(7) Write 99 to address 5.

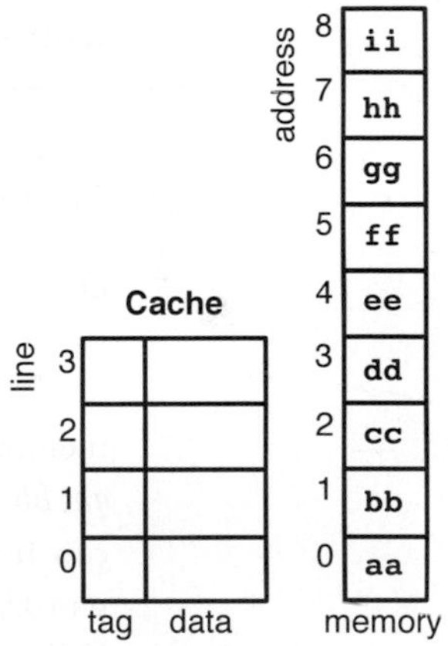

A. We will work step-by-step through the operations and draw the state of the cache in full after steps 5, 6 and 7 to illustrate the actions, in the following diagram:

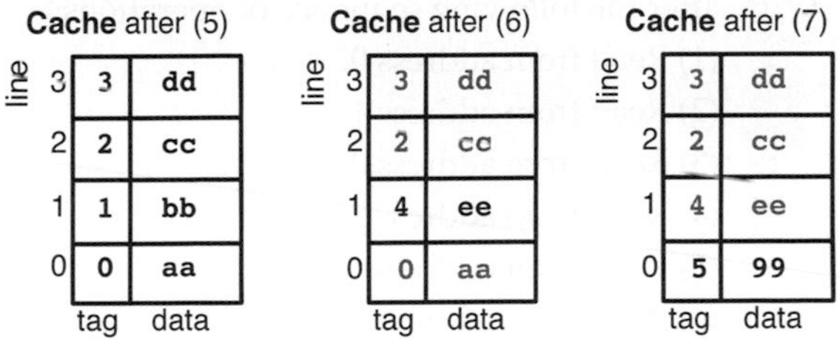

Firstly, (1) is a miss because the cache is empty. So the value *aa* is retrieved from memory and placed in cache line 0 with tag 0 (since a full-associative cache tag is the full memory address). (2) is also a miss and this would result in *bb* being placed in cache line 1. (3) is a hit – address 0 is already present in line 0, so no further action is required. (4) is a miss and would result in *cc* being written to cache line 2. (5) is similarly a miss and this would cause cache line 3 to be filled.

At this point the cache is full, so any new entry will require a retirement. Since we are using LRU (least recently used), we need to take account of the last time each entry is accessed. (6) is a miss, so the value in memory location 4 must be loaded into cache. Looking back, the least recently used line is line 1 in step (2) and not line 0 in step (1)

(Continued)

Box 4.7

Cache replacement algorithm worked example 1 (*Continued*)

because we accessed line 0 after loading line 1, in step (3). Step (6) therefore stores the memory address 4 data, *ee*, to line 1).

Finally, step (7) involves a write from CPU to memory. Since we have a write back system, this value must be placed in the cache as well as in main memory. Applying the LRU algorithm again, we see that line 0 is this time the least recently used location and this is therefore replaced with the new data (it is not retired because we have not written to it since it was loaded).

Box 4.8

Cache replacement algorithm worked example 2

Q. A computer system has cache and main memory as shown in the diagram on the right.

At reset, the cache is empty but the main memory has locations filled with the values *aa*, *bb*, *cc* up to *ii* as shown. Each cache line can hold two memory addresses (in other words, it is a two-way set-associative cache). If the FIFO replacement algorithm is used with a write back system, trace the actions required and draw the final state of the cache after the following sequence of operations:

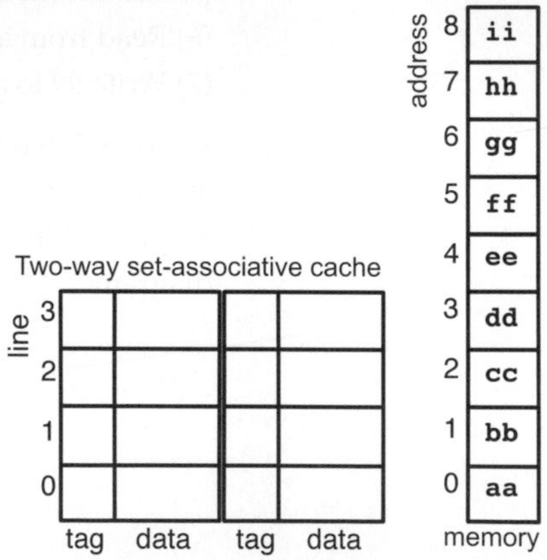

(1) Read from address 0.
(2) Read from address 1.
(3) Read from address 0.
(4) Read from address 2.
(5) Read from address 3.
(6) Read from address 4.
(7) Write 99 to address 5.
(8) Write 88 to address 8.

A. Firstly, it is important to determine the tag range. Since the cache has four lines, memory address range {0–3} resides in tag area 0, {4–7} in tag area 1, {8–11} in tag area 2 and so on. Memory addresses 0, 4 and 8 map to line 0, and 1, 5, 9 map to line 1, and so on.

Working step-by-step through the operations now, (1) will result in a miss and cause *aa* to be loaded into cache line 0. For the sake of readability we will fill the left-hand 'way' first. (2) is also a miss, and will fill line 1. (3) is a hit and will cause the value in cache line 0 on the left-hand side to be read out. (4) and (5) are also cache misses and will fill lines 2 and 3 respectively with data *cc* and *dd*. At this point, every line on the left-hand side of the cache has been filled. So step (6), a read miss from address 4 will cause data

(*Continued*)

Box 4.8

Cache replacement algorithm worked example 2 (*Continued*)

ee to be placed in cache. Address 4 maps to cache line 0 and since line 0 on the left-hand side is full, so it will be written on the right-hand side. Note that address 4 is in tag area 1.

(7) is a write to address 5, which maps to cache line 1 with a tag of 1. We have not accessed address 5 so this is a miss and will cause the written data *99* to be placed in the spare part of cache line 1, namely on the right-hand side. The state of the cache at this point is shown in the diagram below (left cache).

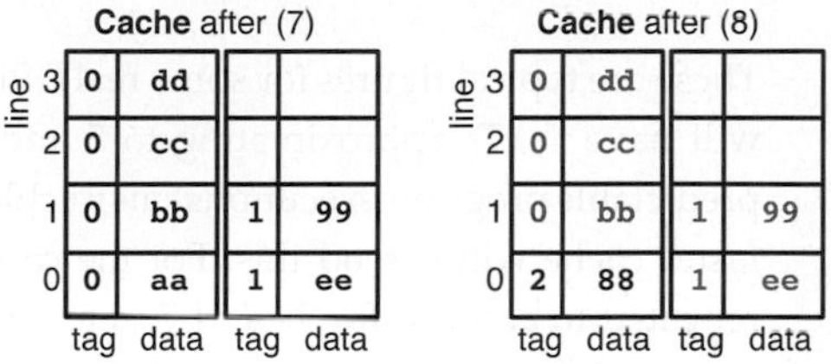

Cache after (7)
Cache after (8)
line
3 0 dd
2 0 cc
1 0 bb 1 99
0 0 aa 1 ee
3 0 dd
2 0 cc
1 0 bb 1 99
0 2 88 1 ee
tag data tag data

The final step (8) is to write *88* to address 8. Address 8 maps to cache line 0 and is in tag area 2. This must be placed in cache since a write back scheme is in use. However, cache line 0 is full. One entry therefore needs to be retired. Applying the FIFO scheme, the first in must be removed. For the case of line 0, the first of the two choices to be loaded was the left-hand side, so this is replaced by *88* (right cache).

4.4.6 Cache Performance

The time taken for a hit equates to the time taken to test for a hit (to access the cache look-up table) plus the time required to retrieve the value from the cache and return to the requesting CPU. It is assumed that updating the runtime part of a replacement algorithm does not add to this timing. Since the cache is, by definition, fast, then the time taken to test for a hit should be minimised.

The time taken for a miss is a little more complicated. This first requires time to test for a hit (access the cache look-up table), then to run the replacement algorithm, then to check for a dirty flag on the chosen line. If set, the time required to retire this unwanted value back to main RAM must be added to the time taken to load the required value from main RAM to the cache plus the time taken to retrieve this from cache into CPU must be factored in.

If cache location M_1 has access time T_1 for a cache hit, but for a cache miss we need to transfer word M_2 from main memory into cache M_1, with transfer time T_2 and hit rate H = number of cache hits/number of requests, then *overall access time* T_S is given by:

$$T_S = H \times T_1 + (1 - H)(T_1 + T_2) = T_1 + (1 - H)T_2$$

As T_1 is much smaller than T_2 (of course a hit is *much* faster than a miss), a large hit ratio is required to move the total access time nearer to T_1 (in other words to try to achieve $H \approx 1$).

Cache

Box 4.9

Access efficiency example

Some typical values of access efficiency for values of T_1/T_S against hit ratio are as follows:

		5	10	20
	0.6	0.33	0.20	0.11
H	0.8	0.50	0.33	0.20
	0.9	0.67	0.50	0.33

These are typical figures for some real CPUs: A 75-MHz ARM7 with 16-MHz memory will have T_2/T_1 approximating to 5 and (with a good cache over fairly benign or predictable program executions) may achieve a 0.75 hit ratio. Other systems with much faster cache will extend this. For the case of multi-level caches, the analysis can be repeated to account for T_3 and T_4, etc. Of course, if the programs being executed all managed to fit within cache, the hit ratio will reach 1.0.

If C is the cost per bit in the cache memory of size S_1 and C_2 is the cost per bit in main memory of size S_2, then the average cost per bit is given by:

$$C_S = (C_1 S_1 + C_2 S_2)/(S_1 + S_2) = C_1 S1/(S_1 + S_2) + C_2 S_2/(S_1 + S_2)$$

Considering that $C_1 >> C_2$, then the cache has to be small, otherwise it is prohibitively expensive. Cache design is all about the three-way trade-off between cost, speed and size (size because low-level cache normally has to fit on the same silicon die as a CPU, sharing valuable space).

Access efficiency is defined as $T_1/T_S = 1/\{1 + (1 - H)(T_2/T_1)\}$, which can be considered to be the ratio between the theoretical maximum speed-up if the hit ratio is 1.0 divided by the actual average access speed derived previously. Some typical values of access efficiency for several values of T_1/T_S with respect to hit ratio are given in Box 4.9.

Note that having a huge cache is not unknown. This is effectively the approach taken in some digital signal processors: a large provision of very fast single-cycle internal RAM allows CPU operation to run at full speed without waiting for memory accesses. A popular example is the Analog Devices ADSP2181 with 80 kbytes of fast on-chip memory. In this case, users are willing to pay the cost of a large block of RAM tied closely together with the CPU, for the benefit of the performance it allows (all operations – including memory accesses – completing within a single cycle).

Note that there are various techniques for improving cache performance, such as predictive read-ahead and adaptive replacement algorithms. A good full-associative cache may provide a hit ratio of up to 0.9, although this might be in a specialised system and achievable only with a small program size.

4.4.7 Cache Coherency

Cache coherency is ensuring that all copies of a memory location in caches hold the same value. We took account of this by simply specifying clean/dirty and valid/invalid flags in the examples shown so far. Cache coherency is important in shared memory multi-processor systems. However, ensuring cache coherency is particularly difficult.

Imagine the case of a shared variable used by two CPUs, A and B. If it is read by both CPUs, it would then end up cached by both. Now, if one of those CPUs, say A, changed the variable (by writing to it), the variable stored in CPU A's cache will be updated. In a write through system the new value of that variable is also immediately written back into memory, so memory will then be up-to-date. However, CPU B still has the old value of the variable in cache. If CPU B reads that variable, it will be a cache hit and will use the old value in its cache, rather than the correct latest value from RAM. The fact that CPU B is now reading an incorrect variable is termed a *coherency* issue: the cached item inside CPU B is not *coherent* with the other stored values of that variable.

An example parallel computer system is shown in Figure 4.18, which could be extended with many more processors. Since bus bandwidth is shared between CPUs, it would quickly become a performance bottleneck, and so the individual cache sizes are made large in order to minimise accesses to shared RAM (and hence bus usage). However, this only exacerbates any coherency problems.

There are a number of techniques in use in modern computer systems to alleviate this problem. A common solution begins with what we term *snooping*. Snooping is the process where a cache 'listens' to accesses put on the shared bus by other caches. This can provide two pieces of useful information: firstly, when another cache reads a location that is also cached locally, and secondly when another cache writes back to memory to a location that is cached locally.

With the information gleaned through snooping, an intelligent cache controller can take some form of action to prevent coherency issues. For example, invalidating a corresponding local cache entry when another cache writes to that location in shared RAM. In fact, there are a number of methods of handling the issue, although something called the *MESI protocol* is one of the most popular.

The MESI protocol, named after its states (modified, exclusive, shared and invalid), is based around the state machine shown in Figure 4.19. An (S) or (E) after the read

Figure 4.18 This diagram illustrates the connectivity of two CPUs, each with an individual cache, to a shared bus architecture with shared main RAM.

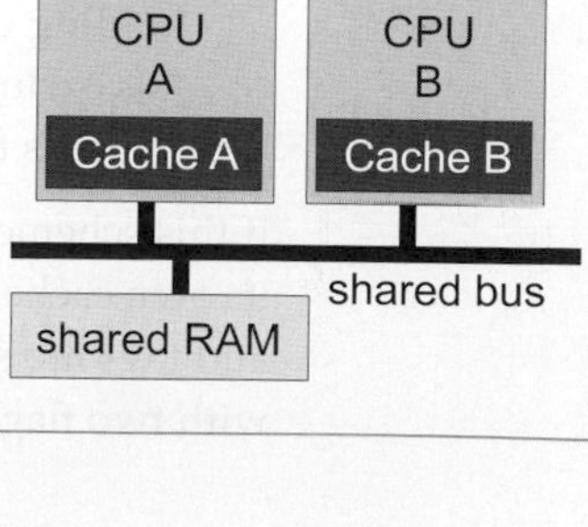

Figure 4.19

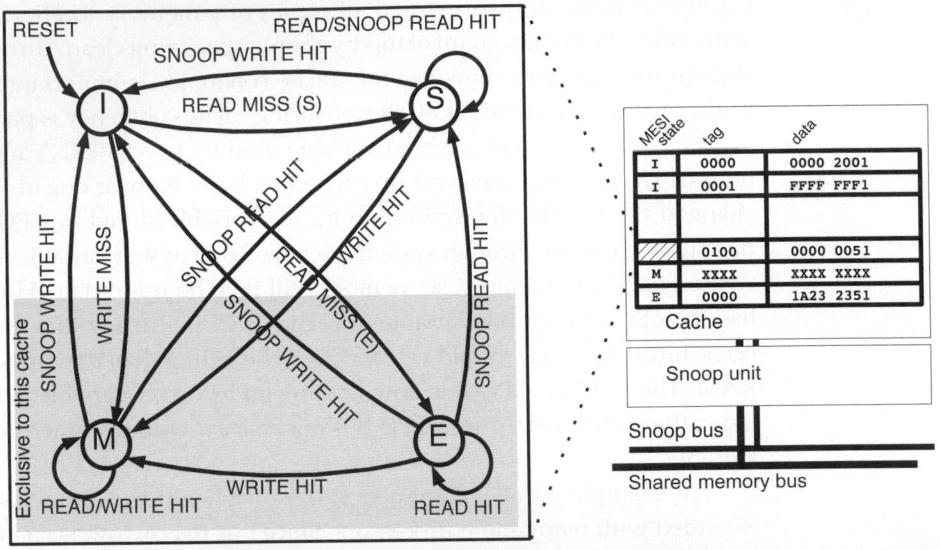

The MESI protocol state transition diagram (left) and a section through cache memory showing where the MESI state identifiers would be located for a particular cache line.

misses in the figure indicates that when the value is fetched from main memory another cache snoop unit indicates that it is also holding a copy (and hence an S for shared) or no other unit indicates it is using it (hence an E for exclusive). It can be seen therefore that snoop units have the responsibility to not only listen to other accesses, but also to inform other processor cache units when they themselves are caching a value that other caches request.

Each cache line can have one of four states associated with it (instead of the two states of valid/invalid and dirty/clean):

- I is invalid, indicating that the data in that line is not correct or is not caching anything.
- S is shared, meaning that *another* CPU is probably also caching this value. A cache can determine this by snooping the shared memory bus. The value in cache is the same as the value in main memory.
- M is modified in that the value has been updated. This means that any other caches holding this value will actually be holding old data.
- E is exclusive, an indication that no other cache is currently holding this value, but that it is the same value as would be found in main memory.

If this scheme is used in a shared memory multi-processor system, then each CPU has its own cache and each cache uses the MESI protocol for control. The usual line number and tags are still required for each line in cache, but the valid/clean flags are replaced with two flag bits that specify the state (invalid, modified, exclusive or shared).

Box 4.10

MESI protocol worked example

To illustrate the operation of the MESI protocol in a twin-CPU shared memory system, the state of the system will be followed through a representative sequence of events. The CPUs are named A and B and their caches begin from reset (so all entries start in the I state).

CPU A reads from location X in shared memory. Since cache is all invalid, this will be a read miss and cause the value to be retrieved from main memory. Cache B will snoop the bus, see the transfer, look internally and see that it is not caching location X. It therefore, will keep quiet. Looking at the state diagram and applying this to cache A, a read miss from state I with no snoop information will lead to state E.

Now, imagine that CPU B also reads location X after that. There is nothing inside cache B and hence it is a read miss. Cache B reads the value from shared RAM, but cache A snoops the bus. Cache A looks internally and sees that it is also caching location X. Cache A will then indicate on the snoop bus to cache B that it is holding location X. Cache B will continue to read the value, but since it is a shared read, the state diagram indicates we must follow the read (S) from state I to state S. Similarly, inside cache A there was a snoop read hit, and so the state of the cache line holding location X moves from E to S. At this time, both caches hold location X and both are in the shared state.

Next, imagine that CPU A writes to location X. Given a write through scheme (where any write is committed directly to main memory), cache A realises that this is a write hit, which from state S moves the line state to E. Cache B snoop unit is monitoring the bus and determines a snoop write hit. Since it is also in state S, this will take it to state I which means invalid. This is correct since the value that it is caching is no longer the latest value – the latest value is in the *other* cache and now back in main memory.

On reset, all cache lines are set to invalid. This means that any data in the cache lines is not correct.

Readers may wish to refer to Box 4.10 for a worked example of the MESI protocol operating in a dual-processor shared memory system.

4.5 Co-Processors

There are certain classes of computational task that are better performed with hardware that is not arranged as a standard CPU. A common example is the processing of floating point numbers, usually faster when handled using a dedicated floating point unit than with a CPU (early personal computers did not provide for floating point calculations in hardware: some readers may remember the sockets provided on Intel 80386-powered PC motherboards for the Intel 80387 floating point co-processor and alternatives). In fact, since the earliest computers, there have been occasions where special-purpose hardware has been used to perform certain functions separately from the CPU, leaving the CPU for general-purpose computing.

Probably the most prominent example of this technique outside the handling of floating point numbers is Intel's MMX extension to the Pentium range of processors, later extended and renamed as *streaming SIMD extensions* (SSE). However, there are others – many modern embedded processors contain dedicated co-processing units for functions such as encryption, audio or video processing and even dedicated input-output handling.

We will examine MMX and SSE later in Section 4.7, but for now, we will consider the most prominent example – the floating point unit. This is something which every modern desktop computer contains, built-in to their CPU, but which is much less often found within processors designed for embedded systems.

4.6 Floating Point Unit

Floating point, as covered in Chapter 2, is the conveyance of numerical information using a mantissa and exponent, for a particular base system. As was explained, IEEE754 standard floating point is by far the most common representation, widely adopted within the computing industry.

Because of this standardisation, devices which implement the standard do not change as often as the other parts of a computer system within which they are used. As an example, the Intel 80486[4] and Pentium processors contained an on-chip FPU that was basically unchanged from the original version that appeared in the mid-1980s as the 80387. This was a separate co-processor chip for the 80386. In those days, a desktop PC could be bought with or without an on-board FPU, and most PCs without FPU could be upgraded by purchasing the chip and inserting it into an empty socket on the motherboard, as mentioned previously.

There was a reason (and still is) for not supplying floating point capabilities, and that is due to the nature of FPUs: large in silicon area and power hungry. Especially for embedded and battery-powered systems, it is often preferred to use a processor with no floating point capabilities and to write all algorithms in fixed point arithmetic, or to use a higher-level language and employ a software floating point emulator.

In use, the CPU loads operands into special registers which are shared between the main CPU and the FPU (whether this is a separate chip or on the same silicon). The FPU is activated through issuing a special instruction. The FPU will then read the shared registers and begin processing the required instruction. Some time later, the FPU returns the result to the special register area and informs the CPU through an interrupt that the process has finished. Many modern processors include the FPU inside an execution pipeline so that the extra interrupt is not required (pipelines will be covered in Section 5.2).

The FPU generally cannot access data in memory or on shared buses directly. It can only operate on what is loaded to those special-purpose shared registers by the main

[4] Some 486-class processors had no floating point capabilities, particularly those made for low-power applications.

Box 4.11

An alternative approach: FPU on the ARM processor

Note the alternative approach to floating point unit design taken by ARM engineers, and described in the book *ARM System Architecture* by Steve Furber:

Engineers first surveyed a large amount of common software to find out what type of floating point operations were used most commonly. Employing the RISC design methodology, they implemented these most common instructions in silicon to design the FPA10, a floating point co-processor to the ARM.

The FPA10 has a four-stage pipeline that allows it to be processing operands every cycle and to have up to four calculations simultaneously being performed. Less common instructions are performed either purely in fixed point software or include elements of fixed point software combined with floating point FPA10 instructions.

CPU, as a slave processor. These registers are long enough to hold multiple IEEE754 double-precision numbers, although internally the extended intermediate formats are used (see Section 2.9.3).

In more recent 586-class processors and above, these registers are shared with an MMX unit, or its descendent the SSE family (Section 4.7). This means that the main CPU loads the values into the registers and then activates either the MMX or the FPU. So in many 586-class processors, *MMX and floating point could not be used together*, and programmers have to choose one mode or another at any particular time.

The limitations of FPU or MMX led to the development of the AMD 3DNow! Extension containing 21 new instructions effectively allowing AMD processors to interleave floating point and MMX instructions in the same piece of code. This then prompted Intel to develop the streaming SIMD extensions (SSE) which we will discuss further as another example of a co-processor in Section 4.7. For an alternative approach, consider the development of the ARM FPU in Box 4.11.

4.6.1 Floating Point Emulation

As we have seen, the FPU is a device capable of operating on floating point numbers. Usually, it provides the standard arithmetic, logic and comparison functions, along with multiplication. Often division and other more specialised operations (such as rounding) are also supported. Most FPUs comply with the IEEE754 standard, which defines their operations, accuracy and so on.

Programmers writing in high-level languages (i.e. the majority) will access an FPU whenever they use floating point data types in their programs. For example, in the C programming language these types are almost always those we have identified in Section 3.4.1, namely:

- `float` – A 32-bit single-precision floating point number comprising sign bit, 8-bit exponent and 23-bit mantissa.
- `double` – A 64-bit double-precision floating point number comprising sign bit, 11-bit exponent and 52-bit mantissa.

There is one further floating point data type in C that is meant to be higher precision than the `double`-precision type, and that is the `long double`. However, `long double` appears to be less standard (as was mentioned briefly in Section 3.4.1), in that it ranges from being the same as a `double`, through the IEEE754 extended intermediate format (see Section 2.9.3) and up to a true quad-precision number.

However, although 'floating point' usually means IEEE754 compliance, it does not necessarily have to. As noted in Section 3.4.5.2, this holds only when the underlying hardware available is IEEE754 compatible. In some embedded systems, where power and size are at a premium, designers made a pragmatic choice to provide floating point with slightly less accuracy than IEEE754. From the point of view of the programmer, the data types of `float` and `double` still exist, however the accuracy of the calculations using these may differ.

Where hardware support for floating point is not available, in other words in the absence of an FPU, instructions specifying floating point operations will be picked up by the CPU, causing an interrupt (or trap – see Section 3.4.5) and handled by specialised code. The code that replaces an FPU is called a floating point emulator (FPE).

Quite often, FPE code is sub-IEEE754 in precision. The time taken to calculate IEEE754 operations using multiple fixed point instructions is so time consuming that it is a trade-off between speed and accuracy. Usually designers favour speed.

Another aspect of this trade-off is illustrated in Figure 4.20 where a processor having a hardware floating point unit and a fixed point processor is shown. The same code is executed on both. In the relatively unlikely event that all other factors are equal (i.e. the only difference between the two is the presence of an FPU co-processor in the first case), the FPU-enabled processor can pass the floating point operations over to the FPU, which consumes a significant amount of power while it operates, while the main CPU performs other, unrelated functions. Once the floating point calculations are completed, the result is passed back to the CPU and operation continues.

In the case of the fixed point processor, the floating point calculations must be emulated by FPE code running on the main CPU. Since there is no co-processor in this case, there is no possibility for the floating point code to be executed in parallel with other code. Obviously, the program will then execute more slowly, even if the FPE code is as quick as the FPU. However, usually an FPE execution is several times, maybe ten or more times, slower than execution in the FPU.

In terms of energy consumed – an important measure in portable electronics where battery life is concerned – energy is shown by the shaded areas in the figure: power multiplied by time. Although the FPU consumes significantly more power than the fixed point CPU, it does so for a shorter period of time,[5] and thus may well be more energy efficient than floating point emulation. Of course, as we have noted previously,

[5] This assumes that when the FPU is not calculating it remains turned off and thus does not consume power. Unfortunately, this assumption is not always true in practice.

Figure 4.20

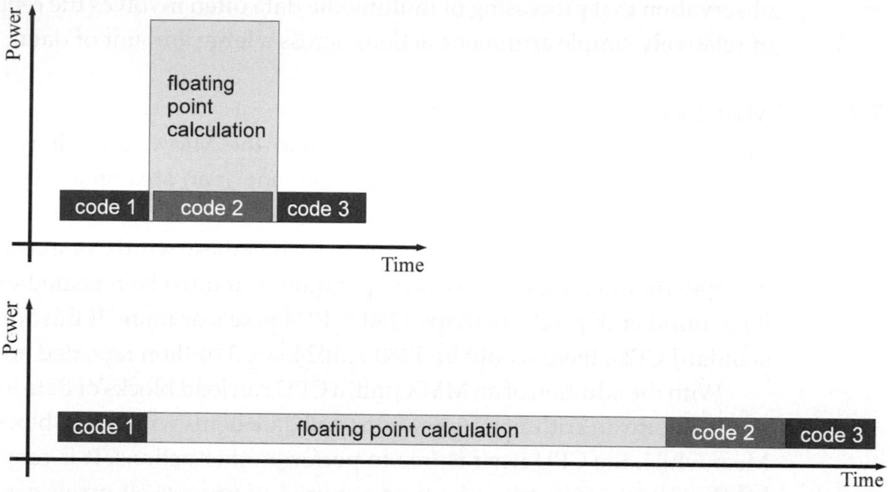

A diagram illustrating the trade-off between (i) executing floating point calculations in a dedicated hardware FPU while fixed point code continues executing in the main CPU (top diagram) and (ii) executing floating point calculations using FPE code which takes longer, but is less power hungry (bottom diagram).

in such a situation the system engineers may well decide to employ lower accuracy floating point routines to speed up the calculations. Even more preferable would be for programmers to refrain from using floating point operations in the first place, and this is often a target of embedded systems developers. Programmers could consider using `long` integers or choose to program in fractional (Q-format) notation (see Section 2.3.7).

4.7 Streaming SIMD Extensions (SSE) and Multimedia Extensions

Multimedia extensions (MMX) was the name given by Intel to a hardware multimedia co-processor for the Pentium processor. The MMX unit was actually an SIMD (single instruction, multiple data) machine as defined in Section 2.1.1. In use, a set of numbers are loaded into the MMX registers, and then a single MMX instruction can be issued to operate on the data in every register, in parallel. An example of this type of processing would be for eight integers to be shifted right by two places simultaneously, or for four of the registers to be added to the other four, and the result overwrite the contents of the first four. There are many variations on this theme, but the important aspect is that each of the separate operations will occur simultaneously, triggered by a single instruction.

After Intel released the MMX, competitors Cyrix and AMD soon offered similar accelerators for their devices, whereas others such as ARM and SUN created custom-designed equivalents for their RISC CPUs. These hardware devices were offered on-chip rather than as an external co-processor. They were derived from the observation that processing of multimedia data often involves the repeated application of relatively simple arithmetic actions across a large amount of data.

4.7.1 Multimedia Extensions (MMX)

An example of the type of processing that the MMX technology was designed to accommodate would be the colour adjustment of an area on a display screen. If each pixel of displayed data on the screen is a byte or word then adjustment of colour may simply be an addition of a fixed value to each of these words, or may be a logical masking operation. Whatever the exact operation is, it must be repeated uniformly across a large number of pixels, perhaps 1280×1024 pixels or more. If this was performed on a standard CPU, there would be $1280 \times 1024 = 1.3$ million repeated additions.

With the addition of an MMX unit, a CPU can load blocks of data into the MMX unit, then perform an arithmetic operation to all data items within that block simultaneously. Meanwhile, the CPU itself is free to perform other actions. It is easy to see that if the MMX unit has 16 entries, the time required to process all pixels can be reduced by a factor of around 1/16.

4.7.2 MMX Implementation

The argument for an MMX extension was convincing, especially in light of the growth in multimedia processing requirements in personal computers during the years of MMX development. However, pertinent questions were asked to find out how to best implement this type of processing and exactly what type of processing to support.

In the case of the Intel Pentium, the implementation problem was primarily that Intel required any new Pentium to be backwards compatible with early 8088 and older 16-bit software as used in DOS and even some surprisingly modern versions of Microsoft windows. There was thus very little possibility of expanding the capabilities of x86 CPUs through changing its instructions – this would have meant that new software could not operate on older machines, something that customers would *not* be happy with (this type of compatibility change needs to be made more gradually, needing time to sink in with customers). In addition, the number of registers could not just suddenly grow from one Pentium version to the next because this would invalidate the process of context save and restore used in older software.

However, Intel engineers found two clever ways to accomplish their aims. The first was to give the Pentium an extra instruction which would place it in MMX mode (and they released simple code that would allow programmers to first check for MMX capabilities and then run one version of code for machines with MMX and another one for machines without MMX). In MMX mode, an extra 57 new instructions were then made available for MMX processing. Older software would not use this mode, and hence not experience the extra instructions. The second innovation by Intel engineers was to re-use the registers of the floating point unit for holding the MMX data. In normal mode, these were used by the FPU, but in MMX mode they could now be used for MMX processing.

Figure 4.21 The MMX registers, parallel functional units (looking like little ALUs) and bus interconnections shown diagrammatically for an MMX-enabled Intel CPU.

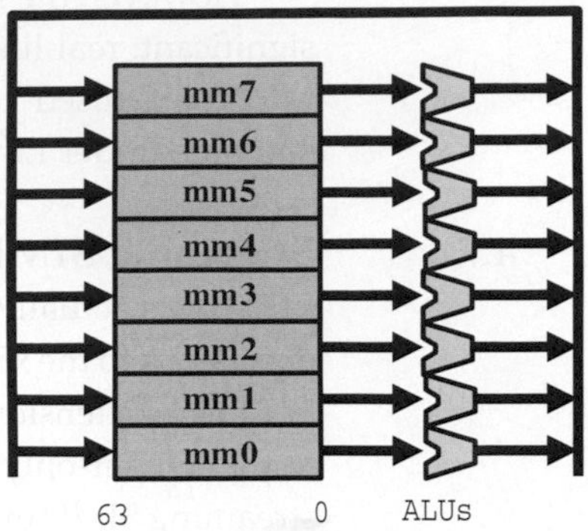

Unfortunately, programmers did not adopt MMX en-masse. There were criticisms relating to the fact (mentioned in Section 4.6) that selecting MMX mode completely removed floating point capability. Ultimately, this led to the AMD 3DNow! inspired SSE. However, before we jump into a discussion on SSE in Section 4.7.4), let us examine how these systems work in general, starting with the venerable MMX.

The logical structure of the MMX unit, showing its eight registers, is illustrated in Figure 4.21 (although it should be noted that this figure is highly stylised – the actual MMX is rather more complex than the one drawn here). Note the bus looping from the output of the eight ALU blocks back into the registers. This is a simplified representation of the internal structure of the MMX unit, but serves to illustrate the parallel nature of the paths from each of the registers. Each line is a separate bus.

In MMX mode, there are eight registers that are 64 bits wide (why 64 bits? Well remember that 64 bits are needed to represent the double-precision floating point values that are normally held in these registers in FPU mode). Instructions operate in parallel and are all from register to register, except the load and store instructions.

Although each register is 64 bits in size, it can hold either 8 bytes or four 16-bit words or two 32-bit double words or a single 64-bit quad word. This is under the control of the programmer and leads to significant flexibility in creating MMX code.

Arithmetic, logical, comparison and conversion operations are supported. These can be applied to whatever data size is known to exist within the transfer registers. Of course, it is the programmer's responsibility to load the correct sized data and choose the correct operations to apply to this data.

4.7.3 Use of MMX

To use MMX capabilities on a suitably-equipped Pentium processor, it is first necessary to check whether the CPU can enter MMX mode (and there is a simple backwards-compatible mechanism to do this). If it can, then MMX mode processing can continue, otherwise, code must be provided to perform the same function using the CPU capabilities alone. This will obviously be far slower, but is needed for backwards compatibility in every portable program.

However, the speed gains for specialised programs using this technology are very significant: real-life testing of MMX capabilities for image processing has shown that MMX optimised code could be at least 14 times faster than non-MMX code in test software under Linux.

4.7.4 Streaming SIMD Extensions (SSE)

MMX was actually an Intel-specific name for single instruction, multiple data (SIMD) extensions to the x86 instruction set, originally launched in 1997. AMD introduced their hardware extensions under the term 3DNow! but had added floating point capabilities to the integer-only hardware from Intel. Not to be outdone, the battle hotted up with streaming SIMD extensions (SSE) of various flavours from Intel and enhanced 3DNow! from AMD.

SSE provides 70 new instructions for the SIMD processing of data and makes available eight new 128-bit registers.[6] These can contain the usual integer values, but now of course allow the use of floating point:

- Four 32-bit integers
- Eight 16-bit short integers
- Sixteen bytes or characters
- Two 64-bit double-precision floating point numbers
- Four 32-bit single-precision floating point numbers

SSE has actually evolved considerably from its initial incarnation through SSE2, SSE3, SSE4 and lately SSE5. Each iteration has brought new capabilities, new instructions and new capabilities for the programmers to learn. Interestingly, from SSE4 onwards, support for using the old MMX registers has been discontinued by Intel.

SSE4 introduced some fast string handling operations and also many floating point operations, such as parallel multiplies, dot products, rounding and so on. There is also now some degree of compatibility between Intel and AMD versions (perhaps more than there is between previous generations of x86 processors), but the ongoing evolution of these capabilities allied with some aggressive marketing tactics make direct comparisons of the capabilities of the two leading x86-style processors quite difficult.

4.7.5 Using SSE and MMX

With so many versions and differing compatibilities among different CPU ranges, let alone between manufacturers, software tools have tended to lag behind capabilities. Many compilers do not support these co-processors by default, or at best provide sparse support across the range of possible hardware inclusions (preferring to restrict support to only the most common options). Although the situation has improved significantly in recent years, especially with the availability of compilers from Intel themselves which

[6] In 64-bit mode this doubles to 16 128-bit registers.

presumably support these extensions, the programming tools do not yet tend to take full advantage of this specialist hardware.

Also, the need to write several versions of code specialised for various different processors has meant that use of these SIMD extensions has tended to be confined to instances of specialised software, rather than general releases of commercial operating systems and applications. However, they exist and are available, especially in desktop or server machines, for absolute maximum processing performance.

4.8 Co-Processing in Embedded Systems

Few embedded systems utilise x86-style processors these days, notwithstanding low power variants such as the Atom: by far the largest proportion are ARM-based or use similar lower-power RISC CPUs. Even among the x86 processors, few have full SSE capabilities (since these co-processors have a reputation for being power hungry). However, those that do may have an advantage over their use in desktop and server systems. The reason being that many embedded systems run controlled or dedicated software, compared with the desktop systems that can run literally any software. While desktop systems need software to be backwards compatible (and as such require code for SSE, code for MMX, code for SSE4 and bare x86 code in case of no extensions at all), in an embedded system, the programmer knows in advance exactly what hardware is available and can develop his or her software appropriately.

The converse is also true – knowing what software is to be run can provide the opportunity to modify or create custom hardware. As an illustration of this process, in Section 4.6, we have met the FPA10, the main ARM floating point co-processor, which was designed based upon an analysis of the most common software requirements.

There are many other co-processors in use within embedded systems, apart from the FPUs and MMX/SSEs already mentioned. Consider the following ARM-specific co-processors:

- **Jazelle** – The name seems to be the 'J' from the Java language, added to a Gazelle, bringing to mind a swift and agile execution of Java code. This is precisely the aim: the ARM engineers who designed Jazelle have created a hardware unit able to directly process many Java instructions (bytecodes) without interpretation, leading to speed and efficiency improvements. A branch to Java (BXJ) instruction enters Jazelle processing, allowing the CPU to natively execute most of the common bytecodes (and trap the rest for execution in optimised software routines).
- **NEON advanced SIMD** – Similar to Intel's SSE, this is a 64-bit or a 128-bit SIMD extension with a very complete instruction set able to process packed integer and floating point operations in parallel. This is probably what SSE would have been if it had been designed from the bottom up, cleanly, for a modern processor (instead of evolving from the MMX addition to a 30-year-old semi-backwards compatible slice of silicon history).

- **VFP** – A vector co-processor for ARM processors enhanced with floating point capabilities (VFP stands for 'vector floating point'). This is used for matrix and vector computation – repetitive sequential operations on arrays of data.

Remember back in Section 3.2.6, we discussed the different rationale behind RISC and CISC processors? CISC processors were presented as the bloated lumbering end-point in an evolutionary process which packed more and more functionality into individual CPU instructions. RISC, by contrast, was lean and swift.

RISC instructions tend to be very simple, but quick. The argument being that even though more instructions are required to do anything useful, those instructions can execute faster and thus overall performance increases compared to a CISC approach. However, the use of a co-processor can allow a RISC processor – small, lean and fast – to hand off specific computational tasks to a separate processing unit. Thus, some of the application-specific instructions available to a CISC processor could be handled by a RISC co-processing unit.

A further refinement, bringing to mind the dual-mode method that Intel used for the early MMX, involves having a co-processor that is reconfigurable. This allows the silicon resources used by the co-processor to be adjusted to suit the computation required at any particular time. Evidently, there will be a cost to the reconfiguration – it will take both time and energy. However, the benefits of having fast accelerated processing for some complex computation could easily outweigh this.

For embedded systems designers, probably the prime example of this would be within a field programmable gate array (FPGA). A 'soft core' processor, residing in an FPGA, is one written in a high-level hardware description language such as Verilog. In fact, we will develop one such processor later in Chapter 8. For now, one of the prime features of FPGAs which we will consider, is their reconfigurability. Many of the free, and commercial, soft cores that are available already implement a co-processor interface, and several researchers have experimented with attaching reconfigurable processing units to these. It is likely that the importance of these approaches to embedded systems will continue to be explored, and consequentially grow in adoption.

4.9 Summary

This chapter investigated the internal elements commonly found within today's general-purpose microprocessors. All of these include the means to transfer data through internal buses to and from various functional units such as ALU, FPU or other co-processors and accelerator units that may be connected.

A memory management unit and cache may be present within the system, and can be thought of as residing on the address and data buses between the processor core and the outside memory system. A cache acts to speed up average memory access time by predicting future memory recall patterns and storing some past memory accesses that match predicted future accesses. Meanwhile, a memory management unit has two important roles. The first is to allow the use of virtual memory which expands the allowable address range and storage space of the processor. The second is to allow memory page and segments to be defined and used – an important benefit of which is the memory protection between running processes (something that prevents a rogue process from overwriting the private memory of other processes, or a kernel, and thus prevents or at least reduces the chances of crashing). The cost of using virtual memory is in a performance hit: it tends to reduce the average memory access time.

The contents of this chapter are commonly found implemented in modern CPUs and are considered standard functional units and capabilities in general-purpose processors. In Chapter 5, we will turn our attention towards improving performance – common speed-ups and acceleration techniques. In the headlong rush by CPU manufacturers to have either faster and faster or lower and lower power devices (but rarely with both characteristics simultaneously), some interesting methods have arisen and been adopted as we shall see.

Problems

4.1 Referring to the ALU design in Section 4.2.2, if each logic gate has a 10 ns propagation delay between any input and any output, what would be the maximum operating frequency of the ALU?

4.2 Referring to the 2-bit ALU in Problem 4.1,

a. Show how four of them can be combined to make an 8-bit ALU (for unsigned numbers).

b. How would you modify the design to cope with two's complement signed numbers?

4.3 The following pseudo-code segment is executed on a RISC processor:

```
loop i = 0,1
read X from memory address 0
read Y from memory address i
Z = X + Y
write Z to memory address i+1
```

The processor takes one cycle to complete all internal operations (including cache accesses). Saving data from cache to RAM takes four cycles. Loading data from RAM to cache takes four cycles (plus one cycle to continue from cache to CPU).

Assume that the system has a *direct* cache which is initially empty. If the cache uses the following policies, how many cycles are required for this code?

a. write back

b. write through with no write allocate (WTNWA)

c. write through with write allocate (WTWA)

4.4 You have a small von Neumann computer with a data cache that can be switched between two-way set-associative and direct mapped. It can hold a single data word in each of its 512 cache lines and all data transfers are word-sized. The following algorithm is to be run on the processor.

```
define data area A from address 0 to 1023
define data area B from address 1024 to 2047
set R0 = 512, R1 = address 0, R2 = address 1024
{
lp [R1]= R0+R0      ; save to address stored in R1
   [R2]=[R1-1]+[R1]
   R1 = R1+1
   R2 = R2+1
   R0 = R0-1
   if R0>0 then goto lp
}
```

Problems

a. Which cache organisation would be best if the system operates with a write back protocol?
b. Name three cache-entry replacement algorithms and comment on their hardware complexity.
c. The algorithm given is run just after a reset that clears the cache and it iterates twice. If the system uses a direct cache with write through (and write allocate), taking 10 ns for CPU-cache transfer and 50 ns for cache-RAM transfer, answer the following questions:
   i. What is the hit rate?
   ii. What is the overall access time for two iterations?

4.5 Rewrite the algorithm of the previous problem to improve hit rate. (Hint: Adjust the data area definitions rather than the loop code itself.)

4.6 An advanced MP3/photo player uses virtual memory to allow the CPU to access 1 Gibyte of logical memory space, although the system only has 1 MiB of RAM. The OS programs the MMU to allow a fixed page size of 4 kbytes. The byte-wide RAM has a 20 ns access time, while the hard disc is limited by its IDE interface to 2.2 Mbytes per second data transfer. The RISC CPU has 32-bit instructions.
a. How many pages can reside in RAM at one time?
b. How many wires must the MMU-to-RAM address bus contain?
c. How much time is required to read each instruction from RAM?

4.7 Using the information from Problem 4.6, calculate how much time is necessary to load a page from disc to RAM (or from RAM to disc). Use the answer to determine two possible timings for the CPU to retrieve an instruction from a retired memory page.

4.8 The MMU-to-RAM address bus in the previous problem is not wide enough to accommodate more memory. Name three (hardware or software) methods of overcoming the address-bus size limitation and connecting more memory on that physical interface.

4.9 A dual-processor machine has a block of shared memory and a snoop bus. Write back caches in each of the processor modules implement the MESI protocol, starting with all cache lines in the invalid (I) state.

Trace the cache states through the following sequence (X, Y and Z are not equal):
1. CPU1 reads from RAM address X.
2. CPU1 writes to address X.
3. CPU2 reads from address Y.
4. CPU1 reads from address Y.

Problems

5. CPU1 writes to address Y.
6. CPU2 reads from address X.
7. CPU2 reads from address Z.
8. CPU1 writes to address Z.

4.10 Consider the block diagram of an ALU and three registers connected in a three-bus CPU as shown below. Assume that this diagram is complete except for a memory interface to each bus, and that memory transfers are much slower than register data movements.

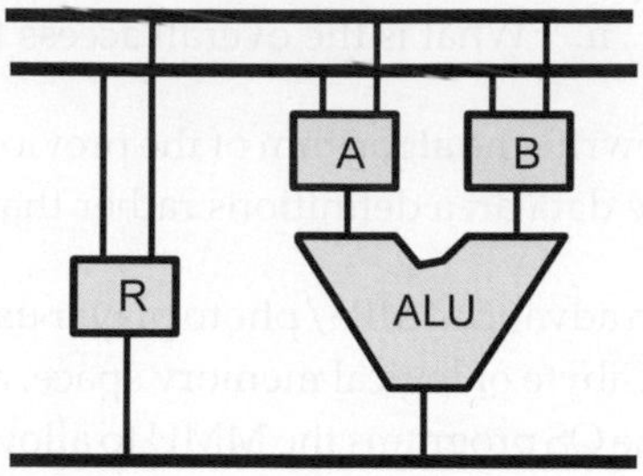

a. Draw arrows on the diagram to indicate allowable data directions for each bus connection.
b. How efficient is the operation X + Y?
c. How efficient is the operation X + X?
d. How efficient is the operation (X + Y) + Z?
e. Suggest an alternative connection arrangement to improve efficiency.

4.11 Identify the two main arithmetic and four basic logic operations that every ALU is likely to be capable of performing (excluding shifts).

4.12 Identify the three different types or directions of bitwise shift that are usually implemented within even simple CPUs, excluding rotate instructions (and can you explain why the question asks for just three types rather than four?).

4.13 Following the propagation delay example of Box 4.1 (page 134), determine the propagation delay of an 8-bit ADD and an 8-bit AND operation. In each case, assume the function-select signals are correct and unchanging (so they do not affect the timings at all). What is the maximum clock speed of this device if the ALU is expected to operate in a single cycle?

4.14 If cache memory can improve processor performance, can you think of any reasons why manufacturers would not simply sell integrated circuits with massive on-chip cache blocks?

Problems

4.15 Calculate the overall access time for a computer system containing a direct cache having a 10 ns access time for hits and a 120 ns access time for misses, when the hit ratio is 0.3.

4.16 Assuming the computer designers of the machine in Problem 4.15 wish to increase performance. They have only three things that they can change in the system (and since each change costs money they only want to do one of these things, and choose the best one). Determine which of the following would most improve overall access time in that system:

a. Fit faster main memory, with a 100 ns access time.
b. Fit faster cache memory, with a 8 ns access time.
c. Increase the hit ratio to 0.4 by squeezing in a much bigger cache with a better arrangement and cleverer replacement algorithm.

4.17 Assuming a small 16-bit embedded system primarily executes integer code, but sometimes needs to quickly process a block of floating point data. This can either be processed using a dedicated FPU, executed in an FPE, or the code converted so that it uses very large integers instead. Discuss the main factors influencing whether the choice of processing solution for this device should contain an FPU or not.

4.18 Chapter 3 has introduced the concept of relative addressing. Briefly discuss how this is related to the principles of spatial and temporal locality as explained in Section 4.4.4.

4.19 In the context of cache memory, what is the meaning of 'write through with write allocate' (WTWA) and how does this differ from 'write through with no write allocate' (WTNWA)? Which would be more appropriate in a system outputting vast amounts of transient graphical data to a memory-mapped display?

4.20 In an embedded system that has a full development and debugging software suite, an experienced programmer has set a memory *watchpoint*[7] on address `0x0000` in RAM while trying to debug a piece of code which occasionally crashes. However, your code, data and variables are located elsewhere in memory: you certainly did not define any variables or code to be located at address `0x0000`. Can you think of a reason why he/she should be interested in this address which is not supposed to be used anyway?

---

[7] A *watchpoint* is a location in memory that the debug software will constantly monitor and will halt program execution whenever the contents of this address change.

CHAPTER 5

Enhancing CPU Performance

It would be unusual to find readers working sequentially through a book such as this, and that is something understood: personally, the author always encourages his students to pick and choose among textbooks where different authors cover different sections in ways that are clearer or otherwise to different readers (and that is what libraries are for). Others may prefer to work sequentially though the various chapters, and for those people – congratulations on having reached this far. I hope that a picture is emerging in your mind of an evolutionary process in computer design. Blocks of required functionality are aggregated into a working CPU and then evaluated. The performance limiting blocks are then adjusted or speeded up. Small speed-ups are common, being stepwise improvements over existing designs. Truly revolutionary change, by contrast, is less common. In most cases, these design changes are driven by performance, which is ultimately driven by the sales department. In embedded systems, power consumption, related to battery lifetime, is a further significant driver, but is often more an excuse *not* to adopt a particular speed-up technique rather than a driver of innovation by itself.

Everybody wants a faster computer. It has been said that there are no speed limits on the information superhighway, and in most cases, users feel that more speed means less wasted time (the author is, however, quite sceptical of this idea – seeing his own students wasting more time with faster computers than their peers did with sluggish machines a generation ago). For embedded systems, especially those requiring real-time processing, there is no doubt that greater speeds lead to greater functionality. For the desktop, however, the suspicion is that much of the speed, memory and storage increases are swallowed by the bloatware of software developers, particularly in regard to the operating system. Still, the mythical 'performance' target is a major driver in the computer industry, and one which has yielded some extremely interesting (wild and wonderful) solutions. In this chapter, we will consider many of the mainstream methods of improving performance.

5.1 Speed-Ups

For early 4th generation computers, the main method of influencing performance was the clock: specifically making it faster and faster. This has led to a number of problems including heat dissipation and high processor costs as it becomes progressively more difficult to improve on existing designs which are themselves often close to the edge of current achievable technology.

Other designers looked elsewhere, and ideas such as RISC processing began to emerge and take hold. Some companies concentrated on increasing the word size, from 4 bits and 8 bits through 16 bits to 32 bits. More recent designs have been 64 bits, 128 bits and even 1024 bits (covered further in Chapter 9).

Not only did clock speeds increase, but an emphasis was placed on achieving more in each clock cycle. This led to parallelism and pipelining (and occasionally a combination of both).

SUN took a different approach with their Java processors which revisit CISC processor design rationale, but this time from a software perspective (and neatly integrate ideas of stack-based and RISC processors into the bargain). In recent times, the PicoJava and similar processors were designed bottom up to accommodate the Java language, rather than a language translated to run on the processor, which was the approach adopted by almost everyone else. Ultimately, this software-first approach seems to have achieved only moderate commercial success. Or perhaps it is another idea whose time is yet to come.

The intention of this chapter is to cover a number of design ideas and approaches that have been explored and adopted into the mainstream, and which trace their ancestry (or rationale) more to profit motive than to academic ideals – in the fight to get faster and cheaper parts out to the customer as quickly as possible. We begin with the biggest and most common speed-up, pipelining.

5.2 Pipelining

Sometimes attributed more to modern industrial manufacturing techniques than to computer evolution, pipelining improves processing *throughput* rather than the time taken to complete *individual* instructions (in fact, this may even increase yet result in better performance). It allows the different stages of instruction processing to overlap and thus process multiple slower instruction concurrently, giving an overall throughput increase.

The *throughput* is the number of operations performed per second: the cycles per instruction benchmark of Section 3.5.2. This measure is much more important than how long each individual instruction takes to complete. To appreciate this fact, let us consider a typical CPU instruction processing flowchart as shown in Figure 5.1.

Figure 5.1

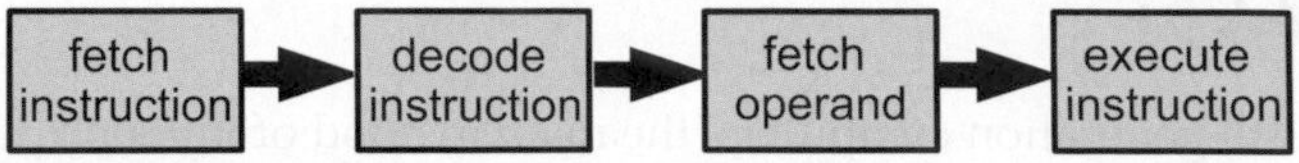

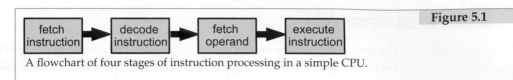

A flowchart of four stages of instruction processing in a simple CPU.

In this example, every instruction is handled in four stages which we will assume are all of a single-clock cycle duration. An instruction must traverse all four stages to complete, thus requiring four clock cycles.

A non-pipelined machine would grab and process one instruction, then wait for that instruction to complete before starting on the next one. We use something called a *reservation table* to visualise this:

Fetch instruction	$Inst_1$				$Inst_2$				$Inst_3$
Decode instruction		$Inst_1$				$Inst_2$			
Fetch operand			$Inst_1$				$Inst_2$		
Execute instruction				$Inst_1$				$Inst_2$	
Clock cycles	1	2	3	4	5	6	7	8	9

The different functional units for handling an instruction are listed on the left side of the table and the clock cycles are shown along the bottom. Inside the table we indicate what is happening in that cycle. The table shown covers nine successive clock cycles.

$Inst_1$ is fetched in the first cycle, then decoded, then its operand fetched and finally the function encoded in that instruction is executed. $Inst_2$ then begins its journey.

But think of this reservation table in a different way: if we consider the rows as being resources and the columns as time slots, it is clear that each resource spends a lot of time slots doing nothing. It would be far more efficient if we allowed instructions to overlap, so that resources spend more of the time doing something. Let us try it out:

Fetch instruction	$Inst_1$	$Inst_2$	$Inst_3$	$Inst_4$	$Inst_5$	$Inst_6$	$Inst_7$	$Inst_8$	$Inst_9$
Decode instruction		$Inst_1$	$Inst_2$	$Inst_3$	$Inst_4$	$Inst_5$	$Inst_6$	$Inst_7$	$Inst_8$
Fetch operand			$Inst_1$	$Inst_2$	$Inst_3$	$Inst_4$	$Inst_5$	$Inst_6$	$Inst_7$
Execute instruction				$Inst_1$	$Inst_2$	$Inst_3$	$Inst_4$	$Inst_5$	$Inst_6$
Clock cycles	1	2	3	4	5	6	7	8	9

The most obvious effect is that instead of getting to the start of $Inst_3$ in the nine clock cycles, the overlapping now covers nine instructions: it processes three times faster. It

Box 5.1

Pipeline speed-up

There are two useful measures of a pipeline: degree of *speed-up* and *efficiency*. Let us consider a program that consists of s sequential instructions, each instruction needing n clock cycles to complete.

In a non-pipelined processor, the program execution time is simply $s \times n$ cycles.

Now, let us pipeline this processor into n stages, each of a single-clock cycle. How long will the program take to execute?

Well, the first instruction takes the usual n cycles, but then each subsequent instruction completes a single cycle later, so the total time is $n + (s - 1)$ cycles.

Speed-up S_n is the ratio of non-pipelined to pipelined operation:

$$S_n = \frac{sn}{n + s - 1}$$

Looking at this, it seems that as $s \to \infty$ then $S_n \to n$ meaning that the bigger the program is, the more efficient it is (because no matter how fast the pipeline is, it starts empty and ends with a single instruction – the final one – inside). In other words, the starting and ending conditions are less efficient.

So a measure of efficiency, on the other hand, must take account of these start and end conditions. Efficiency is the total number of instructions divided by the pipelined operating time:

$$E_n = \frac{s}{n + s - 1}$$

But does this not look similar to the speed-up equation? Yes! $E_n = S_n/n$ and this is also the same as throughput, which is the number of instructions completed per unit time.

---

does this without having to increase clock rate or change processing order, simply by allowing the possibility of overlapping instructions.

This overlap is called *pipelining*. It is a technique used to speed up almost all modern processors. Control of functional units becomes more complex, but the gain in speed tends to outweigh this disadvantage. To determine the actual amount of speed-up, refer to the analysis in Box 5.1.

Later, some more of the difficulties introduced by pipelining will be examined, but first, let us take a look at the different types of pipeline.

5.2.1 Multi-Function Pipelines

Pipelines do not have to be simple strings of functions (*uni-function*). They can allow different instructions to be handled differently, as in *multi-function* pipelines. In fact this is common, but increases the complexity of control. Consider an example shown in Figure 5.2.

Figure 5.2

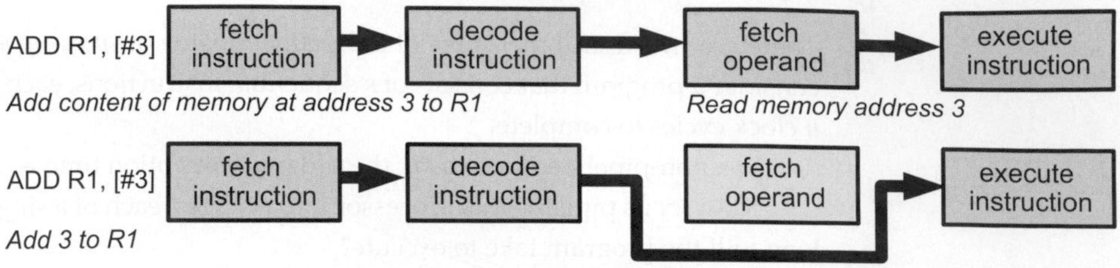

A flowchart of four stages of instruction processing in a simple CPU for two assembler instructions. The top instruction utilises every stage of the pipeline whereas the bottom instruction does not need to fetch an operand from memory, and thus skips the third stage. This illustrates the concept of a multi-functional pipeline where different instructions are handled differently, based upon their needs.

In the top pipeline of Figure 5.2, the first instruction needs to fetch something from memory in order to complete, and thus it needs to use the 'fetch operand' unit. At the bottom the same pipeline is shown at a later time, executing a different instruction. This one does not require an operand fetch (since the immediate value 3 is encoded as part of the instruction and therefore already inside the CPU). So the 'fetch operand' pipeline unit is unnecessary in this case. However, this does not mean that the pipeline skipped a stage and the second instruction was executed more quickly. Consider the reservation table below where these two instructions are executed sequentially:

Fetch	ADD R1, [#3]	ADD R1, #3	$Inst_3$	$Inst_4$	$Inst_5$	$Inst_6$
Decode		ADD R1, [#3]	ADD R1, #3	$Inst_3$	$Inst_4$	$Inst_5$
Fetch			ADD R1, [#3]	**NOP**	$Inst_3$	$Inst_4$
Execute				ADD R1, [#3]	ADD R1, #3	$Inst_3$
Cycles	1	2	3	4	5	6

Clock cycle 4, for the second instruction is marked as a NOP (No Operation). It would not be possible for the CPU to immediately skip from 'decode instruction' to 'execute instruction' because, in cycle 4, the hardware that performs the 'execute instruction' is still handling the previous instruction (ADD R1, [#3]).

This illustrates an interesting point: this pipeline needs to cater for all instruction types, but is limited by the slowest instruction. In a non-pipelined processor, simple instructions could be executed very quickly and difficult ones more slowly. But a pipelined processor generally takes about the same length of time to process anything, unless some very advanced techniques are used.

Designers need to be careful with pipelines. The very argument for having a pipeline is so that processing elements are kept busy for most of the time, however, we now see NOPs creeping into the reservation table. NOPs indicate an unused or

Figure 5.3

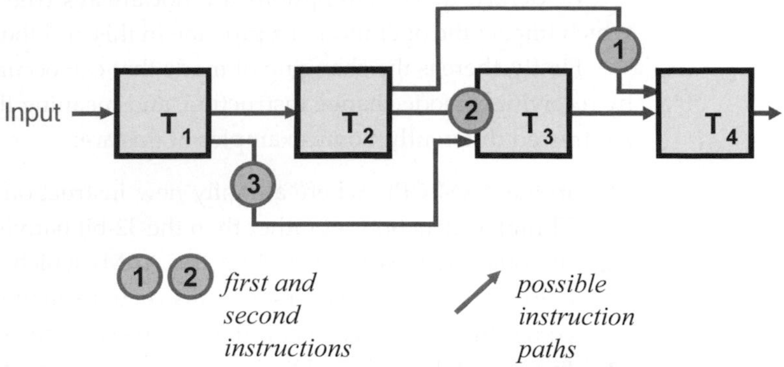

A dynamic pipeline allows different instructions to follow various paths through the pipeline depending upon their execution needs.

wasted resource for a cycle. Judicious examination of instruction requirements and the frequency of occurrence of instructions is needed to ensure that the design of the pipeline minimises these wasted slots.

5.2.2 Dynamic Pipelines

By definition also a *multi-function* pipeline, a *dynamic pipeline* does not simply bypass an unused function, but allows alternative paths to be taken through the pipeline depending on the instruction being processed and the current state of the processor.

This is illustrated in the fictitious example of Figure 5.3, where four unnamed pipelined units (T_1 to T_4) process three instructions which traverse the pipeline through different paths. Not shown is the complex switching control required for this and delay elements that must be used to slow down instructions which skip units (such as instruction 3 bypassing pipeline unit T_2).

The delay elements would also be dynamic: they would only need to be activated to ensure that instructions arrive in-order at the pipeline units. As an example, instruction 3 is about to 'catch up' with instruction 2 and would therefore need to be delayed by one clock cycle to stop both colliding at T_3. Whereas instruction 1 has skipped pipeline unit T_3, but is not about to 'catch up' with any other instruction and therefore does not need to be delayed.

The interested reader will note that some processors are intelligent enough to decide for themselves which instructions need to be processed in-order by pipeline units and those that can be executed out-of-order will not be delayed unduly.

5.2.3 Changing Mode in a Pipeline

Everything that has been written up to now assumes that each instruction that flows through the pipeline is independent and that an instruction can enter the pipeline even before the previous instructions have completed.

Evidently, these assumptions are not always true. We will consider three cases which impact the operation of a pipeline in this and the next two sections.

Firstly, there is the changing of mode that can occur in some processors, triggered by receiving a mode change instruction, and meaning that all subsequent instructions are treated differently. Some examples of this are:

1. In the ARM CPU where a totally new instruction set can be enabled (the 16-bit Thumb instruction set rather than the 32-bit native ARM instruction set).
2. In some processors (including the ARM) which switch between big and little endian operation. The first few instructions may be stored as little endian, then comes the mode switch and then the rest are stored as big endian.
3. In some DSPs such as TMS320 series fixed point processors which change mathematical mode perhaps to turn on or off sign extension, affecting all subsequent instructions.

Although these instructions do occur, they are relatively infrequent. The first two, for example, are likely to be issued at the start of a program only. The third one would be issued once per block of mathematical processing.

Due to the sparse nature of these, most processors will simply *flush the pipeline* once they receive one of these troublesome instructions. That means that all subsequent instructions already being handled in the pipeline will be discarded and the pipeline must begin again as if it were empty. In logic terms, this is a very easy solution, although drastic. It affects pipeline efficiency, but is rare enough in most programs that it is irrelevant to performance.

Consider the example reservation table below, being hit by a mode change instruction (ChM). It is clear that, although instructions 3, 4 and 5 are already being handled by the pipeline, these are discarded, the CPU is switched to its new mode in cycle 6 and then these instructions have to be fetched again.

Fetch instruction	$Inst_1$	*ChM*	$Inst_3$	$Inst_4$	$Inst_5$	**X**	$Inst_3$	$Inst_4$	$Inst_5$
Decode instruction		$Inst_1$	*ChM*	$Inst_3$	$Inst_4$	**X**		$Inst_3$	$Inst_4$
Fetch operand			$Inst_1$	*ChM*	$Inst_3$	**X**			$Inst_3$
Execute instruction				$Inst_1$	*ChM*	**X**			
Clock cycles	1	2	3	4	5	6	7	8	9

This type of reservation table could be the result of a sequence of instructions such as the following:

```
Inst1:   ADD   R0, R0, R1
Inst2:   MODE big_endian
Inst3:   SUB   R4, R1, R0
Inst4:   NOP
Inst5:   NOP
Inst6:   NOP
```

where instructions 3, 4 and 5 are encoded as big endian (this is not shown by the assembler mnemonics, but would be evident if we view a hexadecimal dump of this part of program memory).

Once the mode change is made the pipeline would have to be flushed and the following instructions re-loaded.

In newer processors this would be performed automatically by the CPU, but in older pipelined processors, this may not be automatic and would have to be done by the compiler (or even by a programmer hand-crafting the assembler code). In the example it is fairly easily to perform the mode change pipeline clearing in software. This is done by changing the order of the program:

```
Inst1:    ADD R0, R0, R1
Inst2:    MODE big_endian
Inst4:    NOP
Inst5:    NOP
Inst6:    NOP
Inst3:    SUB R4, R1, R0
```

Otherwise, a sequence of NOP instructions would need to be inserted after the mode change instruction. Ideally, the NOP instruction would be encoded the same if read in big or little endian. For example, instruction words `0x0000` and `0xFFFF` would always be `0x0000` and `0xFFFF` respectively, no matter in which order the bytes were arranged, making it irrelevant what encoding is used for those instructions between when the mode change instruction is read and when the mode change actually occurs.

5.2.4 Data Dependency Hazard

In the same way that a mode change can cause problems by changing the state of the processor part way through a program, the same is true of the continuous changes to internal registers and memory locations when a program is running. Under some circumstances this can complicate matters.

Consider for example the following code sequence:

```
ADD R0, R2, R1     ; R0 = R2 + R1
AND R1, R0, #2     ; R1 = R0 AND 2
```

Clearly in this example, the second instruction relies upon the result of the first instruction to have been written to R0 before it can be read. But in a pipeline this may not always be true. Examine the artificial pipeline construction of Figure 5.4.

Figure 5.4

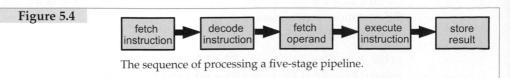

The sequence of processing a five-stage pipeline.

Pipelining

The major difference here to what we encountered previously is the addition of a final pipeline stage that stores the result of whatever calculation has occurred. This is added firstly to help illustrate the data dependency issue, and secondly because many processors really do contain such a final stage.

A reservation table of the two lines of program code given above is reproduced below. Note that below the table there is an indication of the contents of register R0 during each time slot:

Fetch instruction	ADD R0	AND R1				
Decode instruction		ADD R0	AND R1			
Fetch operand			ADD R0	AND R1		
Execute instruction				ADD R0	AND R1	
Store result					ADD R0	AND R1
Clock cycles	1	2	3	4	5	6
R0	x	x	x	x	R2 + R1	R2 + R1

What is important to understand is that the second instruction, the AND, makes use of the content of register R0 as its operand (R1 = R0 AND 2) and this *operand fetch* is the third stage in the pipeline (indicated in bold). In the example shown, the operand fetch for the second instruction occurs in cycle 4, but that is before the first instruction has written its result to register R0 (which occurs only in cycle 5).

As matters stand, the second instruction will therefore perform its operation with an incorrect value from R0.

This is called a RAW hazard (read after write) since register R0 is supposed to be read *after* it is written, but instead was read *before* it was written by the previous instruction.

If you look carefully at the example, there is another hazard there. In this case, a WAR (write after read) anti-dependency on register R1. The first instruction reads R1, the second instruction writes to R1, the hazard being to ensure that the first instruction has finished its read before the second instruction performs its write. With the example pipeline shown, this hazard could not occur, but in certain advanced dynamic pipelines with out-of-order execution, it is something to be aware of.

There is also such a thing as a WAW (write after write) hazard: an example of this is shown in Box 5.2.

5.2.5 Conditional Hazards

Given that some instructions can execute conditionally, there is the question of when the conditions are checked to determine if execution should occur. Here is an example code segment:

```
ADDS R0, R2, R1      ; R0 = R2 + R1 and set condition flags
ANDEQ R1, R0, #2     ; R1 = R0 AND 2 if zero flag set
```

Box 5.2

WAW hazard

This type of hazard is easier to explain than it is to pronounce. A write after write hazard occurs when two nearby instructions write to the same location and a third instruction must read from that location. It must perform the read neither too early nor too late.

Here is an example:

```
ADD R0, R2, R1      ; R0 = R2 + R1
AND R1, R0, #2      ; R1 = R0 AND 2
SUB R0, R3, #1      ; R0 = R3 – 1
```

There is a WAW hazard on R0. Without drawing a reservation table, it should be evident that the second instruction operand fetch much occur after the result store in the first instruction and before the result store in the second instruction.

Note that after this code segment, R0 contains the final value, so the write to R0 by the first instruction is simply a temporary store. It could be changed to any other register or eliminated through data forwarding (see Section 5.2.10), without affecting the final result. WAW hazards sometimes occur in memory systems, where the write back to RAM is slower than the read. Usually it is the responsibility of the cache hardware to ensure that the hazard does not turn into a real problem.

Remember that in the ARM processor, an 'S' at the end of an instruction tells the processor that the result of that instruction should update the condition flags (namely zero flag, negative flag, carry flag and overflow flag, all stored in the CPSR register on an ARM processor – Box 5.3 describes the types of conditional flags possible). The second instruction is conditional – the 'EQ' indicates that this instruction should only happen if the result of the previous condition-setting instruction was zero (in this example, if and only if register R0 is zero).

Next, we can start to populate a reservation table from the example code:

Fetch instruction	ADDS R0	ANDEQ R1	$Inst_3$	$Inst_4$		
Decode instruction		ADDS R0	ANDEQ R1	$Inst_3$		
Fetch operand			ADDS R0	ANDEQ R1		
Execute instruction				ADDS R0		
Store result						
Clock cycles	1	2	3	4	5	6
NZCV	0000	0000	0000	0000		

By the end of cycle 4, the first instruction has been executed and the condition flags updated. Note that the second instruction has already entered the pipeline, even

Box 5.3

Conditional flags

Although some processors have sightly different combinations and names, the following set of condition flags are most commonly found in commercial CPUs:

N or negative flag: the result of the last condition-setting operation was negative.
Z or zero flag: the last condition-setting operation resulted in a zero.
C or carry flag: the last condition-setting operation generated a carry out.
V or overflow flag: the last condition-setting operation caused a sign change.

Some examples of these flags and how they can change are shown in the following code segment. The use of the 'S' flag at the end of an instruction that determines whether or not it will cause the condition flags to be updated.

Instruction	**Meaning**	**N**	**Z**	**C**	**V**
`MOV R0, #0`	`set R0 = 0`	0	0	0	0
`MOV R1, #2`	`set R1 = 2`	0	0	0	0
`SUBS R2, R1, R1`	`R2 = R1 – R1 (result is zero)`	0	1	0	0
`SUBS R3, R0, R1`	`R3 = R0 – R1 (result is negative, 0xFFFFFFFD)`	1	0	0	0
`SUB R2, R1, R1`	`R2 = R1 – R1 (result is zero but 'S' flag not set)`	1	0	0	0
`ADDS R4, R1, R1`	`R4 = R1 + R1 (result is positive, 0x4)`	0	0	0	0
`ADDS R5, R4, R3`	`R5 = R4 + R3 (0x4 + 0xFFFFFFFD)`	0	0	1	0
`MOV R8, #0x7FFFFFFF`	`the largest positive 32-bit signed number`	0	0	0	0
`ADDS R9, R8, R1`	`R9 = R8 + R1 (result is 0x80000001)`	0	0	0	1

Note that zero is usually regarded as a positive number, rather than negative, and that the carry and overflow flag interpretation is used differently depending upon whether we interpret the operands as signed or unsigned numbers. If dealing with signed numbers, the overflow flag is important, whereas only the carry need be considered for unsigned numbers. Please refer to Section 2.4 for more information.

though it is not clear at the present time whether it should be executed or not – the choice is to either allow it to enter the pipeline or *stall* the pipeline, waiting until the first instruction completes. Many processors would use *speculative execution* in this way to load and process the second instruction anyway. Once the conditional flags are known, a decision is made whether to terminate the second instruction or keep it.

We can now complete the reservation table on the basis that the result of the first instruction is not a zero and the second instruction therefore is not executed (or rather it has been executed, but the result ignored):

Fetch instruction	ADDS R0	ANDEQ R1	$Inst_3$	$Inst_4$	$Inst_5$	$Inst_6$
Decode instruction		ADDS R0	ANDEQ R1	$Inst_3$	$Inst_4$	$Inst_5$
Fetch operand			ADDS R0	ANDEQ R1	$Inst_3$	$Inst_4$
Execute instruction				ADDS R0	X	$Inst_3$
Store result					ADDS R0	X
Clock cycles	1	2	3	4	5	6
NZCV	0000	0000	0000	0000	0000	0000

Since the zero flag is not set by cycle 5, the second instruction is effectively removed and replaced by a NOP. This results in an entire wasted diagonal in the reservation table. By contrast, if the pipeline had waited for the first instruction to complete before fetching the next instruction, this would have occurred in cycle 5 and there would have been three wasted diagonals instead.

At this point, the reader should probably be thinking in terms of 'what extra pipeline functionality is needed to support this type of speculative execution?'. We will leave further discussion of that until Section 5.7, apart from a short illustration in Box 5.5 on page 186.

5.2.6 Conditional Branches

The ARM has an instruction set where all (or almost all) instructions are capable of conditional operation. However, most processors support conditional execution with branch instructions only and use these to alter program flow. Here is an example of a conditional branch:

```
loop:   MOV R1, #5          ; R1 = 5
        AND R4, R3, R1      ; R4 = R3 AND R1
        SUBS R2, R0, R1     ; R2 = R0 – R1
        BGT loop            ; if result positive, branch
        NOT R3, R4
```

The important lines are the BGT (branch if condition flags greater than 0) and the line before this which sets the condition flags. Evidently, there is no way of knowing whether the branch should be *taken* or not until the SUBS instruction has finished and the condition flags updated.

Let us run this program through just a small and simplified three-stage pipeline, as shown in Figure 5.5.

Figure 5.5

A flowchart of a very simple three-stage pipeline, where instruction fetch and decode are performed in a single step and no stage is specified for operand fetch.

We then use this pipeline to 'execute' the sequence of operations (up to the branch) in a reservation table:

Fetch and decode instruction	*MOV*	*AND*	*SUBS*	*BGT*					
Execute instruction		*MOV*	*AND*	*SUBS*	*BGT*				
Store result			*MOV*	*AND*	*SUBS*	*BGT*			
Clock cycles	1	2	3	4	5	6	7	8	9

During cycle 5, the result of the SUBS is known, the condition flags are updated and the branch instruction is being executed. Thus, the next instruction can only be fetched in cycle 6 as appropriate, but this gives a wasted diagonal in the pipeline:

Fetch and decode instruction	*MOV*	*AND*	*SUBS*	*BGT*	**X**	*NOT*			
Execute instruction		*MOV*	*AND*	*SUBS*	*BGT*	**X**	*NOT*		
Store result			*MOV*	*AND*	*SUBS*	*BGT*	**X**	*NOT*	
Clock cycles	1	2	3	4	5	6	7	8	9

To reduce this waste, many processors, as mentioned in Section 5.2.5, will perform speculative execution. That means they will start by fetching the NOT instruction anyway. If the branch is to be taken, this is deleted from the pipeline, and if not, execution continues as normal. The following is a reservation table for *speculative execution*, but here the speculation is incorrect:

Fetch and decode instruction	*MOV*	*AND*	*SUBS*	*BGT*	*NOT*	*MOV*			
Execute instruction		*MOV*	*AND*	*SUBS*	*BGT*	*NOT*	*MOV*		
Store result			*MOV*	*AND*	*SUBS*	*BGT*	**X**	*MOV*	
Clock cycles:	1	2	3	4	5	6	7	8	9

Speculative execution, of course, does not always speculate correctly: when it is correct, the pipeline operates at full efficiency, but if it turns out to be wrong, there is a loss of efficiency, but no worse than without speculative execution. There are many weird and wonderful techniques to improve the correctness of speculative execution hardware (see Box 5.4).

Box 5.4

Branch prediction

Given that some CPUs can speculatively execute a branch, it is possible for them to speculate either way – branch taken or branch not taken. A correct speculation results in no loss of efficiency (but an incorrect one results in wasted cycles).

For some CPUs, they always speculate fixed one way, such as 'not taken'. Then a compiler can improve performance if it organises code such that 'not taken' is more common than 'taken'.

More intelligent CPUs keep track of past branches. If most of them were taken then they assume 'taken' for subsequent speculations, otherwise 'not taken'. This is called a *global predictor*. More advanced hardware keeps track of individual branches – or more commonly tracking them by the lowest 5 or 6 address bits, so there is a 'cache' of 32 or 64 branch trackers with perhaps several branches aliased to each tracker. This is a *local predictor*.

The most complex hardware combines a *global predictor* with several *local predictors* and in such cases impressive prediction rates can be observed. As expected, this is a fertile area of performance-led research, but by far the best results are obtained when both the compiler and the hardware work together.

We will explore these topics further in Section 5.7, but note a simple example of speculative hardware in Box 5.5.

5.2.7 Compile-Time Pipeline Remedies

One more point remains before we look at branch remedies, and that is the amount of efficiency reduction caused by pipeline stalls. This obviously depends on the pipeline construction and length, but consider how the two are related.

Three-stage pipelines are rare in modern processors. These days, seven, eight or more stages are commonplace and wildly complex customised pipelines even more so. The single wasted diagonal in our three stage example can become a troublesome seven-stage pipeline stall, dragging down processor performance and efficiency. Maybe this explains the amount of time and effort that has been spent on improving pipelines in recent years.

Compile-time tricks to improve pipeline performance range from the trivial to the highly complex. To illustrate one of the more trivial but useful methods, consider the code example from Section 5.2.6:

```
loop:    MOV R1, #5           ; R1 = 5
         AND R4, R3, R1       ; R4 = R3 AND R1
         SUBS R2, R0, R1      ; R2 = R0 – R1
         BGT loop             ; if result positive, branch
         NOT R3, R4
```

Box 5.5

Speculative execution

Over the years, many forms of speculative execution have been developed. Most notably is the split-pipeline from IBM which, at every conditional branch follows *both* branch paths simultaneously using two identical pipeline paths. One of these paths will be deleted once the conditions for the original branch are resolved. This machine can thus guarantee absolutely no loss in efficiency caused by 'isolated conditional branches' – but at a substantial hardware cost.

Moving down the ability range is the *probabilistic branching* model, in which the processor keeps track of how often a branch is *taken*, as described in Box 5.4, entitled branch prediction, and explored more deeply in Section 5.7.

Despite some very advanced hardware on specialised machines, many speculative branch systems simply fix their speculation to 'always take a branch' or 'never take a branch'. Compilers have to take note of this. They need to order the code to attempt to maximise the proportion of the time that the guess made by the processor is correct. Again, much research has been conducted in this active and important area.

The problem with this code is that there is no way to know whether the branch should be taken or not before the following instruction is due to be fetched. So it must either wait to be fetched or fetched speculatively.

But in this case, we could re-order the code to separate the condition-setting instruction (SUBS) and the conditional instruction (BGT) a little further as follows:

```
loop:    MOV R1, #5          ; R1 = 5
         SUBS R2, R0, R1     ; R2 = R0 – R1
         AND R4, R3, R1      ; R4 = R3 AND R1
         BGT loop            ; if result positive, branch
         NOT R3, R4
```

In this instance, the re-ordering does not change the outcome (because the AND does not depend on anything that the SUBS changes; likewise the SUBS does not depend on anything that the AND changes). The result will be the same, but look at the reservation table:

Fetchand decode instruction	*MOV*	*SUBS*	*AND*	*BGT*	*NOT*				
Execute instruction		*MOV*	*SUBS*	*AND*	*BGT*	*NOT*			
Store result			*MOV*	*SUBS*	*AND*	*BGT*	*NOT*		
Clock cycles	1	2	3	4	5	6	7	8	9

Whether we take the branch or not, the condition flags are updated by the SUBS at the end of cycle 3, and the branch needs to be decided before cycle 5. There is thus sufficient time between the condition flags changing and the branch so that there does not need to be a delay waiting for the conditions to change – and execution can continue at full efficiency.

The changing of code to suit a pipeline can also be performed for the other hazards – data and mode changes. When re-ordering is not possible (perhaps because of two sequential branches or many dependencies), then the compiler is able to either insert a NOP, or simply assume that the pipeline is sufficiently intelligent that it will stall for a short time automatically. This is a reasonable assumption with modern processors, although some of the early pipelined machines relied upon compilers or programmers inserting NOPs in this way for correct execution.

5.2.8 Relative Branching

Examining some of the reservation tables that have been discussed or given in examples above, it is clear that the various pipeline stages are performed by different functional units. The reservation table can indicate which of those functional units are busy at any particular time.

The execution stage includes the ALU (alongside whatever other single-cycle numerical engines are fitted – that is, not an FPU which usually consists of multiple cycles). At first glance it may seem that the ALU has no use during a branch instruction.

However, if a branch instruction requires target address calculation, then perhaps the ALU can be used to perform that calculation? Indeed this is the case for a *relative branch*. That is, to jump forwards or backwards by a set number of locations (see Box 5.6, and refer also to Chapter 3). These branches are relative to the program counter (PC). They require a certain address offset to be added to the PC, and then the PC to be set to this new value.

In fact, the branch becomes an addition just like the add instruction:

```
ADD PC, PC, #24
```

would move 24 address bytes forwards. And similarly:

```
ADD PC, PC, #-18
```

would move 18 bytes backwards. Looking again at the previous reservation table, it should be clear that, when a relative branch occurs, whether it is conditional or not, the processor cannot fetch the next instruction until the branch has completed the 'execute' stage of the pipeline where the address to fetch it from is determined. Here is an example:

```
ADD R2, R0, R1      ; R2 = R0 + R1
B +24               ; branch 24 locations forwards
NOT R3, R4          ; R3 = NOT R4
 ..                  ..
```

Box 5.6

Relative branching

In the ARM processor, instructions are 32 bits in size (as are both the address and data buses, except in the earliest ARM processors that used a 26-bit address bus). Given that each location on the 32-bit address bus can be specified as an address in any instruction such as a branch, then it should be clear that 32 bits are needed to represent any address in full.

It is thus impossible to store a 32-bit address within a branch instruction if some of the other instruction bits are used for other information (such as identifying the instruction words as being a branch and identifying any conditions on the branch). Thus, *absolute* addressing is not used in the ARM. Instead, *relative* addressing is used.

The value stored inside the branch instruction word is therefore a signed offset that needs to be added to the current program counter (PC) to determine the location of the *branch target* address.

In fact, the ARM encodes branch offsets as 24-bit signed numbers. Remember that addresses are on a byte-by-byte basis, but instructions are 4 bytes in size. If all instructions are specified as being aligned to a 4-byte boundary address (such as 0, 4, 8, 12, 1004 and so on), then the lowest two bits of any *branch target* address will always be zero. These two bits need not therefore be stored in the instruction.

In other words, the 24-bit number counts instructions backwards or forwards from the PC rather, than individual bytes. This is a +/−32 Mibyte range: a huge overkill at the time of the ARMs original design when desktop computer memory rarely exceeded 512 Kibytes, but less impressive in today's world of code-bloat.

. .   . .

(24 locations beyond the branch)

`SUB R1, R0, R1` ;R2 = R0 − R1

The simple three-stage reservation table for this unconditional relative branch is as follows:

Fetch and decode instruction	*ADD*	*B*	**X**	*SUB*					
Execute instruction		*ADD*	*B*	**X**	*SUB*				
Store result			*ADD*	*B*	**X**	*SUB*			
Clock cycles	1	2	3	4	5	6	7	8	9

This throws open again the whole nature of pipeline efficiency. Even when a branch is not conditional but is relative, it seems that the pipeline must stall. There are two solutions: one is to include a dedicated ALU solely for relative branch calculations and the other is discussed in the next section.

5.2.9 Instruction-Set Pipeline Remedies

Since the compiler can re-order code (as described in Section 5.2.7) to separate a condition-setting instruction and a branch, it is possible to enforce this in the instruction set. Hence the *delayed branch*, as used in original MIPS processors and some older Texas Instruments DSP processors.

The delayed branch operation does exactly what it says: it delays the branch by a number of cycles – exactly enough cycles to completely solve any problems caused by relative branching or delays due to condition-setting instructions near to a conditional branch. In the author's opinion, it does this at the expense of the unfortunate assembly language programmer. Having written code for both the processors mentioned, he learnt that it is sometimes tempting to negate the improvements generated through the delayed branch mechanism by dropping a couple of NOPs after the instruction, for sanity and safety's sake. As we shall see, failure to observe the delay causes bizarre code problems that have tripped up the best of programmers.

Here is an example of the delayed branch in use:

```
loop:   MOV R1, #5            ; R1 = 5
        SUBS R2, R0, R1       ; R2 = R0 – R1
        BGTD loop             ; conditional branch, delayed
        AND R4, R3, R1        ; R4 = R3 AND R1
        NOT R3, R4            ; R3 = NOT R4
        NOP
```

As in some of the previous examples, this is a conditional branch. It is also a relative branch, such that the assembler will encode the 'BGTD loop' as 'BGTD −2' since the loop label is two instructions before the branch, so at runtime, the machine would actually be doing PC = PC−2 if the branch is to be taken.

Since the branch is delayed, it is necessary to know by how many instructions and this information would be found with details of the instruction set. We shall assume that the branch is delayed by two instructions. What this means is that the branch would not occur at the program line containing the BGTD instruction. Instead, it would actually occur two lines later – between the NOT and the NOP. Let us examine a reservation table in Table 5.1.

Table 5.1

A reservation table capturing 12 clock cycles of the delayed branch example code listed in this section.

Fetch and decode instruction	**MOV**	**SUBS**	**BGTD**	**AND**	**NOT**	*MOV*	*SUBS*	*BGTD*	*AND*	*NOT*	*NOP*	
Execute instruction		**MOV**	**SUBS**	**BGTD**	**AND**	**NOT**	*MOV*	*SUBS*	*BGTD*	*AND*	*NOT*	*NOP*
Store result			**MOV**	**SUBS**	**BGTD**	**AND**	**NOT**	*MOV*	*SUBS*	*BGTD*	*AND*	*NOT*
Cycles	1	2	3	4	5	6	7	8	9	10	11	12

In this 12 clock cycles, the loop is run through twice. During the first iteration (indicated in bold) the branch is taken but during the second iteration the branch is not taken. The first time the branch instruction is encountered, in cycle 3, it loads into the pipeline, and being conditional, waits for the previous condition flag-setting instruction (SUBS) to complete. Although the branch is to be taken, the next two instructions (AND and NOT) are loaded anyway, and the branch is not taken until cycle 6, where the PC returns to the MOV instruction at the *loop*: label.

The second iteration sees an absolutely identical sequence of operations, except that the NOP instruction follows the NOT rather than the MOV instruction to indicate that the branch has *not* been taken in this instance.

Concerning the relative nature of the branch, the first iteration of BGTD claims execution during slot 4 (and hence access to the ALU to perform the branch target calculation), easily in time to provide a complete branch target address to the PC, from which the next instruction in slot 6 is loaded.

There are no spaces in the reservation table, indicating full efficiency, whether branches are taken or not, conditional, unconditional, relative or absolute.

From an assembly language programmer's perspective it is important to remember that the AND and the NOT will always be executed irrespective of whether the branch is taken. Confusing? Yes, which is why the following is all too common:

```
BD somewhere
NOP
NOP
```

This might help the low-level programmer who forgets the branch is delayed, but with such code the efficiency gains possible through using a delayed branch instruction will of course be lost. A compiler, on the other hand, would take care of the delayed branches automatically.

5.2.10 Runtime Pipeline Remedies

Moving back, for a moment to the hazards discussed in Section 5.2.4, namely write after write, read after write and write after read. These can be handled through compile-time measures although most pipelined processors will automatically handle such hazards without compiler intervention. These processors use runtime methods to resolve hazards that are likely to be troublesome.

If O(i) is the set of output locations (including registers, memory addresses and condition flags) affected by instruction i, and I(j) is the set of input locations affecting instruction j, then a hazard between instructions i and j will exist if:

$$O(i) \cap I(j)! = \emptyset for RAW hazard$$
$$I(i) \cap O(j)! = \emptyset for WAR hazard$$
$$O(i) \cap O(j)! = \emptyset for WAW hazard$$

Figure 5.6

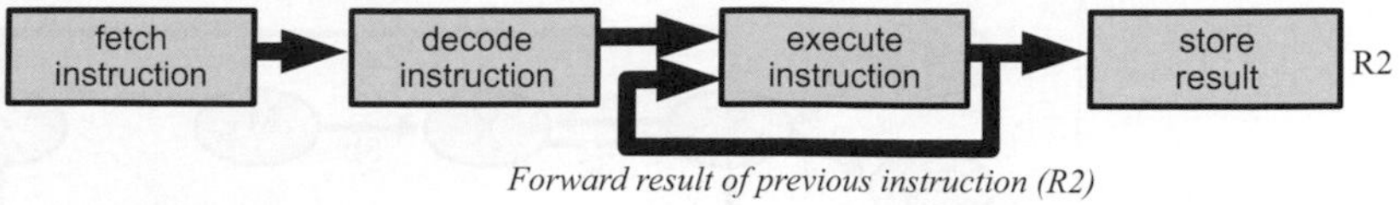

A four-stage pipeline with data forwarding to send the result of one instruction directly into the execution unit for the following instruction, without first storing it to the destination register (R2).

In general, such hazards can be resolved through forwarding: fetch-fetch, store-store and store-fetch. Look at the following RAW hazard example:

```
ADD R2, R0, R3          ; R2 = R0 + R3
AND R1, R2, #2          ; R1 = R2 AND 2
```

The hazard is on R2, which must be written by the first instruction before it is read by the second instruction (something that, given a long pipeline, may not necessarily always be true). However, we can imagine a separate path in hardware that takes the output of the first instruction and feeds it directly into the input of the second instruction, only writing the result to R2 afterwards as illustrated by the separate feedback path from the output of the execution unit (EX) to one of its inputs in the block diagram of Figure 5.6.

This effectively bypasses the store result (SR) stage and mathematically would be equivalent to performing the following transformation:

```
R2 = R0 + R3; R1 = R2 & 2 → R1 =(R0 + R3) & 2; R2 = R0 + R3
```

Forwarding is also used to improve speed of execution through, for example, reducing the number of reads and writes to slow off-chip memory by making greater use of on-chip registers.

For example the following code:

```
LDR R0, [#0x1000]       ; load R0 from mem. address 0x1000
ADD R2, R0, R3          ; R2 = R0 + R3
LDR R1, [#0x1000]       ; load R1 from mem. address 0x1000
ADD R3, R2, R1          ; R3 = R2 + R1
```

can easily be replaced by:

```
LDR R1, [#0x1000]       ; load R1 from mem. address 0x1000
ADD R2, R1, R3          ; R2 = R1 + R3
ADD R3, R2, R1          ; R3 = R2 + R1
```

Pipelining

Figure 5.7

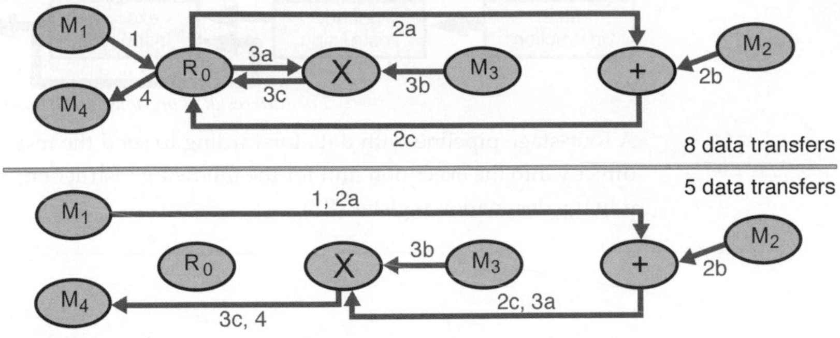

An example of a simple arithmetic calculation performed without data forwarding (top), and with the use of forwarding to reduce memory save/load operations (bottom).

This example of fetch-fetch forwarding improves execution speed by 25% at no cost apart from requiring either a compile-time or run-time code optimisation. Store-store forwarding would perform a similar task for writes to memory.

Note that sometimes multiple reads or writes are communicating with a memory-mapped peripheral such as a UART,[1] where it is entirely reasonable to have multiple writes to the same address (such as serial byte output register), something that would be wasted if it were RAM! In the C programming language, such memory pointers should be marked with the keyword *volatile* to prevent a compiler from optimising them out (the reason for this is described later in Section 7.8.3). For runtime code organisation, an intelligent processor (or well set-up memory areas) would detect such addresses as being outside regular memory pages, and thus not optimise in this way.

A final data forwarding example is provided by the following artificial code segment:

Instruction 1	`LDR R0, [m1]`	; load R0 from address m1
Instruction 2	`ADD R0, R0, [m2]`	; R0 = R0 + content of address m2
Instruction 3	`MUL R0, R0, [m3]`	; R0 = R0 × content of address m3
Instruction 4	`STR R0, [m4]`	; store R4 to address m4

This is represented in the upper half of Figure 5.7, which shows eight data transfers involved in the operation, and again in the lower part of the figure as an optimised code

[1] UART: universal asynchronous receiver/transmitter, usually called simply a 'serial port'.

Pipelining

section involving only five data transfers in total. In both cases, the instruction to which the transfer is associated is identified. The numerical result of the operations would be the same for both, and the original source code is identical, but speed of execution and resource usage will differ markedly. At runtime, the forwarding rules can be determined and applied to accelerate the execution of code by minimising time-consuming and resource-hogging data transfers.

The downside with runtime remedies is that they cost: extra hardware has to be present for them to work, and this increases power consumption, size and therefore the price of each and every processor that is made. However, for pure processing performance, or when backwards compatibility is needed, ruling out compile-time speed-ups, runtime methods alone are suitable.

5.3 Complex and Reduced Instruction Set Computers

Section 3.2.6 introduced the debate between RISC and CISC architectures, and presented RISC processors as the culmination of an evolutionary process that began with a simple control unit, moved through microcode and then applied the microcode (simplified instructions) approach to the entire CPU, resulting in a RISC architecture.

So this led to a RISC processor being loosely defined as any CPU with fewer and simpler instructions than normal. Typically 100 instructions were regarded as the upper limit for a RISC processor. However, over the years since their introduction, several more distinctive features of these devices have come to the forefront, as listed below. Be aware though that there are no hard and fast rules here – much is down to the marketing department of the design company.

- **Single-cycle execution** – All instructions are supposed to complete in a single cycle. Not only does this minimise processor design difficulties and promote regularity in the instruction set, but it also has the side benefit of reducing interrupt response times (discussed later in Section 6.5). In practice, many RISC processors adhere to this loosely, for example, in the ARM, the load/store multiple instructions (LDM/STM) can take many cycles to complete.
- **No interpretation of instructions** – There should be no need for an on-chip interpreter, since instructions should relate directly to the actual physical hardware available on the processor.
- **Regularity of instruction set** – A glance at the instruction set of a common CISC processor will reveal little commonality between instructions. Bit-fields in the instruction word may mean totally different things from one instruction to another. Some instructions can access one register, others cannot. This is troublesome to the assembly language programmer, but also acts to increase the size of the on-chip instruction decode unit. RISC processors by contrast should have a very regular instruction set that is easy to decode.

- **Regularity of registers and buses** – One way to help achieve regularity in the instruction set is to maintain a (preferably large) bank of independent registers, all of which are identical in scope and operation. In some CISC processors it is necessary to visualise the internal bus structure to work out how to transfer a value from one functional unit to another using the minimum number of instructions. In a RISC processor, by contrast, this should be simple: if one register can 'see' the value, then all registers can 'see' it equally as well.
- **Load-store architecture** – Since memory is far slower than registers, it is far more difficult in a fast clock cycle to load a memory location, process that location and then store back to memory. In fact, the best way to prevent the external memory accesses from forming a bottleneck is to ensure that, when an external load or store occurs, nothing else happens to slow that instruction down. Thus, there is precisely one instruction to load from memory and one instruction to store to memory. All data processing instructions thus operate on registers or immediate values only.

As mentioned, there are few rules: there is no global certification authority to decide what is RISC and what is CISC, and many modern designs pragmatically borrow from both camps.

5.4 Superscalar Architectures

The evolution of pipelining in performance-led processors naturally resulted in ever-increasing degrees of pipeline complexity, despite the simplifications promised by the RISC approach. Multi-function dynamic pipelines became more involved, with more customised handling of particular instructions and thus increased control requirements.

Coupling ever-increasing pipeline complexity with the consequent growth in opportunities for hazards, the hazard detection and resolution steps within runtime hardware became more important. These led to significant hardware resources required for the management of pipelines.

5.4.1 Simple Superscalar

One pragmatic alternative to greater pipeline complexity then emerged – an arrangement with a very simple linear pipeline, but augmented with multiple functional units in the execution stage. In this scheme, instructions are issued sequentially, but may follow different paths in the process of execution.

Often, the execution stage is the most time-consuming part of the pipeline, and of course in a pipeline the slowest stage is the bottleneck. For this reason, in a superscalar pipelined system, the instruction fetch unit issues instructions into the pipeline at a faster peak rate than any one individual execution element can process them. Multiple copies of execution elements then accept instructions in turn. Such a system is shown in the five-stage pipeline of Figure 5.8.

Figure 5.8

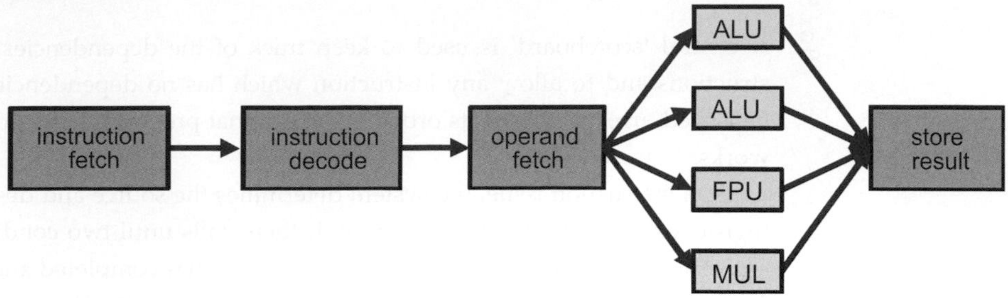

A five-stage superscalar pipeline showing a fairly conventional pipeline augmented with multiple functional units in the execution stage.

This approach was pioneered in DSPs which had more than one multiply-accumulate unit (MAC), but only became formalised as a superscalar approach when applied in general-purpose CPUs.

In the diagram shown in Figure 5.8, the floating point unit (FPU) has been inserted into the superscalar pipeline. FPU devices are notoriously slow: placing an FPU in a linear pipeline (with constant instruction clock rate) would result in a very slow processor, but in a superscalar machine, an instruction issued to the FPU would continue executing in parallel with other instructions being handled by the ALUs, multipliers and so on. Some recent superscalar machines have eight ALUs and 16 MACs, or several ALUs and four FPUs.

A reservation table is given in Table 5.2 for an example superscalar pipeline. In this example, there is a single fetch and decode unit issuing one instruction per clock cycle. Instructions are issued to four functional units (two ALUs, an FPU and a MUL

Table 5.2

A reservation table capturing 12 clock cycles of operation for the superscalar pipeline of Section 5.4. Note that MUL2 cannot be issued in cycle 7, hence it stalls the fetch and decode unit until it is issued in cycle 10.

Fetch & decode	*ADD*	*SUB*	*AND1*	*FADD*	*NOT*	*MUL1*	*MUL2*	–	–	–	*NOR*	*AND2*	*NOT*
ALU		*ADD*		*AND1*		*NOT*						*NOR*	
ALU			*SUB*										*AND2*
FPU					*FADD*								
MUL							*MUL1*				*MUL2*		
Store result				*ADD*	*SUB*	*AND1*		*FADD*	NOT		*MUL1*		
Clock cycles	0	1	2	3	4	5	6	7	8	9	10	11	12

Box 5.7

Scoreboarding

A central 'scoreboard' is used to keep track of the dependencies of all issued instructions and to allow any instruction which has no dependencies at that time to be issued, irrespective of its order in the original program. Let us consider how this works.

On instruction issue, the system determines the source and destination operand registers specified by that instruction. It then stalls until two conditions are met: (i) any other instruction writing to the same register has completed and (ii) the required functional unit is available. These conditions counteract WAW hazards and structural hazards respectively.

Once an instruction is issued to a functional unit, operand(s) are then fetched from the instruction source register(s). However, the fetch process stalls until the completion of any current instructions that will write to the source register(s). This solves RAW hazards.

Having collected all operands, the instruction is then executed (and of course the scoreboard continues to keep track of that instruction until it completes).

Finally, the instruction completes and is ready to write its result to the destination register. However at this point, the write will stall if there are any earlier instructions that have been issued but have not yet fetched their operands, and which the current instruction would overwrite. In other words, if an earlier instruction is still stuck somewhere waiting to execute, and this needs to read from register Rx, but the current instruction is about to write to Rx, then the current instruction will be delayed until the earlier instruction becomes unstuck and completes its reading of Rx. This mechanism avoids WAR hazards.

unit). A single-store stage then completes the pipeline. Examining Table 5.2, it should be noticeable that the instruction fetch unit issues instructions faster than any of the individual pipelined execution units can operate – and also that the stored results can be out-of-order compared to the input sequence. Not all machines are able to cope with out-of-order execution. This feature usually requires complex run-time hazard-avoidance hardware. In fact, we will examine one machine that is excellent at handling out-of-order execution, the Tomasulo method, in Section 5.9, and another method called *scoreboarding* is briefly described in Box 5.7.

Although the example program in Table 5.2 is rather short, it can be seen that the instruction output rate is less than the instruction input rate. Eventually, this system will have to pause the issuance of instructions to wait for pipeline elements to become free. The system thus requires the ability to maintain a higher peak instruction handling rate than the average rate which it achieves when executing real-world code. It is quite possible that when benchmarking such a processor, the manufacturer might choose an instruction sequence that happens to run at peak rate rather than a realistic average rate (we have briefly met this issue in Section 3.5.2).

Unfortunately, this simple view is not the end of the story – and in fact is not the most common view of a superscalar system. For that we need to consider the issuing of multiple instructions in a single cycle, discussed below in Section 5.4.2.

5.4.2 Multiple-Issue Superscalar

In Section 5.4.1, we have considered adding multiple functional units to a scalar pipeline. This does not quite create a full superscalar machine but rather something that is more competent than a scalar machine.

An advance on the simple superscalar machine is the ability to issue multiple instructions per cycle. That is, instead of issuing one instruction per cycle to multiple functional units, we issue multiple instructions per cycle to multiple functional units.

The block diagram of Figure 5.8 may not change significantly, however, the realisation of multiple instructions issued per cycle leads to a different reservation table. This can either appear similar to those drawn previously, albeit with two 'spaces' for fetch and decode each cycle (and for store), or in an entirely different form we will encounter a little later.

The following execution table shows two fetches per cycle. The fetch units are feeding three different execute units which in turn are supported by two result store units. Interestingly, there are two apparent gaps in the pipeline operation, in cycles 3 and 5 respectively. During both of those cycles the second fetch and decode unit cannot fetch a new instruction. The reason is that in each case, the previously fetched instruction has not yet been issued since the required functional unit (execute unit 1 in both instances) is occupied. This illustrates a real and common effect in such processors.

Fetch and decode instruction	I_1	I_3	I_5	I_6	I_8	I_9	I_{11}
Fetch and decode instruction	I_2	I_4	–	I_7	–	I_{10}	I_{12}
Execute unit 1		I_1	I_3	I_4	I_6	I_7	I_{10}
Execute unit 2		I_2				I_8	
Execute unit 3				I_5			I_9
Store result			I_1	I_3	I_4	I_6	I_7
Store result			I_2		I_5		I_8
Clock cycles	1	2	3	4	5	6	7

Throughout this text we have drawn many reservation tables to illustrate pipeline operation. However, there are other ways of drawing reservation tables. One example is given in Figure 5.9. This shows instructions being issued sequentially from the top down and timed along the horizontal axis. In this case, there are no blockages in the pipeline and so instructions are both issued in-order and retired in order. However, this may not necessarily be the case in reality.

Figure 5.9

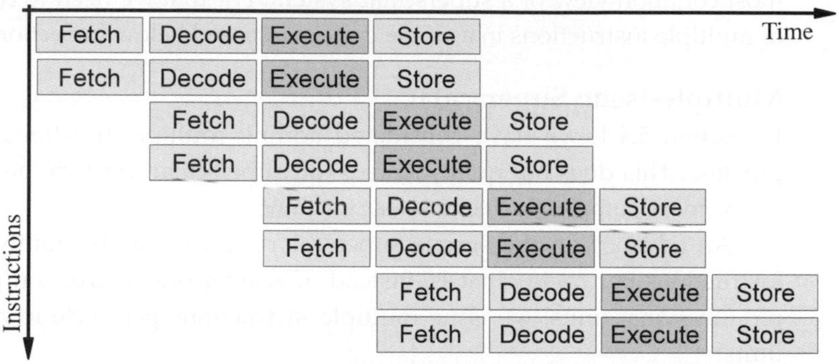

An alternative reservation table format showing instructions being executed sequentially from the top down, moving forwards in time from left to right. A vertical line drawn through the table identifies the operation at a specific time – as it also does in the reservation tables drawn so far.

5.4.3 Superscalar Performance

Superscalar architectures are characterised by the speed at which they issue instructions compared to how quickly they process them. In theory, a superscalar machine does not need to be pipelined, but in reality all, or almost all of them are pipelined.

Everything depends, of course, upon what constitutes the measure of performance (see again Section 3.5.2). We have already noted that superscalar machines need to be capable of high-speed instruction issue, even though the average issue rate in practice may be significantly below this peak – depending primarily upon the occupancy of the execution units. Taking these constraints into consideration, issue rate can be improved through compiler settings to interleave instructions for different functional units. The issue rate depends strongly upon the nature of the task being computed.

At best, and clearly seen in Figure 5.9, a superscalar machine is actually handling instructions in parallel. It is therefore a form of parallel computer (something that we will explore more fully in Section 5.8).

5.5 Instructions Per Cycle

Instructions per cycle (IPC) is a very important measure of how quickly a processor can execute a program, at least in theory. It is not a measure of the amount of work that can be achieved per cycle – because that depends upon how powerful the instructions are, and also upon how intelligent the coder/compiler is. Thus, it is not particularly relevant for comparing the execution speed of code on different machines.

However, IPC is a useful indicator – when averaged carefully over representative code – of the raw processing ability of an architecture. In fact, the ratio of average to peak CPI could be seen as an 'honest measure' – an average close to the peak value indicates an architecture that is very well optimised for the code being executed.

5.5.1 IPC of Difference Architectures

Different types of processors aim for different IPC scores, and naturally fall into certain operating regimes as a result of their structures:

- **CISC processors** exhibit an IPC far below 1.0. This is because instructions tend to be relatively time consuming and there was historically little attempt to simplify instructions in such machines.
- **RISC processors**, by contrast, exhibit an IPC which approaches 1.0, although for various reasons they may not quite achieve such a score. Reasons for falling short include the use of occasional lengthy instructions (such as multiply, divide and so on), and the need to wait for loads/stores to/from slower external memory – RISC machines are almost always load-store machines (Section 3.2.3). This latter effect is particularly prevalent in some DSP devices when using external memory. Pipelining can help to push the IPC of a RISC processor even closer to 1.0.
- **Superscaler processors** as we have seen, aim to issue multiple instructions in parallel. Where there are n issue units (or up to n instructions issued each cycle), then IPC approaches n. However, as we have seen in Section 5.4.2, sequences of instructions that require the same functional unit (hardware dependencies) or having unresolved data dependencies will often cause pipeline stalls. Clearly, the more often a pipeline stalls, the lower will be the achieved IPC.
- **VLIW[2]/EPIC[3] processors**, both of which will be discussed in Section 9.2, aim for an IPC which is significantly greater than 1.0. They are useful in niche areas typically related to media or signal processing.
- **Parallel machines** may include two or more processor cores inside a computer, each of which has a lower IPC, but when operating in parallel exhibits a higher throughput. In effect, the IPC of the entire computer would approach the IPC per core multiplied by the number of cores. We will discuss this a little more below.

Improving IPC has been a major focus for many processor designers in recent years, and has been the prime tool that computer architects have used for increasing performance.

The case of parallel machines is particularly interesting, and currently relevant due to the push of major processor manufacturers such as Intel, at the time of writing, towards dual, quad and higher levels of parallelism. We have briefly met dual-core processors in Section 5.8.1, and indeed will consider parallel processing approaches more fully later in Section 5.8, but suffice it to say that manufacturers appear to have reached a point with increasing clock speed, and in terms of architectural complexities, of decreasing returns: further efforts in either direction do not translate to a

[2] VLIW: very long instruction word.

[3] EPIC: explicitly parallel instruction computing.

commensurate increase in performance. In other words, it has become increasingly difficult to push the performance envelope with today's tools.

As will be revealed as we progress further through descriptions of the remaining items in the above list, the approaches chosen by modern computer architects are increasingly offloading responsibility for increased performance onto compilers and software. Let us recap a little to illustrate this observation: CISC processors performed many functions in hardware. By contrast, the RISC approach simplified (and speeded up) hardware by providing simpler instructions. RISC meant that more software instructions were often required, but these could be processed faster. So RISC programs are typically longer than CISC programs and the compiler has to work just a little harder to create them. Superscalar systems then included some limited parallelism within the pipeline, but issues of handling data dependency became important to prevent pipeline stalls. Thus, to achieve good performance, compilers had to take dependencies into account and have an intimate knowledge of the capabilities of the superscalar pipeline. VLIW and EPIC, as we will discover in Chapter 9, are far more complex to program than anything we have discussed up to now, relying totally upon compiler-level scheduling.

So also with parallel machines. Although the processors themselves may be simple, their interactions can become complex. Furthermore, it is debatable whether the current generation of software engineers is really able to think and program 'in parallel'. Beyond the programmer, there is little debate that the most popular programming languages are not at all optimal when producing code for parallel processors. It seems that two things are needed before parallel machines can be fully exploited: (i) a new generation of programmers who are naturally able to write parallel code and (ii) a new generation of programming languages and tools to support them.

Just one further note on parallel processing. Although 'going parallel' has been the pragmatic response of processor manufacturers to continual demands for increased performance, achieving the promised speed-ups is largely left to programmers. For individual programs, this speed-up is elusive. However, for server and desktop machines in particular, running advanced multi-tasking operating systems such as Linux, it is very common for several *threads* (tasks) of execution to be running simultaneously. Parallel machines can apportion different threads to different processors, and although the individual threads do not execute any faster in terms of CPU time, they will complete quicker because they no longer get time-sliced and preempted as frequently by other tasks. In embedded systems, where typically fewer tasks are running, or perhaps only one major task is active at a time, there is less advantage in moving to a parallel processing solution. In these systems, a significant speed-up would only be evident if the critical tasks themselves were 'parallelised'.[4] This brings the argument back to good parallel-aware tools and languages being written by parallel-aware programmers.

[4] Parallelised: made to run in parallel.

5.5.2 Measuring IPC

As we have already noted in Section 5.4.3 and elsewhere (including through our discussions in Section 3.5.2), performance measures in computing are notoriously unreliable at predicting real performance. An engineer wanting to execute a known algorithm can simply try the algorithm on several architectures to determine which is fastest. However, any prediction of the performance of non-specific code depends upon so many factors that it may be more useful to follow ballpark figures such as dividing a quoted IPC average by the instruction clock frequency and then multiplying this figure by the number of instructions that need to be executed.

As the size and generality of the program increase, the more accurate this type of determination will be. Bear in mind though that embedded systems are more normally characterised by a small fixed collection of computational tasks – by contrast, the code running on desktop and server machines can seldom be predicted at design time.

The question arises as to whether quoted IPC figures are accurate. In any architecture, there are certain tricks that could be used to enhance quoted IPC figures. It is instructive to consider some of these:

- Quote peak IPC figures rather than average IPC, meaning absolutely best case figures are given.
- Quote average IPC, but averaged only over selected test code, not over representative code.
- IPC figures given are for execution from internal memory only.
- IPC has been calculated using external memory, but with the operating clock set very slow (so that the speed of the memory does not affect the figure – the cycle itself is slower!).
- Slow instructions have not been used (or are rarely used) in the code chosen to evaluate IPC.
- Known slow sequences of instructions have been removed.

Every architecture has its advantages and disadvantages, and through the descriptions in this book the reader can begin to appreciate some of these. However, choosing a processor for a particular computational task is often an art rather than a science: it may require intuition. In the view of the author, ignore the sales and marketing information relating to performance. Performance is seldom the most critical criteria and will be outweighed by the ease of programming, expandability, available support and development tools, and product lifetime, in addition to other more technical characteristics.

5.6 Hardware Acceleration

Most of the silicon area in a modern CPU is dedicated to accelerating basic processing operations. Acceleration methods include using a fast cache, adding extra buses to the architecture, pipelining and incorporating dedicated numerical processing units.

Originally, processors contained only a basic ALU for number processing (and it can be shown that *all* processing operations can be performed with an ALU alone – at least if execution speed is not important). Later, multiply-accumulate units were added to speed up multiplication operations, which were previously performed using repeated additions.

Floating point hardware, now deemed mandatory in desktop computers, was originally an extra-cost option requiring insertion of a separate chip. Alongside floating point, desktop processors now routinely contain SIMD hardware (see Section 2.1.1), and are beginning to incorporate various accelerators for wireless networking capabilities.

Other processing accelerators include those for graphics manipulation, cryptography, communications and data compression. It seems that the profusion of these units will continue to increase, as will their application-specific nature – especially in dedicated embedded system-on-chip processors

On the other hand, there are structural improvements to increase processing speed that are not data-processing related. Several have been considered previously, such as pipelining (Section 5.2), caches (Section 4.4), multiple bus architectures (Section 4.1) and customised instructions (Section 3.3). In this section, several further generic architectural support methods are considered.

5.6.1 Zero-Overhead Loops

Many algorithms consist of loops, such as *for()*, *while()* or *do()*. Generally, the loops require some sort of overhead. Consider the case of a loop that iterates a given number of times:

```
i = 20;
while (i-- > 0)
{
        <do something>
}
```

This requires a sequence of steps to its operation:

1. Set i = 20.
2. Compare i and zero.
3. Branch to instruction after loop if equal.
4. i = i–1.
5. Perform the body of the loop.
6. Branch back to the start of the loop (step 2 on this list).

The loop condition could be checked either before or after the body of the loop is executed depending on the type of loop, but what is clear is that when the item inside the loop is very simple, there is a large overhead. Consider the following example from DSP code implementing a digital filter:

```
for(i = 20;i>0;i--)
    y = y + x[i]* coeff[i];
```

The body calculation in the loop, although it appears complicated, can be executed in a single instruction in a modern DSP processor. However, if the six-step loop sequence above is applied, this code will take 1 instruction to set up, then 20 iterations of steps 2 to 6, that is, up to 101 instructions in total.

Since many DSP loops are tight and small like the one illustrated, DSP designers recognised the inefficiency of needing so many extra instructions to support looping and developed the zero-overhead loop (ZOL) concept.

Here is an assembler-style example from the Texas Instruments TMS320C50:

```
          set BRCR to #20
          RPTB loop --1
          ... <body of loop>
loop      ...<now outside loop>
```

In this case, there is a single instruction required to preload the BRCR loop counter, and then a single instruction to launch the looping. The DSP will examine the address of the program counter, and when it reaches a value of (loop – 1) will automatically reset it to the start address of the loop. It will do this 20 times in total. For the 20-iteration loop, this now requires only 22 instructions to complete rather than the 101 needed if the ZOL support was missing.

Analog Devices have a similar concept in their ADSP2181:

```
          set  CNTR to #20
           DO loop UNTIL LE
          ... <body of loop>
loop      ...<now outside loop>
```

It can be seen that the operation principle is the same – but provides the possibility of different loop end conditions (LE means 'less than or equal to' – there are 15 other possible conditions). Section 5.6.2 will expand on the addressing capabilities of the ADSP2181 beyond this.

The hardware required for ZOL support in this way is relatively simple, as can be seen from the block diagram in Figure 5.10.

Figure 5.10 A block diagram showing the hardware and communications needs for implementing zero-overhead loop hardware in a processor.

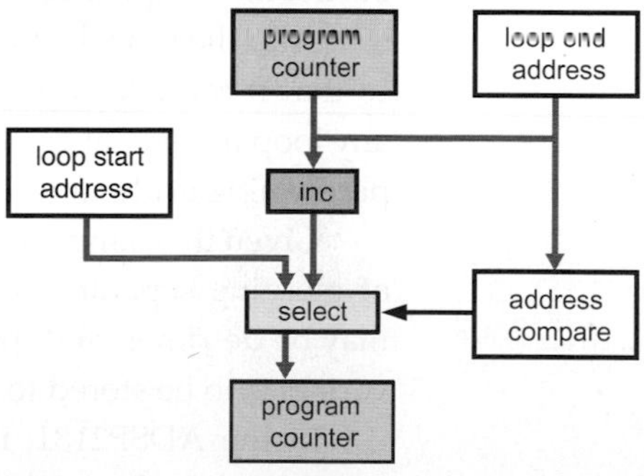

The hardware requirements are namely, somewhere to store the program address at the start of the loop, somewhere to store the address at the end of the loop, a way to determine when the program counter reaches the end of the loop (an address comparator) and a way to branch back to the start of the loop by reloading the program counter from the loop start address. In addition, there needs to be a means of holding the loop counter, decrement this and determine when the end condition is reached (for example, the loop counter has reached zero).

One complication that can occur is when the loop instruction is not a simple one, but perhaps calls other functions which themselves contain loops. Thus, there may be a need to *nest* the loops. In the ADSP, the ZOL registers are actually incorporated inside a stack to allow automatic nesting of loops with the minor proviso that loop end addresses cannot coincide. By contrast, the TMS lacks supporting hardware, and so such nesting has to be accompanied through manually saving and restoring the loop registers.

The second complication is that, although the two ZOL examples were written in assembly language, most code these days is written in C. The C compiler therefore has to recognise opportunities for using the ZOL hardware. Simple C constructs such as the *while* and *for* loops above, and the following, are easy to map to ZOL:

```
k = 20;
do{
      <something>
} while (k-- >0)
```

Note that these examples all have loop counters that count downwards. In the TMS, there is no way for a loop counter to increment, only decrement, so a piece of code such as:

```
for(i = 0;i <20;i++)
{
      <do something>
}
```

would need to be converted to a downwards counting loop (i.e. the counter is decremented from 20 to 0) in the final assembly language code, always assuming that the particular compiler in use is sufficiently intelligent.

Still, the onus is on the software programmer to ensure that C code is structured so that it can take advantage of ZOL hardware. In such hardware, it is best to avoid any loop increment or decrement other than by 1, and to avoid using the loop index for performing arithmetic within the loop.

Given that simple loops can have zero overhead, the old embedded code guideline of merging separate loops together wherever possible is not always true. In fact, it may be detrimental if (perhaps due to a shortage of temporary registers) it forces loop variables to be stored to external memory during the loop.

In the ADSP2181, it is possible to have an infinite hardware loop, but an exit condition can be evaluated manually as part of the loop body. This can actually be highly advantageous for C programs since it generalises to all possible loop constructs.

This type of loop acceleration hardware is called a PC trap. More complex hardware exists to perform similar tasks as described in the next section.

5.6.2 Address Handling Hardware

While the ARM processor has only a single bank of general-purpose registers, many processors differentiate between registers depending upon whether they are for storing data or addresses. In fact, several of these processors force this distinction through having different widths of data and address bus.

The Motorola 68000 series of CPUs, although having uniform 32-bit registers, makes a distinction between the eight data registers D0 to D7 and seven address registers A0 to A6. Although any value can be contained in these, many addressing modes only apply when the address is stored in the correct set of registers. Similarly, many processing instructions cannot store a result directly to an address register. Programmers can take advantage of dedicated hardware attached to the address registers to perform increments and decrements of address values either before or after access, and perform indexing. However, if more complex address calculations are required, they are likely to have to move an address from the A to a D register, perform the arithmetic, and then move the result back to an A register.

The ADSP21xx series of DSPs extends this approach further through the use of data address generators (DAGs). There are two of these in the ADSP2181, each containing four I, L and M registers:

I0	L0	M0
I1	L1	M1
I2	L2	M2
I3	L3	M3

DAG1

I4	L4	M4
I5	L5	M5
I6	L6	M6
I7	L7	M7

DAG2

Each index (I) register contains an actual address used to access memory, the L register holds a memory region length to correspond with those addresses, and the M registers hold modification values.

In assembly language, a read from memory is accomplished through syntax such as:

```
AX0 = DM(I3, M1);
```

This means that a value is read from data memory address pointed to by I3, that value is to be stored in register AX0, and then register I3 modified by adding the content of register M1. If this new value of I3 exceeds the length register L3 + initial I3, then the value in I3 will be stored modulo the initial I3 value (the initial I3 value means the start address of the buffer). If the length register L3 is set to zero, then there is no change to the content of I3. Some examples will clarify this arrangement (see the examples in Box 5.8), but first note that nowhere in the instruction is L3 mentioned. That is because the I and L registers operate in pairs, whereas by contrast the M registers are independent: within each DAG, any M register can be used to modify any I register, but the M registers in one DAG cannot modify I registers in the other DAG. Box 5.8 presents three examples of the ADSP21xx ZOL hardware in action.

Undoubtedly, the ADSP has very capable and advanced address handling, but consider the addressing modes of Section 3.3.4 which are based on those available in the ARM processor. In fact, the ADSP does not really have any capability beyond those addressing modes, despite its advanced addressing hardware.

Thus the DAG, and its extra hardware are useful in maintaining circular buffers and performing synchronised addressing changes (for example, backwards and forwards in predefined steps). However, beyond those efficiency gains, they do not fundamentally improve processor performance. The cost of this efficiency gain is the silicon area needed for hardware such as that shown in Figure 5.11 for one of the DAG units in the ADSP2181 DSP.

It can be seen from the figure that, since at most one of the registers in each DAG is accessed per instruction cycle, each of L, I and M are accessed through shared buses. The DMD bus is data-memory-data which conveys data operands and links to data memory (see Section 4.1.3 for more detail on the unusual internal bus architecture of the ADSP device). In addition to its other abilities, DAG1 (not shown) is able to bit-reverse its address outputs: a significant performance improvement for performing fast Fourier transform (FFT) calculations and several other signal processing techniques.

Figure 5.11

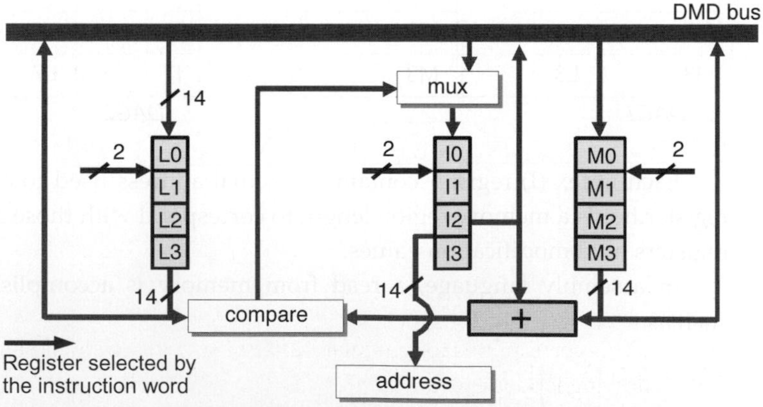

A block diagram of the second data address generator (DAG2) hardware within the ADSP2181 digital signal processor, showing how internal length registers L0 to L3, index registers I0 to I3 and modifier registers M0 to M3 are wired up to a dedicated address adder, and to the internal DMD (data memory data) bus.

Box 5.8

ZOL worked examples

Example 1: Let us use a made-up hybrid of ADSP assembler to access memory and ARM-style assembler for everything else. The exact addresses used in this and the other examples are for illustrative purposes only. Usually, they would be allocated by linker since there are certain constraints not discussed here (but covered in the ADSP21xx manual).

```
            MOV I0, #0x1000      ; Set I0 = 0x1000
            MOV L0, #0x2         ; Set L0 = 2
            MOV M0, #0           ; Set M0 = 0
            MOV M1, #1           ; Set M1 = 1
loop:       AX0 = DM(I0, M0)     ; Load AX0
            ADD AX0, AX0, #8     ; AX0 = AX0+8
            DM(I0, M1) = AX0     ; Store AX0
            B loop
```

Next, we will construct a table showing the values of I0 as the loop is executed:

	After this instruction	I0 is this:
1	MOV M1, #1	0x1000
2	AX0 = DM(I0, M0)	0x1000
3	ADD AX0, AX0, #8	0x1000
4	DM(I0, M1) = AX0	0x1001
5	B loop	0x1001
6	AX0 = DM(I0, M0)	0x1001
7	ADD AX0, AX0, #8	0x1001
8	DM(I0, M1) = AX0	0x1000
9	B loop	0x1000

Note how the value in I0 is first modified by M0 in the second row, but as M0 contains zero, it is unchanged. In the fourth row, I0 is modified by M1. Since M1 = 1 this is an increment. Again, the modification by M0 in row 6 is followed by another increment in the eighth row. Here however, I0 hits `0x1002`, and since L0 = 2, this ends the circular buffer, and the address therefore wraps back to `0x1000`.

Example 2: L1 has been loaded with 0, I1 contains `0x1000` and M0 is `0x10`.

Successive readings from I0 using `AX0 = DM(I1,M0)` will see address register I0 holding the following successive values: `0x1000, 0x1010, 0x1020, 0x1030, 0x1040, 0x1050` and so on. Since L1 holds zero, there will be no wraparound.

Example 3: In this case, L4 has been loaded with 50 and I0 = 0, M4 = 2 and M5 = 10. This corresponds to a circular buffer of size 50 locations, starting at address 0. The following loop is executed:

```
loop:       AX0 = DM(I4, M5)
            AY0 = DM(I4, M4)
            B loop
```

(Continued)

Box 5.8

ZOL worked examples (*Continued*)

As this loop progresses, I4 will take the following values:

0, 10, 12, 22, 24, 34, 36, 46, **48**, **8**, 10, 20, 22 and so on. The numbers of interest are highlighted. Note that from 48, the index I3 would normally increment by 10 to become 58, but since L4 holds 50, this has exceeded buffer length and the register must therefore wrap around to the start. Hence, the value after 48 is 8.

With separate data and program memory on-chip in the ADSP21xx serviced by independent buses, and with the dual DAGs, the device is capable of accessing two DAG-addressed operands in memory indirectly, with dual post-modification and wraparound. Once accessed, these two operands can be processed and stored, all in a single-instruction cycle. The ARM, by contrast, is functionally capable of performing the same operations, but cannot hope to achieve as much in a single cycle. Having said that, the ARM does not ever need to perform two separate addressing operations in a single instruction (since being load-store has at most only one address operand – see Box 5.9 for more detail).

Finally, note that there are no alternate or shadow DAG registers (described in Section 5.6.3) in the ADSP21xx. This means that use of DAGs is dependent on such factors as program context and interrupt servicing: it is likely that direct hand-coding of assembly language is needed to exploit these address handling accelerators to the full.

Box 5.9

Address generation in the ARM

Being a RISC design, the ARM minimises special handling hardware for addresses, but through simplicity tries to streamline instructions so that nevertheless they process very quickly.

As discussed in Section 3.2.3, the ARM has a load-store architecture with one data load and one data store instruction (actually there is also a *swap* instruction intended for multi-processor systems). The address to load or store from can be indexed with pre-offset or post-offset (increment or decrement), and can be direct or indirect.

The ARM utilises the main ALU and shifter for address calculations since these are free for a pipeline slot during load or store (see Section 5.2.8). This also provides an advantage over the DAG of the ADSP in that the main ALU and shifter are more flexible than the dedicated ALUs in the DAG.

Here is an example of that flexibility:

```
LDR  R0,   [R1, R2, LSL#2]
```

This loads the value at memory location (R1 + (R2*4)) into register R0. `LSL` means 'logical shift left', an addressing calculation that is not accessible to the DAGs of the ADSP21xx, despite their evident capabilities.

5.6.3 Shadow Registers

CPU registers are part of the *context* of the processor that is viewable by a running program. Other aspects of context include status flags and viewable memory.

When a program thread is interrupted by an external interrupt signal (a process discussed in Section 6.5.1), an interrupt service routine (ISR) is generally run that responds to that interrupt appropriately. Once the ISR completes, control returns to the original program. 'Control' in this context basically refers to where the program counter is pointing. The program may be happily stepping line-by-line through some assembler code, then an interrupt causes it to fly off to an ISR which it then steps through and completes, before returning to the original program, continuing as if nothing has happened.

Thinking about this process, it is evident that when interrupts are enabled, an ISR could be triggered in between any two instructions of any program! It is therefore vitally important that the ISR, when it returns, tidies things up so that the context is exactly the same as it was when the ISR was called.

A few years ago, programmers would have to perform what is called a context save at the start of the ISR, and then a context restore prior to exit. The save would be to push each register in turn onto a stack, while the restore would be to pop these back off again in the reverse order. This might mean an overhead of 20 or 30 lines of code that would need to be run inside the ISR even before it could do anything useful.

To remove this overhead, the concept of a shadow register set was developed. This being a second set of registers, which is identical in every way and operation to the main set. However, it can be utilised as required (and thus altered) inside an ISR without changing the content of the original registers visible to the main program. On the TMS320C50 for instance, once an interrupt occurs, the processor jumps to the relevant ISR and automatically switches to shadow registers. When the ISR finishes, a special return instruction causes a jump back to wherever the PC was before the interrupt and switches back to the original registers.

With such shadow registers there is no need to perform a manual context save and restore at the beginning and end of an ISR. Any piece of code can be interrupted without any overhead. However, if there is only a single set of shadow registers, interrupts can not be nested. That means that one interrupt cannot interrupt another.

5.7 Branch Prediction

In Section 5.2.6, we investigated the phenomenon whereby pipeline performance will often reduce as a result of branching. We have seen that branching *per se* can be problematic, and is exacerbated by issues such as conditional branching hazards and relative branching. We also briefly met the idea of performing branch prediction (Box 5.4 on page 185) and allowing speculative execution (Box 5.5 on page 186) as methods of reducing this *branch penalty*.

In this section, we will firstly summarise the reasons for branch-induced performance loss, and then discuss methods of branch prediction allied with the capability of speculative execution to mitigate against such losses. As we progress, consider the sheer ingenuity involved in some of the methods we present (and the hardware costs involved), and let this bear testament to how much branch-induced performance loss is a thorn in the flesh to computer architects.

In an ideal world, we could train programmers to avoid branch instructions, but until that happens, specialised hardware presented in this section will continue to be needed, and continue to be the focus of CPU performance research.

5.7.1 The Need for Branch Prediction

First, let us recap some of the issues related to branching. Consider the following code executing on a four-stage (fetch, decode, execute and store) pipeline:

```
i1        ADD R1, R2, R3
i2        B loop1
i3        ADD R0, R2, R3
i4        AND R4, R2, B3
loop1:    STR R1, locationA
```

Without constructing a reservation table, let us follow the first few cycles of operation:

- *i1* is fetched.
- *i2* is fetched while *i1* is decoded.
- *i3* is fetched while *i2* is decoded and *i1* is executed. At the end of this cycle, the CPU 'knows' that *i2* is a branch.

At this point, instruction *i3* has already been fetched and is in the pipeline. However, the correct operation sequence would require the instruction at label `loop1` to be the next one to be executed because *i2* is a branch. *i3* therefore has to be deleted from the pipeline and the correct instruction fetched. This deletion will cause a 'bubble' in the pipeline, consequentially reducing efficiency.

We have also discussed the issue of relative branching in Section 5.2.8: the very common arrangement where the branch target address (i.e. the address of the next instruction to fetch after a branch) is stored within a branch instruction as a relative offset to the current program counter (PC) address. The CPU thus has to perform an ALU operation to add this offset to the PC to obtain the address from which it can fetch the next instruction.

In our example above, if the address to branch to (in this case the address of the instruction at label `loop1`) has to be calculated, this will require another cycle *after* the branch instruction has been decoded. Most likely, processors using this technique will then immediately clear the pipeline and perform the branch. The sequence of operations would look like the following:

- *i1* is fetched.
- *i2* is fetched while *i1* is decoded.
- *i3* is fetched, *i2* is decoded and *i1* is executed.

- *i4* is fetched, *i3* is decoded, *i2* is executed (which means that the branch target address is calculated using the ALU) and the result of *i1* is stored.
- The result of *i2*, the branch target address, is stored – but to the program counter rather than to another register, and the remainder of the pipeline is reset (thus discarding *i3* and *i4*).
- The instruction at the calculated branch address is then fetched.[5]

So far, we have not mentioned the conditional branch hazard situations, where the pipeline needs to wait for the resolution of a previous condition-setting instruction before deciding if a branch should be taken or not.

However, we have discussed the role of speculation in alleviating the problems associated with branching. To recap, *speculative execution* means execution of one path while waiting for the outcome of the conditional operations, and sometimes also for the address calculations to complete. Before the path being speculatively executed is allowed to complete, the processor fully determines whether that speculation is correct (in which case, the speculatively executed instructions can complete) or incorrect (in which case these instructions, and their results, are trashed).

Some processors speculate deterministically, for example, they always speculate that a branch is taken, or perhaps always that it is not taken. Of course, in the absence of any other effects, such a technique cannot really hope to be correct more than 50% of the time. Wherever possible, it also makes sense for a compiler producing code for such a CPU to arrange the generated code so that the speculative path is more commonly taken.

In effect, speculation is guessing: betting that a particular path is taken. A correct guess pays off because usually in this case the processor will have experienced no pipeline stall. An incorrect guess will probably cause a pipeline stall while the remains of the speculative execution are cleared from the pipeline.

A refinement of speculation is *branch prediction*, which means making a more intelligent guess based on information such as:

- Past behaviour.
- Code region/address.
- Hints put in the code by the compiler (for example, a take/don't take bit – TDTB[6]).

Dynamic branch prediction usually relies on some measure of past behaviour to predict a future branch. This was summarised previously in Box 5.4. When the CPU

[5] It should be noted here that many processors would have fetched this instruction in the previous cycle by directly outputting the calculated address from the ALU onto the address bus – a form of data forwarding – while simultaneously loading it into the program counter.

[6] A take/don't take bit (TDTB) is inserted in the program code by a smart compiler to tell the speculation unit what it believes to be the most likely branch outcome at this position. Remember that the compiler has more knowledge available to it than the branch unit – the compiler can 'see' into the future, knows the full extent of loops, functions and programs, and knows what the next instructions will be down each of the alternative paths.

sees a branch it uses a predictor to very quickly make a decision of which path to speculate on. Later, when the actual branch outcome is known, it updates the predictor to hopefully refine the prediction decisions in future to continually improve accuracy.

We will investigate seven different prediction methods in turn, discussing their operation and performance:

- Single T-bit predictor.
- Two-bit predictor.
- The counter and shift registers as predictors.
- Local branch predictor.
- Global branch predictor.
- The gselect predictor.
- The gshare predictor.

Following these subsections, hybrid schemes will be considered (Section 5.7.9), and then the refinement of using a branch target buffer (Section 5.7.10).

5.7.2 Single T-bit Predictor

In the very simple single T-bit prediction scheme, a flag 'T' is set to 1 whenever a branch is confirmed as taken and 0 when it is not. This is updated whenever the CPU has just completed every branch instruction, that is, after all conditionals and other factors have been resolved. The T-bit global predictor has very low hardware overheads – just 1 bit being used to predict the behaviour of the entire CPU.

Whenever a new branch instruction is encountered, the pipeline speculates by following the state of the T bit. In other words, if the last branch was taken ($T = 1$), the next one should be predicted taken. If the last branch was not taken ($T = 0$), the prediction is that the next branch will not be taken either. This is not a particularly intelligent scheme, but can work surprisingly well – especially with compiler support. Primarily, it is a good method where many simple loops exist within the code being executed.

For example, consider the following ARM-style assembler code with initial conditions `R1 = 1` and `R2 = 4`:

```
i1    loop:    SUBS R2, R2, R1    ; R2 = R2 – R1
i2             BGT loop           ; branch if result > 0
```

Now we will 'run' this code through a CPU that has a global T-bit predictor, in order to ascertain how well the predictor copes with the simple loop case:

trace	*i1*	*i2*	*i1*	*i2*	*i1*	*i2*	*i1*	*i2*
R1	1	1	1	1	1	1	1	1
R2	3	3	2	2	1	1	0	0
T-bit	–	1	1	1	1	1	1	0
branch	–	T	–	T	–	T	–	NT
correct	–	–	–	Y	–	Y	–	N

Starting in the leftmost column of the trace table,[7] after instruction *i1* has completed the first time, the register contents will be as shown since `R2` has been decremented from 4 to 3 by the subtraction. In the next cycle, *i2*, the branch instruction, will be taken since the result of the `SUBS` is greater than zero. On this first loop, the predictor is assumed uninitialised and therefore cannot predict anything accurately.

As the trace progresses, the loop repeats two more times and then exits (by virtue of not taking the branch back to the beginning of the loop during the final cycle). By the second loop the predictor has learnt that the previous branch was taken, and therefore correctly predicts that the next branch will be taken. Likewise, the prediction during the third loop is correct. Upon reaching the branch instruction for the final time, however, the prediction is incorrect.

In general, it can be seen that the first branch in such a loop might not be correctly predicted, depending upon the state of the T-bit predictor prior to executing this code. The final branch will be incorrectly predicted, but within the body of the loop – no matter how many times it repeats – the prediction will be correct. This holds true for any size simple loop: no matter what code is placed in between *i1* and *i2*, as long as it contains no branches, the prediction will be as we have described.

Unfortunately, however, loops are rarely as simple as this. There will often be other branches within the loop code. Let us illustrate this, again with another simple example:

```
i1   loop:   SUBS R2, R2, R1    ; R2 = R2 – R1
i2           BLT error          ; branch if result <0
i3           BGT loop           ; branch if result >0
```

We will again 'run' this code through a CPU that has a global T-bit predictor, in order to ascertain how well the predictor copes with the simple loop case. In this case, we will assume an initial condition of `R2 = 3` in order to reduce the number of columns a little. Note that the T-bit used for a branch prediction in the table is the one from the column before the branch because columns show the state after each instruction:

trace	*i1*	*i2*	*i3*	*i1*	*i2*	*i3*	*i1*	*i2*	*i3*
`R1`	1	1	1	1	1	1	1	1	1
`R2`	?	2	2	1	1	1	0	0	0
T-bit	–	0	1	1	0	1	1	0	0
branch	–	NT	T	–	NT	T	–	NT	NT
correct	–	–	N	–	N	N	–	N	Y

In this case, performance is not so good: the predictor fails to correctly predict *any* of the branches. Unfortunately, such a result is all too common with the simple T-bit global predictor. As we can see in subsequent sections, this can be improved by either predicting with a little greater complexity or by applying a separate predictor to each

[7] This trace table cannot take the place of a full reservation table because it neither represents what is happening within the pipeline at a particular time nor indicates how long it takes to execute each instruction. It is simply an indicator of the state of the system after each instruction has completed in-order.

Figure 5.12

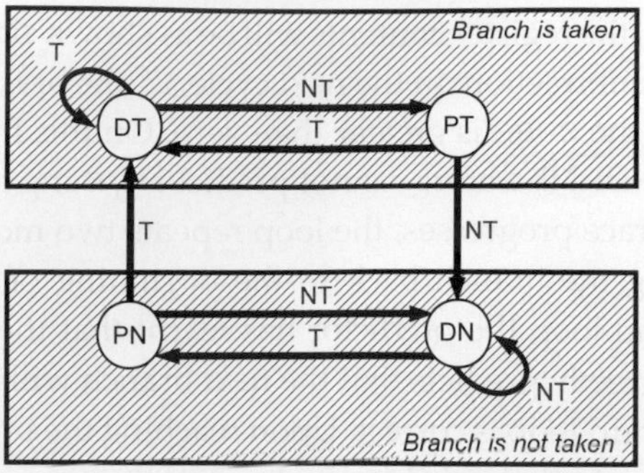

The state diagram of a two-bit predictor, showing states DT (definitely take), PT (probably take), PN (probably not take), and DN (definitely not take). The prediction in the first two states is that the branch will be taken, and in the second two states the prediction is that the branch will not be taken. Following the resolution of the branch conditions, the predictor state is updated based upon the actual branch outcome: T (taken) or NT (not taken).

of the two branch instructions. First though, let us investigate doubling the size of the predictor.

5.7.3 Two-Bit Predictor

The two-bit predictor is conceptually similar to the T-bit, but uses the result of the last *two* branches to predict the next branch, instead of just the last one branch. This method uses a state controller similar to that shown in Figure 5.12. This is also referred to as a bimodal predictor.

Since there are now four states (i.e. two bits to describe the state), one would expect this predictor to be more accurate than the single T-bit. While this is so in general, it is in the nested loop case – the instance where the single T-bit did not fare very well – that the two-bit predictor can provide better performance.

To illustrate this, we will use the same code as used in the previous section:

```
i1   loop:   SUBS R2, R2, R1     ; R2 = R2 – R1
i2           BLT error           ; branch if result < 0
i3           BGT loop            ; branch if result > 0
```

This time we will 'run' the code through a CPU that has a global two-bit predictor. We will again assume an initial condition of R2 = 3, R2 = 1 and that the predictor is initialised to state 'DT':

trace	*i1*	*i2*	*i3*	*i1*	*i2*	*i3*	*i1*	*i2*	*i3*
R1	1	1	1	1	1	1	1	1	1
R2	2	2	2	1	1	1	0	0	0
predictor	DT	**PT**	DT	DT	PT	DT	DT	PT	DN
branch	–	NT	**T**	–	NT	T	–	NT	NT
correct	–	N	**Y**	–	N	Y	–	N	N

The trace table is similar to those in Section 5.7.2. Care should be taken to read the table accurately. Remember that each column shows the state of the processor after the instruction indicated has completed, and that there is no timing information implied in the table, simply the sequence of operations. As an example of reading the table, find the first time instruction *i2* has executed. In this column we see that it has left `R1` and `R2` unchanged, but since it is a branch that is NOT taken, it will have shifted the predictor state from 'DT' to 'PT' (shown in bold). When instruction *i3* has completed, since it is a branch that IS taken (shown in bold), it will have shifted the predictor state back to 'DT'. When *i3* began, the predictor state was still 'PT', thus the prediction was that the branch would be taken, and in fact this was a correct prediction. This correct prediction is shown in bold as the result on the bottom line. Thus, remember to compare the branch outcome in any particular column with the prediction shown in the *previous* column when determining prediction accuracy.

While this predictor has clearly not particularly excelled in its prediction of all branches, it has correctly predicted one of the branches in the loop every cycle apart from the termination cycle. This is half way between the result shown by the T-bit predictor and a perfect result.

Let us now explain this rationale a little more closely: it seems a single-bit predictor has some problems, which can be partially solved by using a two-bit predictor. If a two-bit predictor has problems, can these be solved through applying more bits? Well, the answer is potentially 'yes' because in general spending more resources on the problem results in better performance. However, the quest is to use as small a hardware resource as possible while improving performance as much as possible.

At this point, we need to recognise that it is quite difficult to ever predict the outcome of *i3* based upon the previous outcome of branch instruction *i2*. It is much better to predict the future outcome of *i2* based upon the past history of *i2*, and to predict the future outcome of *i3* based upon the past history of *i3*. In other words, to somehow separate the predictions of the different instructions. In fact, this is what we will encounter starting with the bimodal predictor in Section 5.7.5. However, first we will look at using even more bits for our predictors

5.7.4 The Counter and Shift Registers as Predictors

A simple saturating counter can be incremented each time a branch is taken and decremented each time a branch is not taken. The counter saturates rather than wraps around, so that a long sequence of branches which are taken will lead to the counter hitting maximum value and staying there.

For such a counter, the branch prediction is simply the state of the most significant bit (MSB). That is effectively giving the majority, since the MSB becomes '1' once the counter is half of its maximum value or above, and is '0' when below half its maximum.

The counter is fairly simple hardware, but it can take a long time to 'learn' when switching from a normally-taken to normally-not-taken loop. In addition, it does not work well on a branch within a nested loop.

A similar-sized item of hardware is the shift register. An n-bit shift register holds the results of the past n branches. Whenever a branch instruction is resolved by the processor, the result is fed into the shift register with the contents shuffling along to accommodate it. The oldest stored value is discarded. For example, with a '1' representing a branch that was taken and a '0' representing a branch that was not taken, a shift register storing the result of the past eight branch instructions with a sequence NT, NT, NT, T, T, NT, T, NT would contain `00011010`. If another branch was then taken, the shift register would be updated to `00110101` by shifting every bit along to the left, discarding the leftmost '0' and appending the new '1' to the least significant bit position. It is possible to predict based on shift register content, however, we do not investigate either of these techniques in isolation because they are more normally used when combined together in a prediction mechanism which employs some locality. Four of these mechanisms are now discussed in turn.

5.7.5 Local Branch Predictor

A simple observation in low-level code is that some branches are almost always taken, and some are almost never taken. It seems that the global T-bit and global two-bit predictors treat all branches within a CPU in the same way. A more sensible scheme would be to predict different branches locally, rather than globally. This also relates back in some way to the principle of locality of Section 4.4.4: for example, it is reasonable to assume that the branching behaviour in library code would be different to that in user code and thus both should be predicted differently. Even within user code, different regions of a program would also naturally exhibit different branch patterns.

As mentioned previously, it would seem possible to have a T-bit predictor (or two-bit predictor) for each individual branch. However, there are potentially thousands or even millions of branch instructions in some code. The hardware needed to enable this would be quite significant.

So then perhaps there is some compromise between a single global predictor and a local predictor for each branch. This gives rise to the concept of a bank of predictors. In some ways, this mirrors the hardware arrangement of cache memory (Section 4.4), and also suffers from a similar problem: look-up time. Using such a system, whenever a branch instruction is encountered, the predictor for that branch would need to be 'looked up' and the prediction determined. With more and more predictors to be searched, the look-up time becomes longer and longer, eventually maybe even exceeding the cycle time of the pipeline. Thus, the emphasis of computer architects is actually on having fewer predictors, but making their operation more intelligent.

An arrangement of saturating branch history counters (Section 5.7.4) is shown in Figure 5.13. Instead of having one counter predictor for all branches, there are 2^{k-1} separate counter predictors, each predicting branch instructions at different addresses.

Figure 5.13

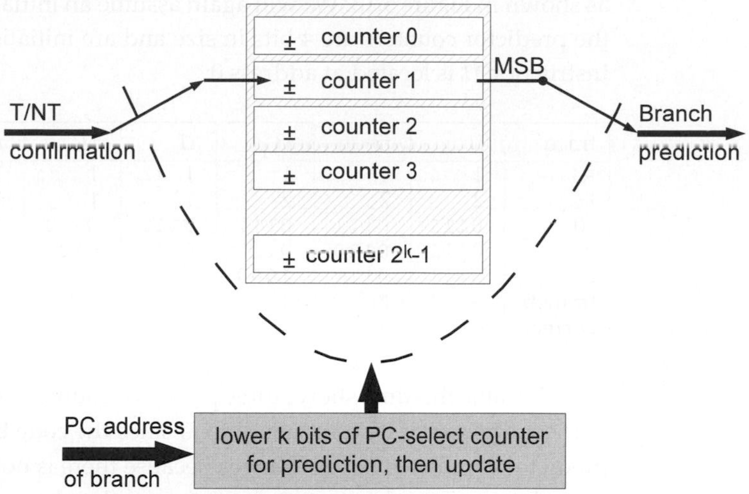

A block diagram of a local branch predictor, showing a bank of saturating branch history counters which are indexed based upon the lower bits of the address of any particular branch (thus the different counters can each map to different groups of branch instructions). The most significant bit of each counter indicates the branch prediction as explained in Section 5.7.4.

Since the lower *k* bits of the address bus[8] are used to select which counter is used for prediction (and of course which counter will later be updated by the outcome of a particular branch instruction once it is resolved), a branch located at address 0 will be predicted by counter 0, a branch located at address 1 will be predicted by counter 1 and so on. If there are only eight counters, then counter 0 would also predict branches at address 8, 16, 32, 64 and so on.

Note that the bank of predictors could instead be a bank of T-bit or bimodal predictors rather than saturating counter predictors. The important thing is that the principle of locality has been brought into play: prediction is based, at least in part, upon address location. We can illustrate the operation of this system using the code we have previously tested for the global T-bit and two-bit predictors:

i1	`loop:`	`SUBS R2, R2, R1`	; R2 = R2 – R1
i2		`BLT error`	; branch if result < 0
i3		`BGT loop`	; branch if result > 0

[8] Some processors, such as the ARM, count addresses in bytes but have instructions which are larger. In this case, since instructions are actually at addresses 0, 4, 8, 16, address-bus bits A0 and A1 will always be set to zero for any instruction in the ARM. These bits are thus ignored and the address bits used by this and subsequent local predictors begin at A2.

This time we will 'run' the code through a CPU that has a local branch predictor as shown in Figure 5.13. We will again assume an initial condition of `R2 = 3`, and that the predictor counters are 4 bits in size and are initialised to `0111` prior to execution. Instruction *i1* is located at address 0:

trace	*i1*	*i2*	*i3*	*i1*	*i2*	*i3*	*i1*	*i2*	*i3*
R1	1	1	1	1	1	1	1	1	1
R2	2	2	2	1	1	1	0	0	0
c0	**0111**	0111	0111	**0111**	0111	0111	**0111**	0111	0111
c1	0111	**0110**	0110	0110	**0101**	0101	0101	**0100**	0100
c2	0111	0111	**1000**	1000	1000	**1001**	1001	1001	**1010**
branch	–	NT	T	–	NT	T	–	NT	NT
correct	–	Y	N	–	Y	Y	–	Y	N

The table this time shows three predictor counters (c0, c1 and c2) which are mapped to the addresses of instructions *i1* to *i3* since the code begins at address 0. In this case, predictor counter c0 never changes because there is no branch instruction at address 0 to update it. The other two counters are updated as a result of the completion of the branch instructions which map to them. The predictor which is selected at each address is shown in bold font.

In each case of a branch instruction the prediction is made by examining the MSB of the corresponding prediction counter from the column before the current instruction (since as always, the columns contain the machine state *after* the respective instruction completes, but the prediction is sought *before* the instruction begins).

The performance of the predictor is rather different from that encountered previously. The first branch instruction is correctly predicted during each loop. The second branch instruction is incorrectly predicted during the first and last loops, but within the loop body – no matter how many times it repeats or how many non-branch instructions it contains – the prediction is always correct. This should be seen as a significant improvement over the case in Section 5.7.3.

Unfortunately, the story does not end here because while this predictor is quite capable, it suffers from aliasing effects as illustrated by the example in Box 5.10.

5.7.6 Global Branch Predictor

The basic global branch predictor is an attempt to improve upon the basic local branch predictor in one particular way. This is namely in the ability to introduce *context* into the branch prediction. We have already seen how the principle of locality has been brought into branch prediction, but the aliasing issue in local branch prediction has branches located in totally different types of software aliased to the same predictor.

In the global branch predictor, a global shift register is used, instead of the least significant address bits, to index into an array of counter predictors (both of these elements were briefly described separately in Section 5.7.4). The overall structure is as shown in Figure 5.14, and appears very similar to the local predictor, with the exception of the counter-select mechanism as we have discussed.

Box 5.10

Aliasing in local prediction

Let us execute the following assembly language code in a processor that has a four-entry local predictor array containing 3-bit saturating counters:

```
0x0000    loop0    DADD R1, R2, R3
0x1001             BGT loop1
0x1002             B loop2
...       ...      ...
0x1020    loop1    DSUB R3, R3, R5
0x1021             B loop0
```

We will assume that on entry `R2 = 0, R3 = 2, R5 = 1`, each of the counters c0, c1, c2, c3 is initialised to `011` and that the code exits with the branch to `loop2`.

address	outcome	branch	predictor	correct
0x0000	R1 ← 2			
0x1001		T	c1 ← 100	N
0x1020	R3 ← 1			
0x1021		T	c1 ← 101	Y
0x0000	R1 ← 1			
0x1001		T	c1 ← 110	Y
0x1020	R3 ← 0			
0x1021		T	c1 ← 111	Y
0x0000	R1 ← 0			
0x1001		NT	c1 ← 110	N
0x1002		T	c2 ← 100	Y

In this table, the address of the instruction just executed is shown in the left-most column. Next is the outcome of the instruction (i.e. whether any registers have been changed). The third column indicates, for branch instructions, whether they have been taken or not taken. Each branch outcome involves the update of a predictor counter in the next column, while the final column tallies the success of the predictor.

Overall, the prediction is fairly successful. However, the most important point to note is that only two predictor counters are used. Counter c1 has actually aliased to represent two branch instructions – at addresses `0x0001` and `0x0021` respectively. Thus, we have hardware capable of local prediction, but we are essentially not utilising it effectively. In order to more effectively 'spread' the available counters among the branches, we need to introduce some other mechanisms. Two of these are described in Sections 5.7.7 and 5.7.8.

Since the counter selected to predict a particular branch is chosen based upon the outcome of the past *k* branch instructions, this scheme is in some ways predicting a

Figure 5.14

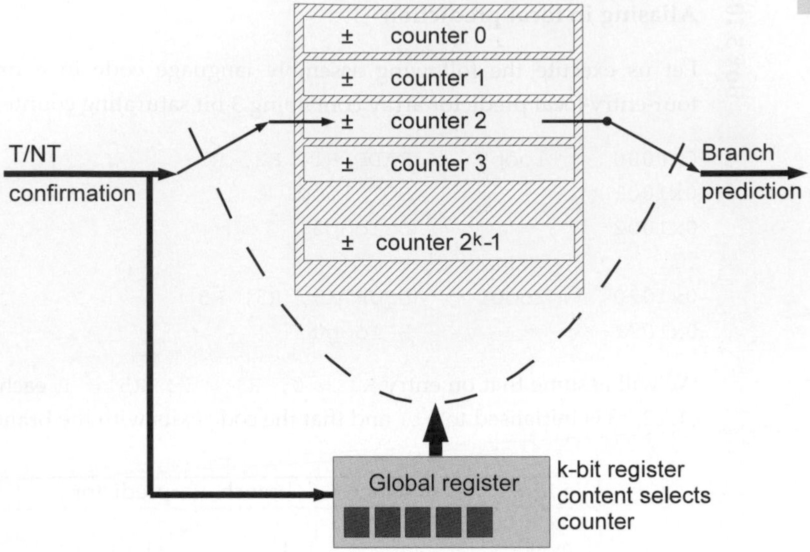

A block diagram of a global predictor, showing a bank of counters which are indexed based upon the content of a shift register which stores the outcome of the previous *k* branches. As usual, each counter increments when a branch related to it is taken and decrements when the branch is not taken. Counters saturate rather than wrap around, so that their most significant bit indicates the branch prediction. The global shift register updates after each and every branch instruction outcome is resolved.

branch based upon *how it was reached* rather than where it is located in memory. In other words, it is more like a trace-based selector.

In some circumstances, this prediction-select mechanism is obviously sensible: for example, a simple library routine can be called many times from different areas of code. How it behaves (in term of its branching behaviour) when called could naturally depend upon what it is asked to do, which in turn depends upon how it was called (and from where). The observation from examining many execution traces of common software is that some quite complex sequences of branches may be executed repetitively. Using this predictor, where the sequence of branches select the predictor, it is considered more likely that individual counters would map more closely to individual branches.

We can examine the operation of the global predictor with another simple example:

```
i1   loop1   ADD R1, R1, R2
i2           BEZ lpend
i3           SUB R8, R8, R1
i4           B loop1
i5   lpend   NOP
```

We will assume that on entry `R1 = 3, R2 = -1, R8 = 10`, and that there is a 4-bit global register (GR, initialised to `0000`), hence 16 counter predictors, each 3 bits and initialised to `011`.

address	outcome	branch	GR	predictor	correct
i1	R1 ← 2		0000		
i2		NT	0000	c0 ← 010	Y
i3	R8 ← 8		0000		
i4		T	0001	c1 ← 100	N
i1	R1 ← 1		0001		
i2		NT	0010	c2 ← 010	Y
i3	R8 ← 7		0010		
i4		T	0101	c5 ← 100	N
i1	R1 ← 0		0101		
i2		T	1011	c11 ← 100	N
i5			1011		

The construction of the above table is similar to those in previous sections, and the GR value is shown in full – there is only one GR and it is updated after every branch instruction. Although this code loops around three times, the interesting fact is that none of the branches aliases to the same counter predictor. Even the subsequent invocation of the same branch instruction has no history in this example.

In general, it shows that the aliasing problem has largely been avoided and that the branch instructions have been 'mixed up' among the counter predictors, but unfortunately the past history has been lost: we could have used that history to predict the branches at *i2* and especially *i4* very well.

It has to be said that in much larger examples than this tiny piece of code, the predictor performs quite well: figures of over 90% accuracy for large global predictors running loop-based benchmark code are not unheard of. However, the basic objection stated above remains: much of the locality information has been lost. We therefore now consider two predictors in turn that combine both the global register trace based behavioural selection with the address-based local selection.

5.7.7 The Gselect Predictor

The gselect predictor, shown in Figure 5.15, updates the global predictor by also considering the address of the branch to be predicted. In fact, the k-bit index which chooses the particular counter predictor (or T-bit or bimodal predictor) to consult for a particular branch is made up from an n-bit global register concatenated with the lowest m bits of the program counter.

For example, where $k = 10$ is made from a 4-bit global register, G, and 6 bits from the address bus, A, the 10-bit index would then be:

G_3	G_2	G_1	G_0	A_5	A_4	A_3	A_2	A_1	A_0

Figure 5.15

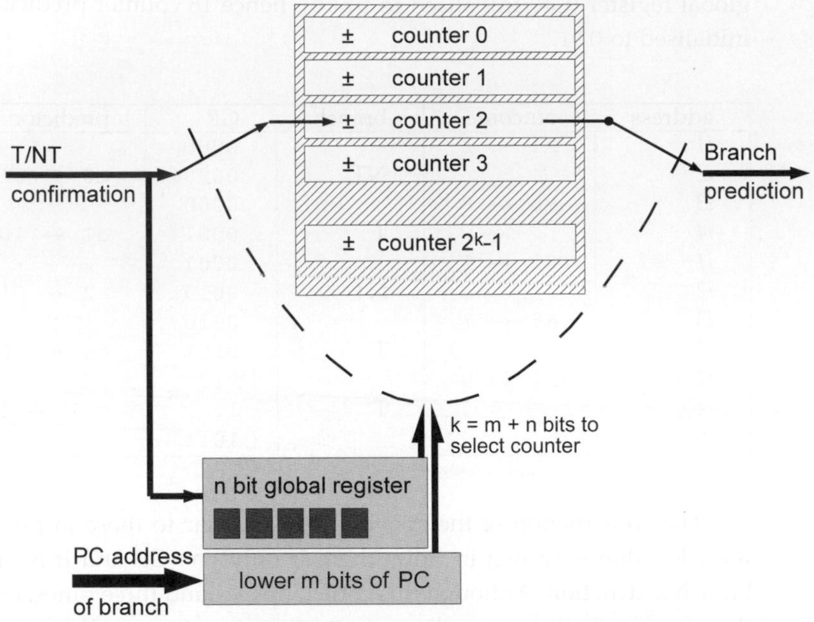

A block diagram of a gselect predictor, showing a bank of counters which are indexed based upon both the content of a shift register which stores the outcome of the previous *n* branches and also the lower *m* bits of the address bus. As usual, each counter increments when a branch related to it is taken and decrements when the branch is not taken. Counters saturate rather than wrap around, so that their most significant bit indicates the branch prediction. The global shift register updates after each and every branch instruction outcome is resolved.

Gselect is reportedly well suited for reasonably small banks of individual predictors – which probably indicates its suitability for a resource-constrained embedded system. Where the bank becomes larger, perhaps $k > 8$ the similar gshare scheme, discussed in the next section, may perform better.[9]

5.7.8 The Gshare Predictor

The gshare predictor is simply a refinement of the gselect predictor of Section 5.7.7. Compare the gselect block diagram in Figure 5.15 to that of the gshare in Figure 5.16: the only difference is that the gshare uses the exclusive-OR of a k-bit global register and the k lowest bits of the program counter to index into the array of individual predictors.

[9] Remember when discussing performance that it is highly dependent upon many factors, not least of which is the particular code that is to be executed. While we can predict performance in general, there is no substitute for actually testing out the schemes with real code.

Figure 5.16

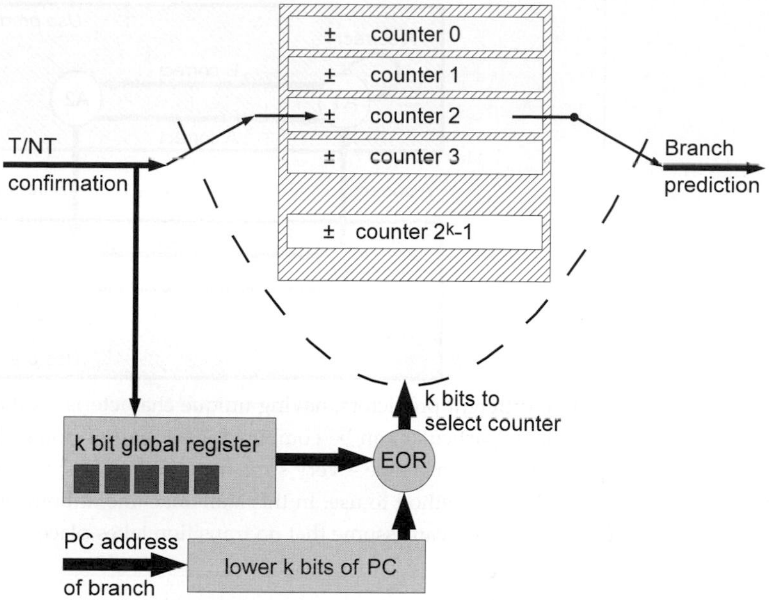

A block diagram of a gshare predictor, showing a bank of counters which are indexed based upon both the content of a shift register which stores the outcome of the previous k branches and also the lower k bits of the address bus (in this case the counter is selected as the exclusive-OR of these two k-bit values). As usual, each counter increments when a branch related to it is taken and decrements when the branch is not taken. Counters saturate rather than wrap around, so that their most significant bit indicates the branch prediction. The global shift register updates after each and every branch instruction outcome is resolved.

Gshare, like gselect and the global branch predictor can exceed 90% accuracy if correctly set up and tuned. However, the beauty of both gshare and gselect is that relatively small bank sizes can perform well. Small bank sizes (i.e. fewer individual prediction counters) means that the look-up process can be very quick. Gshare can outperform gselect in most situations apart from very small bank sizes as it does a better job of distributing branch instructions among the individual prediction counters. In other words, gshare is more likely to see an even distribution of branches to the counters whereas gselect may see just a few counters aliasing to many branch instructions.

5.7.9 Hybrid Predictors

If we pause to think about it, there is a strong likelihood that branch characteristics will probably be different for different programs. Up to now, we have presented many schemes and discussed some of their particular advantages and disadvantages.

Figure 5.17

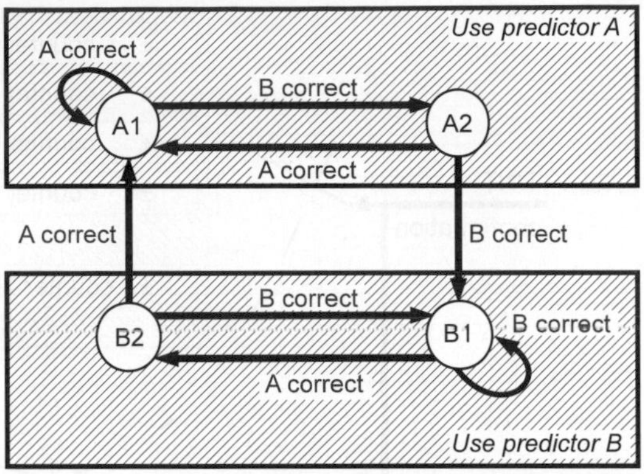

Two different predictors, having unique characteristics that suit certain types of code in particular can be combined. One way of doing that is by employing a two-bit state machine – very similar to the two-bit predictor – to select the best prediction method to use. In this state machine, if both predictors are correct in any state, we can assume that no transition takes place.

The emphasis has been on choosing a branch prediction scheme that seems to work well. However, independent testing of all of these schemes in the academic literature shows that certain types of code are more likely to work better with certain predictors. Thus, perhaps it is useful to combine predictors.

This is precisely the approach of the hybrid predictors. These allow multiple branch predictors to be created, along with logic to select the best one. A scheme for selecting between two predictors A and B is shown in Figure 5.17 (and looks rather like the bimodal predictor of Section 5.7.5). In this scheme, the A/B selector is used to keep track of the prediction accuracy of predictors A and B. Whichever predictor is most accurate will quite quickly be chosen as the overall predictor in the system.

We would expect that different programs, or even different regions within programs, would gravitate towards different predictors, and that is precisely what happens in practice.

One famous example of a hybrid predictor is found in the Alpha 21264 processor. A block diagram of this is shown in Figure 5.18. In the block diagram, an A/B predictor is shown which selects either a global predictor or a two-level local predictor.

The global predictor uses a 12-bit history of previous branches to select one of 4096 2-bit predictors. This predictor is accurate to branch behaviour. In other words, it is sensitive to *along what path* a particular branch instruction was reached (refer to Section 5.7.6).

The local predictor uses the lowest 10 bits of the address bus to select one of 1024 10-bit shift registers. This shift register is a local version of the global register. It keeps track of the history of branches occurring at the current 10-bit address. Do not be

Figure 5.18

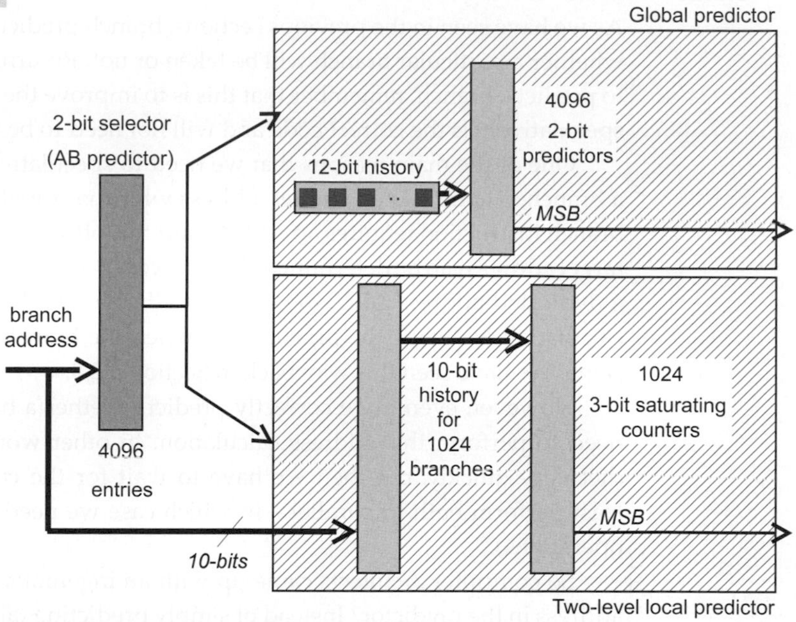

The hybrid predictor used in the Alpha 21264 processor, shown here as a block diagram, uses a state machine similar to the AB predictor of Figure 5.17 (see leftmost block) to choose between either a global predictor or a two-level local predictor, yielding excellent prediction performance.

confused that both the address and the shift register size are 10 bits, they could have been different sizes.

This local shift register value is then used to choose one of 1024 3-bit saturating counters: individual prediction counters. The prediction value is the MSB of those counters.

The predictor in the Alpha 21264 uses both a multi-level structure (for local prediction) and a dynamic selection between two very different predictors. It would seem to ally almost all of the prediction elements discussed up to now.

However, we need to ask how well this performs. Given that a limited amount of hardware within a CPU can be 'spent' on branch prediction, it is appropriate to wonder whether this amount of hardware would be better spent on one type of predictor or on another type – or even on improving some other aspect of the pipeline.

In this case, that question was answered for us back in 1993, the year that the Digital Equipment Corporation (DEC) Alpha 21264 CPU branch prediction unit was being designed. Tests indicated that this hybrid approach outperformed both an equivalent-sized global predictor and an equivalent-sized local predictor. In fact, the branch prediction accuracy of this processor is an amazing 98% on real-world code – a figure that is hard to beat even in the most modern CPUs.

5.7.10 Branch Target Buffer

As we have seen in the previous sections, branch predictors can quite accurately know whether a particular branch will be taken or not. Returning to the reasons for wanting to predict a branch, remember that this is to improve the chance that the code executed speculatively is the correct code and will not need to be flushed from the pipeline.

One of the main reasons that we need to speculatively execute code is that when a branch is to be taken, a target address which is stored as a relative offset within the branch instruction requires an ALU to add this offset to the program counter before the target address can be determined. This process needs an ALU, and in a machine without a dedicated address ALU, the only time the shared ALU is available for the address calculation is during the pipeline slot when the branch instruction is in the 'execute' stage. We have seen this way back in Section 5.2.8.

However, even if we correctly predict whether a branch is taken or not, we still need to perform this address calculation. In other words, we might be able to predict very quickly, but then we have to wait for the calculation to take place (or at least perform both in parallel – in which case we need to wait for the slowest of the operations).

So computer architects came up with an ingenious idea: why not store the target address in the predictor? Instead of simply predicting take/don't take, why not predict the entire target address? After all, there is only one place a branch instruction can branch to, and if we are storing a history of branch behaviour, we could easily store the branch target address at the same time.

This is what a branch target buffer (BTB) does.

Using a BTB means we do not have to wait for the branch target address computation in the ALU if we predict right and have executed the current branch at least

Figure 5.19

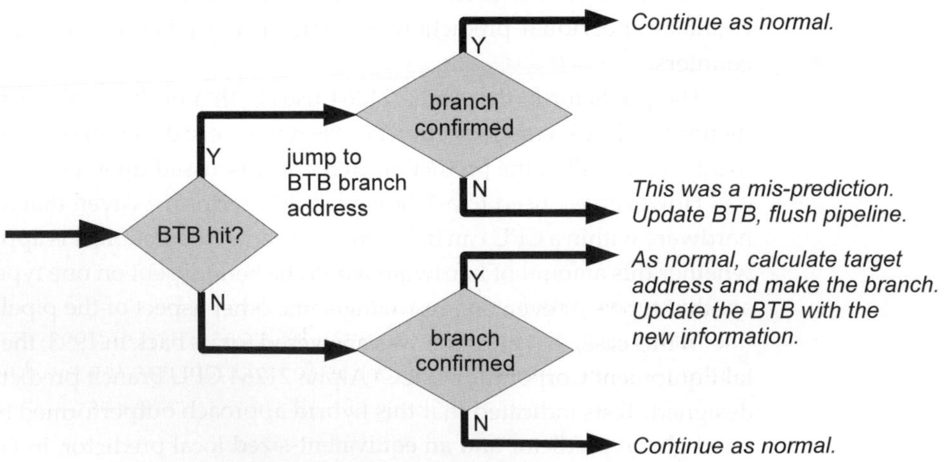
Continue as normal.
Y
branch confirmed
Y
jump to BTB branch address
N
This was a mis-prediction. Update BTB, flush pipeline.
BTB hit?
As normal, calculate target address and make the branch. Update the BTB with the new information.
Y
N
branch confirmed
N
Continue as normal.

A simple flowchart illustrating the operation of a branch target buffer (BTB).

Figure 5.20

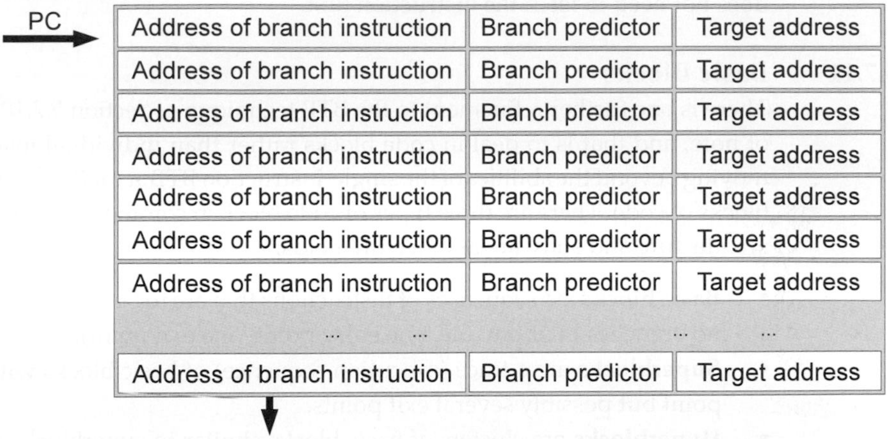

The branch target buffer is organised in a similar way to cache memory and in fact, performs a similar function of reducing the average access time of instructions contained within it.

once before. The decision flowchart within the BTB is given in Figure 5.19. If we need to execute a branch prediction, we first consult the BTB. If we get a BTB hit (i.e. this branch instruction has an entry in the BTB, meaning we have 'seen' it previously), then we simply load the BTB target address into the program counter and begin executing from that address, speculatively.

As soon as the branch is resolved (immediately for an unconditional branch or after the condition-setting instruction has completed for a conditional branch), we know whether to continue with the speculation or to flush the pipeline, update the BTB and fetch the correct instruction.

If we did not have a BTB hit then we speculate 'not taken'. Once the branch has been resolved, if it should have been taken, we update the BTB with the branch target address, flush the pipeline if we have speculated, and then jump to the correct address to continue execution.

In actual fact, the contents of the BTB, shown in Figure 5.20, appear very similar to a cache memory (Section 4.4) with a tag made up from the branch instruction address, an entry to store the branch prediction (using any of the prediction algorithms that we have presented so far) and the target address. Like a cache, the BTB can be full-associative, set-associative or employ more exotic associativity schemes.

However, this is not the end of the story regarding the BTB. There is one further innovation to note: consider what happens when the CPU branches to the target address – it then loads the instruction found there into the pipeline. Around the time that it finishes decoding and executing that instruction, the previous branch will have been resolved so this instruction is either kept or flushed.

But we can speed this process up a little further by storing the actual target *instruction* in the BTB rather than the address of the target instruction. The pipeline then speculates on a BTB hit by loading that stored *instruction* directly into the pipeline. It does not need to fetch the instruction first.

5.7.11 Basic Blocks

There is one further refinement to the BTB technique of Section 5.7.10 which is worthy of note, and that is to deal in code blocks rather than individual instructions. In fact, moving beyond the abilities of the single-instruction BTB actually requires us to work on blocks of code. There are three types of code block in common use within the computer architecture and software architecture fields:

- **Basic blocks** are sequences of instructions that are to be executed sequentially with no branches in or out. (i.e. one entry point, one exit point).
- **Superblocks** are a trace (execution sequence) of basic blocks with only one entry point but possibly several exit points.
- **Hyperblocks** are clusters of basic blocks similar to superblocks in that they have only one entry point, but possibly more exit points. Hyperblocks differ in that they can contain several trace paths (i.e. more than a single control path).

In this text, we will confine our discussion to the simplest of these, basic blocks, as applied within block-based BTB schemes. Imagine a BTB, or even a memory cache, that stores and can feed, blocks of code into the pipeline. For a pipeline able to re-order or execute out-of-order, this allows for maximum flexibility and yields an excellent performance improvement.

Basic blocks are easily formed as the string of instructions between branches and branch targets, and a program trace can identify which path is traversed through a connected graph of basic blocks. An example path through a set of basic blocks is shown in Figure 5.21.

At first we saw how to predict branches as taken/not taken. Next, we predicted branch target address. Then we predicted the branch target instruction. Now we can predict basic block sequences.

Recurring and frequent sequences of basic blocks are identified, and hopefully cached so we can very quickly issue the instructions. For example, with reference to Figure 5.21, a block-BTB could directly issue the instructions contained within B1, B2, B5 and B6 into a pipeline with no branching necessary – assuming we have correctly predicted the trace path through the blocks.

Of course, we still need to check that the branches are correct and flush the pipeline if we get a prediction wrong. In real code, there may be several basic blocks (BB) involved, each potentially containing several tens of instructions (the average BB size is approximately seven instructions, but of course varies widely based upon the computation being performed, the processor and the compiler).

The trace cache is updated over time and whenever the CPU hits the root BB (B1), a branch prediction algorithm predicts the ongoing path. If this matches the second entry in the trace cache (B2) then this is a hit and the CPU starts to follow the basic block contents from the trace prediction (which themselves can be cached).

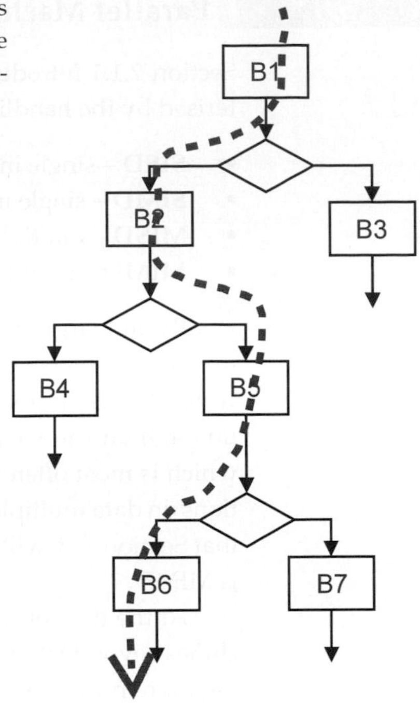

Figure 5.21 A set of interconnected basic blocks (lines of code in between branches) are traversed during execution of a program.

This system was in fact used in the Pentium 4, but with the additional feature that instead of caching the BB instruction contents, it caches the already-decoded instructions themselves, that is, not only can we bypass the pipeline 'fetch' stage, we can also bypass the 'decode' stage.

5.7.12 Branch Prediction Summary

An enormous amount of effort has been spent on trying to keep a hungry pipeline continually 'fed' with instructions to process.

All of this effort on branch prediction, speculation and so on is about making sure instructions are issued at as fast a rate as possible. Pipelining and instruction level parallelism are means of making sure that instructions get executed in as fast and efficient a manner as possible.

We should note that no single performance refinement method alone is supreme. For maximum performance a pragmatic selection of these techniques working in well-tuned harmony is the ideal.

One more caveat is that few hardware speed-ups can make up for a poor compiler,[10] and conversely effort spent in creating a good compiler can provide more benefit than some of the speed-up techniques alone.

[10] The author recommends and uses GCC, the GNU Compiler Collection, himself.

5.8 Parallel Machines

Section 2.1.1 introduced Flynn's classification of processors into four groups characterised by the handling of instructions and data, namely;

- **SISD** – single instruction, single data.
- **SIMD** – single instruction, multiple data.
- **MISD** – multiple instruction, single data.
- **MIMD** – multiple instruction, multiple data.

By and large, up to this point we have considered only SISD machines – the single microprocessors typically found in embedded systems and traditional desktop hardware. We also introduced some elements of SIMD found in MMX and SSE units (Section 4.5) and in some ARM-specific co-processors (Section 4.8). We will skip MISD, which is most often used in fault-tolerant systems such as those that perform calculations on data multiple times, and compare the results from each calculation – something that Section 7.10 will discuss more thoroughly. So the next form to consider after SIMD is MIMD.

At the time of writing, current trends in the processor industry are to extend machines beyond SISD, through SIMD and on to MIMD. MIMD machines are thus becoming more prevalent. We already discussed some common co-processors in Section 4.5, where a main CPU is augmented by an external functional unit capable of performing various specialised functions. Here, we take matters one step further and consider the case of identical processors working together, in parallel, in an MIMD arrangement.

Actually there are several levels of parallelism that can be considered in computers, since the term 'parallel machines' is very loosely defined. Let us briefly run through the scale of these levels:

- **Bit-level parallelism** relates to the size of word that a computer processes. An 8-bit computer processes 8 bits in parallel, but four times as much data can potentially be handled in a 32-bit machine through multiplying the word size four times.
- **Instruction level parallelism** – is a set of techniques that allow multiple instructions to be executed at the same time. As we have seen in many cases, different instructions can be overlapped and processed simultaneously, provided there are no data dependencies between them. Pipelining is a simple example, but superscalar machines, co-processors and Tomasulo's algorithm (Section 5.9) are others.
- **Vector parallelism** relates to SIMD machines that process not just single words of data, but entire vectors at one time. SSE and MMX are examples of this type of parallelism.
- **Task parallelism** means that entire tasks, or program subroutines and functions, can be executed simultaneously by different hardware. We will discuss this throughout this section.

- **Machine parallelism** describes the huge *server farms* used by companies such as Google and Amazon. These are buildings containing hundreds or even thousands of separate computers, each operating towards a certain computational goal, in parallel. We will consider this type of system in Section 9.3.

Each of these levels of parallelism is illustrated diagrammatically in Figure 5.22, showing the encapsulation of bitwise manipulation by instructions into higher and higher levels of parallel activity.

In a discussion of parallel processing it is also useful to distinguish the characteristics of what needs to be processed in terms of 'coupling'. *Loosely coupled* parallel processing means that different parallel threads of execution have few dependencies, and can largely be executed independently. These are very easy to operate in parallel – independent processor cores can handle each task separately. An example might be two different Google search requests, from two independent users, running on two machines in a Google server farm. On the other hand, *tightly coupled* tasks are very interdependent. They may need to share data, communicate frequently and have situations where one task is dependent upon input from the other task. It would be better to run these tasks on the same machine so that communications between the tasks does not become a bottleneck to performance. Naturally, machine architectures can then be either loosely or tightly (closely) coupled to match these tasks.

In terms of computer architecture, the more relevant forms of parallelism are those towards the top of the list given previously. We have already touched upon most of the categories shown and will consider large-scale machine parallelism further in Section 9.3, but for now let us turn our attention to the middle ground – task parallelism. This is higher level than superscalar and vector approaches, but lower level than machine parallelism. It is of growing importance to the architecture of desktop-sized computers and likely to be similarly influential in the field of embedded computer architecture, in the years to come.

There are two major motivations for parallelism which we will discuss in turn. The first is due to the gradual evolution of SISD machines with additional functional units into true MIMD parallel machines. The second is the deliberate adoption of parallelism for reasons of improving raw performance. We will explain both motivations in the following subsections.

5.8.1 Evolution of SISD to MIMD

SISD machines are easy to write programs for – from a programmer's perspective there is usually only one thing happening at any time, and programs execute sequentially, following whatever branches are to be taken. In the early days of stored-program computers this was precisely what the designers required of a computer: load today's program and execute it. Tomorrow they would load a different program and execute that. Switching from one task to another might involve replacing a stack of punched cards.

However, in the decades during which computers have started to find widespread acceptance, software has progressed from predominantly calculation-based operations

Figure 5.22

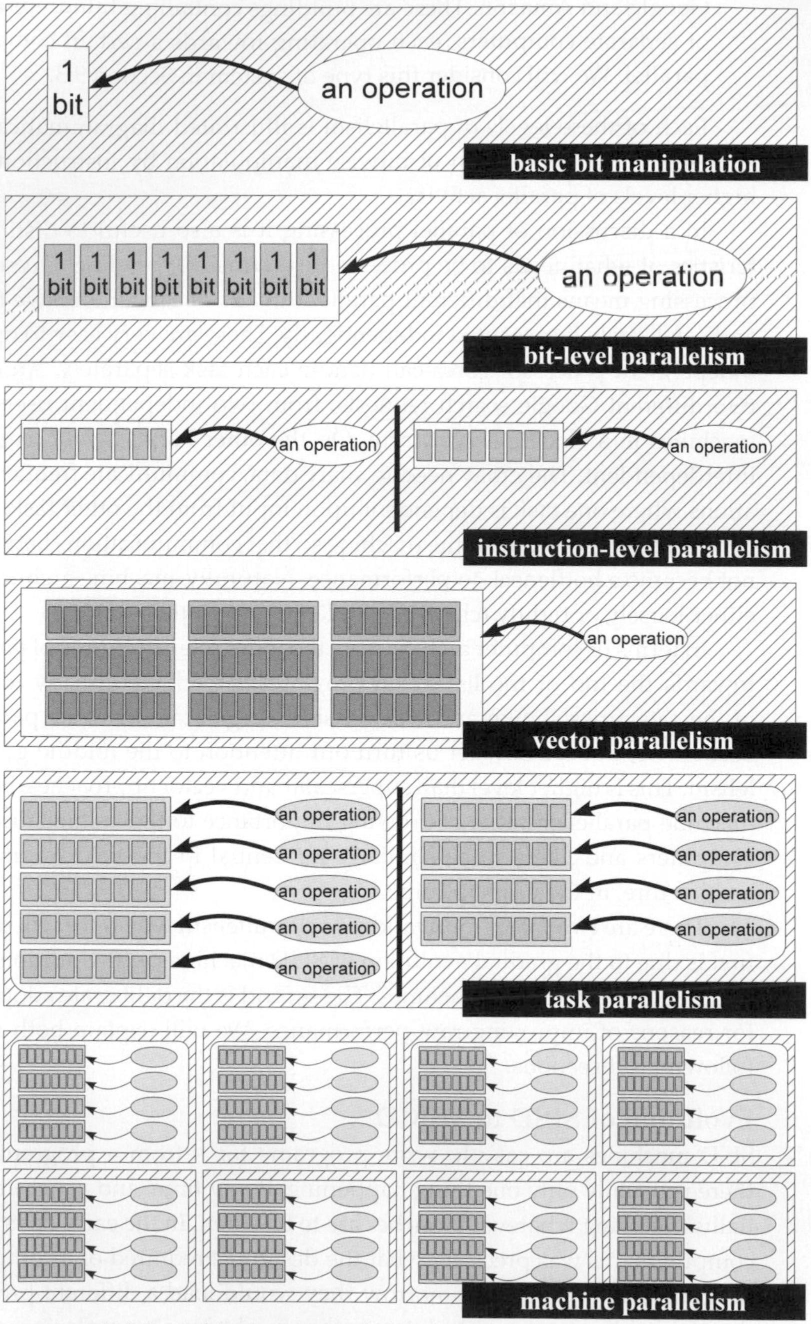

Starting with basic bitwise manipulation, higher and higher levels of parallelism are achieved by encapsulating and repeating the basic operations in parallel.

(accounting, simulation, mathematical formulae), through control (monitoring sensors and adjusting actuators in machinery) towards complex multi-tasking, often involving multi-sensory and immersive human-computer interfacing.

Where once computers were expected to fulfil a single task at any one time, today's machines (desktop *and* embedded) are almost always required to handle multiple concurrent tasks. Such different tasks often imply a range of timing and operating requirements. Section 6.4 will introduce and discuss tasks from a real-time software perspective, but here it is necessary to appreciate that software often requires different sections of code to be executed at different times. Each piece of code can be encapsulated into a separate task, and thus different tasks, performing different functions, can run on the same computer at different times.

Often, these tasks will have strongly individual characteristics and there may even be conflicting requirements between tasks.

In general, when faced with two (or more) conflicting requirements, system architects often respond by partitioning a system – with separate sections of hardware and software dedicated to fulfilling different requirements. The partitioning is almost always done in software: two tasks handle different processing aspects, but share the same CPU. However, the hardware may also be partitioned whereby two processors each handle one task.

A simple example to illustrate conflicting requirements would be a desktop machine running a mouse-controlled windowing desktop display, simultaneously with an MP3 playback system. In this scenario, the MP3 playback requires some mathematical processing and handling of streams of audio. The important requirement here is that individual samples of audio are output on time. Any delay in a sample being output will create a 'click' or maybe even more annoying sounds. A system designer, realising this, may grant the MP3 playback task a high CPU priority so it runs frequently and is seldom waiting for other tasks to finish. Unfortunately the user, controlling the MP3 playback with a mouse, might then find that the mouse pointer movements are not smooth. The solution may well be to make the mouse pointer priority higher than the MP3 priority, or better still, to employ a system capable of adjusting priority dynamically.

There is however a third option: the use of an MIMD machine which allows a single hardware device to contain two (or more) separate streams/tasks of instruction and data and execute these simultaneously. There is no longer any need to time-share on a single processor, but two processors inside the same device, with shared memory and peripherals, can effectively partition tasks.

The hardware choices are illustrated in Figure 5.23 which shows a basic SISD processor, a shared memory MIMD machine and an intermediate form capable of SIMD processing. This basic SISD machine has an ALU, multiplier, I/O block, memory unit, control unit and an instruction fetch/decode unit (IU). A bank of four registers hangs off an internal three-bus arrangement. Given two software tasks, each would have to time-slice, running on the same hardware. In Figure 5.23 (b), extra functional units have been added to the processor for the transition to an SIMD machine where calculations

Figure 5.23

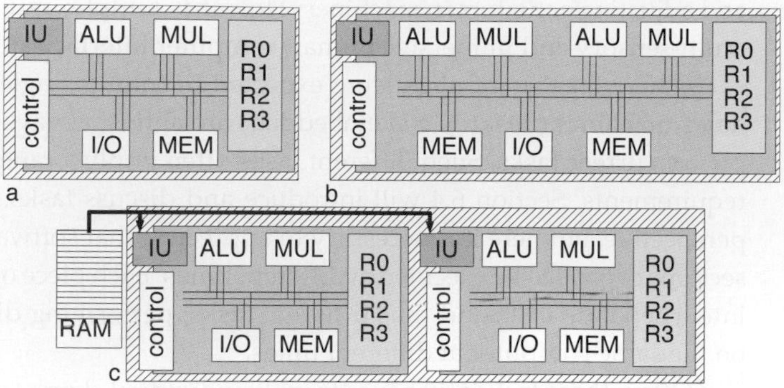

Block diagrams of (a) a basic SISD processor comprising four functional units (ALU, multiplier, I/O block and memory unit), a control unit and an instruction fetch/decode unit (IU) augmented by a bank of registers. In diagram (b), there are extra functional units shown, moving towards an SIMD machine. In diagram (c), a full shared memory MIMD machine is shown containing two complete processors on a single chip.

could potentially be performed in parallel – and which might allow two tasks to be merged together in software. However, this machine has a clear bottleneck in the internal bus arrangement, given that these have not been upgraded from the SISD system. In diagram (c) where a shared memory MIMD machine is illustrated, each individual CPU has an independent internal bus system, allowing for true parallelism. This comprises essentially two complete processors on a single chip. However, the bottleneck in this case would probably be accesses to shared external memory.

As software fragments further into separate threads and designers reach limits of ever-increasing clock speed, data width and so on, the next logical performance improvement is towards increasing parallelism – SISD to SIMD and thence to MIMD.

In the world of embedded computing, one prominent recent addition to the expanding line-up of dual-core solutions is the ARM946 Dual Core Platform (DCP). This is based upon two ARM9 processor cores integrated onto a single chip with shared-memory interfaces and an on-chip communications interface. Figure 5.24 shows a block diagram of the device architecture.

This device is advertised as being a loosely-coupled, pre-integrated dual-core architecture supported by simultaneous debug and program trace in hardware. A large amount of software and firmware is available that is compatible with the system, and operating systems support is readily available for the ARM9. Such support in software would typically include the ability to execute different software threads (tasks) in parallel on the two processing cores, arbitrating between these through the hardware communications port (labelled 'comms' in the figure).

Figure 5.24

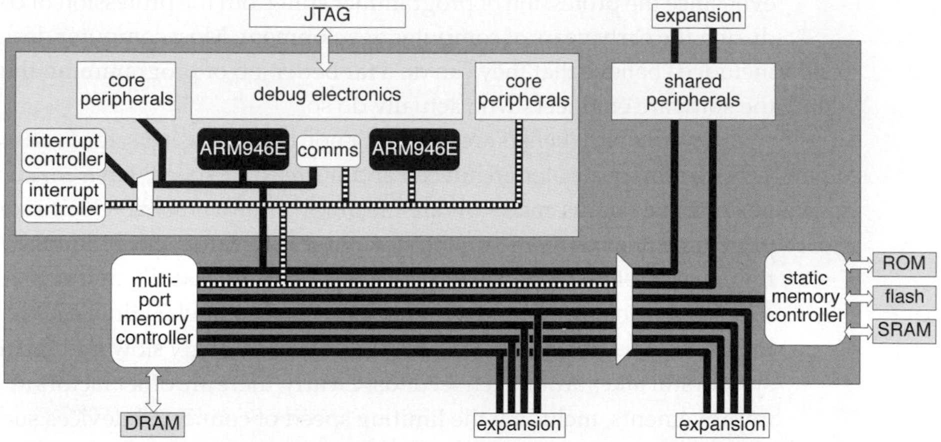

A block diagram of the ARM946 Dual Core Platform.

Although the ARM946 device is being discussed in a section devoted to parallel processing, it is better characterised as a dual-core device rather than a parallel machine. Two processor cores are much easier to synchronise than multiple independent units, and in this case most of the core peripheral devices are simply replicated twice. At the time of writing, a quad-core Cortex-A9 is nearing release. This is yet another step in the direction of embedded parallel processing.

Since these devices are undoubtedly targeted at embedded products, one possible partitioning of a system would be user interface code running on one processor, being triggered as and when necessary by user intervention, and media processing (with critical timing requirements) running on the second processor. Or perhaps MP3 decoding on one processor, and wireless Ethernet processing on the other one, for a wireless LAN-based audio device.

Whatever the application, dual-core devices such as these are currently becoming more popular. They look set to create and occupy a significant niche in the world-wide processor market. Most likely, greater numbers of cores will be clustered together in future, and this is due to the continual and perceived ongoing need for increased performance.

5.8.2 Parallelism for Raw Performance

We have already mentioned the pressure on computer designers to increase performance. The well-known Moore's law has passed into the public consciousness so well that consumers expect ever-increasing power from their computers, and consequently from their computer-powered devices.

Perhaps more concerning is that *software* writers have also learnt to expect that computer power (and memory size) will continue to grow year-on-year. It is traditional for computer architects to direct some blame towards programmers – and has been ever since the profession of programmer split from the profession of computer designer during the early years of computer development. Most computer designers (the author included) believe that they can do a far better job of programming their machines than the software engineers who actually do so.

Whether such beliefs are tenable or not, the increasing size of software (often known as 'bloat' by computer architects) and decreasing speed, have consumed much of the performance gains made by architectural improvements, clock rate increase, clever pipelining techniques and so on. A typical desktop machine of 2009 has a speed[11] that is at least 50 times faster than the computer that the author was using a decade ago. Unfortunately, the current machine does not feel 50 times faster – web pages still load slowly, saving and loading files is still annoyingly slow and booting the operating system still takes around ten seconds. Clearly, there are other factors at work beside CPU improvements, including the limiting speed of connected devices such as the Internet, hard discs and so on. Software-wise there is nothing major that the current computer can do that the old one could not, and yet the operating system has bloated out from being tens of mebibytes to over 1 gibibyte.

This is not to apportion blame on software developers, it is simply to state the fact that software has increased in size and complexity over the years: running much of today's software on a decade-old computer is unthinkable and in many cases would be impossible.

From a position where software grew in step with increases in computer speed and processing capacities, we now have the situation where it is the software itself that is the driving factor for increased computer speed.

Whatever the reasons and driving factors, manufacturers do feel significant pressure to continue increasing performance. This has driven many responses such as increasing clock speed, increasing IPC and so on (see Section 5.5.1). Unfortunately, it is becoming increasingly difficult for manufacturers to improve performance using these means alone. It takes more and more effort and complexity to see performance increase by smaller and smaller amounts. Manufacturers have therefore turned to parallelism to increase performance. It is much easier to design a relatively simple processor and then repeat this 16 times on a single integrated circuit (IC) than it is to design a single processor using all of the resources on that IC that is 16 times faster. It is also easier to use two existing processors in parallel than it is to build a single new processor that executes twice as fast as an existing one.

In theory, having more processors or execution units running in parallel will speed up computation, but only if that computation is inherently able to be executed in parallel pieces. Given m parallel tasks, each requiring T_m seconds to execute, a single CPU will execute these in $m \times T_m$ seconds.

[11]Speed in this case is measured by the execution rate of a simple code loop – namely the infamous Linux bogomips rating of Section 3.5.2.

Where there are more tasks than execution units, n, so that $m > n$ then these tasks will be executed in T_m seconds. Thus, the speed-up achieved is $\{m \times T_m\}/\{T_m\} = m$ times a single execution unit which is called *perfect speed-up*. Of course, this equation does not account for message passing overheads or operating system support needed for parallel processing. It also assumes there are no data dependencies between tasks.

In general, for a program comprising a fraction f of parallel tasks and taking T_p seconds to execute sequentially, sequential tasks require a time of $f \times T_p$ and parallel tasks a time of $(1 - f) \times T_p$. Assuming no overhead, parallel execution using m execution units would thus mean the total time is reduced to $(1 - f) \times T_p/m + f \times T_p$, as speed-up equals original execution time divided by the parallel execution time:

$$speed\text{-}up = n/\{1 + (m - 1) \times f\}$$

When $f = 0$ (i.e. there is no sequential component) the result indicates perfect speed-up as before. The relationship shown, between a speed-up calculation and the number of processors is known as Amdahl's law and indicates the potential gains achievable through parallel processing.

5.8.3 More on Parallel Processing

Symmetrical multi-processing (SMP) systems are those that have two or more identical processing elements connected to a block of shared memory. There are many variations on this theme, including shared cache, individual cache (which may well use the MESI cache coherency protocol – see Section 4.4.7) and so on. The alternative is asymmetrical multi-processing, a term which is not really in such common use, but could refer to something as simple as a co-processor. One of the more common SMP systems, up to quad core at the time of writing, is Intel's Core architecture. The Core 2 duo dual core is shown in Figure 5.25 where its symmetrical nature should be immediately apparent, as is the central role of shared memory (specifically L2 cache) in this architecture.

Multi-core machines combine two or more processing elements (usually entire CPUs) onto a single integrated circuit (IC). Some dual core or quad-core ICs advertised as multi-core machines actually contain two separate silicon dies within a single IC package (this makes it a multi-chip module or MCM). As the number of cores increases, at some point the device can be referred to as a *many-core* machine. It is relatively easy for designers to build both multi-core and many-core machines using soft cores within an FPGA (refer to Chapter 8 for an example of this).

Homogeneous architectures are those in which all cores within a machine are identical. In many ways, this is easier to design and program for. However, sometimes *heterogeneous* architectures are more promising – these are machines comprising one or more different cores. They allow cores to be included which can specialise in different types of processing. Most smartphones currently contain a heterogeneous OMAP processor from Texas Instruments: comprising a fast ARM core and an even faster DSP.

Figure 5.25

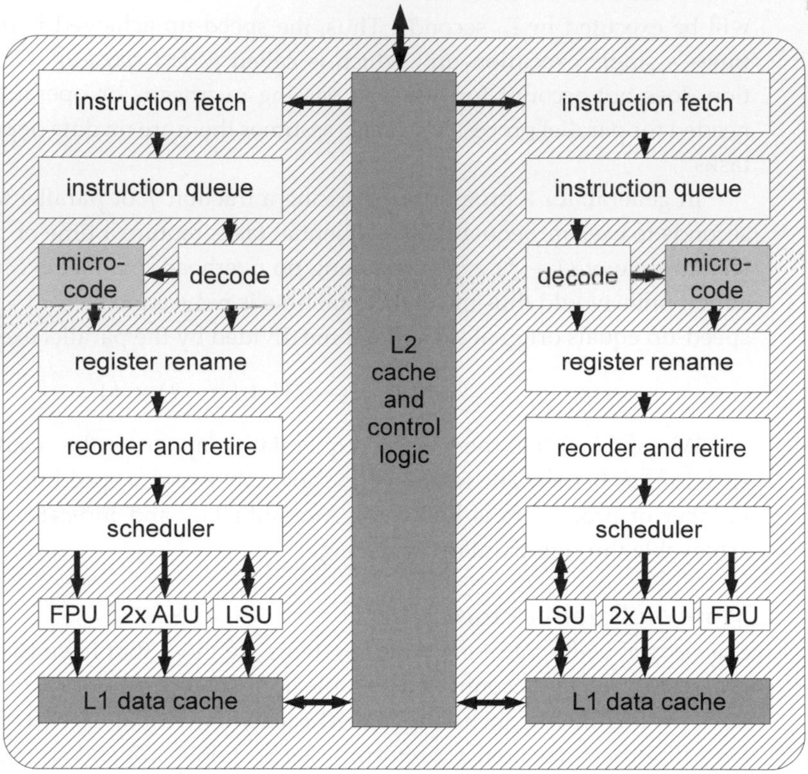

A block diagram of the internals of the Intel Core architecture, showing a symmetrical two-core device with two identical processing units (including the full superscalar pipelines, instruction handling hardware and so on), sharing a level 2 cache which connects outwards to the system bus.

However, one of the neatest examples of a heterogeneous multi-core machine is the Cell processor from IBM, Sony and Toshiba. This processor, which powers several supercomputers and (arguably of more world impact) the millions of Sony Playstation III consoles worldwide, is a remarkable example of combining the power of several unremarkable processors into a remarkable multi-core processor.

The Cell (actually more properly known as the Cell Broadband Engine Architecture), is shown diagrammatically in Figures 5.26 and 5.27.

The Cell processor consists of eight identical and fairly simple, SIMD architecture processors called synergistic processing elements (SPE), augmented with one IBM Power Architecture power processing element (PPE), which is very similar to an off-the-shelf IBM PowerPC RISC processor. The eight SPEs are basic number crunchers controlled by the PPE, which will probably host an operating system.

In itself the Cell processor is not at all appropriate for many embedded systems due to its size, power consumption and thermal dissipation, although it does

Figure 5.26

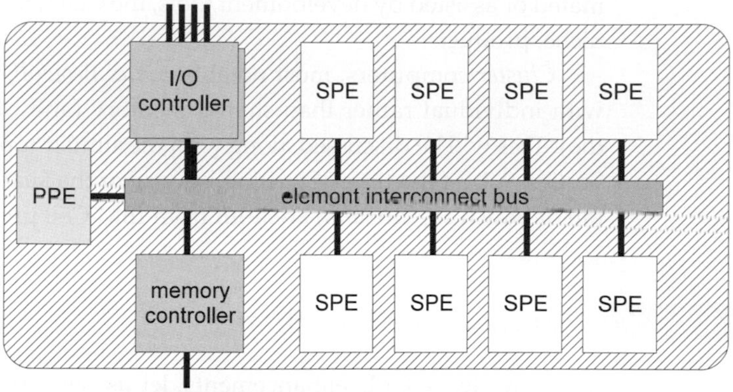

A block diagram of the Cell Broadband Engine Architecture, showing eight synergistic processing elements (SPE) hanging off an element interconnect bus (EIB), along with the obligatory memory and I/O interfaces, plus a single IBM Power Architecture power processing element (PPE).

Figure 5.27

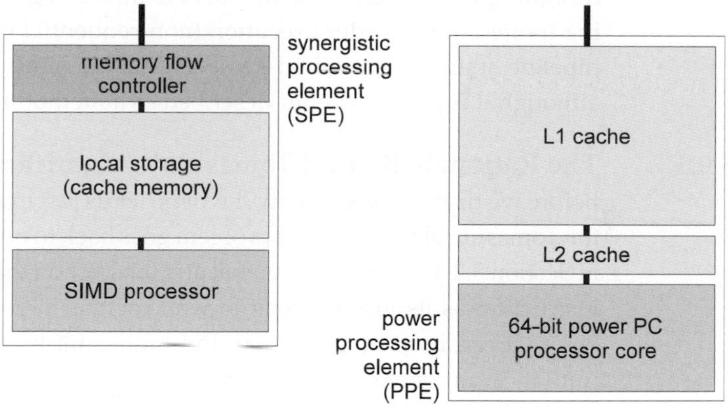

A look inside the PPE and one of the SPEs from the Cell Broadband Engine Architecture processor, showing the important position of local memory/cache in the design.

represent an interesting approach to computer architecture that is likely to make future inroads into the embedded world. Apart from physical and electrical factors, it has also become apparent that the development tools available for the creation of applications on the heterogeneous Cell processor have hindered its adoption. It has been reported that much of the software running on the SPEs has to be hand-coded, the partitioning process between SPEs and PPE, and indeed between the individual SPEs also requires the application of human ingenuity. Until these activities can be better automated or assisted by development tools, the Cell will probably remain an attractive, but niche, product.

Cluster computers, most notably *Linux Beowulf*, comprise entire computers, each with individual rather than shared memory (and often individual hard disc storage too). This will be discussed along with the similar topics of *grid* and *cloud* computing in Section 9.3. At the time of writing, several of the fastest supercomputers in the world[12] (all of which are clusters) are built from IBM Cell processors.

5.9 Tomasulo's Algorithm

Before we leave CPU enhancements, let us wind the clock back a little more than 40 years to an innovation found in the IBM System/360. Although we have constantly stressed the evolutionary development of computer technology throughout this book, we have acknowledged the occasional revolutionary idea. Tomasulo's algorithm is one of those, and one which may have relevance to embedded systems (as we will discuss in Section 5.9.3).

Robert Tomasulo was faced with performance limitations of instruction dependencies stalling programs running in the floating point co-processor unit that he was designing for the IBM System/360. He thus designed an ingenious method of allowing limited out-of-order execution (non-sequential execution) to help 'unblock' many pipeline stalls. This method has been known since then as the Tomasulo algorithm, although it is perhaps better described as a method rather than an algorithm.

5.9.1 The Rationale Behind Tomasulo's Algorithm

Before we discuss exactly how it works, let us just examine the need for something like the Tomasulo algorithm. The problem goes back to our discussion of data dependencies in Section 5.2.4, where we saw that any instruction that uses the output from a previous instruction as its input, needs to wait for that previous instruction to be completed before it can itself be processed. Put more simply, an instruction cannot be executed until its input operands are available.

We have seen how one of the compile-time remedies (Section 5.2.7) to the problem is to re-order instructions, so that neighbouring instructions, as far as possible, have no dependencies. Another method is to allow out-of-order execution, so that the CPU, rather than simply waiting for a dependency to clear, takes a future, unrelated instruction and executes that instead. This allows the CPU to remain busy by executing some future instructions without unmet dependencies (if any are available). For this, of course, the CPU needs to fetch ahead of the current instruction. This is a very strong motivator behind having good branch prediction/speculative execution because otherwise the

[12]The latest list of the world's fastest machines, updated every six months, can be viewed at `www.top500.org`

processor cannot fetch beyond a conditional branch and re-ordering would be limited to small segments of code between branches.

Tomasulo got around these problems by allowing instructions to be 'issued' from the instruction queue with unresolved operands, in this case called *virtual operands*, instead of waiting for them to be resolved. These instructions will proceed to reservation stations (depending upon the functional unit they are destined for), where they wait until the virtual operands are resolved before being handled by their functional unit. This means that the instruction queue is not blocked by each and every data hazard, although some persistent hazards could still block the issuing of instructions.

It is interesting to compare this approach to advances in the healthcare industry. Twenty years ago, patients arriving at a hospital would wait in a large room for a doctor to become available, sometimes for several hours. A doctor would then see them and often specify additional investigations, such as blood tests. While these were being undertaken the patients would remain in the waiting room until the test results returned and they could finally proceed to see a specialist.

Today, the procedure is normally for all patients coming into hospital (the instruction queue) to be seen quite quickly by a triage nurse who then decides where to send the patients. Patients are directed to smaller specialist clinics with their own waiting rooms (reservation stations). They may have blood or urine tests performed, waiting until these test results are available and the specialist doctor is free before entering the consultation room (functional unit).

5.9.2 An Example Tomasulo System

We will now examine a Tomasulo method processor. A Tomasulo-style arrangement for a dynamically scheduled machine with common data bus is considered with reference to Figure 5.28. Separate reservation stations (RS) handle the various functional units: four are shown. These are fed from an instruction queue (IQ) and all are connected to various buses and banks of registers (one register bank is for integer values and one for floating point values).

First, let us examine how this system works. Initially, IQ contains a sequence, or string of instructions which would normally be issued to functional units in the sequence in which they are listed. Each instruction consists of an opcode plus one or more operands. The IQ issues instructions, in sequence, to empty slots in the appropriate RS. For example, an *ADD.D* instruction (double-precision addition) would be issued by the IQ to the RS feeding the FP ALU unit. If the appropriate destination RS is full, then the instruction queue stalls for that cycle and does not issue anything.

Evidently the size or depth of each RS is a design parameter in such systems. The ideal situation is to maintain several slots free in the RS, such that the IQ can issue instructions into one of those slots.

When the IQ issues an instruction (i.e. the opcode plus the operands, if any), it checks for dependencies among the operands. It checks if the instruction being issued requires any operand from prior instructions that have not yet executed, in other words,

Figure 5.28

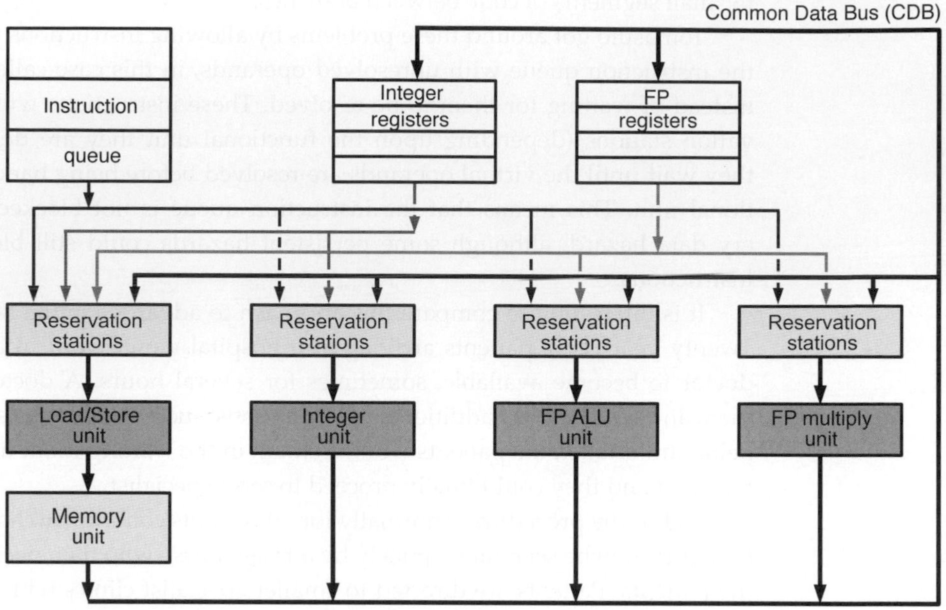

A block diagram of a general CPU structure implementing the Tomasulo algorithm, showing an instruction queue at the top left feeding instructions to four reservation stations each dedicated to a functional unit via several dedicated buses. Two register banks and a common data bus (CDB) feed operands into the functional units. The outputs of all functional units are also connected to the CDB, as are the register banks.

for unresolved data dependencies. If a dependency does exist, the instruction is issued to the RS, but with a 'virtual' operand in place of the missing one. If no dependency exists, then the instruction is issued with real (resolved) operands.

Each RS works independently of the others and can issue an instruction every cycle to its functional unit if the instruction operands are all resolved and the functional unit is not currently busy.

Generally, each functional unit takes a different length of time to process its instructions, so the RSs will empty at different rates. If an RS holds more than one instruction with fully resolved operands so that more than one instruction can be issued, the oldest one should normally be issued first. The common data bus (CDB) writes results back to registers (i.e. it is a load-store machine). But the CDB can carry only one result per cycle, so if two instructions complete in the same cycle, the oldest one needs to be written back first on the CDB.

Every RS continually 'listens' to the CDB. Any RS holding an instruction with a virtual operand will be looking for the register writeback that will resolve that operand and make it real. When it sees what it is waiting for, it grabs the value from the CDB to resolve its virtual operand. Of course, this means that the CDB has to carry more than just the result value and destination register. It has to carry something to inform the instructions waiting in the RSs whether this particular result is the one that resolves their dependency (because an instruction waiting for a value to be written to register R3 may 'see' several CDB writebacks to register R3 – only the writeback that is immediately before that instruction in the original program is the one that conveys the correct value).

A unique tag is provided to each operand issued from the instruction queue. This tag is carried through the RS, through the functional unit, and is conveyed on the CDB along with the result writeback from that instruction. Subsequent instructions dependent upon the output of this first instruction are issued with their virtual operands as we have seen. However, these virtual operands contain two items of information – the register name plus the tag value. The dependent instruction that 'listens' to the CDB is actually 'listening' for a writeback to the correct register that has the correct tag value.

Let us illustrate this entire process with an example. We will define a Tomasulo machine, as shown in Figure 5.28, with the following timing specifications:

Load-store unit:	5 cycles to complete
Floating point adder:	2 cycles to complete
Floating point multiplier:	2 cycles to complete
Integer unit:	1 cycle to complete
Reservation station depth:	1 instruction
Instructions issued per cycle:	1
Number of registers:	32 gpr + 32 fp

The following embedded code is going to be executed on this machine:

```
i1   LOAD.D fp2,(gpr7, 20)
i2   LOAD.D fp3, (gpr8, 23)
i3   MUL.D fp4, fp3, fp2
i4   ADD.D fp5, fp4, fp3         ; meaning fp5 = fp4 + fp3
i5   SAVE.D fp4, (gpr9, 23)      ; meaning save fp4 in address (gpr9 + 23)
i6   ADD gpr5, gpr2, gpr2
i7   SUB gpr6, gpr1, gpr3
```

A full reservation table showing the program operation is provided in Table 5.3. It shows instructions flowing from the queue, through the reservation stations and into functional units when virtual operands are resolved. Results are written back to registers using the CDB.

Note that the program sequence of instructions *i1* to *i7* is not at all reflected in the out-of-order completion sequence: *i1*, *i6*, *i7*, *i2*, *i3*, *i4* and *i5* shown on the CDB. Interestingly, if we had manually re-ordered the code segment to minimise execution time on a simple pipelined processor, it may well have resulted in the same execution sequence. Instructions *i6* and *i7*, having no data dependencies with other instructions, would have been pulled forwards to separate those instructions that do have dependencies.

Table 5.3

A reservation table showing the Tomasulo machine operation beginning with a program stored in an instruction queue (IQ), issuing into several reservation stations (RS) for a load-store unit (LSU), arithmetic logic unit (ALU), floating point ALU (FALU) and floating point multiply unit (FMUL). Completed instructions are written back to the register banks using the common data bus (CDB). Instructions waiting for virtual operands to be resolved, and during multi-cycle processing in functional units, are shown in grey.

	1	2	3	4	5	6	7	8	9	10	11	12	13	14	15	16	17	18	19	20	21
IQ	i1	i2	i3	i4	i5	i5	i5	i6	i7												
RS:lsu		i1	i2	i2	i2	i2	i2	i5	i5	i5	i5	i5	i5	i5	i5	i5					
LSU			i1	i1	i1	i1	i1	i2	i2	i2	i2	i2					i5	i5	i5	i5	i5
RS:alu									i6	i7											
ALU										i6	i7										
RS:falu					i4	i4	i4	i4	i4	i4	i4	i4	i4	i4	i4	i4					
FALU																	i4	i4			
RS:fmul				i3	i3	i3	i3	i3	i3	i3	i3	i3	i3								
FMUL														i3	i3						
CDB								i1			i6	i7	i2			i3			i4		

One final point to note here is that the main cause of latency in this execution is the load-store unit (LSU). Of course, the specification indicated that loads and stores each required five cycles (something that is not at all excessive for a modern processor, although the use of on-chip cache memory could speed up some of them). Given the specification, it is to be expected that the LSU is a bottleneck.

A possible way of overcoming the bottleneck may be to consider adding a second LSU (either having its own reservation station or working off the existing LSU RS). Of course, no matter how many LSUs there are, re-ordering of load-store operations is the major way of resolving such bottlenecks in a Tomasuo machine. However, readers should be aware that dependencies exist in memory access also, and the Tomasulo algorithm does not resolve these. Consider the small code example above: although the three addresses mentioned appear different, they may not be in practice. The three addresses are as follows:

i1 read from `(gpr7, 20)`
i2 read from `(gpr8, 23)`
i5 write to `(gpr9, 23)`

Instruction *i1* reads from address `(gpr7 + 20)`. If `gpr7` happens to hold the value 1003 then the address read from would naturally be 1023. Similarly, if `gpr8` happens to hold the value 1000 then the address read from *i2* would also be 1023, causing a read-after-read hazard: not a particularly worrisome possibility, but still one that could be optimised if detected early.

Perhaps of more concern is the fact that if `gpr8` happens to equal `gpr9` then *i2* and *i5* form a WAR hazard (as described in Section 5.2.4). In the current code segment, with

Figure 5.29

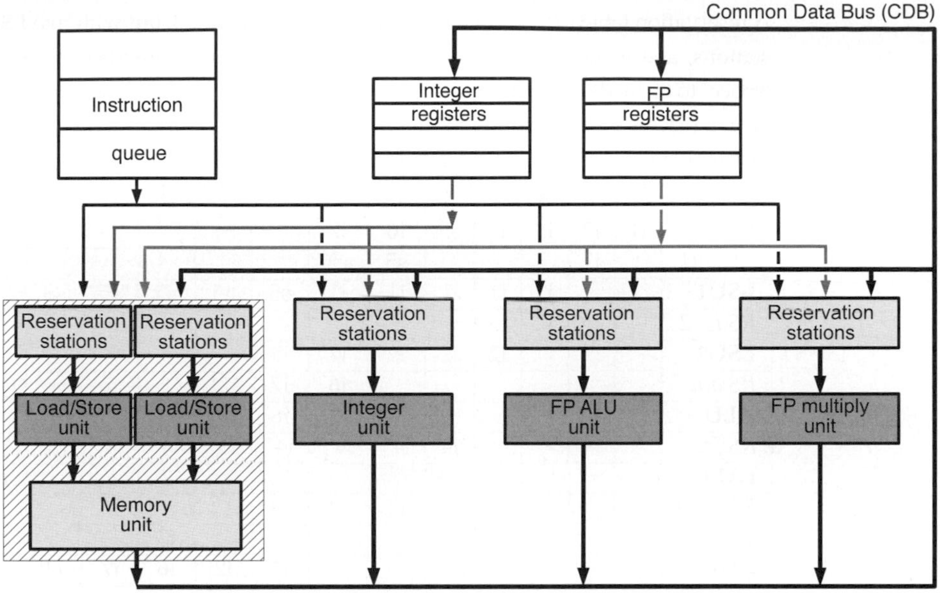

A modification of the basic Tomasulo machine of Figure 5.28 to incorporate dual-memory load-store units and reservation stations.

only a single LSU, it is not possible for *i5* to be re-ordered to before *i2*, and therefore no major problem will be caused by this occurrence. However, that is more due to the good fortune that *i5* has a register dependency than anything else.

Let us examine this claim by changing the code and the machine to highlight the problem. In this case, *i5* becomes *s5*, `SAVE.D fp1, (gpr9, 23)`, so that it has no register dependencies with the rest of the code. We will also add a second LSU and RS, shown in Figure 5.29, and run the following program:

```
i1   LOAD.D fp2,(gpr7, 20)
i2   LOAD.D fp3, (gpr8, 23)
i3   MUL.D fp4, fp3, fp2
i4   ADD.D fp5, fp4, fp3        ; meaning fp5 = fp4 + fp3
s5   SAVE.D fp1, (gpr9, 23)     ; meaning save fp1 in address (gpr9 + 23)
i6   ADD gpr5, gpr2, gpr2
i7   SUB gpr6, gpr1, gpr3
```

In this case, the reservation table of the modified machine, running the new code is given in Table 5.4. It is quite interesting to note that the addition of another LSU has significantly improved program execution. The entire program now completes in 15 cycles instead of 21, and is far more compact.

The speed-up is a good thing, but let us consider the memory accesses in more detail now. Note that s5 enters the first LSU during cycle 8 and begins to write

Table 5.4

A reservation table for the Tomasulo machine as in Table 5.3, but with two LSUs and reservation stations, and a slightly modified program being executed. Instructions that are waiting for a 'space' to be made available, either in the CDB, in the RS or in a functional unit, are marked with an asterisk, as in 'i6*' waiting at the output of the ALU during cycle 9 because the result from instruction i2 is occupying the CDB during that slot.

	1	2	3	4	5	6	7	8	9	10	11	12	13	14	15	16
IQ	i1	i2	i3	i4	s5	i6	i7									
RS:lsu1		i1				s5	s5*									
LSU1			i1	i1	i1	i1	i1	s5	s5	s5	s5	s5	s5			
RS:lsu2			i2													
LSU2				i2	i2	i2	i2	i2								
RS:alu							i6	i7	i7*							
ALU								i6	i6*	i7						
RS:falu					i4	i4*	i4*	i4*	i4*	i4*	i4*	i4*				
FALU													i4	i4		
RS:fmul				i3	i3	i3	i3	i3	i3							
FMUL										i3	i3					
CDB								i1	i2	i6	i7	i3	i2	s5	i4	

to memory address `(gpr9 + 23)`. Simultaneously, *i2* is still reading from address `(gpr8 + 23)`. Clearly, if `gpr8` = `gpr9` the read and the write will be to the same location. As instruction *i2* is reading from that location, instruction *s5* will be writing to it. Quite likely the value read by instruction *i2* would be corrupted or would be incorrect.

Effectively, this type of problem occurs because there is no mechanism here for handling hazards on memory addresses. It is unlikely that a simple solution exists to such problems, except in tracking, and resolving, memory access addresses early or in enforcing in-order execution of unresolved memory reads and writes.

5.9.3 Tomasulo's Algorithm in Embedded Systems

As mentioned, Tomasulo designed his method for a large mainframe computer, the IBM System/360, specifically model 91. We have included a photograph of this monster in Chapter 1 (refer to Figure 1.5 on page 8). Why then is such a method included in a computer architecture book emphasising embedded systems?

The first reason is that out-of-order execution methods are typically not trivial to implement, and for those designing CPUs for use in embedded systems, out-of-order execution may not be something that they are likely to consider possible. However, Tomasulo's method trades resources (extra registers in the reservation stations) for improved performance. It also does not rely upon more sophisticated techniques such as branch prediction, superscalar pipelining and so on. Basically it puts out-of-order execution within reach of fairly simple CPU designs.

Secondly, the Tomasulo algorithm makes distributed decisions concerning instruction execution. There is no real bottleneck in the instruction issue unit, and this is not really limited by clock speed (in fact Tomasulo's method is easy to extend with multiple functional units, requiring only quite minor adjustments to structure). The distributed nature of the system suits an FPGA. The one main bottleneck in the Tomasulo algorithm is the CDB which must stretch to every reservation station and to every register in every register bank. However, this type of global bus is readily implemented inside an FPGA, and to some extent is more convenient than having many 'shorter' parallel buses.

Finally, we have noted in our examples in Section 5.9.2 how additional functional units (in this case a second memory load-store unit) could be added to optimise performance, although we noted the particular memory address dependency issues for the case of additional LSUs. Within embedded systems it is more likely that addresses of variables and arrays can be fixed at compile-time, and not necessarily be specified relative to a base register, something that would solve the problems associated with having additional LSUs. More importantly, it is often possible to know in advance what software will be running on an embedded system, and with this knowledge determine in advance what types of functional units are necessary (and indeed how many there should be).

5.10 Summary

While previous chapters concentrated mostly upon the foundations of computing, the functional units within a computer (and CPU) and the operation of these devices, this chapter has considered performance – mainly because this is one of the major drivers of innovation in the computing industry.

We looked at many types of speed-up, from the traditional increasing clock speed, through the now well-established method of pipelining, CISC versus RISC, superscalar and other hardware accelerations such as zero-overhead looping and dedicated addressing hardware.

A large part of the chapter was devoted to issues related to pipelining, namely hazards and branch penalties, and how to alleviate these potential problems using delayed branching and/or branch prediction.

We have now completed our overview of CPU internal architecture (apart from some more esoteric methods in Chapter 9. Next, we will turn our attention to communicating with the CPU: getting information into and out of the system.

Problems

5.1 On some pipelined processors, a conditional branch can cause a stall or wasted cycle. The following code segment might stall a three-stage pipeline. Why?

```
MOV R0,R3            ;R0 = R3
ORR R4,R3,R5         ;R4 = R3 OR R5
AND R7,R6,R5         ;R7 = R6 AND R5
ADDS R0, R1, R2      ;R0 = R1 + R2, set condition flags
BGT loop             ;branch if the result > 0
```

Note: An 'S' after the instruction means its result will set the condition codes. No 'S' means that condition codes will not be set and assume that every instruction completes in a single pipeline cycle.

5.2 Re-order the code in Problem 5.1 to reduce the likelihood of a stall occurring.

5.3 If a delayed branch was available for the ARM, the BGT could be replaced by a BGTD in the code above. Rewrite the code in Problem 5.1 to use the delayed branch. (*Hint: You only need to move one instruction.*)

5.4 In an 8-bit RISC-style processor, starting from the initial conditions R0 = `0x0`, R1 = `0x1` and R2 = `0xff`, determine the state of the four condition flags after the following ARM-like instructions have completed. Assume that the instructions specified occur in sequence:

Instruction	N	Z	C	V
`MOVS R3, #0x7f`				
`ADDS R4, R3, R1`				
`ANDS R5, R2, R0`				
`MOVS R5, R4, R4`				
`SUBS R5, R4, R1`				
`ORR R5, R4, R2`				

5.5 Identify four hazards in the following segment of ARM-style assembler code which includes a delayed conditional branch:

```
i1    ADD R1, R2, R3
i2    NOTS R1, R2
i3    BEQD loop
i4    SUBS R4, R3, R2
i5    AND R5,R4,R1
i6    NOT R1,R2
```

Problems

5.6 Often, branches can cause pipeline stalls due to dependencies, code ordering and pipeline hardware capabilities. Delayed branches can prevent such stalls. Name two other methods that can be used to improve branch performance.

5.7 Name three general methods of reducing or removing the effect of data hazards in a processor.

5.8 Draw a block diagram of hardware that can multiply any number by a value between 2 and 10. Use data forwarding to apply a feedback path. The blocks you have available are:

- Up to two single-bit shifters.
- Up to two full adders.

Ignore all control logic and storage registers.

5.9 Pipeline the design of the previous question. Use a single adder and a single shifter, again ignore control logic and registers.

5.10 Draw a reservation table for three pipelined multiplication examples from the previous question.

5.11 Identify the main mechanism for transferring data between a CPU and its co-processing unit. State how this differs from a heterogeneous dual processor system.

5.12 List five typical features of RISC processors that differentiate them from their CISC predecessors.

5.13 What range of instructions per cycle (IPC) would be expected for a pure RISC processor? How would that differ for a perfect superscalar machine that can issue three instructions simultaneously?

5.14 A digital signal processor (DSP) implements simple zero-overhead loop hardware that has a loop counter, a start point address register and an endpoint address register. The hardware will detect when the program counter (PC) matches the endpoint address register, and if the loop counter is non-zero will reload the PC with the startpoint address. Identify the types of C loops that can be catered for with this hardware:

a.
```
for (loop = 0; loop <99; loop++){
        <do lots of calculations here>
   }
```

Problems

b.
```
loop = 99;
do{
        <lots of calculations here>
} while (loop-- >0)
```

c.
```
while(x + y != 23){
        <lots of calculations here>
}
```

5.15 Calculate the parallel processing speed-up possible when a program consisting of 1224 tasks (200 of them must be run sequentially but 1024 can be run in parallel) is executed in a 16-way homogeneous perfectly parallel machine. Each task requires 2 ms of CPU time to execute.

5.16 Referring to the pipeline speed-up and efficiency calculations of Box 5.1; if one particular CPU pipeline design is found to have an efficiency of 68% and a speed-up of 3.4, determine the number of stages in that pipeline.

5.17 To implement a digital audio delay, a processor has to continuously read in audio samples, delay them and output them some time later. For 16-bit audio at a sample rate of 8 kHz, how many samples must the wait be for a 1008 ms delay? Implement this on the ADSP2181 using a circular buffer, and write the pseudo code using the instructions. Assume the buffer memory is empty at the beginning:

`<reg>=IO(audioport)`	to read in data to register
`IO(audioport)=<reg>`	to read out data from register
`<reg>=DM(I0,M0)`	to get data from memory location pointed to by I0, and pointer I0 is incremented by the value in M0 after the operation
`DM(I0,M1)=<reg>`	stores value in register to memory location pointed to by I0, and after the operation, I0 = I0 + M1
`I0=buffer_start`	sets I0 to point to a start of buffer in memory
`L0=buffer_end`	sets a circular buffer up (when I0 reaches L0, I0 is reset)
M0=*x*	sets address modifier M0 to contain a value of *x*
M1=*x*	sets address modifier M1 to contain a value of *x*
`B loop`	branches to the program label called *loop*

<reg> can be any register from the set AX0, AX1, AY0 or AX1

Problems

5.18 Identify the conditional flags that need to be set for the following conditional ARM instructions to be executed:

Instruction	Meaning	N	Z	C	V
`BEQ loop`	Branch if equal to zero				
`ADDLT R4, R9, R1`	Add if less than zero				
`ANDGE R1, R8, R0`	AND if greater than or equal to zero				
`BNE temp`	Branch if not zero				

5.19 Briefly explain the circumstance under which shadow registers are used. What method do programmers use in a situation where processors do not have shadow registers?

5.20 Trace the following code through a processor which has a global 2-bit branch predictor initialised to state 'DT':

```
i1          MOV R8, #6          ; load the value 6 into register R8
i2          MOV R5, #2          ; load the value 2 into register R5
i3   lp1:   SUBS R8, R8, R5     ; R8 = R8 – R5
i4          BLE exit            ; branch if result ≤ 0
i5          BGT lp1             ; branch if result > 0
```

CHAPTER 6

Externals

Over the past five chapters the evolutionary, and very occasional revolutionary, heritage of microprocessors have been examined, including the drive for more capable devices with faster processing speeds, the concept of RISC and the architectural or instruction set support for time-consuming programming and operating concepts.

In this chapter, to round off our studies of basic CPUs, we will examine some of the interactions between the core logic and the outside world, in terms of interfaces and buses, and something of particular relevance to many embedded systems – near real-time processing and interaction.

6.1 Interfacing Using a Bus

It is today possible to purchase a computer-on-a-chip which integrates all computer logic along with a CPU on a single integrated circuit.

This chip directly provides all external buses that are required for a computer system. However, as in the pre-integration case, internal buses are present between the CPU and the peripheral handlers – it is simply that these are now on-chip instead of off-chip. These devices are known as 'system-on-chip' or SoC processors.

As an example, consider the diagram in Figure 6.1 that describes a standard personal computer architecture from the late 1990s, showing the central CPU and various items clustered around it. This same architecture can be found implemented across a motherboard with 20 or so support chips, but more recently implemented within a single system-on-chip device. The same standard interfaces are present but are all within the same integrated circuit, shown in the hatched area.

Within ARM-based systems there are typically two standard buses – the AHB (ARM host bus) and the AMBA (Advanced Microcontroller Bus Architecture). Both can be found implemented within many ARM-based integrated circuits from a variety of manufacturers or equally implemented discretely on larger motherboards, such as the ARM integrator platform. The ARM buses have even become a de-facto standard, being used to interface non-ARM processors, such as the SPARC-based ERC32 processor.

Figure 6.1

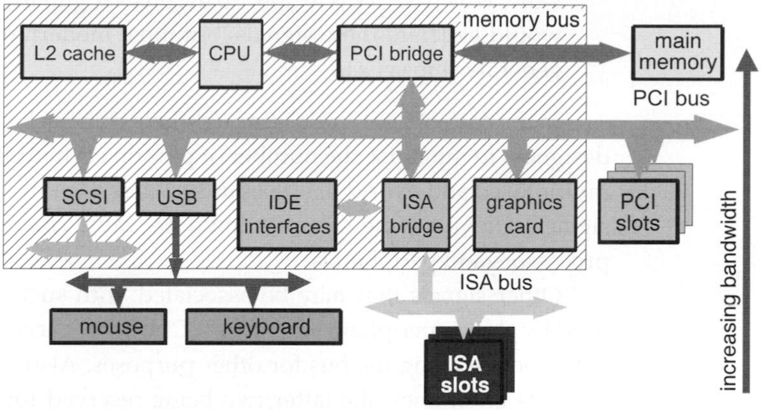

A block diagram of a fairly standard personal computer from the late 1990s.

Such standard buses, whether internal or external, help peripheral manufacturers – either separate IC vendors or internal logic block vendors – to produce standard items for incorporation in systems.

Although it is expected that readers will have been introduced to the concept of a parallel bus previously, it will be reviewed briefly here. Most important is the ability for the same physical resource – the data bus – to be shared by a number of devices for conveying information, either as input or output. A master device, usually the CPU, has the responsibility for controlling the parallel bus using control signals. Where two CPUs share the same bus, arbitration must be performed, either inside the CPUs themselves or using a separate external bus arbiter.

The master device uses bus control signals to tell other devices when to read from, or write to, the bus. Bus-compatible devices must ensure that whenever they are *not* writing to the bus, they do not drive the bus, that is, their bus outputs are in a high-impedance state.

6.1.1 Bus Control Signals

Bus control signals are typically as shown below, where the lower case 'n' indicates an active-low signal:

- **nOE** and **nRD** – Output enable/read enable, indicates that the master controller has allowed some device to write to the bus. The particular device selected is determined by memory address and/or chip-select signals.
- **nWE** and **nWR** – Write enable, indicates that the master controller has itself placed some value on the data bus, and that one or more other devices are to read this. Exactly which devices should read are selected as described for nOE/nRD.
- **RD/nWR** – Read not write. Any valid address or chip select occurring when this is high indicates a read and any occurring when this is low indicates a write.

- **nCS** and **nCE** – Chip enable/select is a one per-device signal indicating, when valid, which device is to 'talk' to the bus. Originally, a separate address decoder chip would generate these signals, but most modern embedded processors internally generate chip selects.

In the days of dual-in-line through-hole chip packaging, there was such pressure on designers to minimise the number of pins on each integrated circuit that some strange multiplexed and hybrid parallel bus schemes were designed, with unusual bus control signals. However, the signals shown are most common among modern embedded processors and peripherals.

Other signals that may be associated with such buses include the nWAIT line, used by slower peripherals to cause a CPU that is accessing them to wait until they are ready before using the bus for other purposes. Also, there are bus ready, bus request and bus grant lines, the latter two being reserved for buses which implement direct memory access (DMA).

6.1.2 Direct Memory Access (DMA)

Direct memory access allows two devices which share a bus to communicate with each other without the continuous intervention of a controlling CPU. Without DMA, a CPU instruction (or several) would be used to first read the external source device, then write to the external destination device. In a load-store architecture machine, this operation would also tie up an internal register for the duration of the transfer.

DMA requires a small amount of CPU intervention for set-up, and then operates almost independently of the CPU. The source device delivers data to the destination device using the external bus. It does not require any CPU instructions per word delivered – excluding the initial set-up, of course – and does not occupy any CPU registers. While the transfer is progressing, the CPU is free to perform any other operations that may be required.

For systems with many devices sharing the same bus, there will be a number of DMA channels, each of which can be assigned different endpoints, and which have ordered priorities, such that if two DMA channels request operation simultaneously, the channel with highest priority will be granted use of the bus first. Box 6.1 examines the workings of the DMA system within one common ARM-based processor.

Although DMA improves processor efficiency in many designs, there are enhancements possible where performance is crucial. In fact, in some CPUs the DMA controller itself is intelligent enough to itself be a simple CPU. An example of this in the ARM-based Intel IXP425 network processor. This contains a number of integrated peripherals such as USB, high-speed serial ports and two Ethernet MACs (Media Access Controller: a component of the Ethernet interface). The main processor clocks at 533 MHz, while three separate slave processors running at 100 MHz are dedicated to handling input/output on the system buses. These are RISC processors designed to free the main ARM CPU from lengthy and inefficient bus handling and memory transfers. Normally, one of these slave processors is dedicated to running the MACs, making this processor very capable at performing network operations.

Box 6.1

DMA in a commercial processor

Let us consider a real example – the ARM9-based S3C2410, a popular system-on-chip processor from Samsung. This has four channels of DMA, with the controller being located between internal and external buses and handling any combination of transitions between these.

The four channels each have five possible source triggers, with each channel being controlled by a three-state finite state machine. If we assume we have selected repetitive operation and set up source and destination addresses correctly, then the operation is as follows:

State 1: DMA controller waits for a DMA request. If seen, it transitions to state 2. DMA ACK and INT REQ are both inactive (0).

State 2: DMA ACK is set and a counter is loaded to indicate the number of cycles to operate for (i.e. the amount of data to be transferred by that channel). Then it transitions to state 3.

State 3: Data is read from the source address and written to the destination address. This repeats, decrementing the counter, until it reaches zero, at which point it optionally interrupts the processor to indicate that it has finished the transfer. Upon finishing, it transitions back to state 1.

6.2 Parallel Bus Specifications

The bus transaction timing for the ARM9-based Samsung S3C2410 system-on-chip device is shown in Figure 6.2. This was chosen for an example because Samsung have done an exceptional job of clarifying the timings and parameters, and matched each of the timings individually into a small number of control registers. With most CPUs, the situation is usually far more complicated – with cycle calculations needed to be done by hand, combined and split parameters, and unusual behaviours being commonplace.

The clock named HCLK is one of the main on-board clocks driving the memory interface and other on-chip devices. It would typically be running at 100 MHz and is not available off chip – it is just reproduced here for reference. The 25-bit external address bus and the nGCS chip select define an interface to an external device, probably a ROM or something similar (including most external bus-interfaced peripheral devices which use the same interface). These signals are active during any bus transaction to that device. The bottom shaded boxes contain the read and write signals and behaviours respectively.

The timing diagram shows several buses in a high-impedance (hi-Z) state – where the line is neither low nor high, but in between. This denotes a floating wire that is not driven by any voltage.

Figure 6.2

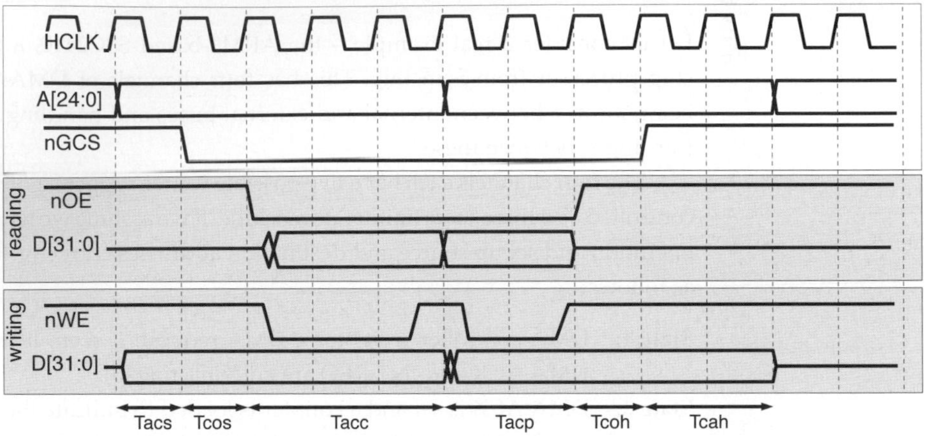

The SRAM bus transactions and timing diagram for the Samsung S3C2410 ARM9-based system-on-chip processor. The top section shows clock and general control signals. The middle section indicates the signals for a read operation (during which nWE would remain – high). The bottom section indicates the signals for a write operation (during which nOE would in turn remain inactive – high). Note: Reading and writing never occur simultaneously, at most only one of these can happen at any one time.

The timings shown apply for both reading and writing, and are set up in the registers of the S3C2410 to control how it accesses external devices connected to that interface. Other peripheral devices would share the data, address, read and write lines, but bus timings are specified individually for each nGCS chip select. Thus, fast and slow devices can co-exist on the same physical bus, but not sharing chip selects.

The table below gives the meanings of the timing signals shown and their settings in the diagram:

Signal	Meaning	Setting shown
Tacs	Address set-up time prior to nGCS active (0, 1, 2 or 4 cycles)	1 cycle
Tcos	Chip select set-up time prior to nOE (0, 1, 2 or 4 cycles)	1 cycle
Tacc	Access cycle (1, 2, 3, 4, 6, 8, 10 or 14 cycles)	3 cycles
Tacp	Page mode access cycle (2, 3, 4 or 6 cycles)	2 cycles
Tcoh	Chip select hold time after nOE deactivates (0, 1, 2, or 4 cycles)	1 cycle
Tcah	Address hold time after nGCS deactivates (0, 1, 2, or 4 cycles)	2 cycles

Page mode is where a whole number of repetitive transactions are done in a quick burst, without accessing any other device in between. Box 6.2 discusses some examples of device connectivity using the bus, and possible settings shown above. Note that some devices, such as SDRAM, are connected very differently – and other devices will drive the nWAIT signal into the CPU which *tells* the CPU exactly how long to extend Tacc (i.e. how long the device needs the CPU to wait).

Box 6.2

Bus settings for peripheral connectivity

Let us now identify a few device connection scenarios and see how we will handle them using the signals shown above, assuming a 100 MHz bus (i.e. a 10 ns cycle time).

Q. A fairly slow memory device that takes 120 ns to look up an internal address.
A. This means that being read or written to, the cycle has to extend over 120 ns. The relevant setting is Tacc, the access time, which would have to be set to 14 cycles, the next biggest after the 120 ns required.

Q. A peripheral where the chip select has to be activated at least 25 ns before the read signal.
A. In this case, the nGCS line has to go low before nOE. The relevant setting is Tacs and this would have to be set to four cycles, which is the smallest setting that waits at least 25 ns.

Q. A peripheral that keeps driving the bus for 12 ns after it is read.
A. In this case, we need to make sure that nothing else can use the bus for at least 12 ns after a read to this device. The relevant setting is either Tcah or Tcoh or both (but most likely Tcoh). To be safe we could set both to be one cycle, giving us a total of 20 ns. This is called the hold-off period.

Usually, the data sheet of whatever peripheral you select will have a timing diagram from which it is possible to derive the required information. But if in doubt, select the longest and slowest values available as a starting point and try to gradually reduce them while ensuring the system still works reliably. As an extra safety measure, make it slightly slower than the fastest settings which work for you – it might work at lab temperature, but once it is out in the cold or hot, or has aged a few years, it might no longer work at those fast settings.

6.3 Standard Interfaces

Modern computers, whether they are embedded, desktop or server, tend to use a limited set of very standard interface types. There is space in this book only to briefly highlight the more common interfaces and their characteristics.

These interfaces are classified according to their usage, whether this is low-speed data transfer, system control or supporting mass storage devices. It should be borne in mind that ingenuity has bent many interfaces to uses different from those envisaged by the original designers.

6.3.1 System Control Interfaces

System control interfaces are those that control and set up various low-speed devices. They are typically pin-and space efficient and usually relatively low speed, but simple in structure. The following are examples of system control interfaces:

- SPI, Serial Peripheral Interconnect, serial multi-drop addressed, 20 MHz.
- IIC, Inter-IC Communications, serial multi-drop addressed, 1 MHz.
- CAN, controller (or car) area network, serial multi-drop addressed, a few MHz.

Other more recent variants now exist, such as Atmel's TWI (Two Wire interface), Dallas Semiconductors 1-wire interface and so on.

6.3.2 System Data Buses

Over the years, there have been many attempts to introduce standard buses and parallel bus architectures. Many of those common parallel buses found in personal computer architecture systems are shown in the following table. It is useful to bear in mind that embedded systems tend to use different bus architectures. Two very commonplace examples are the AMBA (Advanced Microcontroller Bus Architecture) from ARM and GEC Plessey Semiconductors (which later became part of Marconi Ltd and was finally swallowed by Mitel Semiconductors), as discussed in the S3C2410 example in Section 6.2, and the APB (ARM Peripheral Bus). Both AMBA and APB are found in a huge variety of system-on-chip and embedded processor arrangements. These fared far better than the IBM-introduced MCA (microchannel architecture) of the late 1980s, which despite being generally considered a fairly well-defined bus system, was dropped in favour of EISA.

Bus name	Width (bits)	Speed (MHz)	Data rate (MiBytes/s)
8-bit ISA (Industry standard architecture)	8	8	4
16-bit ISA	16	8	8
EISA (Extended ISA)	32	8.33	33.3
32-bit PCI (Peripheral component interconnect)	32	33	132
64-bit PCI	64	33	264
1x AGP (Advanced Graphics Port)	64	66	266
8x AGP	64	533	2100
VL-BUS	33	50	132
SCSI-I & II	8	5	40
Fast SCSI-II	8	10	80
Wide SCSI-II	16	10	60
Ultra SCSI-III	16	20	320
PCIexpress – per lane (up to 32 possible)(using LVDS[1])	1	2500	> 500
RAMBUS (184-pin DRAM interface)	32	1066	4200
IDE[2]/ATA[3]	16[4]	66[4]	133[5]
SATA (Serial ATA) using LVDS	1	1500	150
SATA-600	1	unknown	600

[1] LVDS: low-voltage differential signalling.
[2] IDE: integrated drive electronics, corresponding to the first ATA implementation.
[3] ATA: advanced technology attachment, now renamed to parallel ATA or PATA to distinguish it from SATA.
[4] Assuming ATA-7 operation.
[5] 133 MHz over 45 cm maximum length.

Although there are a vast number of bus systems (those listed are the more common ones), there is a fair degree of commonality since most use the same basic communications and arbitration strategies. There are several voltage and timing standards on offer.

Sometimes, buses which are electrically identical have different names and uses differentiated by the actual communications protocol used on the bus. The OSI layered reference model (see Appendix B) defines the low-level electrical, hardware and timing parameters to be part of the physical layer, whereas the signalling protocol is defined by the data link layer. An example of a physical layer interface is LVDS (low voltage differential signalling), which is increasingly being used for high-speed serial buses in embedded computer systems.

We will examine two of the more common legacy buses here in a little more detail before we consider the physical LVDS layer used by SATA and other schemes.

6.3.2.1 ISA and Its Descendants

The industry standard architecture (ISA) bus was created by IBM in the early 1980s as a bus system for use within personal computers, in particular the IBM personal computers. The 8-bit bus was quickly expanded to 16 bits and then to 32 bits in the EISA extended ISA (EISA) version by 1988. Each new version was backwards compatible with the previous ones.

As mentioned previously, IBM then attempted to move to the microchannel architecture (MCA), but since they did not release the full rights to this closed-standard bus, other computer vendors unsurprisingly preferred to stick with EISA. IBM then effectively backed down, dropping MCA, but two descendants of ISA, peripheral component interconnect (PCI) and VESA local bus, did incorporate some of the IBM MCA features.

As a bus, ISA and EISA performed reasonably well considering their age, however, they suffered from severe usability issues (see Box 6.3). These issues, coupled with relentless pressure to increase bus speeds, soon led to the definition and adoption of PCI in desktop systems.

ISA not only spawned PCI and VESA local bus, but also the ATA standard, which itself led to IDE, enhanced IDE (EIDE), PATA and SATA. In fact, it also led to the PC-card standard interface.[6] Despite being a 30-year-old standard, ISA can still be found in systems today where it is often referred to as a 'legacy' bus.

6.3.2.2 PC/104

In embedded systems perhaps the most enduring legacy of the ISA bus is in the *PC/104 standard* from the PC/104 consortium.[7]

---

[6] PC-card was formerly known as PCMCIA (Personal Computer Memory Card International Association), although it is also known as "People Can't Memorize Computer Industry Acronyms" (see http://www.sucs.swan.ac.uk/cmckenna/humour/computer/acronyms.html).

[7] `http://www.pc104.org`

Box 6.3

The trouble with ISA

ISA, as a product of its time, was reasonable: it was designed for the 8-bit bus Intel 8088 processor, clocking at something like 4.77 MHz and operating with 5 v logic. However, it inherited some severe hardware limitations and usability issues from these pioneering CPUs:

Hardware limitations

The Intel 8086 and 8088 were built in a 40-pin dual in-line package (DIP) with 16-bit and 8-bit external data buses respectively. Due to lack of pins, external buses were multiplexed, meaning that some physical pins were required to perform two functions. Even with this approach, there was only room for 20 address pins, thus only 1 Mbyte (2^{20}) of memory could be accessed. Even more limiting was the fact that use of 16-bit address registers within the 8086 meant that memory could only be accessed in 64 kbyte (2^{16}) windows. Intel also provided two types of external access: memory accesses (using the 20-bit address bus) and I/O accesses (using 16 of the 20 address bits). Interestingly, the split between memory and address accesses is retained today in many systems – in contrast to the welcome simplicity of processors such as the ARM which have only memory-mapped external accesses.

Although the 8088 pins were buffered and demultiplexed before being connected to the ISA bus, the bus retained both the 20-bit address limitation and separate I/O memory accesses (for which separate sets of control pins were provided). On a positive note, the ISA bus did cater for four channels of DMA accesses nicely (Section 6.1.2).

Usability issues

This is not particularly relevant within embedded computer systems, but helps to explain the replacement of ISA by PCI. Many personal computer users were faced with problems when installing ISA (and EISA) cards within their systems. Users would not only need to physically insert and screw down the cards but in most cases would have to inform the installation software what I/O port, DMA channel and IRQ (interrupt request) lines the card connected to, and this is not the sort of information that the average user would be able to provide. This was actually an improvement upon earlier devices where these settings were adjusted through changing tiny switches placed on the plug-in card itself.

Some installation software would scan the ISA bus looking for the installed card. Sometimes this worked, but at other times it would totally crash the system, as would a user entering incorrect details. Some personal computers allowed the ISA slots to be swapped under BIOS control, or automatically at boot time. This meant that a card would work one day, but not the next.

Manufacturers, in exasperation, began to define a standard called 'plug and play' or PnP for short. This would, in theory, allow a card to be inserted and simply work. The fact that the standard quickly became known as 'plug and *pray*' is testament to the eventual demise of that strategy. Thankfully, the replacement of ISA/EISA by the PCI bus heralded a new era of simplification for users, but not for developers.

The PC/104 standard mandates quite a small form factor printed circuit board size of 96 × 60 mm, which is ideal for many embedded systems. The board has, in its basic form, one connector on one edge that carries an 8-bit ISA bus. This 2.5-mm spacing connector has 64 pins arranged in two parallel rows. On the top side, the connector presents a socket, while on the bottom side it presents long pins. This arrangement allows the boards to be stacked, one on top of another. Normally, a second 40-pin connector, J2/P2, placed next to J1/P2, provides the ISA expansion to a 16-bit data bus.

The pin definitions for PC/104 are shown in Table 6.1. Rows A and B are the original ISA signals, encompassing the 8-bit data bus (SD0 to SD7) and the 20-bit address bus (SA0 to SA19) along with memory and I/O read and write (SMEMW*, SMEMR*, IOW*, IOR*), several IRQ pins and DMA signals (those beginning with 'D'). The connector specifies +5 v, −5 v, +12 v and −12 v along with ground (GND), although in practice often only +5 v is used unless items such as EIA232 and other line drivers are present.

The second connector, containing rows C1 and D1, provides a larger address range and expands the data bus to 16 bits (along with providing more DMA functionality). This is a parallel bus and has all signals operating synchronous to SYSCLK.

6.3.2.3 PCI

Peripheral component interconnect (PCI) was a ground-up replacement for ISA/EISA, released in the early 1990s. It is probably the most common of the internal PC buses at the present time, although USB has emerged during recent years as the interface of choice for many peripherals that would once have been internal plug-in cards for a personal computer. The much faster serial-based PCI express (PCIe) system is gradually replacing PCI in more recent systems.

PCI is similar to ISA in being synchronous, this time to a 33 MHz (or 66 MHz) clock, and like EISA is generally 32 bits, although 64-bit versions are available using a longer connector. The connector also differs depending upon the signalling voltage used – both 3.3 v and 5 v versions are available. These versions have different 'notches' on the connector to prevent the wrong connector from being inserted (some 'universal' cards have both notches and thus can plug into both systems). Like ISA, there are also +12 v and −12 v pins, which are similarly not always utilised.

The PCI bus multiplexes the address and data pins, AD0 to AD31 (extending to AD63 in the 64-bit version), allowing for fast data transfer and a large addressable memory space. There is a bus arbitration system defined for PCI allowing any connected device to request control of the bus, and the request to be granted by a central arbiter. A bus master is called an initiator and a slave is called the target, with the bus master being the device that asserts the control signals. Practically, this means that the voltages driving the PCI bus can come from any of the connected devices. This is something that has a major implication on the integrity of electrical signals traversing the PCI bus. Therefore, PCI implements a very strict signal conditioning scheme for all connected devices.

Perhaps bearing in mind some of the usability issues associated with ISA and EISA, PCI devices must implement registers which are accessible over the bus to identify the device class, manufacturer, item numbers and so on. More importantly, these registers define the device I/O addresses, interrupt details and memory range.

Table 6.1

The pin definitions of the PC/104 connector showing the two two-row connectors J1/P1 and J2/P2. Active-low signals are indicated with an asterisk '*'. The two keys shown indicate filled holes in the 0.1-inch connector.

Pin No.	J1/P1 Row A	J1/P1 Row B	J2/P2 Row C1	J2/P2 Row D1
0	–	–	GND	GND
1	IOCHCHK*	GND	SBHE*	MEMCS16*
2	SD7	RESETDRV	LA23	IOCS16*
3	SD6	+5V	LA22	IRQ10
4	SD5	IRQ9	LA21	IRQ11
5	SD4	−5V	LA20	IRQ12
6	SD3	DRQ2	LA19	IRQ15
7	SD2	−12V	LA18	IRQ14
8	SD1	ENDXFR*	LA17	DACK0*
9	SD0	+12V	MEMR*	DRQ0
10	IOCHRDY	*key*	MEMW*	DACK5*
11	AEN	SMEMW*	SD8	DRQ5
12	SA19	SMEMR*	SD9	DACK6*
13	SA18	IOW*	SD10	DRQ6
14	SA17	IOR*	SD11	DACK7*
15	SA16	DACK3*	SD12	DRQ7
16	SA15	DRQ3	SD13	+5V
17	SA14	DACK1*	SD14	MASTER*
18	SA13	DRQ1	SD15	GND
19	SA12	REFRESH*	*key*	GND
20	SA11	SYSCLK		
21	SA10	IRQ7		
22	SA9	IRQ6		
23	SA8	IRQ5		
24	SA7	IRQ4		
25	SA6	IRQ3		
26	SA5	DACK2*		
27	SA4	TC		
28	SA3	BALE		
29	SA2	+5V		
30	SA1	OSC		
31	SA0	GND		
32	GND	GND		

6.3.2.4 LVDS

LVDS (low-voltage differential signalling) is a very high-speed differential serial scheme relying on synchronised small voltage swings to indicate data bits. Advocates of this standard have coined the slogan 'gigabits at milliwatts' because LVDS can reach signalling speeds exceeding 2 Gbits per second.

Note that LVDS is not a bus protocol like ISA or PCI. It is simply a physical layer signalling scheme (see Appendix B to read about the layered view of such systems). LVDS is, however, adopted by many of the bus standards that do exist. An example, which we shall discuss below, is PCI express.

In LVDS, each signal is transmitted over two wires. These are operated differentially, so that it is the difference between the voltage on the two wires which indicates the presence of a logic '0' or logic '1'. Differential transmission schemes are resistant to common-mode noise, that is noise that both wires experience (like power supply noise and interference from nearby devices). In fact, LVDS can routinely cope with levels of common-mode noise that exceed the signalling voltage.

This noise resistance means that lower voltage swings are necessary in LVDS connections. This in turn requires much less power to operate, allows faster signalling, and produces less electromagnetic interference. An illustration of the LVDS signalling scheme can be found in Figure 6.3, It shows the differential nature of the system and the rejection of common-mode noise.

Voltage swings in LVDS are typically around 0.25 v to 0.3 v. Since switching (and data transmission) speed depends upon the time taken for a signal to change from one state to the next, with the very low voltage swings of LVDS, switching can be extremely rapid. Power consumption in transmission systems also depends upon the square of the voltage, so a low-voltage signalling scheme like LVDS is significantly lower power than 3.3 v or 5 v logic systems. Similarly, the low voltage swings lead to low levels of electromagnetic interference generated by LVDS.

Transmission using a differential pair means that as the voltage on one wire increases, the voltage on the other wire decreases. If we relate that to drive current,

Figure 6.3

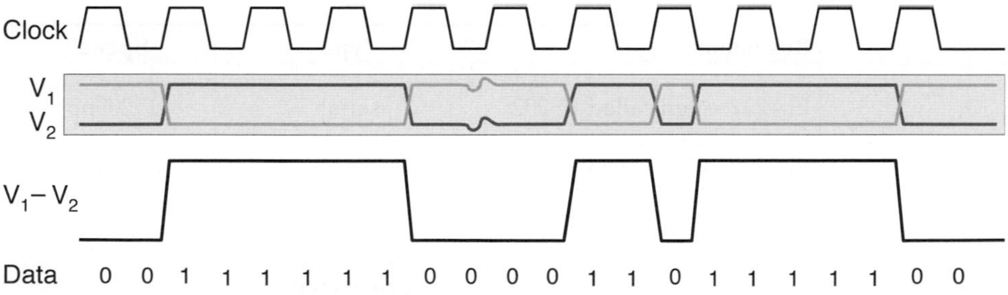

An illustration of low-voltage differential signalling (LVDS) showing two transmitted differential signals. At the receiver, the difference between these signals is calculated ($V_1 - V_2$), and used to determine the transmitted data at each clock cycle (shown at the bottom). Only the two signals, V_1 and V_2 (on grey background) are actually transmitted, although in practice the receiver and transmitter would both need to have accurate, and synchronous, timing information. A small amount of common-mode noise seen on both transmitted signals in the centre of the plot, is completely removed through the differencing process.

at any one time a transmitting device has to drive current into one wire and out of the other wire. When the system is designed correctly, these current flows can actually be made to balance, something which contrasts very strongly to most switching schemes which experience supply current spikes every time a signal is switched. Supply current spikes translates to voltage fluctuations in the power supply voltage – something which can affect other circuitry in such systems.

LVDS receivers normally need to extract a clock signal from the differential data pairs. This clock-recovery process implies that this is not a trivial interface to connect to. However, a separate clock signal – which could also be differential – can be transmitted alongside the data using another two wires, if required. Bus LVDS (BLVDS) is a variant of LVDS to allow for multiple devices to share the same physical differential wires.

PCI express (PCIe), as mentioned previously, is gradually replacing PCI in desktop computer systems. PCIe systems usually specify how many lanes are available. For example, *PCIe 1×* has one lane, *PCIe 4×* has four lanes and *PCIe 32×* has 32, with several intermediate steps being common. Each lane is actually one pair of LVDS transmitters and receivers (i.e. four electrical connections, two in each direction). Each lane operates at 2.5 GHz.

The PCIe 1× connector is rather small, consisting of only 36 pins, and yet delivers a data rate of at least 500 Mbits/s (after taking into account protocol overheads). The common PCIe 16× connector is similar in size to a parallel PCI connector (but is much, much faster of course).

6.3.3 Input/Output Buses

The input/output (I/O) buses shown below are typical communications buses, several being ones commonly found on personal computer architecture systems (apart from USB which is discussed later).

Bus name	Type	Speed	Notes
EIA232, often called RS232	serial	115200bps	−12 v & 0 v
EIA422, often called RS422	balanced serial 32-device multi-drop	up to 10 Mbits/s	1 km at slow speed
EIA485, often called RS485	as 422 but multi-drivers too	up to 10 Mbits/s	1 km at slow speed
DDC, Display Data Channel (monitor info)	serial, data, clk & gnd	based on I^2C bus	
PS/2 (keyboard and mouse)	serial, 6-pin miniDIN	electrically same as AT interface	
IEEE1284 printer port	parallel, 25-pin D	up to 150 kbytes/s	up to 8 m

EIA standards are ratified by the Electronic Industries Alliance (previously known as the Electronic Industries Association), which uses the prefix 'RS' to denote a recommended standard (i.e. proposed standards that have yet to be ratified). As an example, EIA232 was known as RS232 before it became adopted as a standard. However, since it was implemented in almost every home and desktop computer for a generation with the prefix RS, this name has stuck. Perhaps there is a lesson here for the standards bodies, relating to the speed of their internal processes compared to the rate of adoption in the consumer market.

6.3.4 Peripheral Device Buses

Several common peripheral buses are mentioned below. Clearly, the trend in recent years has been towards simple plug-and-play serial-based buses. This is ironic as many older computer engineers will remember the pain of connecting printers to computers in the 1980s, when serial peripherals spelt trouble and the only safe option was considered the parallel bus (also known as IEEE1284, and described in Section 6.3.3).

- USB1.2, Universal serial bus, is a serial format originally envisaged for devices such as keyboard and mouse, but subsequently adopted for a wide variety of peripherals. USB1.2 is limited in distance to about 7 metres and in speed to about 12 Mbits/s raw data rate. Being a serial bus, this bandwidth is shared among connected devices, along with a significant control overhead for each. Perhaps the main driver for adoption of USB has been the fact that it can supply power to the peripheral, freeing up a separate power source and cable.
- USB2.0, appears to have been a response to the introduction of firewire (see below), and significantly improves on the speed of USB1.2 – to 480 Mbits/s. In the gap between USB1.2 and USB2.0, firewire gained a strong foothold in the video market, becoming the de-facto method of transferring video information to a computer.
- Firewire, developed by Apple, and ratified as IEEE standard 1394 is another serial format, originally operating at 400 Mbits/s. IEEE1394b doubles the data rate to 800 Mbits/s but maximum cable length is only 4.5 metres or so. Like USB, Firewire can provide power to peripherals but there does not appear to be a standard voltage or current rating across all providers.
- PCMCIA, The Personal Computer Memory Card International Association (mentioned briefly in Section 6.3.2), developed their card interface in the early 1990s based on the ATA or IDE interface. It is a parallel interface with many variants, but is potentially reasonably high speed. This has evolved into the compact flash (CF) interface.
- Multimedia Card (MMC) is a serial interface adopted primarily for flash memory cards in cameras and portable audio players. This evolved into the Secure Digital (SD and xD) memory card format, which maintains the serial interface nature, but allows more bits to be transferred in parallel. Sony memory stick is a proprietary alternative with similar specification (and similar shrinkage in package dimensions).

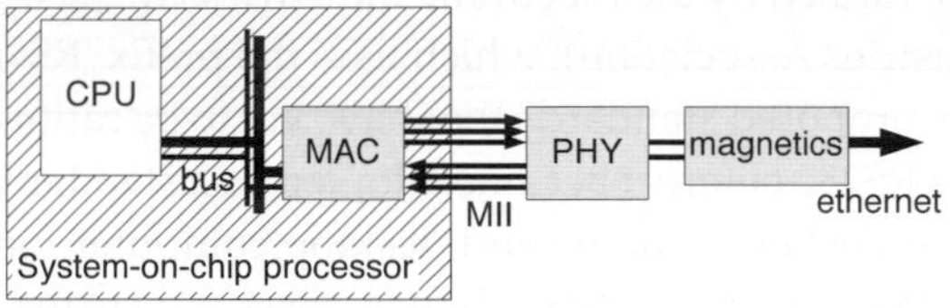

Figure 6.4 A block diagram of a network (Ethernet) data connection to a CPU through a media access controller (MAC).

6.3.5 Interface to Networking Devices

These days networking has become ubiquitous: being off-line for any length of time feels like a bereavement. System-on-chip designers have not ignored this trend, and hardware blocks to handle networking are commonly integrated into modern embedded processors.

Typically, a media access controller (MAC) hardware block is integrated on chip while the physical layer driver (PHY) is not, mainly because of the analogue drive and different voltage requirements of an Ethernet physical interface. It is however, possible to purchase a combined MAC-PHY device, so eventually it is expected that a full MAC and PHY implementation will be possible within a system-on-chip. Current integrations are similar to that shown in Figure 6.4.

Considering that the majority of networked infrastructure is currently Ethernet, magnetics are shown in Figure 6.4 connected to the PHY to give a very common system arrangement. The interface between MAC and PHY is a media-independent interface (MII) indicating that communication is not confined simply to wired Ethernet. It could equally as well be through an optical interface that conforms to the MII standard, and possibly requiring a different PHY device. Wireless is another increasingly common alternative based around the same standards process (to be discussed in Section 6.6).

6.4 Real-Time Issues

Remember the ancestor of today's computers: machines occupying an entire room engaged in abstract mathematical calculations, programmed with discrete switches or punched cards, and delivering results minutes or even hours later? This is far removed from small devices embedded in a human body to adjust blood chemistry or devices controlling the brake system in a family car. The latter examples are *hard* real-time systems of today. Hard in that they must respond to conditions within a certain time and the consequences of not doing so are severe.

The former system has no real-time requirement. Its designers might think in terms of speeding up calculations so that they could go home earlier, but would probably not have envisaged a computer making a millisecond response to an external stimuli. This means that traditional computer architectures and programming languages did not evolve with real-time responses in mind.

Today, with many more embedded processors than PCs sitting on desktops (and many more PCs than room-sized mainframes), the computing world is increasingly running in real time. The vast majority of embedded devices interact with the real world in a timely fashion, and are thus real-time systems, either *hard* or *soft* (soft ones are where the consequence of missing a deadline is not catastrophic).

6.4.1 External Stimuli

External stimuli can take many forms, but are often derived from some form of sensor. Examples include an over-temperature sensor in a nuclear reactor, an accelerometer in a vehicle air-bag controller, a vacuum switch in an engine management system or an optoelectronic gate around a slotted disc in a old-fashioned ball mouse. Each of these could be triggered at almost any time.

Other external stimuli might include data arriving over Ethernet or data sent from a PC via parallel port to a laser printer for printing. Both of these stimuli derive from computers themselves, but since they arrive at the destination at unpredictable times, they appear to be real-time stimuli to the destination processor.

6.4.2 Interrupts

Stimuli arriving at a real-time processor are almost always converted into standard forms to trigger a CPU. These interrupt signals are by convention active-low, attached to an interrupt pin (or possibly an on-chip signal converted to an active-low input to the CPU core in the case of a system-on-chip processor).

Most processors have the ability to support many interrupt signals simultaneously. These signals will be prioritised so that when two or more are triggered together, the highest priority interrupt is serviced first.

Interrupts are discussed more completely in Section 6.5, but here it is only necessary to recognise that once an interrupt stimuli occurs, it takes a short amount of time for a CPU to notice this, then more time until the CPU can begin to service the interrupt, and finally even more time until the servicing has completed. Interrupt servicing is done through an interrupt service routine (ISR) – which was introduced briefly in Section 5.6.3 when discussing shadow registers. When designing a real-time system it is necessary to determine interrupt timings and relate them to the temporal scope of a task (as discussed in Section 6.4.4).

6.4.3 Real-Time Definitions

Soft and *hard* deadlines were mentioned previously and these are both real-time constraints, differentiated by the consequence of missing a required deadline. Missing a hard deadline would be catastrophic to the system, whereas missing a soft deadline is unfortunate but not a critical failure.

These terms can also relate to entire systems: a *hard real-time system* is one that includes some hard deadlines. If all deadlines are soft then it is a *soft real-time system*. When choosing an operating system, it is also possible to consider degree of 'hardness': for example, uCos is capable of meeting hard deadlines whereas embedded Linux is often softer in its response. SymbianOS is relatively hard, but Microsoft windows CE is quite soft – which is why it is generally avoided for 'mission critical' real-time systems.

A *task* is a section of program code dedicated to handling one or more functions, perhaps tied up with a real-time input or output. In a multi-tasking *real-time operating system* (RTOS), there will be several tasks running concurrently, with each task having a priority associated with it.

Most systems are designed around interrupts or timers such that every time a particular interrupt occurs, one task will be triggered to handle it. Other tasks will trigger on expiration of a timer. Tasks can themselves be interrupt service routines, but generally they are separate code (in the interests of keeping the ISR as short as possible), so that when ISRs run they release appropriate tasks using dedicated RTOS functions. These functions, such as *semaphores*, *queues* and *mailboxes* are beyond the scope of this book, but they are covered in most standard texts discussing real-time systems.

Many tasks would spend most of their time sleeping, waiting to be woken up by an ISR or another task, but often a very low-priority background task runs to perform system-related functions and logging. This may also include adjusting prioritisation of tasks yet to be run.

6.4.4 Temporal Scope

The *temporal scope* of a task is a set of five parameters that together describe its real-time requirements. This is a formalism that is very useful in systems with multiple tasks running, each of which have deadlines associated with them.

The following values define the temporal scope, and unless specified are all timed from the event which is supposed to trigger the task:

Minimum delay before task should start	Usually 0, but occasionally specified.
Maximum delay before task must start	Interrupts should be acknowledged as quickly as possible in principle, but a hard upper limit. May be specified.
Maximum time for task processing	Elapsed time between the start and end of the task.
Task CPU time	This may be different to the parameter above since the task could be interrupted, prolonging the time taken but not CPU time.
Maximum task completion time	Elapsed time between the trigger event and the task being completed.

Temporal scope can mostly be determined through analysis of system requirements, although finding the CPU time can only be done either by counting the number of instructions in the task or through OS tools designed to measure processor cycles. A note on CPU timings – remember that sometimes conditional loops might be longer or shorter depending on the data being processed and this should be taken into

Figure 6.5

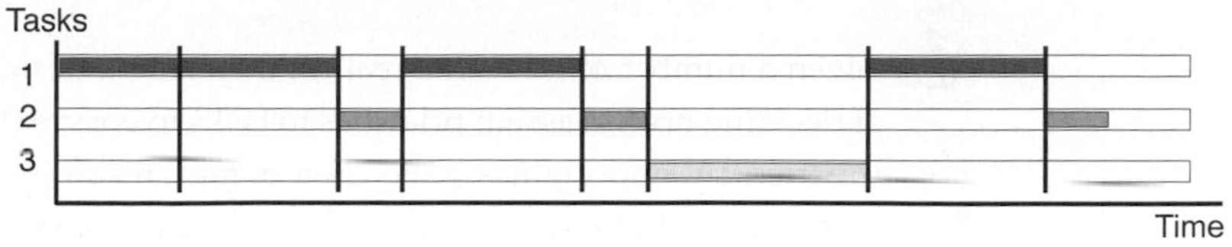

A scheduler diagram for three tasks, executing on a single CPU.

consideration. The CPU time specified is the maximum with all loops being as long as they can possibly be. It therefore stands to reason that writing compact task code is important.

A task diagram is shown in Figure 6.5, which lists three tasks that are available and shows which of these occupies the CPU at any particular time. The vertical lines indicate points at which the scheduler has been run. It is able to switch between tasks if required. The scheduler is often itself implemented in a system task and chooses which user task occupies the CPU at which time. Depending on RTOS type, the scheduler will be invoked in different ways – cooperatively through calls in the software itself, at fixed time intervals or at task despatch points. Task despatch points are usually incorporated in library functions that perform OS-level tasks, sometimes as simple as printf() or similar, but almost always at first-in first-out (FIFO), queue, mailbox and semaphore-related operations. Sometimes a combination of methods is used to invoke a scheduler.

In the task diagram shown in Figure 6.5, the first time the scheduler was invoked (at the first vertical line), task 1 was executing. The scheduler did not switch to another task in this instance, and so task 1 continued. The reason may be because task 1 has the highest priority of the three user tasks shown. Conventionally, that is why task 1 is shown at the top!

Task 2 appears to be about the same length each time, indicating that it is probably doing the same work each time it runs.

This brings us to a brief consideration of how a scheduler decides between tasks. First of all, tasks are allocated a priority. Top may be the scheduler and bottom is the *idle task* that gets executed when nothing else wants to run. In embedded systems, this might handle the low-priority I/O such as printing of debugging information or flashing an activity LED (the use of the low-priority task to print debugging information is very common, but it will not help when debugging a total crash because no debug information will be visible from the task which crashed, since if that task was running, by definition the idle task will not get a chance to run).

A table within the scheduler keeps track of all tasks and maintains the state of each: *running*, *runnable* or *sleeping*. There will only be one running task at each particular instant, but many tasks could be runnable (indicating that they are waiting for a chance to run). Sleeping tasks are those that are halted, perhaps temporarily waiting for a semaphore, or for some data to enter a queue or mailbox. Some methods of ordering scheduling priorities are shown in Box 6.4.

Box 6.4

Scheduling priorities

Given a number of tasks in a real-time system, a designer is faced with the difficulty of deciding how to assign priorities to tasks to ensure that they can be scheduled. This is extremely important – some choices may result in a system that cannot meet the required deadlines (not schedulable), whereas a small change could make the system work. Some common formalised priority orderings are shown below. They all require knowledge of temporal scope of tasks in the system.

Deadline monotonic scheduling: Tasks with tightest deadlines have higher priority.

Rate monotonic scheduling: Tasks that trigger more often have higher priority.

Earliest deadline first scheduling: This is a dynamic scheme that has knowledge of when a deadline will occur and assigns priority to whichever task must complete earliest.

Others include **most important first**, **ad-hoc**, **round robin** and numerous hybrid schemes (most of which claim to be better than all others!)

6.4.5 Hardware Architecture Support for Real-Time Operating Systems

This is a book about computer architecture and not real-time systems, thus it is more important to consider the hardware implications of running a real-time system on a processor than it is to discuss the real-time implications themselves. Let us review again the steps taken when a real-time event occurs:

1	The event causes an interrupt signal to the processor.
2	The processor 'notices' the interrupt.
3	The processor may need a little time to finish what it is currently doing, then branches to an interrupt vector and from there to the address of whatever ISR is registered against that interrupt.
4	The processor switches from what it is currently executing into an interrupt service routine.
5	The ISR acknowledges the interrupt and 'unlocks' a task to handle the event.
6	Any higher priority tasks that are waiting get executed first.
7	Finally, context switches to the task assigned to deal with the event.
8	The task handles the event.

Each of these eight steps (examined in more detail in Section 6.5.2) potentially takes some time, and thereby slows down the real-time response of the system.

Hardware support for interrupts (explored further in Section 6.5) can significantly improve response time. However, the OS functions needed to service the task, particularly switching from previously running code into ISR, and then between tasks, are time consuming and can also be accelerated.

Firstly, shadow registers (Section 5.6.3) speed up the changing of *context* from one piece of code to another. The ARM implements several sets of shadow registers, one of which, called *supervisor*, is dedicated to underlying OS code, such as the scheduler, so that running this does not entail a time-consuming context save and restore process.

Other CPUs take the approach further, implementing several register banks, each of which is allocated to a separate task. With this, switching between tasks is easy. No context save or restore is required, simply a switch to the correct register bank and then jump to the correct code location.

Hardware FIFOs and stacks can be used to implement mailboxes and queues efficiently to communicate between tasks (the alternative is software to move data around a block of memory). These are generally less flexible because of their fixed size, but they can be extremely quick.

It is theoretically feasible to implement a hardware scheduler, although this does not seem to be have been adopted by computer architects. Perhaps the highest performance hardware support for scheduling would be dual-core (or more) processors which can support hyper-threading or a similar technology. In this instance, there is the ability for two tasks to be running in each time instant rather than just one. This is an example of MIMD processing (see Section 2.1.1) that has been adopted in some of the latest processors from Intel in their Centrino Core processors. Other manufacturers are sure to follow (refer to Section 5.8.1 for more details of MIMD and dual cores).

6.5 Interrupts and Interrupt Handling

This section will discuss interrupts, their overheads and consider ways of servicing these quickly. The use of shadow registers for interrupt service routines (ISR) was covered in Section 5.6.3, and so this particular efficiency improvement will not be discussed again here.

6.5.1 The Importance of Interrupts

Interrupts and their handling is one of the most important topics in computer architecture and embedded software engineering. With the degree of interaction between computers and the real world increasing and becoming more critical through the profusion of embedded computer deployments, it is the humble interrupt that is tasked with most of the burden. This burden includes ensuring that a processor responds when necessary and as quickly as necessary to real-time events.

Real-time events were discussed previously, but here it is necessary to remember three important timings associated with an interrupt:

1. The interrupt detection time – How long after the event occurs that the CPU 'notices' and can begin to take action.
2. The interrupt response time – How long after the event occurs that the CPU has 'serviced' the event, that is, worst-case timing before the appropriate action has been taken.

3. The minimum interrupt period – The earliest time after one interrupt that the same interrupt can occur again. If the interrupt is not regular, then take the minimum allowable.

6.5.2 The Interrupt Process

Exactly what happens after an interrupt line asserts is important to understand, since these events have a huge impact on the system architecture as will be discussed. A table of the process already briefly described in Section 6.4.5 is given below:

1	An external event causes an interrupt signal to the processor.
2	The processor 'notices' that the interrupt has occurred.
3	The processor first finishes what it is currently doing, then branches to an interrupt vector and from there to the address of whatever ISR is registered to handle that interrupt.
4	The processor switches from the currently executing code and branches to the appropriate interrupt service routine.
5	The ISR acknowledges the interrupt and ends. It will have 'unlocked' any tasks pending the interrupt event.
6	Any higher priority tasks that are waiting get executed first.
7	Finally, context switches to the task assigned to deal with the event.
8	The task handles the event.

We will look more closely at each of the first five steps in the following subsections since these are strongly influenced by architectural issues.

6.5.2.1 An Interrupt Event Signals the Processor

The interrupt signal to the CPU is, by convention, normally active-low, and can be edge triggered or level triggered. An edge triggered interrupt signals to the CPU by the act of changing state. The processor then responds to this edge as soon as it can – even though the interrupt line may have reset itself in the meantime. Something like a key press might generate this type of interrupt (it should not matter how long the key is held down, the processor will respond in the same way).

A level triggered interrupt will be physically similar – but the processor samples this at predefined times to see what its state is, perhaps once per clock cycle. Once such a signal occurs, it needs to be asserted for a certain length of time before the processor 'notices' it, and this time may be configurable. For example, it should be asserted for three consecutive sample times to be genuine, rather than only once as in the case of a noise spike.

Once an interrupt signal is latched, whether or not the physical interrupt line deactivates again, the internal trigger remains set waiting. Eventually, some code in the processor will get around to servicing that interrupt. The question is, what happens if the interrupt line toggles again before the previous one has been serviced? As always, the answer depends on exactly which processor is being considered, but in general the second interrupt will be ignored. This is because the internal 'interrupt has happened' flag has been set and cannot be reset until it is cleared in software (in the ISR).

However, there have been several processors in the past which have been capable of queuing interrupt signals (especially processors which tended to be fairly slow to respond to interrupts). Queuing interrupt signals sounds like a fine idea, but it significantly complicates real-time handling and is therefore not usually considered these days as a potential hardware solution. The best solution is to handle whatever interrupts occur as quickly as possible.

6.5.2.2 The CPU Finishes What It is Doing

Modern processors cannot be interrupted in the middle of performing an instruction – they have to finish the execution of that instruction first. In the past, with CISC processors taking many cycles to perform some instructions, this was hugely detrimental to interrupt response time. For example, the Digital Equipment Corporation VAX computers are said to have had an instruction that took over 1 ms to complete, which is a long time to wait for an interrupt to be serviced (put in an audio context this means that a sample rate of 1 kHz would have been the maximum that could be supported by individual interrupts, far less than the 48 kHz and 44.1 kHz of today's MP3 players).

Attempts were made to allow sub-instruction interruption for processors using microcode, but this became horrendously complicated and was not popular. Real-time systems designers breathed a sigh of relief with the advent of RISC processors (Section 3.2.6) with their one-instruction-per-clock-cycle design rationale. This means that, in theory, the longest time taken for an instruction to complete is one instruction clock cycle, which tends to be very short on RISC processors. This would mean that the same short time is all that it takes for an interrupt to be 'noticed' and the branch to interrupt vectors.

In practice, this RISC concept is adhered to less strongly by some designers. The ARM for example, has a multi-cycle register load or store instruction which is really useful for fast data moves or for context save and restore, but which takes up to 16 cycles to complete. So the worst-case wait for the interrupt to hit the interrupt vectors is therefore 16 cycles.

One more thing to note is the effect of a pipeline. With pipelined instructions, although one instruction enters the pipeline in each instruction cycle, it takes n cycles to actually complete an instruction, where n is the length of the pipeline. Without complex dedicated hardware support, a shadow register system will have to wait for the current instruction to flow through the pipeline and store any result, before the jump to ISR can occur. Pipelines are great for very fast instruction throughput, but can be slower to respond to interrupts.

6.5.2.3 Branching to an Interrupt Service Routine

The traditional method of handling interrupts is that once one occurs, the program counter is loaded with a preset value, thus causing the CPU to jump to a special place. Typically, there is one of these special places for each type of CPU interrupt in the system. These places in memory are called interrupt vectors.

In the ARM, the interrupt vectors begin at address 0 in memory. Address 0 is called the *reset vector* – it is where the CPU starts at power-up or after reset. Each event and interrupt in the CPU follows in order. What is stored in this vector table is simply a branch instruction to the handler for that event. For the reset vector this will be a branch to something like __start. For IRQ1 it will be to the ISR designated to handle IRQ1 (the use of double underscore is common when translating between C language and assembler).

Here is a typical interrupt vector table for an ARM program:

```
B  __start
B  _undefined_instruction
B  _software_interrupt
B  _prefetch_abort
B  _data_abort
B  _not_used
B  _irq
B  _fiq
```

Figure 6.6 illustrates use of the interrupt vector table to handle an interrupt occurring during execution of a routine.

It can be seen that execution starts at the initial reset vector which branches to the start of the code that is to be run on the processor (B __start). This code progresses as

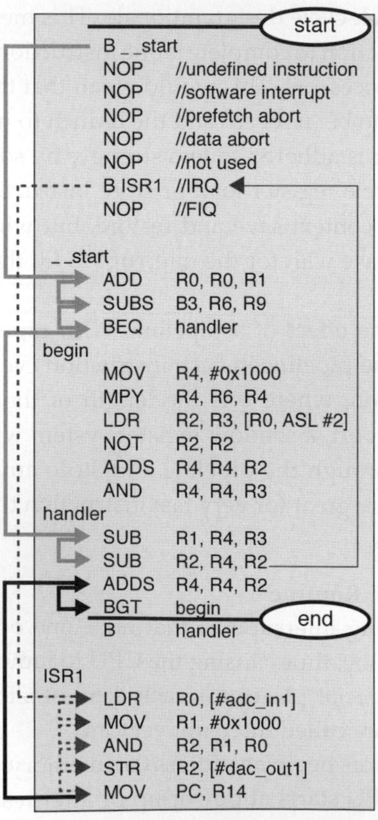

Figure 6.6 An illustration of the calling of an interrupt handler via a branch to the interrupt vector table. In this diagram, execution from power-on involves an initial branching to location __start. The interrupt occurs during the second SUB instruction in the *handler* subroutine, and so the branch to service the interrupt happens before the ADDS instruction. Normal operation is indicated by the solid arrows while control flow during the interrupt handling is shown by dotted arrows.

normal (indicated by the solid arrows on the left-hand side) until an interrupt occurs during the second SUB instruction. This instruction completes and then the processor jumps to the interrupt vector associated with that interrupt, which in this case is the IRQ interrupt. We can assume that, although it is not shown in Figure 6.6, there is a switch to shadow registers during this process. The IRQ interrupt vector contains a branch to the relevant interrupt service routine, which in this case is called ISR1. This services the interrupt and, once complete, returns to the instruction following the one in which the original interrupt occurred. Again, although it is not shown, it is assumed that a switch back from the shadow register set to the main set is performed during this return from interrupt. In some processors this happens automatically, but in others a different return instruction is required (for example the TMS320C50 has a RET to return from subroutine and a RETI to return from interrupt, which automatically POPs the shadow registers when it returns). It is fairly obvious in this case that the machine uses shadow registers. This is indicated by the fact that the ISR and the main code both use the same register names without any explicit context save and restore being performed in the ISR.

One more thing to note here is that the interrupts that are not used in the vector table are populated with NOP instructions, which would mean that if such an interrupt occurred, the NOP would execute, then the next NOP and so on until something happened. For example, if there was a data abort event (caused by some sort of memory error) then control would branch there, do the NOP, then the next NOP and finally reach the branch to ISR. So ISR1 would be executed – even though no IRQ interrupt had occurred. It is thus always better to put interrupt service routines for all interrupts whether they are used or not – and trap them displaying an error so that if the worst does happen and such an interrupt occurs, this error will at least be noted.

The interesting case of interrupt timing within the ARM processor is explored in Box 6.5.

Box 6.5

ARM interrupt timing calculation

The ARM has two external interrupt sources, the standard interrupt (IRQ) and the fast interrupt (FIQ), with the FIQ having higher priority. The shadow register sets provide six usable shadow registers for the FIQ and only one for the IRQ (*assume we need to use four*) registers. Each register load to/from memory takes two cycles because we have a 16-bit external bus, but instructions are 32 bits.

The IRQ interrupt vector is midway in the interrupt vector table, whereas the FIQ vector is at the end (*this means that no jump is needed for FIQ* from the vector table if the interrupt code is simply inserted at *this location onwards*).

The longest instruction on the ARM7 is a multiple load of 16 registers from sequential memory locations, taking 20 clock cycles. It can take up to 3 cycles to latch an interrupt. Assume that 2 cycles are needed for every branch. There is one operation with higher priority than both FIQ and IRQ (and that is an SDRAM refresh operation).

(*Continued*)

Box 6.5

ARM interrupt timing calculation (*Continued*)

Assume that this takes 25 cycles to complete and that the fictitious processor is clocked at 66 MHz.

We can now determine how long it will take to service an IRQ and an FIQ. Counting in cycles, the following events are timed from when the IRQ becomes active:

1. Time to recognise interrupt: 3 cycles.
2. Worst-case current instruction must finish first: 20 cycles.
3. In case SDRAM is being refreshed, wait for that: 25 cycles.

At this point, the CPU is ready to respond.

4. Branch from current location to read line in vector table: 2 cycles.
5. Act on instruction in table: branch to ISR, 2 cycles.

Now we are within the interrupt service routine (ISR).

6. Context save 3 registers (we need 4, 1 is shadowed) $2 \times 3 = 6$ cycles.
7. Execute first instruction to respond to interrupt: 2 cycles.

Total instruction cycles: 60 cycles

Total (66 MHz processor cycle is approximated to 15 ns): 0.9 μs

One microsecond is considered relatively fast in terms of CPU response time. Indeed, interrupt response time is one of the main advantages of the ARM architecture.

Now consider the case of the FIQ. In this instance, there are two main differences. One is the fact that more registers are shadowed and the other is that the FIQ code is resident at the interrupt vector, rather than one jump away. So the differences between FIQ and IRQ (above) are:

8. No need to branch to ISR: 2 cycles.
9. FIQ has 6 shadow registers, so no context saves needed: 6 cycles.

Total instruction cycles: 52 cycles.

Total (66 MHz processor cycle is approximated to 15 ns): 0.78 μs.

Can we do anything to improve this further (without over clocking!)? Yes, we can avoid the 20-cycle longest instruction in our code or change memory technology. Avoiding multiple load/save instructions and removing the SDRAM refresh cycle too, can help us achieve a cycle time of 0.2 μs. Note that ARM7-based processors do not normally use SDRAM, but those based on ARM9 and beyond do tend to.

6.5.2.4 Interrupt Redirection

One more point remains to be explained with regard to the interrupt vector table and that is in cases where the lower part of memory is mapped to non-volatile ROM since it contains a bootloader, and the upper part of the memory map contains RAM. Without some mechanism to alter the interrupt vector table, it means that whatever code is

Box 6.6

Memory remapping during boot

Some processors get around the problem of needing to execute two branches to get to an ISR by using a slightly different method. In the ARM-based Intel IXP425 XScale processors for example, on initial power-up, flash memory or ROM is mapped into memory address space 0 and upwards, intended for storing boot code. A register inside the CPU allows the boot code memory to be mapped upwards in memory, following which SDRAM is mapped at address 0 and upwards.

Thus, the bootloader simply needs to ensure that a program is loaded which contains its own interrupt vectors, and that these are located at the lowest address in RAM. Then the bootloader issues the remap command.

Unfortunately, it is not necessarily that easy since the bootloader itself is executing from an address in ROM, and when the remap occurs, the bootloader code will disappear. In other words, if the program counter (PC) is at address `0x00000104` executing the remap instruction, by the time the PC is incremented to point at the next instruction at `0x00000108` (steps of 4 bytes since each instruction is 32 bits), the instruction will not be there; it will have been remapped into a higher address space!

There is an easy, but tricky solution to this. See if you know what the solution is before reading it below.

We would avoid the problem if, after remap, exactly the same code is at exactly the same address as it was before. In practice, this means saving a copy of the bootloader code to RAM at its higher address before the remapping occurs, and this is the approach used by many XScale bootloaders, such as U-Boot.

Another solution is to split the bootloader into two parts or stages. The first stage exists to copy the second stage to a RAM address that is not affected by the remapping. Then this first stage jumps to the second stage which performs the remapping and, being safely out of the way, is unaffected by it.

loaded into RAM cannot take advantage of the interrupt vectors. This is not at all useful to code in RAM that wants to use an interrupt.

There is thus often a mechanism in hardware to remap the interrupt vectors to another address in memory (Box 6.6 shows an example of this from an ARM processor). This would mean that, on initial reset, a bootloader is executed which then loads some program and runs it. This program would cause the interrupt vector table to be remapped into RAM, into an address range that it occupies itself, can thus write to, and within which it places vectors for whatever interrupts it requires.

Where an RTOS is used, there may be a second layer of vectorisation: all interrupts trigger an appropriate ISR within the OS code itself, but external functions can register themselves with the OS to say that they should be called upon certain events. When such registered events occur, interrupts happen as normal, but the ISR is within the OS and must initiate a further branch out to the registered interrupt handler. This mechanism can provide a handy way to implement shared interrupts on a processor or system-on-chip that does not support hardware interrupt sharing. In this case, it is the responsibility of the OS to decide exactly which of the shared interrupts has occurred and then branch to the relevant handler code. The usual way of interrupt sharing in hardware is covered in Section 6.5.4.

6.5.3 Advanced Interrupt Handling

With the standard interrupt handling procedure in mind, it is instructive to examine one mechanism for efficiency of the process, and that is to preload the interrupt branch address into a register.

Consider the usual situation: when a particular interrupt occurs, the processor will jump to a given location in the interrupt vector table. This will contain a single instruction (or sometimes two) that normally commands the CPU to branch to another address where the relevant ISR resides. The process thus requires two sequential branches, and since Section 5.2 identified the branch instruction as one which is often inefficient in a pipelined machine, this solution is not particularly good.

Thinking about this, it seems that the CPU has to know where to branch in the interrupt vector table for each event. The vector addresses thus need to be stored within the processor – within some sort of register – and copied to the program counter (PC) when the trigger event occurs. Simply making the vector address register writable allows the vector address corresponding to a particular event to be changed. It is then possible to directly load the ISR start address into this vector address register. This would mean that when an event occurs, the processor can branch directly to the ISR without going through the vector table – and this applies to shared interrupts as well as dedicated ones.

The cost of this approach is a set of writeable registers (which occupy more silicon than read-only locations) and a slightly more complex interrupt controller.

6.5.4 Sharing Interrupts

Many computer systems these days implement interrupt sharing. This was initially a consequence of limitation on the number of pins on the integrated circuits used for hardware interrupts and the limited register sizes inside such CPUs to control interrupts. A very small number of physical CPU interrupts would thus be shared by many separate interrupts. For example, the ARM has two separate interrupts: an interrupt request (IRQ) and a fast interrupt request (FIQ) but a typical ARM-based system-on-chip embedded processor may have up to 32 interrupt sources that share the IRQ and FIQ lines.

Upon a shared interrupt occurring, the ISR started in response would then need to read a register identifying which of the shared interrupts had been triggered, and finally trigger the correct code to respond to this. The triggering might be through using RTOS constructs or by issuing a software interrupt. Sometimes, one huge ISR would service many shared interrupts.

Interrupt sharing requires an interrupt controller. This is either a separate integrated circuit dedicated to handling interrupts or more commonly today an

Figure 6.7

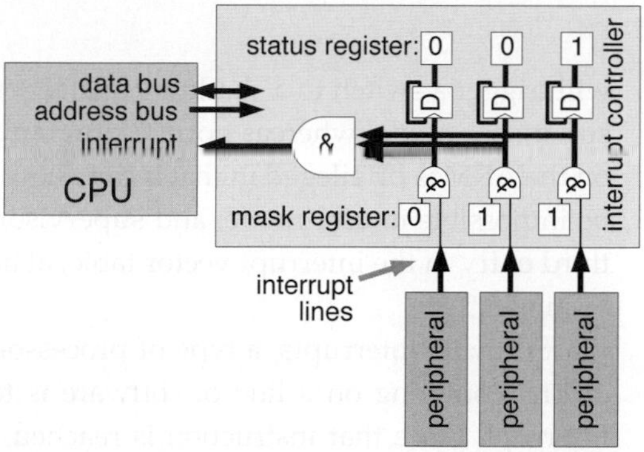

A block diagram of interrupt sharing hardware that might be used within an interrupt control block implemented in a system-on-chip processor.

advanced interrupt controller (AIC) block within a system-on-chip embedded processor. An example is shown in Figure 6.7.

In this example, it can be seen that the CPU itself has only a single interrupt line and this is shared among three peripherals. A CPU-writeable register inside the interrupt controller can mask out any of the shared interrupt line, but those that are not masked can cause the CPU interrupt to be triggered.

When the CPU interrupt is triggered, the CPU is able to read the status register to determine which of the shared interrupt lines caused the event. Usually, the act of reading this status register will clear the register ready for the next interrupt event (logic for which is not shown).

6.5.5 Re-Entrant Code

Although an interrupt that is asserted long enough to trigger an interrupt response and then de-asserts will be physically ready to re-assert, that does not mean that the same interrupt can be triggered again immediately. Although it varies on a processor-by-processor basis, most devices, when servicing one interrupt, do NOT allow that same interrupt to be activated until the ISR has finished (i.e. do not allow *re-entrant* interrupts). A second interrupt event will either be ignored while the first one is being serviced or will cause a re-trigger as soon as the ISR has completed.

Some more advanced processors allow a high priority event to interrupt a lower priority ISR, which requires hardware support through either separate shadow registers for each ISR or a careful context save and restore when it occurs.

6.5.6 Software Interrupts

Software interrupts (SWI) are methods for low-level software to interrupt higher-level code. They are typically reserved for operating system (OS) intervention in task-level code handling in an RTOS. In the ARM processor, issuing a software interrupt command:

```
SWI 0x123456
```

will trigger a switch to a shadow register set. In this case, the processor will also enter supervisor mode (whereas normal programs operate in user mode). Supervisor mode on the ARM is privileged in that it can allow low-level settings to be altered that would be impossible in user mode, and supervisor mode is accompanied by jumping to the third entry in the interrupt vector table, at address 8 (refer to the ARM table shown in Section 6.5.2).

Software interrupts, a type of processor trap, are useful for debugging. One way of breakpointing on a line of software is to replace the instruction with a software interrupt. Once that instruction is reached, the processor will interrupt, jump to the software interrupt vector and on to a software interrupt service routine.

Inside the software interrupt service routine, the conditions of the registers (of user mode) and memory would be communicated to the debug software. The debug software would then wait for commands from the user.

6.6 Wireless

It is unusual to find a section entitled 'wireless' in a computer architecture textbook. However, we purport to be considering computer architecture from the perspective of an embedded system, and embedded systems are increasingly designed around, and for, wireless communications.

Let us therefore briefly consider wireless technology as it relates to computers, especially embedded computer systems. We will classify wireless provision, then discuss the interfacing technology and issues relating to this. Much more information is provided in Appendix D, where specific technologies are surveyed along with suitable solutions for embedded systems.

6.6.1 Wireless Technology

Although wireless engineers have many classifications for wireless technology in terms of radio frequency band (RF), channel bandwidth, power, modulation and so on, for our purposes an embedded engineer would primarily consider different issues:

- **Connectivity to the CPU** – especially whether this is serial or parallel, as will be discussed in Section 6.6.2.
- **Data format** – is data sent in bits, bytes/characters, words or packets? This relates not only to the connectivity, but also whether some standard form of data interchange is used, such as USB or IP (internet protocol) packets.
- **Data rate** – typically measured in bits per second (and note the figure quoted by manufacturers is often before overheads such as packetisation, headers, error control and so on are included, so the rate available for application use may be significantly lower). Of course, it is important to match data rate to the application,

but for real-time use remember that data rate does not necessarily relate to latency. A system sending several megabits per second may respond to a single event slower than a system sending only several kilobits per second.

- **Form factor** – including physical size, number and size of antennae. Lower frequency devices usually require a larger antenna.
- **Range** – also related to power, there will be limits imposed by regulatory authorities (often 0.25 W, and almost always below 1 W, depending upon frequency band and use).
- **Power consumption** – again related to power, range and data rate.
- **Error handling** – are communications 'guaranteed' to be error free, or does the system need to take care of errors itself? This issue is covered more in Section 6.6.3.
- **CPU overhead** – another important factor to consider.

When a designer is given the task of providing wireless functionality for an embedded system, these consideration will need to be resolved and some trade-off point reached between them.

Many wireless standards exist and many are suitable for embedded systems as mentioned previously. Appendix D describes the main choices. In this section, we will consider the major issues that would allow a designer to sensibly analyse and evaluate the choices.

First of all, Figure 6.8 shows a block diagram relating the connection of a wireless solution to an application processor. The application processor is the CPU in the system being connected, and typically this is the only CPU in that application system.

Figure 6.8

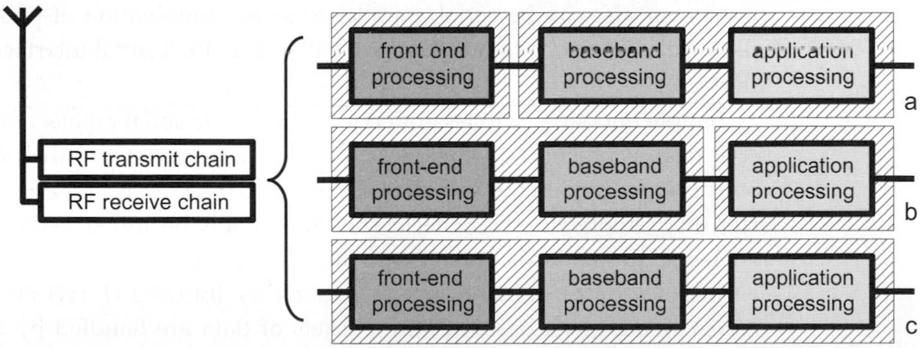

A block diagram of three alternative wireless processing schemes for an embedded computer showing two computational devices for the wireless processing plus one embedded applications process. These devices either handle processing needs separately or the baseband processing is performed together with (a) the applications processing, (b) an add-on device providing wireless functionality to an applications processor and (c) on all-in-one wireless and applications processing device.

Quite clearly, a wireless communication system usually requires a fair degree of signal processing and most of the wireless solutions that embedded systems designers would be considering these days are digital in implementation. Front-end processing (which could be analogue but is becoming more likely to be digital) is the very front-end signal conditioning performed on received and to-be-transmitted wireless symbols. This data may require processing at a MHz or GHz rate, almost always at a multiple of the bit rate. Baseband processing, by contrast, is slower protocol-level computation, such as packet handling, packet error checking, tracking re-tries and re-sends.

When systems designers do not choose to comply with a standard and instead define their own wireless scheme, the baseband processing will probably be performed inside the applications processor (as in Figure 6.8a). It may even be possible to use just a single computational device for *all* processing (Figure 6.8c). While this is also technically possible for simple standard protocols, many involve either a protocol overhead that is too great to be included in the applications processor or is not freely available to embedded systems designers in source code form. Thus, baseband processing needs to be undertaken separately, either in a separate device or together with the front-end processing (as in Figure 6.8b).

Probably the greatest reason to separate the wireless processing out from the applications processor is to not reinvent the wheel. It is truthfully quite difficult to create a reliable wireless communication system. Where a proven working solution is available off-the-shelf, this is a compelling reason to use it!

6.6.2 Wireless Interfacing

Since we have divided CPU buses into serial and parallel in Section 6.1, we can provide the same classification for wireless functionality. Although the actual data conveyed over air may be serial, parallel or some combination of both, at heart every wireless device needs to interface to a CPU either by a serial interface or by a parallel interface.

Simple and slow wireless interfaces tend to be serial connections: if we provide serial data at one end of a wireless link, we can receive it at the other end. If error control is provided in the link, then the received data can be assumed to be (relatively) error free. Otherwise, error checks should probably be added to the application code. Wireless USB standards also fall into this serial category.

Internel protocol-based schemes, such as IEEE802.11 (Wi-Fi) and IEEE802.16 (WiMAX), are block-based. Entire packets of data are handled by the protocols. So wireless solutions for these standards interface to a CPU using a parallel bus and often use direct memory access (see Section 6.1.2) to transfer data and to improve efficiency. In fact, this is much like the interfacing of a standard Ethernet device (Section 6.3.5).

6.6.3 Issues Relating to Wireless

At best, adding wireless functionality to a system simply allows another connection to be made to that system at will. Of course, wireless will obviously impact system power requirements and so on. However, there are other issues that should be considered.

The first of these issues has been touched upon previously: CPU overhead. Obviously, when the protocol handling function is being undertaken in the applications processor, a potentially significant proportion of the processing time will be occupied with that (and as always, consider the worst case – perhaps when every packet is received in error). However, even in the case where a separate device handles all of the wireless processing and protocol handling, even then an applications processor doing nothing but streaming data in and out, may require many CPU cycles to handle the wireless traffic.

When error handling is considered, the issue is that behaviour needs to be identified and coded in the case of the many different error types that are possible. Of course, this is just as true with wired Ethernet. However, wired Ethernet normally suffers extremes – no errors at all, or no packets at all. Wireless, by contrast, normally operates well within these endpoints.

A further issue is that of security – with wired connections, it is fairly easy to know what is connected (just follow the wires). However, a wireless connection is invisible. Designers should note that it is not always the correct recipient who receives data, and who replies. With the rapid growth of computer technology in embedded systems, many more people are entrusting their livelihoods and finances to such systems and some observers feel that security considerations have moved more slowly than the technological advancement in this field.

Finally, the very wireless signals themselves permeate the free space around a transmit antenna. There are many cases where these signals can couple back into the system that is generating them, to become significant sources of electrical noise on the buses and wires within that system. This issue is known as *electromagnetic interference* or EMI, and has been recognised in recent years as a very important contributor to systems unreliability.

There are two main impacts on computer systems designers. The first is that any system which is being designed is a potential source of EMI. Different bus designs cause different levels of EMI. For example, an ISA bus will cause more interference than an LDVS bus by virtue of the larger voltage swings and unbalanced nature of the ISA bus. Memory technology also varies considerably as a cause of EMI. This EMI, created by a computer system, can affect the systems around it (some readers may remember early home computers such as the Sinclair ZX Spectrum which, when turned on, would cause so much EMI that nearby FM radios would stop working), and can affect other parts of the system. The second issue is that embedded system designers probably ought to design their systems so that they can work, even when placed in the vicinity of a vintage ZX Spectrum. How to design such systems is not really a computer architecture issue, so will not be covered here. However, it is well covered in many books and papers on circuit design and PCB layout.

6.7 Summary

While having a wonderful calculating machine (CPU) is a good start to the building of a computer, it absolutely relies upon being provided with data and communicating its output in some way. It is a common axiom in computing that useless input data will generally lead to useless output data. However, this axiom does not just apply to the quality of data, but also to the quantity and timeliness.

In this chapter, we have considered computer interfacing, specifically using buses, both internal and external to convey that information. All computers, of whatever form, from room-sized mainframes to tiny medical diagnostic computers embedded in a pill, require buses to communicate. While there are a large number of standard buses available, more are being invented all the time (and there is nothing to stop an engineer from constructing his or her own bus design).

In this chapter, we tied our consideration of buses with the related discussion of real-time issues that are so important in many of today's human-centric embedded systems, and a separate consideration of wireless technology for embedded computational devices.

With this, we conclude much of our investigation into computer architecture. In the following chapter, we will begin to put much of the techniques we have learnt into practice.

Problems

6.1 An embedded 40 MHz CISC CPU has a slowest instruction (a divide) that takes 100 clock cycles to complete. The fastest instruction (a branch) only requires 2 clock cycles. There are two interrupt pins for high-priority interrupts (HIQ) and low-priority interrupts (LIQ).

Once an interrupt pin is asserted, 4 clock cycles are needed to recognise this fact and begin to initiate a branch to the interrupt vector table. Assume no other interrupts are enabled, and note that an interrupt must wait for the current instruction to complete before being serviced.

a. Calculate the worst-case HIQ interrupt response time, timed from pin assertion until the initiation of a branch to the ISR contained in the interrupt vector table.
b. The HIQ ISR requires 10 ms to complete execution (measured worst-case from when the HIQ pin is asserted). What is the worst-case LIQ response time?

6.2 The CPU in Problem 6.1 contains 16 general-purpose registers. Describe what hardware techniques could be used in the CPU design to improve ISR performance in terms of context save and restore (to reduce the time taken for an ISR to complete).

6.3 Comment on the following four techniques in terms of their effect on interrupt response times:

a. Virtual memory
b. A stack-based processor
c. A RISC design (instead of CISC)
d. A longer CPU pipeline

6.4 Determine the likely real-time requirements of the following systems and decide whether each real-time input or output is hard or soft:

a. A portable MP3 player
b. The anti-lock braking system installed in a family car
c. A fire-alarm control and display panel
d. A desktop personal computer

6.5 Draw a bus transaction diagram for a flash memory device connected to a 100 MHz processor. The flash memory datasheet specifies the following information:

- 40 ns access time
- 20 ns hold-off time
- 20 ns address select time

Problems

6.6 A real-time embedded system monitors the temperature in a pressure vessel. If the temperature exceeds a certain value, the system must flash a warning light at 1 Hz and open a pressure relief valve. The system reads the temperature every 100 ms over a serial line and takes around 10 ms to decode the serial received data into a temperature reading. In the worst case, the temperature can spike rapidly within 150 ms to levels that can cause an explosion.

If the three input and output signals (serial temperature input, pulsed warning light output and pressure relief valve control) are each handled by separate tasks, determine the temporal scope of each of these and classify them by degree of hardness.

6.7 Consider the PC104 interface and its pin definitions shown in Table 6.1. In an embedded system that implements the entire set of connections shown, how wide can the data bus be? When using the expansion connector J2/P2, the system has an extended address bus available. Calculate the maximum addressing space that this would allow, in MiBytes.

6.8 In the LVDS (low-voltage differential signalling) scheme, the voltage swings from representing a logic 0 to representing a logic 1 are much less than in other signalling formats. For example, a voltage difference of 12 v between logic 0 and logic 1 is common in EIA232 (RS232), whereas many LVDS drivers can only output a voltage difference of 0.25 v. Does that mean that EIA232 is likely to be a more reliable choice in systems experiencing high levels of electrical noise? Justify your answer.

6.9 Relate the parts of the Ethernet driver in Section 6.3.5 to the layers in the OSI model in Appendix B (although note that in practice the TCP/IP networking system which is the normal use for Ethernet employs a slightly different layering architecture to the OSI model).

6.10 A simple preemptive multi-tasking embedded computer executes three tasks, T1, T2 and T3, which are prioritised in that order (highest priority first). Task T1 requires 1 ms of CPU time, is triggered every 10 ms and must complete before it is triggered again. Task T2 requires 3 ms of CPU time, is triggered every 9 ms and must complete within 8 ms of being triggered. Task T3 requires 1 ms of CPU time, is triggered every 6 ms and must complete within 4 ms of being triggered.

Assuming that all tasks are triggered at time $t = 0$, draw a scheduler diagram for this system (similar to that shown in Figure 6.5 on page 269), marking the time in ms along the x-axis, from time $t = 0$ up to $t = 40$ ms.

Problems

Determine whether, in the time interval shown, all tasks meet their respective deadlines.

6.11 Repeat Problem 6.10. The only difference is that the tasks are now ordered using rate monotonic scheduling. Does this change make any difference in terms of tasks meeting their deadlines over the first $t = 40$ ms of operation?

6.12 A consumer electronics device requires a small, low-power and medium-speed CPU controller. Discuss whether a parallel-connected data memory storage system or a series-connected data memory storage system would be more appropriate.

6.13 If the system of Problem 6.12 was 'souped up' so that performance and speed became more important than size and power consumption, would that affect the choice of bus you would choose?

6.14 Figure 6.9 shows the timing diagram for the Atmel AT29LV512 flash memory device. The timing parameters shown have the following values from the Atmel datasheet:

Figure 6.9

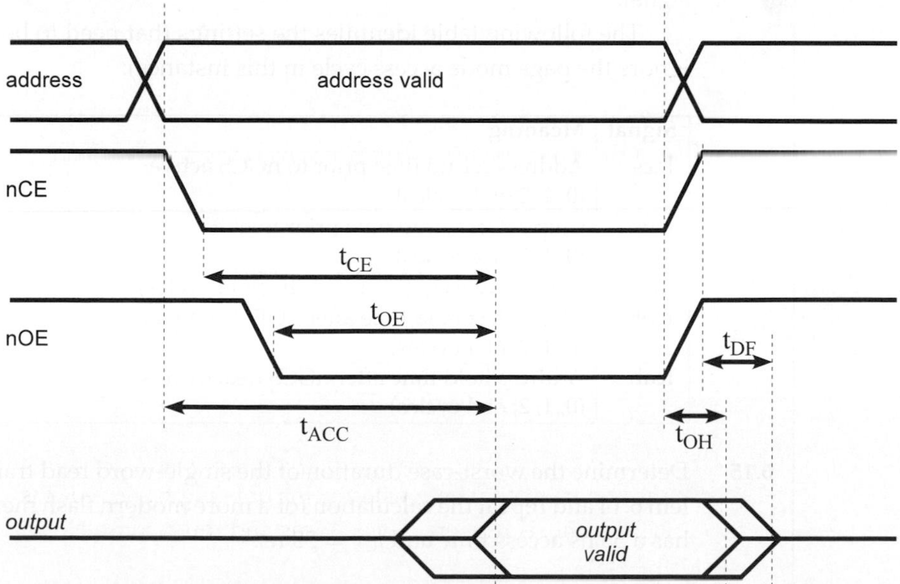

The read cycle of the Atmel AT29LV512 flash memory device (this waveform was drawn from inspection of the Atmel AT29LV512 datasheet).

Problems

Parameter	Meaning	Minimum	Maximum
t_{ACC}	Access time (address valid to output delay)	–	120 ns
t_{CE}	nCE to output delay	–	120 ns
t_{OE}	nOE to output delay	0 ns	50 ns
t_{DF}	when nCE or nOE[1] de-assert to output Hi-Z	0 ns	30 ns
t_{OH}	output hold from address, nCE or nOE[2]	0 ns	–

1: From whichever one was de-asserted first.
2: From whichever one was de-asserted or changed first.

Any values that are not given are assumed to be unimportant. Also, remember that this timing diagram is from the perspective of the flash memory device when being read from something external – presumably a CPU. It shows the timings that the CPU reads *must* comply with for the flash memory device to work correctly.

For this question, determine how to set up the S3C2410 parallel interface timing registers so that it could access a parallel-connected Atmel AT29LV512 device correctly. This will require careful reading of Section 6.2 (and also Box 6.2). Note that the HCLK signal (and hence the entire bus clock) is running at 100 MHz and the Atmel chip enable signal, nCE is connected to the S3C2410 nGCS signal.

The following table identifies the settings that need to be found (note, we ignore the page mode access cycle in this instance):

Signal	Meaning	No. of cycles
Tacs	Address set-up time prior to nGCS active (0, 1, 2 or 4 cycles)	
Tcos	Chip select set-up time prior to nOE (0, 1, 2 or 4 cycles)	
Tacc	Access cycle (1, 2, 3, 4, 6, 8, 10 or 14 cycles)	
Tcoh	Chip-select hold time after nOE deactivates (0, 1, 2, or 4 cycles)	
Tcah	Address hold time after nGCS deactivates (0, 1, 2, or 4 cycles)	

6.15 Determine the worst-case duration of the single-word read transaction in Problem 6.14 and repeat the calculation for a more modern flash memory device that has a 55 ns access time and $t_{CE} = 55$ ns.

6.16 The Atmel AT25DF041A is a 4 Mibit serial flash device, using an SPI interface that runs up to 70 MHz.

Problems

To read a single byte from a selected AT25DF device requires that a controller CPU first outputs a read command (which is the byte `0x0B`), followed by a 24-bit address, followed by a dummy byte. Each of these fields is clocked out serially, at up to 70 MHz from the serial output pin. Without the CPU stopping the SPI clock, the Atmel device will then output the byte stored at that address, serially, over the next eight clock cycles for the CPU to read.

Determine how many clock cycles in total this 'read byte' transaction is, and thus the minimum length of time taken to read a single byte from this device. From this simple calculation, how many times faster was the AT29LV512 single location read of Problem 6.14?

Note: It must be mentioned we are not being particularly fair in either instance. First of all, both devices are more efficient when reading a string of memory locations; the SPI device particularly so. Secondly, the SPI device has a faster read command available which we did not use – by commanding a read using command byte `0x03` instead of `0x0B` it would not have been necessary to insert the dummy byte between the final address bit and the first output bit, although this mode is only specified for clock frequencies up to 33 MHz.

6.17 Match the following applications (a to e) to an appropriate bus technology, taking account of issues such as bandwidth, latency, power consumption, external/internal computer communication, number of wires, noise immunity, distance and so on.

a. A device which is to be connected to an embedded computer for a disabled user to open and close a sliding window, and which has a single LED to warn when the window is open.
b. A graphics output device to be built into a powerful embedded computer which streams video data from a CPU at 1.8 Gibits per second.
c. An industrial automation computer needs to connect to a sensor located 500 m away across an electrically noisy factory (where wireless devices will not work due to interference). The sensor returns temperature data at just a few 10's of Kibits per second.
d. An FPGA co-processor needs to be built into an x86 processor system to stream vast amounts of data as quickly as possible.
e. A small embedded industrial PC needs a peripheral card that can connect to a set of 20 analogue-to-digital converters (ADCs) with a combined data rate of about 6 Mibytes per second.

For these five applications, there are five available bus technologies to choose from, one per application:

- AGP 4x
- USB 1.1

Problems

- PC/104 (16-bit ISA)
- 16x PCIe (16 lane PCI express)
- EIA422

6.18 What are five of the timings that can describe the temporal scope of a task in a real-time system?

6.19 Identify the general sequence of operations that occurs when an interrupt occurs in most embedded-sized CPUs.

6.20 Describe the hardware necessary to implement interrupt sharing for a processor such as the ARM that has only a single general-purpose interrupt signal (IRQ – if we ignore the fast FIQ). Note any additional overhead that this may impose on the software of the interrupt service routine.

CHAPTER 7

Practical Embedded CPUs

7.1 Introduction

Computer architecture has been an academic discipline for decades – taught to generations of engineering students, and reflecting much of the state of the hardware available during the decade prior to it being taught as a subject. A decade gap between course updates was fine when mainframe computers were the norm, but became a little troublesome as personal computers entered the scene.

The author fondly remembers being taught the 8086, 6502 and Z80, and yet he owned a first generation ARM-powered desktop machine (considered blazingly fast in those days). Strangely, the gap also meant that students destined to work in the growing embedded systems industry or exploding consumer electronics industry, were still being taught techniques and technology more suitable for mainframe computers, for many years.

This book has slightly different aims – mainframe-only techniques are covered only in passing, whereas techniques of interest to embedded systems engineers are covered in depth. The focus is on practicalities and encouraging the translation of the knowledge gained into real-world experience.

Up to this point, the book has primarily been foundational and theoretical in nature. However, in this and the following chapter, we plunge boldly into practicalities: we enter the real world of embedded computers. We analyse what needs to be done to make computers work in that world, and in so doing cover several gaps that exist between the theory and reality of embedded computer architecture.

7.2 Microprocessors are Core Plus More

One of the more popular microprocessors that is available at the time of writing (and incidentally is not new, being around five years old) is the ARM9-based S3C2410 from Samsung, which we have mentioned before. Let us turn our attention to this little device for a moment, examining the following list of device features:

- 1.8 v/2.0 v ARM9 processor core, running at up to 200 MHz
- 16 KiB instruction and 16 KiB data cache
- Internal MMU (memory management unit)
- Memory controller for external SDRAM (synchronous dynamic random access memory)
- Colour LCD (liquid crystal display) controller
- Four-channel DMA (direct memory access) mechanism with external request pins
- Three-channel UART (universal asynchronous receiver/transmitter) with support for IrDA1.0, 16-byte Tx FIFO and 16-byte Rx FIFO
- Two-channel SPI (serial peripheral interface)
- One-channel multi-master IIC (inter-integrated circuit) bus driver and controller
- SD (secure digital) and MMC (multimedia card) interfaces
- Two-port USB (universal serial bus) Host plus one-port USB Device (version 1.1)
- Four-channel PWM (pulse width modulation) timers
- Internal timer
- Watchdog timer
- 117-bit general-purpose I/O (input/output) ports
- Twenty-four channel external interrupt sources
- Power control, with states for normal, slow, idle and power-off modes
- Eight-channel, 10-bit ADC (analogue-to-digital converter) and touch-screen interface
- Real-time clock with calendar function
- On-chip clock generator

The S3C2410 is an excellent and feature-packed device, well suited for embedded systems, and consequently adopted by many industry developers over its lifetime so far. As we have seen in Section 6.1, such devices are sometimes called system-on-chip (SoC)[1] processors, to recognise the presence of so many peripheral components. The core at the heart of the system is the ARM processor, identical to that in almost all other ARM9 systems.

Although Samsung probably does not reveal full internal details of the size and arrangements of the S3C2410 components in silicon, we can surmise that the largest part of the silicon integrated circuit (IC) is devoted to cache memory. The component that consumes the next largest area of the silicon die would be the central processing unit (CPU) core. Other large components are the MMU, SDRAM memory handlers and perhaps the ADCs.

[1] Smaller SoC systems are sometimes referred to as single-chip microprocessors or single-chip microcontrollers.

In the early years of ICs, the CPU chip was just that, a single-chip CPU, which was itself an integration of many components that were previously separate. As time progressed, more and more functionality has been subsumed into some of these devices. For embedded systems, semiconductor companies have realised that designers prefer to use fewer individual devices where possible, and hence the many on-chip features. Not all features will be needed in any one embedded system design, but conversely, any design will require at least some of the features mentioned. There are several practical implications of having such highly integrated SoC processors:

1. A reduced chip-count leads to reduced area, and usually reduced product cost.
2. When choosing an SoC, designers can draw up a 'wish list' of features, and then try to find one device which matches this list as well as possible. Any item not integrated can still be incorporated externally.
3. Some hardware design is effectively subsumed into software (in that the designer would ask, 'how can I use this on-chip peripheral?' rather than 'how can I implement this function in hardware?').
4. Occasionally, limitations in the on-chip features can constrain the functionality of products. It is easier to change an externally-implemented feature than it is to change one which is included on-chip.
5. Designers now have to wade through CPU data 'sheets' that can exceed 1000 pages in length (and often hide critically important details in a footnote on page 991).
6. Some functions cannot co-exist. For example, a feature list might proudly proclaim both IIC and UART support, but neglect to mention that the device will support only one of these at a time (either due to insufficient multiplexed device pins or insufficient internal serial hardware).

Even mainstream processors tend to devote more silicon area to cache than they do to normal CPU functionality, since cache memory is seen as an excellent method to improve processor performance. Consider as an example the 64-bit VIA Isaiah Architecture (also known as the VIA Nano), a recent x86-compatible processor, shown in Figure 7.1. It can be seen that the largest area on silicon is devoted to cache memory. There are also separate blocks for clock generation (phase-locked loops – PLLs), very fast floating point (FP), SIMD architecture (specifically, the SSE-3 extensions that the device supports, as discussed in Section 4.7.4, which also explains why they are co-located with the floating point unit – FPU). Other interesting blocks are a section devoted to cryptographic processes, re-order buffer (ROB) for out-of-order execution, extensive branch prediction and retirement hardware at the end of the pipeline, reported to be more than ten stages in length. There are also two 64-bit integer units (IUs) and three load/store units with memory re-order buffer (MOB). Pads along the top and bottom are used to 'wire' the silicon to the lead frame within an IC package. This device, constructed on a 65 nm process has a 64 KiB L1 cache and 1 MiB L2 cache, and uses around 94 million transistors. For reference, compare this to a leading desktop/server CPU, the 450 million transistor quad-core Phenom device from AMD (which also includes 2 MiB of L3 cache), shown in Figure 7.2.

Figure 7.1

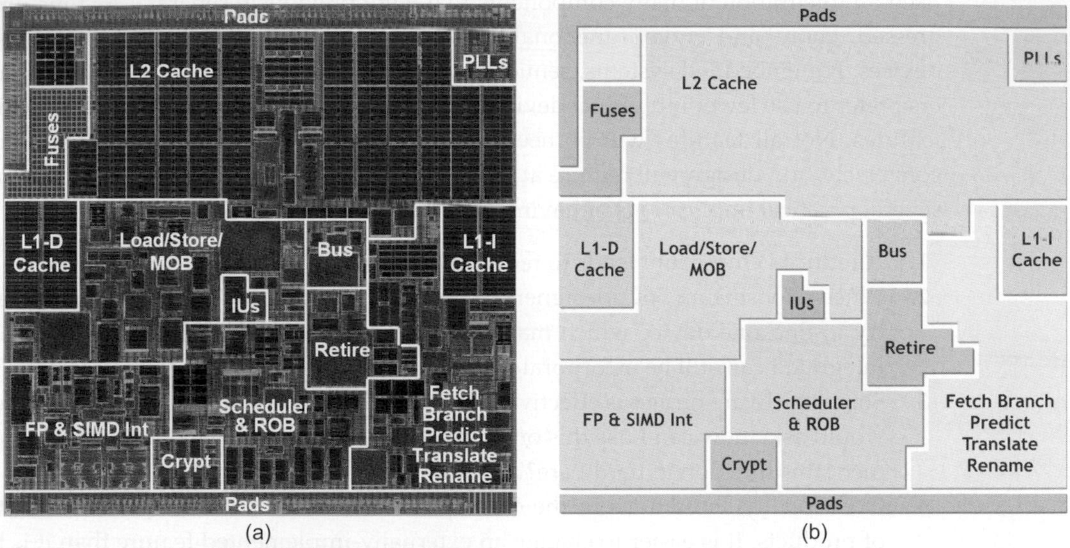

The VIA Isaiah Architecture, a lower-power x86-style CPU, particularly suited for mobile computing applications such as notebook computers, showing the internal arrangement of the device on the silicon (photograph and diagram courtesy of VIA). (a) Die photograph, showing an overlay of functional area blocks. (b) Block diagram of the functional areas fit within the silicon area.

7.3 Required Functionality

In many systems, there are features which are 'nice to have' and features that are essential. Deciding between the two for SoC processors really depends upon the application that they are being considered for. For example, one system may require a serial port, another may require SPI.

For this reason also, SoC manufacturers do not quite agree upon a definitive list of 'must-have' peripherals, and this variety is a good thing for those of us searching for devices to embed within our designs. In fact, the situation is normally consumer device driven: a large company selling millions of systems is likely to be able to convince a semiconductor manufacturer to incorporate exactly what they require, whereas the pleas of a small independent designer to include a particular peripheral are likely to fall upon deaf ears.

However, there are one or two peripheral components that can be considered essential in almost any design and will be found in the majority of SoC processors:

1. *Reset* circuitry (explored in Section 7.11.1) is necessary to ensure that any device starts with registers and state in a predictable, known condition.
2. *Clock* circuitry is needed to distribute a global clock to all parts of a synchronous design. Often a phase-locked loop (PLL) or delay-locked look (DLL) will be used

Figure 7.2

The AMD Phenom^{TM} Quad-core processor die. Note the horizontal and vertical lines of symmetry dividing the silicon into four distinct cores. The non-symmetrical strips along the top and bottom of the device are the interface to double data rate random access memory and 2 MiB shared L-3 cache respectively. The central vertically-oriented rectangle hosts the main bus bridging system for connecting the four cores together, while that on the right and left sides host physical interfaces (photograph courtesy of AMD).

to condition the oscillations generated by an external crystal and to adjust the frequency.

3. *IO* (input/output) drivers to connect to external pins, driving sufficient current to toggle voltages on wires connected to the device. These also have some responsibility for protecting the delicate electronics inside an IC from static charges, shorts and voltage spikes picked up from off-chip sources. Many devices include *GPIO* – general-purpose IO which is programmable in direction, drive characteristics, threshold and so on, discussed in Box 7.1.
4. *Bus* connections, again to the outside world, for connection to external memory, peripheral devices and so on. These are usually implemented as an array of IO drivers acting in concert.
5. *Memory* itself is required either on-chip or off-chip, and normally a combination of volatile storage for variables and stack, plus non-volatile storage of program code.
6. *Power management circuitry* is required for power distribution throughout a device, turning off unused parts of a chip and so on.
7. *Debug* circuitry, such as IEEE1149 JTAG is now considered a requirement rather than a nicety in most cases (we explore this in more detail in Section 7.9.3).

Box 7.1

Configurable I/O pins on the MSP430

The Texas Instruments MSP430 series of devices has, like many processors designed for embedded systems, great configurability in its I/O pins. As evidence, consider the pin definitions for one particular device, the MSP430F1611.

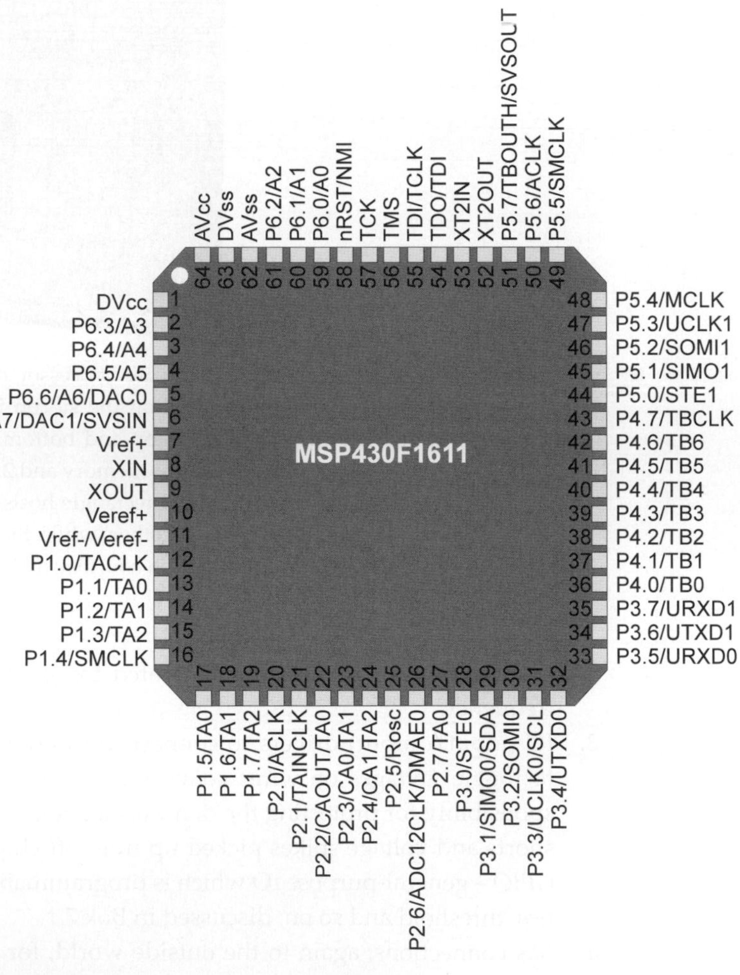

On this 64-pin package device, note that apart from the power and ground connections, voltage reference inputs, crystal oscillator connections and two of the JTAG pins, every pin has multiple possible functions: 51 of the 64 pins are configurable. As an example, refer to pin 5 – this can serve as GPIO port 6-bit 6 (P6.6), as 12-bit ADC input channel 6 or as 12-bit DAC output channel 0, depending upon the particular configuration performed in software by the device programmer.

In Box 7.2, we will explore exactly how these pins can be configured.

Box 7.2

Pin control on the MSP430

Box 7.1 showed the pinout of a Texas Instruments MSP430F1611 to illustrate the ability of a single output pin to have many possible configurations. In fact, these pin configurations are under software control – so let us consider how this mechanism works.

The MSP430 has several pin control registers, arranged in 8-bit ports (such that P1.0 to P1.7 constitute port 1, P2.0 to P2.7 are port 2 and so on). Each port has eight I/O pins individually configurable for input or output, and which can individually be read from or written to. In many cases, they can also be used as interrupt sources. Let us consider the registers for port 2.

Register `P2DIR` is an 8-bit direction register. Each bit in this register controls whether the corresponding pin is configured as an input or as an output. Writing a low value to a particular bit makes that pin an input. Writing a high value configures the pin as an output. For example, writing the value `0x83` would set P2.7, P2.1 and P2.0 as outputs, and the remaining pins as inputs.

Register `P2IN` is an 8-bit register with each bit reflecting the input value on the corresponding pin. So if this register is read, returning a value `0x09`, then we know that the voltage on pins P2.3 and P2.0 is high, and the voltage on all other pins is low. Note that if we had configured P2.0 as an output and P2.3 as an input, then we would now know that P2.0 is currently outputting a logic high value and some other device is providing a logic high input voltage to P2.3.

Register `P2OUT` is another 8-bit register which determines the logic voltage output by each port pin that is currently configured in the output direction. Pins that are configured as inputs will ignore any value written to this register.

There remains one final configuration, and that is to choose between using those pins as a GPIO port, and connecting them to their alternative functions. For this, register `P2SEL` switches the pin between the GPIO port registers and the peripheral modules. Writing a logic low to each bit connects that pin to the GPIO register, and a logic high selects the peripheral function for that pin. For example, writing `0x81` to `P2SEL` will select the following functions:

Device pin	20	21	22	23	24	25	26	27
Function	`ACLK`	`P2.1`	`P2.2`	`P2.3`	`P2.4`	`P2.5`	`P2.6`	`TA0`

Two things should be noted at this point. The first is that the exact meaning of the peripheral function(s) is determined by the peripheral module and its configuration is as specified in the device datasheet. Where some pins have three meanings, one is always the GPIO port and the other two belong to peripheral modules (and choosing between those has nothing to do with the pin-select logic. This must be configured through the peripheral module).

(Continued)

Box 7.2

Pin control on the MSP430 (*Continued*)

The second point is that if a pin is configured for its peripheral function, the direction of the pin must be set appropriately (by writing to `P2DIR`). Some processors will do this automatically, but in the MSP430 it must be done by the programmer. So, for example, if one particular pin is defined as a serial port output and has that function selected by a write to the `P2SEL` register, then the corresponding pin value in the `P2DIR` register should be set to logic 1, otherwise no output will occur.

Most devices also include one or more internal UARTs (universal asynchronous receivers/transmitters) or USARTs (universal synchronous/asyncronous receivers/transmitters), an internal real-time clock module (RTC), several timer-counter devices, internal cache memory and so on.

It is interesting to compare the features of CPUs that have been designed to address different market segments, and we do that in Table 7.1. Each of the three example devices tabulated is characteristic of its class, is in popular use and is of relevance to the embedded system architect. The single-chip microprocessor, a Texas Instruments MSP430F1612, is an exceptionally low-power device (in lowest power modes it can literally be run from the electricity generated by two lemons) and has a wide range of low-level peripherals built into the system. Here, the emphasis is on ensuring a single-chip solution for those who choose this device for their designs. Hence, there is no provision for external memory. The Samsung S3C2410, by contrast, is a reasonably feature-rich ARM9-based SoC that is powerful enough for application as a personal digital assistant, in a smartphone and similar. It not only has an SDRAM interface, an extensive static random access memory (SRAM), read-only memory (ROM) and flash capabilities on its parallel bus (which we had seen exemplified in Section 6.2), but also a wide range of external interfaces – particularly communications and interconnection-based ones. Finally, the VIA Nano, which we also met previously, in Section 7.2, is presented. This is in some ways a standard personal computer processor, although it has been redesigned to be highly power efficient, and much smaller than typical desktop processors. Thus, it is a promising choice for an embedded system that requires an x86-style processor. This device concentrates on being excellent at computation: the emphasis is on performance at lower power. The many peripherals available in the other two devices are absent, although another add-on chip (also available from VIA) can provide most of these, and much more functionality.

We will now examine a few of these 'must-have' CPU requirements in a little more detail, namely clocking, power control and memory. Later (in Section 7.11), we will look at device resetting and in particular, consider watchdog timers, reset supervisors and brownout detectors.

Table 7.1

Example devices from three classes of microprocessor: a single-chip microcontroller, system-on-chip microprocessor and a personal computer CPU, compared in terms of built-in features. Note that the Texas Instruments MSP430 family is available in up to 171 model variants at the time of writing, each having significantly different features and abilities – family devices can clock up to 25 MHz, contain up to 16 KiB of RAM and 256 KiB of flash, and add or drop a wide selection of peripherals. By contrast, both the Samsung and VIA parts have, at most, a small handful of model variants.

	Single-chip micro TI MSP430F1612	**SoC CPU** Samsung S3C2410	**Personal computer CPU** VIA Nano
Clock speed	8 MHz	266 MHz	1.8 GHz
Power	<1 mW	330 mW	5 to 25 W
Package	64-pin LQFN/P	272-pin FGBA	479-pin BGA
Internal cache	None	16 KiB I + 16 KiB D	128 KiB L1 + 1 MiB L2
Internal RAM	5 KiB	None	None
Internal flash	55 KiB	None	None
Internal width	16 bits	32 bits	64 bits
External data bus	None	32 bits	64 bits
External address bus	None	27 bits	Unknown
Memory support	None	ROM to SDRAM	DDR-2 RAM
ALU	1	1	2
FPU	No	No	Yes
SIMD	No	No	SSE-3
Multiply	16 bits	32 bits	Up to 128 bits
ADCs	12 bits	8 × 10 bits	None
DACs	2 × 12 bits	None	None
RTC	No	Yes	No
PWM	No	4	No
GPIO	48 pins	117 pins	None
USARTs	2	3	No
I2C	Yes	Yes	No
SPI	2	2	No
USB	No	2 host, 1 device	No
Watchdog timer	Yes	Yes	No
Brownout detector	Yes	No	No
Timer	2	1	Yes
JTAG	Yes	Yes	Unknown

7.4 Clocking

When looking at control of a CPU in Section 3.2.4, we considered the important role of a system clock in controlling micro-operations. In fact, we have not emphasised the importance of clocking enough: apart from the very rare asynchronous processors (which we will encounter later in Section 9.4), all processors, most peripherals, buses and memory devices rely upon clock-synchronous signals for correct operation.

Clocking is particularly important around CPU blocks containing only combinational logic, such as an arithmetic logic unit. If a clock edge controls the input to an ALU, then the same clock edge cannot be used to capture the output from the ALU (since it takes a certain time for the ALU to do anything). It is necessary to use either a later clock edge or a two-phase clock (two asymmetrical clocks that are non-overlapping and whose edges are separated by the maximum combinational logic delay in the clocked system).

In practice, it is often more convenient to use a single clock, but perform different functions on different edges of the waveform. An example of this is shown in Figure 7.3 where an ALU is operated using different edges of a clock. Starting with the first falling edge, these operations are to (i) drive the single bus from R0, on the first rising edge to (ii) latch this value into the first ALU register and de-assert the bus driver. Following from this, (iii) and (iv) repeat the procedure for R1 into the second ALU register. Having now received stable inputs, some time is required for the ALU signals to propagate through to a result in step (v). Step (vi) then loads this result into register R0.

Figure 7.3 also shows the main clock signal at the bottom of the plot, operating at frequency $F_{clk} = 1/T_{clk}$. The operations fed from this clock, on either the rising or

Figure 7.3

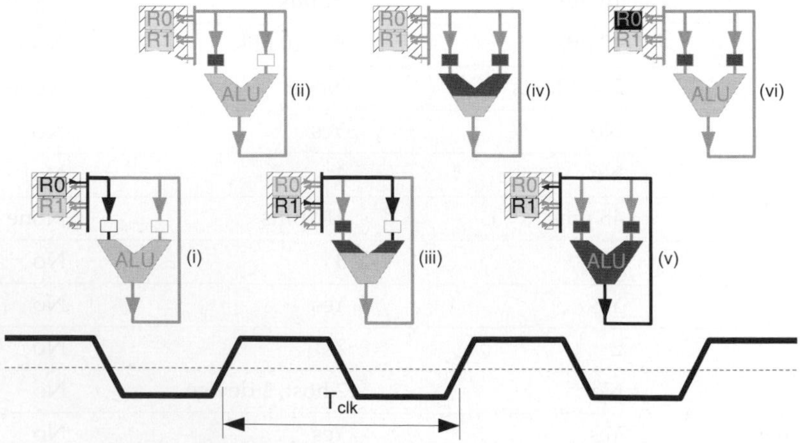

An example of different gates and latches driving an ALU synchronous to a single-phase CPU clock, similar to the cycle-by-cycle timing diagram of Figure 3.3 on page 71. The operation being performed is R0 = R0 + R1, shown divided into six sequential stages.

the falling edge, are performed when the clock crosses some threshold voltage (shown as a dashed line). Note that the edges of this clock are not entirely vertical – there is both a rise time and a fall time associated with the clock. In fact, the point at which the clock crosses the threshold each cycle will vary slightly due to electrical noise, circuit capacitance, inductance, temperature and so on. This is termed *jitter*.

Jitter is also caused by the threshold voltage varying (or more often the threshold staying the same, but the clock voltage varying slowly with time). In turn, jitter causes the value of T_{clk} to change from one cycle to the next. Obviously, if a clock rate had been chosen so that it gave just enough time for a signal to propagate through an ALU, then any major jitter would cause the clock cycle to shorten occasionally and the ALU result to consequentially not be ready in time. The result is erratic behaviour.

Therefore, clock integrity is very important and most systems are clocked slower than the fastest cycle time that they can accommodate. This also means that with a very stable clock and power supply such systems can actually operate faster than their rated frequency (which is one reason why CPU over-clocking was so popular in certain personal computer circles for many years).

7.4.1 Clock Generation

These days, most CPUs and virtually all SoC processors can generate an internal clock frequency from an externally connected crystal oscillator, with at most a couple of tiny external capacitors required.

In order to achieve clock generation, these modern devices must contain phase-locked loop (PLL) circuitry to condition the raw oscillator clock input. Usually, there will also be internal frequency divider and multiplier hardware to allow, for example, the Samsung S3C2410 to clock at 266 MHz using a 12 MHz external clock (in fact, clock divide registers allow a large number of operating frequencies to be generated from any one particular external crystal).

The similar technology of a DLL (delay-locked loop) is slightly less flexible and slightly less accurate, but is simpler and cheaper to construct in silicon. Note also that there is usually a provision for an external oscillator signal to be fed directly into such CPUs, if such a frequency is already available.

Many systems these days require a *real-time clock*, usually provided from a separate 32.768 kHz external crystal (and separate PLL). A 32.768 kHz crystal is a very inexpensive device and can be quite tiny. Often, it is referred to as a watch crystal due to its prevalence in timing circuits: the reason being that the signal can be divided by 2^{15} to yield a one second timing pulse that can drive clock and calendar circuitry (referred to as a 1 pps or 1 pulse per second, signal).

Although very accurate crystals can be sourced, such as oven-controlled crystal oscillators (OCXO) used in radio frequency (RF) circuits, most microprocessors use either a standard quartz crystal or even a ceramic resonator. These have accuracies of around 100 ppm (parts per million), which equates to 0.0001%. This would translate to less than one hour per year inaccuracy, at worst. More expensive parts can easily achieve 10 ppm and OCXOs can achieve accuracies in the range of a small fraction of 1 ppm.

7.5 Clocks and Power

Reading CPU datasheets, one can often find the clock and power control subsystems sharing a chapter, and in many cases sharing system control registers too. There is a very good reason for this, based upon the fact that clocking is the direct cause of most power consumption within a CPU.

Examine, for a moment, where power gets consumed in modern CMOS (complementary metal oxide semiconductor) systems. Without delving too deeply into semiconductor theory, let us briefly consider a simple gate, such as the NAND structure shown in Figure 7.4. The 'complementary' name comes from the fact that the output is connected either directly to Vss or directly to Vdd through the transistors (one path is always on and another path is always off).

In a perfect world, the CMOS system would connect the output to Vss or Vdd with no resistance. However, we know that a 0 Ω resistance is impossible in the real world, and that there will be some wire resistance, some drain-source resistance and so on. The consequence of this resistance is to restrict the flow of current from or to Vss or Vdd, and it thus takes some time to charge up the output (or load) capacitance. Once the gate is switched from one state to another, an electrical current flow is triggered, either charging up or emptying the output capacitance. As the charge level changes, the voltage across the capacitor either rises or falls. This is shown more clearly in Figure 7.5, where the CMOS gate is replaced with a perfect switch. Most important is the logic level output at the bottom of the graph: in a digital circuit such as a NAND gate, the time taken from

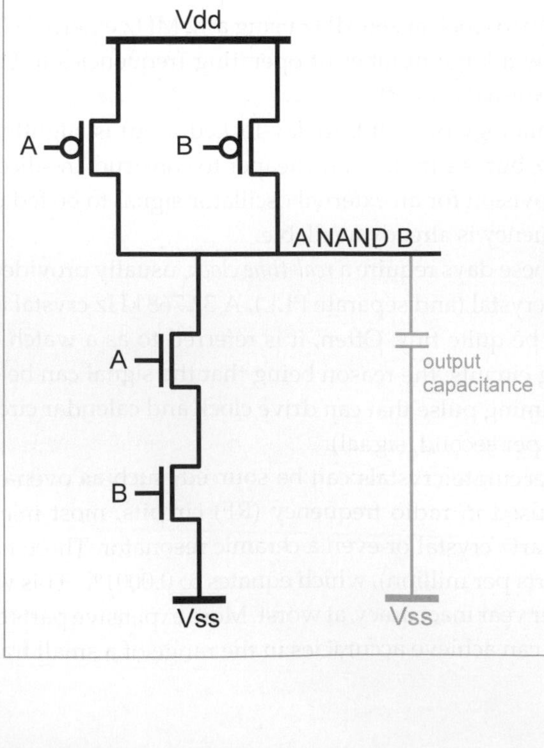

Figure 7.4 Complementary metal oxide semiconductor (CMOS) gate design for a NAND circuit, showing the MOS transistors connecting directly to source and drain voltages. A grey-coloured output capacitor is also shown to reflect the capacitance of the load that is to be switched by the NAND output.

Figure 7.5

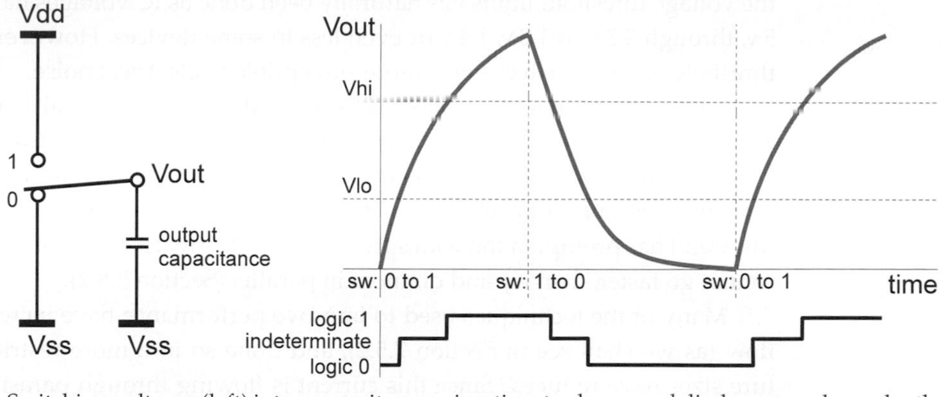

Switching voltages (left) into a capacitor requires time to charge and discharge, as shown by the plot which indicates the capacitor voltage over time as the switch position changes. Note the Vlo and Vhi thresholds for logic voltages, and the corresponding plot along the bottom showing the logic level of the voltage stored in the capacitor over time.

when an event happens (such as a switch position changing) until the output logic level stabilises, causes the propagation delay that we first discussed when considering the carry-propagate adder in Section 2.4.2.

In fact, the situation is actually more complex than we have presented. There are parasitic capacitances within all of the silicon gates (not just on the output), parasitic resistance in each wire, gate connections and so on, and even parasitic inductance in the wires and gates. These, in general, act to exacerbate the issue that we have observed for the load capacitance.

Having understood the basic issue of capacitance in the system, we can note two important consequences of this which we will examine further:

1. *Propagation delay* comes from the time taken to charge up, or discharge these capacitances, through the small resistance present in the wires and conductive tracks in silicon.
2. *Current flow* is caused by gate switching – since current must flow for the capacitors to charge or discharge.

7.5.1 Propagation Delay

To reduce propagation delay (as described in the previous section), silicon designers can do several things: reduce the capacitance (primarily by making the gate smaller, since capacitance is proportional to the area of overlap of the gate structure etched into the silicon), reduce the voltage thresholds so that they are reached quicker or supply more current so the capacitor charges more quickly. Feature sizes of silicon gates have shrunk rapidly over the years and may now be nearing the lower limit of possible sizes, but smaller sizes tend to mean higher resistance, which in turn restricts current flows, and so materials have changed to reduce semiconductor 'on' resistance. Narrowing the voltage threshold limits has naturally been done as IC voltages have reduced from 5 v, through 3.3 v to 1.8 v, 1.2 v or even less in some devices. However, reducing these thresholds makes such systems more susceptible to electrical noise.

Basically, silicon IC designers have squeezed their systems in all ways: carefully balanced trade-offs and reduced propagation delays using all of the easily available means and many difficult ones too. This has led the year-on-year rise in device clock speeds from the 1950s up until 2007 or so. However, the difficulty associated with continuing this trend has prompted the widespread move into greater levels of parallelism – if you cannot go faster, then try and do more in parallel (Section 5.8.2).

Many of the techniques used to improve performance have increased the current flow (as we shall see in Section 7.5.2), and done so in a more restricted area as feature sizes have reduced. Since this current is flowing through parasitic resistors, it is expending energy in the form of heat. Heat dissipation in a resistor is actually proportional to the square of the current multiplied by the resistance (and since the current is proportional to the voltage, the main reason why silicon manufacturers have been keen to reduce supply voltage is to reduce current flow, and thereby reduce power). Unfortunately, resistance is inversely proportional to area, and area has reduced due to feature size shrinkage, so resistance tends to increase. This is one area of significant trade-offs.

Over all, though, resistive losses have increased, and with clock frequencies having risen so that switching is more often, the losses occur more often, and thus amount to a greater rate of power loss. This means that there is less time for heat caused by gate switching to dissipate, and thus temperatures naturally increase. It is not uncommon for silicon junction temperatures to reach or even exceed 125°C in a CPU.

Smaller feature sizes pack more hot junctions into a given volume, and shrinking IC packages mean that it can be more difficult to extract the heat from these. Thus, fans, heat sinks, heat pipes and so on are necessary to remove the heat.

While we will not consider fans and heat sinks further, we will look at methods of reducing power consumption in computers, something of particular relevance to embedded systems that are often required to operate on limited battery power.

7.5.2 The Trouble with Current

Static resistive loss in CMOS gates does consume some power (i.e. even when gates are not switching, there is a tiny current flow which consumes energy), but this is normally dwarfed by the current flow caused by gate switching.

The instantaneous inrush of current caused by a single MOS transistor switch is provided by a power supply circuit, often through a power plane or along wide power tracks on a printed circuit board (PCB). Currents switched to ground are absorbed by a ground (GND) plane on a PCB. Unfortunately, the power tracks, power and ground plane also each have a small resistance. When a very short but significant pulse of current caused by a gate switching passes through these resistors, there will be a compensatory voltage drop.

In reality, of course, there are hundreds of thousands of gates, all being switched at the same time, so the instantaneous current effect becomes multiplied. A sensitive oscilloscope, operating in differential mode, can detect the voltage drops, occurring in time with a system clock, quite easily, when connected between a power supply output and a device power pin. Good circuit design practice is to place external bypass capacitors close to device power and ground pins of digital logic. These act to couple much of the high frequency noise found on a power supply pin directly to ground. In addition, they act as power reservoirs to deliver the short sharp pulses of current that are required synchronous to a system clock.

Switching currents can be very large, perhaps even hundreds of amps for an x86-class device, but they last no more than a few nanoseconds. Another issue caused by this is electromagnetic interference (EMI – mentioned briefly in Section 6.6.3). Any time there is a movement of electrons, there is an associated movement in the electric field exerted by them, and in fact, circuit elements conveying pulses of current can very effectively act as antennae to radiate synchronous noise (or to pick it up from elsewhere).

7.5.3 Solutions for Clock Issues

Without reducing switching frequency, system voltage or changing gate design, current flows will not alter radically, although techniques such as providing bypass and reservoir capacitors can, as we have seen in Section 7.5.2, alleviate some of the problems.

However, we can consider a number of solutions to the issue of clock-induced EMI. The first is to use multiple clocks, each slightly out of phase with each other. If there are four out-of-phase clocks and a circuit is split so that roughly one quarter of the gates are clocked by each of the four clocks, then the peak current flows will drop by a factor of 4 (even though in total the same amount of current will be flowing overall).

Moving to a more steady current will significantly reduce EMI since electromagnetic radiation depends on voltage fluctuations: if we can approach direct current (DC) flow, we solve all EMI issues.

Slightly more ambitious is the concept of a spread-spectrum clock. Essentially, this is either periodically and randomly changing the clock frequency by small discrete steps, so that the energy radiated is spread over several frequency bands, or it is through deliberately introducing jitter into a system to prevent clock edges from 'lining up' exactly.

EMI generated by power or signal lines as a result of current flows can also be counteracted by having a near-identical line running in parallel and carrying an equal but opposite current flow. This is termed a balanced electrical circuit and is commonly used in low voltage differential signalling (LVDS) to reduce EMI.

7.5.4 Low-Power Design

If power consumed in a CPU relates primarily to clock frequency, then one good method to reduce power is to clock the CPU slower. In embedded systems, this is often possible by writing to clock scaling registers that are accessible in many microcontrollers and SoC processors. At certain times, processors may be 'working hard', and at other times may be mostly idle. Peak CPU clock speed, which is matched to the peak workload of a processor, does not need to be maintained at all times.

A simple method of scaling the clock in a real-time system that has many tasks operating, is to dedicate a single background task which runs at the lowest priority. An algorithm within the background task detects how much CPU time that task is occupying over a certain measurement period. If this becomes excessive, the system is evidently idle for most of the time and can scale back clock frequency. However, where the background task CPU time drops to zero, the system is working hard and the clock frequency should be scaled up.

Most major CPU manufacturers, even those designing x86-class processors, now have variations of this system, which are essential for extending battery life in notebook computers.

Another method of reducing the power of a design is even simpler – turn off what is not being used. Surprisingly, this idea took a while to become popular among IC designers, but now most processors designed for embedded systems contain power control registers which can be used to de-power unused circuitry. Where these are used, most programmers simply enable the required blocks and disable the others during the start-up phase of their program. However, it is often better to control these dynamically.

The two methods of power control are illustrated in Figure 7.6 where the current consumption of a SoC processor is plotted as a program is executed which uses

Figure 7.6

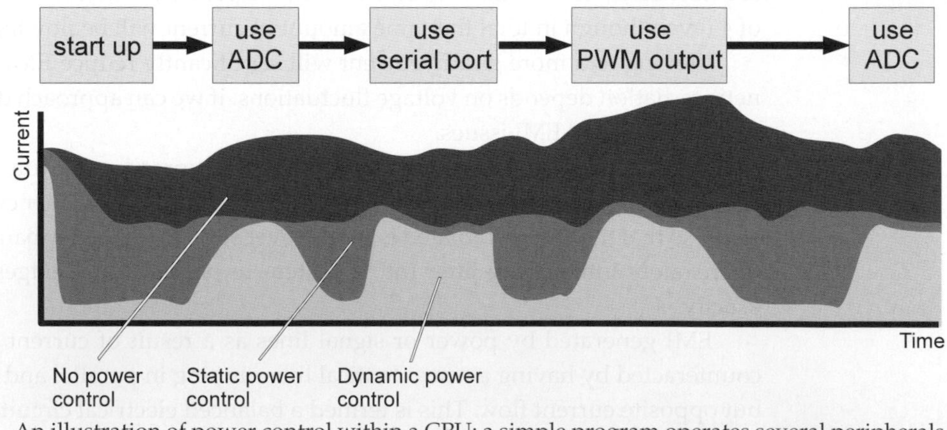

An illustration of power control within a CPU: a simple program operates several peripherals in turn (namely ADC, serial port, PWM and then ADC again), and the current consumed by the device is measured. Three scenarios are shown: no power control, static power control (where all other unused peripherals are turned off during start up) and dynamic power control (where all peripherals are turned off by default during start up, and then are only enabled individually for the duration of their use). The area under each of the curves relates to the total energy consumed under the three scenarios.

a subset of available on-chip peripherals. Static power control reduces current by turning off all peripherals that will not be used, at the beginning of the program. Dynamic power control, by contrast, turns off all peripherals and only turns them on when needed, and only for the duration of their use. In each case, the area under the graphs represents the total energy consumed – if this system was running from a battery, it would indicate the amount of battery power consumed in the three cases.

There are many other useful methods of power control in embedded systems. Consider the following unsorted list of hints and tips for embedded systems designers:

- There is no need to power a light-emitting diode (LED) indicator continually since the human eye will still see a solid light even if it is, for example, turned on for 1 ms every 50 ms (and this will consume only 1/50 of the power).
- Use a combination of clock scaling and intelligent dynamic power control to achieve lowest power consumption.
- When waiting for an event in software, try to find a method of 'sleeping' which can place most processors in a very low-power mode, rather than use a *busy wait* loop which polls repetitively.
- Even if polling is necessary, consider entering a short sleep (which can be exited by a timer interrupt) wherever possible and where the CPU is idling.
- Fixed point calculations are normally lower power than floating point calculations.
- On-chip memory is normally lower power than off-chip memory. Therefore, wherever possible, use on-chip memory for frequently-accessed variables.
- Data moves consume power (and time). Therefore, it is a good idea to maximise operations on data structures in-place that is, by passing a reference to them to operating functions, rather than passing a copy of the entire array.
- Block together operations that use higher-power devices. For example, in the original iPod, the hard disc drive was a major consumer of battery power, so Apple designed a system with a large memory buffer. The system would read one or even two tracks from the hard disc into memory, then power down the hard disc while these tracks are replayed. Later, perhaps after a few minutes, the disc would be re-powered to retrieve the next one or two tracks. In this way, the hard disc was powered for only very short times.

7.6 Memory

We have discussed memory many times in the previous chapters and introduced several acronyms such as SDRAM, double data rate (DDR) and so on. Let us now consider a few types of memory and their characteristics that might be relevant to computer architects and those building embedded computer systems. We shall begin with a recap of computer memory history before looking in detail at ROM and then RAM technologies.

7.6.1 Early Computer Memory

It should be noted that in the early days of computing, there was not a single 'memory' and in particular program storage and variable storage were seldom confused or even considered in any way equivalent. It was only with the advent of von Neumann machines that program and data bytes began to share storage space.

Generally, the earliest programmable computers (such as those mentioned in Chapter 1) were either hard-coded through their wiring or programmed with switches, and tended to use valves or delay lines for bit-level storage. Reprogramming such machines proved inflexible, as resetting wires (or even switches) every day to reprogram a system is time consuming and error prone. Punched cards (or tape) were quickly adopted for program storage – bearing in mind that these had been used effectively for more than 200 years to program looms for textile manufacture.

Data storage was accomplished through delay lines, sometimes with some quite interesting methods (such as cathode-ray tube delay lines, mercury delay lines, acoustic delay lines and so on). These would hold a bit of information for a short time, allowing the computer to work on something else in the meantime: effectively the memory function in a simple digital calculator.

Later, magnetic core memory was invented and magnetic storage was used for both variable storage and program storage, on tape. Magnetic discs were used for both and later evolved into both floppy and hard disc drives.

The greatest advance in memory technology came, as with many other areas, in the integration of circuits onto silicon. This provided rewritable memory storage for variables by the mid-1960s, and read-only memory for code during the same era. However, the higher cost per bit of silicon memory compared to magnetic storage has meant that, although silicon memory conquered most magnetic memory use in computers by the 1980s, the mass storage of data on hard disc drives has remained stubborn. It has only been very recently that hard disc-less computers have been considered viable for anything except the smallest of embedded systems.

Today, however, almost all embedded systems contain flash memory, and several brands of sub-notebook computer are similarly going solid-state: these should in theory be lower power, less susceptible to shock damage and more reliable than their cousins which incorporate hard disc drives.

There is now little to differentiate memory for program code and for data: any of the devices discussed below in this chapter are capable of storing and handling bytes of both types. However, certain characteristics of access for each type of data can match the capabilities of memory types, so we shall consider these in turn.

7.6.2 Read-Only Memory

Read-only memory (ROM) is not a technology, but rather a method of access: data stored in ROM can be read but not written to by the computer. This means that the data is non-volatile and unchanging, a characteristic that is well suited to program code, but could also be useful occasionally for data if that remains constant (e.g. digital filter coefficients or a start-up image for an MP3 player display).

Figure 7.7

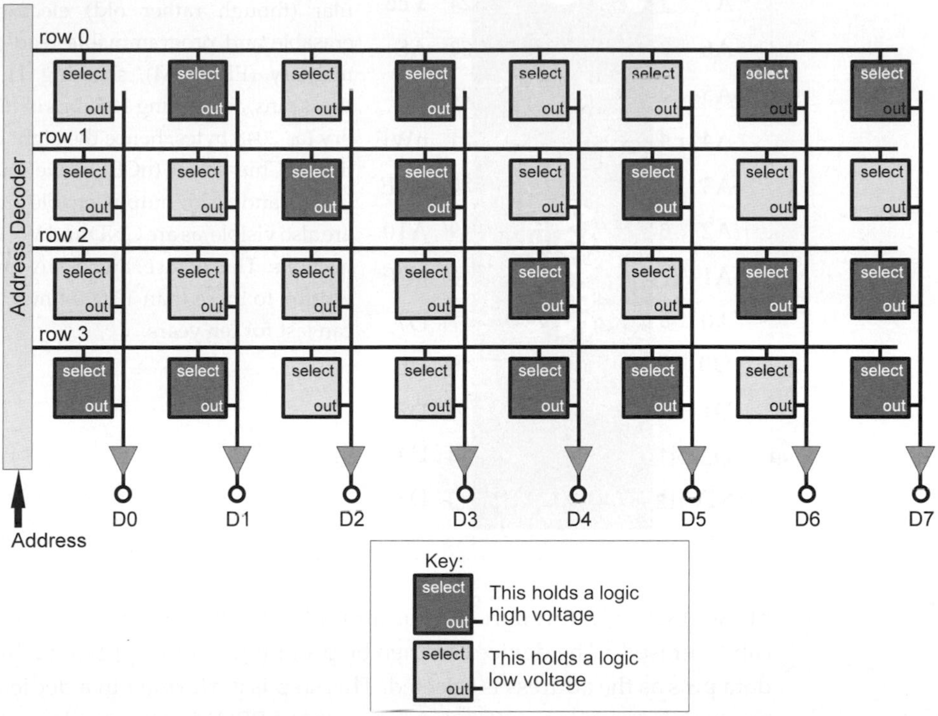

A simplified diagram of a ROM, showing a matrix of logic cells addressed by row and feeding an 8-bit data output. If the dark cells are assumed to contain logic 1 and the light cells logic 0 and output their content when selected, then an address input that selected row 1 would cause a data output of `00110100`b or 0x34 in hexadecimal. For correct operation, only one row should be selected at any one time.

At its basic level, a semiconductor ROM is simply a look-up table implemented in silicon. Given an address input, it selects a gate located 'at' that address, which then outputs its content onto a data wire, with one data wire for each bit. This is shown in Figure 7.7, where a 4-byte ROM is illustrated, although the actual arrangement within ROM devices in use currently is a little more sophisticated than shown.

Some ROM devices are (despite their name) writeable. However, the name indicates that the predominant action is reading, and that writing is either not possible when in-situ or is inconvenient. Let us now consider some varieties of ROM technology.

A basic, or mask *ROM* IC is a simple silicon device having an address bus, chip-select input, read signal input, power and ground pins. It will output the content of the currently selected memory location onto the data bus.

An *EPROM* device – an erasable programmable ROM (PROM) has a small silica 'window' on the top of the device, through which the IC can be seen. By shining

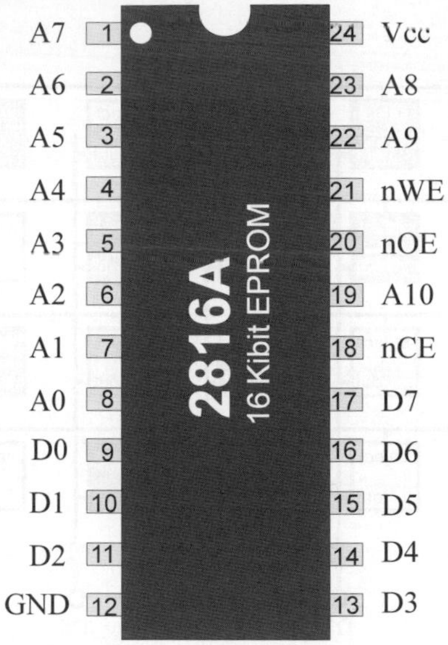

Figure 7.8 A diagram giving the pinout of a popular (though rather old) electrically erasable and programmable read-only memory (EEPROM), showing 11 address pins, addressing 16 Kibits of memory (as 2048 bytes, hence the eight data lines). Chip select (nCE), write enable (nWE) and read/output enable (nOE) are also visible, as are GND and Vcc connections. This device, the 2816A can be written to more than 10,000 times, and can last for ten years.

ultra-violet light through this for around ten minutes, the data stored in the device can be erased.[2] The device can then be programmed by applying a high voltage to the data pins as the address is selected. This step is performed in a dedicated EPROM programming machine, which also means that EPROMs are usually socketed so they can be removed and re-inserted at will. When a device is manufactured without the silica window, it becomes a non-erasable EPROM (which is simply a PROM). Some silicon fuse-based ROMs are also available. In these, the high-voltage inputs blow fuse wires in the silicon to turn on or turn off connections.

As an advancement on the EPROM, the *E²PROM* or *EEPROM* is an electrically erasable PROM, and (depending upon the manufacturer) can be synonymous with *flash memory*. These devices require a programming power supply of approximately 12 v to erase and reprogram their memory contents. However, many modern devices can generate this 12 v internally from a 3.3 v or 5 v power supply. Due to the technology used, these have a finite lifetime, normally specified in terms of data retention and erase cycles, which are typically over ten years and 1000 to 10,000 times. The engineer choosing these devices should note that, while data read times are quick and do not change over time as the devices age, both the erase time and the reprogramming times can lengthen significantly. Figure 7.8 shows the pin arrangements of one of these devices, with a parallel address bus and a parallel data bus. The nWE pin (active-low write enable) is a give-away, indicating that this device can be written to. A true EPROM

[2] Daylight will also erase the device, but it takes a lot longer. Therefore, engineers always have to remember to stick a label over the window if they want their program to last for more than a few days or weeks.

Box 7.3

NAND and NOR flash memory

There are actually two different types of flash memory technology: NAND and NOR flash. They are named after the gate structures used to implement them. NAND flash is a block-based, high density and low-cost device, well suited to mass storage. NAND devices can replace the hard disc drives in embedded computers and are also suitable for storage of data in devices such as MP3 players.

NOR flash, by contrast, may be less dense, and appear to the programmer as a type of ROM. However, through a complicated sequence of data writes, the read-only nature can be unlocked and block-based rewrites performed.

A comparison of the two types of flash technology is shown below:

Feature	NOR	NAND
Capacity	big	bigger
Interface	like SRAM	block-based
Access type	random access	sequential access
Erase cycles	up to 100,000	up to 1,000,000
Erase speed	seconds	milliseconds
Write speed	slow	fast
Read speed	fast	fast
Execute-in-place	yes	no
Price	higher	lower

For embedded computer use, code storage and so on, we will confine our discussion to NOR flash (which is the one we will most likely encounter, especially in parallel-connected devices). Thus, unless otherwise stated, the flash memory devices discussed in this book are NOR flash.

would look similar, and even have the same pin connections, apart from this one (which would probably be marked 'NC' to denote 'no connection').

There are actually two types of flash memory technology. They are NAND flash and NOR flash, as explained in Box 7.3.

Serial flash, shown in Figure 7.9 also contains flash memory, but in this case has a serial interface instead of a parallel interface. Having a 25 MHz serial bus, through which command words, address byte and control signals must run, this is obviously significantly slower than the parallel-bus devices. Because of the nature of the addressing scheme in these devices, where a read/write address is specified (which takes some time to specify serially) followed by any number of reads or byte writes (which happen a lot faster), they particularly suit the storage of information which is to be read off sequentially. They are least efficient when randomly reading or writing individual bytes.

Most flash devices, whether parallel or serially accessed, are arranged internally into a number of *blocks* or pages. When the device is new, every byte within the device

Figure 7.9

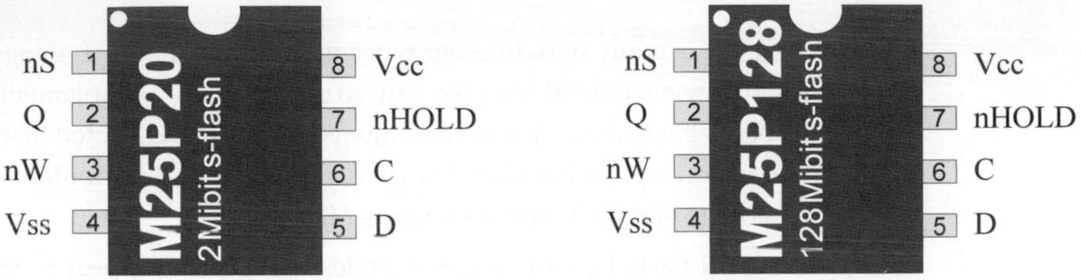

Serial flash devices, by using a serial interface, multiplex control, address and data on the same interface. Thus the size of memory array contained within the device on the right does not require extra dedicated address pins, despite containing 64 times as much data as the device on the left. Note also that this device is tiny – only 6 mm × 5 mm.

is initialised to `0xff`. In other words, every bit stored within the device is initialised to '1'. Any memory location can be addressed and read from and each byte will return with the value `0xff`.

Any location can also be programmed. What happens is that each bit that is a '1' and is programmed with a '0' is cleared to a '0'. Any bit programmed with a '1' stays *unchanged*.

For example, starting with a byte `0xff`, if a value `0xf3` is programmed, then that byte will become `0xf3`. If the same location is programmed again with the value `0xa7`, then the byte will become `0xf3 AND 0xa7`, which is `0xa3` (since `1010 0111 AND 1111 0011 = 1010 0011`). Clearly, if a byte is written to over and over again, it will eventually end up at `0x00`. So developers working with flash memory can see that unerased portions of flash will be filled with `0xff`.

When flash memory is erased, each byte needs to again be set to `0xff`. In fact, the devices are erased block-by-block, so that once the erase command is issued, the entire block selected for erasure will become `0xff`. It is also possible to lock memory blocks against erasure.

Reading flash memory is accomplished in the same way as reading a ROM, and follows a standard bus transaction as seen in Section 6.2. In essence, this means that a CPU connected to external flash can read it by (i) setting the address bus to the desired location, (ii) asserting the chip-select signal, nCE, (iii) asserting output enable, nOE, (iv) allowing the device some time to access the desired location, determine the contents, and output this on the data pins, then (v) reading the data bus before (vi) de-asserting all signals in turn.

A write is physically possible by performing much the same sequence of actions, except this time driving the data bus with the value to be written and asserting write enable (nWE) instead of nOE. If this was performed on an SRAM chip (described in the following section), it would write to the desired address location. However, flash memory is slightly more complicated. It requires a specific command sequence to be written to the device to control it (and before any memory locations can be programmed).

Some of these command sequences for two typical flash memory devices from Atmel and Intel respectively, are shown in the following table:

	Atmel AT29xxx		**Intel 28F008SA**	
	data	address	data	address
Program	`0xaaaa`	`0x5555`	`0x10`	*<addr>*
	`0x5555`	`0x2aaa`	*<data>*	*<addr>*
	`0xa0a0`	`0x5555`		
	<data>	*<addr>*		
Erase sector	`0x00aa`	`0x5555`	`0x20`	*<addr>*
	`0x0055`	`0x2aaa`	`0xd0`	*<addr>*
	`0x0080`	`0x5555`		
	`0x00aa`	`0x5555`		
	`0x0055`	`0x2aaa`		
	0x0050	*<addr>*		
Erase device	`0x00aa`	`0x5555`	not supported	
	`0x0055`	`0x2aaa`		
	`0x0080`	`0x5555`		
	`0x00aa`	`0x5555`		
	`0x0055`	`0x2aaa`		
	`0x0010`	`0x5555`		

Thus, to program a word of value `0x1234` to address `0x1001` in the Atmel device would require four write cycles:

- Write `0xaaaa` to address `0x5555`.
- Write `0x5555` to address `0x2aaa`.
- Write `0xa0a0` to address `0x5555`.
- Finally, the device is set to accept the data by writing `0x1234` to address `0x1001`.

For the Intel device, the sequence is somewhat shortened:

- Write `0x0010` to address `0x1001`.
- Write `0x1234` to address `0x1001`.

The reason for the complicated series of writes is to prevent spurious reprogramming of flash (which could happen when a CPU program operates incorrectly – it is not difficult to create a program that randomly writes data to different address locations!). As a further protection mechanism, these devices carefully sense the voltage of the power supply and if they detect under-voltage or significant fluctuations, will not allow a write to begin. Various status registers can be read from the devices (again by writing a series of commands to place the devices into 'read status register mode' or equivalent, so that the following one or two read commands will return the status register contents). Another command is used to read back a manufacturer and device identifier, so a well-written program can determine the correct programming algorithm for the particular flash memory device that is connected.

Note that different manufacturers have different command sequences to control their flash memory, although the two shown represent the two main classes into which almost all other manufacturers fall (i.e. all other devices are handled similarly to these).

Flash memory is fundamentally a block-based technology – although individual words can be read and programmed as needed, it is entire blocks that get erased (and this is true in any flash-based technology such as compact flash (CF) cards, secure digital (SD) cards, memory sticks and so on, even though this may not be noticeable to the user). The practical implication is that changing a single byte in one 64 KiB block of flash memory will usually require the following steps:

- Read the entire block from flash into RAM.
- Find the byte that needs to be changed in RAM and replace it with the new value.
- Issue the command sequence to erase the flash block.
- (Wait for the above to complete.)
- Issue the command sequence to begin writing and then write the entire block back into flash.

Blocks may be quite large – the 64 KiB mentioned earlier is not uncommon, so flash memory is not a good choice for storing small variables that change frequently!

From a programmer's perspective, it is useful to have different blocks dedicated to storing different types of information. In embedded systems, there are particular concerns over boot memory (we will discuss this further in Section 7.8). A simple scheme is to place items that seldom need to be rewritten into one set of blocks and items that may need to be rewritten more often (such as configuration settings) into another block.

As flash memory ages, it tends to slow down. Both erasing and programming bytes can become time consuming. Obviously, it is better if a flash memory device does not slow down a computer that it is attached to. So the designers of flash memory have come up with some ingenious ways to tackle this problem. The block diagram in Figure 7.10 shows one such technique, that of incorporating a block-sized RAM area into the device. Programmers wishing to write a block of memory to the device can first write the data very quickly into the SRAM-based RAM block, then issue the programming command to cause the device to copy the entire RAM content into a flash memory block. Similarly, when only a single byte needs to be changed, the flash block can be internally copied into the RAM area and the programmer then adjusts the required byte before issuing the command to erase and then reprogram the desired flash block.

The flash memory structure shown in Figure 7.10 is also that which is used inside most parallel flash devices. In the case of serial flash, however, the nOE, nWE and other control signals are generated from a serial interface controller, rather than obtained directly from a parallel interface.

7.6.3 Random Access Memory

The term 'random access memory' (RAM), like ROM, describes a method of access rather than a technology: it means that any memory location can be accessed (i.e. read from or written to) at will. We tend to take this ability for granted in computers

Figure 7.10

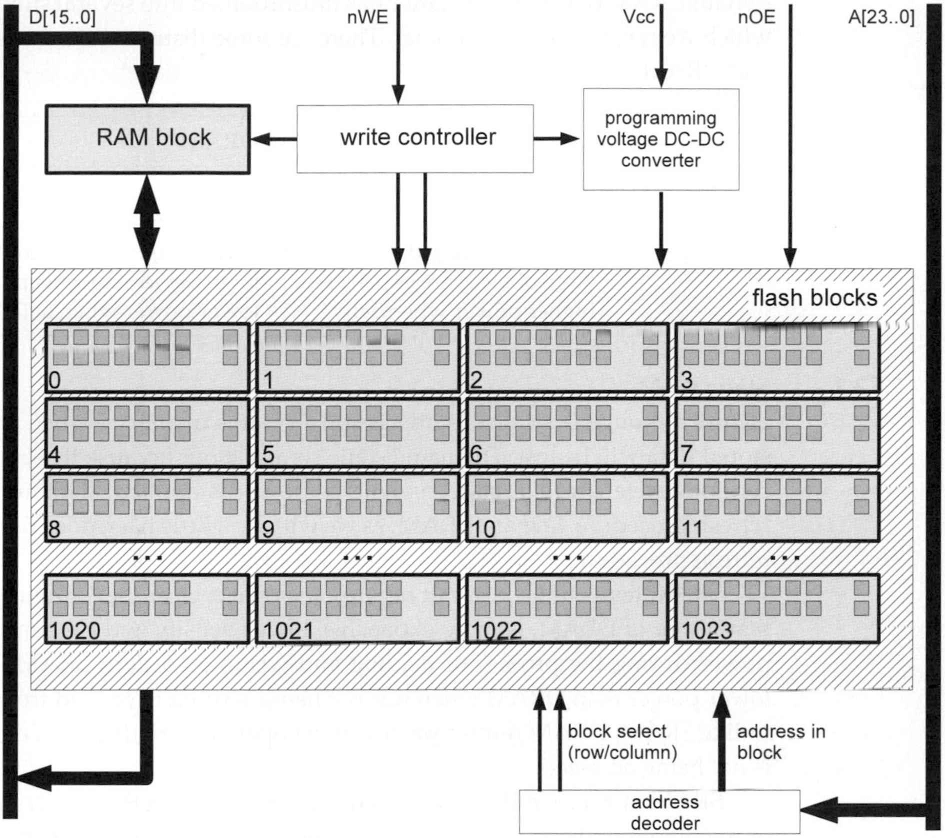

A block diagram of the internal structure of a flash memory device which contains a block-sized area of RAM for storage of programming data. Note the flash array consists of multiple identical blocks. This regular structure makes it very easy for a manufacturer to increase capacity by adding more rows of blocks to the device (and in practice there would probably be more than four columns). Note the direction of arrows connecting to the data bus.

these days, but the alternative is serial access, such as on magnetic tape and certain delay-based memories, in which data is available in the same order that it was written. The constraint of serial data access was not uncommon during the early years of computing.

Of course, there is another difference between serial access and random access memory – the RAM is addressable, and therefore requires an address to be specified to indicate the data locations that require access. For parallel-bus memory, which is most common, this address specification is carried on a dedicated parallel address bus. Sometimes it is multiplexed with a data bus, and for serial memory devices, is conveyed over a serial scheme (as in the serial flash device discussed in Section 7.6.2).

In general, there are two technology classes of RAM: static RAM (SRAM) and dynamic RAM (DRAM). The latter has mushroomed into several subclasses of its own, which we will briefly discuss later. There are some distinct differences between SRAM and DRAM:

SRAM	DRAM
six transistors per bit	one transistor per bit
lower density	higher density
no refresh needed	periodic refresh required
large devices are expensive	large devices are cheap
higher power when active	lower power when active

7.6.3.1 Static RAM

SRAM, although it is called 'static' is still a volatile memory – when power is removed, stored data will be lost. The name static comes about because these memory cells will continually retain their state, as long as power is applied, without the need for the refresh procedure. Dynamic RAM, as we will see a little later, does require this periodic refresh procedure.

SRAM tends to be fast, but because its logic cells are several times more complex than those of DRAM, is more expensive, lower density and consumes more electrical power during the process of reading and writing. Modern SRAM, however, can be lower power than DRAM when it is not being written to or read from. This is because unlike SRAM, DRAM refresh process must operate periodically even when the device is not being accessed.

SRAM is very similar in connectivity and use to ROM. Referring to the example of the pinout of the two SRAM devices shown in Figure 7.11, note the similarity to the EEPROM device of Figure 7.8, in terms of data connections, although the locations of specific pins may differ. Figure 7.11 actually shows two devices, a 16 Kibit and a 1 Mibit device. The former part has 11 address-bus pins (since $2^{11} = 2048 \times 8$ bits = 16,384 bits) while the latter has 6 more, making a total of 17 (`A[16..0]`, since $2^{17} = 131{,}072 \times 8$ bits = 1024 Kibits = 1 Mibit).

SRAM has a regular internal cell-like structure, similar to that of ROM. Figure 7.12 presents a simplified block diagram of an internal SRAM matrix, showing logic cells that can be individually addressed in parallel (to form a connection to an 8-bit parallel bus in the figure), and apart from being selected on the basis of their address, can be read from or written to. Bidirectional buffers connect the external data bus to the internal data lines, and are controlled in terms of directionality to avoid bus contentions with any other items which may be connected to the same external data bus.

SRAM is used for cache memory and for the on-chip memory found in single-chip computers. It is also the external memory of choice for simple and small embedded microcontrollers, where memory sizes on the order of tens of kibibytes are sufficient (since at these low densities, the cost differential between DRAM and SRAM disappears, and because microcontrollers are simple and lack support for DRAM).

Figure 7.11

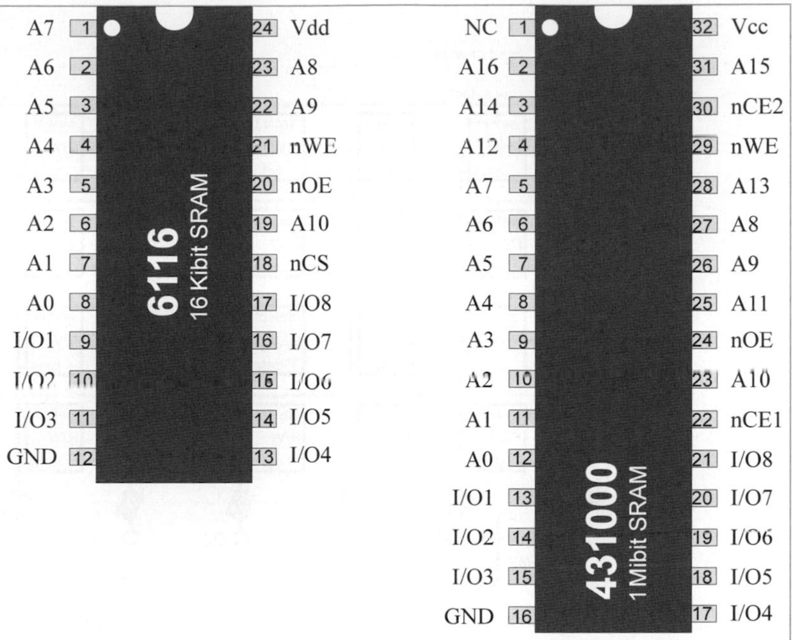

A pinout diagram for two early SRAM chips, the 16 Kibit 6116 and the 1 Mibit 431000. Note that both have the same 8-bit input/output port (usually connected to a data bus), both have power supply, chip select (nCS) and read/write pins. However, the device on the right, containing 64 times as many bytes, requires a further six address pins (A11 to A16) in order to access this.

7.6.3.2 Dynamic RAM

As we have mentioned previously, dynamic RAM is called dynamic because it is constantly in a state of change: the logic value of each cell is determined through the stored charge in a capacitor connected to the single transistor used per bit, and because the gates are 'leaky', these capacitors are continually discharging. A *refresh* process reads each cell in turn and then 'tops up' the stored charge in the capacitor appropriately. Any cell that is not refreshed will lose its charge within a few milliseconds.

The write process simply loads the required charge into the capacitor through the transistor (for a logic high) or discharges the capacitor (for a logic low). Interestingly, the read process, through which the charge in a cell is determined, also refreshes that cell, so reading the entire device in a periodic fashion will refresh it.

Modern DRAM is highly integrated, and most microprocessors (or support ICs) that connect to DRAM will handle the refresh issue automatically although the process may well require several configuration registers to be set up correctly. However, the refresh process takes a little time, which may be time that a CPU must spend waiting for its memory to become free. This can naturally impact CPU performance slightly.

Figure 7.12

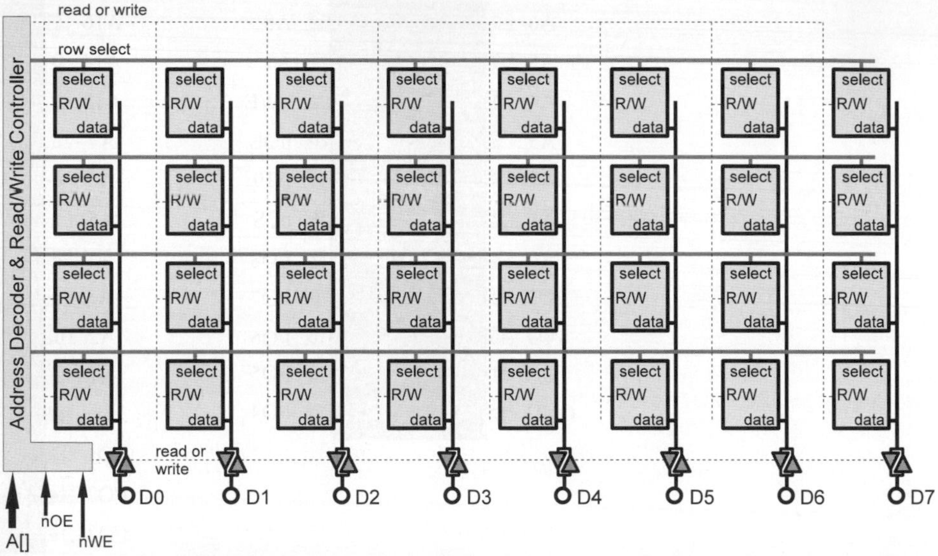

A simplified block diagram of the internal arrangement of an SRAM device, showing an array of memory cells which can be read from and written to, controlled by an address decoder and read/write controller.

DRAM has a very long history, beginning in the mid-1960s, and making several step change improvements along the way. Some of these more important development milestones are shown in Table 7.2, along with their approximate year of release, clock speed and operating voltage.

Table 7.2

Some prominent milestones in the evolution of SDRAM technology.

Name	In use from	Clock speed	Voltage
basic DRAM	1966	–	5 V
fast page mode (FPM)	1990	30 MHz	5 V
extended data out (EDO)	1994	40 MHz	5 V
synchronous DRAM (SDRAM)	1994*	40 MHz	3.3 V
rambus DRAM (RDRAM)	1998	400 MHz	2.5 V
double-data-rate (DDR) SDRAM	2000	266 MHz	2.5 V
DDR2 SDRAM	2003	533 MHz	1.8 V
DDR3 SDRAM	2007	800 MHz	1.5 V

*IBM had used synchronous DRAM much earlier than this, in isolated cases.
Note: RD and DDR RAM devices transfer data on both edges of the clock, so they operate at twice the speed of the rated clock frequency.

Figure 7.13

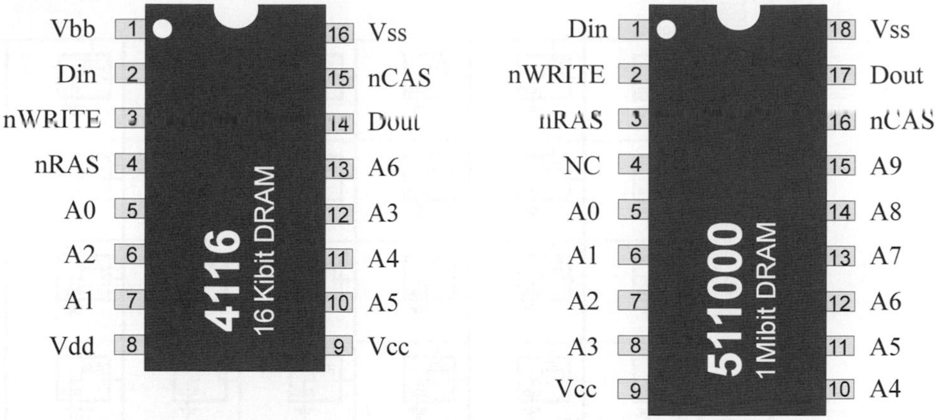

A pinout diagram for two early DRAM chips, the 16 Kibit 4116 and the 1 Mibit 511000. These devices both output a single data bit (and therefore eight of each would be connected in parallel when connected to an 8-bit data bus). Note that both share the same DRAM control signals, but the device on the right, despite containing 64 times as much data, has just three extra address pins (A7 to A9). Vbb, Vcc, Vdd and Vss are various power supply pins.

DRAM differs from SRAM in its dynamic nature, requiring constant refresh. Since DRAM bit memory cells are a lot smaller than those of SRAM, DRAM is cheaper and is available in higher densities. However, DRAM is slower than SRAM, and the constant refresh operations cause the devices to consume power even when they are not being read from or written to (although it must be remembered that SRAM consumes more power during accesses).

There is one other major difference between DRAM devices and SRAM devices, and that is in the addressing scheme of DRAM. Refer to the two early DRAM chip pinouts shown in Figure 7.13, for a 16-Kibit and 1-Mibit device respectively. Firstly, note the several unusual signals named nWRITE, nRAS, nCAS, Din and Dout, which we will discuss in a moment. Secondly, compare the DRAM pinouts to those of the SRAM shown previously in Figure 7.11 (on page 317). In both figures, the two devices have memory content of the same size; in each figure the device on the right contains 64 times as much memory. For the SRAM case, the IC on the right has six more address pins than the one on the left. For the the DRAM case, the IC on the right only has three more address pins than the one on the left. Since a 64 times increase in address space is an expansion of 2^6, this would normally require six extra pins. It seems that there is more than meets the eye inside the DRAM device. We will thus consider this a little further.

7.6.3.3 DRAM Addressing

First of all, let us note that DRAM devices are addressed by row (often called a page) and column. This is unlike the memory structures we presented previously in which only

Figure 7.14

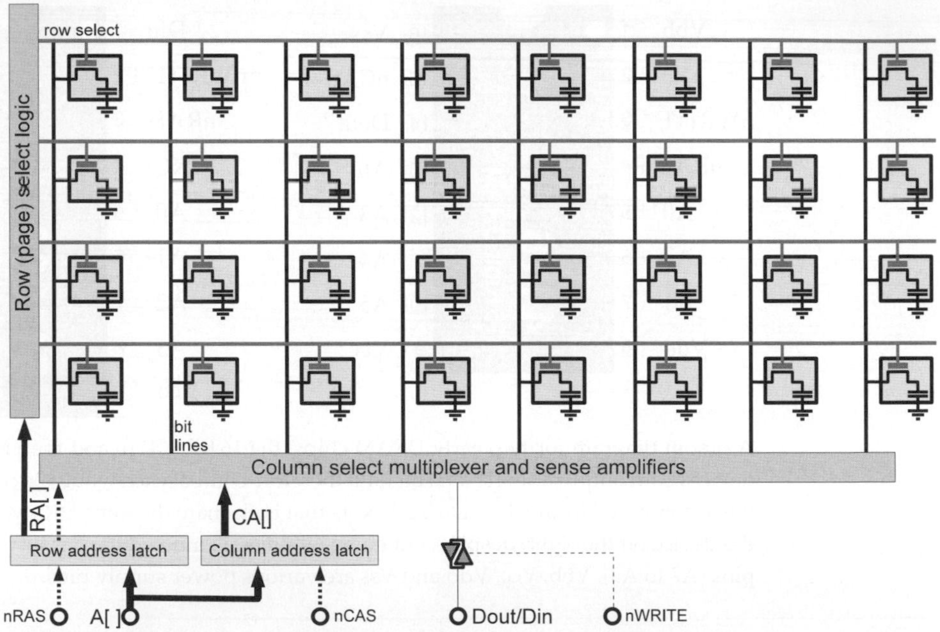

A diagram of the internal row/column select nature of the DRAM device, where a row latch and a column latch hold the row address and column address respectively. Both row and column addresses are conveyed over the same address bus, identified through the row address strobe (nRAS) and column address strobe (nCAS) signals. The array shown connects to a single bit of a data bus.

row addressing was performed. In fact, the devices with pinout shown in Figure 7.13 are 1-bit devices – in order to construct an 8-bit data bus, eight of these would be required to operate in parallel, one per data bit. The Dout pin on these parallel devices would be required to connect to data bus signals D0, D1, D2, D3 and so on, in turn.

A clearer view of this row and column addressing can be seen by examining the internal structure of a DRAM device, shown in Figure 7.14. Internal cells, each consisting of a transistor and a charge storage capacitor, are arranged in a rectangular fashion. The row address strobe (nRAS) when activated, will load the row address latch with the content of the address bus at that time. A demultiplexer maps the row address signal to a particular row (or page) of devices which are then selected to output their stored charge. The column address strobe (nCAS) then causes the column address latch to be loaded with the content of the address bus at that time. The column address determines which of the selected devices is chosen as the single-bit output from the array.

Sense amplifiers, connected to each of the bit lines (columns), detect the charge stored in the capacitors for selected cells and top it up. Thus, after selecting a particular page, if the charge is greater than a certain threshold on one bit line, the sense amplifier outputs a voltage to recharge the capacitor in the cell connected to that line. If the voltage is sensed to be lower than the threshold, then the sense amplifier does not output that voltage.

Actually, the sense amplifiers are triggered after the nRAS signal has selected a row, and this recharging process is entirely automatic. The practical implication is that the 'refreshing' process in DRAM does not need to involve the column addresses – all that is required is for each row to be selected in turn (but as mentioned, most CPUs that support DRAM or SDRAM will perform this automatically). For DRAM that typically needs to be refreshed every 64 ms, each row will have to be selected sequentially within that time.

Of course, many DRAM devices are not single-bit devices, but store bytes or words of data. In that case, the basic DRAM design is replicated on-chip several times. Figure 7.15 shows an example of an 8-bit bus-connected DRAM device, although this is very low density, being only a 256-bit memory! Since the device shown has eight columns and four rows per bit, the row address would consist of 2 bits and the column address would consist of 3 bits.

A 16-Kibit-sized device, such as the 4116 device shown in Figure 7.13, would perhaps have 128 rows and 128 columns (since $128 \times 128 = 16{,}384$), and thus require seven address lines ($2^7 = 128$) to set up the address of the cell to be accessed. The steps required by a bus-connected CPU to read a single bit from this device, starting from the device being inactive (i.e. nRAS, nCAS, nWRITE are inactive; logic high) are as follows:

1. Output the required row on the address bus.
2. Assert nRAS (take it from logic high to logic low, thereby causing the row address latch to capture the row address from the address bus).
3. Output the required column on the address bus.
4. Assert nCAS to latch the column address.
5. The device will, after some time, output the content of the addressed memory cell on to the connected wire of the data bus, which can then be read by the CPU.
6. De-assert nCAS and stop driving the address bus.
7. De-assert nRAS.

Of course, there are some very strict timings to observe when accessing the DRAM device in this way or when performing a write. Clearly, with two address writes per memory access, this is significantly slower than a device that does not use row/column addressing, like an SRAM. This observation is true, but is tolerated for cost and density reasons: as seen in Figure 7.13, moving from a 16 Kibit to a 1 Mibit DRAM device requires just three more address lines, but in SRAM (Figure 7.11) this would require six extra address lines. For larger memory densities, this advantage in pin-count that DRAM has is very significant.

So instead of increasing pin-count, designers have found more intelligent ways of using the row/column addressing scheme. For example, sequential reads from the same row do not require the nRAS signal to be activated (after all, reads from the same row all have the same row address) and read-write or write-read combinations can similarly be simplified.

Figure 7.15

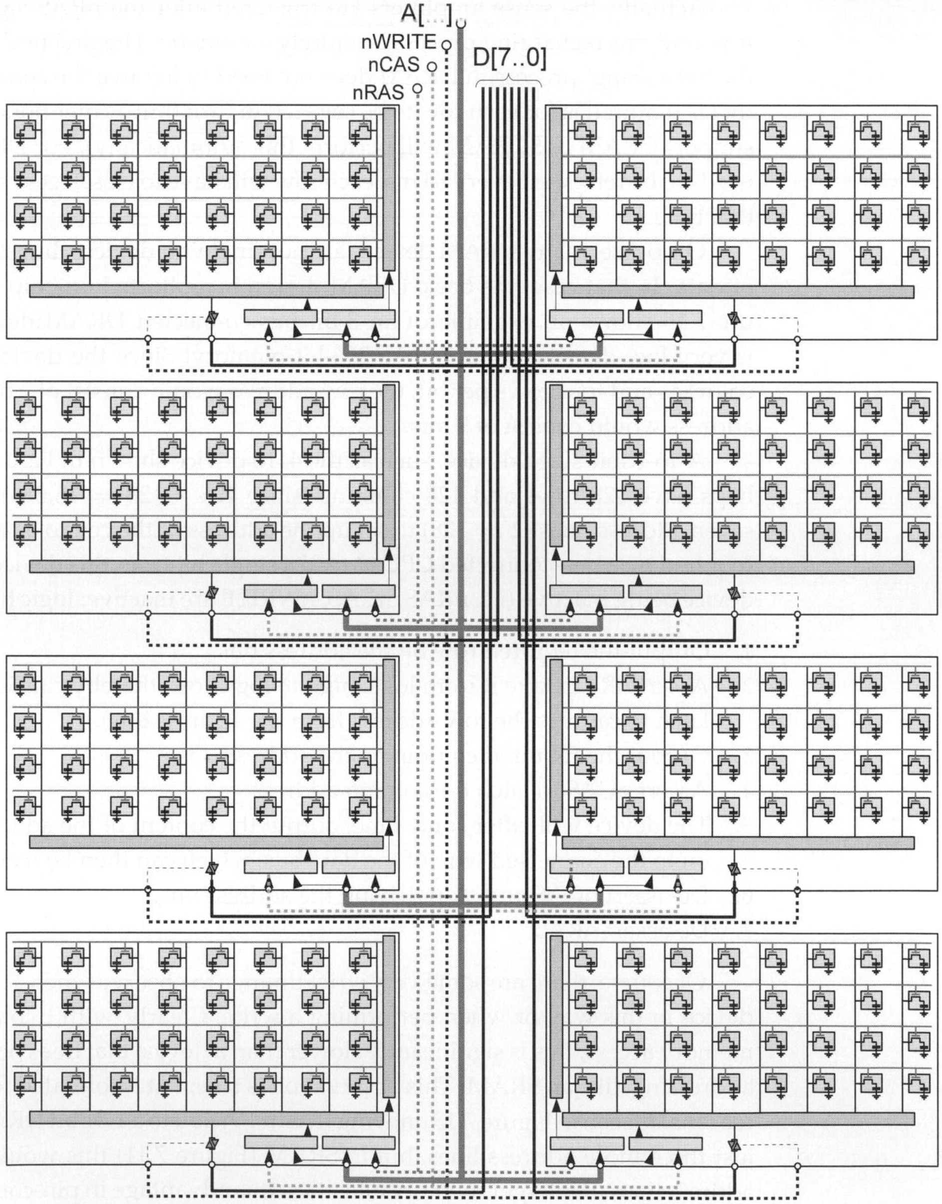

The basic single-bit DRAM array of Figure 7.14 has been replicated eight times to form a DRAM device that connects to an 8-bit bus. All control and addressing signals are common to each of the internal blocks (and in practice the blocks may all share a single common row and a single common column address latch).

In fact, there have been many advances of these kinds, some of which we have listed in Table 7.2. The first innovation was the method of reading many locations from a page without re-asserting nRAS. This technique is called *fast page mode*.

DRAM was also adapted for use in video cards, becoming *video RAM* (VRAM), characterised by having two data ports for reading from the memory array. One port (the one connected to the main CPU) allows the processor to read from and write to this memory. A second part, connected to video DACs (digital-to-analogue converters), was read-only and allowed the data contained in the array to be accessed and read out pixel-by-pixel for display on a screen.

Moving back to general DRAM, *extended data out* (EDO) variants used an internal latch to store page data, so that this could be output and read by a CPU even as the CPU was beginning the process of reading the next page. This is, in fact, a form of pipelining, and was improved further by blocking multiple reads so that they occurred together (up to four at a time in *burst mode* EDO DRAM). In multi-chip memory modules especially, clever use of interleaved memory banks also allowed reads to be staggered across banks, to further speed up access.

Up to now, each of the DRAM variants mentioned has been asynchronous to the CPU, although controlled by the CPU, which is itself synchronous. In fact, it became obvious that squeezing any further performance out of these memory devices required them to have 'knowledge' of the bus clock, and hence *synchronous DRAM* or SDRAM was invented. Being synchronous allows the devices to prefetch data ready for the next clock cycle, to better pipeline their actions through internal memory access interleaving and other tricks.

The major performance improvements to SDRAM have been in increasing clock frequency and allowing data to be transferred on both edges of the memory clock (i.e. instead of one word being transferred each clock cycle, two words can be transferred – one on the falling edge of the clock and one on the rising edge). This is termed *double data rate* or DDR SDRAM.

7.7 Pages and Overlays

Although we have only just looked at real memory devices in Section 7.6, it was way back in Section 4.3 that we introduced memory management using an MMU. MMU configuration is generally considered to be a fairly complex topic (the author can relate from first-hand experience that teaching and writing about it is nowhere near as tricky as having to actually configure a real MMU, in low-level assembly language, on a project with tight deadlines).

In most MMU-enabled systems, pages of memory are swapped in and out to external mass storage, typically provided by hard discs. The memory management system keeps track of which pages are actually resident in memory at any one time and which are on disc, and loads or saves pages as required.

The MMU that controls this is actually the result of a long process of invention and evolutionary improvements, but stepping back now several generations, we can consider life without an MMU. This is not simply a thought-experiment, it is precisely the situation in many very modern embedded processors which have limited on-chip memory – designers very frequently run out of RAM in such devices.

Let us consider a real situation where software engineers are developing control code for an embedded processor that resides in a mobile radio. Nearing the end of their development, they total up the size of the code they have written for that CPU and it requires the following amounts of memory:

- Runtime memory: 18 kibibytes when executing from RAM
- Storage size of code: 15 KiB of ROM (read-only memory)

It happens that the processor has only 16 KiB of internal RAM, which is obviously insufficient to both hold the program code and execute it. If on-chip or parallel external ROM was available in the system then the program could be executed directly from this ROM (but with any read-write code sections located in RAM; in most cases the 'ROM' would actually be flash memory). However, let us suppose that in this case the only flash memory available is a 1 MiB device connected over a 25 MHz SPI (serial peripheral interface) serial port.

Unfortunately, this is far too slow for code to be executed directly from it.

In fact, designers measured the timing characteristics of the system as it was. From power on, the device took approximately 5 ms to transfer the program code from flash memory to RAM before the program would start ($15*1024*8$ bits$/25 \times 10^6$ seconds).

Ignoring the obvious solutions of making the code more efficient or providing more RAM, designers were forced to use overlays to get the system to fit. These followed the principle that not all of the software was in use at any one time – in fact several sections were mutually exclusive. For example, the radio contained software that allowed it to operate in a legacy mode. This mode was selectable during power-up, such that it would either operate in 'normal mode' or 'legacy mode', but never both simultaneously. Bearing this in mind there is no reason why both parts of the code should reside in RAM together, much better to simply load whichever one is required.

Designers therefore split the operating code into two separate executables or overlays. One for 'legacy mode' and one for 'normal mode'. This appeared inefficient at first since the two modes shared quite a few functions, and these functions now had to be provided twice – once for each overlay. Also, an extra start-up code chooser was required to switch between the two overlays (in fact to choose which overlay to use, load it and then execute it). So did this provide a solution?

Examining the memory situation, the code sizes were as follows:

- Runtime memory in 'normal mode': 12 KiB
- Runtime memory in 'legacy mode': 10 KiB
- Storage size of code for overlay chooser: 1 KiB of ROM
- Storage size of code for 'normal mode': 10 KiB of ROM
- Storage size of code for 'legacy mode': 9 KiB of ROM

Total flash memory occupied had become: $1 + 10 + 9 = 20$ KiBs (compared to 15 previously). However, with 1 MiB of flash memory in total, this increase in size was not a concern.

But what about start-up speed? Several engineers were concerned that this approach would make the radio slow to start up. However, tests showed that start-up time was actually faster.

For normal mode it required 3.6 ms to transfer the total 11 KiB of data, ignoring the few instructions of the selection code which might require just a couple of microseconds only (11*1024*8 bits/25 $\times$ 10^6 seconds).

In legacy mode, the start-up time was even less: 3.3 ms (10*1024*8 bits/25 $\times$ 10^6 seconds).

In summary, both start-up time and runtime RAM requirements improved through the use of overlays, although more software and ROM space were needed.

Without an MMU to handle memory management, options for expanding code beyond the RAM limitations are fairly straightforward: either write an overlay loader which could be as simple as a chooser between two executables, or envisage a more complicated device where overlays themselves contain code which chooses and loads the next overlay.

However, for modern embedded processors there is another choice: use of an advanced operating system (OS) that mimics, in part, the functionality provided by an MMU. One such prominent example is uCLinux (this is Linux for processors lacking an MMU), which allows a wide range of standard compiled Linux code to execute – including flash filing systems, execute-in-place (XIP) drivers and so on.

One final point: the overlay approach is finding a new lease of life with FPGA (field programmable gate arrays) technology. These field reprogrammable devices can totally change their firmware functionality upon reprogramming, and as their name implies, they can be reprogrammed just about anywhere (even in a field). A current hot topic applying this concept is software defined radio (SDR). An SDR is a digital radio designed using common hardware. However, it is able to load one of several decoding architectures to match whatever transmission scheme is being used at the frequency of interest. A front-end chooser monitors the wireless signals on the current frequency, decides what sort of modulation is in use within them, and then loads the correct firmware into the FPGA to demodulate and decode those signals. With such techniques likely to find a place in mobile phones over the next few years, it seems that overlay techniques are here to stay.

7.8 Memory in Embedded Systems

Most computer architecture textbooks describe memory subsystems for large computers and some even cover shared memory for parallel processing machines (just as we have done), but they neglect to extend their discussion downwards in dimension to embedded systems.

Embedded systems tend to use memory in a different way to desktop computers, and although embedded systems do come in all shapes and sizes for all manner of application, the majority of modern systems would contain flash memory in place of the hard disc in use within larger systems (as is reflected in the memory pyramid of Section 3.2.2).

At this point, we shall examine a typical embedded system, built around an ARM9 and running embedded Linux. The arrangement we will reveal is actually quite typical of such systems, and forms the majority class of such medium-sized embedded computers. We could also form a class of small systems, ones with up to 100 Kibits of RAM, which would have a monolithic real-time operating system (one which includes an operating system, application code and boot code in a single executable block), and larger PC-style systems which use smaller x86 processors and are basically cut-down low-power PCs.

For the medium-sized system shown in Figure 7.16 (which actually exists, and contains a Samsung S3C2410), non-volatile program code is stored in flash memory, and volatile running code plus data is contained in SDRAM. The flash memory device is 16-bits wide and the SDRAM 32-bits wide (by using two 16-bit wide SDRAM devices in this case).

The lower part of Figure 7.16 shows the content of each type of memory during execution, however, we will consider memory content during three stages of operation.

7.8.1 Non-Volatile Memory

During power-off, only the content of flash memory is preserved: SDRAM is essentially blank. When the ARM processor turns on and reset is de-asserted, the CPU begins to load instructions and thus execute a program from address `0x0000 0000`. In this case, as in most embedded systems, flash memory is located at this position in the memory map. Thus, the first instructions in flash get executed immediately after reset.

At this point the CPU is executing directly from flash. This important *bootloader* code needs to perform tasks such as resetting the processor state, turning off its watchdog timer (Section 7.11) and setting up SDRAM. This is one reason why most embedded developers need to learn about SDRAM: we need to configure it in order to progress beyond this point in the bootloader.

There are many freely available bootloaders to choose from, such as the popular U-boot. However, it is not uncommon for designers to write their own custom-designed boot code to perform the functionality they require. Some of the things a bootloader can be expected to do are as follows:

- Perform power-on self-test (POST).
- Set up memory, particularly SDRAM.
- Set up CPU registers such as clock dividers, power control registers, MMU, cache memory.
- Write a message to serial port, LCD screen or similar.

- Optionally wait for user intervention (such as 'press any key to enter boot menu or wait five seconds to continue').
- Load kernel and/or ramdisk from flash to SDRAM.
- Run executable code (e.g. kernel) by jumping to its start address.

Figure 7.16

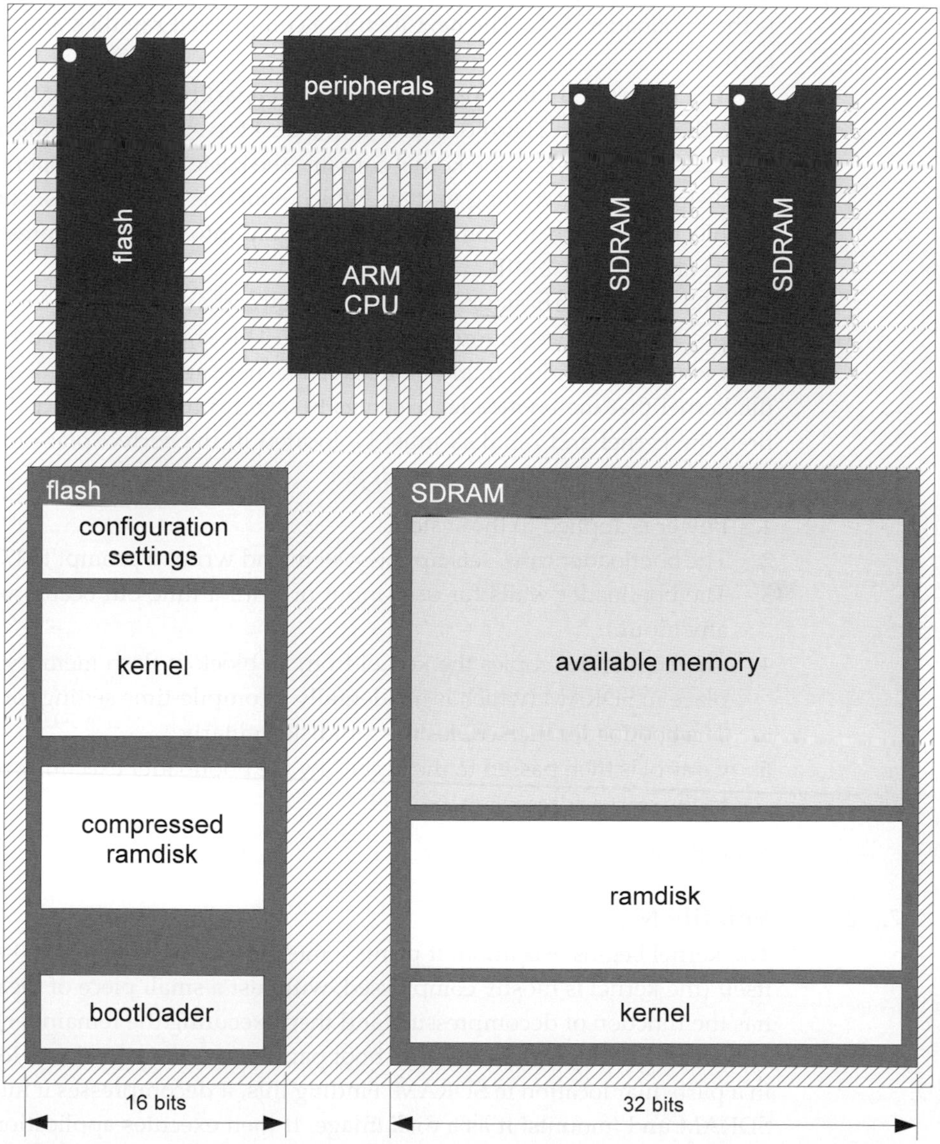

A block diagram illustrating the memory arrangement for an example ARM-based embedded system, with the memory content for both flash and SDRAM shown, during normal system operation.

- Test memory.
- Erase blocks of flash memory.
- Download new kernel or ramdisk to SDRAM.
- Program a kernel or ramdisk from SDRAM into flash memory.

In the case of the system under consideration, there are three items loaded into flash memory. The first, located at the 'bottom' of flash, beginning at address `0x0000 0000`, is the bootloader code. The next item is a compressed ramdisk and the final item is a kernel.

The embedded Linux operating system is partitioned so that the ramdisk (which takes the place of the hard disc found in a desktop system) contains applications software and data, whereas the kernel contains the basic core of the operating system. The ramdisk is actually a filing system, which contains various files, some of them executable, all of which are compressed using gzip into a large compressed file, typically on the order of 1 or 2 MiB in size.

The kernel – the basic OS core – contains all of the system-level functionality, in-built drivers, low-level access routines and so on. This code is designed to be unchanging, even when the ramdisk might be updated as new application code is developed. It is the kernel that the bootloader executes to begin running embedded Linux. However first, the kernel and ramdisk must be located in the correct place in memory. Let us consider the boot process step by step:

1. Power is applied to the system.
2. The bootloader runs, sets up the system and writes a prompt to LCD or serial port.
3. The bootloader waits for user input or until a time-out occurs without receiving any input.
4. The bootloader copies the kernel from its block in flash memory into a particular place in SDRAM (which is incidentally a compile-time setting for the kernel).
5. The bootloader then copies the ramdisk similarly.
6. Control is then passed to the kernel, by the bootloader executing a jump command to the start address of the kernel.

Now, finally, the kernel will run.

7.8.2 Volatile Memory

The kernel begins execution. It prints a message to the screen and then decompresses itself (the kernel is mostly compressed, with just a small piece of 'header' code which has the function of decompressing and then executing the remainder).

Next, and depending upon its boot parameters, the kernel will look for a ramdisk in a particular location in SDRAM. Finding this, it decompresses it into another part of SDRAM and 'mounts' it as a disk image. It then executes applications code found in that disk image according to the normal start-up rules of Linux (which means looking for an `init` program).

The part of the kernel that was previously compressed and the decompressor code are deleted from SDRAM to free up space. The compressed ramdisk image is

Figure 7.17

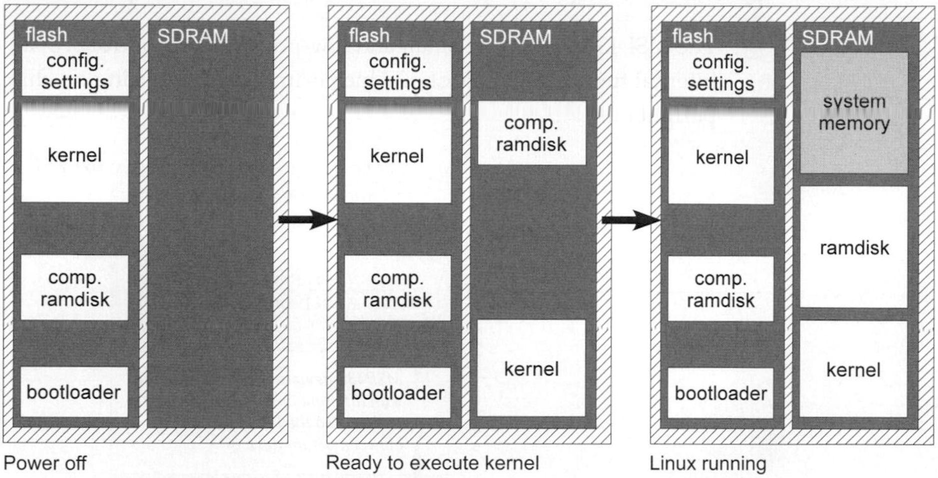

The memory content of the example embedded ARM platform, showing both flash and SDRAM when power is off, during bootloader execution and when embedded Linux is running.

also removed as it is not needed since the decompressed ramdisk is now located in memory.

The remainder of SDRAM is then available for temporary variable and data storage when executing code. This is shown diagrammatically in Figure 7.17.

The memory arrangement in a much smaller embedded processor, the MSP430x1 from Texas Instruments, is far less configurable because it does not have an external data or address bus. However, it is also well constructed to support a very wide selection of internal peripherals and memory block sizes (refer to Box 7.4 for further information).

7.8.3 Other Memory

Many devices having a parallel interface can be added to the memory map of a CPU. These include external devices such as memory, Ethernet chips and hard disc interfaces as well as internal devices such as many of the internal peripherals within an SoC processor.

However, there is one other common entity that is memory mapped, and that is the system and peripheral module control registers. These were identified clearly in the MSP430 memory map in Box 7.4 (at the bottom of the memory map, starting with special function registers and continuing with the peripheral control registers). In fact, if you refer back, for a moment, to the description of pin control system on the MSP430 in Box 7.2 (page 297), you will see several of the MSP430 registers named in our description.

All of these registers, and many more, are specified in the MSP430 data sheet, and all are memory mapped, which means that they occupy specific addresses in the memory

Box 7.4

Memory map in the MSP430

The MSP430 is a typical small and low-power microcontroller with a large amount of internal functionality, most of which is implemented using on-chip memory-mapped peripherals.

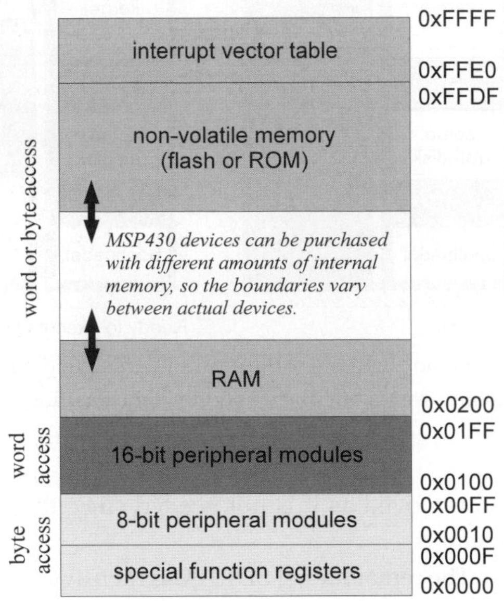

The memory map of the MSP430x1xxx series processors is shown in the diagram above, starting from address 0 at the bottom. Note first that different parts of the memory map have different widths – some of them are 8-bits wide and some are 16-bits wide. Since peripherals handling both data sizes are available in those devices, Texas Instruments has segregated them into different areas of the memory map depending upon their width of access. For example the set-up and data registers of an 8-bit peripheral would lie between address `0x10` and `0xFF`.

Special function registers, at the bottom of the map, control the entire system, processor and so on (such as power and clock control). The interrupt vector table in this processor is actually located at the *top* of memory and that means when the device is reset, it will begin executing the code in that area. For this reason, non-volatile memory (flash or ROM), which will contain boot code, is located at the top of the memory map to overlap this area. RAM is placed lower down.

Interestingly, there are a very wide variety of MSP devices available from Texas Instruments, each with a different selection of features and peripherals and also varying widely in the amount of flash/ROM and RAM provided internally. Among all these parts, the memory maps are the same, apart from the upper boundary of RAM and the lower boundary of ROM, which move depending upon exactly how much of each type of memory is present in the devices.

map of the processor. For the specific registers mentioned in Box 7.2, these registers can be found at the following addresses in memory:

Name	Address
P2DIR	0x02A
P2IN	0x028
P2OUT	0x029
P2SEL	0x02E

Thus, writing to the given addresses or reading from them will control or query the registers.

For the registers we are interested in, referring back to the memory map for a moment, we can see they lie within the '8-bit peripheral modules' section, which is what we should expect since the ports (and hence the registers controlling them) are 8-bits wide.

In C programming language code, the safest way to read from and write to these registers would probably be as follows:

```
unsigned char read_result;
void *addr;
read_result = *((volatile unsigned char *) addr); //to read
*((volatile unsigned char *) addr) = 0xFF;          //to write
```

The use of the `volatile` keyword is interesting. Let us examine why it is required.

Many compilers will detect a write after write within a program and simply delete the first write to improve efficiency. For example, if a program were to save something to memory location X, and then save something to the same location a few clock cycles later without reading from location X in between, then the first write is clearly a waste of time – whatever was written the first time would just be overwritten later.

This may be true when writing to RAM. However, there are some instances where we legitimately need to write after write to the same memory address: such as a flash memory programming algorithm or when the location we are writing to is actually a memory-mapped register.

A case in point is the data output register of a serial port. A programmer wishing to serially output 2 bytes would first set up the serial port, and then write 1 byte after another to the memory-mapped serial transmit register.

The `volatile` keyword tells the compiler that the memory that is being written to is 'volatile', that is, it needs to be refreshed. The compiler will then ensure that the write after write does not become simplified to just a single write.

It is not just the write after write cases that a compiler will detect – often compilers will detect read after read situations and optimise these to a single read if possible. Read after read does legitimately happen in code, in fact, the compiler will often deliberately insert this as part of the addition of spill code (see Section 3.4.4). However, the interpretation for a programmer writing a read after read is that it is unintentional.

Of course, as we have seen, read after read can be just as necessary as write after write. For example, in reading serial data from a serial port input register. Or in polling a serial port status register to detect when the transmit buffer is empty. In each of these cases, just as in the write after write case, the `volatile` keyword is used to tell the compiler that the read after read is deliberate.

The small code snipped above used `volatile` as a cast. It could equally as well have defined a volatile variable type:

```
volatile unsigned char * pointer;
```

7.9 Test and Verification

Test and verification need to be covered in any chapter purporting to address practical issues in computing (and particularly embedded computing). This is primarily because the performance improvements have made processors more and more complex and large over time. This has had the effect of making processor design and manufacture far more difficult. In addition, it has introduced the need for test-support and failure-control mechanisms to be added to the devices themselves.

7.9.1 Integrated Circuit Design and Manufacture Problems

It is no longer possible for a single design engineer to understand and check an entire modern processor as it was in the 1970s. Although good teamwork and excellent design tools have largely taken the place of manual checking, it is easily possible for errors to be incorporated into the design of an integrated circuit (IC). In fact, it is almost impossible to find a processor with no hardware design errors when first released! The vast majority are small inconveniences that can be fixed with a software workaround (e.g. 'always put a NOP after a mode change if the serial port is operating'). Others are more serious.

One high-profile design error was the Intel FDIV bug in the 80486 processor – detected only when the CPUs were sold and installed in thousands, if not millions, of computers. This was literally a one in a million error that could remain undetected for months but nevertheless cost the company dearly in economic and public relations terms.

Manufacturing faults are far more common. A glance at the printed circuit board (PCB) in a modern top-end PC compared to one built in the 1980s would not only reveal the gradual and relentless integration of separate components into silicon, but also that silicon devices that are present on the circuit board today tend to be large with many pins (or rather balls). Figure 7.18 shows a photograph of the BGA (ball grid array) on the underside of an Samsung S3C2410 ARM processor. It clearly shows the small balls of solder that melt when heated in a soldering oven to connect to corresponding pads on the surface of a PCB.

While the BGA is a very compact and efficient method for connecting an IC to a PCB, it is not at all debugging and repair-friendly: with previous generations of IC packaging,

Figure 7.18 Underside of a modern ARM processor, showing the grid array of solder balls (device size is 14 mm × 14 mm).

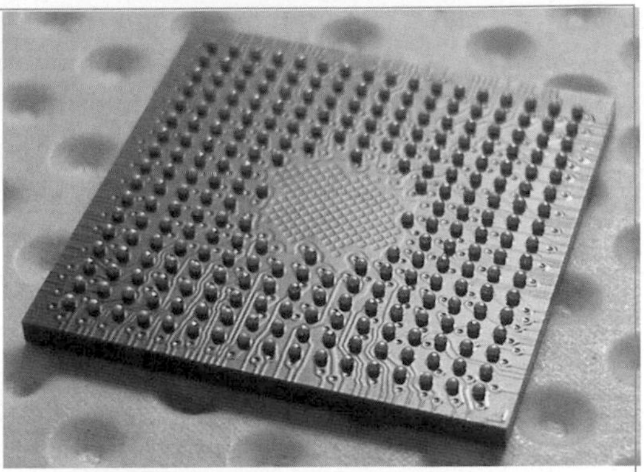

it was possible to probe or test connections which were clustered around the outside of a device, and visible from above). The BGA, by contrast, hides all connections underneath itself – virtually the only way to check each connection physically is by taking an X-ray of the part after it has been placed on the PCB. An example of the ability of X-rays to 'see through' a package is shown in Figure 7.19, where the internal detail of an IC, as well as PCB features below it, are visible.

Figure 7.19

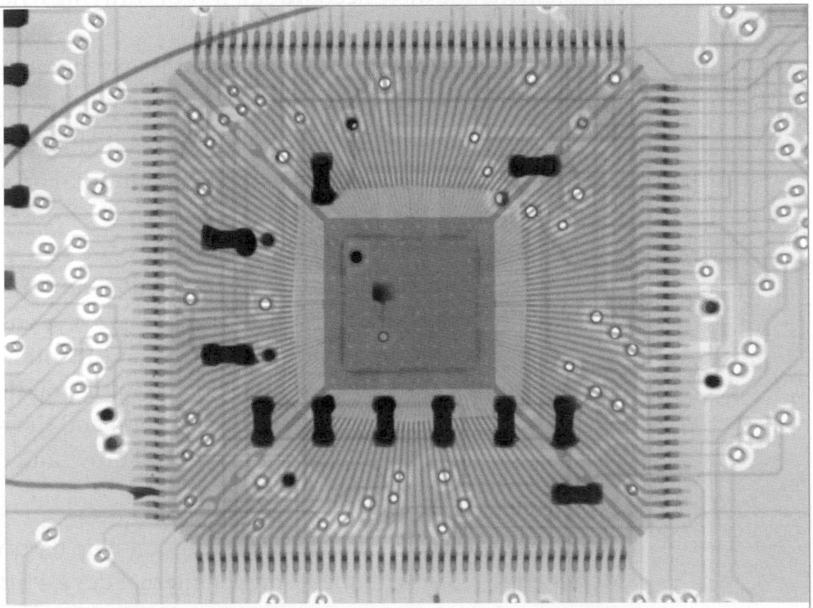

An X-ray photograph of an IC (in this case a quad flat pack package), showing visibility through the package of the IC and revealing the lead-frame and the silicon die inside.

As more design functionality is incorporated into single-silicon devices, such as the SuperIO chip in a modern personal computer, it is of course necessary to integrate whatever external interfaces that the original devices used, and this is one of the major drivers influencing device size. For example, to connect to storage media such as hard discs, CDROMs, floppy drives and so on. However, these use multiple pin interfaces and were designed, in some cases, almost 30 years ago. It is no coincidence that the more recent interfacing techniques of USB (universal serial bus), Firewire and SATA (Serial ATA – Advanced Technology Attachment) use significantly fewer pins, and consequently much of the I/O (input/output) connections are present solely to support legacy interfaces rather than their modern counterparts. It seems likely that in time the older ISA, EISA, IDE, SCSI and floppy disk buses will disappear, allowing a much smaller SuperIO[3] chip footprint.

Getting back to test and verification, there are two main issues with devices having a large number of I/O connections.

Firstly, when an IC is manufactured it generally needs to be tested. Some manufacturers are content with batch testing only, but others prefer zero tolerance to failures, and so will test every device made. These tests need to cover the two main manufacturing steps of making the silicon chip, and then attaching the legs/pins/balls to it.

Secondly, there is a small but finite probability of each solder joint not working, and therefore circuit board manufacturing failure rate is roughly proportional to the number of pins being soldered. Big devices with many I/O connections are thus more problematic and there needs to be a way of verifying whether these soldered connections have been made correctly.

For the sake of clarity, we separate these techniques into two classes, and discuss a number of solutions in the following subsections that apply to computer processors:

1. Device manufacture test – This ensures that an integrated circuit works correctly before it leaves the semiconductor foundry. For more details, see the following sections:
   - Section 7.9.2 – BIST (built-in self-test).
   - Section 7.9.3 – JTAG (Joint Test Action Group).
2. Runtime test and monitoring – These are ways to ensure that the final manufactured system is working correctly (the two ways mentioned above, BIST and JTAG, also serve this purpose). They are explored in the following sections:
   - Section 7.10 – EDAC (Error Detection and Correction).
   - Section 7.11 – watchdog timers and brownout detectors.

7.9.2 Built-in Self-Test

Built-in self-test (BIST) is a device-specific on-chip hardware resource that is specifically designed to assist with the testing of internal device functionality.

[3] The SuperIO chip is the name given to the big IC that sits on a PC motherboard to provide much of the glue logic and functionality of the systems that must surround the CPU for the systems to work, for example, the memory drivers, USB interface, parallel port, serial port and so on.

Figure 7.20 A built-in self-test (BIST) unit can isolate the input and output signals for a device under test, allowing the output to be verified correct for the given input conditions.

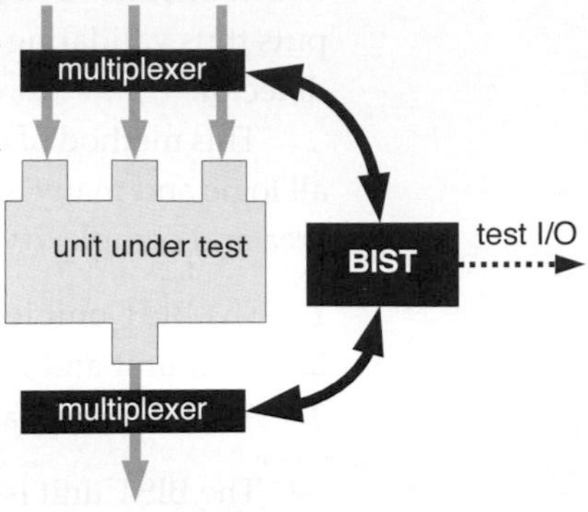

This may be used, for example, by a testing machine as soon as a silicon wafer leaves the silicon etching production line, or perhaps as soon as the individual IC has been packaged and is ready to be shipped to customers. Sometimes customers will also be provided with the ability to access an internal BIST unit to aid in their own design verification.

The requirement of a BIST unit is that it can in some way isolate the part of the IC under test, feed known values and conditions into that part, and then check that the output from that part is correct. This is shown diagrammatically in Figure 7.20 where the multiplexers route data to/from the BIST unit when in test mode.

BIST may also involve an internal program within a CPU that can exercise various peripheral units. In this case, it is usually required that there is some way of validating that the peripheral unit has functioned correctly, such as through a loop-back. This can be accomplished by a BIST unit, as in the diagram of Figure 7.21, where multiplexers will feed back the analogue output signals to the external input port when in test mode.

Feedback of external signals means that a manufacturer can generate a test sequence, output it through the analogue output drivers (e.g. the EIA232 serial port

Figure 7.21

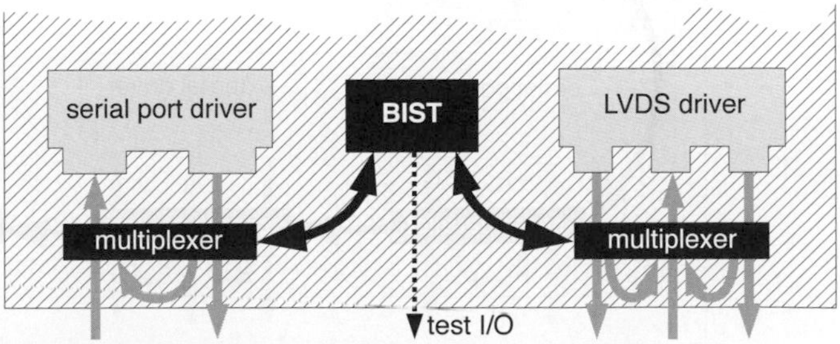

A built-in self-test (BIST) unit could be used to test or set input/output signals travelling between the external pins of a unit and its internal logic.

Test and Verification

which includes a negative voltage signalling level), and then through the analogue inputs thus validating the serial port hardware, the output driver or buffer and the input detector.

This method of on-chip testing is certainly convenient and easily capable of testing all logic and many analogue elements of an IC, but it comes at a cost in terms of silicon area and complexity. There are three components to this cost:

1. The BIST unit itself.
2. Each unit and I/O port to be tested require a multiplexer or similar switch.
3. A switch and data connection from the BIST unit to each multiplexer.

The BIST unit is not overly complex and scales readily to larger designs. For most logic entities, the addition of the input and output multiplexers does not significantly increase the amount of logic in the design. However, it is the data and switch connections from the BIST to each area of the device under test that become troublesome. These may have to operate at the same clock rate as the data paths they test and can require bunches of parallel wires that connect to input and output buses. These wires (or metal/polysilicon tracks in a silicon IC) must run from all extremities of a device to a centralised BIST. Such routing makes designing an IC extremely difficult and adds significantly to the cost. Decentralising the BIST circuitry into a few, or many, smaller units can help, but the problem still remains that as IC design complexity increases, the overall BIST complexity also increases.

One method of decoupling this scaling is through the use of a serial 'scan-path' where the connections between the multiplexers are serial links and the multiplexers themselves are simply parallel/serial registers. This is illustrated in Figure 7.22.

It can be seen that a single chain connects between the scan-path control unit and all of the test points. This is called a scan-chain. Its length is determined by the total number

Figure 7.22

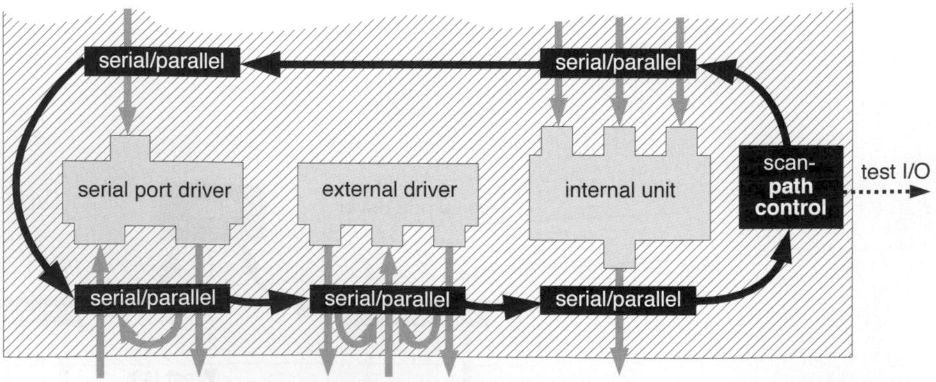

A daisy-chain scan-path unit to be tested, allowing the capability to isolate parts of a design using serial-to-parallel converter logic.

of bits in all of the serial/parallel registers around the chain. The chain consists of clock, data and control line, and is in essence a high-speed serial bus. Most importantly, this is much easier to route around an IC design, and the BIST unit (or scan-path controller) can be located at the periphery of the chip rather than being central.

7.9.3 Joint Test Action Group

The Joint Test Action Group (JTAG) was an IEEE work group which developed what is now IEEE standard 1149, as a common test control unit for scan-chain control in various logic devices. Originally, IEEE1149 applied to boundary scan testing, which is a subset of the scan-path in that it connects to the external input and output of a device, rather than the I/O of internal units.

In fact, JTAG-compliant test units have gathered substantial extra functionality over the years and now commonly include various internal access functions in addition to the boundary scan-path. In many cases, JTAG is the method used to enable hardware debugger access to a target processor, although some very modern processors have both a test JTAG unit and an in-circuit emulator (ICE) JTAG unit, the latter being used for debugging.

JTAG defines a standard test interface comprising the following external signals on the device that implements it:

1. TCK (test clock).
2. TMS (test mode select).
3. TDI (test data input).
4. TDO (test data output).
5. TRST (test reset – optional).

For those JTAG units implementing ICE functionality, there are generally four or perhaps eight other input/output signals that can comprise a high-speed bus to transfer test data rapidly.

Moving back to 'pure' JTAG, the hardware implemented in the unit for something like the ARM processor is shown in Figure 7.23.

The JTAG circuitry – which is definitely not shown to scale in Figure 7.23 – is confined to the bottom half of the picture underneath the CPU internal logic and as a boundary scan connecting to all the inputs and outputs of this block. Using the five JTAG pins, all of the input, output and bidirectional pins connecting to the CPU internal logic can be queried and (where appropriate) adjusted.

JTAG is useful for many things, such as tracking down connectivity issues and soldering faults (see Box 7.5). Another very common application (which is unlikely to have been in the minds of the original designers) is the programming of boot code into flash memory in an embedded system, discussed in Box 7.6.

JTAG control is implemented as a simple state machine. Data is clocked in on the TDI pin on the falling edge of TCK. The TMS pin is used to select and change mode. Several modes exist, which typically include BYPASS which bypasses the scan-chain so that whatever data is clocked in on TDI simply comes straight out on TDO. IDCODE

Figure 7.23

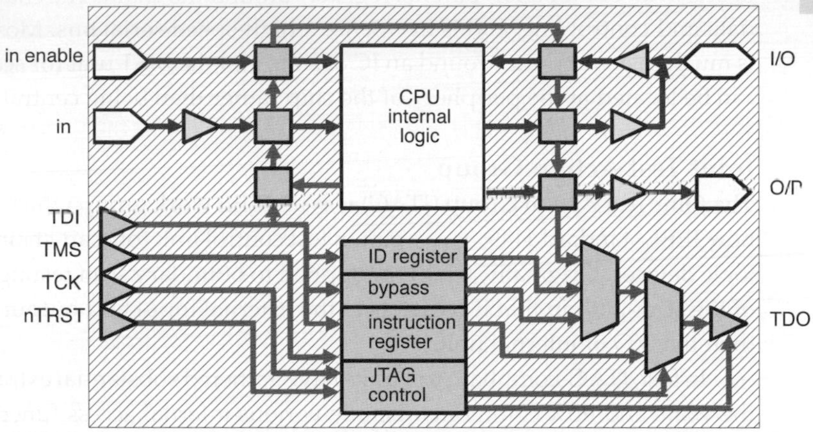

A block diagram of the main JTAG-related registers and examples of the serial data register interconnections in the ARM processor.

Box 7.5

Using JTAG for finding a soldering fault

Imagine you have a newly-made computer motherboard back from the factory. All looks correct: it does not have an over-current fault, the reset and clock signals are fine, but the board simply does not work. Perhaps there is a soldering fault?

Using JTAG, connected to the central CPU device, a test technician could set known values into the pins of the device, and then go around the PCB with a multi-meter checking that these signals are correct. He may set the address bus to `0xAAAA` (which is binary pattern `1010101010101010`) which will reveal whether any of those pins are shorted together, then set it to `0x5555` (which is binary pattern `0101010101010101`) so every pin now changes state and will reveal any pins that cannot drive either high or low correctly. It is important to measure both states because some signals on a PCB will float high if not driven, and some will float low.

Later, the same technician may set various test points on the PCB to known values, and then use JTAG to read back the state of all input pins on the CPU. Then he changes the known value to something else (such as the inverted signals) and repeats the steps.

In this way, all input, output and bidirectional signals on the CPU can be checked. If one pin or ball on the CPU is not soldered correctly, this will show up as the signal not able to be driven by the CPU or as a CPU input being incorrect.

Good as this method is, it has its limitations. Firstly, the pass/fail nature of the test can tell if a solder joint is working, but not how *good* it is (which could help highlight potential future failures). Secondly, there are several pins which cannot be tested – power supply pins, analogue I/O pins and typically phase-locked loop input pins. Thirdly, it is very slow.

Box 7.6

Using JTAG for booting a CPU

Most ARM-based processors that do not contain internal flash memory will start to execute from address 0 following reset. This address relates to chip-select 0 (*nCS0* to indicate it is active low), which is generally wired up to external flash memory.

This external flash would therefore contain a bootloader, which is the first small program run by the CPU after reset or power-up, and which launches the main application or operating system – perhaps mobile Linux for a smartphone or SymbianOS for a basic cell phone.

Before the 1990s, boot code would be in an EPROM (erasable programmable read-only memory) that was typically socketed. It was simply a matter of inserting a programmed EPROM device, turning on the power, and the system would work. Today, EPROM has been superseded by flash memory which is reprogrammable, and a ROM socket is regarded as too expensive and too large to include in most manufactured electronics.

Every new device straight off the production line would have empty flash. There thus needs to be a step of placing the boot code inside the flash memory.

This can easily be accomplished with a JTAG-based programmer. This is driven from an external PC, connected to the CPU JTAG controller. It takes control of the CPU interface pins that connect to the flash memory, and then it drives the flash memory in such a way as to program in the boot code. As far as the flash memory is concerned, it does not know that this is controlled from an external PC: it simply sees the CPU controlling it in the normal way.

The external PC, working through the JTAG to the CPU, and then controlling the CPU interface, uses this to command the external flash device to erase itself, and then byte by byte, programs boot code into flash from address 0 onwards.

clocks the contents of the ID register out to identify the manufacturer and the device. EXTEST and INTEST both clock data through the scan-chain and exist to support testing of external and internal connectivity respectively.

A manufacturer may implement several alternative scan-chains inside a device. One example is where integrated flash memory inside the same IC as the CPU has a separate scan-chain to service it independently of the main CPU (but using the same physical JTAG interface).

Typical scan-chains are several hundred bits long. For example, the Samsung S3C2410 ARM9 processor has 272 BGA balls, but 427 bits in the scan-chain. Each bit position in the scan-chain corresponds to one of:

- Input pin.
- Output pin.
- Bidirectional pin.
- Control pin.
- Reserved or hidden.

Usually, output and bidirectional pins (or groups of similar pins) have a control bit associated with them that determines whether the output buffer is turned on or not. These control bits can be active high or active low – and this information along with everything else needed to control the JTAG of a particular device is stored in a boundary scan data (BSD or BSD logic: BSDL) file, including scan-chain length, command register length, the actual command words themselves and the scan-chain mapping of which bit relates to which pin or function.

Finally, it should be noted that since the JTAG standard is implemented as a serial connection, there is nothing to prevent a single JTAG interface from servicing several separate devices in a long daisy chain. An external test controller can then address and handle each one as required through a single JTAG interface.

JTAG is thus very hardware and resource efficient, and has become increasingly popular on CPUs, FPGAs (Field Programmable Gate Arrays), graphics chips, network controllers and configuration devices, etc. Anyone who can remember the difficulties in debugging and 'running up' new digital hardware in the days before adopting JTAG would probably agree with the author that this technology, although simple, has revolutionised the ability of computer designers to get their prototype designs working!

7.10 Error Detection and Correction

Errors creep into digital systems in a number of ways apart from through incorrect programming. Poor system design may see analogue noise corrupting digital lines, voltage droop occuring on power lines (also called brownout, described in Section 7.11.1), clock jitter (see Section 7.4) causing a digital signal to be sampled at an incorrect time and electromagnetic interference from other devices corrupting signals.

One less commonly discussed cause is through cosmic radiation: so called SEUs (Single Event Upsets) whereby a cosmic ray triggers a random bit-flip in an electronic device. Since the earth's atmosphere attenuates cosmic and solar radiation, SEUs become more prevalent with altitude. Consumer electronics at the altitude of a Galileo or Global Positioning Satellite (around 20,000 km) would be totally unusable, while at a low earth orbit altitude (500 km) they may suffer several events per day. On a high mountain, there may be one or two such events a month, and on the ground, possibly a few per year. This does not sound like a cause for concern, but then imagine designing, for example, a computer to be used in an air traffic control system or for a nuclear reactor control room or a life-support system.

Fortunately, well-established techniques exist to handle such errors, and this is an active research field in space science. Common techniques range from a NASA-like decision to run five separate computers in parallel and then 'majority vote' on the decisions by each one to, at the simpler extreme, the use of parity on a memory bus.

In times gone by, well-engineered UNIX workstations by such giants as DEC (Digital Equipment Corporation), SUN Microsystems and IBM were designed to accept parity memory. Parity memory stored 9 bits for every byte in memory – or 36 bits for a

32-bit data bus. One extra bit was provided for each stored byte to act as a parity check on the byte contents:

7	6	5	4	3	2	1	0	P
1	0	1	1	0	1	0	1	**1**
1	0	1	0	0	1	0	1	**0**

The P bit is a 1 if there is an odd number of 1's in the byte, otherwise it has a value of 0. It is therefore possible to detect if a single-bit error occurs due to an SEU (for example), since the parity bit will then be wrong when compared to the contents of the byte. This applies even if the parity bit is the one affected by the SEU.

While this works well, two bits in error cannot be detected with a single bit of parity. Even more unfortunate is the fact that although it is possible to know that an error has occurred, the scheme does not give any indication of *which* bit is in error, and so the error cannot be corrected.

More capable error detection methods utilise methods such as Hamming codes and Reed-Solomon encoding. One increasingly popular and relatively modern technique is the powerful Turbo Code, often used for satellite communications. Details of these methods are outside the scope of this book, except to note that all the methods increase the amount of data that must be handled, and in return, improve the ability to recover corrupted data. In fact, there is a multi-way trade-off among the following schemes:

- Encoding complexity – *How many MIPs to encode a data stream*
- Decoding complexity – *How many MIPs to decode a data stream*
- Coding overhead – *How many extra bits must be added to the data*
- Correction ability – *How many bits in error can be corrected*
- Detection ability – *How many bits in error can be detected*

It is possible to trade off each of these, and each scheme has its own particular characteristics. In addition, the schemes are based on a unit of data that might range from a single byte (with a repetition code) to several kilobytes or more (Turbo Codes). This has the practical consideration that some schemes will output corrected data after a few bits have been processed, whereas with other schemes it may be necessary to wait until a large block of data has been processed before anything can be decoded.

Some examples are:

- **Triple redundancy** – This is sometimes called repetition code. Under this coding scheme, each bit of data is repeated three times, so the coding overhead is 300% and for that, one error can be corrected in every 3 bits. Encoding and decoding are extremely easy. An example of triple module redundancy (TMR), achieved by performing a 'majority vote' on outputs of three (or more) modules, is shown in Figure 7.24. The signals being voted on do not necessarily have to be bits, but could be bytes, words or even larger blocks of data. Voting can be performed individually for each bit or for the entire item of output data. One example of this is in NASA's space shuttle which has five IBM flight computers. Four of these run identical code

Figure 7.24

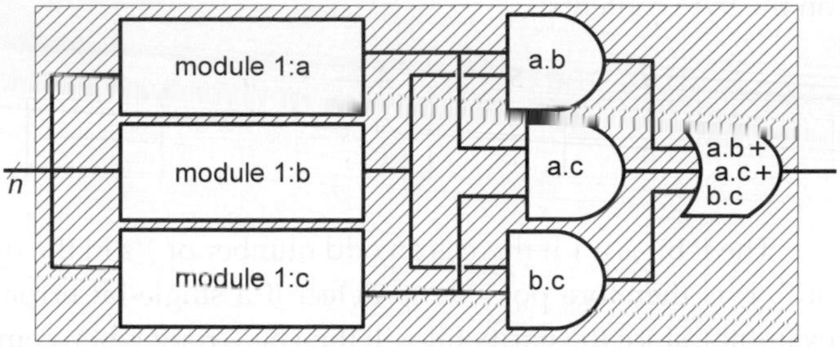

An example of triple module redundancy (TMR) where one processing module is repeated three times. A simple output circuit performs majority voting. For example, if the three modules output 0, 0, 1 respectively at a bit level, then the final output is 0 and we assume that the module which output the 1 is incorrect. Similarly, if the three modules output 1, 0, 1 respectively then the final output will be 1 and we would assume that the middle module is in error. Note that the signals do not necessarily need to be bits, but could be larger items of data.

and all feed a majority voter. The fifth runs software which performs the same tasks, but was developed and written separately (and thus should not be susceptible to a software error common to the other computers).

- **Hamming codes** – A very popular family of codes, with a common choice being the (7, 4) code that adds three parity bits to each four bits of data. This can correct all single-bit errors per block and additionally detect 2-bit errors per block. Encoding and decoding are both relatively trivial – requiring simple modulo-2 arithmetic[4] on matrices of 1's and 0's. Coding overhead is 75% for the (7, 4) code which is explored in Boxes 7.7 and 7.8. Note that there exist many other variants of Hamming code having different overhead, detection and correction characteristics.
- **Reed-Solomon (RS)** – A block-based code characterised by relatively low encoding complexity, but higher decoding complexity. RS is actually a family of possible codes based on block size – with the correction and detection ability set by the size of the block being handled. One common code is RS(255,223) which works in coded blocks of 255 bytes. The coded block contains 223 data bytes and 32 parity bytes and can correct up to 16 bytes in error per 223 byte block. Note that these bytes may each have multiple errors so it is possible to correct significantly more than 16 single bit errors at times. For RS(255,223), coding size overhead is 32 in 223 or 14%.

[4] Modulo-2 means counting with 0's and 1's, and that any value greater than 1 should be represented by the remainder of that value when divided by 2. Thus, modulo-2 values are 0 for even numbers and 1 for odd numbers, for example, $3 = 1 \ (mod\ 2)$ and $26 = 0 \ (mod\ 2)$. Similarly, any number in modulo-n is the remainder of that number divided by n.

Box 7.7

Hamming (7, 4) encoding example

For a 4-bit data word consisting of bits b_0, b_1, b_2, b_3, to be transmitted, we can define four parity bits p_0 to p_3 using modulo-2 arithmetic:

$$p_0 = b_1 + b_2 + b_3$$
$$p_1 = b_0 + b_2 + b_3$$
$$p_2 = b_0 + b_1 + b_3$$
$$p_3 = b_0 + b_1 + b_2$$

The 7-bit word that actually gets transmitted is made up from the four original bits plus any three of the parity bits, such as the following:

b_0	b_1	b_2	b_3	p_0	p_1	p_2

When this 7-bit word is received, it is easy to recalculate the three parity bits and determine whether they are correct. If so, it means that the data has either been received correctly or there is more than a single bit in error. If an error is detected then we can determine (assuming it is only a single bit in error) exactly which bit is affected. For example, if p_1 and p_2 are found to be incorrect, but p_0 is correct, then the data bit common to both must be suspect – in this case either b_0 or b_3. However, b_3 is used to calculate p_0 which is correct, thus the error must be in b_0 alone.

It is more common to use matrices for Hamming (and most other) coding examples – see Box 7.8.

Some CPUs (such as the European Space Agency version of the SPARC processor, called ERC32 – also freely available as the Leon soft core) embed EDAC (error detection and correction) capabilities within themselves, but others rely on an external EDAC unit such as that shown in Figure 7.25.

Figure 7.25

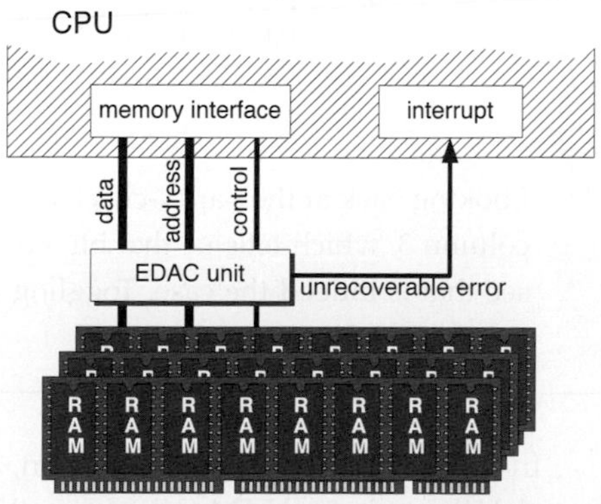

An error detection and correction (EDAC) unit located between a CPU's memory interface and external memory.

Box 7.8

Hamming (7, 4) encoding example using matrices

In practice, Hamming encoding, verification and correction are performed using linear algebra (matrices), defined using a generator matrix, **G**, and a parity-check matrix, **H** defined by Hamming:

$$\mathbf{G} = \begin{bmatrix} 1 & 1 & 0 & 1 \\ 1 & 0 & 1 & 1 \\ 1 & 0 & 0 & 0 \\ 0 & 1 & 1 & 1 \\ 0 & 1 & 0 & 0 \\ 0 & 0 & 1 & 0 \\ 0 & 0 & 0 & 1 \end{bmatrix} \qquad \mathbf{H} = \begin{bmatrix} 1 & 0 & 1 & 0 & 1 & 0 & 1 \\ 0 & 1 & 1 & 0 & 0 & 1 & 1 \\ 0 & 0 & 0 & 1 & 1 & 1 & 1 \end{bmatrix}$$

Let us test this out for an example 4-bit data vector, **d** (`1101`) which first needs to be multiplied by the generator matrix, **G** to form the 7-bit transmitted codeword:

$$\mathbf{x} = \mathbf{Gd} = \begin{bmatrix} 1 & 1 & 0 & 1 \\ 1 & 0 & 1 & 1 \\ 1 & 0 & 0 & 0 \\ 0 & 1 & 1 & 1 \\ 0 & 1 & 0 & 0 \\ 0 & 0 & 1 & 0 \\ 0 & 0 & 0 & 1 \end{bmatrix} \begin{bmatrix} 1 \\ 1 \\ 0 \\ 1 \end{bmatrix} = \begin{bmatrix} 3 \\ 2 \\ 1 \\ 2 \\ 1 \\ 0 \\ 1 \end{bmatrix} \quad \textit{modulo2} => \quad \begin{bmatrix} 1 \\ 0 \\ 1 \\ 0 \\ 1 \\ 0 \\ 1 \end{bmatrix}$$

So the transmitted data *1010101* represents the original data `1101`. Now assume a single-bit error, so we receive something different: **y** = `1000101`. Let us see how to use matrix **H** to check the received word:

$$\mathbf{Hy} = \begin{bmatrix} 1 & 0 & 1 & 0 & 1 & 0 & 1 \\ 0 & 1 & 1 & 0 & 0 & 1 & 1 \\ 0 & 0 & 0 & 1 & 1 & 1 & 1 \end{bmatrix} \begin{bmatrix} 1 \\ 0 \\ 0 \\ 0 \\ 1 \\ 0 \\ 1 \end{bmatrix} = \begin{bmatrix} 3 \\ 1 \\ 2 \end{bmatrix} \quad \textit{modulo2} => \quad \begin{bmatrix} 1 \\ 1 \\ 0 \end{bmatrix}$$

Looking back at the parity-check matrix, **H**, we see that the pattern `[110]` is found in column 3, which tells us that bit 3 of **y** was received in error. Comparing **x** and **y** we see that is indeed the case. Toggling the indicated bit 3 thus corrects **y** and recreates the original message.

In Figure 7.25, the data bus within, and connected to, the CPU is not EDAC protected, but an external EDAC device adds error correcting codes to every memory word written out by the CPU and checks every word read into the CPU from memory. On detecting an unrecoverable error, an interrupt is triggered to inform the CPU. Otherwise, recoverable errors are naturally corrected automatically without intervention required by the CPU.

Note that not all error correcting codes are quick enough to sit between a CPU and memory. For example, Reed-Solomon codewords require a relatively long time to decode and would not be possible in such a scenario without causing the CPU to pause every time it reads an erroneous, but correctable, data word. Hamming, by contrast, is quick, and commonly used for error detection and correction in such systems (see the example of Hamming coding in Boxes 7.7 and 7.8).

In summary, some computer systems are required to be highly reliable, and these are likely to require some form of error detection and correction, either internally or on the external buses that are more susceptible to noise. Similarly, high-density memory, which is more susceptible to SEU errors may need to be protected with an EDAC unit.

7.11 Watchdog Timers and Reset Supervision

While EDAC, apart from straightforward parity checking, is rare in ground-based computers, both watchdog timers and brownout detectors (Section 7.11.1) are extremely common and are often implemented inside a dedicated CPU support IC.

A watchdog to a processor is like a pacemaker to a human heart: a watchdog needs to be reassured constantly that a processor is executing its code correctly. If a certain period expires without such a reassurance, the watchdog will assume that the processor has 'hung' and will assert the reset line – just like a pacemaker delivering a small electric shock to a heart that has stopped beating.

From a programmer's perspective, a processor has to write to, or read from, a watchdog timer (WDT) repeatedly, within a time-out period. It can write or read as often as it likes, but failure to read or write at least once within the specified period, will cause the reset.

Internal WDTs usually allow the programmer to specify the time-out period by writing to an internal configuration register, which is usually memory-mapped. The devices are constructed as countdown timers fed by a divided-down system clock, with the divide ratio also being configurable in many cases. On system reset, the value in the watchdog count configuration register will be loaded into a hardware counter. Once out of reset, this counter is decremented by the clock. A comparator determines when it reaches zero, in which case the reset signal is asserted. Any time the CPU reads from, or writes to, the WDT registers, the counter is reloaded with the value in the count configuration register.

An external watchdog timer can be constructed from a capacitor, resistor and a comparator. This works in a similar way to an external reset circuit (see Section 7.11.1), although the CPU can periodically 'write' a logic high to the capacitor to keep it charged up, and thus present the reset.

Typically, the watchdog time-out period is a few hundred milliseconds or perhaps a few seconds – anything too short would mean too many wasted CPU cycles as the code periodically accesses the WDT. Servicing this is best accomplished inside some periodic low-level code such as an operating system (OS) timer process that is executed every 100 ms. If this stops, we can assume that the OS has crashed, and the result will be the watchdog resetting the processor. The watchdog thereby ensures that the OS remains operational, otherwise it will reset the CPU and restart the OS code cleanly.

7.11.1 Reset Supervisors and Brownout Detectors

Many veterans of the computer industry will remember the 'big red switch' on the early IBM PCs and the prominent reset buttons sported by the machines. The prominence of these conveniences was probably a reflection of the reliability of the operating systems running on the machines, namely MS-DOS (Microsoft Disk Operating System) and Microsoft Windows. While MS-DOS is, thankfully, no longer with us in a meaningful way, Windows unfortunately remains – although is not normally used in 'mission critical' applications where reliability is paramount.

Embedded systems, by contrast, are unlikely to sport large reset switches, and often have 'soft' rather than 'hard' power switches (i.e. those that are under software control, rather than ones that physically interrupt the power to the systems). It follows that embedded systems need to be more reliable, especially those in physically remote locations. For example, it would not be particularly useful to have a 'big red switch' on the side of the Mars Rover.

In their quest to improve system reliability, embedded systems thus tend to make extensive use of watchdog timers (explained previously in Section 7.11) and also have supervisory circuits for power and reset.

Reset circuitry, usually driven by an external reset input, is important in ensuring that a device begins its operation in a known state. The lack of a clean reset signal has been the cause of many system failures, whether in CPU, SoC, FPGA or discrete hardware systems.

An external reset controller device, or supervisory IC, shown in Figure 7.26, normally 'asserts' a reset signal as soon as power is applied to a system. Some time later, the reset signal is de-asserted, allowing the device to operate, from a known starting position. A few SoC processors contain all of this reset logic and timing internally. Other devices may allow a designer to simply wire the reset pin to a capacitor connected to GND, and a resistor connected to Vcc, but note that this can be dangerous in many cases, so beware.[5]

[5] The reason for the danger is in the way the reset is triggered. As power is applied to the system the voltage across the capacitor will initially be zero, meaning that the reset pin is held low. As the capacitor slowly charges up through the Vcc-connected resistor, the voltage will rise until it reaches a threshold on the reset input pin, which then interprets it as a logic high, taking the device out of reset. Unfortunately, however, there is always electrical noise in any system, causing small fluctuations in voltage which, as the rising capacitor voltage passes the reset pin threshold, causes the device to rapidly toggle into and out of reset. The effect is often to 'scramble' the reset action, prompting most manufacturers to specify a minimum time that their device should be held in reset.

Figure 7.26

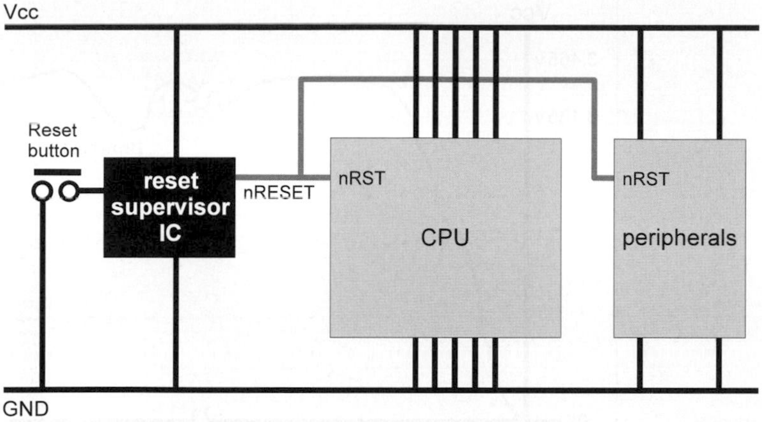

A reset supervisory IC connects between Vcc and ground (GND) to generate an active-low nRESET signal for a CPU and any peripherals that require it. By convention, the reset signal is active low to ensure that devices are in reset when first powered on. If a reset button is required in a design, this is also supported as an input to the reset supervisor.

A *brownout* is a voltage droop on a power rail.[6] Since CPUs are only specified to operate within a very narrow range of power rail voltages, these droops can cause malfunction when they occur. External reset chips will assert the reset line if the power drops completely (i.e. once the power restores they will hold the CPU in reset for at least the length of time specified by the manufacturer before de-asserting the reset). However, only reset chips with a brownout detector will do the same whenever the supply voltage goes outside of the specified operating range.

In addition, some brownout detecting reset chips can give an immediate power fail interrupt to a processor. This could allow the processor a few milliseconds to take action before the power fails totally, and thus power down cleanly. The process of reset supervision and brownout detection is illustrated in Figure 7.27, where the voltage of the Vcc power supply to a processor is plotted over time. The operating voltage of this device is 3.3 v +/ − 5%, and thus a reset supervisory system has been configured to detect any excursion of the Vcc voltage outside this range. In the event a voltage excursion is detected, the system will trigger a reset condition. The reset condition is held for 10 ms in each case (in reality, this would be set to comfortably exceed the minimum time specified by the processor manufacturer, which is normally significantly less than 10 ms). The brownout device will be connected and used in the same way as the standard reset supervisory IC that was shown in Figure 7.26.

[6] A 'brownout' is like a 'blackout' but a little less severe. Perhaps we can follow the colour analogies further and refer to a power surge as a 'whiteout'.

Figure 7.27

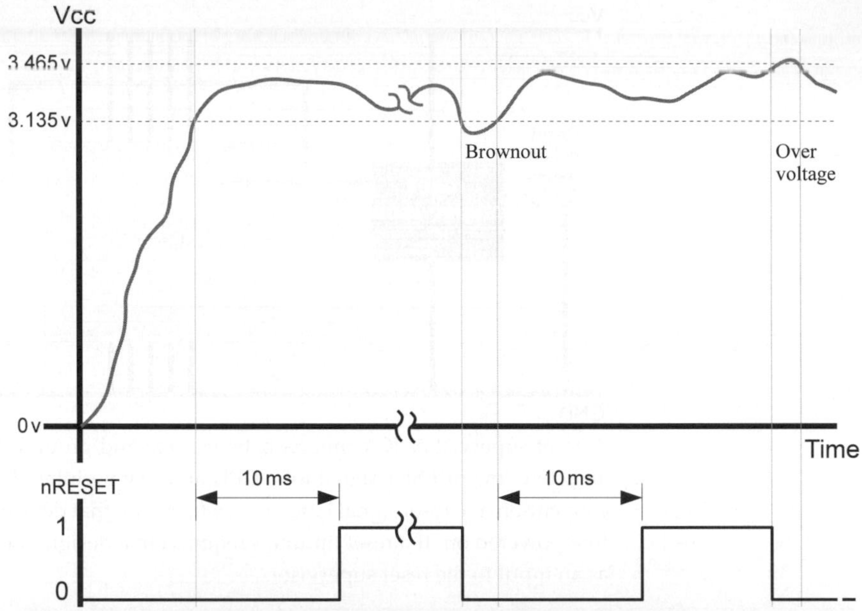

An illustration of a reset supervisory chip holding a device in reset (shown as the state of the nRESET signal on the lower axis) as the power supply (shown on the upper axis) rises to the nominal 3.3 v level. After some time of normal operation, a brownout occurs when the power rail voltage drops. The supervisory chip consequentially resets the processor cleanly until after the voltage has again risen to the nominal level. Later, the beginning of an over-voltage condition occurs, which will be handled similarly.

7.12 Reverse Engineering

The consumers of embedded technology developments see desirable and breathtaking new products, but for the developers these are often the culmination of a long, arduous and expensive design process. Of course, any pioneering inventor of new embedded systems can expect there to be some competition in time, which may improve upon their original design. However, companies may often rely upon the first few months of sales in an uncrowded market to recoup large up-front design and manufacturing costs. Usually, competitor products will have a similar costing to the pioneer products – since these would have incurred similar development expense.

However, the economics changes substantially when a competitor cheaply and rapidly reverse engineers[7] a pioneering design. Their development costs are largely

[7] 'Reverse engineering' is normally defined as a process involving the analysis and understanding of the functionality, architecture and technology of a device, and then representing these in some manner which allows reuse or duplication of the original product, its architecture or technology.

replaced by reverse engineering costs and, if we assume that these are significantly less, then the competitor would easily be able to undercut the pioneer device in price. The effects are twofold: firstly, the market lead of the pioneer company has been curtailed, and secondly, their market share will reduce due to the lower pricing of the competitor product. The assumption that the reverse engineering (RE) process can be shorter and less expensive than a full prototype-development project is borne out by the evidence of commercial examples of product piracy. The larger the differential between up-front development cost and RE cost, the greater the risk to a pioneering company and the greater the reward to a nefarious competitor intent on pirating their products. The differential is greatest in the case of a truly revolutionary product which is simple to reverse engineer.

Of course, it should be noted that reverse engineering to understand how something works is a time-honoured engineering approach. It is even a valid research area and something that many engineers love to do. However, design piracy through reverse engineering is a real concern in the embedded industry, and one which has led to some computer architecture-related challenges and responses which we will discuss.

First, however, it is useful to briefly survey the RE process itself, since this is the activity which prompts the later discussion.

7.12.1 The Reverse Engineering Process

In this section, we will work from the viewpoint of an offending company intent on reverse engineering an unprotected embedded system. The intention is to examine the difficulty, specialised equipment and effort needed for each step, to allow determination of the cost structure of the process and how this relates to the architecture of the system under 'attack'.

The RE process involves both top-down and bottom-up analysis of a system. The hierarchy of information which describes an embedded system is shown diagrammatically in Figure 7.28, where the system itself can be seen to potentially comprise different sub-assemblies each of which contain a module or modules of one or more printed circuit boards (PCBs). Top down means beginning with overall system functionality, and working down, partitioning the design as the process progresses, in order to elucidate more and more of the design functionality as a lower level is approached. Bottom up would most usually include identifying critical devices early and then inferring information from them. An example would be finding a known CPU on one PCB and thus inferring that much of the 'intelligence' within the system is concentrated within that module.

Top-down RE of embedded systems typically involves several analytical steps. Although in practice a particular RE attack may not necessarily involve each step, or be in a particular sequence, a logical listing of RE stages would be as follows:

A: System functionality

B: Physical structure analysis

- B.1: electro-mechanical arrangement
- B.2: enclosure design

Figure 7.28

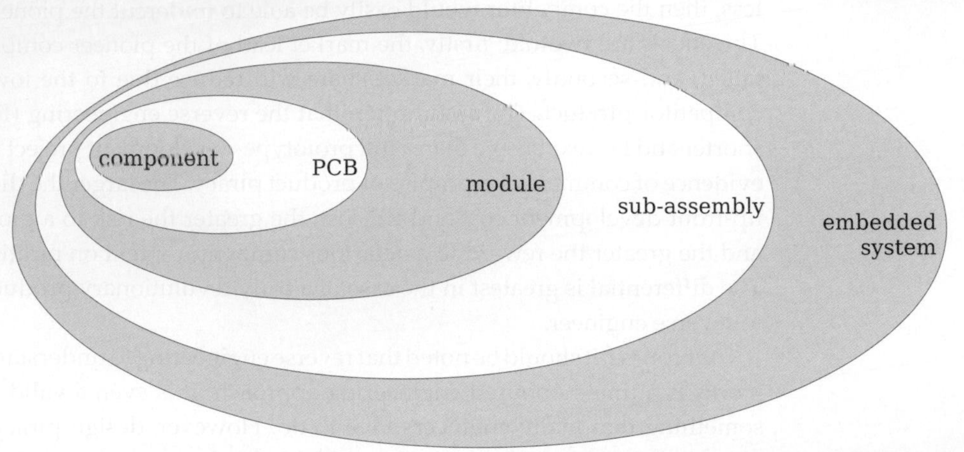

The hierarchy of information that will be revealed when reverse engineering an embedded system comprises, from the outside in, analysis of the system as a whole, one or more sub-assemblies (including wiring looms), modules (and their fixtures), comprising one or more PCBs (including daughterboards, plug-in cards and so on), down to the individual components mounted on the PCBs or located elsewhere within the system.

- B.3: printed circuit board layout
- B.4: wiring looms and connectors
- B.5: assembly instructions

C: Bill of materials

- C.1: active electronic components
- C.2: passive electronic components
- C.3: interconnect wires and connectors
- C.4: mechanical items

D: System architecture

- D.1: functional blocks and their interfaces
- D.2: connectivity

E: Detailed physical layout

- E.1: placement of individual components
- E.2: electrical connectivity between components
- E.3: impedance-controlled and location-aware orientation

F: Schematic of electrical connectivity

G: Object/executable code

- G.1: isolation of code processors
- G.2: isolation of firmware code for reconfigurable logic

H: Software analysis

In order to highlight the process, each RE stage will be discussed in relation to an unprotected/unhardened embedded system with a very generic system level diagram as

Figure 7.29

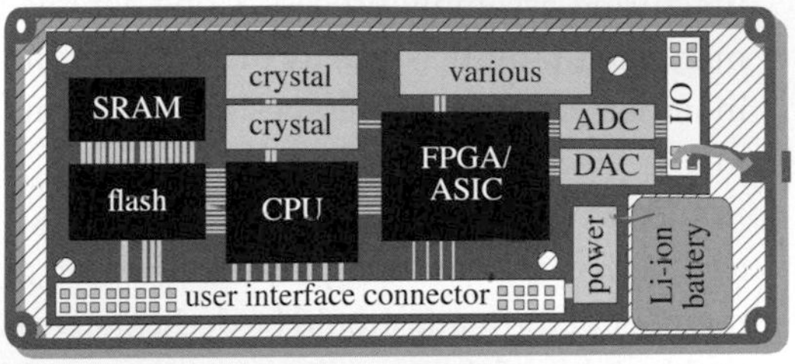

A block diagram of an example embedded system under analysis, showing two active ICs (loosely identified as CPU and FPGA/ASIC), two memory elements (volatile being SRAM and non-volatile being flash), plus several connectors, power circuitry, crystals and interfacing devices.

shown in Figure 7.29. This consists of a large integrated circuit (IC) connected to volatile memory (SRAM in this case), non-volatile memory (flash), a field programmable gate array (FPGA), a user interface of some kind, connectors and some devices to interface with the outside world, generically termed analogue-to-digital converter (ADC) and digital-to-analogue converter (DAC) in this instance. Specific systems may differ, but as a general class, embedded systems often comprise a CPU booted from flash, executing out of SRAM (both of which are increasingly likely to be internal to the IC), connected to discrete or programmed logic (FPGA, programmable logic device and so on) or application-specific integrated circuit (ASIC). A user interface of some kind, and interfaces to the outside, analogue, world. Larger systems would tend to use DRAM, SDRAM or even hard disc storage. More integrated systems tend to incorporate a CPU soft core within an FPGA or ASIC.

Let us now discuss each stage of the RE process of the example system shown in Figure 7.29. We will assume that the system has not been protected or deliberately hardened in any way.

7.12.1.1 Functionality

An RE team would normally receive several of the units to be reverse engineered. The process would begin by consulting user documentation, repair manuals, product briefs and so on. At minimum, a list of functionality is required to double-check that subsequent analysis has revealed sufficient hardware and software to provide each of the functions identified.

This is relatively simple work and can be augmented by searching the Internet for information on newsgroups, blogs, hacking sites and so on. Knowing the manufacturer and any original equipment manufacturer (OEM), postings by individuals from these email domains can be tracked and correlated.

7.12.1.2 Physical Structure Analysis

Disassembly may be as simple as removing a few screws to open a box or as difficult as having to work through layers of micromachinery. In many cases, documentation of a complex disassembly process is the key to determining the corresponding manufacturing assembly process. Considerable time and effort may have been devoted to manufacturability issues by the designers and as such there is likely to be implicit value in understanding these issues. Such information may also be found ready documented in a service manual.

Order and location of removed parts should be recorded – perhaps most easily accomplished by having a photographic or video record of the process. Ideally, one member of the team should be dedicated to documenting the process. Any observations and insights of those performing disassembly should also be noted at this stage. While detailed mechanical drawings for replicating enclosures, internal structures, wiring diagrams and so on, can be obtained from static analysis of the parts, assembly drawings need to be made through disassembly followed by reassembly. The analysis of the physical structure is unlikely to be an expensive component of the RE. However, the reasons behind unusual mechanical arrangements and structures may at first be non-obvious and require brainstorming.

7.12.1.3 Bill of Materials

A bill of materials (BOM), listing all components used in the design, can be as simple as counting the number of screws, resistors and so on. However, it may transpire that some components are difficult to identify, particularly semi-custom ICs and devices in highly miniaturised packages (which do not have sufficient surface area for identification marks). If simplified codes are shown, these may follow the standardised formats from JEDEC, JIS or Pro-Electron. Discrete parts may have to be removed to be tested and their characteristics painstakingly matched to known devices. However, with tolerances of 5% or more being common, it may be necessary to remove and test parts from a number of systems before an accurate determination can be made.

Some parts can be copied as-is, a genuine field of academic research, especially in cases where obsolete parts need to be recreated. In general, solid models from physical measurement can be combined with materials analysis to completely describe many parts including structural items, fixings and passive components.

PCB silk screen markings often provide useful clues to the identity of tiny unmarked parts (e.g. Z12 may well be a Zener diode and L101 an inductor). ICs with unusual or missing markings are more troublesome, especially where the manufacturer is not identified. Sometimes, system-on-chip processing cores are more likely to be identified with certain manufacturers than others. If a fabrication process can be identified, this can often be related to other known deliveries from that process.

Otherwise, subsequent system analysis (such as location and size of data bus, address bus, control signals and power connections) can aid in identifying parts that are not immediately obvious.

Most embedded systems will incorporate off-the-shelf parts and even provide helpful silk screen annotations, kindly assisting in allowing an inexpensive RE process. The most common difficulty appears to be associated with custom silicon devices, either from an OEM or in-house development of large-scale integrated (LSI) devices.

However, while OEM silicon is often undocumented, it can sometimes be traceable online in Chinese, Korean or Japanese documents. In addition, in-house LSI devices may be offered for sale by a commercialisation arm of the parent company, in which case a feature list will be published somewhere – but a non-disclosure agreement (NDA) may be required before a full datasheet can be viewed.

Clearly, the identification of major ICs during a cursory inspection process is preferable, but even if identification is not immediate, the process does not end there. Detailed and costly analysis can be performed to identify exact inputs and outputs and from there infer internal functionality. This may include examining voltage levels (such as CPU core voltage), clock frequencies, bus connectivity, decoupling arrangements and so on. More destructively, the device casing can be opened and painstakingly analysed silicon layer by silicon layer. IC reverse engineering will be discussed further in Section 7.12.2.2.

7.12.1.4 System Architecture

System architecture analysis reveals a rough block diagram of connectivity and subsystems responsible for various items of functionality: this involves understanding the partitioning of a design among the modules, boards and devices within the system. Another important aspect to determine at this stage is the identification of power or ground planes and the power distribution to areas of the system. Equally necessary is an identification of bus connectivity within the system. The presence of a debug port or IEEE1149 JTAG (see Section 7.9.3) interface can be very significant in assisting the RE process, so any indication of this is an important find. Clues may include a set of five test points with pull-up resistors located close to the CPU.

In most systems, circuit continuity tests and visual inspection of parts and their arrangements can be performed and conclusions subsequently drawn. For example, it is likely in an embedded system that the same CPU data bus connects both flash memory and SRAM. Continuity tests in conjunction with device data sheets easily reveal this type of arrangement. Such tests are complicated with modern packages such as ball grid arrays, but are still possible with some difficulty. Power pin locations, often predictable in advance, are easily tested for. For most embedded systems, this type of analysis is simple and inexpensive, but as we shall see in Section 7.13.1, it can be deliberately complicated by designers.

7.12.2 Detailed Physical Layout

Where silk screen layout annotations are not present, photography of component placement and orientation can reveal required placement information for both outer layers. Next, all components are removed and drilled hole positions noted. As a quick check, the locations of holes on the top and bottom layers can be compared: if these are identical then there are no blind vias and it is unlikely, although not impossible, that there are any buried vias.

The next stage is PCB delamination (peeling apart layer by layer) with photography of each layer from a constant reference position. This can be used to build a photographically correct layer stack-up. From this point, it is relatively simple to copy the PCB, however, the composition and thickness of copper and each PCB layer are also required. In practice, this can be found by examining a section of the PCB where copper is present on every layer (many PCBs have a test coupon area designed for this purpose, since manufacturing process changes can affect copper thickness in particular, which in turn affects system performance and thus may need to be tested for).

Normally, a multi-layer area is cut out from the PCB test coupon and placed end-on into a hockey-puck shaped mould, which is then filled with epoxy. When set, a lens grinding machine can be used to prepare an end-on section of the PCB for examination under a measuring microscope. Copper and layer thicknesses can simply be read off.

For large circuit boards, cut-outs from several areas on a PCB might have to be examined since variations may exist in the copper etching bath during manufacture (e.g. the edge of a PCB nearer to the top corner of the bath would have etched differently to an area nearer to the bottom centre, and in either case local copper coverage density would similarly affect etching).

A growing number of embedded systems require track impedance control for high speed or radio frequency related signals. In this case, the exact characteristics of the PCB are important, including dielectric constant, the prepreg weave thickness and resin type. Overall, impedance can be determined through time-domain reflectometry or use of a network analyser. The prepreg type and characteristic can be found through microscopy, and some determination of resin type can be made by looking at the overall figures.

An example of the information required for the recreation of electrically equivalent PCBs, apart from the photographically correct layer stack-up, is shown in Table 7.3.

X-rays may also be a viable method of extracting layout information, and can even provide useful information on the internals of unknown ICs. As an example, Figure 7.19

Table 7.3

Example layer characteristics of four-layer PCBs

Name	Composition	Thickness
L1 signal	1/4 oz copper foil	0.0176 mm
prepreg	7628 × 2	0.3551 mm
L2 signal	1/4 oz copper	0.0177 mm
laminate	FR4	0.91 mm
L3 signal	1/4 oz copper	0.0177 mm
prepreg	7628 × 2	0.3543 mm
L4 signal	1/4 oz copper foil	0.0176 mm
Total		**1.69 mm**

(on page 333) showed a low-magnification X-ray of an FPGA device mounted on a PCB within which electrical tracks, decoupling capacitors (on the underside of the PCB) and the internal lead-frame of the FPGA mounted on the top side of the board can be seen clearly. The solid circles are test points, whereas the hollow circles are vias interconnecting tracks on different PCB layers. The hair-like line across the top left is a thin wire soldered to one of the pins on the IC.

Although some specialised equipment (such as measuring microscope and reflectometer) may be required for the physical layout analysis stage, unless impedance control is involved, copying a PCB layout and stack-up is neither difficult nor expensive.

7.12.2.1 Schematic of Electrical Connectivity

Electrical connectivity is most commonly represented as a netlist. This specifies the electrical connectivity between various nodes, and usually also specifies devices connected to those nodes. The netlist itself does not take account of actual physical positioning. It is only concerned with the connectivity relationship between nodes, although in real systems the physical positioning itself can be important (perhaps keep-out areas to reduce interference, or for safety reasons when high voltages may be present). The nodes are normally the pads and holes to which components are connected, and the connections are normally either wires or PCB tracks.

A netlist can be generated from the connectivity check, by inspection of X-ray photographs or photographs of a delaminated PCB. This is a time-consuming and error-prone business, but is at least simple to verify by means such as (i) testing for expected continuity on the original board, (ii) referring to expected connectivity found on device datasheets and (iii) searching for hanging vertices and unexpected shorts, such as a two-pin component with only one pin connected, or both pins of a two-pin component commoned.

Once a netlist has been found and the devices identified within a BOM, the next step would be to recreate a schematic diagram to represent the system. Netlist to schematic generation is an established research area, and there are even commercial tools available to assist in the process. However, in reality most RE attempts will involve a complete redrawing of a schematic directly from the revealed information. A forwards netlist generation of this schematic can be compared to the deduced system netlist as a check of correctness.

Note also that a BOM and known schematic allow the possibility of simulation tools to be used, which can assist in the verification of both BOM and netlist accuracy.

7.12.2.2 Stored Program

Where multiple programmable devices are used (such as CPU and FPGA), the simplest electrical arrangement would be for each to have individual flash memory storage devices (with parallel and serial connections for CPU and FPGA respectively). However, normally all non-volatile program storage within a system is clustered into a single device for cost reasons. In modern embedded systems, this device is often flash memory – serial connected if possible, otherwise parallel connected.

Items of storage within the non-volatile memory could include separate boot code and operating code for a CPU, system configuration settings, FPGA configuration data or other system-specific items. In this subsection, we consider methods of determining the memory location of stored programs, with a view to enabling individual extraction of these (in subsequent sections, we will discuss reverse engineering of the firmware/software programs themselves).

Mask-programmed gate arrays, non-volatile PLDs and of course ASICs require no external non-volatile devices, having their configuration stored internally. In some cases, it is possible to isolate a programmable device and read out its internal configuration code. In cases where such readout is not possible or device security measures are in force, the device will need to be either subject to extensive black box analysis or examined internally. The latter can be accomplished through dissolving its plastic case and/or carefully grinding through layers of silicon, reading the state of each stored bit with an electron microscope or a reflected laser.

Undoubtedly, stored-program devices with security settings in place are far more troublesome and expensive to reverse engineer than the majority systems containing a single non-volatile storage block. The example system here falls into the majority category, where the CPU is responsible for programming the FPGA, and both in turn derive their code from the flash memory.

7.12.2.3 Software

Software obtained from a memory dump can easily be copied as-is. Changes may involve simple adjustments such as rewriting the content of strings to change a manufacturer's name, serial number and version codes. Executable code pieces can, with care, also be cut-and-pasted.

In contrast to embedded systems hardware RE, software RE of all scales is a very well-researched field. At the benign end of the scale, software RE is a useful means to achieve the potential reuse of object-oriented code, whereas at the nefarious extreme, it is applied in the circumvention of copy protection schemes, leading to software piracy and theft. There is no indication that these conclusions are confined to software only. It is also the experience of the author that embedded system cloning and design theft are more prevalent in some regions than others. This may be due to such attitude differences or more likely to variations in legal protection against design theft.

Software plays an increasingly important role in embedded systems, and although it is advisable for manufacturers to consider software RE and software security, in general it is a subset of general RE and protection.

However, an important subset of embedded system-specific software reverse engineering remains to be discussed. This includes the embedded operating system, bootloader and non-volatile memory storage arrangement of software in a typical embedded system. Consider a typical embedded system such as that discussed previously in Figure 7.29. A generic real-time operating system running on that hardware may contain a monolithic block of boot, operating system and applications code stored in flash. However, the growing use of embedded Linux in embedded systems would usually present a different picture. Such embedded Linux systems normally contain separate instances in memory of the following items:

- Boot code.
- Operating system.
- Filesystem.
- System configuration settings.
- FPGA configuration data.

Non-volatile memory content can easily be extracted by either removing the device and dumping its content (static analysis) or by tapping off bus signals with a logic analyser during operation (dynamic analysis). The logic analyser method can give useful clues regarding context – for example, memory read signals detected immediately following power-up are likely to constitute boot code. However, this method obviously only reveals the content of memory addresses that are accessed during the analysis - in effect the current trace of execution/access, determining the entirety of stored code in this manner would be next to impossible in most real systems. It would require operating the system in every possible operating mode with every possible combination and timing of input signals in order to guarantee 100% code coverage. Nevertheless, a combination of both techniques is a powerful analytical tool.

Address and data bus lines are commonly jumbled on dense PCBs to aid in routing (see Box 7.9 for an explanation of this). This needs to be borne in mind with both methods, thus complicating the analysis slightly.

Static flash memory analysis first needs to determine the extent, boundaries and identity of different storage areas. Where delimiters of erased flash are present (namely long strings of `0xFFFF` or `0xFF` ending on a block boundary), then this process is trivial. Otherwise, boot code is likely to begin with a vector table and is most likely to reside at the lowest address in flash or in a specific boot block. An FPGA programming image will be approximately of the size specified in the FPGA data sheet, or compressed using a standard algorithm (which if zip, gzip or compress, will begin with a signature byte that can be searched for). A filesystem will be identifiable through its structure (and on a Linux desktop computer the `file` command is available to rapidly identify the nature of many of these items once they are dumped in the computer for analysis). The Linux kernel, along with other operating system kernels, contains distinct signature code and may even contain readable strings (on a Linux desktop computer the `strings` command will find and display these).

The combination of static and dynamic analysis is very powerful and can provide significant information on memory content. For example, system configuration data may be stored anywhere in flash memory and may be difficult to identify by content alone. However, simply operating the device and changing a single configuration setting will cause a change in memory content. This can be identified by comparing content before and after, or by tracking the address of specific writes to flash memory with a logic analyser.

Box 7.9

Bus line pin swapping

For ICs such as quad-operational amplifiers that contain more than one amplifier per package, it usually does not matter which one gets used for any particular part of a circuit. So, during layout, even though the schematic would have connected individual amplifiers to different parts of the circuit, the designer is free to swap these to improve routing. This is a well-established technique.

In fact, the same can be true of memory devices. For example, while we would naturally connect D0, D1, D2 and D3 on a CPU to D0, D1, D2 and D3 on a memory device, we are at liberty to swap the bit lines. In fact, we are also at liberty to swap address pins if we want (as long as the CPU always accesses memory with the same width – otherwise we can swap within individual bytes, but not between bytes). For example, consider the byte connection between a CPU and memory device:

CPU data pins	Memory data pins	Example bits
D0	D6	1
D1	D0	1
D2	D1	0
D3	D5	0
D4	D4	1
D5	D3	0
D6	D7	0
D7	D2	1

If this does not make sense, consider that as long as the CPU writes a byte B to location A, and receives the same byte B when reading back from location A, it will operate correctly. The exact way that byte B gets stored in memory is unimportant. The same is true of the address bus, when writing to SRAM:

CPU address pins	Memory address pins	Example bits
A0	A3	1
A1	A2	0
A2	A1	1
A3	A6	0
A4	A5	1
A5	A4	0
A6	A9	0
A7	A8	0
A8	A7	1
A9	A10	0
A10	A0	0

(Continued)

Box 7.9

Bus line pin swapping (*Continued*)

This works great with SRAM, but there are issues with flash memory. Remember the programming algorithms in Section 7.6.2? Well, the flash expects to be receiving particular byte patterns, which means specific bits on specific pins. If the system designer has scrambled the data bus, then the programmer has to descramble the flash command words and addresses to suit. For example, using the above scrambling scheme, if flash memory expects a byte `0x55` on address `0x0AA` then the programmer would need to write byte `0x93` to address `0x115` (as shown in the tables above).

The type of bus scrambling shown here is very common as a means to solve tricky PCB routing problems. However, be very careful with SDRAM; some address pins are dedicated as column addresses and some as row addresses (refer to Section 7.6.3.3). Furthermore, some SDRAM pins have other special meanings: for SDRAM in particular, which is actually programmed though a write state machine within the SDRAM controller, this is similar to the flash memory programming algorithms, except that it is *not under the programmers' control*, and so cannot be descrambled in software.

In the extreme case, flash memory can be copied as-is and replicated in a copied product. Overall, unless designers have specifically taken measures to protect their embedded system software, the process of reverse engineering non-volatile memory to reveal stored programs is not difficult.

7.13 Preventing Reverse Engineering

Since RE cannot be prevented *per se*, the issue becomes an economic one: how we can maximise the RE cost experienced by competitors at minimal additional cost to ourselves. For determining this, the description of embedded systems RE from Section 7.12 will be drawn upon, related to an embedded context and then classified. First, mitigation methods are rated based upon their implementation complexity and cost, plus the economic impact of their implementation upon a RE-based attacker. We will first classify *all* methods of interest to embedded systems designers, before narrowing in on those with particular relevance to computer architecture.

To begin the classification, RE mitigation techniques are divided into categories of *passive methods* which are fixed at design time, and *active methods* of resisting RE during an attack. The former tend to be structural changes that are less expensive to implement than the latter. We will explore both in turn.

Cost multipliers to the reverse engineers due to RE protection, come about through three major factors:

- Increased labour cost incurred as a result of greater time taken to RE the system.
- Increased labour cost due to higher levels of RE expertise required.

- Increased cost spent on purchase of specialised equipment required for the RE process.

In some cases, there will also be an increased BOM cost, if extra components are required.

Following the RE process of Section 7.12.1, the first level of protection can be applied to the functionality assessment: RE stage A. In this case, restricting the release of service manuals and documentation can reduce the degree of information available to an RE team. Manufacturers should control, monitor and ideally limit, information inadvertently provided by employees, especially when posting online. This will undoubtedly increase the time and effort needed to RE a system.

Stage B, the physical structure analysis can be made marginally more difficult through the use of tamper-proof fittings for enclosures such as torx and custom screw shapes which would require purchase of specialised equipment. One-way screws and adhesively bonded enclosures work similarly. Fully potting the space around a PCB provides another level of protection. At minimal cost, the primary detraction to the use of these methods comes from any requirement for product serviceability, which would normally necessitate ease of access.

Wiring which is not colour coded may complicate the manufacturing and servicing process, but will cause even greater difficulty and delay to an RE team working on a heavily wired system.

Unusual, custom and anonymous parts complicate the RE of a system's BOM in stage C. However, passive devices (stage C.2) can easily be removed and tested in isolation. A missing silk screen causes some difficulty in manufacturing and servicing, but limits the information provided to the RE team. for stages C.3, E.1, E.2 and F. However, by far the most effective method of preventing BOM RE is through the use of custom silicon (or silicon that is not available for sale to the RE team). Reverse engineers in stage C.1 confronted by a large unmarked IC surrounded by minimal passive components, no silk screen and with no further information would face a very difficult and expensive RE process indeed. The need to identify and/or replicate custom silicon adds significant expense as well as great up-front cost to the RE process, and so may be economical only for large production runs.

For best security, JTAG (Section 7.9.3) and other debug ports should be eliminated from semi-custom silicon, and not routed from standard parts to connectors or test pads, and certainly not labelled *TDI, TDO, TMS, TCK*. For device packages with exposed pins these can still easily be accessed, so BGA (ball grid array) devices are preferred. But even for BGA devices, unrouted JTAG pins can often be accessed by controlled depth drilling through the PCB from the opposite side, meaning that back-to-back BGA placement is most secure (such as a BGA processor on one side of a PCB with a BGA flash memory device directly underneath on the other side). The disadvantage here is that manufacturing cost increases by having double-sided component placement. Double-sided BGA placement is yet one step more expensive, but there is still no guarantee that reverse engineering can be prevented since it is possible, although extremely difficult, to remove a BGA device, reform the solder balls, and then refit this into a carrier which is soldered to the PCB. The intermediate signals through the carrier can then be made available for analysis.

Back-to-back BGA packaging generally necessitates blind and/or buried vias, which can increase PCB manufacturing costs (rule of thumb: by 10%), complicate the layout process and significantly impact on any hardware debugging or modifications needed. It does, however, result in a very compact PCB which might itself be a useful product feature. Similarly, the number of PCB layers would often need to increase to accommodate back-to-back placement, therefore also increasing the RE cost to perform delamination and layer-by-layer analysis. Use of X-ray analysis to reveal layout details for stages E.2 and E.3 is difficult in multi-layer PCB designs, and can be complicated further by the useful practice of filling all available space on all layers with power plane fills. These can even be crosshatched on internal layers to mask individual tracking details on other layers on an X-ray photograph.

Electrical connectivity, stage E.2, can be difficult to ascertain when devices are operated in an unusual fashion such as jumbled address and data buses. Wiring unused pins to unused pins can add nothing to manufacturing cost, but it can complicate the RE process.

7.13.1 Passive Obfuscation of Stored Programs

There is much that can be done structurally to obfuscate the stored code in the flash memory of an embedded system, thus complicating RE stages G.1 and G.2. We will not consider that further since it is an active research area. However, there are some architectural aspects we can work on.

Firstly, and as mentioned previously, the gaps between code sections (of unerased flash) can very easily be filled with random numbers or dummy code such that detection of separate memory areas is non-trivial. Apart from initial boot code, other sections of flash can also be encrypted if execute-from-flash is not required. This will cause difficulties in analysing an image of flash contents. However, the unencrypted boot code may well be small and simple enough to trace and disassemble, revealing an unencrypted entry point to the system, and hence the security of such encryption is questionable.

Scattering code, data and configuration sections throughout flash memory will cause some programming difficulty but is primarily another means of protecting against stored-program analysis. If an FPGA image is stored in flash, simple methods of obfuscating this apart from encryption include performing an exclusive-OR on every data byte with some other area of flash and storing a custom compressed FPGA image (not gzip, zip or similar which have identifiable signatures).

A summary of various of the discussed RE mitigation methods are shown in Table 7.4, where the design cost effectiveness at increasing RE cost and manufacturing impact are identified using a five-point subjective scaling for the example embedded system.

Table 7.4

Passive methods of increasing hardware reverse engineering cost rated on several criteria, 5 = most, 0 = least.

	Design cost	RE cost	Manufacturing impact
Tamper proof screws	2	0	1
Bonded case	1	1	1
Potting	1	1	2
No silk screen	1	1	1
Erased component identifiers	1	1	2
Use of BGA packages	1	3	3
Inner layer routing only	2	2	3
Blind or buried vias	2	2	4
Bus signal jumbling	1	1	0
ASIC signal router	5	3	2
FPGA signal router	2	2	2
No debug port	1	1	2
Random padding of unused memory	2	2	0

7.13.2 Programmable Logic Families

SRAM-based FPGAs normally require a configuration bitstream to be provided from an external device – such as a serial flash configurator, or provided by a microprocessor, such as the case in the example system. Since this bitstream can be accessed physically with little difficulty, this firmware can always be copied by tapping off and replicating the bitstream.

EEPROM-based programmable logic devices (PLDs), the otherwise obsolete EPROM versions, and newer flash-based products, are more secure since the configuration program resides internally and does not need to be transferred to the device following reset. Note that some flash-containing devices actually encapsulate two silicon dies in one chip – a memory die and a logic die, and thus are less secure since the configuration bitstream can always be tapped once the encapsulation is removed. In general, devices that are configured right after exiting reset are those which contain non-volatile memory cells distributed around the silicon, and those that become configured several milliseconds after exiting reset are those in which a configuration bitstream may be accessible. In either case, many devices, including those from Altera and Xilinx, provide security settings which may prevent readout of program bitstream from a configured device. Use of this feature is highly recommended.

In regular cell-structure devices, including the mask-programmed gate array (MPGA), the location of memory configuration elements is known, determined by the manufacturer for all devices in that class. Using the methods of Section 7.12.2.2, this configuration data, and thus the original 'program' can be retrieved – although this requires sophisticated technology.

A full-custom ASIC can be reverse engineered by analysing silicon layer by layer (similar to the PCB delamination, but with layers revealed through careful grinding), but even this technique can be complicated through countermeasures such as inserting mesh overlay layers. Antifuse FPGAs are generally considered to be the most secure of the standard programmable logic devices, due to the location of fuses buried deep below layers of silicon routing, rather than being exposed near the surface.

It is not impossible to RE systems incorporating ASICs or secured antifuse FPGAs, but this requires significant levels of expertise and the use of expensive specialised equipment and is time consuming.

7.13.3 Active RE Mitigation

Many of the passive electronic methods given in Section 7.13.1 have active variants. Electrical connectivity can be confused by using spare inputs and outputs from processors to route signals which are not timing critical but which are functionally critical.

While jumbled address and data buses are more difficult to reverse engineer, dynamically jumbled buses provide one further level of complication, but add to the cost of preventing RE in that active devices will have to be incorporated to perform the jumbling/de-jumbling.

ASICs are probably the ultimate tool in mitigating RE attempts, but even the humble FPGA can be quite effective. In either case, IP cores (which will be discussed in Chapter 8) implemented within logic are not easy to identify or isolate, and can access any externally stored program in a variety of ways – whether linearly, non-linearly or using some form of substitution or encryption. A CPU core which is completely custom, and without any public documentation, adds another layer of security through not revealing any details of its instruction set architecture. Furthermore, the instruction set could be deliberately changed in every implementation among several product versions to prevent repeated RE of the cores program. This would be an inexpensive software/firmware-only protection.

7.13.4 Active RE Mitigation Classification

The basic forms of RE mitigation can be subdivided into two dimensions: methods of active confusion, hiding or obfuscation, and temporal or spatial methods of achieving confusion. Any real system may employ a combination of these methods to maximum effect.

Information hiding uses existing resources in ways that attempt to conceal information from an attacker. This may involve combining code and data through concealing operating software within data arrays such as start-up boot images, or by sharing information across data reads in a non-obvious fashion. It may also include operating electronics at marginal voltage levels, relying upon unusual signalling or data handling schemes.

Obfuscation, normally a passive method (such as swapping the names of labels and functions within code, or jumbling the PCB silk screen annotations) can also be active in arrangements such as those that change bus connectivity or device pin usage (e.g. multiplexing an interrupt input pin with a signal output function). This again uses existing resources in ways specifically designed to complicate the RE process by misdirecting the RE team.

Protection by confusion adds resources specifically to deliberately mislead or confuse an attacking RE team. This could include large pseudo-random data transfers, out-of-order code reading and so on. There may be signal interconnections that employ current signalling but overlay a randomly modulated voltage signal upon the wire, or perhaps a meaningful signal driving a redundant signal wire. In a dynamic sense, this may include mode changes on tamper-detection or even a more extreme response of device erasure on tamper detection.

Spatial methods are those which operate at a placement or connectivity level, such as scrambling bus order depending upon memory address, turning on or off signal path routing devices in a non-obvious fashion or similar.

Temporal methods confuse through altering the sequence and/or timing of events. One example would be a boot loader that deliberately executes only a subset of fetched instructions. Another would be a memory management device able to prefetch code pages from memory and access these in non-linear fashion, especially if these are out of sequence with respect to device operation.

The combination of these classifications is shown in Table 7.5 where their relative strength is categorised.

In terms of costs, dynamic methods are likely to cost more to develop, debug and test. They also increase both manufacturing and probably servicing costs, more than fixed timing methods. Both information hiding and obfuscation could well be of similar development cost – mostly adding to NRE. However, deliberate confusion methods will undoubtedly cost more to develop than either hiding or obfuscation, and will add to manufacturing cost.

Table 7.5

Relative strength of active protection methods, 5 = most, 0 = least.

	Fixed timing	Dynamic timing
Information hiding	0	2
Obfuscation	1	3
Deliberate confusion	4	5

What is clear is that custom silicon, implementing active confusion and protection means, provides the greatest degree of protection. A developer concerned by the costs involved in creating a full-custom ASIC for security purposes, could develop a generic security ASIC which can be used across a range of products. For the reverse engineers, the active protection methods in each category, particularly the dynamic timing cases, will require employing a highly skilled and flexible RE team. This team will require access to specialised equipment. For example, marginally operating timing signals may require analysis by high-speed digital oscilloscopes with very low capacitance active probes that do not load the signal lines, or even the use of a superconducting quantum interference device (SQUID). A multi-channel vector signal analyser may be required for some of the more unusual signalling schemes.

7.14 Summary

This chapter has considered many of the practical aspects of computing, such as memory technology, on-chip peripherals, clocking strategies and the provision of reset signals. Embedded systems in particular often suffer from memory shortages, which can be alleviated through the use of memory pages and overlays (and we also examined the memory structure of a typical embedded system using the popular embedded Linux operating system).

Watchdog timers were described, as useful means of ensuring overall reliability in real-time and embedded systems, and for this aim we also discussed error detection and correction.

As CPUs have become faster and more complex over the years, manufacturing and development difficulties abound due to this complexity. This has highlighted the need for test and verification in such systems – so we split this into methods of provision during IC manufacture, system manufacture and at runtime.

Finally, the issue of reverse engineering was surveyed. This is a particularly relevant issue in many embedded systems, especially those within consumer devices. As such, we looked at how nefarious reverse engineering is performed, and with this in mind, surveyed methods to prevent this.

Problems

7.1 Identify four factors that would argue for the use of system-on-chip (SoC) processors in an embedded system.

7.2 List the minimum set of control register settings necessary to implement programmable I/O pins on a microcontroller given that these are required to support the following functionality:

- Can be configured as either general-purpose input/output (GPIO) or as a dedicated output from an in-built peripheral device such as a UART.
- When in GPIO mode, can be configured as either an input or an output.
- Each pin can be individually read from, and written to.

7.3 Indicate whether you would expect a single-chip microcontroller or a quad-core high-speed server processor to devote a greater proportion of its silicon area to memory. Justify your answer by noting the primary use of that area in both machines.

7.4 List a few of the approaches that semiconductor designers have taken to reducing propagation delay in CPUs over the past two or three decades.

7.5 What changes can be made to a computer system clocking strategy (or to the clock itself) to reduce the amount of electromagnetic interference (EMI) generated by that system?

7.6 What external devices, located close to the power pins of a CPU, can reduce the amount of EMI generated? Explain the mechanism that causes EMI, and how these devices can reduce it.

7.7 Identify the most appropriate memory technologies, from those listed below for the following applications:

a. An MP3 player needs to access audio data from 8 Gibyte memory at a rate up to 350 Kibits per second. The data (your songs) should remain in memory even when the power is turned off.

b. The program memory within a small and simple embedded system is designed to do one thing, and one thing only. The manufacturer will build millions of these devices, which have no provision for reprogramming.

c. The 256 Mibyte system memory within an ARM9 embedded system, built to run an advanced embedded operating system such as embedded Linux, in a personal digital assistant.

d. The 16 Mibyte non-volatile program memory in the above system – assuming that many of the OS routines remain in flash memory, and are executed directly from there.

Problems

e. A 4 kibyte runtime memory to be connected to a medium size microcontroller in a small embedded system.

The set of memory technologies (one to be used for each application) is as follows:

- Serial flash
- Parallel flash
- SDRAM
- SRAM
- ROM

7.8 Note seven common functions that can be found in an embedded system bootloader such as u-Boot.

7.9 A typical embedded system CPU, implemented in a BGA package, is mounted on the PCB of a prototype embedded system. The designer suspects that a soldering fault is preventing the system from operating correctly. List two methods by which the potential system problems can be identified.

7.10 A byte `0xF3` is to be transmitted over a noisy wireless channel as two nibbles, each encoded using Hamming (7, 4). Refer to the method shown in Box 7.7 on page 343 and identify the two 7-bit transmit words in hexadecimal.

7.11 Repeat the Hamming encoding of Problem 7.10, this time transmitting byte `0xB7` using the method of Box 7.8 on page 344.

7.12 Identify the three main reasons why, although it is sometimes necessary to incorporate reverse engineering protection in an embedded system, it may lead to slightly reduced profitability to the manufacturer.

7.13 In what ways would a working JTAG connection to the CPU in an embedded system be usable by a reverse engineering team trying to determine:

a. The identity of that CPU.
b. Circuit connectivity and system schematic.
c. The content of the non-volatile (flash) memory installed in the system.

7.14 Why do so many SoC microprocessors have 32.768 kHz crystals connected to them?

7.15 What is clock jitter, and how does this influence the determination of the maximum clock speed that a processor is capable of?

Problems

7.16 If a byte `0xa7` is programmed to one location in parallel flash memory, and later another byte `0x9a` is programmed to the same location (without it being erased in between), what value would the location then contain?

7.17 EPROM memory devices have a small glass window which can be used to expose the silicon die to ultraviolet light in order to erase the memory array. Flash memory devices (and EEPROM), by contrast, can erase their memory electronically. Identify two major advantages that flash memory technology offers over the EPROM.

7.18 Imagine you are leading a small design team for a new embedded product: the hardware is ready and the software engineers are putting the finishing touches to the system code. There is a huge amount of serial flash memory in the system, but only a small amount of SRAM available. Just weeks before product launch, the software team reveals that the runtime code cannot fit within the SRAM, and there is no way of reducing the code size. Without changing the hardware, suggest a method of memory handling that will provide a way around this problem.

7.19 A JTAG scan-chain may be several hundred bits long. This chain can be serially clocked into a CPU's JTAG scan-path to change the device behaviour or clocked out to read the device state. What are the meanings of some of the bit positions (i.e. what behaviour they can change and what state they can determine)?

7.20 How can triple module redundancy be used to determine the correct output of a calculation? Illustrate your answer by considering three supposedly-identical blocks in a malfunctioning system that output bytes `0xB9`, `0x33` and `0x2B` respectively. If these were wired to a bitwise majority voter, what would the final corrected output byte from the system be?

CHAPTER 8

CPU Design

The earlier chapters of this book have presented many ideas and introduced concepts which have been used in microprocessors, both simple and advanced, throughout the short lifespan of the engineering discipline of computer architecture.

In this chapter, we build and consolidate this knowledge into a practical focus – real processors that we, as embedded engineers, can design, modify, use and reuse. We will discuss this through considering the use of soft cores in embedded systems.

8.1 Soft-Core Processors

A soft core (or soft processor) is a CPU design that is written in a logic description language that allows it to be synthesised within a programmable logic device. Typically, a high-level language such as Verilog or VHDL[1] is used, and the end product synthesised on a field programmable gate array (FPGA).

This differs from the position of most processor manufacturers, who tend to create low-level designs that are specific to the semiconductor manufacturing process of their semiconductor fabrication partners. This happens mainly due to the need to squeeze maximum performance from the silicon that is being worked on. Sometimes, there are both custom and soft-core designs available for a particular processor, for example the ARM. In such cases, the soft-core design will usually provide inferior performance (slower, higher power), but be more flexible in where it can be used.

There are very many soft-core processors on hand, many of them freely available[2] although few could compare in efficiency, speed or cost when implemented in FPGAs, to dedicated microprocessors.

Other possibilities are the use of a commercial core – the main FPGA vendors each have such cores – and designing your own core. We will

[1] VHDL stands for VHSIC hardware description language, where VHSIC refers to a very high-speed integrated circuit.

[2] Refer to the project collection in `www.opencores.org` for free processor and other 'IP' cores, where IP refers to intellectual property.

consider the anatomy of soft cores, then each of the three main possibilities of obtaining a core, ending up with a design exercise to create a completely custom core, making use of many of the techniques described earlier in the book.

8.1.1 Microprocessors are More Than Cores

A soft-core processor, implemented on an FPGA, is a block of logic that can operate as a CPU. At its simplest, this block of logic, when reset and fed with a clock, will load in data and process it as specified by a program. The program could reside internally within the FPGA, or could reside in external memory, either RAM or flash, as in most embedded systems.

This arrangement is fine, however, microprocessors are more than just cores. Refer back to the features available in the popular Samsung S3C2410 ARM-based microprocessor, discussed in Section 7.2. A long list of internal features and peripherals was presented, including the following more major ones:

- 16 KiB instruction and 16 KiB data cache plus internal MMU.
- Memory controller for external SDRAM.
- Colour LCD controller.
- Many serial ports, UARTs, SPI, IrDA, USB, IIC, etc.
- SD (secure digital) and MMC (multimedia card) interfaces.
- An eight-channel, 10-bit ADC (analogue-to-digital converter) and touch-screen interface.
- Real-time clock with calendar function.

Clearly, the processor core itself (which incidentally is the one item that was not listed in Samsung's own documentation) makes up only a small part of the integrated circuit named an S3C2410 which is purchased and included in an embedded system.

To clarify further, if an engineer somehow managed to obtain an ARM processor core written in a high-level hardware description language (HDL) and loaded this into an FPGA, he would not have a fully functioning microprocessor. Furthermore, this would be unlikely to operate at anything approaching the S3C2410's 200 MHz in an FPGA (even in an FPGA advertised as supporting a 1 GHz clock speed).

The extra effort required to implement all of the other peripherals and interfaces on the FPGA would be excessive, and remember that the final result would be slower, more power hungry and far more expensive than an off-the-shelf ARM.

So given such disadvantages, why would anyone consider using a soft core?

8.1.2 The Advantages of Soft-Core Processors

There are probably millions of systems worldwide powered by soft cores, and although that is far less than the estimated 10 billion ARM devices shipped worldwide, there must be some good reasons for opting for soft-core processors. Let us consider a few of those good reasons under headings of performance, availability and efficiency.

8.1.2.1 Performance

Performance should clearly be on the side of standard microprocessors, since we mentioned that soft cores are usually slower than dedicated devices. While that is true, remember that there are some performance issues that are more important than clock speed:

- Parallel systems allow multiple processors, or processor cores, to be implemented and run in parallel. It is quite easy to include several or even many soft cores inside a single FPGA and thus create a parallel system. As always, learning how to use these multiple cores effectively, is a task not to be overlooked.
- The complex instruction set computer (CISC) approach is known for creating custom instructions required by programmers. The reduced instruction set computer (RISC) approach, by contrast, eliminates the more complex or less common instructions and concentrates on making the most common instructions faster (so that the complex CISC instructions can be performed by multiple simple RISC instructions). However, in an embedded system where code is often small and unchanging, it is quite possible that a different set of instructions would be chosen to be implemented. For example, in a system performing many division calculations and no logic operations, the optimal RISC processor may have a divider, but very few logic instructions. Where code is known and fixed in advance, there is something to be said for custom-designing an instruction set specifically for the purpose of executing that code quickly.
- Even where the instruction set is not modified to suit a particular piece of code, it is always possible to add a dedicated functional unit or co-processor to a given core inside an FPGA. In the example above, we could opt to add a division unit to a standard core. Off-the-shelf parts cannot be modified in this way, although some do have external co-processor interfaces.
- Soft cores are supplied in VHDL or Verilog. They usually do not contain sophisticated buses and are without memory (sometimes even without a cache). The designer who uses these in an FPGA thus has to build buses and memory around them. While this fact appears to be a disadvantage, it is quite possible to turn it into an advantage by creating a dedicated bus that matches the application. By contrast, an off-the-shelf standard part may implement a bus scheme that does not match the application perfectly.

8.1.2.2 Availability

Availability has two meanings in the context of a soft core. The first relates to how easy it is to procure and use a device, and the second relates to ensuring that a processor works correctly when needed. We will cover both meanings:

- It is the bane of product designers (including the author, in an earlier life) to standardise on a CPU in their design, to work towards a product release, and then days from the launch to receive a notification from the CPU vendor that the device they are using is now EOL (end of life). This requires a very fundamental redesign of both software and hardware. While such a situation is unlikely to occur for designers selling mass-market products, it is all too common for small and medium embedded systems companies. With this in mind, consider the attraction of having *your own* CPU design: it is yours to keep forever and can never be dropped by a cost-cutting semiconductor vendor. You can program this, reuse code, reuse hardware, extend and modify at will, in as many designs as you wish. Although it is synthesised in an FPGA, and the specific FPGA may go EOL, you can simply switch to another FPGA and the same code, same processor, will run there – perhaps even a little quicker.

- Similar issues are felt by designers in countries outside Europe and North America. New CPUs take time to become available in those markets and stocks are usually slow or difficult to access. Again, for a company wishing to purchase several tens of thousands of devices, this is usually not a problem, but for small and medium embedded companies, it can be. In Singapore, for example, it is almost impossible for the author to purchase anything less than about 100 devices, something which effectively discourages prototyping. Thankfully, the FPGA vendors are a little more considerate to smaller companies.
- Availability in an electronic system means ensuring that the system is working correctly and is working when you need it. Good design is the key to ensuring reliability, but sometimes, in order to ensure that a CPU is working and available, it is necessary to replicate it. Thus, two CPUs can be better than one. In fact, three are better than two and so on. A soft core can be replicated and parallelised as often as necessary, consuming just FPGA resources and power when turned on. By contrast, a replicated dedicated processor means, for a start, twice as many ICs, also twice the cost.

8.1.2.3 Efficiency

Efficiency can be measured in respects such as power, cost, space and so on. It turns out that there are arguments for each of these for soft cores, however, all relate to the same basic reasoning:

- The impressive list of S3C2410 features in Section 8.1.1 is hard for any designer to replicate in a custom soft-core design. However, are all of these features really necessary? The answer is 'yes' when designing a one-size-fits-all SoC solution that is to be used by almost everyone. However, in individual cases, only a small subset of these features would probably be necessary and therefore the answer is probably a 'no'. Soft cores only tend to include those features, interfaces and peripherals that are absolutely necessary. They do not waste silicon space (or FPGA cells) on unused functionality in the way that a standard part may well do, and because of this will, at times, be more efficient than their standard cousins.
- Glue logic is the name given to those devices holding microprocessors and other parts together. Examples are inverters and AND gates. Sometimes, a large requirement for glue logic would be fulfilled by using a small FPGA. Given that glue logic is so ubiquitous, and is required almost everywhere, replacing a standard microprocessor with an FPGA-implemented soft core can also allow the designer to fold all of the glue logic into the same FPGA. Sometimes the result will be

reduced PCB space, lower manufacturing cost and so on, over the dedicated CPU design.

8.1.2.4 Human Factors

Human factors are often overlooked by engineers, however, these are as big a motivation as any technical reasons. Just witness how upset and irrational some engineers can be when faced with the elimination of their ideas in a group design session. Some human factor reasons for considering soft cores might include the following:

- It is fun to develop your own computer! Well-motivated designer engineers are efficient and hard-working design engineers. Motivation comes, in part, from doing something interesting, and building a custom soft core is something most engineers consider very interesting – something that most managers might not realise.
- Ownership of a design, while running the risk of the irrational behaviour mentioned above, is another great motivator for engineers, and aids in the pursuit of design perfection. You can easily design and own your own soft core.
- When embarking on a new embedded design project, there is usually a time to consider which embedded processor should power the new project. The 'degree of fit' will be determined of various devices to the design requirements, and the best fit chosen, at least in theory (this process may well trigger more of that irrational behaviour as various parties push their own agendas). However, something that is less often considered is the 'learning curve' required to retrain engineers to use a new microprocessor. Sometimes the need to switch to a totally new device will incur months of delay while designers familiarise themselves with new features and ways of working, or may lengthen the design process through unanticipated beginner mistakes. It is often better to use a device that the team is familiar with, but is a less optimal fit. The use of soft cores can help here in that once a team is familiar with that soft core, it can be used in many successive designs. Small changes to the FPGA-implemented peripherals, functional units and co-processors can be made to ensure that the core remains an optimal choice for new projects, and yet does not need to involve the team in lengthy retraining activities.

8.2 Hardware-Software Co-Design

Hardware-software co-design is the term given to the process of designing a system that contains both hardware and software. It is particularly relevant to embedded systems, since such systems normally entail custom hardware and custom software.

When writing software for a desktop PC, programmers will normally expect that the hardware is error free and will function correctly. When designing a new PC, designers are able to run diagnostic software which has been proven correct and error free on working hardware (such as on the previous generation of PCs).

In embedded systems, the potential problem area is that both the hardware and the software are usually developed together – neither can be proven error free without

Figure 8.1

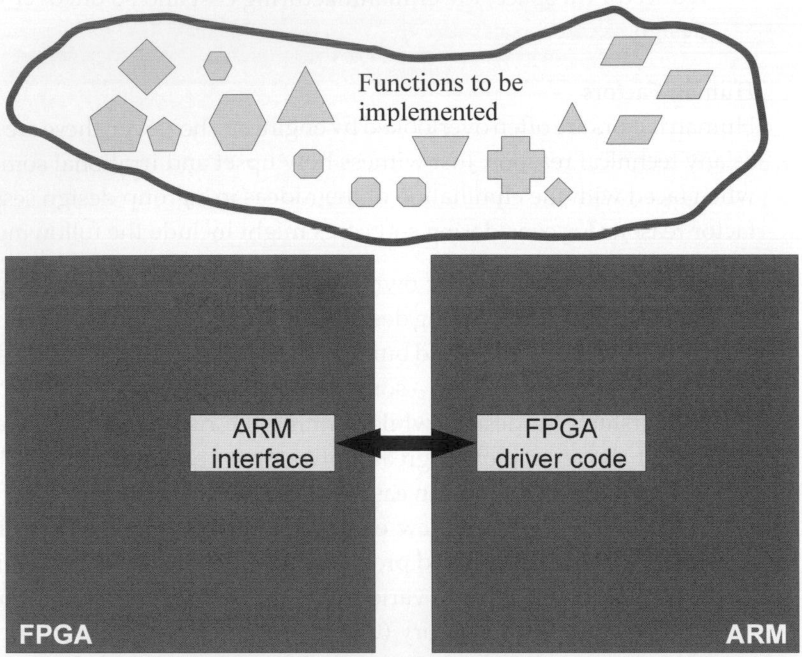

The process of designing an embedded system that contains both a CPU and an FPGA involves identifying the tasks to be performed and allocating these to one of the two processing units. Of course, this presupposes that a working CPU-FPGA interface exists.

the other, and so the process of debugging and making a working system is mired in problems that may lie in either domain (or even cross domains).[3]

Given a system containing an FPGA and a CPU, such as that shown in Figure 8.1, an embedded systems designer, knowing the requirements for the system being designed, must decide how to implement each of those requirements. Some will be implemented in software, some in hardware, and many will require a little of both. In general, software implementations are more flexible, easier to debug and change and easier to add features, whereas hardware implementation are higher performance and potentially lower power.

Some tasks are more naturally FPGA-oriented (e.g. bit-level manipulation, serial processing or parallelism) and some suited for high-level software on a CPU (e.g. control software, high-level protocols, textual manipulation and so on). Knowing the size of

[3] There is a great tradition among hardware designers to blame programmers when something does not work correctly. There is a great tradition among programmers to 'blame the hardware' when code crashes. This makes for an interesting development environment but is not particularly productive from a management perspective.

FPGA and MIPS/memory constraints in the processor will assist the designer in the partitioning process. There are many other issues that must be considered, and usually there will be an element of trade-off required. These issues include questions such as: 'Who will do the coding?' 'How maintainable does the code need to be?' and 'Will the system need to be upgraded later?'

One particular area of concern could be in the connection between FPGA and CPU. This connection will have both bandwidth and latency constraints: it can only support a certain amount of data flow and will naturally involve a small delay in message passing (an important consideration in real-time systems). Also, it would be normal for one device (usually the CPU) to be a master and the other a slave. Messages and data are initiated from the master, and so latency may well be different for messages in the two directions. Bandwidth could differ too. Most probably, the two devices are not clock-synchronous, and so any data that is streaming between the two may have to be buffered, possibly on both sides – adding to the data transfer latency.

The situation is exacerbated also when an FPGA (field programmable gate array) becomes available that could contain a soft-core processor. This means a further decision needs to be made regarding whether tasks will be implemented in the CPU, in the FPGA as logic functions/state machine or in the FPGA executed by a soft-core processor.

Despite the difficulties, a partitioned design will eventually be agreed upon, such as that shown in Figure 8.2. Separate specifications for this system including interface specifications, would then be drawn up and handed to the software team, and to the hardware (or firmware) team which would then go away and implement their parts of the system.

Some time later, *integration* would start – the process of fitting together the hardware and software designs, and (typically) discovering that the system does not work. At this point, the two teams tend to apportion some element of blame, before setting out on the long and hard process of getting their domains to 'talk' to each other and work together.

Figure 8.2

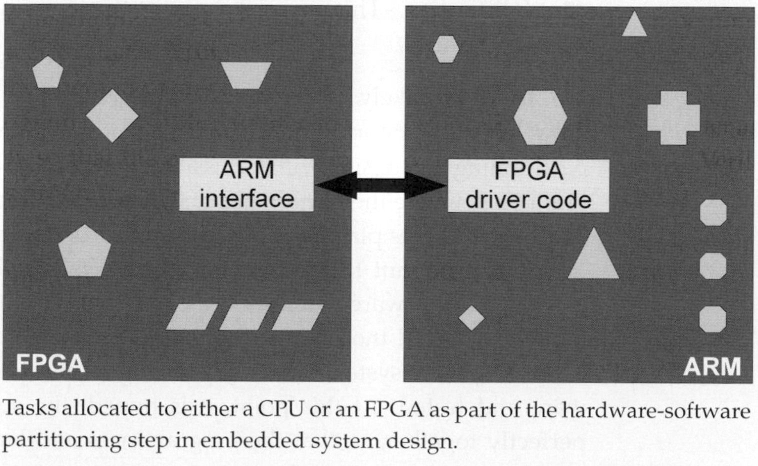

Tasks allocated to either a CPU or an FPGA as part of the hardware-software partitioning step in embedded system design.

Unfortunately, even when the system does finally work, it will seldom be an optimal solution because there is just too much human subjectivity involved in the original partitioning process, and the subsequent implementation.

Hardware-software co-design has emerged relatively recently as a response to these design difficulties in systems that involve both hardware and software design. Co-design methodologies are implemented as a type of computer-aided design (CAD) tool, with the aim of simplifying the design process (to reduce time, money and errors), optimising the partitioning between hardware and software and easing the integration process.

Hardware-software co-design involves the following stages, assuming we are targetting a mixed FPGA/CPU system:

1. Modelling – Here, some specification of what the system must do is created in a machine-readible format. This might be a formal design language (which we, thankfully, will not consider further here) or a simple program in C or MATLAB that emulates the output of the system to given input. This model will be used later to verify that the new system works correctly.
2. Partitioning – As mentioned above, and probably best performed by a human aided with information describing the system. Sometimes it is easy to split a system into different blocks, but usually there is at least some difficulty, and may require the original model to be rewritten slightly.
3. Co-synthesis – Uses CAD tools to create a model of three items: the FPGA code, the C programming language code and the interface between the two. FPGA code is synthesised in FPGA design tools, C code is compiled and loaded into a processor emulator, and the interface between the two is often file-based.
4. Co-simulation – This means running the three above-mentioned items together within the design tools. Ideally, this would be in real time, but often it is thousands of times slower than the real hardware, however, it is bit-level accurate to an actual hardware implementation.
5. Verification – This means comparing the co-simulated system to the original model for veracity.

There are likely to be several iterations in this process: as errors are found (or more likely as opportunities for greater optimisation are identified), slight changes to partitioning and design will be possible. A flowchart depicting these stages is shown in Figure 8.3, where the importance of the system model is clear through the verification process that takes place at every stage in the design process.

The important fact is that *everything gets simulated together*: the hardware (usually FPGA), software and interface between them can be developed using the design tools, and tested thoroughly in simulation. Problems can be identified and rectified early. When the system is finally working as modelled, it can be constructed in hardware and tested. At this point, it is hoped, the software and hardware will work perfectly together, so that the programmers and hardware developers can celebrate together.

Figure 8.3

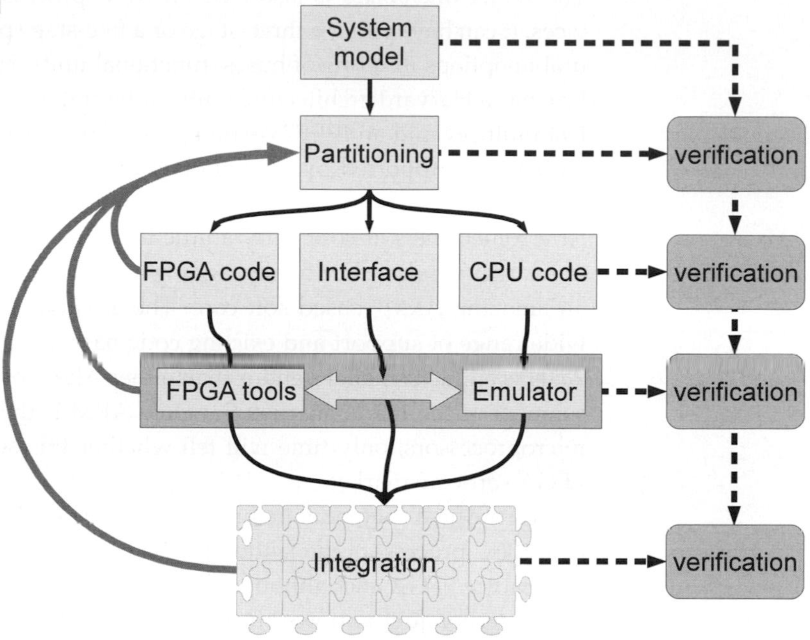

An illustration of the hardware-software co-design process, showing the sequential development flow, with verification performed at each step and iteration back to previous steps in the case of errors detected.

8.3 Off-The-Shelf Cores

Earlier in this chapter, we have seen that many free processing cores are available for synthesis within FPGAs. In the following section (Section 8.4), we will discuss building our own custom core. It is also possible to use commercial cores from several vendors, not least the main FPGA manufacturers, so let us take a moment to consider these offerings as they exist at the time of writing:

- The *Altera Nios II* is a 32-bit RISC processor optimised for Altera FPGAs. It is built upon the original Nios core. In many ways, it is seen as a response to the widely popular ARM processor. A single instruction set can be executed by the Nios II in one of many sized configurations ranging from 700 logic elements (LEs) upwards. The largest, and fastest configuration, with a six-stage pipeline, separate data and instruction caches, dedicated multiplier, branch predictor unit and even an optional divider and MMU, is quite powerful.

  Most usefully, from an embedded computer architect's perspective, the core allows up to 256 custom instructions to access dedicated blocks of custom logic, and for dedicated hardware accelerators to be included within the pipeline. Nios II is supported by a variety of operating systems, including embedded Linux.

- The *Xilinx MicroBlaze* is also a 32-bit RISC processor, for use within Xilinx devices. It can have either a three-stage or a five-stage pipeline and has many configurable options in terms of buses, functional units, MMU and so on. The MicroBlaze has a Harvard architecture with configurable cache sizes. Hardware division, fast multiply and an IEEE754-compatible FPU are available, and like Nios II, MicroBlaze is supported by several operating systems, again including embedded Linux.
- *Actel* joined the soft-core party a little later, initially not having a response to the two larger vendors, but finally signing a significant agreement with *ARM* to ship an amazing *ARM7*-based soft core. The advantage of this approach is the very wide range of support and existing code base available for the ARM7. However, Actel is a much smaller vendor than either Altera or Xilinx and targets a different segment of the FPGA market. So while ARM is the clear winner in off-the-shelf microprocessors, only time will tell whether this success is repeated within the FPGA soft-core market.
- *Lattice*, the final contender in this market, also developed and released a 32-bit soft-core RISC processor. The *LatticeMico32* uses less than 2000 look-up tables (LUTs) in a Lattice FPGA and, although not quite as configurable as the Xilinx and Altera offerings, nor quite as powerful, is small and fast. Various peripherals such as UART and bus interfaces are available, and configurable. Furthermore, it is completely open, meaning that it can be used and modified anywhere. It does not need to be licensed when used and sold within a design.

Apart from these cores, there are a few companies specialising in the IP-cores market, selling their cores for use on any FPGA. Even ARM has released a small soft-core ARM Cortex device. Clearly this field is active, and of growing importance to embedded systems.

A final note of importance: remember that these cores do not exist in isolation. Yes, we have seen that they require synthesising with an FPGA, require external buses, peripherals such as memory, clock signals and other facilities in order to operate. However, they also need programs.

Software development for soft-core processors is an integral part of ensuring that they can operate correctly within a design. Therefore, important issues to resolve are whether a toolchain is available (which is used to develop software), whether an operating system (OS) is available for that processor and what types of debug tools are available.

A standard embedded toolchain, such as the GNU toolchain incorporates several elements which include a C (and possibly C++) compiler, assembler and linker. There is often a need for library management tools, object file tools, a stripper (to remove debugging comments from within an object file in order to reduce its size), analytical tools and so on. A debugger, such as GDB, is highly recommended for debugging, since it can execute, single step, breakpoint, watch point and monitor running code. The GNU toolchain also contains software to allow running code to be profiled (i.e. to determine the amount of CPU time spent within each function, the program trace and the number of loops executed).

An operating system, particularly a real-time operating system (RTOS), is often required in many developments. Unfortunately, it can be difficult writing or porting an OS to a new processor, and this is one major argument in favour of choosing a core that is already supported by a good OS such as embedded Linux. Despite this, there are reasons to custom design a soft core, for example, when only small items of code, such as hand-written assembly language are used.

In fact, over the next few sections of this book, we will create a custom soft core and later develop an assembler for this (we will also introduce a basic C-like compiler).

8.4 Making Our Own Soft Core

In this section, and those following, we will cement together much of the knowledge gained up to this point, by following the design of a simple CPU. Actually, we will plan the design of this, and then create a real Verilog executable which can be used inside an FPGA. The CPU which we will describe is in fact named TinyCPU, and is the invention of Professor Koji Nakano[4] of the Department of Information Engineering, School of Engineering, Hiroshima University, Japan. TinyCPU consists of only about 420 lines of Verilog hardware description language source code.

Although this design is included here specifically for the purpose of teaching and illustrating basic computer architecture features, TinyCPU is a fully working CPU. Since it is written in Verilog it can be included inside most common FPGAs, such as those from Altera, Xilinx and Actel and programmed to perform real-world tasks. Professor Nakano and his team have also released both a simple assembler for TinyCPU and a compiler for a subset of the C programming language (i.e. basic C commands are supported but not some of the esoteric and advanced features).

For readers who are seeking a processing core for their FPGA designs, TinyCPU may well work. However, far better would be for readers to first understand, and then experiment with TinyCPU: rather than adopt this design as-is for a project, why not extend it or use this knowledge to create or choose a custom processing core? TinyCPU may not be the most efficient or suitable design for a particular application, but with the practical CPU design knowledge that this chapter presents plus the foundational material presented in earlier chapters, readers will have the skills needed to create a custom solution or to choose from existing available solutions.

A word of warning though – sometimes it will be better to use a common processing core for several designs, even when the core is clearly sub-optimal, because of the shared benefits that this allows: the possibility of code/library reuse, shared development

[4] The source code and design of TinyCPU are used with the kind permission of Professor Nakano. More information relating to TinyCPU can be found on his HDL wiki pages at `http://www.cs.hiroshima-u.ac.jp/~nakano/wiki/`

tools, shared development skills and knowledge. The time-consuming learning curve that must be traversed when transferring development knowledge from one processor to another, is one reason to stick with a known, and standard processor rather than design a custom core.

For those who require power/space efficiency and/or performance above all other considerations, a full custom processing core may well be the best choice.

CPU design will be presented in this chapter as a step-by-step hands-on approach culminating in the fully working TinyCPU. Even those who are unfamiliar with hardware description languages (HDL) should be able to follow this, and all features of the design will be described as the chapter progresses. In fact, following this CPU design also provides an easy path to building foundational knowledge of Verilog.[5]

8.5 CPU Design Specification

The CPU designed in this chapter, is clearly to be an educational tool. However, it must also be a fully working system in its own right. Let us then define some key features of this TinyCPU:

- A fully working CPU, synthesisable into FPGA.
- Should be as simple as possible, consistent with correct operation.
- Should require a minimum amount of source code and be written in Verilog.[6]
- Programmable by assembly language programming (and preferably also the C programming language).
- Have a simple, but full-featured instruction set.
- Have at least a 16-bit architecture.
- Capable of input and output.
- Capable of the usual conditional operations (e.g. NE, GZ, EQ and so on).
- Employ a stack architecture for simplicity (see Section 3.3.5).

With the feature set established, it should now be possible to logically define and describe the CPU structure and operation. Of course, in any engineering problem there are several possible solutions, and here we will follow the approach of the TinyCPU.

The remaining parts of this chapter build the TinyCPU design linearly. We first consider the CPU architecture, discuss instruction handling and then control before the Verilog design is presented. However at this point, readers who are more practically inclined may prefer to skip forwards to Section 8.7 to view and test out the design, before going back to Sections 8.5.1 to 8.6.1 to analyse the design choices.

[5] See also the serialised articles by Professor K. Nakano and Y. Ito in *Design Wave Magazine* from 2007–2009 entitled "Verilog HDL & FPGA design learned from basics".

[6] Although the author of this book is himself a long-time VHDL user and advocate, it seems that many educators now recognise that Verilog is easier to learn, and is a more 'forgiving' language for novice users.

8.5.1 CPU Architecture

Referring back to Chapter 3, Section 3.2, note that a computer or CPU is simply a device to transfer information (data) and perform logical operations upon this data, and which does so according to some sequence of instructions.

If we are to design a CPU then, we shall need at least four elements. Firstly, some method of transferring information. Secondly, some method of storing data and programs. Thirdly, some method of performing logical operations. And fourthly, some method of allowing a sequence of instructions to specify the operations and transfers.

Let us examine each in turn, and then in Section 8.6.1 begin to code the structure in Verilog.

8.5.2 Buses

The first item required in our CPU example, the method of transferring data, is of course a bus: Chapter 4 began with a comprehensive discussion about bus architectures and the implications upon instruction set design and efficiency. In this case, we shall begin with the simplest bus arrangement, namely the single-bus architecture (described in Section 4.1.6).

TinyCPU therefore has a single data bus. At the present time the width of this is not particularly important, but clearly everything involved in data processing and handling will need to be wired up to this common bus. The bus structure for TinyCPU is shown in Figure 8.4, and will be augmented with additional functional units and connections as our design progresses.

In TinyCPU, the main data bus is imaginatively named `dbus`, and is 16 bits in width to match the design specification. The width impacts the CPU resources required to implement the design, and may have a follow-on impact upon the instruction set if an immediate load operation is to be provided, but apart from this it is relatively unimportant at this stage.

Figure 8.4

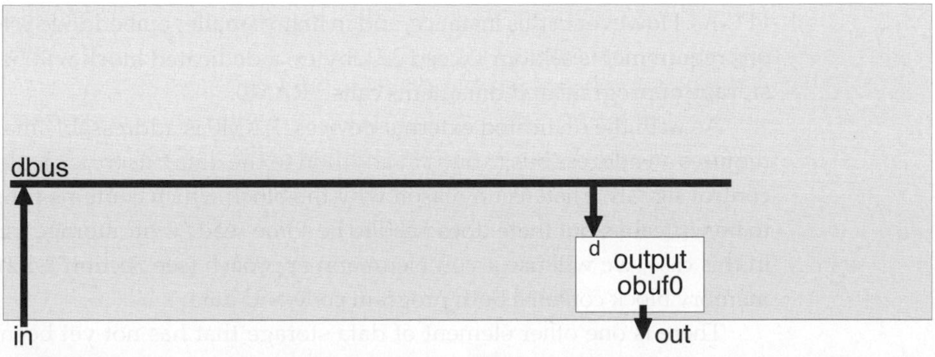

A block diagram of the TinyCPU single internal bus arrangement, showing its data bus, dbus, an input port, output buffer and output port. Control logic is omitted.

We mentioned also input and output from this device. Quite clearly, both input and output words are to be conveyed over `dbus`. This arrangement is shown in Figure 8.4, but some explanation of bus arbitration must be given first.

Since `in` is something driven from the outside world, the voltage (logic level) signal applied to the wires on the bus can enter the CPU at unpredictable times. This could evidently upset normal operation of the CPU, so there is a need for some type of gateway between the `in` signal and `dbus`. This is achieved with a buffer: a specific CPU instruction then allows the programmer to read the logic values on the `in` lines. This instruction will turn on the buffer to connect the `in` wires with the `dbus` wires. The input signal then flows into the bus, where some other logic (not yet shown) will cause the signal to be stored somewhere (also not shown yet).

Similarly, a specific CPU instruction allows the content of the data bus to be output on the `out` wires. This instruction is active only for a fraction of a second: it triggers the output buffer (`obuf0`) to sample the logic values on `dbus` at that time, and then latch them onto the output buffer.

Clearly, there are large amounts of CPU design still missing, although we have now defined the input, output and data transfer backbone of the design.

8.5.3 Storage of Program and Data

Some form of program memory is needed to store a sequence of instructions that will control the eventual CPU. For this, as in almost all other computers, we shall assume a program of binary machine code instructions. Again, in common with many modern, especially RISC processors, we will use a fixed instruction size for simplicity. For the same reason, all instructions will be stored within the Verilog source code directly.

In a real FPGA-based implementation, designers may wish to physically connect up an external memory device (SRAM, SDRAM, flash or similar). In that case, the TinyCPU program could reside within the external memory device and be conveyed over a bus into the FPGA. This approach may sometimes be necessary if the program code size exceeds the relatively small dedicated memory space available within typical FPGA devices. At the time of writing this may be around 1 Mibyte for the largest FPGAs. However in this instance, and in many smaller embedded systems where memory requirements seldom exceed 32 kibytes, a dedicated block will be specified for the storage of program and data items called RAM0.

As with the dedicated external devices, RAM0 is addressable memory, and thus it requires an address bus (`abus`) in addition to the data bus (`dbus`), plus read and write control signals. There is no reason why the block which contains program code needs to be writeable, but there does need to be some read/write storage for variables. Thus, in this case, we will use a von Neumann approach (see Section 2.1.2) where the same memory block contains both program code and data.

There is one other element of data storage that has not yet been mentioned, and that is the stack. Stack machines were briefly discussed in Section 3.3.5, where they were shown to provide temporary storage for variables for use in operations. In fact, the example given showed the connection of a stack to an ALU.

Figure 8.5

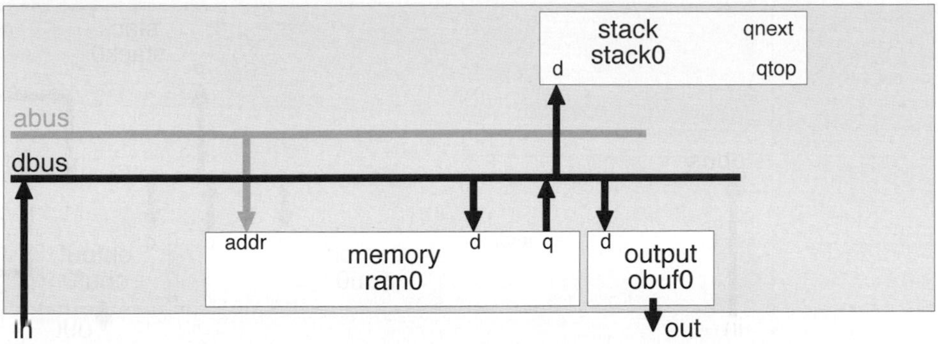

A block diagram of TinyCPU showing memory, stack and output port.

To load data onto a stack its input will need to be connected to `dbus`. A stack requires two outputs to feed logic operations (since these operations have at most two arguments), and these are the content of the top two stack entries respectively.

We define a stack named `stack0` that is fed from `dbus`, and which outputs its top two stack entries. This, together with `ram0` and the address bus `abus` are now added to the CPU design in Figure 8.5.

Note in the figure we use the convention, common in digital logic designs, that the letter *d* represents the data input to a block and *q* represents the data output. It is worth mentioning also that the stack output `qnext` and `qtop` will need to be connected to `dbus` eventually. However, this detail will only be added once the ALU has been connected to the system.

8.5.4 Logical Operations

Section 4.2 presented the ALU, in terms of both functionality and design, and demonstrated the logical and arithmetical operations it provides. Clearly, an ALU is required for performing logical operations within this CPU, as shown in Figure 8.6.

In a stack architecture system, the ALU A and B inputs are always fed from the top two stack entries (named `qtop` and `qnext` in the current design), and the output

Figure 8.6 A general-purpose arithmetic logic unit (ALU) symbol, which will be interconnected within TinyCPU.

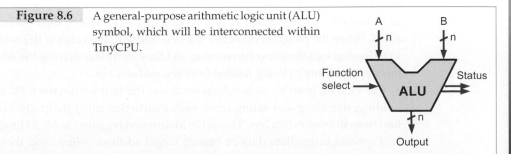

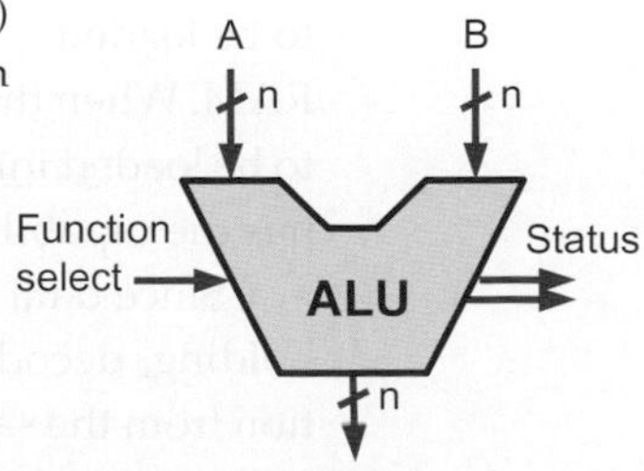

Figure 8.7

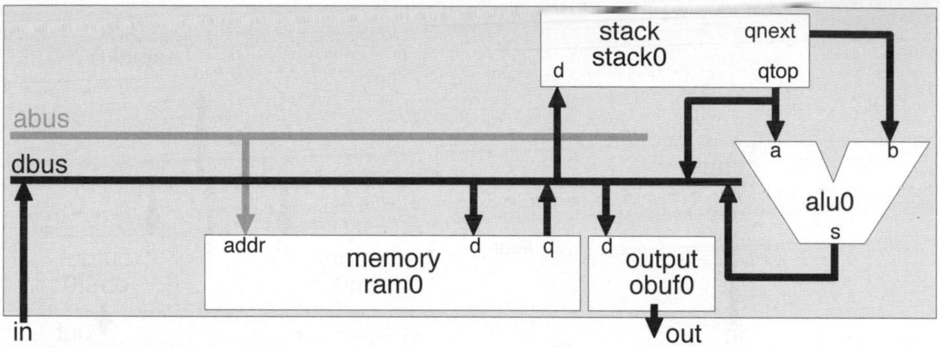

A block diagram of TinyCPU now with an ALU (`alu0`) connected to the internal bus and stack unit. The ALU input ports are labelled `a` and `b`, and output port as `s`.

always feeds back into the stack. In TinyCPU the stack input is conveyed on `dbus` and hence the ALU (`alu0`) output connects to the main bus. This is shown in Figure 8.7, where the top stack output has also been wired so that it can feed `dbus` directly when required.

There is also a need to collect the status output from the ALU, which will be required by subsequent conditional instructions, and a need to specify which ALU function is to be performed with the data from the stack. Neither of these connections has been included in the system block diagram, but it is worth remembering that these signals will need to be there, along with signals controlling each of the latches and buffers that arbitrate connection to and from the buses.

We shall see later that the TinyCPU ALU is actually a little more intelligent than the basic ALU discussed in Section 4.2.2, and this relates to the way in which conditional instructions are handled in TinyCPU. This enhanced intelligence does not affect the data paths in the block diagram above, but does affect the control signals.

8.5.5 Instruction Handling

We noted previously that instructions are located within `ram0`, and that these instructions are binary machine code. Instructions are identified in memory by their address, and as in most CPUs, a program counter (`pc0`) holds the address of the next instruction to be loaded. `pc0` will drive the address bus when accessing the next instruction from RAM. When the program branches to a new address, the value of this address will need to be loaded into the program counter, and thus as well as driving the address bus, `pc0` has the capability of being loaded from the address bus.

Since data from `ram0` is output on `dbus`, the unit within the CPU responsible for holding, decoding and acting upon each instruction must naturally load the instruction from the same data bus. This is the instruction register (`ir0`). At times, instructions will contain immediate data or branch target address values, and these will need to be conveyed to `stack0` and `pc0`, over `dbus` and `abus` respectively. Thus, the instruc-

Figure 8.8

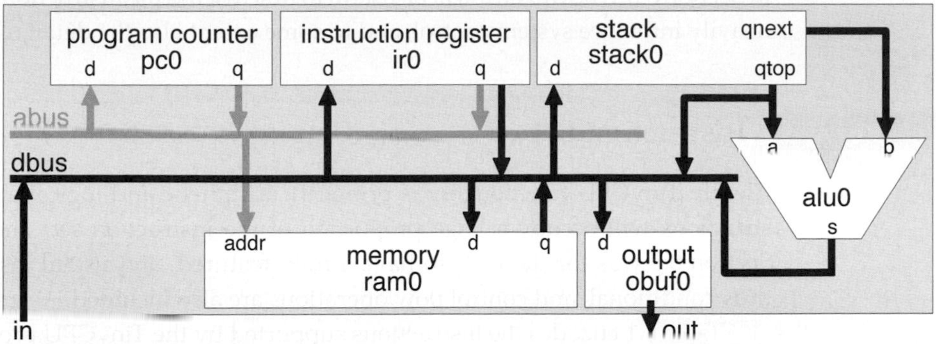

A block diagram of TinyCPU now showing an instruction register (`ir0`) and a program counter (`pc0`).

tion register requires the ability to output to either the data bus or address bus at the appropriate times. This structure can be seen in Figure 8.8.

8.5.6 System Control

TinyCPU is almost complete – at least as far as the data and address path are concerned. However, there are several items that are still necessary for CPU operation. These are the control buses to turn buffers and latches on and off (which we omit for clarity) and a controller to use these to regulate the sequence of operations within the CPU.

The diagram in Figure 8.9 thus contains one more block, the state machine controller (`state0`). It is shown unconnected to the other units within the CPU, and it is true that `state0` does not connect to the data or address buses. However, it does connect widely to almost every unit and bus driver within TinyCPU.

Figure 8.9

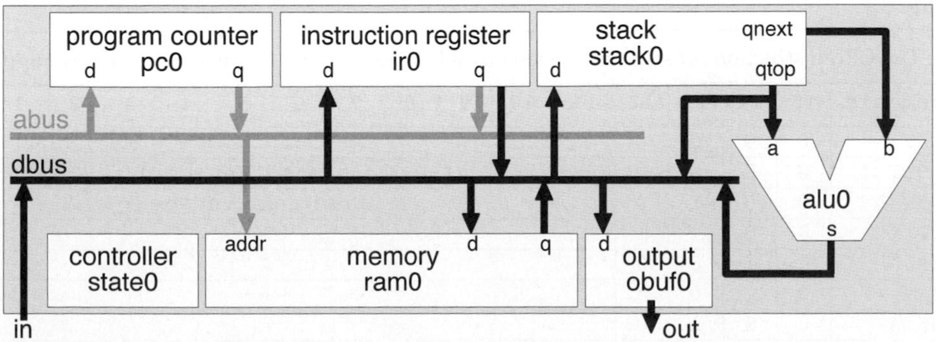

A complete block diagram of the internal structure and interconnection arrangements of TinyCPU, showing everything apart from the control signals.

We will examine the sequence of operations within this CPU and its control aspects in Section 8.6.1, however, it will be useful to first discuss the instruction set since this will heavily influence system control, and to some extent also the detail of the architecture.

8.6 Instruction Set

Clearly TinyCPU functionality is primarily arithmetic and logical and thus these instructions will occupy a large proportion of the instruction set. The requirement in Section 8.5 was for the CPU to have a fully featured, and useful instruction set, and thus conditional, and control flow operations are also included.

Table 8.1 encodes the instructions supported by the TinyCPU processor.

It can be seen that the instruction set is very regular, with the most significant 4 bits determining the instruction type, and any immediate or absolute address values being encoded in the lower 12-bit positions. Let us examine each instruction in turn.

- HALT is used to discontinue processor operation. This is a legitimate event that occurs at the termination of a program. In addition, it is a safety feature that may come into play when an unintended program branch causes the CPU to jump outside of its program code. In this case, a jump to uninitialised memory would likely result in an 'instruction' being read in with the numerical value of zero – causing the processor to halt rather than continue operation incorrectly.
- PUSHI I pushes the immediate operand onto the stack. However, the value of I can be a maximum of 12 bits, and yet the machine (including stack) is 16-bits wide. Thus, the immediate value which is loaded into the stack is first sign extended, otherwise it would be impossible to load a negative value to stack!
- PUSH A retrieves the content of memory location A from `ram0` and pushes this onto the stack.
- POP A performs the reverse operation, popping the top value from the stack and storing it in RAM address A.

Table 8.1

The TinyCPU instruction set showing the ten possible types of 16-bit instructions currently supported.

<table>
<tr><th>Mnemonic</th><th>15</th><th>14</th><th>13</th><th>12</th><th>11</th><th>10</th><th>9</th><th>8</th><th>7</th><th>6</th><th>5</th><th>4</th><th>3</th><th>2</th><th>1</th><th>0</th><th>Hex</th></tr>
<tr><td>HALT</td><td>0</td><td>0</td><td>0</td><td>0</td><td colspan="12">X (don't care)</td><td>0XXX</td></tr>
<tr><td>PUSHI I</td><td>0</td><td>0</td><td>0</td><td>1</td><td colspan="12">I (signed integer)</td><td>1000+I</td></tr>
<tr><td>PUSH A</td><td>0</td><td>0</td><td>1</td><td>0</td><td colspan="12">A (unsigned integer)</td><td>2000+A</td></tr>
<tr><td>POP A</td><td>0</td><td>0</td><td>1</td><td>1</td><td colspan="12">A</td><td>3000+A</td></tr>
<tr><td>JMP A</td><td>0</td><td>1</td><td>0</td><td>0</td><td colspan="12">A</td><td>4000+A</td></tr>
<tr><td>JZ A</td><td>0</td><td>1</td><td>0</td><td>1</td><td colspan="12">A</td><td>5000+A</td></tr>
<tr><td>JNZ A</td><td>0</td><td>1</td><td>1</td><td>0</td><td colspan="12">A</td><td>6000+A</td></tr>
<tr><td>IN</td><td>1</td><td>1</td><td>0</td><td>1</td><td colspan="12">X</td><td>D000</td></tr>
<tr><td>OUT</td><td>1</td><td>1</td><td>1</td><td>0</td><td colspan="12">X</td><td>E000</td></tr>
<tr><td>OP f</td><td>1</td><td>1</td><td>1</td><td>1</td><td colspan="7">X</td><td colspan="5">f</td><td>F000+f</td></tr>
</table>

- JMP A, JZ A and JNZ A each jump to execute the next instruction from address A either always, or only when a data item popped from the top of the stack is zero (JZ) or non-zero (JNZ) respectively. The process of jumping involves the absolute address A encoded in the machine code program being loaded into the program counter. Note that no other conditionals apart from NZ and Z are supported in the jump command, and thus the full range of traditional conditionals (such as GT, LE and so on) must be supported in another way (see later).
- IN reads the input port and pushes the value found there onto the stack.
- OUT pops the top item from the stack and latches it into the output buffer.
- *OP* f is not an instruction in itself, it is a class of instructions. These instructions cause the ALU to perform the requested function encoded in f. Since the ALU is wired to the top two stack locations, the function can use either of these stack values.

The `OP f` instruction class currently encodes 19 separate operations (although with 5 bits reserved for identifying the operation in the f bit-fields, up to 13 more could potentially be added). Most of the operations are self-explanatory through their mnemonic: 16 of them involve two operands (from the stack `qtop` and `qnext` outputs), and will thus pop the stack before writing the result output back into the stack.

Three operations are unary – taking only the stack `qtop`, operating on this, and then loading back into stack. In this case, no pop is required since the single value from the stack top used in the instruction will be directly overwritten by the result.

Table 8.2 identifies the data operations currently available in TinyCPU.

The several logical comparisons (AND, OR, EQ, NE, GE, LE, GT, LT, NOT) push a value of zero onto the stack in the case that the comparison is true and a non-zero value in the case that the comparison is false. In this way, a jump to subroutine if A is greater than B would be performed using the following sequence of instructions:

```
PUSHI valueA
PUSHI valueB
EQ
JZ subroutine
```

An examination of the instruction set above can reveal several structural opportunities and limitations, just as it can do in any other CPU.

First, consider expansion possibilities for TinyCPU. We have already noted that there are several possible f bit combinations that are not used – up to 13 more operations could be added. In the same way, the four most significant bits in the machine code instruction set could encode 16 possible variations, and yet only 10 are used – therefore up to 6 more could be added.

Input and output instructions only require the top 4 bits in the machine code word: the bottom 12 bits (which are currently unused in those instructions) could potentially specify further information, such as allowing the output of immediate values, allowing the output of data from a specified memory address and the input of data to a specified memory address. Alternatively, several input and output ports could be supported or the instructions could even be made conditional.

Table 8.2

The format of the TinyCPU *OP* instruction class, showing the arithmetic, logic and a single multiply instruction, plus the more unusual use of comparison instructions.

Mnemonic	**4**	**3**	**2**	**1**	**0**	**Hex**	**Stack top becomes**	**Popped?**
ADD	0	0	0	0	0	F000	next + top	Y
SUB	0	0	0	0	1	F001	next - top	Y
MUL	0	0	0	1	0	F002	next * top	Y
SHL	0	0	0	1	1	F003	next >> top	Y
SHR	0	0	1	0	0	F004	next << top	Y
BAND	0	0	1	0	1	F005	next & top	Y
BOR	0	0	1	1	0	F006	next | top	Y
BXOR	0	0	1	1	1	F007	next ^ top	Y
AND	0	1	0	0	0	F008	next && top	Y
OR	0	1	0	0	1	F009	next || top	Y
EQ	0	1	0	1	0	F00A	next == top	Y
NE	0	1	0	1	1	F00B	next != top	Y
GE	0	1	1	0	0	F00C	next >= top	Y
LE	0	1	1	0	1	F00D	next <= top	Y
GT	0	1	1	1	0	F00E	next > top	Y
LT	0	1	1	1	1	F00F	next < top	Y
NEG	1	0	0	0	0	F010	-top	N
BNOT	1	0	0	0	1	F011	~top	N
NOT	1	0	0	1	0	F012	!top	N

There are thus many opportunities for future expansion within the instruction set, provided any new instructions can be supported within the single-bus stack architecture. Supporting instructions within a given architecture then becomes predominantly a question of what operands and functional units the instructions require. This is the realm of the control system.

8.6.1 CPU Control

Section 3.2.4 presented the control unit of the CPU as the spider in a web of interconnected control signals and timing units. This is potentially a complex issue even in a simple processor like TinyCPU. In this case, to maintain simplicity, a very simple state machine controller will be used to synchronise the operation of the CPU. The basic state machine, implemented in module `state0`, is shown in Figure 8.10.

8.6.1.1 The Idle State

On power-up the CPU is in an idle state, meaning that the CPU is not operating. There are several reasons for this, not least the fact that an implementation connecting to external devices (such as flash memory) will need to wait for these memory devices to become available before operation can begin.

A `run` signal causes the CPU to begin normal operation, fetching the first instruction from memory. Once the CPU enters this normal operating mode, it will execute

Figure 8.10

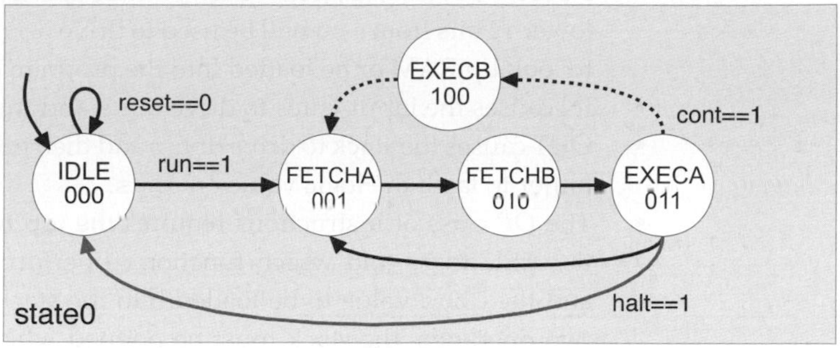

The states used within TinyCPU, showing the transitions between them and the three-bit state codes implemented within `state0`.

instructions one at a time. Only the issuing of a HALT instruction (or an unrecognised instruction) from RAM will cause the CPU to re-enter IDLE state. This normally indicates the endpoint of a program.

8.6.1.2 The Fetch States

FETCHA is the first state encountered during normal operation. FETCHA causes the address in the program counter (`pc0`, initially set to zero), to be output on the address bus, `abus`. The `ram0` module will then look up the content of that memory address. Once that is found `ram0` will output it.

FETCHA will automatically be followed one clock cycle later by FETCHB state, to conclude the instruction fetch process. In state FETCHB, the memory content that `ram0` has found will be allowed to drive `dbus`, and `ir0` will latch this in. At this point, register `ir0` will contain the instruction machine code from the `ram0` address that `pc0` pointed to.

In fact, the program counter `pc0` will have automatically been incremented in the transition from state FETCHA to FETCHB.

FETCHB is followed one clock cycle later by the first of the execution states, EXECA.

8.6.1.3 The Execute States

EXECA has the general responsibility of beginning the execution of the instruction by first performing an instruction decode function. Note from the machine code instruction bit-fields given in Table 8.1 that differentiating instructions classes requires only that the top 4 bits be examined in state EXECA.

Depending upon the class of instruction, the values driving the various buses differ as follows:

- PUSHI instruction – `dbus` will be driven by the lower 12 bits from `ir0` (the immediate value to be pushed onto the stack) and the sign bit from this immediate value will be extended into the top 4 bits of the data bus.

- PUSH, POP, JMP, JZ, JNZ – Each of these specify an absolute address, and thus the lower 12 bits from `ir0` will be used to drive `abus`. In turn, `abus` will either be used to look up RAM or be loaded into the program counter.
- IN causes the input wires to drive `dbus` and this then gets pushed onto the stack.
- OUT causes the stack to drive `dbus`, and then to be popped. Next, it tells the output buffer to latch the logic value on `dbus`.
- The *OP* class of instructions requires the top two stack entries to feed the ALU, the ALU to be told which function to perform, the ALU output to drive `dbus` and the `dbus` value to be loaded into the stack. In the case of instructions using two operands, the stack must be popped when it drives the ALU (and this can be performed easily since all unary instructions are identified by `ir0[4] = 1`, as shown in Table 8.2).

For some instructions, EXECA will need to be followed by a continuation state EXECB, but at other times the CPU will be ready to execute the next instruction, and thus transition back to FETCHA. Where the instruction stored in `ir0` is zero, this indicates the HALT instruction has been executed, and so the CPU must transition to IDLE mode in this case.

For the CPU design illustrated here, a continuation state (EXECB) is only necessary for the `PUSH` instruction. The reason is that there is a memory look-up required as part of this instruction (just like the memory look-up for instruction loading which requires two fetch states). Remember that `PUSH A` loads the value from memory address `A` into the stack. On entry to state EXECA, the instruction will already have been loaded into `ir0`. During EXECA, the value of memory address A is output from the instruction register to `abus`. The `ram0` module then looks up the content of this memory address, but cannot drive this value onto `dbus` immediately as it will take some short time to retrieve it from the memory array. Thus, a second execution state EXECB exists during which RAM drives this value onto `dbus` and the stack is simultaneously instructed to push the current `dbus` content.

EXECB state is always followed by a fetch of the next instruction, FETCHA.

8.7 CPU Implementation

Since TinyCPU will be implemented in Verilog, the first step in implementation is to have a working Verilog compiler available. Freely downloadable FPGA design tools from Altera and Xilinx (named Quartus and ISE respectively at the time of writing) are suitable. However, both are large and cumbersome to install and get started with. In general, the author prefers to use ModelSim for simulation and testing of VHDL and Verilog. However, since this tool may not be available free of charge for many readers,[7] a lightweight open source alternative is presented in Appendix E.

[7] At the time of writing, a six-month student evaluation version is available free of charge.

In this book, TinyCPU will be implemented and tested within a simulation environment only. However, once the simulation is working, it is easily ported to operate on an FPGA system in hardware. Again, the reader is referred to Professor Nakano's website where examples can be found to map the CPU onto a Xilinx Spartan-3E starter kit, including input key driver and both LED and LCD output code.

8.7.1 The Importance of Testing

HDL code is generally developed in a modular fashion. Modules have well-defined input and output ports, and perform their specified functions independent of other modules, apart from interacting through those inputs and outputs.

When code is developed, typically one module is written at a time and tested in accordance with its interface definition. Only tested and working modules are then incorporated within a larger design. Each of these modules may in turn include more modules, in a strongly hierarchical design structure.

The method of testing modules is to create a testbench. For those familiar with C programming, think of this as a main() function which calls a module, supplying the various input parameters to that module and examining the various output parameters as the module runs. A good test bench also encodes its expected behaviour and will compare actual module outputs to this expected behaviour, drawing attention to any discrepancies.

In this way, if a module incorporated within a larger design is modified slightly at a later date, it can still be 'plugged' back in to its test bench and its behaviour verified in isolation.

We will make sure that test benches are provided throughout our design process. However, the recommendation for now is to read the following sections as a design process relating to the main Verilog source. Subsequently, in Section 8.8, we will examine the process of using the test benches to verify the code.

8.7.2 Defining Operations and States: defs.v

First of all, before any logic definitions begin, there is a need to define a common language of bit definitions to be used between logic blocks. In Section 8.6, the instruction set was presented, along with the bitwise definitions of each machine code instruction class. To aid readability of the TinyCPU code, we can define some constants with names and bit definitions corresponding to the assembler mnemonics. Similarly, Section 8.6.1 introduced the various operational states used in the processor, and these can also be defined by name.

All of these constant definitions allow us to create a *header* file which can be included in all of the other Verilog source files, in just the same way we use a .h file in the C programming language. These definitions are stored in a file named 'defs.v', reproduced in Listing 8.1.

8.7.3 Starting Small: counter.v

Since TinyCPU contains many registers and buffers inside its design, it makes sense to use a standard component for implementing these items. The first step in doing that is

Listing 8.1 defs.v

```
`define IDLE   3'b000
`define FETCHA 3'b001
`define FETCHB 3'b010
`define EXECA  3'b011
`define EXECB  3'b100

`define  ADD  5'b00000
`define  SUB  5'b00001
`define  MUL  5'b00010
`define  SHL  5'b00011
`define  SHR  5'b00100
`define  BAND 5'b00101
`define  BOR  5'b00110
`define  BXOR 5'b00111
`define  AND  5'b01000
`define  OR   5'b01001
`define  EQ   5'b01010
`define  NE   5'b01011
`define  GE   5'b01100
`define  LE   5'b01101
`define  GT   5'b01110
`define  LT   5'b01111
`define  NEG  5'b10000
`define  BNOT 5'b10001
`define  NOT  5'b10010

`define HALT  4'b0000
`define PUSHI 4'b0001
`define PUSH  4'b0010
`define POP   4'b0011
`define JMP   4'b0100
`define JZ    4'b0101
`define JNZ   4'b0110
`define IN    4'b1101
`define OUT   4'b1110
`define OP    4'b1111
```

to work out what they need to do. Primarily, the various registers need to store a binary word, output this on bus wires, load a new value in from another bus and be reset to zero on demand. In the case of the program counter, `pc0`, the register also needs to increment the address (so that it is ready to fetch the next instruction) at the appropriate time.

It does not matter too much that some registers will not use some of the available functions: if these are hard wired in an inactive state when the module is instantiated, the Verilog compiler will simply ignore the logic for that function.

With these requirements in mind, the input and output specification for a simple counter able to do this is shown below:

Signal	Direction	Meaning
clk	in	System clock
reset	in	Active-low reset, enter idle state
d	in	The input data bus
load	in	A signal to trigger the counter to store the current logic values on the input data bus
inc	in	A signal to increment the stored logic values
q	out	The output bus, reflecting the stored logic values

Note that TinyCPU, like almost all other CPUs, is a synchronous design, and thus the system clock plays a major part in its design – it defines the timing of the system throughout, and thus needs to be fed into almost every Verilog module. Apart from this timing aspect, the Verilog source code for the counter is quite simple, as shown in Listing 8.2. The parameter *N* allows the same counter.v module to be defined for different bus widths. In this case we have a 16-bit architecture, so *N* is set to 16 by default.

As mentioned above, this counter will be instantiated and used in many places within the CPU design, including the following units:

- Program counter (pc0)
- Instruction register (ir0)
- Output buffer (obuf0)

A simple test bench to exercise this counter is provided in Listing 8.3.

Listing 8.2 counter.v

```
module counter(clk,reset,load,inc,d,q);
  parameter N = 16;

  input clk,reset,load,inc;
  input [N-1:0] d;
  output [N-1:0] q;
  reg [N-1:0] q;

  always @(posedge clk or negedge reset)
    if(!reset) q <= 0;
    else if(load) q <= d;
    else if(inc) q <= q + 1;

endmodule
```

Listing 8.3 counter_tb.v

```
`timescale 1ns / 1ps
module counter_tb;
reg clk, reset, load, inc;
reg [15:0] d;
wire [15:0] q;
counter counter0(.clk(clk), .reset(reset), .load(load),
    .inc(inc), .d(d), .q(q));

initial begin
  clk=0;
  forever
    #50 clk = ~clk;
end

initial begin
  reset=0; load=0; inc=0; d=16'h0000;
  #100 reset=1;
  #100 inc=1;
  #300 inc=0; load=1; d=16'h1234;
  #100 inc=1; load=0; d=16'h0000;
  #500 reset=0;
end
endmodule
```

Simulating the counter, plotting a waveform, and comparing the values of d and g should indicate the load, increment and reset functionality as well as demonstrate the output, q.

Next, we consider the sequence of operations in TinyCPU and how this is controlled.

8.7.4 CPU Control: state.v

The state machine, `state0`, described in Sections 8.5.6 and 8.6.1, controls the operation of TinyCPU: it consists of five states (and thus requires 3 bits to encode these), and transitions between states based upon the system clock, `clk`, plus several control signals as shown in the following interface definition table:

Signal	Direction	Meaning
clk	in	System clock
reset	in	Active-low reset, enter idle state
run	in	A trigger to begin CPU operation if in idle state
cont	in	Continuation signal for instructions needing a second execution state
halt	in	End CPU operation, but dropping back to idle state
cs[2:0]	out	3-bit state output

There is only a single output from this module: the current processor state reflected on the three `cs` wires. The sequence of operations in TinyCPU is completely defined by the current state – all items must work together at the appropriate times in order for the system to function correctly. In the Verilog source code for state.v given in Listing 8.4, note the programmed transitions between states using the case statement.

Listing 8.4 state.v

```
`include "defs.v"

module state(clk,reset,run,cont,halt,cs);

  input clk, reset, run, cont, halt;
  output [2:0] cs;
  reg [2:0]cs;

  always @(posedge clk or negedge reset)
    if(!reset) cs <= `IDLE;
    else
      case(cs)
        `IDLE: if(run) cs <= `FETCHA;
        `FETCHA: cs <= `FETCHB;
        `FETCHB: cs <= `EXECA;
        `EXECA: if(halt) cs <= `IDLE;
                else if(cont) cs <= `EXECB;
                else cs <= `FETCHA;
        `EXECB: cs <= `FETCHA;
        default: cs <= 3'bxxx;
      endcase

endmodule
```

The test bench for the state machine needs to exercise the operation of the 3-bit state output, with the expected sequences of input control signals `reset`, `run`, `cont` and `halt`. A minimal test bench is given in Listing 8.5.

Listing 8.5 state_tb.v

```
`timescale 1ns / 1ps
module state_tb;
reg clk, reset, run, halt, cont;
wire [2:0] cs;
state state0(.clk(clk), .reset(reset), .run(run), .cont(cont),
   .halt(halt), .cs(cs));

initial begin
  clk=0;
```

(Continued)

Listing 8.5 state_tb.v (*Continued*)

```
  forever
    #50 clk = ~clk;
end

initial begin
  reset=0; run=0; halt=0; cont=0;
  #100 reset=1; run=1
  #100 run=0;
  #200 cont=1;
  #100 cont=0;
  #600 halt=1;
  #100 halt=0;
end
endmodule
```

8.7.5 Program and Variable Storage: ram.v

The RAM module serves two purposes in TinyCPU, as discussed in Section 8.5.3: firstly, as a storage area for program code to be retrieved during the FETCH states, and secondly, as a storage area for variables. TinyCPU does not contain a register bank. Instead, it relies upon a stack architecture. If there are more variables used within the code than the stack can hold, or large blocks of data, or variables used in an order that is not necessarily convenient for stack processing, then these variables would be stored elsewhere. Thus, any memory address can be used to either hold data or to store variables.

The practical implication of this is that `ram0` needs to be a read-write addressable memory. Most modern FPGAs contain dedicated RAM elements within their structure which could be used for this purpose, but the default and simplest method is to use the flip-flop elements within FPGA logic blocks for encoding bits. However, this is relatively 'expensive' because although each logic block or logic cell (note that different manufacturers have different names for these smallest programmable units within an FPGA) might contain just a single flip-flop, it will also contain a configurable block of combinatorial logic, various buffers, and possibly a look-up-table, most of which will be wasted if the flip-flop is being used to store a single bit in memory.

The RAM module is, like the rest of the CPU, synchronous, and requires a very simple interface to the outside world:

Signal	Direction	Meaning
clk	in	System clock
load	in	A trigger to store data word currently on bus d into memory at address specified on addr
addr	in	The address bus
d	in	The input data bus
q	out	Outputs the data word stored at address addr

The source code given in Listing 8.6 implements the RAM module in a very simple way. The data and address width parameters are configurable, although here set to a 16-bit data bus and 12-bit address bus. The entire memory area of 4096 words is reset to 0 initially, and then some values are loaded into the first few addresses.

For example, note the line loading `12'h001`. This is the second address location and `16'h3010`, the value we specify, will be stored in that location initially. From our discussion of the instruction set in Section 8.6, we know that machine code `0x3010` corresponds to a POP instruction, with parameter `0x10`. The parameter is the memory address that the value from the stack should be popped into. In this case, looking at the specification for address `12'h010`, we note that a zero value is being loaded in there initially (which we will now be overwriting), and from the comment see that we are reserving that location for storage of variable n.

Listing 8.6 ram.v

```
module ram(clk, load, addr, d, q);
 parameter DWIDTH=16,AWIDTH=12,WORDS=4096;

 input clk,load;
 input [AWIDTH-1:0] addr;
 input [DWIDTH-1:0] d;
 output [DWIDTH-1:0] q;
 reg [DWIDTH-1:0] q;
 reg [DWIDTH-1:0] mem [WORDS-1:0];

 always @(posedge clk)
   begin
     if(load) mem[addr] <= d;
     q <= mem[addr];
   end

 integer i;
 initial begin
    for(i=0;i<WORDS;i=i+1)
       mem[i]=0;
mem[12'h000] = 16'hD000;          //        IN
mem[12'h001] = 16'h3010;          //        POP n
mem[12'h002] = 16'h2010;          //        L1:       PUSH n
mem[12'h003] = 16'hE000;          //        OUT
mem[12'h004] = 16'h2010;          //        PUSH n
mem[12'h005] = 16'h500F;          //        JZ L2
mem[12'h006] = 16'h2010;          //        PUSH n
mem[12'h007] = 16'h1001;          //        PUSHI 1
mem[12'h008] = 16'hF001;          //        SUB
mem[12'h009] = 16'h3010;          //        POP n
mem[12'h00A] = 16'hD000;          //        IN
```

(*Continued*)

Listing 8.6 ram.v (*Continued*)

```
mem[12'h00B] = 16'h1005;        //      PUSHI 5
mem[12'h00C] = 16'hF001;        //      SUB
mem[12'h00D] = 16'hE000;        //      OUT
mem[12'h00E] = 16'h4002;        //      JMP L1
mem[12'h00F] = 16'h0000;        //      L2:      HALT
mem[12'h010] = 16'h0000;        //      n: 0
end

endmodule
```

A simple test bench to verify the operation of the RAM simply needs to read back some of the predefined locations and then test the read-write operation on data variables. The test bench, shown in Listing 8.7, first reads back some of the instructions that should be predefined in RAM, then writes to the variable location n. It then reads back from location n. During the read operations, the value of data on output wire q

Listing 8.7 ram_tb.v

```
`timescale 1ns / 1ps
module ram_tb;
reg clk, load;
reg [7:0] addr;
reg [15:0] d;
wire [15:0] q;

ram ram0(.clk(clk), .load(load), .addr(addr), .d(d), .q(q));

initial begin
   clk=0;
   forever
      #50 clk = ~clk;
end

initial begin
   reset=0; load=0; d=0;
   #100 reset=1; addr=12'h000;
   #100 addr=12'h001;
   #100 addr=12'h006;
   #100 addr=12'h010; load=1; d=8'h55;
   #100 addr=12'h00D;  load=0; d=0;
   #100 addr=12'h010;
end
endmodule
```

should be verified to ensure it correctly matches the required machine code instruction words and variable n content respectively.

8.7.6 The Stack: stack.v

The stack module, discussed in Section 8.5.3, is responsible for storage of data that is currently in the context of a sequence of operations – typically that means data which has either just been output from a calculation or which is just about to be used in a calculation or a combination of both.

The TinyCPU stack supports the standard pop and push operations. In addition, it is able to load a value into the top of the stack, overwriting the value that is there: something which can be useful for certain situations. The top and second stack entries are always visible on outputs `qtop` and `qnext` respectively:

Signal	Direction	Meaning
clk	in	System clock
reset	in	Clears the content of the stack
load	in	Places the data item currently on bus d into the top stack location, leaving other entries unchanged
push	in	Pushes all items down by one level: the item that is on top goes into the second position, the previous second item goes into the third position and so on. The bottom stack entry drops off the stack. The data item currently on bus d will *only* enter into the top stack location if `load` is also set.
pop	in	Replaces the item at the top of the stack with the one from the second position and so on
d	in	The input data bus
qtop	out	Outputs the data word stored in the top stack location
qnext	out	Outputs the data word stored in the second stack location

The interface to the outside world shown above supports a little more functionality than the RAM module. However, the storage space is much smaller in this instance. In fact, the stack depth shown in Listing 8.8 is only eight (since `N = 8`), however, it could be made deeper if required.

Listing 8.8 stack.v

```
module stack(clk, reset, load, push, pop, d, qtop, qnext);
  parameter N = 8;

  input clk, reset, load, push, pop;
  input [15:0] d;
  output [15:0] qtop, qnext;
  reg [15:0] q [0:N-1];

```

(Continued)

Listing 8.8 stack.v (*Continued*)

```
  assign qtop = q[0];
  assign qnext = q[1];

  always @(posedge clk or negedge reset)
    if(!reset) q[0] <= 0;
    else if(load) q[0] <= d;
    else if(pop) q[0] <= q[1];

  integer i;
  always @(posedge clk or negedge reset)
    for(i=1;i< N-1;i=i+1)
      if(!reset) q[i] <= 0;
      else if(push) q[i] <= q[i-1];
      else if(pop) q[i] <= q[i+1];

  always @(posedge clk or negedge reset)
    if(!reset) q[N-1] <= 0;
    else if(push) q[N-1] <= q[N-2];

endmodule
```

The operation of the stack can of course be tested by pushing data onto the stack and then popping it back out again. A more comprehensive test might examine different sequences of push and pop operations. However, since the stack code is fairly simple in this instance we will only perform the straightforward push then pop sequence plus a single load, as shown in Listing 8.9.

Listing 8.9 stack_tb.v

```
`timescale 1ns / 1ps
module  stack_tb;
reg clk, reset, load, push, pop;
reg [15:0] d;
wire [15:0] qtop;
wire [15:0] qnext;

stack stack0(.clk(clk), .reset(reset), .load(load), .push(push),
      .pop(pop), .d(d), .qtop(qtop), .qnext(qnext));

initial begin
  clk=0;
  forever
    #50 clk = ~clk;
end

```

(*Continued*)

Listing 8.9 stack_tb.v (*Continued*)

```
initial begin
  reset=0; load=0; push=0; pop=0; d=0;
  #100 reset=1; push=1; d=16'h1111;
  #100 push=1; d=16'h2222;
  #100 push=1; d=16'h3333;
  #100 push=1; d=16'h4444;
  #100 push=1; d=16'h5555;
  #100 push=1; d=16'h6666;
  #100 push=1; d=16'h7777;
  #100 push=1; d=16'h8888;
  #100 push=1; d=16'hEEEE;
  #100 push=0; pop=1;
  #100 pop=1;
  #100 pop=1;
  #100 pop=1;
  #100 pop=1;
  #100 pop=1;
  #100 pop=1;
  #100 pop=1;
  #100 pop=0; load=1;  d=16'h1234;
  #100 load=0; pop=1;
end
endmodule
```

8.7.7 Arithmetic, Logic and Multiply Unit: alu.v

The ALU, or more properly the 'arithmetic, logic and multiply unit', is responsible for performing each of those operations. In section 8.5.4, we discussed the ALU requirements as it interfaces with the single-bus stack architecture TinyCPU. The traditional ALU-shaped block symbol was even given. However, the shape of the symbol and its description bear very little resemblance to the Verilog code for the ALU, as we shall see shortly. First, we will define the inputs and outputs of this code module:

Signal	Direction	Meaning
a	in	First operand data input
b	in	Second operand data input
f	in	Multiplex lines to define the function to be performed
s	out	Result output port

The table shows that the ALU has no clock signal – it is asynchronous in its operation. In fact, the worst-case propagation delay of the slowest of these ALU operations is used to define the maximum clock frequency that this design can operate at.[8]

[8] Note, however, that where external RAM is used, the load/store operations to external RAM may constitute the limiting factor in clock frequency.

As mentioned, the ALU code bears little resemblance to its symbolic block. It does, however, resemble very closely the specification of the OP functions in Section 8.6. Compare that specification to the code in Listing 8.10.

Listing 8.10 alu.v

```
`include "defs.v"

module alu(a, b, f, s);

 input [15:0] a, b;
 input [4:0]  f;
 output [15:0] s;
 reg  [15:0]   s;
 wire [15:0] x, y;

 assign x = a + 16'h8000;
 assign y = b + 16'h8000;

 always @(a or b or x or y or f)
   case(f)
     `ADD : s = b + a;
     `SUB : s = b - a;
     `MUL : s = b * a;
     `SHL : s = b << a;
     `SHR : s = b >> a;
     `BAND: s = b & a;
     `BOR : s = b | a;
     `BXOR: s = b ^ a;
     `AND : s = b && a;
     `OR  : s = b || a;
     `EQ  : s = b == a;
     `NE  : s = b != a;
     `GE  : s = y >= x;
     `LE  : s = y <= x;
     `GT  : s = y > x;
     `LT  : s = y < x;
     `NEG : s = -a;
     `BNOT : s = ~a;
     `NOT : s = !a;
     default : s = 16'hxxxx;
   endcase

endmodule
```

It is not difficult to test the operation of this ALU: simply create a test bench where some signals are loaded into the a and b inputs of the module, the function, f, is selected appropriately and the output checked for correctness. Note that the ALU is asynchronous – no clock is required, as it is limited by propagation delay. However, a test bench probably requires a clock (otherwise all inputs would quickly get pushed into the module right at time zero). Where this CPU is to be used in a real-world project, it would be a good idea to first exhaustively test many combinations of inputs and functions. However, here we will simply construct a test that samples a few of the possible functions, shown in Listing 8.11.

Listing 8.11 alu_tb.v

```
`timescale 1ns / 1ps
module alu_tb;
reg clk;
reg [15:0] a;
reg [15:0] b;
reg [4:0] f;
wire [15:0] s;

alu alu0(.a(a), .b(b), .f(f), .s(s));

initial begin
  clk=0;
  forever
    #50 clk = ~clk;
end

initial begin

       a=16'h0000; b=16'h1234; f=5'b00000;   //ADD
  #100 a=16'h000A; b=16'h0100; f=5'b00010;   //MUL
  #100 a=16'h1010; b=16'hFFFF; f=5'b01000;   //AND
  #100 a=16'h0008; b=16'h1234; f=5'b00100;   //SHR
  #100 a=16'h0003; b=16'h0100; f=5'b00011;   //SHL
  #100 a=16'h0010; b=16'h0001; f=5'b00001;   //SUB
  #100 a=16'h0000; b=16'h1234; f=5'b10010;   //NOT
  #100 a=16'h0005; b=16'h0004; f=5'b01100;   //GE
  #100 a=16'h0003; b=16'h0004; f=5'b01100;   //GE
  #100 $finish;
end
endmodule
```

8.7.8 Tying It All Together: tinycpu.v

TinyCPU, as a working processor, with code stored internally, simply presents two interfaces to the outside world: its input port and its output port. However, there are several signals required by the Verilog module to enable operation. These are firstly the system clock, secondly a global active-low reset signal, and finally a trigger to cause the CPU to begin operation (called 'run').

In this particular implementation, since TinyCPU is a research machine which is designed to instruct and educate, several of the internal signals are revealed at the top level interface. In the original system designed by Professor Nakano and implemented upon an FPGA development board, these signals can be displayed on an array of seven segment LEDs.

The following table separately identifies the required signals, and also those 'brought out' to the top layer for visibility.

Signal	Direction	Meaning
clk	in	System clock
reset	in	Active-low reset for the entire CPU
run	in	A control signal to trigger the CPU to begin execution (shown in Figure 8.10)
in	in	The input port (can be read using the IN instruction)
out	out	The 16-bit output buffer
Signals made visible in order to examine internal operations:		
cs	out	Indicates the current CPU state
pcout	out	The 12-bit program counter
irout	out	The instruction register content
qtop	out	The content of the top location in the stack
abus	out	The 12-bit internal address bus
dbus	out	The internal data bus

The final source code for TinyCPU is given in Listing 8.12. For a fully-functional 16-bit CPU this is not particularly long. In fact, the entire source code, including all modules, is less than 500 lines of code, hence the prefix 'Tiny' in its name!

TinyCPU is also very logically ordered and thus easy to comment upon. We shall highlight several points here:

- After importing the definitions file and defining the top level inputs and outputs for the CPU, the various signal and bus names are defined.
- The top level instantiates all of the previously discussed modules (excluding their test benches), namely counter.v, state.v, stack.v, alu.v and ram.v. The counter is actually used three times within the design, serving as the program counter, the instruction register and the output buffer.
- Several assignments are then made to connect up various buses and ports when specified by control signals (e.g. `ir2dbus` is the control signal specifying when the data bus should be driven by the sign extended lower 12 bits of the instruction register, presumably driven during the `PUSHI` instruction).
- Next, the main body of the code is executed depending upon the current state. In the EXECA state, the operation is specified based upon the instruction currently located within the instruction register (or to be more accurate, based upon bits

[15:12] of the instruction register – those bits which identify the nature of the current instruction).

Listing 8.12 tinycpu.v

```
`include "defs.v"

module tinycpu(clk, reset, run, in, cs, pcout, irout, qtop,
    abus, dbus, out);

  input clk,reset,run;
  input [15:0] in;
  output [2:0] cs;
  output [15:0] irout, qtop, dbus, out;
  output [11:0] pcout, abus;
  wire [15:0] qnext, ramout, aluout;
  reg [11:0] abus;
  reg halt, cont, pcinc, push, pop, abus2pc, dbus2ir, dbus2qtop,
       dbus2ram, dbus2obuf, pc2abus, ir2abus, ir2dbus,
      qtop2dbus, alu2dbus, ram2dbus, in2dbus;

  counter #(12) pc0(.clk(clk), .reset(reset), .load(abus2pc),
      .inc(pcinc), .d(abus), .q(pcout));
  counter #(16) ir0(.clk(clk), .reset(reset), .load(dbus2ir),
      .inc(0), .d(dbus), .q(irout));
  state state0(.clk(clk), .reset(reset), .run(run), .cont(cont),
      .halt(halt), .cs(cs));
  stack stack0(.clk(clk), .reset(reset), .load(dbus2qtop),
      .push(push), .pop(pop), .d(dbus), .qtop(qtop),
      .qnext(qnext));
  alu alu0(.a(qtop), .b(qnext), .f(irout[4:0]), .s(aluout));
  ram #(16,12,4096) ram0(.clk(clk), .load(dbus2ram),
      .addr(abus[11:0]), .d(dbus), .q(ramout));
  counter #(16) obuf0(.clk(clk), .reset(reset),
      .load(dbus2obuf), .inc(0), .d(dbus), .q(out));

  always @(pc2abus or ir2abus or pcout or irout)
    if(pc2abus) abus <= pcout;
    else if(ir2abus) abus <= irout[11:0];
    else abus <= 12'hxxx;

  assign dbus = ir2dbus ? {{4{irout[11]}},irout[11:0]} :
      16'hzzzz;
  assign dbus = qtop2dbus ? qtop : 16'hzzzz;
  assign dbus = alu2dbus ? aluout : 16'hzzzz;
  assign dbus = ram2dbus ? ramout : 16'hzzzz;
```

(Continued)

Listing 8.12 tinycpu.v (*Continued*)

```
assign dbus = in2dbus ? in : 16'hzzzz;

always @(cs or irout or qtop)
  begin
    halt = 0; pcinc = 0; push = 0; pop = 0; cont = 0; abus2pc = 0; dbus2ir = 0; dbus2qtop = 0; dbus2ram = 0; dbus2obuf = 0; pc2abus = 0; ir2abus = 0; ir2dbus = 0; qtop2dbus = 0; alu2dbus = 0; ram2dbus = 0; in2dbus = 0;
    if(cs == `FETCHA)
      begin
        pcinc = 1; pc2abus = 1;
      end
    else if(cs == `FETCHB)
      begin
        ram2dbus = 1; dbus2ir = 1;
      end
    else if(cs == `EXECA)
      case(irout[15:12])
      `PUSHI:
         begin
           ir2dbus = 1; dbus2qtop = 1; push = 1;
         end
      `PUSH:
         begin
           ir2abus = 1; cont = 1;
         end
      `POP:
         begin
           ir2abus = 1; qtop2dbus = 1; dbus2ram = 1; pop = 1;
         end
      `JMP:
         begin
           ir2abus = 1; abus2pc = 1;
         end
      `JZ:
         begin
           if(qtop == 0)
             begin
               ir2abus = 1; abus2pc = 1;
             end
           pop = 1;
         end
```

(*Continued*)

Listing 8.12 tinycpu.v (*Continued*)

```
         `JNZ:
            begin
               if(qtop != 0)
                 begin
                   ir2abus = 1; abus2pc = 1;
                 end
               pop = 1;
            end
         `IN:
            begin
               in2dbus = 1; dbus2qtop = 1; push = 1;
            end
         `OUT:
            begin
               qtop2dbus = 1; dbus2obuf = 1; pop = 1;
            end
         `OP:
            begin
               alu2dbus = 1; dbus2qtop = 1;
               if(irout[4] == 0) pop = 1;
            end
         default:
            halt = 1;
         endcase
       else if(cs == `EXECB)
         if(irout[15:12]==`PUSH)
           begin
           ram2dbus = 1; dbus2qtop = 1; push = 1;
         end
     end

endmodule
```

TinyCPU, as it is defined here and in the sections above, is a module that can be incorporated within the top-level design of an FPGA, fed with a clock signal, a reset and wired up to input and output pins. Once the CPU begins operation (which is when the run signal is taken to logic '1'), it will execute the internal program until a HALT instruction is read or the system is reset.

As the code has been written, all memory, which comprises volatile memory for runtime storage of variables as well as program instructions, is defined internally. It would be equally possible to connect the CPU to external memory. With internal definition of program code, new programs must be entered, by hand, into the ram.v Verilog source file, and then the entire CPU recompiled.

When using an FPGA, a design incorporating a new program would have to be built using logic design tools such as Altera's Quartus-II or Xilinx ISE. The output, a programming file, would then need to be loaded into the FPGA through a programming cable (or equivalent) before operation can commence. This entire cycle can be time consuming, sometimes requiring over an hour to complete for a complex design, although the basic TinyCPU alone should require no more than a few minutes.

Use of external program memory, by contrast, would require only that memory device to be reprogrammed rather than the entire Verilog design to be rebuilt with each change in TinyCPU program code.

In Section 8.9, the programming and use of TinyCPU will be explored, but before that we will examine the overall testing and operation of the CPU.

8.8 CPU Testing and Operation

Up to this point, we have explained the design of TinyCPU in terms of architectural elements (Section 8.5), program operation (Section 8.6) and through presentation and discussion of the implementation using Verilog (Section 8.7). For each of the six Verilog modules that make up TinyCPU (tinycpu.v, state.v, stack.v, ram.v, counter.v and alu.v), a small and basic test bench was created, after we had highlighted the importance of testing and using a test bench in Section 8.7.

So far we have not explored how to use these test benches to test the system. We will be doing so only at a simulation level, rather than at a hardware level in an FPGA. It should be noted, however, that in a real industrial development where this code is to be deployed in an FPGA, it would be crucial to verify the code not only through extensive simulation but also by operating and testing the system at a hardware level. Both Altera and Xilinx provide JTAG-based (see Section 7.9.3) tools, which make the collection and insertion of test vectors from operating hardware, a convenient process. At the time of writing these tools are, respectively, called SignalTap/SignalTap II and ChipScope/ChipScope Pro. SignalTap II in particular is available in the free web edition download of Quartus II (as long as TalkBack is enabled – which basically allows the Quartus software to provide Altera with limited information regarding the use of the software). In the days before such tools became available, the usual solution was to wire up from the FPGA I/O pins to a digital storage oscilloscope (DSO) or logic analyser, and then internally route these outputs to the signals requiring test inside the VHDL/Verilog code. The disadvantage of course, was that a lengthy recompilation was necessary whenever a different signal was to be tested.

As mentioned, however, here the emphasis will be on simulation. There are at least two levels of simulation available for Verilog prior to running it on an FPGA. The first is a *functional simulation* where the basic operation and logical correctness of the code can be evaluated. The second is *timing simulation* which takes account of the propagation delays and timings of individual wires and elements within a target

FPGA.[9] The first simulation method outputs cycle-accurate results. In other words, if there is a clock being used to make the system synchronous, the cycle-by-cycle operation of the device is tested, and one cycle is evaluated independently from the next. If there is combinational logic in the design, it will output a result instantaneously, once its input changes. The second simulation method produces results that are, at best, very similar to the actual timings experienced by the target FPGA. Combinational logic outputs take some time to propagate through the logic. In this case, an event occurring in one clock cycle may not complete in time before the start of the next cycle. This type of analysis is the means by which designers can estimate the maximum clock speed of a design. Either several timing simulations can be performed with faster and faster clocks until the system fails, or more normally a *critical path* analysis is formed which determines the *slowest* path through the logic, and which in turn sets the limitation on the fastest cycle time that can be supported.

Since timing simulation is entirely device-specific, we will confine our testing here to functional simulation. Functional simulation is much faster and easier than timing simulation, and can also be performed by using a wider variety of tools.

The tools we require for this are namely a compiler for the Verilog source code, a functional simulation tool and a method of displaying the results (preferably by viewing waveforms graphically). Both the free downloadable web versions of Quartus II and ISE support both methods of simulation (although only for a particular range of devices, usually excluding the very newest). ModelSim, if it can be obtained, is another excellent tool for functional simulation. It can also be used for timing simulation if device-specific timing libraries are available. Appendix E describes the use of open source tools for Verilog compilation, simulation and waveform viewing.

8.9 CPU Programming and Use

Professor Koji Nakano, the inventor of TinyCPU, has created both an assembler and a C compiler for this processor. Although compilers and assemblers are probably outside the scope of a text on computer architecture, it is recognised that both are necessary for the real-world usefulness of these devices and so we will take an opportunity to explore these in brief. First, however, we will consider hand assembly and the code-writing process for TinyCPU.

8.9.1 Writing TinyCPU Programs

The first thing any programmer of a new device wants to do is to gain an understanding of that device – particularly in regard to both its limitations and internal architecture. We have seen in Chapter 3 (primarily in Section 3.3.4) how the internal architecture of a machine affects its instruction set, and ultimately determines how efficiently that machine performs certain operations.

[9] Target FPGA: the particular device name, package and speed grade that has been chosen to implement this design in hardware.

For a programmer to write efficient low-level code, knowledge of the architecture and its limitations are thus crucial. For the case of TinyCPU, we have discussed the architecture (Section 8.5.1 and beyond) and the instruction set (Section 8.6). No matter how flexible the architecture, it is ultimately the instruction set that limits exactly *what* the programmer can do with the machine.

Beyond that, a TinyCPU programmer needs to remember that there is a single input port (in) and output register (out), a single ALU capable of all the usual logical operations and multiplication. All program code and memory storage are 16 bits, and there is a limit of 4096 words in memory as implemented. Any constants are to be either loaded using `PUSHI` (for anything up to a 12-bit signed integer) or stored in program memory, where they can be retrieved by their label name.

Above all, TinyCPU is a stack machine. The eight stack locations currently implemented will restrict calculations not involving memory to eight levels deep. This means that all operands and results are 16 bits in size (note that this includes the multiply unit, thus `MUL` can only operate correctly on eight significant bit-sized input operands). Obviously, it also implies that calculations need to be formulated for a stack architecture (see Reverse Polish notation – Section 3.3.5), something which may require a little forethought.

As an example, let us develop a very simple program to read a value from the input port, subtract a constant from that, and then load the result into the output register. We will assume that the constant is located in memory with a label 'const'.

Reading from the input port is not difficult: a quick check with the TinyCPU instruction set on page 386 reveals that the `IN` command will read something from the input port and place it onto the stack:

```
IN
```

In order to subtract a constant from that, we need to also load the constant into the stack. If this was an immediate constant we would use `PUSHI`, but in this case the constant resides in memory, so we need to retrieve a value from memory and push it onto the stack, instead using `PUSH`:

```
PUSH const
```

Next, we perform the subtraction operation:

```
SUB
```

which will pop the two input operands off the stack, perform the subtraction, and then push the result back onto the stack. So finally, we can load the result into the output register:

```
OUT
```

Notice that there are almost no operands required in this simple program! That is one of the characteristic 'trademarks' of a stack architecture machine – we do not need to specify registers if there are none.

Putting this all together, we also need to add a location to store the constant. The full program source code is shown in Listing 8.13, where we have set the constant to a value of 3.

Listing 8.13 subtract.asm

```
1           IN
2           PUSH cnst
3           SUB
4           OUT
5           HALT
6   cnst: 3
```

Next, we determine the machine code (hexadecimal) identifiers for each of the instructions in turn from the instruction set tables given in Section 8.6 (specifically Tables 8.1 and 8.2 on pages 386 and 388 respectively). For example, looking up the `IN` instruction in Table 8.1, we can see that it is represented by the hexadecimal value `D000`. The second instruction, `PUSH const` is represented by the hexadecimal value `2000+A` where A is the address at which the constant is stored. In this case, we need to convert the label 'const' to an address – and we can do this by simply counting which address this is at. From the listing it is the sixth line, but since the computer counts address locations starting at zero, then the address of the constant is actually 5. Thus, the hexadecimal value of this instruction would become `2005`.

Repeating this process for the remaining instructions, we would end up with a machine code as shown in Listing 8.14.

Listing 8.14 subtract.hex

```
D000 \\         IN
2005 \\         PUSH cnst
F001 \\         SUB
E000 \\         OUT
0000 \\         HALT
0003 \\ cnst: 3
```

At this point, those who have conscientiously performed the conversion themselves will realise how tedious this process is, even for a simple program (and maybe how error prone it can be). That is why Professor Nakano has created an assembler (and a simple compiler) and why today almost nobody writes machine code directly. We will introduce the TinyCPU programming tools in Section 8.9.2, but for now it is important to understand the process before we start taking short-cuts.

The next stage will be to format this program to the correct syntax and insert into `ram.v`. We can do that by examining the syntax in Section 8.7.5, deleting the program given there originally and inserting our subtraction code. This is shown in Listing 8.15.

Listing 8.15 ram_subtract.v

```
module ram(clk, load, addr, d, q);
 parameter DWIDTH=16,AWIDTH=12,WORDS=4096;

 input clk,load;
 input [AWIDTH-1:0] addr;
 input [DWIDTH-1:0] d;
 output [DWIDTH-1:0] q;
 reg [DWIDTH-1:0] q;
 reg [DWIDTH-1:0] mem [WORDS-1:0];

 always @(posedge clk)
   begin
     if(load) mem[addr] <= d;
     q <= mem[addr];
   end

 integer i;
 initial begin
    for(i=0;i<WORDS;i=i+1)
       mem[i]=0;
mem[12'h000] = 16'hD000; //  IN
mem[12'h001] = 16'h2005; //  PUSH cnst
mem[12'h002] = 16'hF001; //  SUB
mem[12'h003] = 16'hE000; //  OUT
mem[12'h004] = 16'h0000; //  HALT
mem[12'h005] = 16'h0003; //  cnst: 3
end

endmodule
```

Let us now simulate and test this code. First of all, we would need to ensure that our test bench has been set up correctly. In this case, to provide a value on the input port from which the constant will be subtracted, we choose a value of 7. The original TinyCPU test bench has been modified appropriately in Listing 8.16.

Listing 8.16 tinycpu_tb_subtract.v

```
`timescale 1ns / 1ps
module tinycpu_tb;

 reg clk, reset, run;
 reg [15:0] in;
 wire [2:0] cs;
```

(Continued)

Listing 8.16 tinycpu_tb_subtract.v (*Continued*)

```
 wire [15:0] irout, qtop, dbus, out;
 wire [11:0] pcout, abus;

 tinycpu tinycpu0(.clk(clk), .reset(reset), .run(run), .in(in),
       .cs(cs), .pcout(pcout), .irout(irout), .qtop(qtop),
       .abus(abus), .dbus(dbus), .out(out));

initial begin
    clk=0;
    forever #50 clk = ~clk;
end


initial begin
    reset=0; run=0; in=3;
    #100 reset=1; run=1;
    #100 run=0; in=7;
    #12000 $finish;
end

endmodule
```

If we were now to simulate this code, using the methods shown in Appendix E (Icarus Verilog and GTKwave), we would obtain operating waveforms as shown in Figure 8.11.

The figure shows the input port having a constant value of 7. Following the assertion of the run signal, instructions 0 through to 5 are loaded in turn (look at the abus value). qtop shows the top value on the stack: 0, then a 7 from the input port, then constant 3 from memory, and finally the result of the subtraction 4. This result is then loaded into the output register, as marked by the cursor position.

Clearly, $7 - 3 = 4$ is correct, however, readers may feel that there exist many easier methods of performing such a calculation!

8.9.2 TinyCPU Programming Tools

Having discussed the method of creating a machine code output by hand, loading it into TinyCPU and using it to perform a simulation, in Section 8.9.1, readers will realise that the assembly process is actually quite mechanical, requiring (i) resolving of labels in the code to actual addresses, (ii) conversion of assembly language mnemonics to hexadecimal machine code and (iii) incorporating any operands (such as inserting the address of our constant variable into the appropriate bit-fields of the PUSH instruction).

Figure 8.11

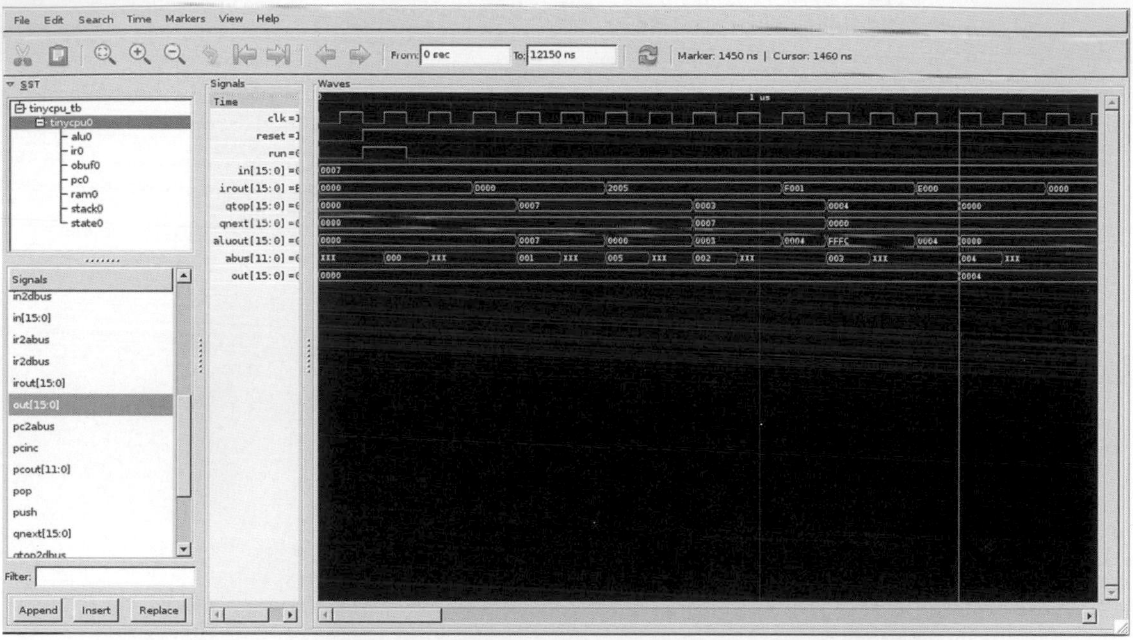

A screenshot of the GTKwave viewer for the subtract example, showing several of the important signals available within the simulation.

It is not difficult to write an assembler. In fact, Professor Nakano has done just that – written an assembler, and also a simple compiler. The reader is referred to his several publications,[10] and website for further information.

The assembler, presented in full in Appendix E, is a Perl program that performs two-pass assembly. The first pass scans through the input code, determining instruction addresses and the address of each label in the code. The second pass then converts assembler mnemonics into hexadecimal machine code, inserting label address values obtained from the first scan as appropriate.

Assembler output from this tool is formatted by a second helper application to produce an output form which is capable of being directly inserted into the program space within `ram.v`.

[10]Koji Nakano, Yasuaki Ito, "Processor, Assembler and Compiler Design Education using FPGA", Proc. International Conference on Parallel and Distributed Systems (ICPADS), Melbourne, Australia, Dec. 2008

8.10 Summary

This chapter has first built upon the foundations of earlier chapters in considering the design of microprocessors for programmable systems such as FPGAs. We discussed the taxonomy of these systems in general, then presented off-the-shelf cores and mentioned that several good open and free cores are also available.

Primarily, in applying many of the concepts we have learnt throughout this book, we have explored the techniques required to build a complete working CPU in Verilog. Specifically, we followed the design of TinyCPU, originally the brainchild of Professor Koji Nakano of Hiroshima University, Japan. TinyCPU (as the name implies) is a small and self-contained CPU. This stack-based processor can easily be used inside an FPGA to run simple programs.

In this chapter, we first discussed the idea of using a soft-core microprocessor, including making use of a downloaded core or one purchased from an IP-core vendor. In addition, we examined the in-house cores from the four main FPGA manufacturers. Finally, we embarked upon a full-custom core design of our own. We did this by first setting out a design specification for an example CPU, then developed the architecture step by step. Next, we created an instruction set, before coding the entire system in just six small Verilog code modules. Along the way we re-explored the issue of testing and developed test benches for every part of our CPU design.

Finally, we created an example program for TinyCPU and simulated its operation.

TinyCPU does a perfect job: it is a simple home-made CPU that is visible and open enough to allow us to explore its inner workings. However, it should be regarded as simply a beginning: readers are invited to extend, adapt, rewrite, improve and experiment with the original code. Let these be lessons that will lead, in time, to the invention of a new generation of application-specific custom processors.

Problems

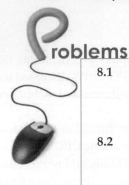

8.1 An off-the-shelf CPU can usually be clocked faster than a similar architecture CPU implemented on even the fastest of FPGAs. Does this mean that the off-the-shelf solution will always be faster? Justify your answer.

8.2 What is meant by the term *hardware-software co-design*, and why is this arguably more important in embedded system development than it is in the development of a new desktop PC?

8.3 Identify the steps involved in the hardware-software co-design process. Estimate which step requires the greatest level of system knowledge and which step is most important to get right.

8.4 What are the main advantages in choosing an off-the-shelf or commercial soft core over and above designing your own? What are the main disadvantages?

8.5 Manufacturers of niche small-volume products with long lifetimes are often hit particularly hard by end-of-life notifications from semiconductor manufacturers. How does the use of a soft core for their computation needs help such manufacturers? What factors contribute to the up-fronts costs involved in switching from an existing mass-market CPU to an in-house designed soft-core solution?

8.6 Does TinyCPU always follow FETCHA with FETCHB? Why does TinyCPU require two fetch states (FETCHA and FETCHB – refer to Section 8.6.1.2)?

8.7 Why does the TinyCPU stack have both a `qtop` output and a `qnext` output? Could it function with only the `qtop` output?

8.8 Does the TinyCPU implement a one-, two- or three-bus architecture according to the definitions given in Section 4.1.1? How does that impact the instruction set?

8.9 What is the difference in operation between the TinyCPU `PUSHI` and `PUSH` instructions, and why are these two both instructions available? Summarise the hardware differences between the implementation of these two instructions.

Enhancements and Upgrades to TinyCPU

The following questions assume a working TinyCPU implementation in Verilog, and propose various different upgrades, enhancements and adjustments to TinyCPU, its instruction set and the way it works. Attempting these questions will give an excellent grounding in the issues involved in do-it-yourself soft-core computing and impart a deep appreciation of the trade-offs involved in such systems.

For each change, a new TinyCPU program (or test bench) should be written, and the new code thoroughly tested for correctness, as well as to ensure the additions have not invalidated the *existing* code. For readers with full FPGA development systems who are able to implement TinyCPU in hardware as well as in simulation, it would be useful to examine the difference that the changes make in the implementation cost of TinyCPU (i.e. what proportion of device memory and area resources it occupies).

8.10 Enhance TinyCPU with a rotate right and rotate left instruction (`ROR`, `ROL`), implemented similarly to the existing instructions `SHL` and `SHR`.

8.11 TinyCPU can currently only handle 16-bit data. Upgrade the internal data paths, the ports, RAM and the stack to 32 bits. This may require a method (i.e. a new instruction) to push an immediate value into the upper 16 bits of a stack location. However, there is more than one way to achieve this 32-bit enhancement, so the readers are free to implement their own method of achieving the aim of 32-bit data handling.

8.12 TinyCPU has only one input and one output port. Implement new instructions to increase the number of ports accessible to four.

8.13 Add an interrupt to TinyCPU (and maybe also an interrupt vector table).

8.14 Shadow registers, as we have discussed in Section 5.6.3, can improve the speed of interrupt service routines. Implement a shadow *stack* for TinyCPU in conjunction with the interrupt capability of Problem 8.13. Is such an enhancement necessary or useful?

8.15 Implement a basic repeat instruction for TinyCPU, similar to that in Section 5.6.1.

8.16 Consider how the repeat instruction of Problem 8.15 could be extended to a full zero-overhead loop.

8.17 Extend the stack by implementing an SIMD input trigger to stack.v that can increment the top four entries. Add a new instruction to TinyCPU to drive this trigger. Consider how this differs from a similar single SIMD instruction that

Problems

would automatically POP the stack four times, increment the output from each POP and then PUSH them back onto the stack in the original order. Which is faster? Which requires most additional FPGA resources?

8.18 Implement a co-processor on TinyCPU. First, create a new 16-bit output port that TinyCPU can write to, and an input port that can be read from. These ports should connect to a simple 'co-processor' that will, when triggered, read a16-bit word from the TinyCPU output port, reverse the endiness (by swapping bit 0 with bit 15, swapping bit 1 with bit 14 and so on), and then output the result to the TinyCPU input port, which can then be read by TinyCPU.

8.19 For readers able to implement TinyCPU within an FPGA, design a system containing two of the processors operating in parallel. Next, implement a port and register on both processors which will allow them to communicate with each other (this will be similar to the co-processor interface of Problem 8.18).

8.20 Introduce a simple *pipeline* to TinyCPU and show that this can improve throughput of at least some types of instruction (note: for this, it would be good to implement on FPGA design tools which can give an estimate of the longest-path timing in the system (i.e. which automatically calculate the maximum clocking speed of the design).

CHAPTER 9

The Future

As the title suggests, this chapter is concerned with the next steps in the continuing evolution of computers and their architecture. As we have noted many times previously, the future emphasis in computing is likely to be embedded in the near future, but emerging topics include ambient intelligence (the idea of computers all around us), pervasive and cloud computing (similarly distributed), quantum computers, biological computers and so on. Many proponents also believe that parallel computing is overdue for a renaissance.

In trying to chart a future that differs from mainstream computing, some of this chapter is definitely with us already: it is included here to indicate growing importance and potentially a wide impact in the future computing world. Some of the so-called future techniques are those which have been tried and forgotten, but are now being revisited. Others, such as quantum computers, sound more at home in a science fiction novel than a computer architecture text book.

Whatever the future holds, it is entirely possible that you, the reader currently studying computer architecture, will have a part in building it and making it happen.

9.1 Single-Bit Architectures

In Section 4.2.2, we designed an ALU from a combination of separate 1-bit ALUs. This approach is quite common (for instance, the ARM core historically used it) and can be called bit-slicing. In effect, each bit is dealt with separately in parallel because the bus to the ALU is parallel.

Alternatively, the ALU could accept bits in a serial fashion, process these and output its result serially. In fact, serial CPUs exist that do all processing with a bit-serial architecture.

This means higher on-chip clock speed, but fewer on-chip bus connections. However, the CPU is not always simplified because a serial controller has to route all the serial operands around the CPU – this means complex timing circuitry. One big advantage is that the same CPU can cope with different word lengths with no ALU changes (just different timings).

Figure 9.1

An example of two serial streams of binary digits being added together bitwise. The carry in for each bitwise addition is the fed-back carry output from the previous bit calculation.

For some serial operations, processing can occur as the serial bits are being fed into the ALU. For other operators, all bits must be fed in before processing can begin.

9.1.1 Bit-Serial Addition

As an example, consider the addition of two bit-serial numbers. These are presented to the adder with the least significant bit first, and added bitwise, with the carry from a particular add being fed back ready for the subsequent add.

In the example shown in Figure 9.1, the first four bits have been added so far, and thus four answer bits have been produced. The logic within this adder need not be complex, in fact, it may be somewhat similar to the block diagram of Figure 9.2.

Within Figure 9.2, the two bit-streams are presented at A and B. These are added together with the carry feedback to produce a sum and a carry. The least significant bit (LSB) control signal is used to inhibit any carry feedback, so that there is no carry going in to the least significant bit position (as expected). The latch delays the output of the adder to be synchronous with a bit clock and delays the carry to be ready for the next bit additions.

With this scheme there is no need for any gap between one set of inputs and the next, as long as the LSB control signal prevents any inappropriate carry from being transferred from one sum to the next. The beauty of this is that literally *any* word length numbers can be added with exactly the same hardware, as long as the timing of the LSB control signal demarcates between input words, as shown in Figure 9.3.

Figure 9.2

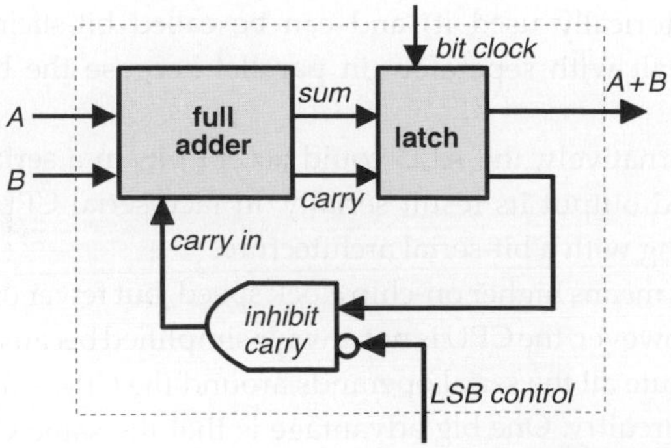

The full adder circuitry required by a bit-serial adder unit.

Figure 9.3

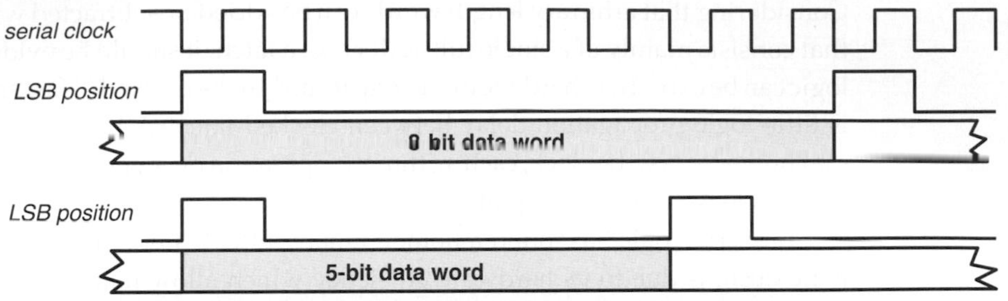

Timing waveforms relating to bit clocks, the LSB position flag and the data words.

An accumulator is equally simple to implement – this is left as an exercise for the reader.

9.1.2 Bit-Serial Subtraction

Consider the adder of Section 9.1.1 and note that any carry is naturally propagated from beginning to end. Since a subtraction may involve a *borrow* instead of a carry, there could be an analogous process. However, it is likely that a simple trick can make the process easier.

Remember from Chapter 2 that changing the sign of a two's complement number is relatively easy (although not quite as easy as it is for a sign-magnitude number): it is necessarily to simply swap all 1's with 0's and 0's with 1's then add a 1 to the least significant bit position. Then we use the fact that A − B is equivalent to A + (−B), so we simply need to perform an addition with one operand negated.

Inverting all the bits in the bit-serial input is as easy as placing a not gate at the input signal. Similarly, adding a 1 to the least significant bit position is as simple as ensuring that the first carry is set rather than clear (i.e. the LSB control signal causes the carry to be set instead of cleared).

The logic required to perform a bit-serial subtraction is shown in the diagram of Figure 9.4. Comparing this and the hardware in Section 9.1.1, it should be fairly easy to convert the system such that it can perform either add or subtract dependent upon an external control signal.

Figure 9.4 The full adder modified to perform the subtraction B − A.

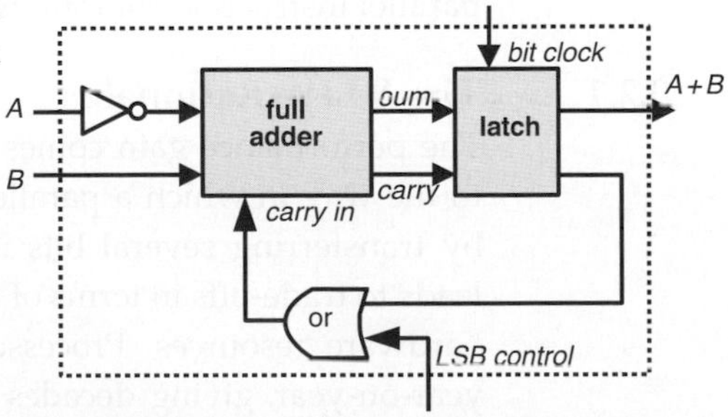

9.1.3 Bit-Serial Logic and Processing

Considering that arbitrary length words can be added or subtracted with this hardware that consists mainly of a single full adder and a latch, it should be evident that bit-serial logic can be extremely hardware efficient. It can also be clocked at fast speeds (since there is little logic propagation delay between clocked latches), but with the disadvantage that however fast the clock, each arithmetic operation on length n-bit words, will require $(n + 1)$ clock cycles to complete.

Bit-serial logic has found a home in many FPGA (field programmable gate array) logic designs due to its hardware efficiency which allow many streams of processing to occur simultaneously. It also matches the hardware architecture of an FPGA where the logic described in 9.1.1 and 9.1.2 (or indeed the selectable version of both) can be implemented in a single cell of the device. Such a cell may be called a logic element (LE), logic cell (LC) or similar name by different manufacturers, but the important point is that each cell contains a look-up-table with the ability to perform as a full adder, allied with a flip-flop (which can implement a latch) or sometimes two of each. Interconnects between such cells are slower than within cell, with the speed being inversely proportional to the geographical distance between cells.

The interconnect delay can become crippling in an FPGA as the width of numbers being added increases. This, along with carry propagate issues, means that once numbers of around 256 bits or more are added together, it becomes extremely difficult to do so at any reasonable speed. Moreover, current generation mid-range devices may not even contain sufficient routing interconnects to implement such functionality (which incidentally is not an obscure requirement, but rather a common function in many encryption algorithms). Under these circumstances, the single cell required for a bit-serial implementation becomes highly attractive.

9.2 Very-Long Instruction Word Architectures

Very-long instruction word architectures (VLIW) can make CPUs much faster by allowing instruction-level parallelism (ILP) – shifting the responsibility for efficient instruction ordering from the processor to the compiler. This ordering includes grouping instructions that can be executed in parallel.

As we have mentioned previously, VLIW is sometimes also referred to as explicitly parallel instruction computing (EPIC).

9.2.1 The VLIW Rationale

The performance gain comes about through execution in parallel. This is analogous to the way in which a parallel bus can transfer information faster than a serial bus, by transferring several bits in a single clock cycle: and like the bus example, this leads to trade-offs in terms of a greater instruction bandwidth required and additional hardware resources. Processor manufacturers have tried to increase clock speeds year-on-year, giving decades of relentless processing gains. However, VLIW allows the speed to remain constant, but the number of operations executed per clock cycle to increase, thus improving overall performance significantly. We will explore some of the disadvantages of this approach in Section 9.2.2, but first consider the rationale and its advantages.

Although performing operations in parallel is not a new idea, VLIW as a concept really began with multimedia-based DSP processors from Texas Instruments in the late 1980s, resulting in some very fast modern processors from companies such as TI, Philips (most notably the Tri-media range) and Mitsubishi (initially with the V30 processor). It is likely that, although initial take-up has been relatively slow, VLIW will gradually become a mainstream processor technique over time simply because it helps to break the tight relationship between processing performance and clock speed. VLIW has become a good solution for media – streaming audio and video in particular, and such content is continually increasing within processing system. Intel has also adopted the VLIW architecture, although in typical marketing fashion, usually refer to it as EPIC. It is heavily used in their IA-64-architecture machines.

VLIW is an extension of the RISC philosophy into parallel dimensions. It is inherently RISC-like in that individual sub-instructions are themselves simple and regular, and typically execute in a single cycle. Separate RISC-style sub-instructions are folded together by the compiler into a long instruction word that is to be executed in parallel by using:

- Independent CPU functional units (such as ADSP2181).
- Multiple copies of functional units (many DSPs and later Pentiums).
- Pipelined functional units.

One question arises as to how VLIW differs from a superscalar architecture (Section 5.4), since both include multiple functional units and parallelism within the processor hardware. There are several differences, but most importantly the superscalar instruction fetch unit has to be able to *issue* instructions faster than individual execution units can process them, and instructions may have to wait to be processed. This is because the processor schedules what each instruction unit is doing, and which of the parallel execution units it is sent to, at runtime. By contrast, the VLIW processor relies on the compiler to do the scheduling. It is the compiler that directs exactly what each execution unit is doing at every instant, where it gets its data from and where it writes it to. Parallel instructions are issued and executed at a regular rate and the processor instruction handling hardware is less complex, and therefore potentially works faster. An example of VLIW hardware is given in Box 9.1.

The VLIW compiler output for the example presented in Box 9.1 would look like the following:

	ALU 1	ALU 2	ALU 3	FPU 1	LOAD/STORE
Instruction 1	ADD	ADD	ADD	FMUL	NOP
Instruction 2	ADD	NOP	NOP	FMUL	STORE
Instruction 3	NOP	NOP	NOP	NOP	STORE

Box 9.1

Example of a VLIW hardware

Consider an example code segment derived with permission from "VLIW Architecture For Media Processing" by K. Konstantinides, *IEEE Signal Processing Magazine*, March 1998 (© 1998IEEE):

Standard processor		**VLIW processor**	
Cycle	Operation	Cycle	Operation
1	`add t3 = t1, t2`	1	`add t3 = t1,t2`
2	`store [addr0] = t3`		`add t5 = p2,p10`
3	`fmul f6 = f7,f14`		`add t1 = p2,p7`
4	...waiting...		`fmul f6 = f7,f14`
5	...waiting...	2	`add t4 = t1,t5`
6	`fmul f7 = f7,f15`		`fmul f7 = f7,f15`
7	...waiting...		`store [addr0] = t3`
8	...waiting...	3	`store [addr1] = t4`
9	`add t1 = p2,p7`		
10	`add t5 = p2,p10`		
11	`store [addr1] = t4`		

This example uses some form of pseudo-code to indicate how a normal processor (on the left) would perform some adds, floating point multiplies and stores. Including the waits for the multiplies to complete, 11 instruction cycles are required to perform the operations. A VLIW processor, on the right, with multiple functional units programmed in parallel from a long instruction word, could perform the same operations in only 3 instruction cycles – and there is no reason to expect that these cycles will be any slower than the non-VLIW processor.

Consider for a minute the parallel hardware blocks required for the VLIW processor on the right – these are explored in Section 9.2.1 as part of the rationale behind the use of VLIW.

A superscalar machine such as in this example would instead issue eight sequential instructions (ignoring the NOPs). They would *possibly* be parallelised to some degree depending on hardware flexibility and the current state of the system.

VLIW instructions are commonly 1024-bits long and directly control multiple hardware units, such as 16 ALUs, four FPUs and four branch units.

9.2.2 Difficulties with VLIW

As the discussion in the previous section has revealed, VLIW hardware is actually more regular, and simplified over and above an equivalent superscalar machine, but much of the complexity moves into the compiler.

To efficiently compile for VLIW machines, the compiler has to consider separate data flows – it rearranges the sequence of instructions in the user's program to improve instruction throughput, taking care where later instructions depend on the output from previous instructions. In other words, the compiler particularly needs to avoid pipeline hazards (such as those mentioned in Section 5.2).

Some of the other potential issues associated with VLIW code include the following:

- Poor code density – Sometimes it is not possible to make a program fully parallel, in such cases VLIW code contains many NOPs 'padding' out the instruction word.
- Complex compilers are required – This is simply a matter of transferring 'difficulty' from a hardware domain to a software domain.
- High-bandwidth memory needed – On average, a VLIW processor will require more instruction bandwidth than other processors, such as superscalar, exacerbated by the padding of extra NOPs. The usual solution is for instruction memory to be 64-bits, 128-bits or even 256-bits wide. This means more memory chips are needed, more printed circuit board (PCB) space to route buses and more pins on the processor IC.
- VLIW is very hard to code in assembly language – Use of a high-level language (HLL) is almost an essential prerequisite for using VLIW processors.

The compiler complexity issue is one reason why VLIW has not generally been used in PC-architecture systems where backwards code compatibility is required. If VLIW were to be adopted then compilers would need to be replaced by much more intelligent versions – object code would change and existing low-level tools would need to be replaced. By contrast, superscalar techniques are entirely compatible with legacy code. They require more complex instruction-handling hardware, but the compiler can remain simple.

Where companies such as Mitsubishi and Philips have designed totally new architectures with no legacy code issues, they have been free to adopt VLIW with some success.

9.3 Parallel and Massively Parallel Machines

With smaller and smaller CPUs or cores becoming available, and the convenience of interconnection by means such as Ethernet, it has become easy to cluster computers together with the aim of having them co-operate. Writing efficient software for such a system is another question, but from a hardware point of view, simply wiring together several off-the-shelf PCs constitutes a cluster computer.

Previously in Section 5.8, we have outlined some of the many levels of parallelism that could be found within computers and met the distinction between loosely and tightly coupled systems in that chapter. Here, we will concentrate on the biggest level of parallelism that was listed, namely machine parallelism.

For computational problems with many loosely coupled tasks (such as groups of code functions that perform difficult and complex processing, but communicate between each other with relatively low bandwidth), parallel execution of each function into separate tasks can speed up completion time.

On the other hand, a system with tasks that communicate between each other either very frequently or with high bandwidth, may not run faster with parallel execution, due to bottlenecks in communications between CPUs. However, there are sufficient tasks which *can* be parallelised to have driven forward the parallel processing agenda over the past decade or so.

In large-scale parallel processing systems, tasks typically execute on physically separate CPUs, and this is what we will consider: groups of separate CPUs or perhaps PCs, rack servers or blade servers. The argument could even be extended to clusters-of-clusters, but that is outside the realm of computer architecture and is best left to textbooks devoted to parallel and distributed computing.

Here, we will first consider this type of processing from a generalised computing perspective, before delving into the particular implications for embedded systems.

9.3.1 Clusters of Big Machines

The concept of shared computing resources scattered everywhere around us is known as *pervasive computing* (and most of us *are* surrounded by many computerised devices that could potentially co-operate in such a pervasive way). It is also described by the term *ambient intelligence* when acting in concert to provide services and, more recently, by the term *everywhere* computing.

Cloud computing is a little more down-to-earth, being where multiple distributed machines connected, usually by the Internet, co-operate to share processing. The cloud is dynamically changing, with machines joining and leaving, and yet the overall computing service continues (or at least should do so). Sometimes *virtualisation* technology is run on the different connected computers to make them appear uniform within the cloud. Thus, the virtualised machines form the cluster. The analogy of the cloud comes from the way in which the Internet is depicted as a cloud in many network diagrams. Where this type of arrangement is more formalised it is referred to as *grid computing*. This is a form of organised cluster where the networked machines may be distributed and may, as in cloud computing, actually be PCs sitting on people's desks. The analogy of a grid comes from the idea of a power grid, which interconnects producers and consumers so as to share resources and balance loads more evenly.

Many of the companies operating the largest clouds or grids, will sell computing time on these systems, priced in terms of CPU seconds or similar. The idea is that the entire cost of these services should be lower than the cost incurred by a company setting up and running its own cluster computing service. Some of the server farms which provide these services are huge, occupying areas larger than a football field. One of the smaller, but more aesthetic examples of a cluster machine is the Barcelona Supercomputer, the Mare Nostrum, shown in Section 1.4.

9.3.2 Clusters of Small Machines

Even a decade ago it was almost unthinkable to combine the topics of parallel computing and embedded systems. However, today there are more and more examples of overlap between the two fields.

There are in fact two major impacts of large-scale parallelism on embedded systems that we will consider here. The first is when embedded (usually portable) systems offload their computing needs onto a fixed centralised computer. The second is the opposite; when hitherto centralised computation becomes portable as the parallel processing itself becomes embedded.

9.3.2.1 Offloading Processing from Embedded Systems

So firstly, the idea of pervasive computing is that of computing being everywhere, and connected. Given that we are surrounded by always-on computing resource, this should be used when appropriate. Rather than designing a power-hungry computer inside an embedded device, the argument goes, it is better to have a wirelessly connected embedded device – the computing happens in powerful fixed computers, and the result is conveyed wirelessly to the embedded device. Consider the case of a portable media player. This carries a display and audio hardware, however, the actual material being presented could be stored and processed elsewhere and simply conveyed to the player using wireless.

This is an attractive vision of remote processing. It helps enormously to overcome the power limitations of portable systems (battery technology has not progressed at the same rate as the increase in processor power). However, the wireless technology necessary to achieve such a vision in a reliable and cost-effective way is currently lacking. Furthermore, it is interesting to note that all of the current potential contenders for providing such advanced wireless links, are themselves very complex and computationally intensive (in many cases, these are more computationally intensive than the main computer processing being conducted in the portable devices themselves).

Undoubtedly, there will be popular examples of future embedded systems offloading computing. However, issues of cost, reliability and availability probably mean that in the near future these will be confined more to niche applications, apart from the existing modes of connection in the mobile telephony industry.

The second impact of large-scale parallelism on embedded systems, the incorporation of parallel processing into the embedded systems themselves, is here with us today. We discussed the dual-core ARM946 in Section 5.8.1, and can find many cases of multiple soft cores implemented in embedded FPGA designs. However, true embedded cluster computers are more limited, but will become more prevalent in time. We will discuss one of the earliest embedded cluster processing designs to be built, the parallel processing unit (PPU).

9.3.2.2 The Parallel Processing Unit

The parallel processing unit (PPU) was designed to provide high-reliability computer services in a microsatellite (i.e. a satellite weighing up to 100 kg). The satellite was designed to capture images from a 500 km high orbit, process these on board and then downlink them to the ground.

We know from Section 7.10 that the space environment contains cosmic radiation that makes electronics unreliable, and so most satellite designers choose to design using radiation hardened or radiation-tolerant CPUs. Unfortunately, due to the manufacturing, testing and qualification processes involved, these devices tend to be very expensive, difficult to procure, not at all power efficient and rather slow. Most microsatellites contain 8086-era processors and few exceed operating speeds of 10 MIPS. Even so, satellite computer designers are a conservative bunch (albeit with good reason – few would want to risk wasting a million dollar launch to a risky on-board computer), and typically derate processors so that they operate at half of the maximum clock speed specified by the manufacturer.

With such feeble on-board computers, it is no wonder that satellites do not tend to perform processing on board. Most simply capture information and then download this to ground-based computers for processing. Clearly this runs counter to the trend for more powerful computing at the mobile end of a communications link. This is not the forum to argue the advantages and disadvantages of such approaches, but only to note the small but growing movement towards improving the capability of satellite on-board computers using commercial off-the-shelf (COTS) CPUs.

The PPU uses this approach. It is designed around Intel StrongARM (SA1110 CPUs, now sadly discontinued by Intel) which operate at 200 MHz and are arbitrated through two radiation-tolerant field programmable gate arrays (FPGAs). Since any COTS processor is unlikely to survive long in space, there are in fact 20 separate CPUs provided in the PPU, and the system is designed to accommodate the expected gradual failure of these over time. Using published radiation-tolerance information, the PPU is designed so that at the end of its designated lifetime of three years, sufficient CPUs will still be alive for the PPU to maintain its mission objectives.

A PPU is shown in block diagram form in Figure 9.5. It can be seen that the two Actel AX1000 FPGAs each accommodate ten processing nodes (PNs). Each PN connects to its FPGA over a dedicated parallel bus which will be explained a little later. Within the FPGAs, a time-slotted global backplane (TGB) bus, operating like a token-ring system, sends messages and data between nodes. Each PN has its own dedicated TGB node, as do external connections, internal configurable processing modules (PM) and status register (SR). The external connections are to solid-state recorder, a large array of flash memory storage, and to a controller area network (CAN) bus, arbitrated by C515C controllers. The CAN bus conveys control information to and from the PPU. The two FPGAs connect together using low-voltage differential signalling (LVDS – see Section 6.3.2), over which the TGB normally traverses, and LVDS is also used for fast data connections to the solid-state recorders (and incidentally also to the camera module and high-speed data download radio).

Operating code for the PNs is stored in flash memory. There are three identical copies of the code connected to each FPGA in a triple redundant fashion (see Section 7.10).

The entire design showcases the concept of 'reliability through redundancy' and is built from the bottom up with reliability in mind. Consider some of the reliability features of the design:

- Replicated PNs – With so many PNs, failure of a few can be tolerated so that the system will continue working.

Figure 9.5

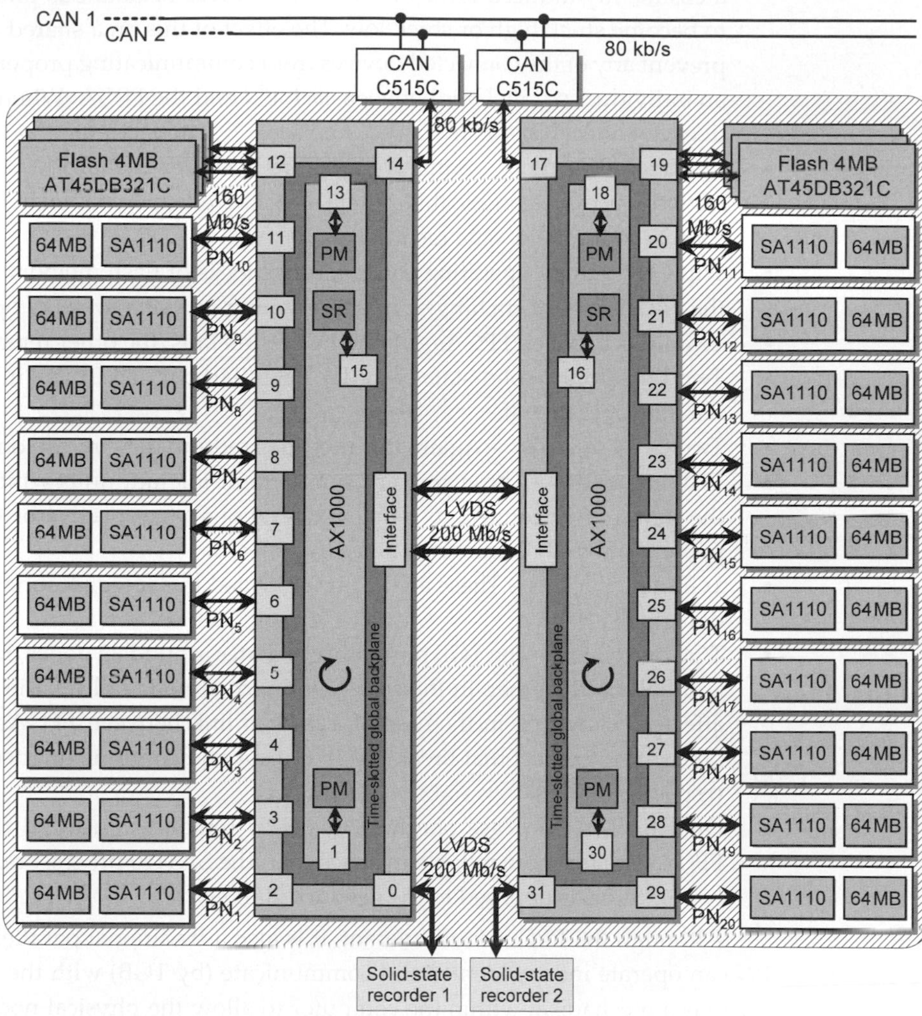

A block diagram of a parallel processing unit (PPU), showing 20 processing nodes (PNs), each containing an SA1110 CPU and 64 Mbytes of local memory connected to a local Actel AX1000 FPGA using dedicated buses. Two FPGAs each host 10 PNs and connect to one solid-state recorder and one controller area network (CAN) bus. The two FPGAs inter-link using dual bidirectional low-voltage differential signalling (LVDS) connections. A time-slotted global backplane bus conveys data between PNs, external links, internal configurable processing modules (PM) and internal status registers (SR).

- Individual buses – If the PNs shared a common bus, then it is quite possible for a cosmic ray induced error to cause the address or data bus pins to fail, usually to become stuck high or stuck low. The effect of this on a shared bus would be to prevent any of the connected devices from communicating properly. Thus, there is an individual parallel bus between each PN and the FPGA. When a PN 'dies', this does not affect other PNs.
- Distributed memory – Similarly, a failure in shared memory would affect all connected processors, and so this system does not rely upon any shared memory except for that in the solid-state recorder.
- Triple redundant operating code – Three blocks of flash memory per FPGA allow the FPGA to perform bitwise majority voting on every word of operating code.
- Two links between FPGAs – If one LVDS link fails, the other remains operational.
- Two links to the solid-state recorder – Similarly, if one LVDS link fails, the other remains operational.
- Two CAN bus links – Again, this provides redundancy in case one fails.
- TGB bus nodes – These are very simple fault-tolerant units which track whether the device they connect to remains operational. Irrespective of this, they do not prevent onwards communications on the TGB.
- TGB data packets – These are parity protected in source, destination address and data fields.
- TGB bus circuit – The TGB normally circulates around 32 nodes, half on one FPGA and half on the other. In the case of individual node failure, the bus remains unaffected. However, in the case of a broken link between FPGAs, the TGB buses on each side detect that break, 'heal' the cut and continue unaffected within their respective halves.
- Dual FPGAs – In case one fails, the PPU remains. Since the radiation-tolerant FPGAs are far more reliable in space than the SA1110 processors, we only require two of these as opposed to the need for 20 PNs.

Although the PPU is fault tolerant, it is also a traditional parallel processor. Each PN can operate independently and communicate (by TGB) with the nodes around it. There is a mechanism within the computer to allow the physical node numbers (0, 1, 2, up to 31) to be remapped into various types of logical connection, including any of those we will encounter in Section 9.3.4.

In fact, an example of this remapping can be seen in Figure 9.6. The node which 'launches' any PN by handing it a computational task can restrict the connectivity of that PN to just itself, or to other PNs, leading to a very flexible set of operating arrangements.

At start-of-life, when all resources are operating correctly, the PPU has a respectable specification for an embedded computer (especially one that was designed almost a decade ago), of 4000 MIPS, consuming 6 Watts of electrical power in a 1800 cm^2 package (about the same size as a small notebook computer). A typical microsatellite on-board computer will be 200 times slower, two or three times as big and consume a similar amount of power. In addition, it would cost around ten times as much – although cost is rarely the primary consideration during satellite design.

Figure 9.6

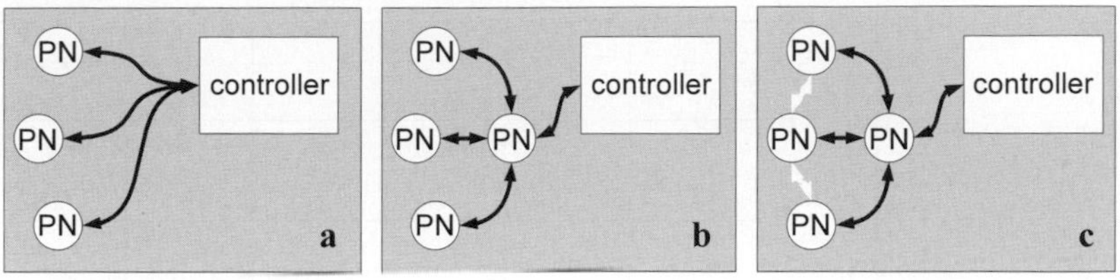

The remapping of PNs within a PPU and the establishment of links between the PNs can result in several alternative interconnection strategies to be used. In this case, diagram (a) shows three PNs operating independently, perhaps as a three-way majority voter arbitrated by an external controller. Diagram (b) shows that the majority voting process itself has been offloaded from the controller onto a PN which has in turn called upon three other PNs to co-operate. Diagram (c) then shows four PNs fully interconnected, with one responsible for interactions with the controller.

Although there are several further interesting design features of the PPU, including an unusual 17-bit parallel data bus arrangement for optimal data transfer speed, it is the parallelism that is the focus of this section. With that in mind, consider Figure 9.7 in which the speed-up has been plotted for an image processing job shared across several processors. Speed-up, defined in Section 5.8.2, indicates how well a system is able to parallelise its computation. Perfect speed-up (shown as a diagonal line in Figure 9.7) means that a job will run n times faster on n processors than it does on one. The example algorithm running on the PPU does not achieve perfect speed-up, but does very clearly benefit from increased parallelism.

9.3.3 Parallel and Cluster Processing Considerations

Parallel processing system design issues might include the following:

- How many processors are required?
- How should they be interconnected?
- What capabilities should each processor have?
- Should the system be homogeneous or heterogeneous, that is, should all CPUs be the same or should there be a mixture?

If n processors are in use, then the completion time, as we have seen, may not equal an nth of the time taken by a single processor – even in a homogeneous system. The actual time may be more or even less than an nth of the time taken by a single processor. It all depends on the original *single-thread* implementation and the parallel implementation. Some calculation problems can be divided easily into a number of subtasks where the data transfer between these subtasks is small. Given this, each subtask could be allocated to a different processing unit. In other systems this process may not be so simple.

Figure 9.7

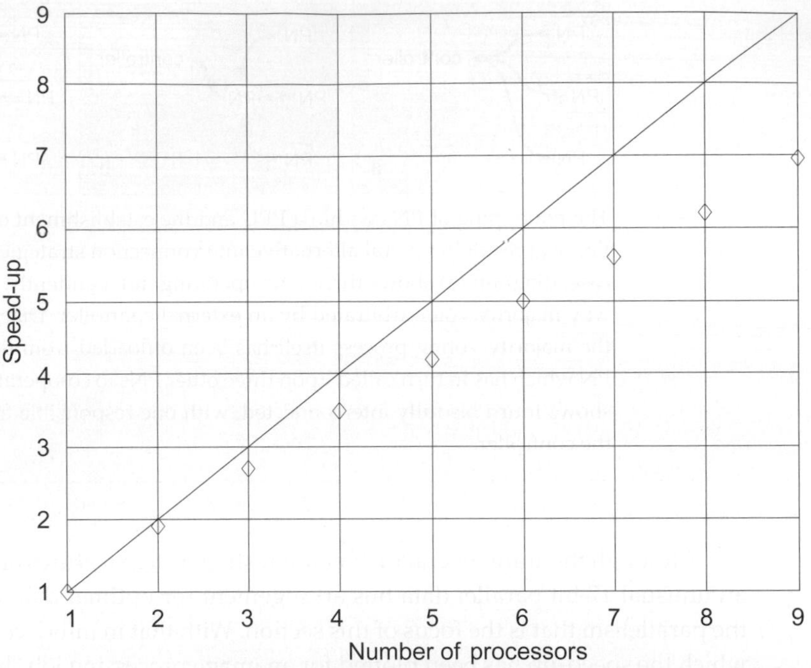

The degree of speed-up achieved within a PPU by sharing an image processing job among up to nine PNs, with perfect speed-up indicated by the diagonal line. Clearly, the PPU does not achieve perfect speed-up, but does evidently benefit from parallel processing. This result was obtained by PPU co-inventor Dr Timo Bretschneider and his students for processing involving unsupervised image classification tasks.

With subtasks of unequal complexity, the system could benefit from being heterogeneous – consisting of processors of different capabilities. The inter-linking of processors could even follow the requirements of the calculation to be solved, that is, heterogeneous interconnection is also possible. However, the control of such a system becomes more complex – especially if the dividing up of tasks is to be accomplished dynamically, and given different types of processors which are themselves being dynamically chosen.

9.3.4 Interconnection Strategies

Let us consider a more general system with identical (homogeneous) processors, which we shall refer to as *nodes*. If these nodes are linked in a regular fashion, two main system design issues are the type of interconnection used and the number or arrangement of interconnections.

Interconnection type will define the bandwidth of data which can travel over the link and the latency of messages passed. Example types are Ethernet, ATM

Figure 9.8 Six different parallel interconnection arrangements, showing computational nodes as dots and links between these as lines.

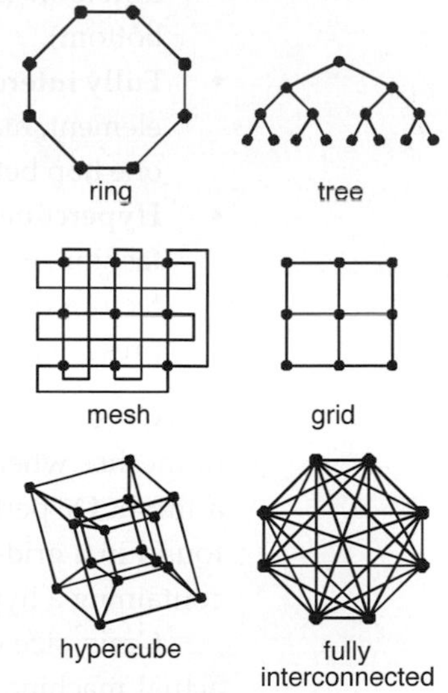

(asynchronous transfer mode), optical interconnects and InfiniBand. These vary widely by both bandwidth and cost.

In addition, there are two paradigms of distributed parallel processing systems, with many variations in between – these paradigms are shared memory and message passing. Message passing uses structured methods to communicate between nodes, such as message passing interface (MPI), and is well-suited to loosely coupled tasks that require low-bandwidth data interconnects. Shared memory is useful when separate processors operate on the same source data or need to communicate with high bandwidth. Shared memory systems of this type were considered in the discussion of the MESI cache coherence protocol in Section 4.4.7.

The number of interconnections that each node possesses limits the number of other nodes that it can be connected with. At one extreme is the possibility of being fully connected to all other nodes. On the premise that connection between processors is relatively slow, a fully-linked system minimises data transfer duration since each transfer is one hop. At the other extreme is a ring structure where each node connects to two others. These, and several other common interconnection strategies are shown in Figure 9.8 and explained below.

- **Ring** – Each element needs to support two connections. It is scalable with no changes in the elements. There are potentially many data hops between target nodes.
- **Tree** – Each element (apart from the top and bottom layers) needs to support three connections. It is easily scalable and software data paths are simplified, but may require many data hops between nodes.
- **Mesh** – Each element needs to support four connections. It is easily scalable, but the data paths can be complex and require many hops. A *grid* is similar but

differs in the provision of wraparound edge connections (i.e. left right and top bottom).

- **Fully interconnected** – Each element needs to support a connection to every other element, making this very difficult to scale. However, there is a maximum of only one hop between nodes.
- **Hypercube** – Each element needs to support only four connections in a tetrahedral fashion, while data path hops are also minimised. In many cases, this is the architecture of choice: sometimes simply because it sounds so high-tech in company press releases.

Of course, there is no reason why hybrid schemes cannot exist. For example, a ring of meshes where each 'node' around the ring is itself a set of machines connected as a mesh. Or perhaps a more common example is a grid of hypercubes that could be found in a grid-connected parallel processing centre with each vertex within the grid containing a hypercube processor.

Grain size describes the level of parallelism. In the most fine-grained machines, actual machine instructions are issued in parallel (such as vector machines or VLIW processors) while course-grained machines can run large software routines in parallel. This relates to the discussion in Section 5.8.

With an abstraction such as MPI, course-grained parallel algorithms can execute in different program instances. It does not matter whether these are run all on one CPU or across multiple CPUs. Similarly, it does not matter whether these CPUs reside in a single box, in several boxes with a data centre or in several geographical locations within a cloud or grid computer.

Course-gained machines tend to be loosely coupled, whereas fine-grained machines tend to be more tightly coupled. The amount of data transfer between elements specifies the speed of the data connection between them, and the number of hops the data must traverse has both bandwidth and latency considerations (i.e. if inter-processor data must traverse two hops then each hop must be capable of twice the bandwidth). Data transfer requirements also have a bearing on memory architecture such as whether each processing element should use local memory or shared memory as mentioned previously. Local memory machines may have distributed memory or may simply use multiple copies of cached memory. Some examples of large-scale parallel processing machines are shown in Box 9.2.

9.4 Asynchronous Processors

All common modern CPUs are synchronous in operation, meaning that they are clocked by one or more global clocks (and domains) such as a processor clock, memory clock, system clock, instruction clock, bus clock and so on.

Within a particular clock domain – being the physical area on-chip that contains elements acted upon by the same clock – flip-flops and units built upon the basic flip-flop, will be synchronous, operating together. The speed of clock is determined for a

Box 9.2

Examples of parallel processing machines

Roadrunner, the fastest supercomputer at the time of writing, lives in Los Alamos Labs, New Mexico, USA. It is actually a cluster of IBM machines, comprising 6912 dual-core 1.8 GHz AMD Opteron processors and 12,960 IBM PowerXCell 8i Cell processors (Section 5.8.3) running at 3.2 GHz. There is slightly over 103 Tibytes of RAM split evenly between the Opteron and Cell units, and all machines are interconnected by Infiniband. The total number of cores (remember each Cell processor contains nine and each Opteron two), is over 130,000. The operating system powering this computer is, of course, Linux. Overall, this system can achieve a peak speed of 1.71 petaFLOPS (1 petaFLOP is 10^{15} FLOPS – see Section 3.5.2), but consumes 2.35 MWatts of electricity, about as much as a small UK town.

Eka, India's fastest supercomputer (and the current number 13 worldwide), built for prominent conglomerate Tata, achieves about 172 TeraFLOPS using 0.786 MWatts of electricity. Comprising 14,240 cores spread over 1800 nodes of 3 GHz Intel Xeon 53xx processors, this Linux-powered computer is said to have been built as a money-making venture on the basis that companies would pay to run their jobs on such a powerful beast.

DeepComp 7000 is China's most prominent supercomputer, installed at the Computer Network Information Center, Chinese Academy of Science. This Linux machine consists of 12,216 cores of Infiniband-connected 3 GHz Intel Xeon E54xx processors currently and ranks as the world's 19th fastest supercomputer. It peaks around 145 TeraFLOPS. In recent years, Chinese machines have been making great progress up the league table, and are clearly set to leapfrog the UK and USA, the traditional supercomputer leaders.

Conspicuously absent are Google's server farms. If these ran as a cluster they would in all likelihood top any list of powerful computers. However, Google and its competitors are secretive concerning their installations. Little is said publicly, and Google reveals almost nothing itself. Thus, the Tata Eka remains as one of the few private industry machines open to public scrutiny.

particular domain with the upper limit being set by the *slowest* individual element. Typically, this means that many individual elements could operate faster, but are held back by the slowest one.

For example, an ALU takes its input from two holding registers, and one clock cycle later, latches the result into an output register. If performing an ADD, the operation may be completed only just in time – perhaps the result is ready only 0.01 clock cycle early. However, if the operation is something simpler, such as an AND which has no carry propagation, then the operation may be ready far earlier – perhaps 0.9 clock cycle early. So depending upon what the ALU is doing, it is either almost fully occupied or is sitting waiting for its result to be collected. Irrespective, the fixed processor clock which controls it will be set to the slowest operation.

An analysis of ALU operation would then probably reveal that for a substantial amount of time, the unit lies idle. This indicates a low usage efficiency. There are several techniques to overcome these efficiency limitations, including allowing parallel operation (i.e. several events occur simultaneously rather than sequentially) and pipelining. Pipelining breaks up the individual elements into smaller, faster, elements which then overlap with each other in operation. Since each individual element is now faster, the overall clock speed can increase.

One very unusual technique is to allow asynchronous operation. An asynchronous processor allows each operation to perform at full speed without wasting parts of a clock cycle. In fact, there may be no need to have a clock at all since each individual element operates at maximum speed, informing the control hardware when the operation is complete.

The following are advantages of the synchronous approach:

- Simpler to design and there is more design experience of this approach.
- Almost, if not all, CPU design tools assume a clocked design.
- Eliminates race conditions.
- Predictable delays.

The synchronous approach is not without its disadvantages:

- At higher speeds, clock skew becomes a problem.
- Almost all latches and gates switch in time with the clock (whether or not there is any new data to process). Since complementary metal oxide semiconductor (CMOS) power usage is mostly caused by switching, this leads to relatively high power dissipation.
- Performance is less than the theoretical maximum (parts of cycles wasted due to operation at the speed of the slowest element).
- Large areas of silicon are devoted to clock generation and distribution.

Moving to an asynchronous approach makes sense, although each individual asynchronous element still has to be interfaced with its neighbours – and this requires some form of synchronisation, but not necessarily with a global clock. Such synchronisation may be relatively simple, but being replicated across an integrated circuit for many elements will result in extra logic.

In theory, an asynchronous processor should operate at lower power but at higher speed than the similar synchronous processor. However, the designer has to pay careful attention to the possibility of race conditions occurring. Avoiding these may actually make the asynchronous processor slightly larger than the synchronous processor.

One example of an asynchronous processor (in fact the world's only commercial asynchronous architecture at the time of writing) is the AMULET. This was designed at Manchester University in the UK, based on the very popular ARM processor. In the design of the AMULET, certain problems had to be overcome. We will consider some of these and the approach the designers used to solve them in the following sections.

Figure 9.9

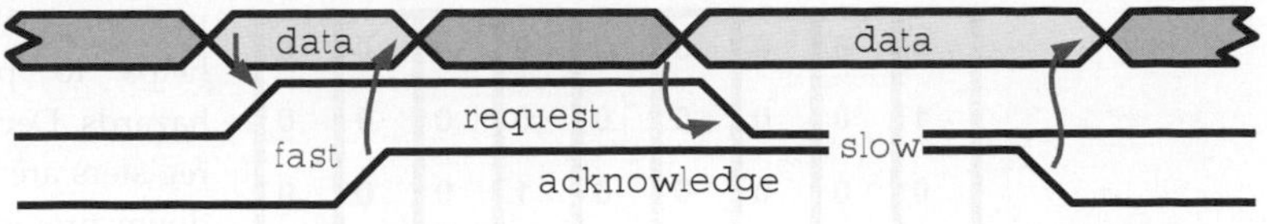

Request-acknowledge bus transactions for asynchronous bus communications.

9.4.1 Data Flow Control

If there is no reference clock within the processor, then how can data flow from one unit to the next be controlled? AMULET uses a technique known as request-acknowledge handshaking, which follows the following sequence of events for a unidirectional parallel bus:

1. Sender drives its data onto the bus.
2. Sender issues a request event.
3. When ready, receiver reads the data from the bus.
4. Receiver then issues an acknowledge event.
5. Sender can then remove data from the bus.

The request and acknowledge signals are two separate wires running alongside a standard bus. Figure 9.9 illustrates these edge-sensitive (transition encoded) signals in use.

Use of request-acknowledge signalling allows each element to be self-timed. The AMULET pipeline elements each operate at different (optimal) speeds depending on the actual instructions being executed. In other words, a unit performing a simple operation will complete very quickly, whereas one performing a more complex operation will take longer. In the worst case, the pipeline is the same speed as if it was synchronously clocked (which means it is clocked as slow as the slowest element – so it is performing a continuous sequence of the slowest instruction). However, in any real-world application, the pipeline would operate faster than the fully synchronous version.

9.4.2 Avoiding Pipeline Hazards

If instructions complete at different, possibly unknown, times, how can read after write hazards be avoided within the pipeline?

Since the processor shares a load-store architecture with its parent, the ARM, almost all CPU operands are register-to-register. So a method is needed to prevent an instruction reading from a register that has not yet been updated by the result of a previous instruction.

The solution is a method of register locking based on a register-lock first-in first-out (FIFO). When an instruction is issued that needs to write to a particular register, it places a lock in the FIFO, and then clears this when the result is written. When an instruction needs to read a register, the FIFO is examined to look for locks associated with that register. If a lock exists, the register read is paused until that register entry in the FIFO clears.

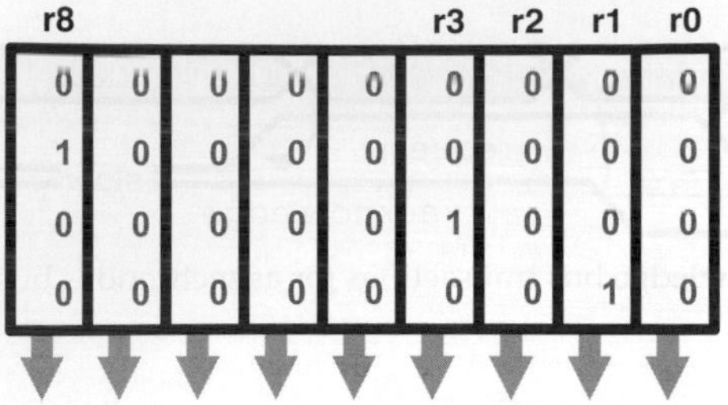

Figure 9.10 The register-locking hardware in the AMULET processor helps to prevent pipeline hazards. Decoded destination registers are fed from the top down, providing an indication of the sequence of following register writes at any one time.

An example is given in Figure 9.10 which shows the first eight register-lock FIFOs, and the locks corresponding to pipeline position being entered from the top and flowing downwards in step with the corresponding flow through the pipeline. In the program that is running, the result of the first instruction goes to r1 (and the lock is then removed). The result of the second instruction goes to r3 (and that lock is then cleared). The result of the third instruction goes to r8 (and that lock too is cleared). At the current time, instructions that read from r1, r3 or r8 will pause until the instructions currently in the pipeline that write to any of those registers have completed.

While register locking solves potential read-after-write hazards, it has been shown to result in frequent pipeline stalls, so more recent AMULET processor developments utilise register forwarding techniques that have been adapted for asynchronous use.

9.5 Alternative Number Format Systems

Looking at the world of computers and CPUs today, we see a profusion of binary logic devices, where a logic 1 is represented by a high voltage level and a logic 0 by a low voltage level. A binary word consists of several such bits – typically 4, 8, 16, 24, 32 or 64. Whether two's complement or unsigned numbers are used, the weighting of each bit in the binary word represents a power of 2. Floating point extends the concept further to represent mantissa and exponent separately, but these are also binary words, with weightings based on powers of 2.

Analogue computers were a refreshing alternative, but these were phased out in the 1980s as digital computers became faster, cheaper, smaller and more accurate. It seems that the world has converged on digital binary systems for their computing needs.

However, there are some research alternatives with niche applications that may well become mainstream in time. These will be explored in the following sections.

9.5.1 Multiple-Valued Logic

Faster and faster clock speeds have been the rule for several years in the computing industry, but there are limits. True, these limits shift outwards regularly, but they do constrain progress. As we have seen in Chapter 6, if clock rate is constrained, more data can be shifted down a bus by having more wires in parallel. Or by clocking data on both edges of a clock (known as double data rate or DDR).

There is another alternative though, and this is to allow voltage changes so that each wire can carry more information. This can be done by using multiple-valued logic. For example, encoding two bits of a word into a range of four voltages:

`00`	0.0 v
`01`	1.7 v
`10`	3.3 v
`11`	5.0 v

This is rather different from the CMOS voltage levels commonly used in electronics, and requires more complicated driver and detection circuitry, but doubles the amount of data that can be represented on a single wire. It does reduce the noise immunity of the data when compared to a system utilising two (binary) voltage levels. A CPU that uses such logic would need to consider analogue as well as digital design issues. With reduced noise immunity it would also be less tolerant to noise and interference spikes, but could convey more data faster.

Although the author knows of no commercial CPUs utilising such methods at present, this technique has found a niche application in memory storage. Intel, in common with other vendors of flash memory, is continually under pressure to deliver 'larger' devices – meaning devices that can store more bits of memory in a given volume. Manufacturers have typically relied on reduced silicon feature sizes to allow smaller transistors which can be packed more densely into an integrated circuit. However, Intel produced a more radical design several years ago, which allows two bits of data to be stored in a single transistor cell, using a multiple-valued logic approach. Intel markets such devices as StrataFlash (® Intel) which have found widespread adoption in mobile phones, MP3 players and personal digital assistants (PDAs).

Note that there are diminishing gains as the number of multiple values increases – moving from 1 to 2 bits means halving the voltage threshold (but doubling the amount of data that can be represented). Moving from 2 to 3 bits means halving the threshold again (but only increasing data representation by 50%). This shows the decreasing returns, coupled with increased noise sensitivity that tend to limit the technique in practice to 2 bits per cell/transistor/wire.

One final point here is the effect of cosmic ray irradiation as mentioned briefly in Section 7.10, where the occurrence of Single Event Upsets (SEU) was discussed. Since a cosmic ray impinging on a silicon gate induces a change in stored charge, this manifests itself as a voltage fluctuation. Multiple-valued logic devices exhibit reduced immunity to voltage noise, implying that such devices are best avoided in systems that may be used in high-altitude locations such as on aeroplanes, in electronic climbing equipment and in consumer electronics destined for Mexico City or Lhasa.

9.5.2 Signed Digit Number Representation

Signed digit (SD) is an extension of binary representation such that there is redundancy (i.e. there is more than one way to represent each number). The redundancy comes about by introducing the possibility of a sign for each digit, and gives a degree of freedom to represent a number.

By sign, this means that each bit position in a digital word using SD could hold a '1', a '0' or a '−1', although the actual bit position weightings are the same as for a standard binary number. Of course, there is an obvious disadvantage with this: negative digits must be handled in every bit position (rather than just in the most significant bit for two's complement). However, this disadvantage is negligible because binary adders perform both addition and subtraction in almost identical ways with no extra hardware needed.

Some SD examples are shown in the table below which gives some of the many alternative ways that the number equivalent to decimal value 3 could be written:

SD vector	Value	Weight
(0 0 0 0 1 1)	$2+1=3$	2
(0 0 0 1 0 −1)	$4-1=3$	2
(0 0 1 −1 0 −1)	$8-4-1=3$	3
(0 1 −1 −1 0 −1)	$16-8-4-1=3$	4
(1 −1 −1 −1 0 −1)	$32-16-8-4-1=3$	5
(0 0 1 −1 −1 1)	$8-4-2+1=3$	4
(0 1 −1 −1 −1 1)	$16-8-4-2+1=3$	5
(1 −1 −1 −1 −1 1)	$32-16-8-4-2+1=3$	6

We shall see later that choosing an alternative with more zero digits will require fewer operations when implementing adders and, particularly, multipliers. We define the *weight* of a signed digit number as the total number of non-zero digits used to represent that number. A lower weight is better because it would result in a faster partial product multiply.

A radix-2 binary number can be converted to SD representation using the following algorithm:

Let $a_{-1}, a_{-2}, ...a_b$ denote a binary number, and the desired SD representation be $c_{-1}, c_{-2}, ...c_b$. Each bit in the SD representation may be determined through:

$$c_{-1} = a_{-i-1} - a_{-1} \text{ where } i = b, b{-}1, ..., 1$$

where $a_{-b-1} = 0$.

In order to better exploit the redundancy involved in this representation when it is used in an FPGA or similar system, ensure that there are as few non-zero digits as possible within the number representation. This can be achieved through the employment of a *minimal signed digit vector*. This is the one (or possibly many) SD representation among the alternatives that has the minimum weight.

All the examples in the table shown earlier represent the same number (3), with the first or second entries in the table having the minimum weight (2) and are thus the minimum signed digit vectors for decimal 3. Note the second row (0 0 0 1 0 −1) which is a minimum signed digit vector. Additionally, there is a zero digit between the two non-zero digits. It is, in fact, possible to prove that for every number a SD alternative exists where there are no non-zero digits next to each other. Sometimes there is more than one alternative where this is the case. These numbers are called canonical.

Hence, canonical signed digit (CSD) numbers are minimum signed digit vectors that are guaranteed to have at least one zero between any two non-zero digits.

Apart from the reduction in hardware that results from having many zeros in a calculation, there is another excellent reason for selecting a CSD number. This relates to the parallel adder of Section 2.4.2 where the maximum speed at which additions can occur is limited by the propagation of a carry bit upwards. Of course, there is the carry look-ahead or prediction technique, but this requires large amounts of logic when the number of bits in the operand words becomes large. However, if we can guarantee that for a non-zero digit the next most significant digit is always a zero, there can be no upwards carry propagation from that point.

In this way, performing addition calculations using CSD numbers is extremely fast: there is no carry propagation problem.

Let us now look at one method of generating such a number (this method is discussed in the excellent *Computer Arithmetic: Principles, Architecture and Design* by Kai Hwang, published in 1979).

We start with an $(n+1)$ digit binary number denoted by vector $B = b_n b_{n-1} \ldots b_1 b_0$ where $b_n = 0$ and each element $b_i \in \{0, 1\}$ for $0 \leq i \leq n-1$. From this, we want to find the $(n+1)$ length canonical signed digit (CSD) vector $D = d_n d_{n-1} \ldots d_1 d_0$ with $d_n = 0$ and $d_i \in \{1, 0, -1\}$. Within their own formats, both B and D should represent the same value.

Remember that in terms of determining the value of a number (and in fact any signed digit vector including SD, CSD and so on), the normal rules of binary apply in relation to the weighting value of each bit position:

$$\alpha = \sum_{i=0}^{n} b_i \times 2^i = \sum_{i=0}^{n} d_i \times 2^i$$

The heuristic described below, based on the method by Hwang, is a simple but logical method of obtaining the CSD representation of a binary number:

Step 1	Start with the least significant bit in B and set the index $i = 0$ and initial carry $c_0 = 0$.
Step 2	Take two adjacent bits from B, b_{i+1} and b_i and the carry c_i and use these to generate the next carry c_{i+1}. The carry is generated in the same way as for full addition: thus, $c_{i+1} = 1$ iff[1] there are two or three 1's among $\{b_{i+1}, b_i, c_i\}$.
Step 3	Calculate the current digit in the CSD word from $d_i = b_i + c_i - 2c_{i+1}$.
Step 4	Increment i and go to step 2. Terminate when $i = n$.

Notice that before the calculation, the most significant bit of the original binary number is fixed at 0 (and thus the number of bit positions is effectively lengthened by one bit). Thus, the CSD representation may have one extra digit over and above binary. See Box 9.3 for another example of a CSD number.

[1] 'iff' means 'if and only if'.

Alternative Number Format Systems

Box 9.3

Example of a CSD number

Let us consider the following 8-bit binary number:
`(0 1 0 1 0 1 1 1)` which has a value in decimal of 87.

Applying Hwang's heuristic, the CSD representation becomes

`(0 1 0 -1 0 -1 0 0 -1)` with a value of 128 – 32 – 8 – 1 = 87.

In his example, since it is canonical, there are no adjacent non-zero digits in the resulting number and the weight of the CSD number is 4.

9.6 Optical Computation

Advanced researchers have turned to some novel technologies to try and improve CPU performance. In this section two interesting ideas based on optical processing are presented.

Any digital computer needs to rely on the existence of a switch. Optical switching technologies have received significant amounts of research effort over the past two decades or so, however, miniature all-optical switches are still elusive laboratory creations for the most part. Integrated optics is a branch of optical technology that attempts to build optical circuitry on silicon and other substrates using fabrication technology similar to electronic integrated circuits (and sometimes mixed with electronics on the same substrate). Current commercial devices using such technology include multiplexers and filters.

Although all-optical computers is the major research goal, hybrid electro-optical systems have found several applications in recent years inside computers. The driving factor behind the adoption of optical signals is their speed: signals travel at the speed of light. Several signals can co-exist in the same physical location without interfering with each other (i.e. crossed beams of light) and optical interference is easier to control than electrical.

9.6.1 The Electro-Optical Full Adder

Remember the carry-propagate delay in the full adder of Section 2.4.2? The problem encountered was that the output is not available until the carry has propagated from the least to the most significant bit. This upwards propagation delay then becomes the major limiting factor on adder speed.

The electro-optical full adder works on the principle of making the carry operate at the speed of light. The carry circuitry is shown in Figure 9.11, where the important things to note are that bits x and y are input as electrical signals, whereas the carry in and carry out are optical (light beams).

$$c_{OUT} = x.y + x.c_{IN} + y.c_{IN}$$

For such a structure arranged as a parallel adder, C_{in} is fed from the C_{out} of the

Figure 9.11

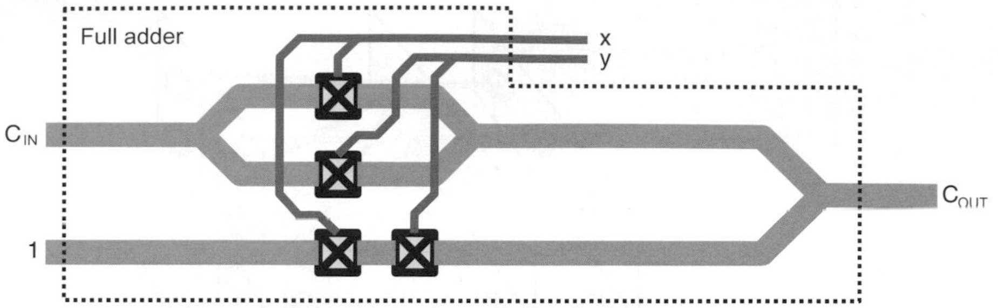

The electro-optical full adder combines electronic switches and light paths to create a very fast adder not limited by the propagation speed through layers of logic gates.

next less significant bit. There are two switch elements per bit, and these switch as soon as the input bits are present. In other words, all switches, for all bit calculations happen simultaneously. The optical carries propagate at the speed of light through the entire structure. Further circuitry (not shown) is used to calculate the output result for each bit position (which depends upon the input bits and the C_{in}, which has just been determined). This is less important because, once the carries have all been resolved, at the speed of light, the actual bit additions can take place as normal.

Compare this technique to the propagation delay of a standard n-bit full adder, which is n times the delay of a single add element (which itself is the propagation delay of several AND and OR gates). This is one technique of many optically-assisted elements that comprise current research topics in computer architecture.

9.6.2 The Electro-Optical Backplane

As buses become wider (64 bits or more for both data and address), a larger number of signals have to be connected between modules or blocks within a computer. These are also becoming faster clocked, therefore both causing more electromagnetic interference (EMI), and more signals to be susceptible to EMI. This complicates the job of designing buses, such that 12 or 16 layer printed circuit boards (PCBs) are not uncommon for embedded computer designs. In particular, it can be difficult on PCBs in regions where large buses must cross, or worst of all (from an EMI perspective) the presence of long parallel runs of bus lines.

One solution to this involves electro-optical technology. In this case, the big advantage of optics is the ability of beams of light to intersect or run close together without causing mutual interference. The advantages of optical interconnects have been demonstrated in optical backplanes. These use individual laser diodes for every signal output and individual photodiodes for every signal input. Transmission holograms are used to route signals to receiver arrays as shown in Figure 9.12.

Optical backplanes have no maximum clock speed (they are limited only by the laser diode modulation and photodiode bandwidth), and the clock speed can be very fast – at least in the GHz range. They also allow hot-insertion (multiple cards can be

Figure 9.12

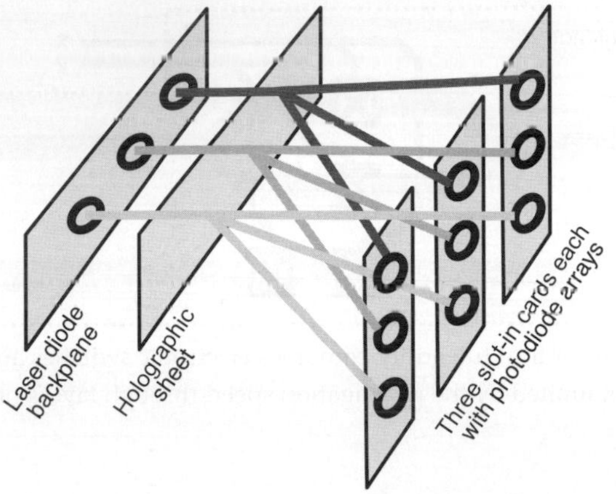

The electro-optical backplane uses a holographic sheet to split optical signal beams in free space from laser diode (or LED) transmitters into multiple receiver arrays, perhaps located on physically separate slot-in cards.

unslotted, and slotted in while the system is running but the backplane signals do not change). By contrast, fast electrical buses require termination which varies with the load so that fast buses generally cannot support hot-insertion.

With no electrical contacts to corrode, degrade, or become mechanically worn, such systems can achieve very high reliability.

However, careful alignment of slot-in cards is required so that the signal beams hit only the correct photodiode. This assumes that the beams propagate through free space, although it is entirely possible that the same technique could be used in other optically-transparent media, such as silicates.

9.7 Science Fiction or Future Reality?

Maybe this section should not exist. It cannot be examined and is not core syllabus for any computer architecture course that the author has seen. However, let us consider this your reward for reaching here after working through the entire book: a glimpse of some of the wild and wonderful ideas taking shape at the fringes of the computing research arena.

9.7.1 Distributed Computing

As mentioned in the preface, the world of computing is becoming more and more embedded. It is interesting that this trend coincides with another – the shift towards wireless connectivity. As technology progresses, the logical convergence point is a future in which humans may be outnumbered several thousand to one by miniaturised processing units that are interconnected by wireless networks. Even though most of these processors will be nominally dedicated to particular functions (such as a microwave processor, a telephone processor or a central heating/air conditioning processor), it is quite likely that at any given time many of them will not be required for their nominal functions.

Simply allowing idle processors to communicate and co-operate would make available an aggregate computing power several orders of magnitude greater than that available in a current desktop PC. Given new forms of human-computer interfacing and advances in software, we may each expect to be able to interact with our own dedicated computer personality. This personality would be hosted on a constantly changing set of basic processors, but would present a consistent interface to the user. It would be a distributed computer program, remotely accessible and existing as our personal assistants.

Does this sound like science fiction? The basic technology exists today.

9.7.2 Wetware

Perhaps moving further into the realm of science fiction, if current advances in genetics and bio-computation continue, we could start to see viable computation performed on biological machines during the next decade.

This is not so far-fetched when we consider that the most complex and capable computer available today is located inside our heads. In addition, advances in medical analysis techniques are constantly unveiling more and more details on the operation of the human, and mammalian, brain. The attraction here is computing capability: human ingenuity, despite decades of progress, has not yet invented a computer that can approach the abilities of his own brain, except in the single area of fast computation of fixed calculating tasks. In almost all other processing comparisons, the human (or even mammalian) brain wins. Since nature has designed such amazing computing machines biologically, perhaps we can either emulate these designs, or learn to harness them directly.

Several potential futures can be identified here. Most simple is the use of biological and/or chemical building blocks for performing computation. Something like an artificial biological computer, where processing is performed on artificial biological neurones, perhaps based on the structure of the human brain. At the very least, a biological transistor (controlled switch) has already been demonstrated, so we know that logic functionality is possible. However, it is likely that novel structures would be better suited to biological computation rather than simply copying the methods used with silicon into a biological construct. For example, fuzzy associative sets rather than discrete binary computation.

The second potential future is the augmentation of the human brain with artificial intelligence. Direct interfacing with the brain and nervous system has been performed for decades using electrical sensors and stimulators. Examples include vision systems for the blind and cochlear implants for the hearing-impaired. It does not require a wild imagination to envisage the interfacing of computer units to the brain in a kind of 'co-processor' arrangement. At the very least this could aid in the ever-present research topic of human-computer interaction.

Personally, the author is quite happy with his brain the way it is, but a natural progression into the future could see artificial neural aids being developed for people with disabilities, including learning disabilities, and then shifting into augmentation of non-disabled people. Such augmentation could take many forms, but might include a higher-bandwidth computer interface for realistic gaming, a memory-recall device and access to senses beyond the five natural ones of sight, sound, smell, touch and taste. The possibilities are endless once the basic problems of making a brain-compatible interface are solved, but the real advance will be augmentation with an artificial all-biological computer (at least that means you do not have to carry a battery around).

9.8 Summary

In this chapter, we have tried to plumb the depths of the future of computers. We began with some fairly safe bets – single-bit architectures, VLIW, parallel and asynchronous systems (safe in that each of these is an established technique, already with us, albeit largely confined to specialist processing applications these days). Parallel processing seems to be on the agenda for Intel's future: with dual-core, quad-core and eight-core processors being available, it does not take a large leap of imagination to see this trend continuing. Massively parallel computing is also a safe bet since most of us enjoy the benefits that such computation bring to the world, used by the likes of Google and Amazon.com.

This chapter also provided an overview of alternative number formats, encompassing another class of techniques that not only have significant penetration in niche computing areas but also the potential for impacting the future of mainstream computing.

Beyond this, we considered electro-optical hybrids which, despite having been technically feasible for over two decades, have yet to make any major impact in the computing world.

Finally, science fiction. Let us be honest: science fiction was the path that led many of us into the study of science and engineering in the first place. Whether it is the sonic screwdriver and TARDIS of Dr Who, the phasor arrays and transporter of the Starship Enterprise or the droids and lightsabres in Star Wars, most engineers have been impacted strongly by technologically-inspired imaginations. Let us try and maintain that 'cool' technology factor, and while self-aware computers may be a little beyond our reach, we can and will collectively make great, inspired leaps that are *revolutionary* rather than just *evolutionary*.

APPENDIX A

Standard Notation for Memory Size

Most people are taught the International System of Units (abbreviated SI) at school, in which the prefix of the unit denotes the power of 10. For example, a millimetre is 10^{-3} metre, a centimetre is 10^{-2} metre and a kilometre is 10^{3} metres.

Here are some of the more useful prefixes:

Prefix name	Prefix letter	Multiplier
exa	E	10^{18}
peta	P	10^{15}
tera	T	10^{12}
giga	G	10^{9}
mega	M	10^{6}
kilo	k	10^{3}
milli	m	10^{-3}
micro	μ	10^{-6}
nano	n	10^{-9}
pico	p	10^{-12}

However, when it comes to counting computer memory sizes, which are constructed in powers of 2: 2, 4, 8, 16, 32, 64 and so on, the SI units are inconvenient and confusing.

The reason is that it turns out 2^{10}, being equal to 1024, is too close to 1000 and so the value of 2^{10} has come to be referred to as a 'kilo'. Thus, in popular usage 1 kbyte is actually 1024 bytes, which is not the correct SI definition of a 'kilo'. While this discrepancy may be fine for everyday usage, there are many occasions when it is necessary to be more precise and where the non-SI usage can become confusing.

Thus, the International Electrotechnical Commission (IEC) has introduced a new and non-ambiguous set of terms for the storage of computer data, similar to, but distinct from the SI units. In the range of sizes useful for computers, these prefixes are as follows:

Prefix name	Prefix letter	Multiplier
exbi	Ei	2^{60}
pebi	Pi	2^{50}
tebi	Ti	2^{40}
gibi	Gi	2^{30}
mebi	Mi	2^{20}
kibi	Ki	2^{10}

Thus, a computer hard disc having a capacity of 1 TiByte (tebibyte), actually contains 1,099,511,627,776 bytes, which is almost 10% more than a hard disc having a 1 TByte (terabyte) capacity (1,000,000,000,000 bytes).

Throughout this book, the IEC units, ratified by the IEEE and others, have been adopted wherever appropriate.

Examples

128 Kibytes
128 KiB
128 Kibibytes
Means $128 \times 2^{10} = 131{,}072$ bytes

20 Mibytes
20 MiB
20 Mebibytes
Means $20 \times 2^{20} = 20{,}971{,}520$ bytes

500 Pibytes
500 PiB
500 Pebibytes
Means $500 \times 2^{50} = 562.96 \times 10^{15}$ bytes

APPENDIX B

Open Systems Interconnection Model

B.1 Introduction

The Open Systems Interconnection (OSI) model or reference system, was formalised by the Open Systems Interconnection (OSI) initiative of the ITU (International Telecommunications Union), recommendation X.200 working with the ISO (International Standards Organisation) as a way of classifying computer interconnections.

Now that we know the various abbreviations, we will use 'OSI' to refer to the model itself. This model has a number of layers which are used to divide up computer connections by their logical connectivity and functionality. These layers can be referred to by layer number or by their name, as we will see later.

The OSI model is commonly applied to networking protocols, but in this book we restricted our use of the model to the 'lower layers', that is, those closer to the hardware. It is used in discussion of communications and bus systems in particular, to separate out protocols from low-level hardware and voltage details.

To those readers who have not yet encountered the OSI model, this type of classification may seem a little unnecessary. However, be assured that it does simplify systems design and understanding when things get complicated in embedded systems, hence our brief introduction.

B.2 The OSI Layers

The basic OSI model consists of seven layers, stacked horizontally. From the bottom up, these encompass everything from bit-level signalling to the application which makes use of that signalling (e.g. spanning the intermediate steps from voltage transitions on a 1000BASE-T Ethernet cable up to an Internet banking system).[1]

[1] Note that the TCP/IP layered model and the OSI model apply the same principles but slightly different naming and layering.

OSI layer	Layer name	Data unit
7	Application	Data
6	Presentation	Data
5	Session	Data
4	Transport	Segment
3	Network	Packet
2	Data link	Frame
1	Physical	Bit

The idea is that each layer communicates only with the layers immediately above and below them on the stack, and that such communications are strictly defined. Thus, developers of one layer need only be concerned with the communications to neighbouring layers. These subdivisions allow for more regularity in communications, and in theory higher reliability.

Layers 1, 2 and 3 are concerned with transmission media, whereas layers 4 to 7 are termed host layers. There is a greater tendency for lower layers to be implemented in hardware and for higher layers to be implemented in software (and some would say that code size increases from the bottom up). Next, let us consider the media layers individually.

Layer 1: Physical

The physical layer encompasses the electrical connectivity of a unit to a communications medium, for example, the wires, timings and voltages within a data bus. The physical layer is responsible for ensuring that the unit can 'talk to' and 'listen to' the medium of transmission (which could be wire transmission, wireless transmission, optical transmission and so on).

This layer is responsible for establishing a connection to a medium, to participate in a scheme allowing units to share that medium (where appropriate), in converting outgoing signals from logical bits into the format expected by the medium, and in converting received signals to logical bits.

Basically, it translates logical requests for communication originating with the data link layer into the hardware-specific transmission or reception of signals. In computer networking, the device which handles the physical layer is often called a 'PHY'.

Layer 2: Data Link

The data link layer (DLL) imposes a point-to-point or (multi)point-to-multipoint structure onto the physical communications handled by layer 1. Often, it is required to handle errors that occur in the physical layer so that in such cases it presents an error-free frame interface to the network layer.

There are actually two sub-layers in the DLL: the media access control (MAC) and logical link control (LLC). If these are present, the MAC interfaces with the physical layer and the LLC interfaces with the network layer. The MAC layer frames up data to be transmitted, verifies the frames of received data and provides arbitration, flow control and so on for situations where the media of transmission is shared by multiple units. The LLC, by contrast, handles errors and flow control within the higher layers.

Some physical (PHY) devices also contain a MAC, and thus are called 'MACPHY' devices.

Layer 3: Network

The network layer allows for the transmission or reception of information packets, which could be of variable sizes. The communications here is end to end, in that the network layer can send and receive packets to and from a specified recipient. The actual means of achieving such requests are the functions of lower layers.

Layers 1 to 3, and Beyond

The layers above these three are termed the host layers. They are responsible for transporting quanta of information between specified hosts, establishing and maintaining communications sessions between these hosts, allowing for different information to share links and for interfacing to a particular application. Although these are highly important to Internet-based applications, they tend to fall outside the realm of embedded computer architecture, thus we concentrate instead upon the lower three layers.

As an example of the OSI system, consider a packet of information that is to be transmitted. This is passed to the data link layer along with addressing information to indicate where it is to go. The data link layer splits the message into frames and maybe codes this message before passing bits to the physical layer for transmission. The physical layer then modulates the wires by driving high and low voltages along the wires in a specific way at a given timing to transmit the data, either in parallel or in serial.

B.3 Summary

Several layer 1 examples have been described in this book, primarily in Section 6.3, including LVDS, EIA232 and so on. We have also discussed one or two layer 2 examples such as Ethernet. However, many of the bus systems we discussed, such as USB, SCSI and so on, actually encompass the lower two or three layers of the model.

The important point here is that, although systems such as EIA232 and USB define physical connections, abstractions such as the OSI model allow them to be transparent to whatever the higher layers wish to transmit. For example, both EIA232 and USB can allow a PC to connect to the Internet and communicate TCP/IP packets (which in turn can convey hypertext transport protocol, HTTP web pages). USB can also convey files to a thumb drive, or audio data to or from external sound hardware.

It is this flexibility – thinking in terms of abstract layers – that is characteristic of many modern systems, particularly so as networking interconnection becomes increasingly ubiquitous.

APPENDIX C

Exploring Trade-Offs in Cache Size and Arrangement

C.1 Introduction

This appendix will describe the use of two software tools, Dinero and Cacti, to evaluate and investigate cache configurations.[1] Cacti is an integrated model describing cache access time, cycle time, area, aspect ratio and power consumption. It is intended for use by computer architects to better understand performance trade-offs inherent in different cache sizes and arrangements. Dinero is a trace-driven cache simulator that uses an input trace plus cache design parameters to determine performance (primarily measured in terms of hit rate). A trace is a sequence of memory references accessed by a program (which can include both instruction and data memory), either obtained by the interpretative execution of a program or through the incorporation of debugging code into the program by a compiler.

The authors of both Cacti and Dinero: Premkishore Shivakumar and Norm Jouppi at Hewlett-Packard Research labs and Mark Hill and Jan Edler, respectively are to be acknowledged for creating and releasing these tools. Note that both Dinero and Cacti are copyrighted software rather than open source. However, the respective authors have made the code available for non-commerical and academic use.

C.2 Preparation

As in other examples in this book, the reader is assumed to have access to a standard computer running Linux. Any modern version of the operating system will suffice, although the author tends to prefer either Kubuntu or Mandrake. It is also possible (although not as easy) to run these tools under MacOS-X and on Cygwin in Microsoft Windows. All 'action' occurs on the command line.

[1] The particular versions we introduce, Dinero IV and Cacti 3.2 will advance over time, so naturally the specific options and instructions may change. However, the performance investigation remains valid.

1. Download the Cacti 3.2 source distribution from:
   `http://www.hpl.hp.com/personal/Norman_Jouppi/cacti4.html`
   The required file is **cacti3.2.tar.gz**, which can be found under the link called gzip'ed tar file in the section relating to Cacti 3.2. Other repositories for this file can also be found using an Internet search engine.
2. Download the Dinero IV source distribution from:
   `http://www.cs.wisc.edu/markhill/DineroIV`
   The required file is **d4-7.tar.gz**, located under the link labeled Wisconsin. This file can also be found elsewhere through an Internet search.

There is also an online version of Cacti, available at:
`http://www.ece.ubc.ca/~stevew/cacti/`

C.3 Installing Cacti and Dinero

1. **Copy** the source files (**cacti3.2.tar.gz** and **d4-7.tar.gz**) to a working directory.
2. **Building Cacti:**

   Create a new directory called cacti:

   ```
   mkdir cacti
   cd cacti
   tar xvzf  ../cacti3.2.tar.gz
   make
   ```

   This produces the Cacti executable.

   ```
   cd ../
   ```

3. **Building Dinero:**

   ```
   tar xvzf d4-7.tar.gz
   ```

   This creates a sub-directory called d4-7.

   ```
   cd d4-7
   ./configure
   make
   ```

   This produces the Dinero IV executable.

   ```
   cd ../
   ```

C.4 Meet the Tools

In order to illustrate both Cacti and Dinero, we will construct an experiment in which we will be designing separate instruction and data caches as if we were designing a cache for an embedded processor. We will specify an area constraint for each cache, and using this we will need to maximise the cache performance when it runs a test program.

First, we will run through the design process that will be used.

1. Cacti can be used to 'create' a cache:

   ```
   ./cacti/cacti C B A X Y
   ```

   where C is the size of the cache in bytes (i.e. its capacity), B is the block size and A is the associativity. In this case, we will set X = Y = 1.
2. We can execute Cacti on an example cache, giving some parameters for C and B. Note that it prints out a lot of information when it runs. Looking over this information we will see the **Total area One subbank** output field. This gives the area that the specified cache design will occupy.
3. Often, we will need to produce several cache designs using different input parameters, in each case noting down the cache area for each design.
4. To run Dinero IV, we use the following command (all on one line):

   ```
   ./d4-7/dineroIV cache-config -informat p
   < d4-7/testing/mm.32
   ```

   where *cache-config* is one of the following two lines:

   For I-cache: `-l1-isize` *`capacity`* `-l1-ibsize` *`block-size`* `-l1-iassoc` *`associativity`*

   For D-cache: `-l1-dsize` *`capacity`* `-l1-dbsize` *`block-size`* `-l1-dassoc` *`associativity`*

   `-l1` means level 1, `-isize` means instruction cache size and `-dassoc` means data cache associativity. The input `mm.32` is our test file to run on the cache, and is included within the Dinero IV package.

   If we execute Dinero IV on the example cache (from item 2), we will see that again, a lot of information is produced by this program. Dinero IV can simulate an instruction cache and a data cache simultaneously. However, to prevent confusion we will be looking at each separately (because we will look at the number of misses as our performance measure, and so each cache works independently – except that they both have to share in the limited area constraints. The important field to look for is **Total Demand misses**.
5. As we progress and attempt different designs in order to explore trade-offs, we will need to note down the Total Demand misses from each of the designs we try.

C.5 Experimenting with Different Trade-Offs

In order to illustrate how these tools can be used, we will specify that we wish to use an area of no more than 0.90 cm^2 for each cache. This is a realistic approach for designers of 'real' CPUs who are trying to allocate silicon area on their integrated circuits. It is also a realistic approach for FPGA designers who are specifying cache memory for a soft-core processor within an FPGA – and we believe that this is the more usual scenario for readers of this book. The units, in this case, square centimetres, will change for each usage case, but the trade-offs will remain the same.

Assuming a Harvard architecture (see Section 2.1.2), we will create both an *I-cache* and a *D-cache*. We will adjust the design parameters to obtain maximum performance (measured as total number of misses, $I_{misses} + D_{misses}$).

The parameters we will vary for each cache are: *cache size*, *associativity* and *block size*. These parameters define a multi-dimensional design exploration space. An exhaustive test would have us tying every combination (however, that truly is exhausting rather than exhaustive), so usually it is possible to run several designs to identify how the results vary over the exploration space, and then subsequently 'narrow in' on an optimal design.

In this case, we can simplify matters by restricting the values we use. Firstly, we should only use values that are *powers of* 2 (e.g. 1, 4, ..., 8192 and so on). Secondly, given the size specified, some experience would dictate that we restrict the associativity to a *maximum of 32* and the block size to values in the range of *8 to 64 bytes*. All other values can safely be left as the defaults used by the tools.

A solution will be specified as the design parameters for the instruction and data cache, the total cache area and the total number of misses, when running the trace file `mm.32` on the specified cache. In an embedded system, we could specify a 'real' trace file obtained from the code that is to be executed in the system. We would therefore be determining the absolutely best cache design for the actual software running on our hardware with the given area constraints.

C.6 Further Information in Cache Design

The following are a few useful hints that may help with the cache design process:

- *Hint 1*: First determine the combinations of cache design parameters that lead to the largest caches subject to the area constraints. One of them is probably the solution with the best possible performance.
- *Hint 2*: Since we are only considering the number of misses as the main performance measure, the measured performance of the two caches are independent of each other. Therefore, we run Dinero separately on the I-cache and the D-cache (i.e. we run Dinero with only an I-cache specified, then run Dinero with only a D-cache specified; combining the results would be equivalent to running Dinero with both I-cache and D-cache specified). If we consider other performance measures, we may wish to combine the cache search process.
- *Hint 3:* There are readme files for both Cacti and Dinero IV that provide information. Moreover, Dinero IV has some built-in help:

```
./dineroIV -help
```

It is also important to realise that we are ignoring several real-world performance factors in this appendix. Most important is the cache access time (ns per access, which is reported by Cacti), which varies with our design parameters and would affect the execution speed of the program just as much – if not more than the miss rate!

Also, the default settings used by Dinero IV and Cacti are reasonable assumptions, but in the real world we would need to set these based on the silicon feature size and characteristics of our silicon foundry, or separately upon FPGA design parameters.

In the real world we would also need to adjust parameters such as bus width and clock speed!

Despite this caution, the appendix does accurately portray the major trade-offs in cache design. It shows how these two tools can be used to explore the design space and to determine an optimal cache design given real constraints.

Problems

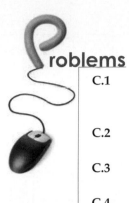

C.1 Complete the entries in Table C.1 with the sequence of solutions tested across the design space, and from this, determine the optimum cache design.

C.2 Note how cache design parameters relate to cache area across the design space.

C.3 Provide a reason, and justification for these observations.

C.4 What is the smallest area cache you can design that is no worse in performance than 95% of the best solution from question C.1?

Table C.1

Design exploration space record sheet for cache trade-off determination.

I-Cache Capacity (bytes)	I-Cache Block size (bytes)	I-Cache Assoc.	D-Cache Capacity (bytes)	D-Cache Block size (bytes)	D-Cache Assoc.	I-Cache Area (cm^2)	D-Cache Area (cm^2)	Total Area (cm^2)	I-Cache Misses	D-Cache Misses	Total Misses

APPENDIX D

Wireless Technology for Embedded Computers

D.1 Introduction

Wireless is a field that is advancing and evolving as fast as embedded computing. Although it is far from being a computer architecture topic, wireless is nevertheless a very important topic for embedded systems, as these are increasingly required to achieve wireless connectivity. It is indeed possible that wireless connectivity will become as ubiquitous as embedded computers are in the near future.

While large mainframe computers are designed for one purpose – number crunching – embedded systems are designed primarily for their application. If their design requirement is for connectivity, then this must be catered for from the architectural perspective in the same way that mainframes cater to data transfer and processing.

This appendix is dedicated to presenting the most important and prominent of the wireless connectivity systems in use today. Each will be described in general overview, and there is a discussion on available devices for use in an embedded computational system. Areas of particular interest (such as protocol stack requirements) will also be highlighted.

Unfortunately, the selection of wireless devices is very fluid – data rates and communication ranges seem to be increasing annually at the same time as power consumption is decreasing. New devices are introduced and old devices retired. Even in the time taken to read this appendix, it is likely that another new wireless device has been developed somewhere in the world.

This appendix will run through the main contenders for wireless connectivity (and some more unusual ones), ending with a summary table of devices, ranges, bandwidths and so on. Finally, a small application example will be given to consider adding wireless connectivity to a standard system-on-chip processor (in this case the ARM9-based Samsung S3C2410).

D.2 802.11a, b and g

The most famous of wireless network standards were approved by IEEE in late 1999 as part of the 802.11b standardisation effort. Shortly after that, the 802.11a standard was ratified, using a new encoding scheme – orthogonal frequency division multiplexing (OFDM) – to enable higher data rates and wireless channel availability. 802.11a is much faster than 802.11b, with a 54 Mbps maximum data rate in the 5 GHz frequency range, to 802.11b's 11 Mbps rate at 2.45 GHz.

The peak data rate of 802.11g networks sounds very promising, supposedly 54 Mbps. However, nearly half of the available bandwidth is consumed by transmission overheads. A Wi-Fi device typically requires between 30 to 100 mW of power to operate and has a maximum range of 50 to 100 m.

D.2.1 802.11a/b/g Solutions for Embedded Systems

Some currently available single-chip 802.11a/b/g Wi-Fi solutions include the following:

- Atheros have many devices for both fixed and mobile applications (e.g. AR54xx family – FBGA[1]: 13 mm × 13 mm).
- Broadcom BCM 4xxx and 5xxx series devices (e.g. BCM4328 – FBGA: 10 mm × 10 mm).
- CSR UniFi family (e.g. UF6026 in WLCSP[2]: 3.7 mm × 4.2 mm).
- Texas Instruments WiLink versions 4.0, 5.0 and 6.0 (e.g. WL1253 – BGA: 6 mm × 6 mm).

D.3 802.11n

Draft 802.11n products have been available on the market for some time and embedded in many consumer devices. IEEE 802.11n advertises data rates of 600 Mbps and guarantees a minimum throughput of 100 Mbps (after subtracting protocol management features like preambles, inter-frame spacing, acknowledgments and other overheads). It does this by using MIMO (Multiple in, Multiple out) technology.

Current 802.11n solutions tend to claim data rates of around 300 Mbps and a range of 50 m. At these speeds, access points (APs) need Gigabit Ethernet connections to the infrastructure to keep up with the air link.

D.3.1 Draft 802.11n Solutions for Embedded Systems

Chipsets that support draft 802.11n of the WLAN standard are available from each of the manufacturers listed in Section D.2.1, plus the following:

- Marvell TopDog.

[1] FBGA: fine pitch ball grid array.

[2] WLCSP: wafer-level chip scale packaging.

- Metalink (MtW8171/MtW8151).
- Qualcomm/Airgo (WFB4030/WFB4031).

Some of these are multi-chip solutions, but these days most are becoming available in a single-chip solution.

D.4 802.20

802.20, also known as Mobile Broadband Wireless Access (MBWA), is for operation in licensed frequency bands below 3.5 GHz, with peak data rate per user in excess of 1 Mbps. It supports various vehicular mobility classes up to 250 km/h in a metropolitan area network (MAN) environment with a range of up to 8 km.

D.5 802.16

802.16, also known as Worldwide Interoperability for Microwave Access (WiMAX), is a wireless broadband technology, supporting point to multi-point (PMP) wireless access. 802.16 was published in 2002 as a fixed-wireless standard based on line-of-sight (LOS) technology in order to provide T1/T3 levels of service to enterprises operating in locations where it was infeasible to run a physical fibre or copper infrastructure.

802.16 is targeted at business users and operates on licensed bands in the 10 to 66 GHz range over 20, 25 or 28 MHz channel widths and requires LOS between base station and user. Data rates of up to 134 Mbps can be achieved, but limited to a range of 2 to 5 km around the base station. There are several other variants of this technology, having different operating parameters, frequency bands, data rates, ranges and so on.

D.5.1 802.16 Solutions

Some manufacturers with currently available chipsets supporting the 802.16a/d standard are listed below:

- Atmel (e.g. AT86RF535B QFN-56: 8 mm × 8 mm).
- Fujitsu Microelectronics America, Inc. (e.g. MB87M3550 in a BGA-436 package).
- Intel (e.g. Intel PRO/Wireless 5116: PBGA-360).
- Sequans Communication (e.g. SQN1010 – PBGA-420: 23mm × 23mm).
- TeleCIS (e.g. TCW1620).

Some currently available chipsets that support 802.16e standard are listed below:

- Altair Semiconductor (e.g. ALT2150).
- Intel (e.g. Intel WiMAX Connection 2250: PBGA-360).
- NXP (e.g. UXF234XX – HVQFN48: 7 mm × 7 mm).
- Runcom Technologies Ltd (e.g. RNA2000/RNF2000).
- Sequans Communication (e.g. SQN1130 – VBGA-256: 11 mm × 11 mm).
- Wavesat (e.g. UMobile WiMAX Series).

D.6 Bluetooth

Bluetooth,[3] originally developed by Ericsson, but now a world standard, is a short-range communications technology intended to replace the cables connecting portable and/or fixed devices while maintaining high levels of security. Bluetooth-enabled devices connect and communicate wirelessly through short range, ad-hoc networks known as piconets.

Each device can simultaneously communicate with up to seven other devices within a single piconet. In addition, each device can belong to several piconets simultaneously. The piconets are established dynamically and automatically as Bluetooth-enabled devices enter and leave radio proximity. Version 2.0 + Enhanced Data Rate (EDR), adopted in November 2004, has a data rate of 3 Mbps.

Bluetooth technology operates in the unlicensed industrial, scientific and medical (ISM) band at 2.4 to 2.485 GHz and comes in several flavours or classes:

- Class 3 radios have a range of up to 1 m (maximum transmitter power is 1 mW).
- Class 2 radios, usually found in mobile devices, have a range of 10 m (maximum transmitter power is 2.5 mW).
- Class 1 radios, used mostly in industry, have a range of 100 m (maximum transmitter power is 100 mW).

There are also three security modes for Bluetooth access between two devices: Mode 1 which is actually non-secure, mode 2 which describes service level enforced security and mode 3 which enforces security at the link level.

Each Bluetooth device has two parameters that are involved in practically all aspects of Bluetooth communications. The first one is a unique 48-bit address assigned to each Bluetooth radio at manufacture time. The Bluetooth device address (BD_ADDR) is engraved on the Bluetooth hardware and it cannot be modified. The second parameter is a free-running 28-bit clock that ticks once every 312.5μs. which corresponds to half the residence time in a frequency when the radio hops at the nominal rate of 1600 hops/sec.

A Bluetooth device consumes around 30μA when in power save mode, and then takes a couple of seconds to wake up and respond. Having adopted the TCP/IP protocol, Bluetooth devices can actually communicate with any other device connected to the Internet.

D.6.1 Bluetooth Solutions

Some embedded Bluetooth chipsets are listed below:

- Broadcom (BCM20XX).
- CSR (BlueCore Series).

[3] Bluetooth is named after a mythical Norse 10th century king who united the far-flung Scandinavian tribes into a unified kingdom, presumably matching the ambitions of Ericsson towards Scandinavian neighbour Nokia.

- Infineon (PMB8753 – WFSGA-65: 5 mm × 5 mm and PBA31308).
- NXP (BGB210S – TFBGA-44: 3.0 mm × 5.0 mm).
- STMicroelectronic (STLC2500C – WFBGA-48: 4.5mm × 4.5mm).
- Texas Instruments (BRF6300 BlueLink 5.0).

Bluetooth 3.0 has been proposed at the time of writing, which could see data rates rise beyond 400 Mbps.

D.7 GSM

In 1982, the Conference of European Posts and Telegraphs (CEPT) convened a research group charged with developing a standard for a mobile telephone system that could be used across Europe. This group was called Groupe Speciale Mobile (GSM). By 1989, with a working system, the GSM group was transferred to the European Telecommunication Standards Institute (ETSI).

The acronym 'GSM' then changed from Groupe Speciale Mobile to Global System for Mobile Communications (to reflect new global ambitions as the standard spread out of Europe). GSM is now easily the most widely-used cell phone system in the world: an open, digital cellular technology used for transmitting mobile voice and data services. It is classed as a second generation (2G) cellular communication system.

Although GSM is great for voice communications, it only supports data transfer speeds of up to 9.6 kbps natively. It allows the transmission of basic data services in the SMS (Short Message Service), which can send 140 bytes, or when packed together in the usual way, allows 160 ASCII characters (140 × 8 bits/7 bits).

GSM was designed with a moderate level of security. It is able to authenticate the subscriber using shared secret cryptography. Communications between the subscriber and the base station can be encrypted. GSM only authenticates the user to the network (and not vice versa). The security model therefore offers confidentiality and authentication, but limited authorisation capabilities, and no non-repudiation. GSM uses several cryptographic algorithms for security, and although it is of reasonable strength, can be broken with some effort.

D.7.1 GSM Solutions

Some currently available GSM chipsets are listed below:

- Broadcom (e.g. BCM2124 – FBGA-296: 10 mm × 10 mm).
- Infineon E-GOLD series.
- NXP AeroFONE (PNX490 – PBGA: 10 mm × 10 mm and PNX4905 – PBGA: 12 mm × 12 mm).
- Texas Instruments (e.g. LoCosto ULCGSM TCS2305 and LoCosto ULCGSM TCS2315).

All the above chipsets also support General Packet Radio Service (GPRS).

D.8 GPRS

The extension of GSM to 2.5G is largely due to the General Packet Radio Service (GPRS). GPRS adds packet switching capability to GSM. With a GPRS connection, the phone is 'always on' and can transfer data immediately, giving users an access speed similar to that of a dial-up modem, but with the convenience of being able to connect from anywhere and at higher speeds: typically 32 to 48 kbps. Unlike basic GSM, data can be transferred at the same time as making a voice call. GPRS is a network overlay to the existing cellular network and uses the nature of IP (Internet protocol) transmissions to its advantage.

Since IP traffic is made of packets, the network does not need to have continuous data transmission. Thus, IP traffic can easily share channels. A user may be receiving or transmitting data while another one is reading information. The second user does not need to use the channel during this time. Hence, it makes packet networks more efficient than circuit switched networks (2G), where the channel would be in use, regardless of whether the user is transmitting data or not.

The class of a GPRS phone determines the speed at which data can be transferred. Technically, the class refers to the number of time slots available for uploads (sending data from the phone) or downloads (receiving data from the network). Each channel is divided into eight time slots, with a maximum sustained data transmission rate of 13.4 kbps. One of these time slots is used for control and normal allocation would reserve two slots for voice traffic as well.

The theoretically maximum possible speed is up to 171.2 kbps when eight slots are assigned at the same time to a single user. The maximum rate a user can have using a Type 4 + 1 device (four downlink time-slot and one uplink time-slot) is 53.6 kbps but in reality, speeds of 40 to 50 kbps can be expected. GPRS devices also have a classification related to their ability to handle GSM voice calls and GPRS connections: Class A mobile phones can be connected to both GPRS and GSM services simultaneously. Class B mobile phones can be attached to both GPRS and GSM services, using one service at a time. Class B enables making or receiving a voice call, or sending/receiving an SMS during a GPRS connection. During voice calls or SMS messaging, GPRS services are suspended and then resumed automatically after the call or SMS session has ended. Class C mobile phones are attached to either GPRS or GSM voice service. The user needs to switch manually between services.

D.9 ZigBee

Formally known as the IEEE 802.15.4 wireless personal area network (WPAN) standard, ZigBee, ratified in 2004 is targeted at embedded applications. ZigBee layers on top of 802.15.4 with mesh networking, security and applications control. The focus of network applications under ZigBee includes the aim of low power consumption, high density of nodes per network, low cost and simple implementation.

Three device types are specified, namely: Network Coordinator, Full Function Device (FFD) and Reduced Function Device (RFD). Only the FFD defines the full ZigBee functionality and can become a network co-ordinator. The RFD has limited resources and does not allow some advanced functions (such as routing) since it is a low-cost endpoint solution. Each ZigBee network has a designated FFD that is a network co-ordinator.

The co-ordinator acts as the administrator and takes care of organisation of the network. ZigBee has addressing space of up to 64-bit IEEE address devices and supports up to 65,535 separate networks. The different network topologies supported include: star, peer-to-peer and mesh. ZigBee has a master-slave configuration, well suited to networks of many infrequently used devices that talk via small data packets. This aspect means that ZigBee is well suited to building automation systems, the control of lighting, security sensors and so on.

Low latency is another important feature of ZigBee: when a ZigBee device is powered down (all circuitry switched off apart from a 32 kHz clock), it can wake up and transmit a packet in 15 ms. The latency also gives power consumption advantages (i.e. it is possible to blip a device on, transmit and then return to sleep mode almost immediately, for very low average power consumption).

The defined channels are numbered 0 (868 MHz), 1 to 10 (915 MHz) and 11 to 26 (2.4 GHz). Maximum data rates allowed for each of these frequency bands are fixed at 250 kbps (at 2405 to 2480 MHz worldwide), 40 kbps (at 902 to 928 MHz in the Americas), and 20 kbps (at 868.3 MHz in Europe). These are, of course, theoretical raw data rates rather than achievable ones. Due to the protocol overhead, the actual data rates will be lower than these.

The ZigBee packet length is up to 127 bytes including header and 16 bit checksum, with a data payload up to 104 bytes in length. The maximum output power of the radios is generally 1 mW giving a range of up to 75 m. ZigBee includes configurable options in software for encryption and authentication, key handling and frame protection. In terms of protocol stack size when connected to a controlling CPU, ZigBee requires about 32 KiB, but can define a limited variant down to about 4 KiB (which is considered very small).

D.9.1 ZigBee Solutions

Some ZigBee chipsets suitable for use in embedded computing systems are manufactured by the following companies:

- Atmel (e.g. AT86RF230 in PQFN-32 package: 5 mm × 5 mm).
- Freescale (e.g. MC132XX in LGA-64 package: 9 mm × 9 mm).
- Microchip (e.g. MRF24J40 in QFN-40 package: 6 mm × 6 mm).
- Texas Instruments (e.g. CC2420 in QLP-48 package: 7 mm × 7 mm).

D.10 Wireless USB

Wireless USB (WUSB) aims to expand upon the success of the wired USB standard: wired USB is generally considered to be user-friendly and reliable, and the wireless USB promoters group presumably hopes for a similar perception of their standard.

WUSB is designed for room-size ranges in a point-to-point 127-channel architecture (where one end of the link can be a 'hub' that services many other endpoints). Data rates of up to 480 Mbps are achievable at distances of up to 3 m, and 110 Mbps can be achieved over 10 m in a frequency band starting around 3 GHz (which means that this technology may not be licensed for use in quite a few territories).

In most respects, WUSB is similar to USB: easy to use, 127 addressable devices, same hub and spoke topology, same maximum data rate of 480 Mbps, same computer interface and so on.

D.10.1 Wireless USB Solutions

Some of the first few WUSB chipsets are available from the following companies:

- Alereon (e.g. AL5100 wireless transceiver plus AL5300 ARM-powered baseband processor and MAC).
- Atmel (e.g. AT76C503A in a 128-pin TQFP: 14 mm × 14 mm – and which contains an ARM7 processor for the baseband processing).
- Samsung (e.g. S3CR650B in a FBGA 8 mm × 8 mm package – interestingly, the 'S3' prefix to the part number is shared by the Samsung S3C2410, which we have discussed many times, and gives away the fact that the S3CR650B also contains an ARM processor core, specifically for the WUSB baseband processing).
- Wisair single-chip solution (WSR610 in a TFBGA package: 13 mm × 13 mm – guess which processor this contains? No prizes, it is also an ARM).

D.11 Near Field Communication

Near Field Communication (NFC) is one of the newest of the wirelesses networking technologies, providing dedicated short-range connectivity. NFC was jointly developed by Sony and NXP and provides intuitive, simple and safe communication between electronic devices over distances up to about 4 cm. It was approved as an ISO standard in 2003.

NFC operates at 13.56 MHz with a data rate up to 424 kbps, and is compatible with some other contactless approaches, such as ISO 14443A and ISO 14443B (used with Sony's FeliCa technology). Like NFC, both operate in the 13.56 MHz frequency range.

An NFC interface can operate in several modes which determine whether a device generates a radio frequency field of its own, or whether a device harvests its power from a radio frequency field generated by another device. If the device generates its own field it is called an *active* device, otherwise it is called a *passive* device.

NFC technology is probably aimed at mobile phone applications, but could be extended elsewhere for short distance communications (such as RFID – radio frequency identification tasks).

D.11.1 NFC Solutions

Some currently available chipsets are as follows:

- NXP (e.g. PN511 in a HVQFN40 package and PN531 in either HVQFN40 or TSSOP38 packages).
- Sony FeliCa family.

RedTacton is another low-power technology, but one which uses the human skin as a conductor. Hence, this is a protocol for human area networking (HAN). It was first demonstrated in 1996 by Thomas Zimmerman and Neil Gershenfeld of MIT MediaLab Based on their work, Nippon Telegraph and Telephone Corporation (NTT) conducted further research and development to create ElectAura-Net, which became RedTacton.

RedTacton safely turns the surface of the human body into a data transmission path at speeds up to 10 Mbps between body-mounted points. The three major functional features of RedTacton are highlighted below:

- A communications path can be created with a physical touch, triggering data flow between, for example, a body-mounted electronic sensor and an embedded computer. As another example, two people equipped with RedTacton devices could exchange data simply by shaking hands.
- RedTacton can utilise many materials as transmission medium apart from the human body so long as the material is conductive and dielectric, such as water and many other liquids, metallic fabric, some plastics, etc.
- Unlike wireless technologies, the transmission speed does not deteriorate even in the presence of large crowds of people all communicating at the same time in meeting rooms, auditoriums, stores, etc. This makes for an inherently reliable communications system. It would mean, for example, that an embedded computer device in one pocket could 'talk' to a device in another pocket, or query body-mounted sensors, shoe-mounted sensors, hearing aids and so on.

D.12 WiBro

Moving up the scale in terms of speed and complexity, Korea's WiBro (short for Wireless Broadband) is a wireless broadband service based on mobile WiMAX technology (IEEE 802.16e TDD OFDMA standard). This is a high-speed service delivering voice, data and video to users travelling at speeds of up to 120 km/h.

The WiBro specification is a subset of IEEE 802.16-2004, P802.16e and P802.16-2004 standards. In 2002, the South Korean Government allocated 100 MHz of spectrum in the 2.3 GHz region for this, allowing WiBro to offer an aggregate data throughput of 20 to 30 Mbps from base stations with a cell site radius of 1 to 5 km (in 10 MHz channels).

Samsung provides a PCMCIA-based WiBro access card, although several other manufacturers are developing chipsets for use by WiBro developers.

D.13 Wireless Device Summary

Table D.1 summarises much of the information presented in the previous sections. However, as mentioned in the introduction, this is a rapidly evolving field. The information in the table is up to date at the time of writing but will age rapidly as technology continues to advance. This is especially true of the information in the lower part of the table.

D.14 Application Example

To exemplify the selection criteria, imagine that we have been given an embedded ARM system, and it is required that this be augmented with wireless technology.

The system requirements include the following:

- A 200 MHz Samsung S3C2410 microprocessor having a 32-bit parallel bus interface and serial ports which support speeds up to 4 Mbps. (For the wide range of peripheral connectivity to the S3C2410, refer to Section 7.2 on page 291.)
- 32 MiB of SDRAM and 16 MiB of parallel-connected flash memory.
- A power budget that is no more than 1.5 W consumption.
- A data rate of 4 Mibits/s over 10 m around an office.
- We do not want to buy spectrum. Instead, an ISM band is preferred.
- A 3.3 v power supply rail.

We are quite fortunate in this instance: cost is not an issue (unlike in most 'real-world' developments). In terms of the 3.3 v power supply, one could use a linear regulator to reduce the voltage or step it up using a switched-mode regulator (which could approach 80% efficiency).

The frequency used needs to be in unlicensed ISM band. Since this involves public frequency, spectral efficiency is relatively unimportant, as are latency, security and start-up time. Potentially all the 200 MIPS of the microprocessor could be used to support wireless communications (since no upper figure for MIPS is given to support this), although a low-cost standalone single-chip solution would definitely be preferred, since that involves less development work (no software protocol writing or extensive testing required).

Based on the requirement of a 4 Mbps data transfer rate, one can eliminate many of the wireless technologies given in Table D.1. One is left with 802.11a/b/g/n, 802.16a/d/e, ElectAura-Net, WUSB and WiBro. WUSB is eliminated due to the use of a non-public frequency range.

Based on the distance requirement of 10 m, one can further eliminate ElectAura-Net from the list and, with a power budget of 1.5 W, one would probably choose the

Table D.1

Several of the more prominent wireless standards that are likely to be used within forthcoming embedded computer systems, along with several of their important operating parameters.

Technology	Frequency	Channel bandwidth	Maximum data rate	Typical data rate	Power requirement	Typical range
802.11a	5.0 GHz	20 MHz	54 Mbps	25 Mbps	50-1000 mW	25 m
802.11b	2.4 GHz	25 MHz	11 Mbps	5.5 Mbps	10-1000 mW	30 m
802.11g	2.4 GHz	25 MHz	54 Mbps	25 Mbps	10-1000 mw	50 m
802.11n	2.4/5 GHz	20/40 MHz	600 Mbps	300 Mbps	50-1000 mW	50 m
802.20	< 3.5 GHz	1.25/2.5 MHz	1 Mbps	-	-	3-8 km
802.16	10-66 GHz	20, 25, 28 MHz	33-134 Mbps	-	-	2-5 km
802.16a/d	2-11 GHz	1.5-22 MHz	75 Mbps	40 Mbps	250-2500 mW	10 km
802.16e	2-11 GHz	1.5-22 MHz	75 Mbps	15 Mbps	250-2500 mW	3 km
WiBro	2.6 GHz	10 MHz	20-30 Mbps	1-3 Mbps	250-2500 mW	1-5 km
Bluetooth	2.4 GHz	1 MHz	1-3 Mbps	0.7-2.1 Mbps	1-100 mW	1-100 m
GSM	0.8/0.9,1.8/1.9GHz	200 kHz	9.6-19.2 kbps	-	20-3000 mW	100 m-35 km
GPRS	0.8/0.9,1.8/1.9GHz	200 kHz	171 kbps	40-50 kbps	20-3000 mW	100 m-35 km
ZigBee	868-868.9 MHz	300/600 kHz	20 kpbs	-	1-1000 mW	10-75 m
ZigBee	902-928 MHz	300/600 kHz	40 kpbs	-	1-1000 mW	10-75 m
ZigBee	2400-2483.5 MHz	2 MHz	250kbps	-	1-1000 mW	10-75 m
WUSB	3.1-10.6 GHz	ultra wideband	480 Mbps	-	100-300 mW	10 m
NFC	13.56 MHz	-	424 kbps	-	-	0-20 cm
PAN	0.1-1 MHz	400 kHz	417 kbps	2400 bps	1.5 mW	0 cm
RedTacton	-	-	10 Mbps	-	> 100 mW	0 cm

802.11a/b/g technologies for implementation in this application example as they are the most power efficient based on distance requirement.

802.16a/d/e and WiBro might also exceed the power budget given. The 802.11n standard has not been finalised, thus it is also eliminated from the list. The added advantage of choosing 802.11a/b/g is that it is TCP/IP compatible.

To find a suitable single-chip solution, we can look up Section D.2.1. We should then refer to the datasheets of the devices listed, as well as search the Internet for any newer alternatives. Having searched among the available choices shown, the Broadcom BCM4328 looks interesting: it is a single chip supporting the IEEE802.11a/b/g standards with an integrated CPU to handle the communications protocols. The BCM4328 power requirement is for a 3.3 v power rail. This means that no step-up or step-down power supply regulation is needed. The BCM4328 also supports secure digital and USB2.0 host interfaces – the S3C2410 too supports secure digital, and USB1.1 interface. One would therefore be able to use the USB interface if the data rate does not exceed its maximum speed of 12 Mbps, otherwise one would need to use the secure digital interface which supports data rates of over 100 Mbps.

D.15 Summary

This appendix has taken a brief tour through the topic of adding wireless connectivity to an embedded computer system. Most of the common wireless contenders were presented and briefly described in turn, leading to a table summarising the various offerings.

Finally, a simple application example was presented showing how to add wireless connectivity to a Samsung S3C2410-based embedded system.

APPENDIX E

Tools for Compiling and Simulating TinyCPU

Many advanced tools exist currently for FPGA development. The main FPGA vendors provide their own software, often with a web version freely available for download, while the professional chip development companies supply their own tools, which are often used in industry, running on UNIX and Linux workstations, to develop the most advanced projects. Mentor Graphics ModelSim is perhaps the most common of these tools.

It is the author's recommendation that ModelSim be chosen for larger or more critical design projects. However, for rapid evaluation and lightweight testing we will present here a simple open source solution: Icarus Verilog,[1] combined with GTKwave[2] waveform viewer. Alternative options, especially for the waveform viewer, are also available.

E.1 Preparation and Obtaining Software

The software runs best, and of course fastest, on a Linux computer, preferably running `Kubuntu` or `Ubuntu` Linux. Since some readers may not have upgraded their PCs from Windows to Linux, they can first install `Wubi`[3] – this will create a large file on their 'C' drive and add an option to the Windows bootup menu, so that next time they reboot they can choose to run `Kubuntu`. To uninstall is equally easy. The large file can simply be deleted to remove the software. Mac operating system users can obtain and run both versions on their computers, or more competent users could simply build the software from source.

At this point, it is assumed that readers have a working Linux distribution or similar. `Kubuntu`/`Ubuntu` users can now proceed to install both items of software. At a shell window, type the following:

```
sudo apt-get install verilog gtkwave
```

1 http://www.icarus.com/eda/verilog/

2 http://gtkwave.sourceforge.net/

3 Simply download and run the `wubi` installer from http://wubi-installer.org, and then follow all instructions, choosing `kubuntu` or `ubuntu` as the distribution to install.

When prompted, provide your password. If this fails with the warning that you are not on the 'sudoers' list, then you will need to approach the administrator or root user of that computer. If apt fails to find or download the software, then simply perform a web search for 'gtkwave ubuntu package' or 'verilog ubuntu package', download the `.deb` file to your desktop, right click the mouse on this and choose the 'install package' option.

If all this works without error, you now have a working Verilog compiler and simulator (Icarus) and waveform viewer (GTKwave).

E.2 How to Compile and Simulate Your Verilog

As an example, let us use the TinyCPU stack from Section 8.7.6, reproduced in Listing E.1.

Listing E.1 stack.v

```
module stack(clk, reset, load, push, pop, d, qtop, qnext);
  parameter N = 8;

  input clk, reset, load, push, pop;
  input [15:0] d;
  output [15:0] qtop, qnext;
  reg [15:0] q [0:N-1];

  assign qtop = q[0];
  assign qnext = q[1];

  always @(posedge clk or negedge reset)
    if(!reset) q[0] <= 0;
    else if(load) q[0] <= d;
    else if(pop) q[0] <= q[1];

  integer i;
  always @(posedge clk or negedge reset)
    for(i=1;i< N-1;i=i+1)
      if(!reset) q[i] <= 0;
      else if(push) q[i] <= q[i-1];
      else if(pop) q[i] <= q[i+1];

  always @(posedge clk or negedge reset)
    if(!reset) q[N-1] <= 0;
    else if(push) q[N-1] <= q[N-2];

endmodule
```

Assuming that this was saved to a text file named 'stack.v' in the current directory, we would use Icarus Verilog to compile the Verilog source at a shell prompt as follows:

```
iverilog  -o stack  stack.v
```

This is telling the Icarus Verilog compiler (`iverilog`) to compile the Verilog source program `stack.v` and produce an output executable named `stack`, also in the current directory.

Unfortunately, this alone is not particularly useful; we have to specify the inputs or outputs for the program: doing so is the role of the test bench. Thus, we need to write a test bench to 'exercise' the Verilog module. Fortunately, we had created a test bench when we wrote the original code in Section 8.7.6.

This test bench could be used *as-is* if we were performing the simulation using ModelSim. However, for Icarus Verilog and some other tools, we would need to carefully specify which signals within the source code we want to examine during simulation, and where we want to store this information. The latter can be easily done with the Verilog `$dumpfile` simulation command:

```
$dumpfile("stack_tb.vcd")
```

whereas the former specification can be made within the clause that contains the signals being exercised using the Verilog `$dumpvars` simulation command:

```
$dumpvars(0, stack_tb);
```

There is one final point worthy of mention. Within all of our test benches, we had created a clock that runs forever. In the absence of any other information, our simulation (which runs until the completion of the activity specified in the test bench) would therefore also run forever. Thus, we can use another Verilog simulation command to end the simulation:

```
$finish;
```

The original test bench, modified with these operators, is shown in Listing E.2:

Listing E.2 stack_tb.v

```
`timescale 1ns / 1ps
module stack_tb;
reg clk, reset, load, push, pop;
reg [15:0] d;
wire [15:0] qtop;
wire [15:0] qnext;

stack stack0(.clk(clk), .reset(reset), .load(load), .push(push),
      .pop(pop), .d(d), .qtop(qtop), .qnext(qnext));

initial begin
```

(Continued)

Listing E.2 stack_tb.v (*Continued*)

```
  clk=0;
  forever
    #50 clk = ~clk;
end

initial begin

  $dumpfile("stack_tb.vcd");
  $dumpvars(0,stack_tb);

  reset=0; load=0; push=0; pop=0; d=0;
  #100 reset=1; push=1; d=16'h1111;
  #100 push=1; d=16'h2222;
  #100 push=1; d=16'h3333;
  #100 push=1; d=16'h4444;
  #100 push=1; d=16'h5555;
  #100 push=1; d=16'h6666;
  #100 push=1; d=16'h7777;
  #100 push=1; d=16'h8888;
  #100 push=1; d=16'hEEEE;
  #100 push=0; pop=1;
  #100 pop=1;
  #100 pop=1;
  #100 pop=1;
  #100 pop=1;
  #100 pop=1;
  #100 pop=1;
  #100 pop=1;
  #100 pop=0; load=1;  d=16'h1234;
  #100 load=0; pop=1;
  #100 $finish;
end
endmodule
```

We then need to compile this test bench together with the stack module being tested:

```
iverilog  -o stack_tb  stack.v stack_tb.v
```

which, as we had seen earlier, produces an executable output file, this time called `stack_tb`. Next, we perform the simulation of `stack_tb` using the Icarus Verilog `vvp` command:

```
vvp stack_tb
```

Once the simulation completes, and this should be quite quickly, a file will have been produced with the name that we had given in the `$dumpfile` command:

Figure E.1

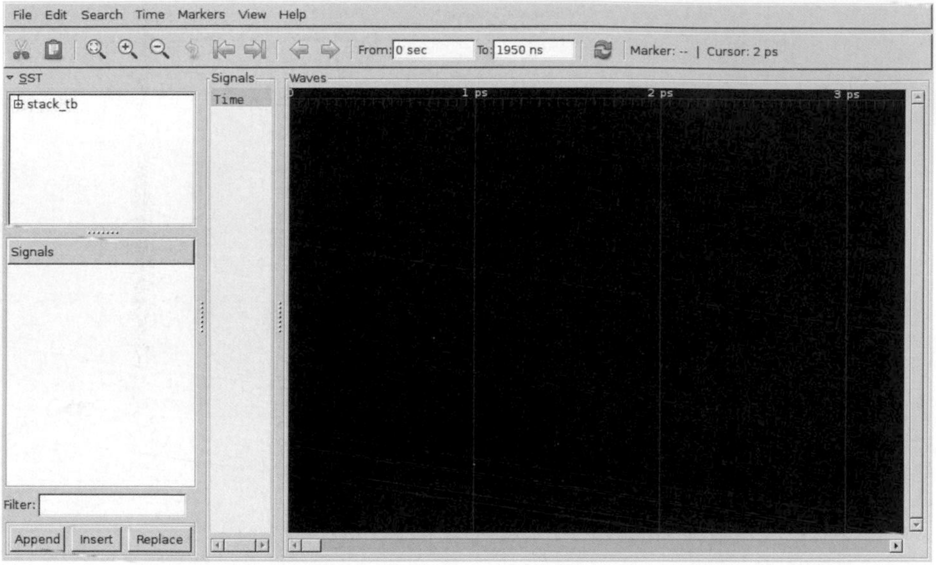

A screenshot of the GTKwave display prior to specifying signals to view.

`stack_tb.vcd` in this case. This value change dump (VCD) file, part of the Verilog standard, can be opened using a number of viewers. In our case, we will use GTKwave to open and display it:

```
gtkwave stack_tb.vcd &
```

This results in a blank waveform window display, as shown in Figure E.1. It is then necessary to expand the signals shown in the 'SST' box on the left-hand side of the display, and click on the '*stack0*' identifier that is then revealed, as shown in Figure E.2.

By selecting the required signals and clicking on 'Append', these can be added to the main display area. It is also usually a good idea to zoom this display out to the maximum extents by selecting **Time -> Zoom Full** from the main menu (or clicking on the magnifying glass icon containing the square frame-like symbol). Figure E.3 shows seven of the main signals added to the display, which has been zoomed out in the manner indicated.

E.3 How to View Simulation Outputs

The most basic, and error-prone, method of ensuring that a simulation using a test bench has worked as planned, is to view the waveforms by eye. It is rather slow where large simulations are concerned (the human eye is certainly not designed to view large amounts of information in the way presented in the waveform viewer). Experience reveals that errors can very easily be missed using this method.

Figure E.2

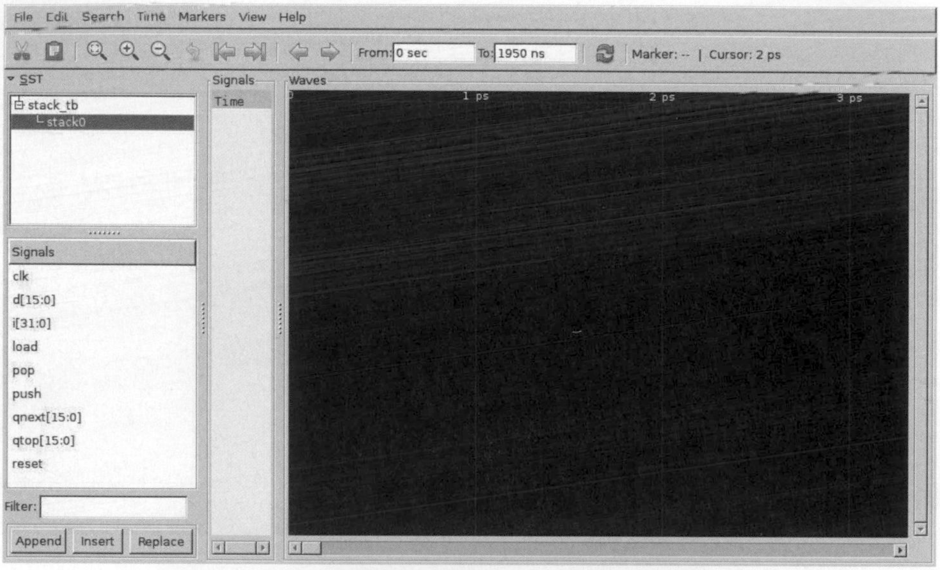

A screenshot of the GTKwave display now listing the available signals.

Figure E.3

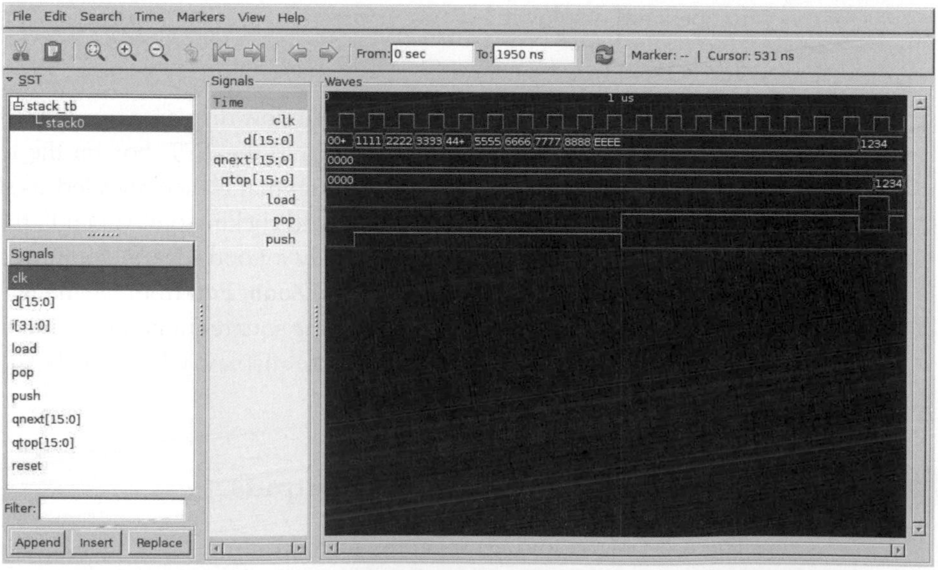

A screenshot of the GTKwave display showing the clock generated in the test bench plus six of the control and data signals available in the VCD file, zoomed out to the maximum $2\mu s$ extent of the simulation.

It is far better to use the waveform viewer for obtaining smaller amounts of information, but to use a separate tool for a pass/fail test of a module.

However, to enable this, we need to learn a few of the Verilog simulation commands. We had met three earlier in Section E.2. Here are a few of the more useful commands:

Command	Meaning
`$monitor`	print stuff when signal changes
`$input`	read commands from file
`$display`	equivalent to printf
`$stop`	halt simulation
`$finish`	terminate process
`$time`	simulation time
`$readmemh`	load a hexadecimal formatted array from a file into memory
`$readmemb`	load a binary array from a file into memory
`$dumpfile`	specify VCD file to write output to
`$dumpvars`	specify variables to monitor and dump

The Verilog `$display` command can work just like a `printf()` in C, outputting required information during simulation (and all but ignored when the code is compiled up for FPGA).[4]

To illustrate the use of input and output text data for verifying the operation of a module in Verilog simulation, we will return again to the example of the stack. In this case, we can reformulate the test bench so that it reads its data from a file instead of hand-coding the data items inside the body of the Verilog.

Listing E.3 stack_file_tb.v

```
`timescale 1ns / 1ps
module stack_tb;
reg clk, reset, load, push, pop;
reg [15:0] d;
wire [15:0] qtop;
wire [15:0] qnext;
stack stack0(.clk(clk), .reset(reset), .load(load), .push(push),
      .pop(pop), .d(d), .qtop(qtop), .qnext(qnext));

reg [500:0] data [0:100];  // each line of input data has 5
     words.  We have 20 lines, 20x5=100

initial $readmemh("infile.txt", data);
integer i;
```

(Continued)

[4] Note that Verilog 2001 has input/output functions available beyond those listed here, but not all are supported by Icarus Verilog.

Listing E.3 stack_file_tb.v (*Continued*)

```
initial begin
  clk=0;
  forever
    #50 clk = ~clk;
end

initial begin
  $dumpfile("stack_tb.vcd");
  $dumpvars(0,stack_tb);
end

initial begin
   reset=0; load=0; push=0; pop=0; d=0;
   $display("\t\t\ttime\treset\tload\tpush\tpop\td\tqtop\tqnext");
   for(i=0;i<5*20;i=i+5) begin
   #100
   reset=data[i];
   load=data[i+1];
   push=data[i+2];
   pop=data[i+3];
   d=data[i+4];
   $display("\t%d\t%b\t%b\t%b\t%b\t%04h\t%04h\t%04h",$time,
      reset, load, push, pop, d, qtop, qnext);
   end
#100 $finish;
end
endmodule
```

Listing E.3 shows this test bench. In this case, a register has been defined near the beginning of the test bench called *data* which is to store the input test vector files. *readmemh* is then used to load the data from an input file into this register (which is really a memory structure). The format of the data file should match this arrangement in memory. In this case, our data file, arranged with each line from left to right, contains input for *reset*, *load*, *push*, *pop* and *d*. There are thus five items per line in the input vector file, as shown in Listing E.4.

Listing E.4 infile.txt

```
0 0 0 0 0
1 0 1 0 1111
1 0 1 0 2222
1 0 1 0 3333
1 0 1 0 4444
```

(*Continued*)

Listing E.4 infile.txt (*Continued*)

```
1 0 1 0 5555
1 0 1 0 6666
1 0 1 0 7777
1 0 1 0 8888
1 0 1 0 EEEE
1 0 0 1 XXXX
1 0 0 1 XXXX
1 0 0 1 XXXX
1 0 0 1 XXXX
1 0 0 1 XXXX
1 0 0 1 XXXX
1 0 0 1 XXXX
1 1 0 0 1234
1 0 0 1 XXXX
```

Referring back to the test bench in Listing E.3, the register contains space for 500 elements, arranged in a 5 × 100 table. This could therefore cater for 100 lines of text vectors. However, in the main loop where we read in test vectors, we read in only 20 lines (each containing the 5 elements).

So next we compile up and simulate this:

```
iverilog  -o stack_file_tb stack.v stack_file_tb.v

vvp stack_file_tb
```

This time, since we have used the *$display* command, there will be information printed on the display, which should look similar to the following:

```
VCD info: dumpfile stack_tb.vcd opened for output.
time     reset    load     push     pop      d        qtop     qnext
 100       0        0        0       0        0        0        0
 200       1        0        1       0     1111        0        0
 300       1        0        1       0     2222        0        0
 400       1        0        1       0     3333        0        0
 500       1        0        1       0     4444        0        0
 600       1        0        1       0     5555        0        0
 700       1        0        1       0     6666        0        0
 800       1        0        1       0     7777        0        0
 900       1        0        1       0     8888        0        0
1000       1        0        1       0     eeee        0        0
1100       1        0        0       1     xxxx        0        0
1200       1        0        0       1     xxxx        0        0
1300       1        0        0       1     xxxx        0        0
1400       1        0        0       1     xxxx        0        0
```

```
1500    1    0    0    1    xxxx       0    0
1600    1    0    0    1    xxxx       0    0
1700    1    0    0    1    xxxx       0    0
1800    1    1    0    0    1234       0    0
1900    1    0    0    1    xxxx    1234    0
2000    x    x    x    x    xxxx       0    0
```

These printed columns were those specified in the test bench, and provided the time, followed by the text vector input information, and then the resulting output from the `stack.v` module: `qtop` and `qnext`. If required, this information can simply be captured into a file. In fact, that can best be accomplished by executing the simulator using the UNIX syntax to redirect its output to a file:

```
vvp stack_file_tb  > dump.txt
```

So now turning our attention to the test vectors that had been output, we can see firstly that the input parameters are, unsurprisingly, the same as specified in `infile.txt`. Looking at the output columns, `qtop` shows the data currently at the top of the stack. However, there appears to be a problem – we can see that `qtop` gets loaded with `1234` at time 1800, but why are the values `1111`, `2222` and so on, not pushed onto the stack?

The immediate suspicion would be an error in either the `infile.txt` input vectors or the test bench itself. Let us go back and examine the *original* test bench and simulation output in Figure E.3 on page 476. Examining the waveform display carefully, it is obvious now that the same error is present: `qtop` only ever holds the value `1234`, and that is near the end of the simulation.

One or two sharp-eyed readers might have realised the error already. Cast your mind back to Section 8.7.6 (page 399) where we had first defined the stack. Look at the table defining the inputs and outputs plus the stack behaviour. Note that a PUSH signal by itself does not cause data to enter the stack, it only ripples the data one level down the stack. To load data, both PUSH and LOAD must be set. Examining our test vectors, we can see the problem – we had only PUSH set and not LOAD. We now correct this in our test vectors, as shown in Listing E.5.

Listing E.5 infile.txt

```
0 0 0 0 0
1 0 1 0 1111
1 1 1 0 2222
1 1 1 0 3333
1 1 1 0 4444
1 1 1 0 5555
1 1 1 0 6666
1 1 1 0 7777
1 1 1 0 8888
1 1 1 0 EEEE
```

(*Continued*)

Listing F.6 mac2mem.perl output for the subtract code

```
mem[12'h000] = 16'hD000; // IN
mem[12'h001] = 16'h2005; // PUSH cnst
mem[12'h002] = 16'hF001; // SUB
mem[12'h003] = 16'hE000; // OUT
mem[12'h004] = 16'h0000; // HALT
mem[12'h005] = 16'h0003; // cnst: 3
```

F.5 The Compiler

The inventor of TinyCPU, Professor Nakano, has even created a compiler.[4] In fact, there are two compilers – with different levels of functionality.

The main TinyCPU compiler, called `tinyc` is written using the standard compiler generation tools *flex* and *bison*, and interested readers are referred to the wiki pages for detail of how that is performed. The compiler code is not reproduced here, but can be downloaded from the wiki pages mentioned above (as `tinyc.l` and `tinyc.y` which, when processed by flex and bison respectively, generate a C language source which can be compiled into an executable called `tinyc` which is in fact the compiler). TinyC actually supports compilation of a subset of the C language, written with C syntax but using several simplifications and built-in operators. As an example, consider the C source code shown in Listing F.7 that performs the same subtract example used previously.

Listing F.7 subtract.c

```
out(in-cnst);
halt;
int cnst=3;
```

Note that although the syntax is C-like, there are several differences immediately obvious: built-in function `out()` sets the output buffer, built-in variable `in` reads the input port and the `halt` instruction is used. In addition, the variable declaration is at the end of the program (which is most unlike C) – if we had placed the variable declaration at the start of the program, then the first location in memory would be occupied by that variable, and once TinyCPU began to run, it would begin by reading that constant and trying to execute it as if it were an instruction.

Still, despite these differences, the syntax should be immediately familiar to C programmers, and the code is a lot easier to write than assembler. In particular, the main strength of the *tinyc* compiler is in formulating stack-based equations (which is not

[4] Refer to his wiki pages `http://www.cs.hiroshima-u.ac.jp/~nakano/wiki/` for more details.

really shown in this example). In fact, it is very capable when it comes to transforming complex equations into the Reverse Polish notation required by TinyCPU.

The output from compiling the `subtract.c` source with `tinycpu` is shown in Listing F.8.

Listing F.8 subtract.out

```
        IN
        PUSH cnst
        SUB
        OUT
        HALT
cnst: 3
```

This is indistinguishable from the assembler code we had started with in Listing F.1: the output of the C compiler is actually assembler code! We then use the `tinyasm.perl` Perl assembler in the usual way to create machine code, and `mac2mem.perl` to format this into Verilog syntax.

F.6 Summary

This appendix began by assembling a short TinyCPU program by hand. Noting the tedious and repetitive nature of this process, we introduced an assembler. This performed an almost one-for-one conversion of assembler mnemonics into hexadecimal machine code, in addition to resolving label locations.

Although the assembler is a great improvement over the hand-assembly process, a higher-level language compiler would provide yet further improvement. Thus, we introduced the TinyCPU compiler which uses C language syntax, with some additions and exclusions, to significantly ease the process of creating TinyCPU programs, especially those involving mathematical calculations.

These tools, particularly the compiler, may not be complete final solutions: there is room for improvement in both, and thus the interested reader is encouraged to adapt and extend these. Most importantly, the author of this book would like to repeat his message at the end of Chapter 8 to encourage readers to use the knowledge they have gained to not only enhance TinyCPU (and its assembler/compiler), but also create their own custom solutions.

Index

6502, 10, 78, 79, 99, 127, 291
8086, *See Intel 8086*

A

Absolute addressing, 188
Acorn, 5, 8, 78, 79, 112
Actel
  ARM core, 378
  AX1000 FPGA, 428
Adder
  ripple carry, 30, 130
Address
  bus architecture, 206
  handling hardware, 205–206
ADSP2181, 17, 81, 82, 90, 94, 130, 204–205
Advanced graphics port, 258
Advanced interrupt controller, 279
Advanced microcontroller bus architecture, 252, 258
Advanced technology attachment, 258
  parallel (PATA), 258, 259
  serial, 334
  serial (SATA), 258, 259
AGP, *See Advanced graphics port*
AHB, *See ARM host bus*
Altera, 362
  Nios II, 377
  Quartus-II, 408
ALU, *See Arithmetic logic unit*
AMBA, *See Advanced microcontroller bus architecture*
AMD, 11, 112, 161, 164
  3DNow, 159, 163, 164
  Phenom, 293, 295
Amdahl's law, 237
AMULET, 436, 437, 438
Analog Devices, 41
  ADSP21xx, 67, 80, 81, 82, 84, 123, 124, 203, 205, 207, 208, 423
Analytical difference machine, 1, 2, 4
ANSI C, 99
Apple, 112, 265, 307
  iMac, 9, 10
  iPhone, 10, 13
  iPod, 104
  Newton, 34
Application specific integrated circuit, 351
Architecture
  bit serial, 419
  dual bus, 127–129
  electro-optical, 442
  load store, 69, 79, 86, 194
  multiple bus, 121–130, 202
  regular, 69
  related to IPC, 199–200
  single bus, 129–130
architecture
  von Neumann, 17, 143
Arithmetic
  binary addition, 29–30
  binary subtraction, 30–33
  logical, 18, 19, 23, 107, 130
  reverse Polish notation, 96–98
  stack, 96, 97
Arithmetic logic unit, 19, 29, 67, 72, 130–132, 244
ARM, 10, 11, 13, 22, 34, 67, 77–80, 83, 86, 90, 99, 106, 110, 112, 122, 127, 143, 165, 207, 252, 254 610, 34
  address handling, 208

ARM (*Cont.*)
ARM 7, 21, 34, 82, 84, 130, 140, 275
ARM 9, 83, 298
ARM7TDMI, 83
ARM946, 234, 235
branching, 86, 187–188
condition codes, 87
conditional instructions, 110, 183–185
Cortex, 83, 235, 378
desktop computer, 291
dual core, 234, 235
FIQ, 275, 276, 278
floating point unit, 159
FPA10, 159, 165
immediate constants, 89, 90
indirect addressing, 94
instruction format, 81–98, 121
interrupt response, 273
interrupt timing, 275–276
IRQ, 275–276, 278
Jazelle, 165
JTAG scanchain, 339
Linux, 326
MOV instruction, 89–90
NEON, 165
on FPGA, 378
registers, 205
S-flag, 85, 181, 182, 190
shadow registers, 271
Thumb, 178
Thumb mode, 84, 90
vector table, 274
VFP, 166
ARM host bus, 252, 258
ASCII, 110
ASIC, *See Application specific integrated circuit*
Asymmetrical multi-processing, 237
Asynchronous computer, 74
Asynchronous processors, 434–438
ATA, *See Advanced technology attachment*
Atanasoff-Berry machine, 4
Atmel, 258
Atom, 165

B

Babbage, Charles, 1, 4
Baby, *See SSEM*
Barcelona supercomputer, 11, 426
BASIC, 112
Basic blocks, 228–229
Basic input/output stream, 18
BBC, *See British Broadcasting Corporation*
BCD, *See Number, binary coded decimal*
Bell Labs, 4
Berkeley University, 78
Bill of materials, 352–353
BIOS, *See Basic input/output stream*
BIST, *See Built in self test*
Bit-serial
addition, 420–421
architecture, 419–420
arithmetic, 420–422
logic and processing, 422
subtraction, 421
word size, 422
Blanket, electric, 66
Bletchley Park, 3
Bloat, 141, 236
Bluetooth, 462–463
BODMAS, 96
Bogomips, 111, 236
Bootloader, 277, 326
Branch
conditional, 183–185, 211
delayed, 189
global prediction, 218–221
global predictor, 185
gselect predictor, 221–222
gshare predictor, 222–223
hybrid predictor, 223–225
instruction, 86, 88
local prediction, 216–218
prediction, 209–212
prediction algorithms, 212–225
prediction counter, 215–216
probabilistic, 186
speculation, 185, 211
target buffer, 226–228
to relative address, 187–188, 210
British Broadcasting Corporation, 79
British Standards Institute, 112
Brownout, 340, 346–348
Built in self test, 334–337
Bus arbitration, 73, 261
Busch, Adrian, 130

C

Cache
area trade-offs, 454–455
coherency, 155–157
design tools, 452
direct, 144–145
efficiency, 154
full associative, 147–148
layering, 144
MESI protocol, 155–156
performance of, 153–154
replacement algorithms, 149–153
set associative, 145–147
tag, 145
worked example, 146, 147, 151, 152
Cache memory, 68, 104, 111, 121, 143–144
Cacti, 452–454
Cambridge University, 4, 75
CAN, *See Controller area network*
Canonical signed digit, 441
Carry
look-ahead, 30
propagation, 30
propagation example, 31
CDC6000, 7
Cell processor, 238, 239, 240
Churchill, William, 3
CISC, *See Complex instruction set computer*
Clock
asynchronous, 434
cycle, 110
delay locked loop, 301
domain, 434
double edged, 110
generation of, 301
oscillator, 301
phase locked loop, 301
solutions, 305
speed, 110
synchronous logic, 300
system, 294–295

Cloud computing, 426
Cluster computers, 240, 425
Co-processor, 157–158, 165–166
Co-simulation, 376
Co-synthesis, 376
Colossus, 3, 4, 6
Commercial-off-the-shelf, 428
Common mode noise, 263
Communications hardware, 203
Compiler
  error trapping, 142
  handling of stored data, 105
  loop handing, 204
  optimisations, 105
  support for branch prediction, 185
  support for VLIW, 425
Complex instruction set computer, 20, 76–79, 80, 93, 95, 166, 193, 199, 371
Computer design, 373–377
Computer generation, 5–10
  fifth, 9–10
  first, 6
  fourth, 8–9, 173
  second, 7
  third, 7–8
Computer system bus, 259
Condition
  codes, 87
  flags, 182
  simple flags, 380
Control
  self-timed, 72, 73–74
  distributed, 72
  of a pipeline, 175
  of asynchronous machine, 437
  simplified, 72
Control program for microcomputers, 8
Control unit, 70–75
Controller area network, 258, 428, 429
COTS, *See Commercial-off-the-shelf*
CPI, *See Cycles per instruction*
CP/M, *See Control program for microcomputers*
Cryptography, 202
CSD, *See Canonical signed digit*
Cycles per instruction, 111, 198–201
Cyrix, 161

D

DAG, *See Data address generator*
Dallas Semiconductor, 258
Data
  compression, 202
  format and representation, 99–103
  handling, 98–109
  stream, 16–17, 341
Data address generator, 205, 206
Data dependency, 179–180, 196, 200
Data link layer, 450–451
DDC, *See Display data channel*
Debug, 295
  using serial port, 335–336
DEC, 7, 112, 340
  Alpha 21264, 225
  StrongARM, *See StrongARM*
Design ownership, 373
Design partitioning, 353, 375, 376
Dhrystone, benchmark, 112–113
Differential signalling, 262–264
Digital filter, 38, 202
Digital signal processor, 110, 112, 123, 126, 140
Dinero, 452, 453–455
Direct memory access, 104, 254–255, 261
Disk operating system, 8, 162, 346
Display data channel, 264
Distributed computing, 444–445
Division, 41–43
DMA, *See Direct memory access*
DOS, *See Disk operating system*
DRAM, 76, 114, 144, 258, 316, 317–323
DSP, *See Digital signal processor*
Dual core processor, 234, 271

E

EDAC, *See Error detection and correction*
EDSAC, 4
EDVAC, 4
EEPROM, 67, 310
EIA232 interface, 264, 265, 335, 451
EIA422 interface, 264
EIA485 interface, 264
EISA, *See Extended industry standard architecture*
Electromagnetic interference, 283, 305
Electronically erasable programmable read only memory, *See EEPROM*
Embedded
  future, 66
Embedded designs, 115
EMI, *See Electromagnetic interference*
Endian
  big, 20–21
  little, 20–21
  switching, 179
  worked example, 20–23
ENIAC, 3, 4, 6
Enigma code, 3, 6
EPIC, *See Explicitly parallel instruction computing*
EPROM, 69, 309–310
Erasable programmable read only memory, *See EPROM*
ERC32, 252, 343
Error detection and correction, 340–345
Ethernet, 254
  interface, 266
  memory mapped driver, 329
  processing, 235
  service layers, 449
European Space Agency, 343
Execution
  out of order, 180, 196, 228, 240, 246, 293
Explicitly parallel instruction computing, 199, 422
Extended industry standard architecture, 258, 259

F

FDIV bug, 332
Ferranti, 112
  Mark 1, 5

Field programmable gate array, 166, 237, 247, 325, 340, 346, 351, 355, 356, 357, 362, 363, 369, 370, 371, 372, 374, 375, 376, 379, 380, 382, 396, 408, 427, 428, 429, 430, 471
Finite impulse response filter, 125
Finite state machine, 70
FIR, *See Finite impulse response filter*
Firewire, 265
Flash memory, 67, 265, 310, 311, 312, 314, 326, 339
Floating point, 46–54, 106
  data types, 159
  emulation, 108, 159–161
  hardware, 202
  power consumption, 160
  processing, 54–60, 108
  unit, 19, 54, 82, 108, 121, 157, 158–161, 162, 163, 195
Flowers, Tommy, 3
Flynn
  classification, 16–17
  Michael, 15, 16–17, 230
  MIMD, 16, 17, 230, 231–235, 271
  MISD, 16, 17, 230
  SIMD, 16, 17, 18, 161, 164, 165, 230, 233, 293
  SISD, 16–17, 230, 231–235
FORTRAN, 109
Forwarding
  fetch-fetch, 191, 192
  store-store, 191, 192
FPGA, *See Field programmable gate array*
FPU, *See Floating point unit*
Fragmentation
  external, 138–139
  internal, 138
Freescale, 80
FSM, *See Finite state machine*
Full adder, 29
Furber
  Steve, 159

G

GEC Plessey, 258
GFLOPS, 111
Glue logic, 372–373
Google, 10, 83, 230, 435
gprof, 115
GPRS, 463, 464
Graphics processing, 202
Grid computing, 426
GSM, 34, 463
GTKwave, 414, 471, 472, 476, 481
Guard bit, 59

H

Half adder, 29
Hamming code, 341, 342
Hardware acceleration, 201–209
Hardware software co-design, 373–377
Harvard architecture, 17, 125, 126, 143
Hazard
  avoidance in asynchronous machine, 437–438
  data, 179–180, 196
  pipeline remedies for, 190
  read after write, 190, 196
  structural, 196
  write after read, 180, 190, 196
  write after write, 180, 181, 190, 196
Heterogeneous architecture, 237
High level language, 81, 90, 369, 425
Homogeneous architecture, 237
Huffman coding, 90, 91, 92
Hyperblocks, 228
Hypercube, 434

I

I/O pins
  configuration, 297–298
  multiplexing, 296
IA-64 architecture, 423
IBM, 5, 78, 79, 112, 238, 258, 259, 340, 435
  Cell processor, *See Cell processor*
  PC, 79, 346
  power architecture, 238, 239
  RS6000, 5
  System/360, 8, 75, 240, 246
Icarus Verilog, 471, 473, 474
ICE, *See In-circuit emulator*
IDE, *See Integrated drive electronics*
IEEE 802.11n, 460–461
IEEE 802.16, 461
IEEE1149 JTAG, 295, 296, 337, 353, 408
IEEE1284 interface, 264, 265
IEEE754, 19, 46–47
  arithmetic, 55–56, 57, 58
  denormalised mode, 49–50, 52–53
  division, 56
  double precision, 159
  extended intermediate format, 56, 57–60, 159
  in industry, 158
  infinity, 50, 51
  modes, 47–51
  multiplication, 56, 108
  NaN, 50, 51
  normalised mode, 48–49, 51–52
  number range, 51–54
  on fixed point CPU, 108
  processing, 54–60
  rounding, 60
  single precision, 53–54
  standard, 159
  worked example, 48–49, 50, 54, 57–58
  zero, 50, 51
IEEE802.11 a, b and g, 460, 470
IIC, *See Inter-IC communications*
IIR, *See Infinite impulse response filter*
Immediate constants, 88–90
In-circuit emulator, 337
Indirect addressing, 94
Industry standard architecture, 258, 259
Infinite impulse response filter, 125
Information hiding, 363, 364
Instruction
  application specific, 166
  condition setting bit, 82, 85
  custom, 202
  decode, 84–90
  fetch, 84–90
  format, 80
  handling, 81–98
  level parallelism, 229, 230, 422

microcode, 75–77
set, 81–84, 95
set regularity, 193
stream, 16
translation, 76
Instructions per cycle, 198–201, 236
Integrated drive electronics, 69, 258
Integration, 375
Intel, 10, 11, 78, 79, 112, 159, 161, 164, 165, 313, 423, 439
4004, 5
8086, 1, 75, 260, 291, 428
8088, 162, 260
80386, 157
80387, 157
80486, 143, 158, 332
Core, 237, 271
IXP425, 254, 277
Pentium, 161–163, 423
Pentium Pro, 143
SA1110, 428
StrongARM, *See StrongARM*
XScale, 143, 277
Inter-IC communications, 258, 292
Interrupt
advanced handlers, 278
and real time, 267
event, 272
flag, 272
handlers and memory management, 141
handling, 271–280
importance of, 271–272
queue, 273
redirection, 276–278
service routine, 209, 268, 277
sharing, 278–279
software, 279–280
Interrupt vector, 273
IPC, *See Instructions per cycle*
ISA, *See Industry standard architecture*

J

Java, 109, 165, 173
JTAG, *See IEEE1149 JTAG*
JTAG for booting a CPU, 339

K

Kernel, 142, 167, 327, 328, 357

L

Lattice
Mico32, 378
Linux, 83, 142, 164, 200, 329, 435, 471
Beowulf, 240
determination of MIPS, 111
embedded, 142, 326, 356, 377, 378
uCLinux, 325
Load store architecture, 194
Loosely coupled tasks, 425
Low voltage differential signalling, 259, 262–264
LVDS, *See Low voltage differential signalling*

M

MAC, *See Multiply accumulate unit*
Machine parallelism, 231
Manchester University, 4, 5, 132
Marconi, 258
MareNostrum, 11
Massachusetts Institute of Technology, 4, 5
MCA, 258, 259
MCM, *See Multi-chip module*
Media independent interface, 266
Memory
access, 125
access in C, 331
background, 307
burst mode, 110
cycle, 126
DRAM, 316, 317–319
DRAM addressing, 319–323
DRAM refresh, 317, 319
DRAM structure, 320
EDO DRAM, 323
EEPROM, 362
EPROM, 309, 339, 362
flash, 311, 351
flash blocks, 314
flash memory control, 313
for an FPGA core, 382
fragmentation, 138
in embedded systems, 325–332
map of ARM 9, 326
map of MSP430, 330
mapped registers, 329
NAND flash, 311
NOR flash, 311
on-chip, 114, 126
overlays, 323–325
pages, 323–325
parity checking, 340, 341
pin swapping of, 358–359
PROM, 309
protection, 140–142
RAM, 314–323
remapping, 277
ROM, 308–314
SDRAM, 323, 359
serial flash, 311
SRAM, 316, 351, 359, 362
stack, 138
VRAM, 323
Memory management unit, 19, 68, 104, 121, 292, 323–324
address translation cache, 140
advanced designs, 139–140
operation, 133, 135–137
rationale, 133
translation look-aside buffer, 140
worked example, 137
Mesh, 433–434
MESI
in shared memory system, 433
protocol, 155
worked example, 157
MFLOPS, 111
Micro channel architecture, *See MCA*
Microcode, 75–77
Microprogramming, 75
MIMO, 460
MIPS, 67, 78, 111, 114, 140, 189, 341
Mitel, 258
MMC, *See Multimedia card*
MMU, *See Memory management unit*
MMX, *See Multimedia extensions*
ModelSim, 409, 471
Moore's law, 1, 77, 235
Motorola, 79
68000, 20, 67, 80, 205
Coldfire, 80

MP3, 66, 115, 233
MS-DOS, 346
Multi-chip module, 237
Multi-core, 237
Multimedia card, 265, 292
Multimedia extensions, 17, 82, 158, 159, 161–165, 230
Multiple-valued logic, 438–439
Multiplication, 34–41
  Booth's method, 34, 38–41
  on a small machine, 106
  partial products, 35–38, 440
  repeated addition, 34
  Robertson's method, 34, 38
  shift and add, 38
Multiplication, by repeated addition, 34
Multiply accumulate unit, 123, 195, 202

N

NASA
  computers, 340
  space shuttle, 8, 341
Near field communication, 466–467
Network layer, 451
Newton, Isaac, 14
Number
  alternative formats, 438–442
  binary coded decimal, 26
  complex, 109
  conversion examples, 25–26
  excess-n, 24, 26
  (m.n) format, 26
  format, 23–28
  fractional, 27
  fractional arithmetic, 44
  fractional examples, 27, 44
  fractional multiply, 45
  fractional notation, 26–27
  negative two's complement, 24, 25
  one's complement, 24
  Q-format, 26, 43, 161
  sign extension, 27–28
  signed digit representation, 439–442
  two's complement, 24
  unsigned binary, 23–24

O

Obfuscation, 364
  of software, 361
OFDM, *See Orthogonal frequency division multiplexing*
Open systems interconnection, 259, 449–451
Orthogonal frequency division multiplexing, 460
OSI, *See Open systems interconnection*

P

Parallel
  at different levels, 230
  considerations, 431
  coupling, 425
  for performance, 235–237
  grain size, 434
  interconnecting links, 432–434
  machines, 199, 230, 425
  processing, 200
  speedup, 237
  worlds biggest machines, 435
Parallel adder, 29–31
Parallel architectures, 433
Parallel port, 103
Parallel processing unit, 427–431
Parallel topology, 433
PC-card, 265
PC/104, 259, 261
PCB characteristics, 354
PCI, *See Peripheral component interconnect*
PCI express, 258, 264
PCMCIA, *See Personal computer memory card international association*
PDA, *See Personal digital assistant*
PDP-1, 7
Performance
  assessing, 113–115
  measures, 111–113
Peripheral
  memory mapped, 192
Peripheral component interconnect, 258, 261
Personal computer memory card international association, 259, 265
Personal digital assistant, 15, 34, 439
Pervasive computing, 426
PFLOPS, 111
Phase locked loop, 293
Physical layer, 450
PIC, 67
Pin swapping during layout, 358–359
Pipeline, 175
  compiler support for, 185
  dynamic, 177, 194
  efficiency, 188
  FPU, 158
  mode change, 177–179
  multi-function, 175–177, 194
  multiple issue superscalar, 197
  speedup, 175
  split, 186
  stall, 187
  superscalar, 195, 197
  superscalar performance, 198
  throughput, 173
PLL, *See Phase locked loop*
Plug and play, 260
Power
  due to current switching, 304
  ideas for reduction of, 307
  in semiconductors, 302
  low power design, 305–307
  on self test, 326
PPU, *See Parallel processing unit*
Principles
  of locality, 148–149
Programmable logic device, 362
Propagation delay, 303
Propagation delay, example, 134
PS/2, 264
Pyramidal, view of memory, 68

Q

Quad core processor, 237, 295
Quake, 112

R

Radiation damage, 340
RAM, 67, 69, 76, 314–323

RAMBUS, 258
Ramdisk, 327, 328–329
Random access memory, *See RAM*
RDRAM, 144
Re-entrant code, 279
Read only memory, *See ROM*
Real-time, 113
  definitions, 267–268
  hard or soft system, 266–267
  issues, 266–271
  operating system, 268, 270–271, 326, 356, 379
  scheduling, 270
  stimuli, 267
  task, 268
Reconfigurability, 166
Reduced instruction set computer, 20, 67, 72, 76, 79, 80, 85, 93, 95, 111, 159, 161, 173, 193, 199, 273, 371
Reed-Solomon, 342
Register
  shadow, 209, 280
Relative addressing, 188
Remote processing, 427
Reservation station, 241
Reservation table, 174, 181, 184
Reset
  circuitry, 294
  controller, 346
  supervisory IC, 346
Retirement algorithm, 137–138
Reverse engineering
  analytical steps, 349
  mitigation, 363
  of computer devices, 349
  of software, 356
  structure anaysis, 351–352
  the process of, 349–353
Reverse Polish notation, 96–98
RISC, *See Reduced instruction set computer*
Rockwell 6502, 10, 79
ROM, 67, 76, 308–314
RPN, *See Reverse Polish notation*
RS232, *See EIA232 interface*
RS422, *See EIA422 interface*
RS485, *See EIA485 interface*

S

S3C2410, *See Samsung S3C2410*
Samsung
  S3C2410, 255, 256, 288, 291, 298, 326, 339, 370, 459
  S3CR650B, 466
Scan path, 336
Scheduling
  deadline monotonic, 270
  earliest deadline first, 270
  most important first, 270
  rate monotonic, 270
Scoreboard, 196
Scoreboarding, 196
Scrambling of bus signals, 359
SCSI, *See Small computer systems interface*
SD, *See Secure digital*
SDRAM, 76, 126, 127, 144, 275, 292, 326
Secure digital, 265, 292
Segmentation, 138
Serial peripheral interface, 258, 324
Serial port, 103, 331, 370
Sign extension, 27–28
Signed digit, 439–442
Simulation
  of FPGA code, 471
  of Verilog designs, 475
Sinclair, 112
  Sir Clive, 79
  ZX Spectrum, 79, 283
  ZX-79, 5
Single chip computer, 293, 316
Single event upset, 340
Single T-bit branch predictor, 212–214
Slave processor, 159
Small computer systems interface, 69
SMP, *See Symmetrical multi-processing*
Snooping, 155, 157
SoC, *See System-on-chip*
Soft core, 166, 369–373
Software
  in embedded systems, 328
  real time, 267
  support for zero overhead loops, 204
Sony playstation, 238
SPECint and SPECfp, 112
Speculation, 182–186
SPI, *See Serial peripheral interface*
Spill code, 105
SRAM, 115, 126, 316–317
SSE, *See Streaming SIMD extensions*
SSEM, 4
Stack computer, 96, 380
Stanford University, 78
Streaming SIMD extensions, 17, 158, 164–165, 230, 293
StrongARM, 17, 143, 428
SUN, 5, 161
  Java processor, 173
  picoJAVA, 5
  picoJAVA II, 19
  SPARC, 20, 78, 252, 343
Superblocks, 228
Superscalar processors, 199
Supervisor mode, 280
Symmetrical multi-processing, 237
System International, 447
System modelling, 376
System-on-chip, 15, 252, 266, 292, 352

T

Task parallelism, 230
Temporal scope, 268–269
Test, 332
  benches, 482–483
  by development stage, 334
Testing, 391
Texas Instruments, 77
  DSP processor, 189
  MSP430, 296–298, 330
  TMS320, 80, 178
  TMS32C50, 275
  TMS320C50, 203, 209
TinyCPU
  ALU, 383–384, 401–403
  `alu.v`, 401–403
  architecture, 381
  assembler, 484–488
  comparison operations, 387
  compiler, 489–490

TinyCPU (*Cont.*)
control system, 385–386, 388
counter.v, 391–394
data bus, 381–382
defs.v, 391
design specification, 380–386
execution state, 389–390
implementation, 390–408
instruction handling, 384–385
instruction set, 386–390
instruction types, 386–387
inventor, 379
memory space, 382–383, 396
overview, 403–408
programming, 409–414
programming tools, 413–414
RAM, 382–383
ram.v, 396–399
stack, 382, 399–401
stack.v, 399–401
state machine, 388
state.v, 394–396
testing, 408–409
tinycpu.v, 403–408
writing code for, 409, 484
Tomasulo algorithm, 196, 240–247
Trace table, 213, 215
Transistor computer, 4, 5
Trap
of program counter, 205
Triple redundancy, 341–342, 430
Tristate buffer, 19, 70, 71, 72, 73, 122
Turbo code, 341
Turing, Alan, 3
TWI, *See Two wire interface*
Two wire interface, 258
Two-bit branch predictor, 214–215
TX-0 computer, 4

U

U-boot, 277, 326
UART/USART, 192, 292, 298
UltraSPARC II, 140
Unicode, 103
Universal serial bus, 69, 254, 265, 451
UNIX, 69, 340, 480
USB, *See Universal serial bus*

V

VAX, 20, 273
Vector parallelism, 230
Vector processor, 104, 166
Verification, 376, 391, 482
Verilog, 369, 379, 471
Very large scale integration, 8
Very long instruction word, 199, 422
VHDL, 369, 371, 390, 408
VIA
Isaiah architecture, 293–294, 298
Nano, 293–294, 298
Virtual memory, 19, 132–133
VLIW, *See Very long instruction word*
VLSI, *See Very large scale integration*
Volatile, 192, 331, 332
Voltage droop, 340, 347
von Neumann, 17, 143, 308

W

Watchdog timer, 345–347
Wetware, 445–446
Whetstone, benchmark, 113
Whirlwind 1, 5
WiBro, 467–468
Wilkes, Maurice, 4, 75
Wireless
features, 280
for embedded systems, 459–470
interfacing, 282
issues, 282–283
technology, 280–282
USB, 466

X

X-ray of circuit, 333, 354
x86, 21, 80, 140, 162, 164, 165, 305
Xilinx, 363, 379, 390, 408
ISE, 408
MicroBlaze, 378

Z

Zero overhead loop, 110, 202–205
worked example, 207–208
Zero padding, 28
ZigBee, 464–465
Zilog
Z80, 291
ZOL, *See Zero overhead loop*
Zuse, Konrad, 4